SOUTHEAST
ASIA

SOUTHEAST ASIA

PAST AND PRESENT

Sixth Edition

D. R. SarDesai

University of California at Los Angeles

A Member of the Perseus Books Group

959
Sa 24

Designed by Pauline Brown

Library of Congress Cataloging-in-Publication Data

SarDesai, D. R.
  Southeast Asia : past and present / D.R. SarDesai. — 6th ed.
     p. cm.
  Includes bibliographical references and index.
  ISBN 978-0-8133-4434-8 (alk. paper)
  1. Southeast Asia—History. I. Title.
  DS525.S27 2009
  959—dc22

                                                             2009014006

10 9 8 7 6 5 4 3

SOUTHEAST ASIA

PAST AND PRESENT

Sixth Edition

D. R. SarDesai
University of California at Los Angeles

A Member of the Perseus Books Group

Copyright © 2010 by Westview Press
Published by Westview Press,
A Member of the Perseus Books Group

All rights reserved. Printed in the United States of America. No part of this book may be reproduced in any manner whatsoever without written permission except in the case of brief quotations embodied in critical articles and reviews. For information, address Westview Press, 2465 Central Avenue, Boulder, CO 80301.

Find us on the World Wide Web at www.westviewpress.com.

Westview Press books are available at special discounts for bulk purchases in the United States by corporations, institutions, and other organizations. For more information, please contact the Special Markets Department at the Perseus Books Group, 2300 Chestnut Street, Suite 200, Philadelphia, PA 19103, or call (800) 810-4145, ext. 5000, or e-mail special.markets@perseusbooks.com.

Designed by Pauline Brown

Library of Congress Cataloging-in-Publication Data

SarDesai, D. R.
   Southeast Asia : past and present / D.R. SarDesai. — 6th ed.
      p. cm.
   Includes bibliographical references and index.
   ISBN 978-0-8133-4434-8 (alk. paper)
   1. Southeast Asia—History. I. Title.
   DS525.S27 2009
   959—dc22
                                                                    2009014006

10 9 8 7 6 5 4 3

*For
Vandana and
Archana*

Contents

Preface

Most general historians of Southeast Asia, with the notable exceptions of D. G. E. Hall, Georges Coedes, and John F. Cady, have given an undue emphasis to the period of European rule. They have consequently treated the pre-European period merely as a prologue to the understanding of colonial rule. Such a treatment, condemned first by the Dutch scholar J. C. van Leur as providing a Eurocentric view regarding Indonesian history, for example, "from the deck of the ship, the ramparts of the fortress, the high gallery of the trading house," is unacceptable to most contemporary historians. On the other hand, the Indian historian-diplomat K. M. Panikkar, a well-known partisan of the Asiacentric viewpoint, has conceded that, qualitatively speaking, the changes brought by Western rule could only be described as "revolutionary." There is no denying that most of the present-day economic, communications, and educational patterns of the region's independent states owe much to the colonial period. Therefore, while focusing on the activities of the indigenous people, I have felt compelled to treat the colonial period as more than an "interlude." A fairly large section of the book consequently is concerned with Western activity in the region and the indigenous reaction to it.

This book is the product of four decades of teaching courses in Southeast Asian history and separately on Vietnam, at the University of California, Los Angeles. I appreciate the contribution of many a bright student who raised questions or offered comments during innumerable discussions in and out of the classroom. These have helped immensely in clarifying my ideas on a wide range of historical problems concerning Southeast Asia. I am also thankful to the many scholars whose monographs, translations, and articles provided a research base for much of what is included in this book. The notes, which I have deliberately kept to the minimum, are an inadequate acknowledgement of my debt to those scholars; the bibliography at the end of the volume is a truer measure of it.

In a treatment of a region like Southeast Asia, with its diverse ethnic units, states, and two millennia of historical development, there are bound to be gaps in information. In fact, I have tried not to clutter the book with too many details unless they represent major historical landmarks or have relevance for illuminating a point. After all, modern history writing is not just a record of every event so much as a recollection of and reflection upon the more significant of the happenings. What is attempted here is a broad survey of trends and currents in the historical panorama of the region, combining thematic and chronological approaches.

In the aftermath of the dissolution of Western colonial regimes and the advent of independence, many newly freed peoples adopted new place-names. Thus, some of the previous editions of this book used the changed nomenclature: from the

Dutch East Indies to Indonesia, Celebes to Sulawesi, and Dutch Borneo to Kalimantan. A resurgent Thailand, which never fell formally under Western colonial domination, dropped its old name, Siam, twice—in the 1930s and 1940s—finally to settle in 1949 on Prathet Thai or Thailand. When Cambodia became Communist in 1975, its name was changed to Kampuchea; on April 30, 1989, contrary to the general trend, its colonial name, Cambodia, was readopted. The Vietnamese Communists marked their victory in 1975 by renaming Saigon after Ho Chi Minh. Burma became Myanmar on June 18, 1989, and its capital, Rangoon, became Yangon. Most scholars, journalists, and even Myanmar government publications, however, continue to refer to the people of that country as Burmese and the majority community as Burmans.

I must record here my appreciation of the assistance received from several persons. Drafts of this manuscript were read in part or as a whole by several professional colleagues and graduate students. I am particularly thankful to Professors Mark McLeod and the late Ingelise Lanman and Professors Arnold Kaminsky and Damon Woods, who read the entire manuscript from a student's angle and later from an instructor's standpoint and made most valuable suggestions for improvement. I am also grateful to Charlotte Spence of UCLA's Research Library for extensive bibliographical assistance and to Jane Bitar, manager, Word Processing for Social Sciences and Humanities, and Nancy Rhan at UCLA for their technical assistance with a smile. My gratitude to Hubert Ho of UCLA's History Department Computer Laboratory for helping with the mysteries of computers, particularly in preparing a revised edition. My deepest appreciation to my wife for her unfailing inspiration and encouragement at all times throughout what will next year be a half century of life partnership.

—*D. R. SarDesai*

Part One

Cultural Heritage

This part entitled "Cultural Heritage" covers traditional Southeast Asia from the time small kingdoms arose in mainland Southeast Asia (the area covered by modern Myanmar, Thailand, Laos, Cambodia, and Vietnam) and in insular Southeast Asia (covering modern Malaysia, Brunei, Singapore, Indonesia, East Timor, and the Philippines).

Historians of the ancient times in Southeast Asia—whether they were French, Dutch, Indian, or Chinese—for long labored on the division of the region into two cultural spheres influenced deeply by India and China. The rulers and the ruled may not then have seen the entire region as a whole as we do in modern times, particularly after World War II and even more so since the birth of the Association of Southeast Asian Nations (ASEAN) in 1967 with Malaysia, Singapore, Indonesia, and the Philippines as founding members and subsequent enrollment of Laos, Cambodia, Vietnam, Brunei, Myanmar, and East Timor. True, two different styles of housing, dress, communications, and cuisine developed, but the region shared many common factors, such as the monsoons and the cultivation and consumption of rice as a staple.

Imperial China, since the Han times, was satisfied with the acknowledgment by the Southeast Asian polities, both mainland and insular, of Chinese hegemony through its celebrated tributary system and of direct rule over the Tongking region for very long periods (111 B.C. to A.D. 939 and for a decade and a half in the fifteenth century). With a single exception in the eleventh century of direct rule over Srivijaya in West Indonesia for more than two decades, the Indian influence was pervasive throughout the region from about the beginning of the common era when small states were born and chose to invite Indian Brahmans and other conduits of culture to their courts. North Vietnam was possibly the only exception to resist Indian control, instead falling under the spell of Chinese literature, court etiquette, and Confucian political philosophy, to mention only a few aspects of life and culture.

Another distinction made by analysts, historical or political, has hinged on the major religions in Southeast Asia. Roughly speaking, considerable parts of insular Southeast Asia—including Malaysia, Indonesia, and the southern Philippines—are overwhelmingly Muslim. The conversion of such large numbers beginning in the 13th century and becoming a massive wave in the 15th and 16th centuries applied in two contexts. First was the conversion of people from Hinduism and Buddhism in Malaya and Indonesia without abandoning the predominant Hindu-Buddhist culture. Those who were responsible for the conversion came from India, a land conventionally acceptable to Southeast Asians as a cultural source. The shift occurred in the same way Hinduism and Buddhism had taken hold in the first millennium C.E.: without the use of force or political pressure. Second, as the Portuguese advanced through Southeast Asian waters seeking "spices and Christians," as Vasco da Gama had declared when he first landed in Calicut in South India, the people and their rulers living along the path of the Portuguese advance converted to Islam to escape forcible conversion to Christianity. Eventually, Southeast Asia became home to more Muslims than lived in any other region, such as the Middle East or South Asia.

Post–World War II historiography and the emergence of independent states in Southeast Asia not only underline the existence of a cultural infrastructure prior to the advent of the Indian culture, but also highlight that Indian influence arose through a deliberate choice by the region's numerous rulers to prohibit adoption of certain Indian cultural elements, particularly its caste system and the declining importance of women in India. The pervasive Indian influence in art and architecture, language and literature, dance and music, and court etiquette and legal structure has not been denied by modern writers. Indeed, these commentators have rightly underlined the substructure already existing. This was true not only in art and architecture but also in music and dress, notably in the Indonesian gamelan (musical group) and batik (hand-printed fabric). The predominantly Hindu-Buddhist culture in both the mainland and insular regions was not replaced in cultural terms by the advent of Islam, mainly in the insular region from about the 13th to the 15th centuries.

The whole of Southeast Asia never came under the rule of a single person or dynasty. On the mainland, the Khmers created the largest empire, which at its height in the 9th to the 13th centuries embraced the region from Lower Burma (Myanmar), Thailand, Laos, Cambodia, and South Vietnam. There were large polities in insular Southeast Asia, but they did not cover the entire region, although modern historians of Indonesia cite an exception among the early Majapahit rulers, notably under the prime minister, Gajah Mada (1331–1364). In addition, during one short period in the second half of the eighth century, an insular ruler from Java's Sailendra dynasty apparently conquered and ruled over large portions of Cambodia and Central and South Vietnam. As discussed in the second part of this book, none of the Western colonial powers was able to bring all of Southeast Asia under a common rule.

Important sources for historians of Southeast Asia's early past are Chinese records, both governmental and travelers' accounts. Although inscriptions appeared in South Burma, Thailand, Cambodia, and Central Vietnam, they were much fewer than the Chinese accounts. The Chinese tradition of maintaining court records, including the accounts of tribute-bearers from the "barbarian" vassal kingdoms in Southeast Asia, has yielded a mine of valuable information for historians. This does not mean the Southeast Asians lacked regard for history; they too produced documents, notably in "independent" Vietnam after it overthrew the millennium-long Chinese direct rule. The shorter Chinese direct rule (1407–1428) over Vietnam after the Ming invasion was condemned by the Vietnamese for many reasons, one of which was the brutal and systematic removal by the Chinese and, in some cases, destruction of all Vietnamese books, which were replaced with Chinese classics. The periodic Cham invasions from the South also helped to destroy Vietnamese documentation.

Part 1 sets the tone for the book inasmuch as it deals with the traditions of the peoples of Southeast Asia, traditions that, in most parts, apply to both urban and rural populations, especially the latter. Rural dwellers account for more than 75 percent of the population, a demographic that modernity has not overtaken.

Part 1 also includes the early European intrusion in insular Southeast Asia. It began with the Portuguese conquest of Malacca in 1510 and was followed, after almost a century, by the English, the Dutch, the French, and even by the Spaniards in the Philippines. Except for the last, European contacts with the indigenous people were overwhelmingly coastal and commercial in this early period. Because there was only minor cultural contact, Europeans had only negligible influence over the region. This changed from the middle of the 18th century when territorial conquest replaced what was until then predominantly a trading activity.

MAP 1.1 Southeast Asia Today

1

The Land and Its People

THE REGION'S NAME AND SIGNIFICANCE

The term *Southeast Asia* is of recent origin. It became popular during World War II, when the territories south of the Tropic of Cancer were placed under Lord Louis Mountbatten's Southeast Asia command. The command included Sri Lanka, and at least one study covers that island country along with Southeast Asia because of "similar" experience with Portuguese, Dutch, and British colonialism and because it is "closely related to the Malay Archipelago."[1] On the other hand, D. G. E. Hall excluded the Philippines in the first edition of his monumental history of Southeast Asia because that country lay outside the region's mainstream of historical developments.[2] Most scholars presently use the term *Southeast Asia* to include the geographical areas bounded by the states of Myanmar (formerly Burma), Thailand, Malaysia, Singapore, Brunei, Indonesia, East Timor, Laos, Cambodia, Vietnam, and the Philippines.

Older books on Southeast Asia designated it variously but mostly in reference to either of the two large neighboring countries. Thus, many British, French, and Indian scholars called it Farther India, Greater India, L'Inde Exterieure, and the Hinduized or Indianized States. On the other hand, most Chinese writings identified the region as Kun Lun or Nan Yang (Little China). Still others have referred to the land mass between India and China as Indo-China, from the term *French Indochina,* to include Laos, Vietnam, and Cambodia. The noted geographer George B. Cressey has suggested that the region be called "Indo-Pacific," since it lies between two oceans and cultures.[3]

The variety of terms is perhaps suggestive of the minimal role Southeast Asia played in world affairs until well into the twentieth century. For the famous British political geographer Halford Mackinder, Southeast Asia was a peripheral region, a part of the "rimland." A series of events—beginning with the Japanese occupation of Southeast Asia during World War II, the emergence of the People's Republic of China, and the long, drawn-out conflict and eventual unification of Vietnam—has transformed the entire region into one of the most strategic and sensitive areas of the world. To use Mackinder's geopolitical term, it is the "heartland" of our times. Until the collapse of the Soviet Union in the early 1990s, both the superpowers were vitally interested in the politics and the economic potential of the region. Neither of them would permit Beijing to bring the states of Southeast Asia into a subservient relationship as China had done periodically over the previous two millennia. Such an eventuality would enlarge the parameters of the Communist world, enhance China's power, and deny the Southeast Asian peoples the fruits of freedom that most of them secured after a bitter struggle against Western rule. Besides, dominance by any single power might deprive the rest of the world of the largely unexploited, immense, and precious mineral and oil deposits of the area in addition to denying an easy access from the Pacific to the Indian Ocean. The last is a matter of the gravest concern for Japan, whose survival as an economic and industrial giant depends upon the transport of oil and raw materials from the Middle East, Africa, India, and Southeast Asia as well as the ability to dispatch finished goods to the markets of all these areas and Europe through the Southeast Asian sea-lanes. It should be noted that at any given time, there is a Japanese tanker or freighter situated almost every one hundred nautical miles in the Indian Ocean area. Thus, Southeast Asia may have been a marginal area during most of recorded history, but the various factors briefly outlined here have underlined its strategic importance and made it (along with the Middle East) a potential tinderbox of a global conflict in the past three decades.

The Southeast Asian region is not a unit in the religious, historical, geographical, or ethnic senses. There are at least four different religions in Southeast Asia: Islam, Hinduism, Buddhism, and Christianity. Historically, the region never underwent political consolidation as India or China did. In fact, colonial history has only helped to enhance separatist development among Southeast Asian peoples. Five non-Asian powers ruled the region until various times in the twentieth century: the British in Myanmar, Malaysia, and Singapore; the Dutch in Indonesia; the French in Laos, Cambodia, and Vietnam; the Americans in the Philippines; and the Portuguese in East Timor. Only Thailand managed to remain free. The differing orientations of each of these colonies in the spheres of administration, education, trade, currency, and shipping, to mention only the most important aspects, have been responsible for erecting additional barriers between Southeast Asian people that impede easy and effective communication among them.

ECOLOGICAL SETTING

Geographically, Southeast Asia is included in the monsoon belt and, except for a small portion of Myanmar, located between the tropics. However, nature has divided the land here as nowhere else in any of the Asian segments, effectively fractionalizing it into diverse social and political units. This fragmentation complicates any attempt to develop a common approach to the entire region.

Southeast Asia can be seen as two geographical regions: "mainland" Southeast Asia, to include the countries of Myanmar, Thailand, Laos, Cambodia, and Vietnam; and "insular" Southeast Asia, comprising Malaysia, Singapore, Brunei, Indonesia, East Timor, and the Philippines. The inclusion of Malaysia in the latter group is justified by the Malay Peninsula's greater exposure to the sea and its eth-nic, cultural, religious, and geographical affinities with Sumatra and Java. Indone-sia and the Philippines are groups of islands, large and small, fertile and barren; there are 17,000 in Indonesia and 7,000 in the Philippines. Along with Malaysia and the Philippines, the Indonesian islands constitute the Malay world.

Some physiographers advocate a separate treatment for the Philippines and Sulawesi (the Celebes) because of their location between two geological shelves: the Sunda platform, covering Borneo, Sumatra, Java, and the Malay Peninsula in the west; and the Sahul platform, linking New Guinea and Australia. Between these two "massifs" lies a transitional zone of deep valleys in the seas around the Philippines and Sulawesi, at least partly responsible for the unusual configuration of those islands. In the Sunda platform area, the sea is often only a few hundred feet deep, in contrast to the six- or seven-mile depth of ocean troughs east of the Philippines. This geographical factor explains why the Philippines lacked much historical relationship with the rest of Southeast Asia before the advent of Islam in the middle of the second millennium of the Christian era.

Mainland Southeast Asia is noted for its diverse mountain ranges and rivers running north-south, most of them originating in Tibet. Following George Cressey, one might imagine eastern Tibet as a "complex knot or core area from which great mountain ranges radiate like the arms of an octopus,"[4] dividing the Asian peoples. Thus, the Arakan Mountains stand between India and Myanmar; the Dawna, the Bilauktaung, and the Tenasserim between Myanmar and Thailand, passing farther through Malaya; and the Annam range between Laos and Vietnam, cutting the latter in two. Finally, such ranges as Nu Shan, Kaolikung Shan, Wu-liang Shan, and Ailao Shan together separate Southeast Asia from China. The prin-cipal rivers and streams also flow north-south, providing little help in east-west communications. The numerous river basins, which have become the principal areas of human settlement, are hundreds of miles apart. The primary rivers of mainland Southeast Asia are the Irrawaddy, the Chindwin, and the Salween in Myanmar; the Chao Phraya in Thailand; the Song Koi (Red River) and Song Bo (Black River) in North Vietnam; and the international stream of the Mekong, passing through Laos, Thailand, Cambodia, and South Vietnam. These rivers meander over hundreds of miles, bringing rich alluvial deposits to the deltas, which are like gateways open to the Indian Ocean. Four richly fertile deltas created by these rivers—Lower Myanmar, central Thailand, Tongking, and Mekong deltas—constitute the most populous areas of mainland Southeast Asia but are hundreds of miles apart. On the other hand, rapids in the northern reaches of the rivers obstruct intraregional travel and trade. Thus, the physical features of main-land Southeast Asia, with its numerous mountains and valleys, rivers and rapids, have militated against the development of a common focal point in the region.

Except for equatorial latitudes, where rainfall is well distributed throughout the year, most of the Southeast Asian region is affected by the monsoons. The monsoons—southwest and northeast—are a factor the region's inhabitants must reckon with in cultivating their crops and navigating in open seas. Precipitation averaging 100 inches annually comes with the southwest monsoon winds that hit the leeward side of the various mountain ranges between late May and middle

September, and with the northeast monsoons that bring the much-needed rains between December and February. The accompanying gusty winds, developing at times into devastating hurricanes and typhoons, compel the mostly nonpowered boats to sail only in the direction of the winds and at times wait three to four months for a change of winds before resuming their return journeys. The monsoon belt is generally synonymous with the rice belt; most of Southeast Asia is known for both dry- and wet-rice cultivation. Rice is the principal crop and staple diet of the people of the region. Rice cultivation began in Myanmar and Thailand around 3500 B.C., though the technique of wet-rice cultivation may not have been known in Southeast Asia until after the impact of Indian culture in the beginning of the Christian era.[5] The much-awaited monsoons are often erratic, requiring sophisticated hydraulic controls to ensure water supply. Such equipment and techniques were devised and mastered in ancient times by agrarian leaders, who often assumed political and spiritual leadership as well. The location of houses and temples preferably on elevated ground, the tapering design of the roofs, and the drainage and irrigation systems are conditioned by the often merciless monsoons flooding the dwelling areas and causing untold miseries to the population.

PREHISTORIC ROOTS

Early Man in Java

Archaeological discoveries in the past one hundred years, notably in Java, have pushed our knowledge of Southeast Asia to a couple of million years ago. The oldest of the skulls found was that of a child, at Mojokerto in eastern Java, belonging to the species *Homo erectus,* which is deemed to have evolved from the first tool-making ancestor of the human species, *Homo habilis,* some 1.5 million years ago. The skull was found with the Jetis mammalian fauna along riverbeds dating between 3 million and 1 million years old. Archaeologists also found, at Sangiran in central Java, mandible fragments of a very large-jawed creature named *Meganthropus palaeojavanicus.* Although some scholars have opined that this being might have been contemporaneous with *Homo habilis,* whose remains were found in Olduvai Gorge in Tanzania (and whose estimated age is 1.5–2 million years), it is considered more likely that *Meganthropus palaeojavanicus* falls within the category of *Homo erectus.*[6]

Most of the fossils were discovered, however, at Trinil on the bank of the Solo River in central Java in 1892 and are dated roughly between 1 million and 300,000 years ago. Estimates of the cranial capacity of the skulls in this group range between 750 and 1,125 cc. It is supposed that "Java man" had an almost upright body stance and may have been a contemporary of the ten-foot-tall pongids called *Gigantopithecus blacki,* who lived over a wider region, from southern Kwansi to the fairly open expanses of western Indonesia, from the Pliocene to the Middle Pleistocene epochs. According to Franz Weidenrich, these giant ancestors of man were the progenitors of a series of diminishing forms evolving into *Meganthropus* and *Pithecanthropus (Homo erectus).*[7]

There is only one fossil group of eleven calvaria (partial skulls) and two tibiae (the tibia is the inner bone of the lower leg) found in Java to represent the gap between *Homo erectus* and modern man. This find, made in the early 1930s at Ngandong on the bank of the Solo River, also yielded extensive remains of fauna—25,000 mammalian bones—indicating cohabitation of a wide variety of animals including cattle, elephants, panthers, pigs, deer, and hippopotamuses in what must have been a grassland environment. Estimates of the age of "Solo man" vary considerably. T. Jacob places him between 100,000 and 60,000 years ago;[8] Peter Bellwood hypothesizes that he may be of much older vintage, perhaps the progenitor in "the direct line of evolution of modern men, particularly the Australoids, in Southeast Asia."[9] He agrees with Weidenrich and Carleton Coon that the Australoids (and the Mongoloids) are lineal descendants in Southeast Asia of *Homo erectus*,[10] with Solo man and the Wajak man of Java marking the intermediate stages in the transition. This would imply that Solo man did not become extinct and that his genes could be flowing in modern Australoids, such as the Sakais of Malaya and the populations of southern Celebes and Enggano and of the Mentawai islands off the coast of Sumatra.

As for the larger picture of distribution of prehistoric humans in Southeast Asia, it would appear that Mongoloids and Australoids mingled in the region for a long time. According to Bellwood, because of the lack of major barriers to north-south movements, the population of *Homo sapiens sapiens,* or modern man, "evolved in a pre-existing situation of clinal variation," with predominantly Mongoloid characteristics in the North and Australoid in the South and without a distinct line of separation as such. Eventually, the Mongoloids replaced the Australoid population, which had predominated in Southeast Asia, Papua, and Australia for a long time. The Australoid population survives to this date in Southeast Asia as isolated pockets of Negritos, known as the Semang in Kedah and Perak, the Pangan in Kelantan, and the Aetas in the Philippines. Bellwood, however, warns us:

> We should interpret the idea of replacement with care, by envisaging a complex situation with gene flow between the two already highly varied human races, who may have been part of a single clinal distribution in the first place. It would be naive in the extreme to envisage mass migrations of identical Mongoloid populations swamping and exterminating their Australoid predecessors.[11]

The Hoabinhian Technocomplex

An early stage of the social and economic evolution of societies in Southeast Asia is provided by the Hoabinhian culture, first discovered in North Vietnam but later known to have existed over an extensive area from southern China to northern Sumatra.

The term *Hoabinhian* was first used in 1927 when Madeleine Colani reported on excavations in nine rock shelters in the North Vietnamese province of Hoa-Binh, southwest of Hanoi. Since then, additional limestone rock shelters have been excavated in North Vietnam, central and northern Malaya, Thailand, Cambodia, northern Sumatra, and southern China. Noted for pebble and flake-tool industry, most of these sites have yielded evidence of the beginnings of horticulture, pottery, and edge-grinding of stone tools roughly falling in the pre-Neolithic period, from

13,000 to 4000 B.C. It is suggested that a similar economy and technocomplex may have covered a much larger area in western parts of insular Southeast Asia, which may have been obliterated during the last glaciation, between 14,000 and 7,000 years ago. Some variations in the components of the Hoabinhian techno-complex are seen, for example, in North Vietnam in the more recent excavations in the coastal shell midden at Quynh-Van; there tools are of flaked basalt, and pebble tools and edge-ground tools are missing or absent.

In general, it may be said that the Hoabinhians engaged both on land and at sea in hunting, food-gathering, and fishing. They were the first to practice the art of horticulture in Southeast Asia, though it is not firmly established whether they carried out intentional planting or whether the plants underwent genetic changes from their former wild forms. In the Spirit Cave in northeast Thailand, archaeologists found remains of a variety of edible plants and nuts, including the betel nut, providing perhaps the earliest evidence of the common South and Southeast Asian practice of chewing betel nut. Also in evidence at the site are remains of mammals like cattle, rhinoceroses, pigs, and deer, and coastal and lake sites have varieties of shellfish. No evidence of rice cultivation exists among the Hoabinhians, although the roots of such a practice may lie in the incipient horticulture, particularly closer in time to the Neolithic age. There is also some evidence that the Hoabinhians domesticated pigs. The Hoabinhian sites also testify to contracted or flexed burials, mostly with the pottery of the time.

THE HUMAN FABRIC IN HISTORICAL TIMES

Just as Tibet is the source of the major rivers of mainland Southeast Asia, southern China and eastern Tibet were sources of the region's population. Indeed, some migration southward had been taking place for nearly two millennia before the Chinese political consolidation in the third century B.C. Thus, the Miao, Lolo, and Yao people, who today inhabit the mountainous terrain of North Vietnam, northern Thailand, Hainan, and southern China, may have moved from their habitat in the lower-middle Yangtze River sometime prior to the Han rule in China (202 B.C.–A.D. 220). Chinese records around 110 B.C. indicate the presence of Kadai speakers (Kadai is linguistically related to Thai) dwelling in the areas of Gweichow, Hunan, and Gwangsi, from where they most likely moved to North Vietnam. Such migration was limited in numbers compared with the large-scale exodus from China during the first millennium of the Christian era. It was during the latter period that most of the ancestors of the people of Myanmar, Vietnam, Malaysia, Indonesia, and Thailand migrated, mostly along the course of the rivers to the fertile plains and islands of Southeast Asia.

The largest ethnic element in today's Southeast Asia is the brown-skinned Malay, inhabiting Malaysia, Brunei, Indonesia, and the Philippines. It is believed that the original home of the Malays was southern China, from where they moved southward at two different times. First, the Proto-Malays, having a clearer Mongoloid strain, arrived in Southeast Asia in about 2500 B.C., bringing with them elements of Neolithic culture. They were followed by the Deutero-Malays, who migrated in around 300 B.C. and probably introduced bronze and iron to the area. Ancestors of the bulk of the present population of Malaya and Indonesia, the Deutero-Malays soon acquired control of the coastal districts as they pushed the Proto-Malays into the interior. In the process, very few groups successfully resisted the loss of cultural identity. Such were the ancestors of the Bataks of Sumatra, the Dyaks of Borneo, and the Alfurs of the Celebes and of the Moluccas. The Deutero-Malays spread throughout insular Southeast Asia, diffusing a common culture and a related language.

Closest to the source of migrations was Burma, renamed Myanmar in 1989, which received a variety of ethnic groups from Tibet and southern China. Among dozens of such groups, six stand out significantly because of their numbers and historical roles: the Mons, Shans, Karens, Chins, Kachins, and Burmans. Burmans, from whom the country took its name and who account for three-fourths of its population, are predominant in the lowlands, in urban centers, and in all avenues of public life. Not all the Burmese minorities have easily identifiable separate physical characteristics, yet there are distinct differences in their way of life that have fostered a sense of separatism among them. With the exception of the Mons, the minorities are clustered in the frontier highland states named after them, which under the British administration were called "excluded districts" and placed under special frontier political jurisdiction. Independent Myanmar's efforts, both under civilian and military regimes, to bring about an emotional integration of the country's diverse ethnic groups have not succeeded so far.

There is no agreement among scholars on the chronology of migrations of these ethnic groups into Myanmar. The Mons from southwest China or northeast India and the Karens from eastern Tibet migrated to Myanmar sometime before the beginning of the Christian era. After some period of settlement in the fertile Kyaukse plain of northern Myanmar, the Mons moved southward, occupying Lower Myanmar and the districts east of the Salween River in present-day Thailand; the Karens lived in the mountains separating the two Mon settlements. Next to arrive were the Chins, who probably crossed the lower Himalayan hills into western Myanmar in the early centuries of the first millennium A.D. Their movement into the river valleys was stalled by the pressure of the Burmans, who began filtering in from eastern Tibet and Yunnan around A.D. 500. Two centuries later, the Thai migrations began from Yunnan. One of the directions they took was toward the eastern hills of Myanmar, where they came to be known as the Shans. Last, the Kachins moved into northern Myanmar, where they are still predominant in the hilly province named after them.

A people closely related in language and race to the Mons were the Khmers, whose original home has been a subject of controversy among scholars. They migrated along with their cousins, the Mons, sometime around 2000 B.C., either from southwest China or from the Khasi hills in northeast India. While the Mons followed the course of the Salween into Lower Myanmar and central Thailand, the Khmers moved along the Mekong into Cambodia. Here they mixed with people of Malay stock who already inhabited the area, driving most of them into the highlands. The Khmers eventually spread into the eastern littoral of mainland Southeast Asia, concentrating for the most part in Cambodia and South Vietnam. Over 85 percent of the present Cambodian population claims Khmer ancestry.

T'ai, or Thai, is an ethnic term applicable to diverse peoples in Asia. Presently numbering over 50 million, they are known by different ethnic names in the areas of their settlement: as Lao in Laos and northeast Thailand; Shan in northeast Myanmar; Yunnan Thai in south China; Tribal Thai in North Vietnam; and Thais in Thailand. The Thai movement southward from their original home in south China was slow but steady, covering the period between the eighth and thirteenth centuries of the Christian era. For a considerable time, they occupied the vast plateau extending over eastern Myanmar, northern Thailand, and northern Laos. They filtered along the Salween into the Shan region of Myanmar along the Mae Ping and the Chao Phraya in Thailand and along the Mekong in Laos. Of the various communities that migrated from China to Southeast Asia, only the Thais and the Vietnamese had significant contact with the Chinese civilization before migration.

The Vietnamese were long believed to have migrated from Tibet. More modern theories point to a mixture of many stocks, Mongoloid and non-Mongoloid. According to these hypotheses, an Austro-Indonesian tribe inhabiting the Chinese provinces of Guangdong and Guangxi mixed with the Mongoloid ancestors of the Viets (known to the Chinese as Yueh). The Viets, who migrated into the Red River Delta around the third century B.C., came into contact with the Mongoloid Thai because the latter invaded the Tongking Delta in the eighth century A.D. The mixed heritage of the Vietnamese is certainly responsible for the monotonic Indonesian and the variotonic Mongoloid elements in the Vietnamese language. It also explains why the Vietnamese share a variety of animistic beliefs, which are common to all Austro-Indonesian peoples.

No demographic picture of Southeast Asia would be complete without the mention of the two numerically small but economically important communities: the Indians and the Chinese. Indian minorities are found in every country of the region, most notably in Myanmar, Malaysia, and Singapore, which were, like India, parts of the British empire. Most of them migrated in the nineteenth century as laborers in rubber plantations, rice fields, docks, and government construction projects. Others followed them as traders and moneylenders. Among the region's total population, those of Indian origin account for less than 2 million, whereas the Chinese are seven times the number, forming the preponderant majority in Singapore and an important minority in every other country of Southeast Asia. Chinese migrations date from the second century B.C. in Vietnam but were insignificant in other Southeast Asian countries until the seventeenth century, reaching a peak in the latter half of the nineteenth century. Intelligent and industrious, most of them arrived penniless by sea from the coastal provinces of China. Hence, they are known as "overseas" Chinese. Through a variety of vicissitudes, trials, and tribulations, the Chinese have managed to occupy the highest economic positions in most countries of Southeast Asia.

Tables 1.1 and 1.2 indicate the ethnic distribution in Southeast Asia. Unfortunately, due to the unsettled political conditions in some of these nations, data for both ethnic and total populations may be incorrect. This is particularly so for Cambodia, where an estimated 1 million to 3 million people have died of starvation or were killed during the Pol Pot regime (1975–1978), and for Vietnam, whose population may have been reduced by a million "boat people" leaving Vietnam after 1975 for different shores.

TABLE 1.1 Distribution of Population in Mainland Southeast Asia (in thousands), 2008 (estimate)

	Myanmar 47,749	Cambodia 13,104	Laos 5,279	Thailand 62,806	Vietnam 78,137	Total 207,075
Burmans	32,468					
Thais			1,055	50,244		
Vietnamese		655			65,635	
Montagnards					8,595	
Lao			2,639			
Kha, Meo, etc.			1,583			
Shans	4,297					
Karens	3,342					
Rakhine	1,909					
Chinese	1,432	131		7,536	2,344	
Mons	954					
Indians	954					
Malays				2,512		
Khmers		11,793		1,884	781	
Chams		500				
Tay					781	
Others	2,387			628		

TABLE 1.2 Distribution of Population in Insular Southeast Asia (in thousands), 2008 (estimate)

	Malaysia 22,218	Singapore 4,018	Brunei 328	Indonesia 212,092	Philippines 75,653	East Timor 750	Total 315,059
Javanese				84,000			
Sundanese				31,800			
Bahasa Indo				25,400			
Madurese				10,600			
Tagalogs					22,695		
Cebuanese					18,156		
Bocano					7,565		
Hiligaynon Hongo					6,808		
Bicol					4,539		
Samar-Leyte					3,026		
Malays	13,775	566	219				
Chinese	6,221	3,093	51			17	
Indians	1,999	281					
Timorese						663	
Indonesians						70	
Caucasians		40					
Others			37	59,360	12,864		

Total Population of Southeast Asia: 522,134,000 (2008 estimate)

Based on: World Health Organization, *Reports*, United Nations *Demographic Yearbooks*, and *Statesman's Yearbooks*.

THE CULTURAL CONTEXT

Prehistoric Culture

There is no doubt that before the Indian cultural influence became widespread, Southeast Asia had fostered an indigenous culture. To be sure, it was not homogeneous, nor was it evenly spread. Yet certain common characteristics linked the peoples who developed a culture in the mainland deltas and those in the fertile, low-lying plains of Java. Long before the historical era, they had built up a society and organization of their own, based on irrigated cultivation, sharing the benefits and problems common to the inhabitants of monsoon Asia.

A good example of the level these societies attained before the influence of Indian and Chinese cultures is provided by the Dong-son civilization, discovered in the village of that name in the Tongking Delta. This bronze-using civilization, evidenced by their bronze drums as well as axes, knives, and plates of armor, spread not only along the Vietnamese coastline but as far away as Malaya and the Flores in the Moluccas. Dating around 300 B.C.,[12] the Dong-son people were excellent farmers who had developed irrigation and who knew the ox, buffalo, pig, and dog. Notably, they were seafarers who built canoes and guided their navigational movements with some knowledge of astronomy. Their trading contacts with the outside world must have brought them the knowledge of metallurgy. The earlier theory that bronze was introduced by China (where iron was not used until the third century B.C.) and that the use of iron came with later Indian traders and settlers must now be laid to rest.[13] As for religion, the art of Dong-son demonstrates the people's practice of ancestor worship and animism. Gods were related to agriculture; temples were built on hills or elevated platforms. The ashes of the dead were buried in jars or in megalithic dolmens, although the people seemed to believe that the dead "sailed away" to some place in the direction of the sinking sun. There was also an elaborate cosmologically oriented mythology in which the dualistic elements of mountain and sea, winged beings and water beings, and mountain dwellers and plains people provided the core themes. According to the Dutch scholar N. J. Krom, before the Javanese had contact with India, they had developed three of the well-known aspects of Indonesian cultural life: the wayang, or shadow puppet theater, the gamelan orchestra, and batik work in textiles.

Sino-Indian Influences

It is on such an indigenous substratum that the later cultural superstructure, based on Indian and Chinese influences, was erected in many parts of Southeast Asia. Yet because of the earlier separate development, the indigenous cultures never lost their identity, even as they developed similarities derived from their common borrowings, mostly Indian. Large-scale penetration by Indian and Chinese cultures began around the commencement of the Christian era, two or three centuries after the first major political consolidations in those countries in the third century B.C.—China under Shi Huang Di and India under Ashoka Maurya.

Succeeding centuries saw the gradual spread of the Indian cultural and commercial domain in Southeast Asia, except in the Tongking Delta. Here, Chinese

MAP 1.2 Southeast Asia: Principal Crops and Minerals

cultural and political dominance was evident. The Sino-Indian cultural demarcation was noted by a French scholar-diplomat, Reginald Le May:

> On the map of Asia, there is a range of mountains running down the spine of Annam, and this range marks the boundary or dividing line between Chinese and Indian culture. Everything North and East of this range is culturally based on China, while everything West and South is based on India, and the two neither overlap nor clash.[14]

China succeeded in having a major effect on all of Southeast Asia in the political sphere. Beginning with the Han dynasty (202 B.C.–A.D. 220), the Chinese empire bordered Southeast Asia, whose rulers recognized China's political superiority by sending periodic tribute as a mark of vassalage. Throughout most of China's history, its rulers followed a policy of keeping the peoples on the periphery of the empire in a weak and fragmented state. In general, periods of political consolidation, stability, and strength in China coincided with periods of active intervention in and political subordination of most of the states of Southeast Asia. Conversely, there was a greater measure of autonomy and independence in Southeast Asian states when the central authority in China was questioned by the Chinese people. China required its vassals to send periodic, usually triennial, tribute to the emperor, who reciprocated with gifts of a larger value. China regarded the tribute as a symbol of political subordination and a possible channel for cultural Sinicization of the "barbarians." The delegation carrying the tribute often consisted of a caravan of merchants, whom China offered hospitality and facilities for trading along the long and arduous route to the emperor's court. The tributary system, which China enforced for long periods of time until the end of the twentieth century, assured the imperial power of its paramount position while offering some economic benefits and military protection for the vassals.

Southeast Asia did not become a cultural battlefield between China and India. In the field of religion, for instance, there was no rivalry between the two great Asian peoples to save souls in Southeast Asia. On the contrary, the Chinese adopted Buddhism, which was introduced from India by way of central Asia at the court of the eastern Han emperor in the first century A.D. Throughout the first millennium, scholars and pilgrims from China as well as Southeast Asia visited places of worship and scholarship in India. Many Chinese scholars and pilgrims stopped halfway in Borneo or Sumatra to learn Sanskrit and Pali before proceeding to India for advanced study. Both China and Southeast Asia were areas of Indian religious influence in this period.

Apart from religion, however, there were many aspects of the rich Chinese culture that the Southeast Asians could have adopted. But with the exception of the Vietnamese, most of Southeast Asia followed the Indian cultural patterns. The absorptive, syncretic quality of Indian culture, itself enriched by numerous strands imported by series of invaders of the Indian subcontinent, succeeded in striking roots in the Southeast Asian region, which adopted the alien cultural traits without losing its identity in the process. The relative acceptability of Indian culture may be further attributed to geographical commonness, relative lack of Indian political ambition in the region, and the state of commerce between India and Southeast Asia. At the same time, it should be noted that the exact beginnings of the Indian culture in Southeast Asia, the agency of its transmission, and the administrative mechanism of its implantation or implementation are still matters of scholarly speculation. As Ian W. Mabbett has pointed out, the process of Indianization "is nowhere reliably portrayed; what is portrayed by the earliest evidence is the operation of kingdoms already Indianized."[15]

Geographically, India and Southeast Asia share the tropical monsoon climate, with all its implications for a way of life based on irrigated agriculture. In India, in the second millennium B.C., the immigrant Aryans had adopted some of the cultural traits of the pre-Aryan society. When Aryanized Indians migrated to Southeast Asia in the first millennium A.D., the people there discovered among the Indian immigrants a similar cultural base, a shared substratum, some of whose traits were pre-Aryan and common to all peoples of monsoon Asia.[16] In addition, apart from the solitary instance of invasion of the Srivijaya kingdom in Sumatra by the Indian king, Rajendra Chola, in the eleventh century A.D., India did not show any political ambitions or expansionist tendency in neighboring Southeast Asia. Indian culture was welcome in Southeast Asia because it came without political strings. Finally, it should be noted that commerce has been an important carrier of culture throughout history. In Southeast Asia, diverse maritime peoples of the region—the Mons, the Funanese, the Chams, the Javanese, the Sumatrans, the Bugis, and others—participated in the lucrative trade among China, India, and the Western world. Traditional Chinese wariness about the sea left maritime trade largely to Indians at first and, later, to the Arabs, Persians, and Southeast Asians themselves. The overwhelming Indian participation in east-west trade brought large numbers of Indian seafarers and merchants to Southeast Asia, where the rulers were also the principal traders. Commercial contacts with the Indians must have developed in the Southeast Asian ruling elite an interest in the Indian culture.

However, the large-scale acculturation of the Southeast Asian elite on the Indian pattern could not have been the work of Indian traders, who belonged to the Vaishya class, or of sailors, who came from the Shudra group. Indeed, the prime agents of the process of Indianization were the Brahmans, the priestly class, who had monopolized knowledge of the sacred lore, the rites and rituals, and customs and laws. The initiative for the Indianizing process in Southeast Asia most certainly came from the region's ruling classes, who invited Brahmans to serve at their courts as priests, astrologers, and advisers. The Indian priesthood was used "for the magical, sacred legitimation of dynastic interests and the domestication of subjects, and probably for the organization of the ruler's territory into a state."[17] The Brahmans introduced Indian court customs and ensured their proper observance. They also underlined the divine nature of monarchy through a variety of ritual sacrifices and ceremonies, thereby enhancing the prestige and power of the Southeast Asian rulers in the eyes of their subjects. The Brahmans also promoted administrative organization on the Indian pattern and introduced laws based on the Code of Manu, the Indian lawgiver. The process of Indianization also included the alphabetical basis (except for Vietnam) of the Southeast Asian scripts; importance of Sanskrit in the vocabulary; introduction of the Indian epics *Ramayana* and *Mahabharata* and works on a variety of subjects like philosophy, astrology, medicine, mathematics, and the arts; and finally, the religious lore—Brahmanic, Buddhistic, or a combination of both.

Religions and Their Role

As previously noted, at least four different religions have sizable numbers of adherents in Southeast Asia. Thus, Malaysia and Indonesia (except Bali, which follows Hinduism), Brunei, and southern Philippines are overwhelmingly Muslim; Myanmar, Laos, Cambodia, and Thailand follow Theravada Buddhism and have more cultural borrowings from Indian influences than does Vietnam, which is culturally Chinese-oriented and mostly follows Mahayana Buddhism; and the Philippines is predominantly Catholic, except in the south. A short introduction on the origins of Buddhism, Hinduism, and Islam and the timing of their dissemination in Southeast Asia is useful for an appreciation of the historical developments in the region.

Buddhism. Buddhism was founded in India in the sixth century B.C. When its founder, Gautama, was born in a royal family, it was predicted that he would become either a universal king or, if he saw misery, a universal teacher. His father trained Gautama to be a great prince and kept him away from miseries. Despite such precautions, Gautama experienced four "sights": an old man, a sick man, a corpse—all representations of pain and misery—but the fourth "sight" was an ascetic, calm and serene. Gautama left his home, wife, and son and repaired to the forests, where after years of fasting, study, and meditation, he had "enlightenment." He became a Buddha, or the Enlightened.

The Four Noble Truths of Buddhism state that existence is pain. Craving for delights and passions leads to rebirth and, therefore, is the cause of pain. It is essential to end the pain. This can be done through the Noble Eightfold Path of an ethical life in thought and deed. A person would then end the cycle of birth and death and attain Nirvana.

Buddhism was a religion of equality. It did not recognize idolatry or the fourfold class system of Hinduism. It had no church. Its affairs were managed democratically by a body of *bhikus* (monks). Among its influential converts in the third century B.C. was King Ashoka of India, who sent emissaries to distant countries, including Myanmar and Sri Lanka, to spread the message of Buddhism.

By the first century A.D., a major schism had divided the Buddhist faith into the Mahayana (greater vehicle, or conveyance to salvation) and Theravada (lesser vehicle). The principal difference between the two sects hinged on the Mahayana concept of *bodhisattva* (Buddha in the becoming), according to which a meritorious person could "save" others. Such great souls would be reborn in a higher order until they attain Nirvana, or the state of Buddha. *Bodhisattvas* could be worshiped and temples built for them. The Mahayana faith naturally appealed to the kings, nobility, scholars, and the elite because they could appear superior to others by virtue of the extra merit they earned through good works toward others. Mahayana used Sanskrit, whereas Theravada used the languages of the masses, including Pali and Magadhi in India. Mahayana employed pomp and pageantry and imagery in sculptured panels around the temples; Theravada had only images of Buddha in simpler religious edifices. Mahayana followers could save themselves as well as others through good meritorious deeds; Theravada followers believed that each individual had to work for personal salvation and that all human beings were equal. Beginning in the second century A.D., the Mahayana faith spread to China and then to Korea, Japan, and Vietnam. By the end of the first millennium, Buddhism was completely overwhelmed by resurgent Hinduism within India. Only pockets of Buddhism remained on the Indian subcontinent, although Theravada Buddhism flourished in Sri Lanka and Lower Myanmar.

Along with Hinduism, Buddhism—Mahayana and Theravada—spread from India to Funan, Angkor, Sumatra, and Java in the first millennium. However, after the eleventh-century conversion of a Burmese monarch, Anawratha, to Theravada, the latter spread rapidly in mainland Southeast Asia and became the dominant faith of the people of Myanmar, Thailand, Laos, and Cambodia, whereas most of the Vietnamese followed a modified form of Mahayana Buddhism.

Hinduism. Hinduism evolved in India over centuries of development of religious life and thought. It began with the four Vedas (books of knowledge) and the commentaries thereon dated between 1500 B.C. and 500 B.C. Despite the multiplicity of gods, there is a monotheistic strain in its belief in the Supreme Being, Brahma (the Creator), and its twin manifestations, Vishnu (the Preserver) and Shiva (the Destroyer), together forming the Trinity. Its cosmology includes the sacrifice of the primeval being from whose limbs sprang the four *varnas* (classes): the Brahmans (priests, scholars, astrologers) from the mouth; the Kshatriyas (warriors) from the arms; the Vaishyas (traders) from the thighs; and the Shudras (menials) from the feet. Around the eighth century B.C., the classes became somewhat rigid, and the religion came to be controlled by Brahmans, who emphasized sacrifice and its attendant rituals at which they officiated as being essential to maintain the *rita* (world order). Around the sixth to fifth century B.C., a number of philosophical treatises—the Upanishads—raised fundamental questions of the meaning of life and death, the microworld of the soul (Atman), and the macrocosmos of the world spirit (Brahman). The Ultimate Reality involved the blending of the Atman and the Brahman.

Central to the evolving Hinduism were the doctrine of the transmigration of souls and the doctrine of karma, the fundamental law of cause and effect by which one's deeds in the present birth are rewarded or punished in the next birth, which may correspondingly be in happier or unhappier conditions. Karma did not exclude free will, since one's karma could be improved upon through a life based on ethical values and the pursuit of knowledge, meditation, or devotion to God. Such a life could also be the "path" to destroy the cycle of births, deaths, and rebirths and thus to attain *moksha* (salvation).

Around the beginning of the Christian era, when India's contacts with Southeast Asia increased, the Hindu social system had rigidified in terms of its four *varnas* and had evolved further into microfunctional groups of castes and subcastes. The place of women in society had slipped, and a fifth class, the Untouchables, largely involving "unclean" occupations, such as disposal of carcasses, tanning, and scavenging, had emerged.

The Hindu society, overwhelmingly the Brahmans, produced a prolific and profound literature in many genres, including epic stories, systems of philosophy, and theoretical treatises on fine arts and music. Among the peak periods of Hindu cultural efflorescence and its spread in Southeast Asia was the Gupta period (A.D. 320–550).

Islam. The founder of Islam, Mohammed, was born in Mecca, Arabia, in A.D. 570. He had divine revelations while leading trading caravans in the desert. His preachings infuriated influential people in Mecca, leading to Mohammed's *hegira* (flight) to Medina in 622, a date that marks the commencement of the Islamic era. Eight years later, Mohammed returned to Mecca at the head of his armed believers. In 632, two years after he had made Mecca headquarters of his religion, Mohammed died.

The religion Mohammed preached was simple and easy to follow. The Five Pillars of Islam required profession of faith in Allah (Arabic name of God) and Mohammed as the only prophet; prayers five times a day; the giving of alms; fasting during the month of Ramadan (no eating or drinking between sunrise and sunset); and the making of a pilgrimage to Mecca at least once in a lifetime. Islam preached brotherhood of all believers and equality of men before God, irrespective of color, race, or class (but not gender). There were specific injunctions against the use of intoxicants and the consumption of pork. By 651, the series of divine revelations made to the Prophet were compiled in the *Koran*. The book has remained ever since the ultimate authority in political, economic, legal, and ethical matters of Muslims.

Mohammed maintained that God had finally and completely revealed Himself only to him. Christianity and Judaism were partial revelations; as such, their followers should be tolerated as "people of the book." Others were termed infidels, to be put to death if they refused to convert to Islam. Mohammed's inspiration led hordes of Arabs out of their homeland "with Koran in one hand and sword in the other" to reduce *dar-ul-harb* (country at war) to *dar-ul-Islam* all over the Middle East, North Africa, and the Iberian Peninsula within a century of Islam's birth.

Islam had no priests or formal church hierarchy. The Prophet was succeeded by a caliph, who was both the spiritual and temporal head of the Muslim community. The followers of Islam were divided between two sects—the Shia, who believed caliphs had to be blood relatives of the Prophet, and the Sunni, who did not. The Sunnis followed four different schools of law: the Hanafi, Maliki, Shafi'i, and Hanbali, named after prominent Islamic scholars in jurisprudence and theology. The Shafi'i school was most dominant among Southeast Asian Muslims. From the twelfth century on, a new sect called the Sufis developed. They were mystics, who believed salvation could be attained through personal devotion to God. Sufi missionaries came closest to Indian spiritual approaches and were instrumental in bringing about large-scale conversions in India and Southeast Asia from the thirteenth century. Islam spread even faster in the fifteenth and sixteenth centuries in large portions of insular Southeast Asia. Today, it is the dominant religion of the people of Malaysia, Brunei, Indonesia, and the southern Philippines.

2

Early Kingdoms in Mainland Southeast Asia

FACTORS HELPING STATE FORMATION

Among the several factors responsible for the rise of principalities and kingdoms in early Southeast Asia, agriculture and maritime trade must be deemed the most important. Clusters of population and political power arose where agricultural surpluses, contributing to trade, could be built up. The vagaries of the monsoons and the physical characteristics of the land provided a challenge to people's ingenuity and skill in organizing water control and soil conservation. Where this was achieved, agriculture prospered, as in the silt-rich deltas in mainland Southeast Asia, the plains of central Myanmar, the region around Tonle Sap Lake in Cambodia, and the central and eastern parts of Java. The relationship between agricultural prosperity and the rise of states in these areas is obvious. On the other hand, certain principalities, whose main source of revenue was trade, sprang up in relatively infertile areas of southeast Sumatra and coastal Malaya. Their asset was their location on the India-China trade route. Among the many locations where early states emerged, the greatest advantage accrued to the delta regions of Southeast Asia, where a combination of fertile soil and proximity to the sea helped both agriculture and commerce.

The importance of trade as a factor was derived from the strategic location of the Southeast Asian realm.[1] Navigation in the region was governed by the monsoons. The southwest monsoon prevailed from May to early October; the northeast monsoon between November and March. Ships from India and the western countries sailed to Southeast Asia by the southwest monsoon and halted there until the northeast monsoon would make their return journey easy. In the same fashion, ships from the east of the Malay Peninsula and beyond would take advantage of the northeast monsoon for their westward journey. From about the seventh century, the Strait of Malacca as well as the Sunda Strait became the most popular routes. Earlier, both straits were considered unsafe because of piracy; the longer distance involved in the use of the Sunda Strait made that route uneconomic as well. Shippers and traders instead favored the narrow neck of the Malay Peninsula, which provided many portage routes across the Isthmus of Kra. Goods could be unloaded on its western side and carried overland to ships waiting on the eastern side.

The earliest kingdoms known to have existed in Southeast Asia were of the Malay people, who profited as intermediaries in the east-west and Sino-Indian trade. Many small states came into being along the Malay Peninsula, some of them established by Indian adventurers, others by indigenous Malays with Indian encouragement and guidance. Two of the most notable kingdoms arose in the southern part of the Gulf of Thailand: the kingdom of Langasuka with its capital at Patani and a little northeast of it, and the kingdom of Tambralinga in the Ligor-Sri Thammarat area. The prosperity of these kingdoms was short-lived. Although strategically important for navigation and commerce, the region's infertile soil could not sustain a large population. Larger and more powerful prosperous kingdoms—Funan and Champa—therefore grew up elsewhere on the eastern littoral of the Indo-Chinese peninsula.

FUNAN

Funan and Champa were Hindu kingdoms. The Funanese were probably earlier arrivals of the Mon-Khmer people, speaking an Austro-Asiatic language, while the Chams belonged to the Malay race and used a language of Indonesian origin. Funan is a Chinese form of an old Khmer word, *bnam* (modern Khmer *phnom*), meaning mountain. Our information about early Funan is derived from two sources, both belonging to the third century: a Sanskrit inscription discovered near Nha Trang in South Vietnam and fragments of an account left by two Chinese envoys to Funan, K'ang T'ai and Chu Ying.

The foundation of Funan is ascribed to an Indian Brahman, Kaundinya, who in the first century, following instructions in a dream, picked a magic bow from a temple, embarked on a merchant vessel, and reached Funan. There he defeated the local queen, Soma, daughter of the king of the Nagas (cobras), married her, and began a royal line. This legend of the mystical union between the Brahman and the serpent, giving the dynasty a dual legitimacy of Indian origin as well as roots in the popular indigenous mythology in which belief in earth, water, and snakes was important, was adopted by several Southeast Asian kingdoms, including Champa, Angkor, and Kedah, to name only a few. The cobra was regarded the lord of the earth and therefore commanded reverence from agricultural people. The Indian Brahmans continued to be held in high esteem. According to Chinese sources, a second Kaundinya, this time from the nearby Isthmus of Kra, was welcomed in the fourth century by the Funanese, who chose him as their king, whereupon he proceeded to modify their laws to conform with the usage in India.[2]

Funan soon surpassed every other state in the area. With its capital at Vyadhapura (near the present Cambodian capital of Phnom Penh), it extended under its greatest ruler, Fan Shih-man (early third century), to South Vietnam, Cambodia, central Thailand, northern Malaya, and southern Myanmar. Vyadhapura and nearby Angkor remained the most important political focal points in the history of Southeast Asia for the first twelve to thirteen centuries of the Christian era. With a great fleet at its command and a fairly firm control over the sea-lanes, Funan emerged as the most important maritime intermediary in the Sino-Indian trade. Fan Shih-man promoted shipbuilding, navigation, and foreign trade. During his successor's reign, the first embassies were sent to India and China. These missions were reciprocated; K'ang T'ai, who left a valuable account of Funan, was a Chinese envoy to that country in the middle of the third century. There is no doubt that the Funanese kings exploited the strategic position of their empire to build a commercial monopoly, setting a model for the later Srivijaya, Sailendra, and Malacca rulers to follow. Their reign, however, weighed lightly on the subject peoples in distant parts of the realm so long as they did not challenge or obstruct Funan's predominant role in commerce. It is very likely that the Funanese monarchs adopted the quasi-feudal pattern of an Indian *maharajadhiraja* (king of kings) to whom the vassals paid homage.

The tendency of the vassal states to emulate the court and customs of their overlord must have resulted, to a certain extent, in the development of a common culture. Funan's adoption of Sanskrit as the court language and its encouragement to Hinduism and, after the fifth century, to Buddhism as well aided the process of Indianization of the whole area. According to K'ang T'ai, the principal cities in Funan were walled with brick, unlike the less prosperous ones in the Malay isthmus area, which had wooden barriers. The people in Funan were barbarian, "ugly, black, frizzy-haired," and moved about naked and bare-footed. They knew agriculture and metalworking. Taxes were paid in silver, gold, pearls, and perfumed wood. Slavery existed. The gap between the court and the elite on the one hand and the common people on the other was wide. The king lived in a multistoried palace, while his subjects lived in thatched houses built on piles. Justice was rendered through trial by ordeal, which involved such practices as carrying a red-hot iron chain in hand and retrieving gold rings and eggs from boiling water.

K'ang T'ai's account was grossly prejudiced and unfair to the Funanese, who were a highly cultured people. Chinese court annals mention a group of musicians from Funan visiting China as part of an official delegation in A.D. 263. Their performance was of such a high quality that the Chinese emperor ordered the establishment of an institute for Funanese music near Nanking. As K'ang T'ai himself reported, the Funanese had books and archives. How could such people be described as "barbarians"?

Funan's relations with China did not always remain friendly. In 270 they were strained because Funan joined neighboring Champa in attacking Tongking, at the time a province of the Chinese empire. Commercial relations were resumed in 280. Later, in 357 Funan established a tributary relationship with China that continued until the fall of Funan in the middle of the sixth century.

CHAMPA

Champa, or Lin-yi in Chinese records, was the Sanskrit name of a kingdom in Southeast Asia, contemporaneous with Funan. Early Chinese records refer to the rebellion in 192 of a local official, Kiu-lien, who overthrew the Chinese authority and established the independent kingdom of Lin-yi near the present city of Hue.

Champa included the present provinces of Quang Nam, Quang Tin, Binh Dinh, Nha Trang, Phan Rang, and Binh Tuan. The history of the relationship between China and Champa was one of alternating hostility and subservience on Champa's part. With the reconsolidation of China under the Tsin dynasty, Champa sent the first embassy to the Chinese emperor's court in 283. But whenever the Chinese authority in Tongking slackened, the Chams seized the opportunity and raided the northern province.

Champa came under Indian influence later than Funan, around the middle of the fourth century, when Champa absorbed the Funanese province of Panduranga (modern Phan Rang). Tall towers of kilned brick in Phan Rang, Nha Trang, Qui Nhon, Quang Tri, and Da Nang are surviving vestiges of the once-powerful Cham kingdom. Champa's expansion southward in the areas previously controlled by Funan may have introduced the Chams to Indian culture, which they embraced enthusiastically. The kings of Champa assumed the Pallava style, their names ending with -varman, as in Bhadravarman, who built the first temple of the Hindu god Shiva. The famous Cham archaeological sites of Tra Kieu, Mison, and Dong Duong in the Quang Nam province indicate profound Pallava impact of the Amravati school of art. The Chams withstood for more than a thousand years the political and cultural pressures of China and Vietnam.

Despite the fact that the kingdom was divided into several units separated from each other by mountains, the Chams rallied dozens of times in defense of freedom against attacks by the Chinese, the Vietnamese, the Khmers, and later the Mongols. In such conflicts, Champa's mountainous terrain and easy access to the sea provided considerable scope for military maneuvers. The Chams at last suffered a severe defeat at the hands of the Vietnamese in 1471, which restricted them to the small area south of Cap Varella around Nha Trang. More than 60,000 Chams were killed and about half that number carried into captivity. The remnant state lingered until 1720, when it was finally absorbed by the Vietnamese, with the last Cham king and a large number of his subjects fleeing into Cambodia.

The Cham society was and is matriarchal, with daughters having the right of inheritance. Following the Hindu tradition, Chams cremated their dead, collected the ashes in an urn, and cast them into the waters. Their way of life resembled that of the Funanese. Men and women wrapped a length of cloth around their waists and mostly went barefoot. Their weapons included bows, arrows, sabers, lances, and crossbows of bamboo. Their musical instruments included the flute, drums, conches, and stringed instruments. Today about 40,000 South Vietnamese and about 85,000 Cambodians claim Cham ancestry.

THE KHMER EMPIRE

Rise of the Khmers

The people who supplanted the Funanese supremacy were the Khmers, ethnically related to the Mons of Lower Myanmar. It is not certain whether they were an altogether new ethnic group or later arrivals of the same stock to which the Funanese belonged. They called themselves the Khmers, descendants of their mythical ancestors, the wise hermit Kambu and the celestial nymph Mera. The kingdom was

MAP 2.1 Southeast Asia About A.D. 800

called Kambuja. Their ancestral home was southwest China or northeast India. While the Mons followed the Salween-Sittang river route into Myanmar, the Khmers moved eastward along the Mekong into southern Laos and the Korat Plateau in Thailand. Here the Khmers established the state of Chenla, which became a vassal of the Funanese empire. Their new habitat was mountainous, unsuited for intensive agriculture; a drive southward toward the Mekong Delta was inevitable. By the middle of the seventh century, the restive Khmers had overthrown the Funanese overlordship. However, conquest did not bring major cultural changes because the Khmers had already assimilated Indian culture both from their Mon kinsmen to the west and from their Funanese superiors to the south.

With the conquest of Funan, the Khmers became the political successors of the Funanese, extending their authority over Lower Myanmar, the upper Malay Peninsula, central Thailand, Cambodia, and South Vietnam. They were incapable, however, of carrying on the Funanese legacy of the greatest maritime and commercial power in all Southeast Asia. Being land-oriented, the Chenla Khmers were ill-equipped for their important role as intermediaries in the large-scale seaborne trade between China, India, and the West. Besides, they were divided among themselves. In 706, their kingdom was split into Upper (Land) Chenla, situated in the middle of the Mekong Valley north of the Dangrek mountain range, and Lower (Water) Chenla, covering the present Cambodia and the Mekong Delta of South Vietnam. The fragmented and disunited Khmers became exposed to threats of military and political subjugation from outside. The threat became a reality when an insular power attacked Chenla in the last decade of the eighth century.

Two different kingdoms in insular Southeast Asia attempted to exploit the situation for political and commercial benefits. The China trade, always lucrative, had increased many times over during the T'ang dynasty. The vision of subduing small trading kingdoms in mainland Southeast Asia, formerly under the Funanese sway, and incorporating them in an extended empire was intoxicating to the rulers of the islands. The rival powers were the Sumatran kingdom of Srivijaya and the Sailendra rulers of Java. Like the Funanese monarchs, the Sailendras had styled themselves "the kings of the mountain." It was no wonder then that they vied to succeed to the symbolic role and substantial maritime and trading power that the Funanese had once enjoyed. Sailendras were the first group in Southeast Asian history to aspire to bring the insular and mainland territories under a common control. According to a tenth-century Arab traveler-writer, Sulayman, a Chenla king expressed the desire to have the head of a Javanese king brought before him on a dish. News of this reached the Sailendra king of Java, who in 790, under the pretext of a pleasure cruise, armed his fleet, invaded Lower Chenla, killed its king, appointed a successor to the throne, embalmed the decapitated head, placed it in an urn, and sent it to the king of Upper Chenla.

The Sailendra attacks and bid for power on mainland Southeast Asia acted as a catalyst to Khmer unity. The divided Khmers rallied under the leadership of a remarkable young man, Jayavarman II, who had spent some time at the Sailendra court as a hostage. He expelled the Sailendras and brought the dissident Khmer groups together in a common polity. Jayavarman's long reign (802–850) helped to consolidate these early gains and lent a solid foundation to the Khmer kingdom. There were several innovations: Jayavarman shifted the focus of Khmer activity from the Mekong Delta to the region around Tonle Sap Lake in western Cambodia; and with control over the passes leading to Korat Plateau and the Menam Basin, he opened prospects for further expansion westward and northward. For the next five centuries, Angkor and its environs represented the base of Khmer power and glory.

The Devaraja Cult

An even more important decision of Jayavarman II was to revive the Devaraja (god-king) cult of Indian origin, intended to legitimize and bolster his authority over all the dissident groups among the Khmer people.[3] At his capital, Mount Mahendra (modern Koulen in western Cambodia), he invited an Indian Brahman to perform an elaborate ritual, which allegedly infused into the royal person the divine essence of kingship, making him in effect a manifestation of Shiva. On top of the mountain stood numerous temples, the principal one being a pyramidal structure housing Shiva's phallic symbol, the *linga*. On the death of the king, the temple would serve as the funerary site, enabling the deceased to be one with Shiva himself. The mountain temple was, like Mount Meru of the Hindu sacred tradition, regarded as the center of the universe. The king was styled *chakravartin* (ruler of the universe).

Closely linked with the Devaraja cult was the concept of the universe. The plan of the royal capital at Angkor reflected the world structure according to the Hindu cosmology. The capital was surrounded by a wall and a moat, just as the universe was believed to be encircled by rock and ocean. Exactly at the middle point of the capital city stood the pyramidal temple, representing the sacred mountain, with the *linga* at the center. The edifice was a symbol of the union between king and God, establishing harmony between the microcosmos of the human world and the macrocosmos of the divine world. Such an identity was believed to assure the prosperity of the kingdom and its people. In practical terms, to ensure against the vagaries of nature, the king took pains to regulate the water supply through control of the elaborate hydraulic system on Tonle Sap Lake.

All this should not be taken to mean that the Khmer monarchs were exclusively followers of Shiva. In Southeast Asia in general and in the Khmer kingdom in particular, there was no conflict of loyalties in the minds of the devotees, who worshipped Shiva, Vishnu, and Buddha in the same shrine complex. Thus, in Angkor, the kings were portrayed through statuary as *avatars* (reincarnations of Shiva or Vishnu) or, as in the most famous of all the Khmer temples, the Bayon, as *bodhisattva* (Buddha in the becoming). Existing knowledge is insufficient to explain the exact religious beliefs of the Khmers. It is possible that they did not comprehend the finer points of evolving Hinduism in India or did not want to, instead seeking extra spiritual insurance through the pursuit of Hindu, Buddhist, and indigenous beliefs.

The Basis of Khmer Power

Khmer power was centered on the king, who was the divine source of all authority. He was the upholder of the established order, the defender of the faith, and the patron of the myriad religious foundations. The Khmer kings divided the society into numerous classes and corporations according to occupation. The monarchs held absolute control over social organization by virtue of their ritual position; they were social engineers who could and did appoint favored individuals to privileged social orders.[4] Important state offices were held by members of the royal family. The inscriptions of the time reveal a whole hierarchy of officials, indicative of a fairly centralized and well-organized bureaucracy. Although this was true of the Angkor kingdom, the outlying provinces were at best held by loose feudal ties, more or less on the Chinese pattern of tributary states.

Apart from the royal family and high nobility, the only other group that shared power seems to have been the priestly class. Descended from families originally imported from India, the group was periodically replenished by arrivals from the same source. These were Brahmans, who intermarried with the high nobility or Kshatriya group and formed an elite class, which largely followed a Sanskrit culture. Their rank was determined by the gold or silver shafts of the palanquin poles or the gold or silver handles of the parasols of different colors; only the king could have the white umbrella, symbolic of sovereignty, held over his head.

The economic basis of the Khmer power must have been agriculture in the rich Tonle Sap Lake region, tribute from numerous vassal states, and participation in the east-west trade. It may be assumed that the Khmers shared with insular states the extensive, international trade once carried on by their predecessor state, Funan. There is no conclusive evidence of this, although Khmer records have spotty references to Indian and Chinese textiles and other imported products.

KHMER HYDRAULIC SYSTEM

Agriculture, therefore, must have been the most important pillar of the kingdom's prosperity. The well-planned irrigation system, which exploited Tonle Sap Lake and brought large land areas under intensive cultivation, was crucial to Khmer economic well-being and power. The Khmer kings must have had an army of engineers and supervisory staff to build and maintain this magnificent hydraulic system.[5] With the help of aerial photography, Bernard Philippe Groslier established details of this sophisticated system of water utilization. According to him, it was based on Funanese antecedents, designed "to solve the problem posed by too much and too heavy monsoon rain within too short a time." Immense storage tanks, or *barays,* were constructed, one of them with a capacity of 30 million cubic meters, equipped with an ingenious device for letting off the water according to the need. Some 12.5 million acres of land were covered, carefully divided into square paddy fields and capable of yielding three or four harvests a year.[6]

Groslier's thesis became the subject of a vigorous debate in the past thirty years, triggered by W. J. van Liere in 1980,[7] who asserted that the management of water in Angkor was "either not necessary for irrigation nor did it have the characteristics required to be an irrigation system."[8] As Roland Fletcher pointed out, "the issue polarized . . . into an English-speaking non-utilitarian ritual posture and a 'French' supposedly utilitarian, hydraulic civilization."[9] This was a serious challenge to Groslier and the understanding at the time of the Khmer empire and the basis of Khmer power in the capital of Angkor and the rest of its empire extending over most of mainland Southeast Asia for several centuries.

The meticulous work done by C. Pottier[10] and Eileen Lustig[11] has not only demolished the anti-Groslier writing but has furnished an extensive empirical, archaeological basis for Groslier's work. The Greater Angkor Project has located the inlets and outlets of the *barays* and excavated an over 100-feet-wide "masonry spillway" at Bam Pen Reach in northern Angkor. In Lustig's view, the hydraulic network was not created for yield intensification but for risk mitigation. In other words, the Khmer kings managed through the critical component of the hydraulic system an assured crop to avert a famine and guarantee the kingdom's stability. To quote Fletcher, "A small, secure yield from irrigation" was crucial "to avoid the risk of crop losses in a year with a low monsoon rainfall. The Angkor network sufficed to make up the liable shortfall."[12]

The intricately designed network of canals, dams, and dikes prevented overflow of Tonle Sap Lake, protected the soil from erosion, and provided means for travel. Linked with moats of the cities, the waterways enabled transportation of materials from the quarries to the sites of the monuments. The hydraulic system thus constituted the lifeline of the Khmer economy.

Khmer greatness and glory were based on territorial conquest and commemorated in monuments. Yasovarman I, who reigned 889–900, founded the first city of Angkor, built the great reservoir at the present eastern Baray, and erected a number of temple hermitages for devotees of Shiva, Vishnu, and Buddha. Suryavarman I (1002–1050) extended the Khmer power in the Menam Valley, establishing religious foundations and making large grants of land to them so they could undertake major irrigation works to raise production and revenues for building monasteries. Suryavarman II's (1113–1150) building of the Vishnu temple at Angkor Wat marked the high point of the Angkor civilization. He conquered and occupied Champa for two decades. During his reign, the Khmer empire extended from the frontiers of Myanmar to the south of the Red River Delta. But the greatest builder of them all was Jayavarman VII (1181–1219), who constructed a new capital city, Angkor Thom, with its famous Buddhist temple, the Bayon. The statue of the *bodhisattva* Lokeswara in this temple resembles the king himself. The main temple is surrounded by numerous smaller edifices adorned with statues of Buddha, *bodhisattvas,* Vishnu, Shiva, and a host of Hindu gods and goddesses, which are actually portraits of members of the royal family and the lesser nobility. This was an extension of the Devaraja cult, a manifestation of the belief that statues combining features of the living and the divine would help the former achieve immortality. The statues bear the names of the persons who desired their descendants to worship them after death. The city was surrounded with a thick stone wall and a moat measuring two miles along each of its four sides. During Jayavarman's reign, the empire reached its zenith, although it might be said in retrospect that the roots of the Khmer decline were sown during his rule.

Decline of the Khmers

A number of factors led to the decline of the Khmers, among them Jayavarman VII's building projects that laid a heavy burden on the kingdom's economy. It is estimated that during his time the Khmer state built and supported 102 hospitals, 101 rest houses for pilgrims, and 20,000 shrines. He constructed roads linking the capital with the principal provincial centers, where temples were built and furnished with images. There were nearly 300,000 priests and monks supported by the state treasury. The burden of monument-building on the population was too severe to bear. Thousands of villages, tens of thousands of officials, and an army of laborers and artisans were assigned to the uneconomic tasks of building monuments to glorify the royalty.

Jayavarman's punitive wars against Champa and recalcitrant vassal kingdoms further drained the empire. As in the past, the Chams continued to pose a threat on the northeast frontier. Even more serious was the progressive movement southward of the Thai people, who carved out new states in the territory formerly ruled by the Khmers. Thus, Sukhotai in the upper Menam declared its independence of Khmer rule in 1219, the year of Jayavarman VII's death. Later, in the thirteenth century, the Mongol rulers of China helped weaken the Khmer power by encouraging the Thais to move farther into Southeast Asia.

A religious factor that undermined the Khmer authority was the spread of Theravada Buddhism in the empire. This version of Buddhism did not permit belief in *bodhisattvas* or in the divine basis of kingship. It came to Burma from Sri Lanka in the eleventh century, and through the Mons and Thais it spread in the Khmer empire, where the masses seem to have appreciated its egalitarian character. No more would they regard the kings as divine. The great extension of the god-king cult under Jayavarman VII might have been a response to this threat.

Such forces continued to act against Khmer power throughout the period after Jayavarman's death. The Chams in the east and the Thais in the west took large chunks of the Khmer empire; in 1431, Angkor itself was captured by the Thais. The Khmers regained their former capital for a brief period, but in 1434 they abandoned it and established a new capital near Phnom Penh. In sum, the Khmer empire developed a civilization that dominated the southern and central areas of mainland Southeast Asia for several centuries. Though its political authority clearly declined from the fourteenth century, many of its main features in the social, cultural, and administrative domains were transmitted to the new states that were built on its ruins.

MYANMAR

Like the kingdom of the Khmers, Myanmar was a vital link in the spread of Indian culture to mainland Southeast Asia. Geographically closest to India, its earliest inhabitants must have been the first in Southeast Asia to receive elements of Indian culture. Among these were the religions, Hinduism and Buddhism, and the corpus of Sanskrit literature, including doctrines of administration, theories of kingship, and the Code of Manu. In the adoption of Indian practices, the Burmese exercised discretion, rejecting the Indian hierarchical caste system and giving women a high place in society.

The earliest Burmese to come into contact with India must have been the Mons, a minority kindred to the Khmers in language and appearance, living in Lower Myanmar today. Before their further migration southward, the Mons lived in the Kyaukse plain in central Myanmar. Shortly before the Christian era, they moved into two areas: Lower Myanmar and the region to the east of the Salween in Thailand. The Mons were the preceptors of the other Burmese ethnic groups, including the dominant Burmans, in art, religion, and administration. Numerous Mon words for articles of ordinary use are found in all the Burmese languages.

Indian traders and adventurers following the eastern coastline of Bengal to Suvarnabhumi, or the Land of Gold (identified with Lower Burma and the Malay Peninsula), first carried the knowledge of Indian culture to the Mons. In the third century B.C., Emperor Ashoka sent two Buddhist missionaries to Myanmar to propagate the faith. The Mons used Sanskrit and Pali and modeled their script after the Granthi script of southern India. After Buddhism declined in most parts of India, the Mons remained in frequent contact with Sri Lanka, where Theravada Buddhism has thrived in an unbroken tradition since Ashoka's time. Another point of contact with Theravada Buddhism, at least until the eleventh century, was Conjeevaram in southern India.

The Pyus

The first historically significant ethnic people in Myanmar were the Pyus, who probably migrated from southwest China in about the third century. The ruins of their capital city, Sri Kshetra, six miles east of Prome, testify to a flourishing culture between the fourth and eighth centuries. The Pyus followed Hinduism as well as Theravada and Mahayana Buddhism. By the seventh century, however, Theravada faith had become the dominant element in Pyu society and government. According to Chinese sources, the Pyus lived in cities with circular brick enclosures and were among the most peace-loving people in Southeast Asia. They were nonviolent to a fault. As an example, the Pyus spurned the use of silk because the extraction of silk involved killing the silkworms. The crime rate was negligible, and punishments were mild except in cases involving homicide. The mild manners of the Pyus must have cost them their independence. The Pyus were defeated by the Mons in the eighth century. They fled northward and became the vassals of the Thai kingdom of Nan Chao. In 832, the Thais attacked the new Pyu capital and took a large number of Pyu subjects captive.

The Pyu monarchs officially encouraged Buddhist learning. Boys and girls had their heads completely shaved at seven years of age when they entered schools run by Buddhist monks. They remained there until their twentieth year. Burmese society was distinguished in all of Asia for its high rate of literacy and the low incidence of crime well until the end of the nineteenth century, characteristics that date to the Pyus' time. Among Pyu contributions was the Vikrama era (named after the Pyu Vikrama dynasty), beginning in 638, which was later adopted in Thailand and Cambodia and is still used in Myanmar and Thailand.

The Pyus have remarkably beautiful monuments at Prome. These include Buddhist stupas, cylindrical with a pointed dome, indicating Oriyan architectural influence from the northeast coast of India. Characteristic of Pyu architecture is employment of the *sikhara* (tower), which gives the temples a feeling of strength and solidity as is found in the somewhat later Bhubaneshwar temples of Orissa.

The Burmans

The people responsible for the defeat of the Pyus were the Burmans, or Tibeto-Burmans, whose descendants form the majority of Myanmar's population today. They were probably pushed out of their home in the northwest Chinese province of Kansu by ethnic Chinese in the second millennium B.C. to eastern Tibet, from where they moved through Yunnan to Myanmar over several centuries. According to Burman tradition, they arrived in the second century A.D. in the fertile plain of Kyaukse, where the rivers Irrawaddy and Chindwin meet. The Kyaukse plain, now renamed the Ledwin (rice country), remained the base of Burman power for centuries. Before they moved into the Pyu state, the Burmans had adopted Mahayana

Buddhism, which continued to be the dominant faith of Upper Myanmar until the middle of the eleventh century.

The Burmans founded their kingdom around their chief city, Pagan, around 849. In that year, according to Burmese chronicles, a leader brought a group of nineteen villages, each possessing its own *nat* (local spirit), into one kingdom with a common spirit for all the inhabitants. He also set up two spirits representing two virtuous siblings, a brother and a sister, viciously killed by some tyrannical king in the past, on the site of the ancient volcano Mount Poppa, a mountain sacred to all Burmans. A tree into which the two spirits were supposedly incarnated was carried a little distance northeast of Pagan, which was then established as the capital of the new state. The derivation of divine royal authority from a sacred mountain was similar to Funanese and Khmer beliefs. In the same way the installation of the sacred *linga* on Mount Mahendra by the founder of the Angkor monarchy, Jayavarman II, had symbolized the union of the divided Khmer peoples, so did Pagan and its monarch represent the unification of the Tibeto-Burman people. Despite the Indianization of Tibeto-Burmans and their later adoption of Theravada Buddhism as the state religion in the eleventh century, the *nat* cult continued its hold over the Burmese mind.

Through the maze of legends of bloodshed, intrigue, and usurpations clouding the early history of Pagan emerges the figure of the greatest ruler of the time, King Anawratha, or Aniruddha (1044–1077). He was founder of Myanmar, and the boundaries of his kingdom matched those of the modern state of Myanmar from Bhamo in the north to the Gulf of Martaban in the south. This was achieved by defeat and incorporation of non-Burman peoples, including the culturally advanced Mons in the south, into his kingdom. At this time, the Mons were divided into two rival centers of power, one based in Pegu and the other in Thaton. A Khmer invasion of Pegu led to the latter's appeal for help from King Anawratha, whose forces expelled the foe. The campaign had far-reaching consequences for the political and cultural history of Myanmar. Prior to the campaign, King Anawratha had received Shin Arahan, an illustrious Mon monk, who had aroused the monarch's interest in the older form of the Buddhist faith. Anawratha's readiness to help the Mons in repulsing the Khmer invaders was partly attributable to the hope of getting some of the rarest Buddhist sacred writings in Pali, which were then in the possession of the rival Mon monarch in Thaton. Refusing to comply with the Burman demand, the Thaton king found himself a Burman prisoner, transported to Pagan along with a priceless booty of 30 sets of the Buddhist canon (Tripitaka) and about 30,000 Mon monks and artisans. The cultural plunder left indelible scars on the Mon mind, and the people never became reconciled to the Burman domination of their land.

The most important consequence of Anawratha's conquest of the Mon country was the conversion of his people to Theravada Buddhism and the assimilation of the more refined Mon culture by the Burmans. Not for the first time in history was the political victor vanquished by a culturally superior subjugated population. Anawratha became the most ardent propagator of the Theravada faith, which quickly spread throughout Myanmar and eventually to all of mainland Southeast Asia, with the exception of Vietnam. He also sent artisans to the island kingdom of

Sri Lanka to assist in the restoration of ancient Buddhist monuments. In return, the Sinhalese (Sri Lanka's) monarch sent to Anawratha a replica of Buddha's tooth, which was then enshrined in the newly built Shwezigon pagoda in Pagan.

Of the two centuries of Pagan rule following Anawratha's death in 1077, the first century was culturally dominated by the Mons both at the court and in the countryside. The Mon monk-scholar Shin Arahan, who was to be the chief spiritual counsel to Anawratha, continued that function for Kyanzittha, Anawratha's son, who ascended the Pagan throne in 1084. Mon monks helped Burman conversion to Theravada Buddhism. Pagodas proliferated in Pagan during this period, most of them built and carved by Mon artisans and sculptors. The Mon script became the basis of Burmese script and the vehicle for the dissemination of the Indianized Mon culture, law, and literature. Burman monarchs adopted the Indian concept of kingship, royal duties and powers, and court etiquette. While the Burmans enjoyed the exercise of political power, the Mons carried Myanmar's trade with the outside world.

The large-scale assimilation of Mon culture by the Burmans may have helped to diminish some of the Mon hostility, but it did not completely overcome their bitterness over the extinction of their independence. In fact, the Burman kings following Anawratha took several steps politically to conciliate the Mons, even at the cost of arousing discontent among the Burman population. Thus, Kyanzittha, who had given his daughter in marriage to the Mon prince at Thaton, nominated her son rather than his own to succeed him to the Pagan throne. The succession in the Pagan-Mon line continued until the accession in 1174 of Cansu II, a descendant from the Anawratha line, ended the Mon domination at court. Burman moves at political conciliation with the Mons were hardly reciprocated by the Mons. The experiment of composite polity begun by Anawratha, however, provided an ambition and a frustration for every Burman government thereafter.

VIETNAM

Early History

One of the most persistent themes throughout Vietnamese history is the existence of a love-hate relationship between China and Vietnam. Whereas Chinese culture was appreciated, admired, and adopted, Chinese political domination was despised, dreaded, and rejected.

The Vietnamese have attempted to give their country a history as hoary as China's. According to one of the numerous legends concerning the origin of their state, a Vietnamese prince named Lac Long Quan married a fairy named Au Co sometime around 2800 B.C. Instead of the commonplace results of such a union, the fairy princess laid 100 eggs; when they hatched, a son emerged from each of them. For some unknown reason, the parents separated, the mother leading half the progeny across the northern mountains, while the remaining fifty followed the father into the Red River Delta. The legend symbolizes the two branches of the historical Vietnamese race.

Discounting such myths, one might state that the Vietnamese very likely migrated from their original home in the lower Yangtze Valley. They were pushed southward by the advancing Chinese into the Red River Delta, where they established the kingdom of Au Lac. In 207 B.C., in the aftermath of the collapse of the Chin dynasty in China, Trieu Da, a Chinese general commanding the Guangdong and Guangxi provinces, brought the Red River Delta as well under his jurisdiction, carving out an independent kingdom called Nan Yueh, or Nam Viet. The capital of the new state was near Canton, with the territory of Au Lac forming the southern part of the state. Nam Viet was thus ethnically a composite Sino-Vietnamese state. Under the Han dynasty, the independence of Nam Viet was liquidated in 111 B.C., when it was turned into a province of the Chinese empire. Nam Viet remained an integral part of the Chinese empire for the next millennium. For administrative purposes, the Han emperors divided Nam Viet into three commanderies: Chiao Chih (or Tongking, Chinese for Hanoi, the eastern capital), Chiu Chen (Than Hoa), and Jenan (North Annam).

The two essential elements that contributed to the molding of the early Vietnamese social organization have been the struggle with nature and the conflict with the neighbor to the north. In the process, the Vietnamese have developed into one of the most determined, persistent, and tenacious peoples anywhere. The vagaries of nature have brought fortunes and disasters to the people of the Red River Delta. In a dry year, the supply of water may drop by five-sixths; in wet periods, floods may raise the water level to forty times the normal height of the Red River. Early in Vietnamese history, possibly before the Christian era, the Vietnamese had developed an elaborate system of dikes and canals and the rudiments of government authority to control and channel water supplies. The dikes cover an area of more than 1,500 square miles in the Tongking Delta today, assuring the peasants of sustenance but exposing the populace to the risks of an avalanche if they are damaged. The collective work on the building of dams and the regularly compartmentalized field system, which provided protection against flooding, were Chinese techniques introduced by Chinese rulers. They may have also been responsible for the Vietnamese use of human excrement as field manure, intensive pig-rearing, and market-gardening techniques, which contribute substantially to alleviation of the peasants' financial stringencies in China and Vietnam to this date.

The Chinese Millennium

The long period of direct Chinese rule extending over a millennium accounts for the Sinicization of the Vietnamese. Even before Chinese rule began, as inhabitants of the composite state of Nam Viet, the Vietnamese had come into contact with the Chinese people and their culture. However, large-scale introduction of Chinese culture came about with floods of refugees from China into the Red River Delta in the first century A.D. These were not needy peasants but well-accomplished scholars and officials, who disagreed with the successors of the Han dynasty and who were welcomed by the Chinese governor of Tongking. They were responsible for the intensive Sinicization of the Vietnamese people through the introduction of Chinese classics, Confucian ethical principles, and Chinese ideographs. Until the widespread use of the romanized *quoc-ngu* form of writing in the twentieth century, Vietnamese was the only script in Southeast Asia based on the Chinese characters and it was therefore not alphabetical. Beginning in the fifth century, Mahayana

Buddhism was introduced to Vietnam through China by Chinese scholars and preachers, some of whom passed through Vietnam on their way to India for higher studies in Buddhism or pilgrimage to Buddhist holy places. The Chinese traveler I-Ching attested that Hanoi had become a great intellectual center of Buddhism by the seventh century.

It is difficult, however, to estimate the depth of assimilation of Chinese culture by the Vietnamese. As among the other Southeast Asian peoples, probably only the court and the elite were able to appreciate and absorb these alien cultural importations. The Chinese mandarin system with its Confucian values helped the elite to erect a wall of authority, which further buttressed their social and economic position vis-à-vis the peasantry. The masses retained their language, customs, and religious beliefs rooted in animism and ancestor worship.

Paradoxically, the Sinicization of the Vietnamese elite resulted in the latter's desire and ability to acquire and retain their independence of China. As Joseph Buttinger put it:

> The more they [the Vietnamese] absorbed of the skills, customs, and ideas of the Chinese, the smaller grew the likelihood of their ever becoming part of the Chinese people. In fact, it was during the centuries of intensive efforts to turn them into Chinese that the Vietnamese came into their own as a separate people with political and cultural aspects of their own.[13]

The Chinese rule and intensive efforts to Sinicize may have promoted Vietnamese dependence, but it promoted resistance as well.

The Chinese rule of a millennium was punctuated by several violent expressions of hostility on the part of the Vietnamese subjects. Resentment was first expressed by members of the old feudal class, whose positions had been endangered and, in many cases, abolished by the Chinese officials. Vietnamese revolts occurred not coincidentally during periods when the central government in China was weak and its authority consequently less effective in the outlying province of Tongking. The first of these uprisings occurred in A.D. 39 and is notable for giving Vietnam two heroines remembered for their bravery and patriotism. The occasion was triggered by the execution of a local lord as a warning to other recalcitrant chiefs. His widow and her sister, Trung Trac and Trung Nhi, raised troops, pushed the Chinese out, and ruled as joint queens for a brief two years. When the Chinese retaliated and crushed the revolt, the two sisters jumped in the Day River and committed suicide. The Vietnamese have almost deified the two martyrs. The repression that followed won the Chinese obedience but not the loyalty or love of their subjects. Minor revolts occurred at intervals, but it was not until the collapse of the powerful T'ang dynasty in China in the tenth century that Vietnamese efforts to overthrow the hated yoke were successful. In 939, the Chinese were pushed out as the leader of the movement, Ngo Quyen, declared himself ruler of the kingdom of Dai Viet.

Independent Dai Viet

Between 939 and the imposition of French colonial rule in the nineteenth century, Vietnam enjoyed nearly a thousand years of freedom from alien rule. The only exception was a short period of two decades from 1407 to 1428, during which the Ming armies overran Vietnam and brought it under direct Chinese rule. The millennium of freedom from alien domination followed a millennium of intensely hated Chinese rule. One would have naturally expected a revulsion for Chinese political and cultural institutions in the new era of freedom. The reaction was mixed, however. As David Marr has observed, there was "the subtle interplay of resistance and dependence which appeared often to stand at the root of historical Vietnamese attitudes toward the Chinese."[14]

As a means of political expediency, Vietnam maintained formal though nominal links with China during the period and in fact sent triennial tribute to the Chinese court until 1885. The expediency can be explained on several grounds. First, the long Chinese rule had produced a Chinese-Vietnamese aristocracy with intellectual and institutional loyalties to a Confucian court. These elites perceived their vested interests to be more secure within the Chinese political system to which they were by then accustomed rather than in a completely independent monarchy. Second, the new Vietnamese state had reasons to be concerned about potential attacks from the Thai state of Nan Chao, which had previously overrun Tongking in the eighth and ninth centuries. Indeed, there also was Champa, the perpetual thorn in the Vietnamese side. The Vietnamese rulers therefore felt that an overlord-vassal relationship with China would serve as a deterrent against any potential aggressive designs of its enemies.

There was the ticklish question, however, of how to designate the ruler of Dai Viet, who, although a vassal, wanted to be designated emperor. The Chinese preferred that the Vietnamese monarch be called governor. Realizing that it would be difficult if not impossible to reestablish control over Dai Viet, the Chinese finally agreed to a compromise: The Vietnamese ruler would be designated a "vassal king" of China. He could style himself "emperor" in relation to his own subjects and in dealing with his own vassals.

Dai Viet was plagued by internal conflicts for quite some time after its founding. The first seventy years brought the rise and fall of three dynasties. Real stability had to await the establishment of the Ly dynasty (1009–1225), followed by the Tran dynasty, both having excellent rulers at least for the first hundred years.

The power of the court and the civilization the Ly dynasty created lasted four centuries. The Ly rulers moved the capital to Thang Long (present-day Hanoi) and gave the country a strong centralized government. In order to facilitate closer administrative ties, a network of roads linking the provincial capitals to the royal capital was built by 1044. A postal courier service was also established by the middle of the century. The Lys created an elaborate apparatus to promote the Confucian cult at the court. Thus, during the last quarter of the eleventh century, they established a Confucian Temple of Literature and the Han-lin Academy for Study in Confucianism for studies at the highest level. In 1076, the National College was founded to train civil service officials. Only scholars well versed in Confucian classics would be able to pass these examinations. Consequently, the principles underlying the government were Confucian, and the mandarins, who were regarded as social and intellectual leaders, would through their personal example propagate Confucian values among the Vietnamese elite. The Chinese model of hierarchical bureaucracy was adopted in 1089, creating nine levels of civil and military officials. Thus, despite strong political hostility toward the Chinese, the Vietnamese deliberately set their nation on a course of Sinicization.

The Tran dynasty produced a number of great rulers, the most notable being Tran Thai Tong (1225–1258). The many innovative, administrative, agrarian, and economic measures he introduced were extended more or less along the same continuum by his successors. The kingdom was divided into twelve provinces, ably administered by scholar-officials. Tran Thai Tong revamped the taxation system by classifying the rice fields into different categories depending on quality and by imposing a land tax. During his reign and almost throughout the Tran dynasty, rulers energetically pursued public works. Embankments were constructed all along the Red River, even down to where it emptied into the sea. Many other irrigation and water control projects were undertaken, thus assuring good crops and general prosperity for most of the long period of the Tran dynasty.

Mongols Invade Dai Viet and Champa

A great show of strength and resistance toward the end of Tran Thai Tong's reign was the repulsion of the Mongol invasion in 1257 (see Chapter 4). When the Mongols sent an ambassador to Dai Viet demanding tribute, Tran Thai Tong imprisoned him. The Mongol armies launched an attack in retaliation and reached the Vietnamese capital of Thang Long (Hanoi) in 1257, but were pushed by Tran Thai Tong and his heir apparent, Tran Thanh Tong, across the border into China.

Champa, to the south of Dai Viet, also opposed the Mongols. The Cham king, Indravarman V, sent tribute to Beijing, but did not comply with the Mongol emperor's invitation to appear there in person. Thereupon, Kublai Khan sent a punitive expedition under General Sogetu by sea because Dai Viet refused to allow Mongol troops to pass through its territory. In the face of superior forces, the Cham king withdrew from his capital and from his refuge engaged two separate Mongol expeditions for several years in guerrilla warfare.

In 1285, Kublai Khan sent a third expedition numbering 500,000 men under his son, Prince Toghani, which forced itself by land through Dai Viet to help Sogetu's naval expedition. The Mongol troops suffered heavy casualties both in the Tongking Delta as well as in Cham territory. The guerrillas killed General Sogetu; Prince Toghani suffered an ignoble defeat. Kublai's troops finally withdrew without getting the Cham king to appear in person at Beijing. Both Dai Viet and Champa, however, agreed to send embassies to the Mongol emperor, just as they had done with previous Chinese emperors.

During the Mongol attack the Vietnamese monarch, like the Cham king, vacated his capital and repaired to the countryside to fight the invaders. The hero of the resistance was Prince Tran Quoc Toan, who is deified to this day by the Vietnamese by his posthumous name, Tran Hung Dao. His valiant exploits are among the most celebrated in the annals of Vietnamese history of resistance against China. The proud Vietnamese king refused to agree to Mongol demands that he send his sons as hostages to Beijing and to supply troops for the Mongol army. After defeat, the Mongols adopted discretion and meekly accepted the Vietnamese and Cham triennial tribute in return for mutually peaceful relations.

Chinese Reoccupation and the Birth of the Le Dynasty

In the fifteenth century, in 1407, tiny Vietnam had once again to suffer a Chinese invasion and occupation. This was followed by the most intensive Sinicization efforts ever. Chinese civil service officials were imported and imposed on the Vietnamese. A census was undertaken as a means to facilitate conscription into the Chinese army and to levy heavy taxes. The Vietnamese way of life and religious practices were banned, and the language was not allowed to be taught in schools. Those Vietnamese who resisted, about 10,000 intellectuals and artisans, were exiled to Beijing, where they were drafted to serve the empire. All Vietnamese were treated as suspects and were required to carry an identity card on their persons. Such actions naturally provoked the Vietnamese spirit of nationalism and age-old hostility against China. In 1418, Le Loi, an aristocratic landowner from Thanh Hoa, emerged to lead an army of resistance employing guerrilla tactics that a decade later captured Hanoi and expelled Chinese troops as well as civilian officials. The Le dynasty later produced a remarkable leader in Le Thanh Ton. His conquest of most of Champa made possible the Vietnamese expansion in central Vietnam. Le Thanh Ton (1460–1497) also made Laos (then Lan Chang) a vassal of Vietnam. While the Vietnamese thus received tribute from their vassals, they in turn sent tribute to the Chinese emperors, who recognized them as kings of Annam, "pacified south."

Le Thanh Ton consciously and deliberately adopted the Chinese system of administration, including its recruitment method of the competitive Confucian-style civil service examination. Whether this mode of cultural acceptance was designed simply to flatter the Chinese into abandoning thoughts of conquest, or whether it was born of a genuine belief that such Chinese institutions lent social and political stability to the state, is controversial. The range of reforms introduced in Vietnam in the fifteenth century was, according to Keith Taylor, of far greater magnitude and intensity than in the thousand years of direct Chinese rule.[15] Chinese language, the art of writing, spatial arts, and Mahayana Buddhism were adopted. The central administration was patterned on the Chinese model with six ministries: finance, rites, justice, personnel, army, and public works. The civilian bureaucracy and military establishment were divided into nine grades each. The bureaucracy did not reach the village level, where the local affairs were managed through a Council of Notables, whose charge was to maintain order, execute official decrees, collect taxes for the imperial government, and recruit conscripts for the imperial army.

Recruitment to the civil service was dependent upon success in the examinations specially conducted for the purpose. They were based on the Confucian classics and were held annually at the provincial level, triennially at the regional and national levels. As in China, the candidates successful at the national level were granted an audience with the emperor and were posted to high positions in the administration. Since the social and economic status of elites was dependent upon their administrative rank, Vietnam became and remained until the nineteenth century a Confucian state dominated by mandarins.

The intense cultural impact of China on Vietnam was a mixed blessing. The civil service examination system produced an educated elite, encouraged a family-oriented hierarchical loyalty, and promoted a well-regulated mandarin bureaucracy, all of which resulted in a relatively stable social, political, and administrative order. On the other hand, the same factors bred an attitude of condescension toward people of other walks of life and a tendency to look to the past for precedents to solve present and future problems.

At the same time, Le Thanh Ton sought consciously to move away from Vietnam's intellectual bondage to the Chinese in at least two respects. The code of Hong-Duc promulgated in 1483 brought together within a single conceptual and legal framework all the laws, rules, and regulations issued from time to time by previous Vietnamese emperors. In addition, the Vietnamese asserted themselves in art. The Le dynasty undertook a large-scale program of construction of temples, tombs, and ceremonial halls all over the kingdom, notably in Hanoi, Lamson in Thanh Hoa province, and Hue. These edifices, along with steles, balustrades, and ornamental gateways, still survive and attest to significant Vietnamese variation of traditional Chinese themes.

3

Early Kingdoms of Sumatra and Java

Insular Southeast Asia was far more exposed than mainland to influences from distant countries like India, Arabia, Persia, China, and, in more recent times, Europe. International commerce brought in its wake cultural contacts including, of course, religion. Unlike mainland Southeast Asia, people in the insular region followed a variety of religions: Buddhism and Hinduism held sway during the first millennium in Malaya and Indonesia, giving way after the thirteenth century to Islam, which spread rapidly in the archipelago in the fifteenth and sixteenth centuries. The sixteenth century opened doors to Christianity, which became the dominant religion of the Philippines. Only the people of picturesque Bali adhered to Hinduism despite such large-scale conversions around them. If Theravada Buddhism is the dominant religion of mainland Southeast Asia, Islam is that of the insular region, with Indonesia the largest Muslim nation on earth.

HISTORICAL SOURCES

Sources of information for the early history of Indonesia are varied, though scantier and more ambiguous than those for mainland Southeast Asia. Stone and copper inscriptions have been found in Sanskrit, old Malay, old Javanese, old Balinese, old Sundanese, and in Sumatra, in Indian languages other than Sanskrit.[1] A few texts on palm leaves (*lontar*) have survived the ravages of tropical weather, the most notable being *The Nagarkertagama* and *The Pararaton*. The first, dealing with the founding of Singhasari in 1222, was composed in 1365 by Prapanca, the court poet during the reign of King Rajasanagara of Majapahit. *The Pararaton* is an older chronicle from which Prapanca borrowed considerably, although modern knowledge about it is based on a version dating from the sixteenth century.

Besides these indigenous accounts, considerable information on the early history of Sumatra and Java is found in Indian and Chinese sources. Chinese sources in regard to the archipelago are not as numerous as for mainland Southeast Asia.

The imperial annals provide information on various kingdoms, their rulers, and the embassies they sent to the Chinese emperor's court. Obviously, the insular kingdoms sent tribute or embassies to the Chinese court far less frequently than did the kingdoms of mainland Southeast Asia. A second category of Chinese sources is the travel accounts of Chinese pilgrims who stopped in Southeast Asia on their way to India. Last is the valuable account of Marco Polo, who visited the archipelago in 1292, coinciding with the time of Mongol invasion.

EARLY KINGDOMS

Two kinds of states developed in the Indonesian archipelago: those based on maritime commerce and those capable of large-scale cultivation of agricultural products for consumption and export. Whereas Srivijaya in southeastern Sumatra belonged to the first category, most of the Javanese states, particularly those in the volcanic and sawah-cultivating central and eastern parts of the island, belonged to the latter kind. Sumatra's only advantage was topographic, deriving from its location on the shortest sea route through the Strait of Malacca. Java's strong points were a central location among the myriads of islands; access to and control of the products of the archipelago, particularly spices and sandalwood; fertile soil capable of sustaining a large population and yielding substantial surpluses; and finally, its control over an alternate east-west trade route through the Sunda Strait.

It is no wonder, then, that rivalry between Java and Sumatra for the control of the straits of Malacca and Sunda persisted in the history of the region. With its natural advantages, Java had longer periods of dominance in the archipelago than Sumatra. On the other hand, Java experienced a disastrous pattern of rise and fall of kingdoms brought on not only by human factors such as excessive local ambition or dynastic disputes but also by natural disasters, including earthquakes and volcanoes that prompted demographic dislocations on a massive scale. The cycle of dynastic changes and the rapid shifts of power alternating mostly between central and eastern Java must have caused considerable chaos and untold hardships to the hapless peasantry. Of the dozens of polities that thus emerged in Java in the millennium beginning about 700, a few stand out for their superior attainments: the Srivijaya, Sailendras, Mataram, Kediri, Singhasari, and Majapahit.

SRIVIJAYA

Perhaps the oldest among the more durable of the Indonesian kingdoms was Srivijaya, whose capital was Palembang in southeast Sumatra. Thanks go to Georges Coedes for "discovering" Srivijaya.[2] Its rise as the greatest maritime power in the region from about the seventh to the thirteenth centuries was most certainly a consequence of the fall of Funan and the inability of its successor kingdom, Chenla, to serve as an effective trading intermediary in the extensive east-west trade. Clearly, there was a great opportunity for a new power to make enormous profits from engaging in the lucrative international trade as well as by simply providing port facilities in the western part of the archipelago.

42

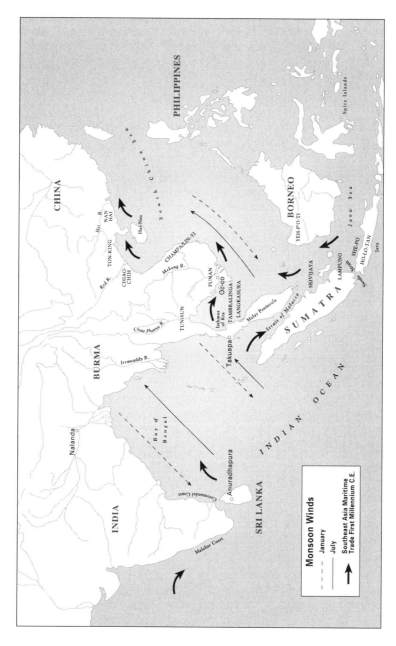

MAP 3.1 Southeast Asia Maritime Trade, First Millennium C.E.

Located halfway between the two principal maritime passages, namely, the straits of Malacca and Sunda, Srivijaya's Palembang port provided an excellent harbor sheltered from the fury of the northeast and southwest monsoons by the mountain ranges of Sumatra and Malaya. Srivijaya's prosperity was helped by the phenomenal rise in the revived Chinese maritime trade during the T'ang dynasty (seventh to the tenth centuries). In the opinion of O. W. Wolters, Srivijaya's rapid growth could also be attributed to sales of Indonesian, in particular north Sumatran, substitutes of pine resin and benjamin gum for frankincense and myrrh, supplies of which from Arabia and eastern Africa were not adequate to meet the increasing demand for these commodities in west Asia and China.[3]

Srivijaya attracted international shipping to its harbors by suppressing piracy in the Strait of Malacca and providing excellent anchorage, storage, and recreational facilities in Palembang. The well-known Chinese traveler-pilgrim I-Ching noted the arrival of as many as thirty-five ships from Persia alone during his six-month stay in Srivijaya in 671. According to such accounts, porcelains, jades, and silks from China; camphor, sandalwood, spices, and resins from the Moluccas; and textiles from India found eager buyers in the hustle and bustle of the Srivijayan ports of Malayu and Palembang.

The fortified city of Palembang was also an important center of Mahayana Buddhist learning. According to I-Ching, who was on his way to India for a ten-year period of study and who spent four years again in Srivijaya on his return trip, Palembang's monasteries had more than a thousand inmates. He recommended that his countrymen planning travel to India for higher studies in Buddhism spend one or two years in Srivijaya.

To ensure its prosperity, Srivijaya employed a powerful fleet, compelling all shipping passing through the region to touch its ports and pay dues and taxes, thus marking a precedent for the hated impositions later made familiar to the region by the Portuguese and the Dutch. In order to enforce such a monopoly over the trade route between India and China, Srivijaya acquired territorial control over the strategic areas around the Strait of Malacca and the Isthmus of Kra. According to an Arab chronicler, Sulayman, the Srivijayan empire extended by the middle of the ninth century over all of Sumatra, Kedah, and western Java. Another Arab traveler, Masudi, testified in 995 that it took two years to go around all the islands of the Srivijayan empire in the fastest vessel.

Srivijaya's domination of the Sino-Indian trade route remained almost unchallenged for two to three centuries. Its high-handed practice of forcing ships to use and pay excessive charges for its port facilities tried the patience of the region's traders and rulers. The first major challenge came from the Mataram rulers of eastern Java in the last quarter of the tenth century. A few decades later, in 1025, however, Rajendra Chola of south India dealt a crushing blow to Srivijaya's maritime might and monopoly. Apparently, the Cholas conquered and administered large portions of the Srivijayan empire, including its ports of Ligor, Kedah, and Tumasik, although that lasted only two decades. In the end, logistical problems of political control from Chola's distant base in south India must have worked to Srivijaya's advantage. Besides, Srivijaya acknowledged Chola's suzerainty and promised good behavior, which apparently met the Chola king's demands.

THE SAILENDRAS

A century after Srivijaya was established, central Java developed a dynasty that became its competitor in the east-west trade for the next one hundred years. These were the Sailendras. According to Coedes and de Casparis,[4] the Funanese descendants lived in Java for two centuries in obscurity until, in the middle of the eighth century, one of their leaders, Bhanu, acquired a kingdom. He called himself a Sailendra (king of the mountain), a title held by his Funanese ancestors. In what may have been an attempt to retrieve their patrimony, the Sailendras raided Tongking and Champa, defeated the divided Chenlas, captured and beheaded the king of water Chenla, and briefly ruled that mainland kingdom from insular Java during the last decades of the eighth century. Thus, the Sailendras became the only indigenous power in history to rule over substantial territory in both mainland and insular Southeast Asia. As noted in the previous chapter, the Sailendra rule over Chenla was quickly extinguished in 802 by Jayavarman II, the founder of the Angkor monarchy. The Sailendras, however, left their mark on mainland Southeast Asia in the form of Javanese art patterns and graceful scrolls in Champa and Angkor.[5]

The Sailendras participated actively, though on a much lower scale than Srivijaya, in the east-west trade; their principal base of power and prosperity was agricultural. Agriculture helped them to build surplus wealth, which they expended mostly in constructing palaces, temples, and Buddhist monuments, including the world-famous Borobodur, the greatest architectural monument in all of Southeast Asia.

The Borobodur was begun in 778 by King Vishnu and completed in 824 by a grandson, Samaratunga. Along the same cosmological lines as the later Angkor monuments, the Sailendras selected Borobodur as the Mount Meru of their kingdom to erect thereon a miniature cosmos dedicated to the Buddha. The Borobodur's nine terraces carved out of a single hill represented the nine previous lives of Gautama before he attained the Buddhahood. Seen from a distance, the immense structure looks like a single Buddhist stupa.

The Borobodur is the best example of Indo-Javanese art. The galleries around the terraces measure about three miles, their sides fully adorned with nearly two thousand intricately detailed bas-relief sculptures. These include four hundred statues of the Buddha in various moods, encapsulating in stone the saga of Mahayana Buddhism. The structure, undoubtedly Indian in conception and reflecting the best forms of art of the Gupta period, was at the same time representative of Javanese artistic skills. A few Indian artists may have been invited to assist, but the work was principally executed by indigenous people. The faces are typically of Javanese people engaged in diverse occupations from princes to peasants, carpenters, pottery makers, weavers, fishermen, merchants, dancers, and seafarers. Their dress and jewelry are distinctively Javanese, as are some of the musical instruments and items of furniture and utensils. Taken together with scores of other smaller buildings around Borobodur, the Sailendra construction activity is truly stupefying, a remarkable testimony of the culture's wealth, taste, and organizational abilities.

According to an alternate interpretation given by J. G. de Casparis,[6] the Borobodur was built to serve as a tomb for the soul of Sailendra's King Indra (782–

812), during whose rule most of the construction work on the monument was carried out. His ashes, after cremation, were to be placed in a reliquary at the basement level. The upper nine levels were meant for the souls of his nine ancestors, all of them *bodhisattvas* in the Mahayanist tradition, on their way to attain the blissful state of Nirvana. The basement level, also elaborately sculptured, was covered to await the day of Indra's death. For some unknown reason, the ceremonial placement of his ashes there never occurred. The basement remained in that state until World War II, when the Japanese uncovered a part of the casing.

The Sailendras were matrimonially related to the old Sanjaya family in north-central Java as well as to the Srivijaya ruling house in Sumatra. In 832, a Sanjaya prince, Patapan, usurped the Sailendra throne. The infant Sailendra prince, Balaputra, remained in a political wilderness until 850, when he attempted to regain his patrimony, failed, and consequently fled to Srivijaya. There he ascended the throne almost unchallenged. Thus, the Sailendra line was extinguished in Java but continued in Srivijaya. There, the Sailendras adopted the Srivijayan policy of giving primary attention to trade and commerce to the neglect of their traditional devotion to building Buddhist monuments.

MATARAM AND KEDIRI

The successors of Patapan of the Sanjaya dynasty ruled over the former Sailendra kingdom of central Java for nearly one hundred years before moving the capital to Mataram in 929, possibly because of an earthquake or an epidemic. The Mataram rulers emulated the vanquished Sailendras in every way except religion. Beginning from Patapan, Hinduism reasserted itself over Mahayana Buddhism. In trying to rival the Sailendra Buddhist monuments, the Mataram rulers energetically built numerous temples dedicated to Hindu gods. The ruins of their capital at Prambanan, near modern Jogjakarta, show three central temples (*chandis*) dedicated to the Hindu trinity of Brahma, Vishnu, and Shiva, with a number of smaller temples surrounding them. The temples were adorned with sculptures elaborating stories from the *Ramayana* epic. Like Borobodur and Angkor, the Prambanan temples may have served as mausoleums for princes and higher nobility. The reassertion of Hinduism did not mean intolerance of Buddhism, which coexisted just as in contemporary Angkor, though on a much lower key. As Coedes observed, a syncretic cult of Shiva-Buddha evolved both in Mataram and Angkor.[7] Reflective of such eclecticism was the appearance of two great literary works on Hinduism and Buddhism in the tenth century under the patronage of the Mataram ruler Sindok (929–948). These were the Javanese *Ramayana* and the Tantric Buddhist treatise *Sang Hyang Kamahayanikan,* which give valuable insights into the artistic concepts, iconography, and architecture of the Javanese of the time.[8]

The Mataram rulers participated actively in the region's trade with China, taking full advantage of the economic boom during the T'ang dynasty. They developed trade in spices from the Moluccas, for which there was an increasing demand both from China and the Arab world. Trade with the latter necessitated the use of the port facilities around the Strait of Malacca, which was at that time under the firm control of Srivijaya. As mentioned before, Srivijaya's tax and other exactions irked a number of states, including Mataram. Around the end of the first millennium, when Mataram was apparently at the peak of its political and economic power, it challenged Srivijaya's hated monopolistic practices. The Mataram navy, however, was no match for Srivijaya's. In 1006, Srivijaya completely defeated Mataram, sacked its capital, and put large numbers of its inhabitants to a merciless end.

East Java's political misfortune, however, proved temporary despite what had appeared to be a total debacle at Srivijaya's hands. The revival of political power in Java was helped by at least two factors: the defeat of Srivijaya in 1026 by Rajendra Chola of south India, and the leadership of Prince Airlangga, son of a Balinese prince and a Mataram princess. His qualities of heroism and tact so impressed the Mataram nobility and the Brahmans that they persuaded him to accept the Mataram crown. Within a decade of his coronation in 1019 at the age of nineteen, Airlangga was able to restore Mataram to its former political strength. His statesmanship was evident in his decision to forget and forgive Srivijaya's past acts and instead propose his own marriage with a Srivijayan princess to initiate a policy of cordial relationship between Java and Sumatra.[9] In the field of religion, he scotched the rivalries between Hinduism and Mahayana Buddhism by recognizing both, though he and his successors represented themselves as incarnations of Vishnu. More astutely, he weakened the hold of the Brahman priests and Buddhist monks by appropriating the vast estates they managed on behalf of their religious organizations. The peace and prosperity Airlangga thus brought to Mataram have earned him a high place in the history of Java. Unfortunately, his lifelong work, particularly in creating unity among his subjects, was undone by his own action in 1042. Having no direct heir and fearing a contest between two children born of rival concubines with equally dubitable claims to the throne, he divided his state just before his death into two kingdoms: Janggala and Kediri.

Of the two kingdoms, only Kediri attained prominence. A Chinese writer, Chou Chu-fei, referred to it in 1178 as the greatest maritime power in Southeast Asia, ranking it higher than Srivijaya. Its political control then extended over Bali, southwest Borneo, and southern Sulawesi, while its ports attracted most of the spices exported from the Moluccas. In the fast-developing spice trade between India and the Mediterranean after the Crusades, the Gujarati merchants from west India at first preferred Kediri ports to Srivijayan, because of both the easier access to Moluccan spices as well as lower port duties. By all accounts, Kediri flourished and was at the zenith of its political and economic power in the first quarter of the thirteenth century when Ken Angrok (literally, "he who upsets everything"), an adventurer who first captured the less important state of Janggala, attacked Kediri, killed its ruler, and established a new dynasty in eastern Java in 1222. Three decades later, his successors changed the name of the capital, Kuttaraja, to Singhasari (the name of Angrok's birthplace), by which name his dynasty came to be known to history.[10]

The Singhasari dynasty's greatest king, Kertanagara (1268–1292), the hero of the Javanese epic poem *The Nagarkertagama,* was a great warrior, fine scholar, and devotee of Shiva as well as of Tantric Buddhism. He promoted a syncretic cult of Shiva-Buddha, which claimed to work for the redemption of the souls of the dead and was very much in tune with the Indonesian practice of ancestor worship.[11]

MAP 3.2 Kingdoms of Southeast Asia About A.D. 1200

All this made Kertanagara a legendary figure able to rally large numbers of supporters in the realization of his plans to make Java the center of power in the entire archipelago. By 1290, he attained his dream of subjugating Singhasari's longtime rival, Srivijaya, and making himself master of both the principal maritime passages of Southeast Asia, the straits of Malacca and Sunda. Srivijaya had been in decline for some time, its northern Malay territories having been appropriated during this same time by the Thais. The Singhasari dynasty proved short-lived, as Kertanagara was killed by a rival during the Mongol invasion.

4

The Rise of New States: Ayuthaya, Majapahit, and Malacca

Beginning late in the thirteenth century, two factors markedly altered the power configuration in Southeast Asia: The first factor was the Mongol invasion of Southeast Asia and the consequent rise of the Thais and of the Majapahit empire; the second was the advent of Islam and the rise of Malacca. For well over a millennium, the major power center of Southeast Asia had been in the region of present-day Cambodia and South Vietnam. The Mongol invasions and the development of the Thai state upset the Khmer supremacy in mainland Southeast Asia. In the fourteenth century, Thailand and the Majapahit empire competed for maritime trade. In the following century, the trade rivalry became triangular, with Malacca as the third competitor.

THE MONGOL INVASIONS

In the thirteenth century, the descendants of the Mongol empire-builder, Genghis Khan, invaded China and Southeast Asia, bringing about major changes. Having destroyed the age-old Thai state of Nan Chao in southern China in 1253, the Mongols completed the conquest of China in 1279. Thereafter, they followed the traditional Chinese policy of demanding loyalty and tribute from the peoples on China's borders, including those in Southeast Asia. Most of the Southeast Asian rulers refused to recognize the Mongol upstarts, reneged on traditional tribute owed to the Chinese throne, and even heroically confronted the huge Mongol forces sent to secure their capitulation. The Mongols followed the Chinese policy of leaving the border states in a fragmented and weak condition in order to ensure the security of their middle regions. In that context, the image of a strong Khmer empire in Southeast Asia, with its own tributary system extending to principalities all the way through present-day Thailand and Laos to the Chinese borders, must have been galling to the Mongol pride. The steadfast resistance of Vietnam, Champa, and Myanmar to Mongol overlordship made the chances of securing the subjugation of the Angkor kingdom even more dismal and distant. Myanmar (Pagan) was defeated and broken up by the Mongols in 1287, and the Vietnamese and the Cham capitals were overrun, but the resistance itself continued in all three countries through guerrilla warfare in the countryside. The conflict marked a precedent for similar struggles in later Southeast Asian history, particularly in Vietnam. The Mongol military moves seriously disturbed the political picture of all Southeast Asia, mainland as well as the archipelago. Thus, Mongol destruction of Pagan led to the ascendancy of Thai power on mainland Southeast Asia, and the Mongol defeat of the Singhasari kingdom in Java gave rise to the Majapahit empire. Both Thailand and Majapahit were to become the dominant powers of the two respective regions of Southeast Asia for at least the succeeding three centuries.

The Thais and Ayuthaya

The rapid rise of the Thais in the thirteenth and fourteenth centuries has been attributed by some historians largely to the encouragement given them by the Mongols. It is true that the Thais were compelled to move into Southeast Asia because of the Mongol conquest of their ancient homeland in Yunnan. It is also a fact that the Mongol destruction of the Pagan kingdom in 1287 eliminated a chief obstacle to the southward expansion of the Thais. Even so, it cannot be said that the establishment of the new Thai kingdom was entirely the result of Mongol policies. The political decline of the Khmers and the topography of the region also contributed to Thai success.

The first direct role the Mongols played in Thai affairs was through the conquest of the Thai state of Nan Chao (in modern Yunnan) in 1253. Rather than endure foreign domination, the Thais, traditionally a freedom-loving people (the word Thai means "free"), preferred to migrate en masse to Southeast Asia. At first, they established small principalities in the northern parts of the Khmer empire. It is unlikely the Thais did this to help their erstwhile enemies, the Mongols. From the viewpoint of Mongol political goals, however, the rise of new Thai principalities served as a counterbalance against Khmer power. Because the emergence of Thai power served Mongol interests of weakening the Khmers, the Mongols tolerated and, to a certain extent, even encouraged further accretion of Thai power in mainland Southeast Asia.

On the other hand, it should be noted that the beginnings of Thai migration southward long predated the Mongols. Early exploits of the Thais of Nan Chao included successful raids in the eighth century in distant Tongking and defeat of a southern Chinese dynasty in the ninth. As for their southward movement, trickles of Thais had ventured into the northwestern portions of the Khmer empire as early as the tenth century, establishing tiny principalities and sending tribute to the regional Khmer commanders. The Mongol conquest of the Thai homeland only helped to accelerate the migratory process, turning the trickle into a tide. Further Thai territorial expansion owed more to Khmer weakness than to Mongol aid. In fact, the Thais had begun to chip away at the Khmer empire in the thirteenth century soon after Jayavarman VII's death (1219) and long before the Mongol conquest of Nan Chao. The Thai expansionist movement built momentum over the next century when the Khmer political system lapsed into an irreversible decline.

In a sense, the Thai conquests were facilitated by geography. Moving southward along the Menam, the Thais had no major geographical obstacles to surmount, whereas the north-south mountain range made it difficult for the Khmer armies to maneuver in defense of the western parts of their empire. In addition, the new lands conquered by the Thais were fertile, providing an economic surplus that enabled them to build larger armies. Thus, the political and economic decline of the Khmers and the advantages of geography favored the Thai position in the thirteenth century. Thai success was much more than a product of Mongol politics.

The three centuries from the thirteenth to the fifteenth marked the formative stage of Thai history in Southeast Asia. During this period, the Thais had three great monarchs—Rama Khamheng (1283–1317), Ramadhipati (1350–1369), and Trailok (1448–1488)—whose contributions to Thai society and polity were remarkably distinctive. Some of their accomplishments, notably in language, script, and religion, have remained an integral part of Thai culture to this date, and their impact on administration and law persisted almost to the end of the nineteenth century, giving Thailand a more stable base than any other state in Southeast Asia.

Rama Khamheng, justly remembered by Thais as one of their greatest monarchs, had both an adoptive and innovative genius. He was also a political pragmatist, who sensed the new power wave symbolized by the Mongols and decided to exploit it for the establishment of an independent Thai state. Beginning in 1287, the year of Pagan's fall, Rama Khamheng, then chief of the small principality of Sukhotai, or Sukhodaya, extended his hegemony over the upper Menam, the upper Mekong, and the lower Salween valleys, the last of which was a principal center of Mon population. The enlarged Sukhotai borrowed from the Khmers their art forms as well as political and administrative apparatus, including the concept of divine monarchy. From the Burmans and the Mons, the Thais received their legal tradition and the Theravada form of Buddhism. Rama Khamheng created, based on a south Indian script, a new alphabet, which with some minor modifications is still used in Thailand.

Sukhotai had certain ecological advantages over the other Thai principalities (*muangs*). Its location at the apex of the principal flood basin gave it control over the allocation of water to the entire Menam Basin extending to Ayuthaya. The latter could be connected to the Gulf of Thailand by canals cut from the Menam River through the marshy delta surrounding present-day Bangkok.[1]

Such a development took place barely half a century after Rama Khamheng's death. By the middle of the fourteenth century, the center of Thai power shifted to central Thailand, where it remained for the next four centuries. The founder of the new kingdom and capital of Ayuthaya (after the name of Rama's capital, Ayodhya, in the Indian epic *Ramayana*) reigned under the title of Ramadhipati (1350–1369). Situated in the agricultural heartland, Ayuthaya assured prosperity to the kingdom: Its strategic location, with easy access to Angkor in the east, Lower Myanmar in the west, and the Gulf of Siam and Isthmus of Kra in the south, opened prospects for future Thai hegemony over most of mainland Southeast Asia.

King Ramadhipati's greatest contribution was in the field of common law. The Thai customary law was found inadequate for a more complex society that now included non-Thai populations such as the Mons, the Malays, and the Khmers. Ramadhipati combined ancient Thai practices and the Code of Manu, the Indian lawgiver, which had been the basis of the Mon-Khmer legal system for centuries.

Ramadhipati's laws throw considerable light on the social structure and mores of the time. Slavery flourished. There were severe penalties for slaves attempting to escape. The society was hierarchical. Polygamy was legal and divorce easy. There were severe penalties for misappropriation of funds by a government official; bribery or corruption could invite one of eight punishments, ranging from ordinary suspension from office to death by strokes of rattan.

If King Ramadhipati is remembered as the first lawgiver, King Trailok is known for a lasting impact on the country's administrative and social structure. By Trailok's time, the Thai state had expanded phenomenally, to over 200,000 square miles with the conquest and inclusion of the Khmer kingdom in 1431. The administrative system he introduced for this immense area was comprehensive; it endured with only minor modifications until the revolutionary changes of the nineteenth century. Large numbers of former Khmer bureaucrats brought to Ayuthaya helped the reorganization of the administrative system.

Trailok's reforms can be grouped in several categories: centralization of government and administration on a departmental basis; distinction between civilian and military functions of government; creation of a social and judicial system based on economic holdings; and a code to govern the royal household, including the issue of succession to the throne. The resulting system lent Thailand a stability unsurpassed anywhere in Southeast Asia.

Before Trailok's time, the Thais were divided into a number of principalities, whose chiefs paid nominal homage to the king of Ayuthaya. Trailok brought all the Thai principalities under his control and divided his kingdom into provinces, each headed by a *chao phraya* (governor), usually a prince. The separate military forces of the various principalities were amalgamated into a single army under central control.

The civilian administration was divided into five departments: the Department of the Interior; the Department of Local Government, in charge of the capital of Ayuthaya, which had by then an estimated population of 150,000; the Department of Finance, including foreign trade; the Department of Agriculture; and the Department of Palace Affairs and Justice. The military administration was also divided into several departments, each under a *kalahom*, who enjoyed a ministerial rank on a par with heads of the civilian ministries.

King Trailok also reorganized the society based on *sakdi na* (literally, field power) grades, an old Thai practice relating landholdings to an individual's social position and linking it to the judicial system. The punishments and compensations depended on a person's status. Trailok codified the system, laying down specifically how much land could be held by different classes of people. The highest official held as much as 4,000 acres, the lowest commoner 10 acres. The princes ranked above the highest officials and were entitled to more land, the heir apparent holding as much as 40,000 acres.[2] The commoners were obligated to give a portion of their time to work on government projects and to the cultivation of their local lord's lands. Only high officials and monks were exempted from these corvée obligations. Slaves and prisoners of war helped the Thai nobility and the free people to cultivate the extensive lands granted them by the state.

The system had its merits. All nobles and officials had an income on which to live, while the common people were assured of subsistence. Land was fertile and plentifully available. The system kept corruption to a minimum. The laws of inheritance enabled social mobility and prevented rigid social stratification. After five generations, titles of nobility, along with their assigned lands, lapsed to the state.

Another area of codification was the royal household. The Palatine Law of 1458 was a detailed enactment concerning members of the royal family and tributary states. It defined five classes of members of the extended royal family and indicated the privileges and duties of each class. The law prescribed penalties for violations of law. Thus, princes of high rank were to be restrained with golden fetters, the less-important ones with silver shackles. When a member of the royal family was to be executed, the person was placed in a sack and beaten to death with a fragrant sandalwood club. A lady of the palace charged with adultery was to be executed, her suitor tortured for three days and then killed. Penalties for even suspected conspiracy against the king were very severe. To enable a smooth transition, Trailok created the office of heir apparent, *brah maha uparaja* (vice-king). From this time on, it became customary to appoint the king's younger brother or the eldest son as vice-king, with a separate palace and ten times the land given to the highest official.

The Rise of Majapahit

The Mongol emperor of China, Kublai Khan, also sent his emissaries in 1289 to Singhasari kingdom in Java, demanding tribute and ordering Kertanagara to appear in person at his court in Beijing. Kertanagara did not heed the Mongol demands. Given the long distance, he doubted Mongol ability to overcome the well-built Singhasari defenses. Undaunted, he sent the Chinese ambassadors back to Beijing with their faces mutilated. Kertanagara had miscalculated the Mongol might—Kublai was truly outraged. In 1292, he sent a huge punitive fleet of 1,000 ships and 20,000 men to teach Kertanagara a lesson. Meanwhile, the Mongol pressure had already generated dissidence among Kertanagara's vassals. A prince of the rival old house of Kediri Jayakatwang revolted, seized Singhasari, and killed Kertanagara. The latter's heir and son-in-law, Vijaya, managed to flee with some of his troops to a village called Majapahit (literally, bitter fruit) on the river Brantas.

When the Mongol fleet arrived, it found Singhasari in disarray. The proud, defiant ruler Kertanagara was dead, and the bulk of his fleet was away in Malayu on an expedition. The rebel prince of Kediri was barely in control of his sprawling empire. The Mongols could not, however, return to China without a proper political settlement, including acknowledgment by the island rulers of the Chinese emperor's suzerain status. The fugitive prince, Vijaya, perceived the Mongol predicament. He promised to become a vassal of China in return for assistance in overthrowing the Kediri usurper. While the negotiations were in progress, the Singhasari fleet returned from Malayu. Vijaya quickly turned against his unwary

Mongol "allies" and expelled them. The Mongol expedition designed to castigate Kertanagara thus had the unintended result of placing his legitimate heir on the throne. Vijaya himself was destined to be the founder of a great empire. Out of sentimental attachment for the village that had given him shelter and refuge in the days of his erstwhile adversity, he made Majapahit his capital and adopted the same name for his dynasty. The Majapahit empire became, in the course of time, the greatest ever of all the states in insular Southeast Asia, claiming political control over most of the archipelago, the only indigenous power to do so in the pre-Dutch history of the region.

The credit—some have argued it is misplaced—was given to Gajah Mada, the *patih* (prime minister) from 1331 to 1364 and certainly the most remarkable figure in Indonesian history before the Dutch conquest. During the first part of his premiership, a regency was established in the name of Vijaya's widow, Raja-patni Gayatri. Her grandson, Hayam Wuruk, ascended the throne on her death in 1350, assuming the reigning title of Rajasanagara. With Gajah Mada's aid, he became the greatest king of the Majapahit dynasty, and he continued Gajah Mada's work after the latter's death in 1364.

Gajah Mada united the archipelago, not through a confederate alliance as Kertanagara had tried but through direct conquest. The celebrated Javanese epic *Nagarkertagama* perhaps gives him more credit than was due as an empire-builder. Thus, it speaks of the Majapahit hegemony extending not only over the entire archipelago (except western Sunda) but also over Champa, Thailand, and Cambodia, comparing its domain with China's. Modernly, most historians discount the premise that an extended Majapahit empire could include territories on mainland Southeast Asia. In their view, the Majapahit empire was limited to the Indonesian archipelago except western Sunda, which retained its independence until early in the sixteenth century. During the nationalist movement in the twentieth century, some of the Indonesian leaders, including Sukarno, argued that Indonesia had historically been a united state under Gajah Mada, thus refuting Dutch claims that Western colonial rule had brought the people of the archipelago together for the first time. Independent Indonesia has honored Gajah Mada's memory by naming the main street of Djakarta and the university at Jogjakarta after this much-admired administrator of the fourteenth century.

The period politically dominated by Gajah Mada and King Rajasanagara marked the golden age of Javanese history, known for literary and cultural efflorescence. Most notable of the literary works produced under extensive royal patronage were *The Nagarkertagama* by the poet Prapanca and *Arjunavivaha* and *Purushadasanta* (or *Sutasoma*) by the poet Tantular. The fourteenth century also brought major construction, including of many religious edifices dedicated to the syncretic cult of Shiva-Buddhism, noted for their bas-reliefs depicting scenes from *The Ramayana* and *The Krishnayana*. These monuments represent an advanced stage in the evolution of Indo-Javanese art, in which the Indian forms became more completely assimilated and the Indonesian elements and attitudes asserted themselves most clearly.

The Majapahit glory lasted only about seventy-five years, although the state lingered on until it was slowly liquidated by the advance of Islam in the first quarter of the sixteenth century. The Majapahit was the last great Hindu kingdom of Southeast Asia. A war of succession between 1401 and 1406 weakened it at a time when a new state, Malacca, which would eventually be the most responsible for its decline, emerged. After the establishment of Malacca in 1402, the trader-rulers of many small states converted to Islam in the hope of better promoting their trade prospects, thereby severing their ties with Hindu Majapahit. Majapahit's central position in international commerce then passed increasingly to Malacca. The Thais also showed an urge to expand in the Malay Peninsula and to secure for themselves a more important commercial role, thereby making the contest for supremacy triangular. By the early sixteenth century, Majapahit had sunk to being just one of a number of small Javanese states whose glory had become only a distant memory.

THE ADVENT OF ISLAM IN SOUTHEAST ASIA

Although the Chams are known to have embraced Islam in the tenth century, that religion did not attract a large number of adherents in Southeast Asia until the end of the thirteenth century. What accounted for such delay in the conversion of Southeast Asians to Islam? After all, their contacts with the Arab world predated Islam. Arab traders and sailors had been visiting Southeast Asian ports or passing through the region on their way to China long before Islam was born. The Arabs continued their traffic with China and Southeast Asia after their conversion. By the eighth century, there were large communities of Arabs in the ports of China and western India and smaller ones in Sumatra and Java. However, they lived separately from the rest of the people and made no effort to convert them for fear of jeopardizing the trade and their relationship with the local authorities.

Large-scale propagation and acceptance of Islam in insular Southeast Asia became possible only after a similar development had taken place in India. Although a Muslim dynasty came to power in Delhi by 1208, it was only later in the century that substantial numbers of traders and others from Gujarat and from the Coromandel coast were converted to Islam. Merchants from these regions had historically been engaged in trade with Southeast Asia and had been partly responsible for carrying Indian culture there. In keeping with such traditional patterns, Islam became acceptable to Southeast Asians only when it came through Indian intermediaries. The new religion appealed to Southeast Asians also because, like Hinduism and Buddhism before, it came in a relatively peaceful fashion and made some accommodations. Scholars have noted that many Arabic words in Malaysian languages indicate an Indian origin.

By the thirteenth century, following increased European contacts with the Middle East because of the Crusades, European demand for Asian goods grew phenomenally. Persian and Arab traders found Gujarat strategically well suited to take advantage of the spiraling trade in sugar, spices, textiles, and luxury goods produced in India, Southeast Asia, and China. Gujarati merchants in search of spices visited Southeast Asian ports far more frequently than before and found it necessary and convenient for reasons of trade to take up residence there. However, Gujarat alone could not be responsible for the initial spread of Islam in Southeast Asia. Most Gujarati Muslims followed the Hanafi school of Islamic law. A considerable

MAP 4.1 Spread of Islam in Southeast Asia

movement for conversion must have originated from the Coromandel coast where, as in Indonesia later, the Shafi'i school was prominent.[3] Some Indian Muslim traders, on account of their great wealth, were able to marry the daughters of prominent merchant-rulers of Sumatra and settle down. Their offspring were raised as Muslims. They also encouraged the spread of Islam by offering better terms of trade to Muslims in the region. The superior position of the Indian Muslims in trade and business inspired the local rulers to convert to their faith. It was no wonder that Islam spread rapidly in the western part of the archipelago as subjects followed their rulers' example. Trade was combined with transmission of religion and culture. A rather morbid example of this was the practice of Gujarati Muslim merchants exporting tombstones from Gujarat, beautifully inscribed in classical Arabic with blank spaces for insertion of names of the deceased in Southeast Asia.

The subsequent spread of Islam in the Malay archipelago was the result of several factors, including trade rivalry with the Hindu Majapahit kingdom, development of Malacca as a center for the spread of Islam, advent of Christianity in the region under the aggressive Portuguese, and the patient work of the Sufi missionaries. Most important, however, was the compromising spirit of the advocates of the new religion, who did not at all insist on the abandonment by the peoples of the region of their Hindu-Buddhist cultural heritage. Thus, the Hindu ceremony of royal coronation[4] and marriage continued unchanged. In the Malay world, the animistic belief in *keramat,* a place or object inhabited by spirits, remained. Even today, most Indonesian personal names have retained their Sanskrit origin; the Javanese ballet and shadow theater continue to draw their themes from the Hindu epic *Ramayana;* and their traditional music, contrary to Islamic injunctions, is avidly enjoyed by millions. If one accepts the judgment of the Dutch scholar J. C. van Leur, Islam brought no changes of any great consequence in Indonesian polity, economy, or culture. Outside of theology and some alterations in ceremonies, Islam was "only a thin, easily flaking glaze on the massive body of indigenous civilization,"[5] which by that time included Hindu-Buddhist influences.

Establishment of Malacca

The conversion of Malaya and the diffusion of Islam in the archipelago as a whole came about with the establishment of a new empire based on a new city, Malacca. Its strategic location at the narrowest point of the Strait of Malacca enabled the city to watch and control maritime traffic. Sheltered from the monsoon by the massive island of Sumatra, Malacca provided a safe harbor for ships at the mercy of the prevailing winds. Ships from the west sailed to Malacca across the Indian Ocean aided by southwest winds, spending several months in Malacca until the change of winds facilitated their return voyage.

Stories indicating the founding of Malacca several centuries before the fifteenth century may now be discounted. Evidence from Portuguese and Malay sources uncovered since 1940 prove that it was no more than a fishing village before 1402.[6] A few years before this, Parameshwara, prince of Palembang across the straits in Sumatra, disclaimed allegiance to his king, who was also his father-in-law, and was forced to flee. He tried to establish himself in Singapore by killing the local prince, only to be expelled by the latter's suzerain, Ayuthaya (Thailand).

Parameshwara fled from Singapore northward to Malacca. Using his previous contacts in Palembang, he persuaded some traders and shipowners to use the port of Malacca. He also used force to compel ships to call at Malacca, where he offered them an entrepôt for exchange of goods from the East and the West, warehousing facilities, and excellent accommodation for merchants and seamen awaiting a change of monsoon winds to resume their return journeys. Within a few years, Malacca became a great port city and an emporium where merchants from India, Pegu, Java, China, and Arabia jostled in its busy streets.

For its success, Malacca had to contend with three rival forces: Thailand, Majapahit, and the Muslim principalities of northeast Sumatra. Of these, the Thais were a rising, strong power, whereas Majapahit was past its prime. Early Malaccan rulers sent tribute to the Thai court, at the same time establishing and maintaining a cordial tributary relationship with Beijing as a counterpoise to Ayuthaya. Parameshwara visited Beijing in 1404 and two years later received from China a seal, a set of robes, and a yellow umbrella, the Chinese symbols of kingship.

Attempts to improve relations with the Muslim states of Sumatra led to Malacca's conversion to Islam. The sultan of Pasai demanded the conversion of Parameshwara's son, Megat, and the latter's marriage to his daughter as the price of recognition of Malacca. Megat assumed the Persian title, shah, and made Malacca a spearhead for the further spread of Islam. He employed royal marriages between Malacca and the ruling houses of the peninsula and in the archipelago as a device to convert the elite of the region. Another tactic was the conversion of Malacca's army, composed largely of Javanese mercenaries, whose families back in Java then were converted by the soldiers when they were home on leave. In the same manner, thousands of Javanese slaves of merchants in Malacca were also converted to Islam. Malacca's success and prosperity provided an inspiration to merchants in the rest of the archipelago to convert to Islam. Malacca also became the foremost seat of Muslim learning, attracting hundreds of Islamic divines from all over the Muslim world.

Administration of Malacca

Despite such an active policy of Islamization, Malacca encouraged all merchants, irrespective of their race or religion, to use the port facilities. At the head of the state was the sultan. Although a Muslim, his coronation ceremony and court etiquette were indistinguishable from the divine-monarchy concept followed by his counterparts in the rest of Southeast Asia. In keeping with the practice of Hindu-Buddhist courts, he had a council of four principal ministers, eight ministers of middle rank, and sixteen of lower rank. The head of the council was the chief minister *(bendahara)*, which became almost a hereditary office. Next was the *temenggong,* in charge of law and order and weights and measures. The port authority was under four harbor-masters called by their Persian title of *shahbunders,* selected from the four principal merchant communities from China, Java, Bengal, and Gujarat.[7]

Within a half century of its birth, Malacca became the best port and emporium in all Southeast Asia. It became the seat of an empire, largely as a result of the initiative and dynamism of its greatest *bendahara,* Tun Perak (1456–1498). This included Pahang, known for its natural reserves of gold; Johor; the Carimon Islands; Rhio-Linga Archipelago; and several small Sumatran kingdoms, including

Kampar, Indragiri, and Siak. Patani and Kedah were added to the empire during the decade following Tun Perak's death.

Tun Perak's long tenure as *bendahara* had its good and bad points. His predominance in all state matters stifled the initiative of the sultans and other court officials. Besides, in later years he overlooked the corrupt practices and exactions of the ruling elites as a price of their loyalty. During his lifetime, Tun Perak was able to placate the rival *bendahara* family of Tamil Muslim origin, largely through patronage and matrimony. Within two years of his death, however, Tun Mutahir of the rival family succeeded to the office of *bendahara*.

Such factional disputes, corruption, and a parasitical way of life of the elite weakened the Malacca sultanate. Tun Mutahir's administration witnessed more nepotism, bribery, and exactions than ever before. He was finally suspected of harboring ambitions of capturing the throne and was arrested and beheaded along with most of the male members of his family. Although Malacca was militarily and economically very strong, its internecine struggles had left it weak when the Portuguese arrived in the year after Tun Mutahir's execution.

The Muslim domination of trade in the western part of the Malay archipelago was first undermined by the Portuguese. By the end of the seventeenth century, it had become extinct because of the Dutch maritime and trading supremacy in the entire archipelago.

5

European Intrusion in the Indian Archipelago: The Early Phase

PREMODERN EUROPEAN ROLE

Although European political contacts with Southeast Asia began with the Portuguese conquest of Malacca in 1511, there was no major political or cultural European impact on the region until well into the nineteenth century. An exception to this was the Philippines. It was not that the population was completely Europeanized, but that the degree of religious and cultural penetration by the Europeans in the Philippines was greater than anywhere else in Asia.

Elsewhere, the pre-nineteenth-century European contacts remained largely coastal and commercial, affecting a small segment of the population. On the mainland, the influence was negligible. Even in insular Southeast Asia, Europeans limited themselves principally to islands producing or exporting spices. European influence in the archipelago reached only the fringes, while the bulk of the island population continued to be governed by indigenous rulers and their time-tested traditions.

Most of the earlier works on Southeast Asian history placed a disproportionate emphasis on the role of this miniscule body of Europeans in the pre-nineteenth-century period. It is amazing that such a distorted view of the region's history, condemned by a brilliant young Dutch historian, J. C. van Leur, as "observed from the deck of the ship, the ramparts of the fortress, the high gallery of the trading house," persisted as long as it did.[1] A balanced treatment of the pre-nineteenth-century history should include a more intensive coverage of the developments in the indigenous states and societies and their interrelationships with each other. Unfortunately, the general paucity of materials in respect to indigenous states, as opposed to the abundance of documentation concerning the activities of the European trading companies, has handicapped historians' efforts in providing a proper balance and perspective to Southeast Asian history.

THE PORTUGUESE

In the fifteenth century, two Iberian powers—Spain and Portugal—both Catholic, rivaled each other in exploring routes to the East. Impelled by the twin urges of acquisition and proselytization, their courts patronized cartographers and mariners. The poorer and more fanatic of the two were the Portuguese, who were as much inspired by the missionary spirit as by the prospect of acquiring wealth from the East to build a glorious state rivaling the Italian city-states such as Venice, Genoa, and Milan, which fattened themselves with profits of trade with the Arabs in products of the East. The increase in the European demand for oriental goods, particularly spices, had swelled since the Crusades. The demand and prices of spices had risen, thanks to their growing use in medicine and food preparation and preservation. The Italian merchants also made feigned pleas that the flow of Eastern commodities to European markets was severely impeded by the advance of the Turks and the fall of Constantinople in 1453. Portuguese morale was boosted by Pope Nicholas V's Bull of 1454 urging Christians to go to India (erroneously believed to be a Christian country, perhaps because of the knowledge that the Apostle Saint Thomas had gone there in the first century A.D.) and secure its assistance against the Ottoman Turks advancing toward Europe. Portuguese explorations and conquest were inspired by the three Gs: gospel, gold, and glory for their king. India, known as a land of spices and textiles, lured both Columbus and Vasco da Gama. The latter, after arriving in 1498 at Calicut on the southwest coast of India (from which the English word *calico* is derived), declared that he had come "to seek Christians and spices." Trade and religion were two sides of the same coin; to deprive the Arabs of trade profits and to kill them as enemies of Christianity became the passion of the Portuguese for the next several decades.

The man who truly enunciated and pursued the early Portuguese goals was Alfonso de Albuquerque, the second viceroy of the "State of India" (1509–1515). Seeking a monopoly of trade with the South and Southeast Asian regions, the Portuguese acquired strategic locations in the Indian Ocean and Arabian Sea—Malacca, Sri Lanka, Goa, Diu, Socotra, Ormuz—to plug the arteries of Arab and Persian trade.

Malacca was, at the time of the Portuguese arrival in Southeast Asia, the most prosperous port of the region. In June 1511, Alfonso de Albuquerque himself led the fleet against Malacca. Two attacks failed. The Portuguese then divided the merchant community by burning Arab and Indian Muslim shipping, sparing the Chinese and non-Muslim. Crucial help from the latter in the form of landing craft enabled the Portuguese to cross a vital bridge at night and enter Malacca. The sultan and his mostly mercenary army fled, leaving the civilian Muslim population—men, women, and children—to be mercilessly butchered by the Portuguese. Albuquerque's speech to his men emphasized "the great service which we shall perform to our Lord in casting the Moors out of this country and of quenching the fire of the sect of Mohammet so that it may never burst out again hereafter." As for trade, he added: "I hold it certain that if we take this trade of Malacca away from them [the Muslims], Cairo and Mecca will be entirely ruined and Venice will receive no spiceries unless her merchants go and buy them in Portugal."[2]

The Portuguese held Malacca for 130 years, often precariously because of the hostility of Muslim rulers of nearby Johor, Acheh, and Java. Apart from controlling the Strait of Malacca, they were not interested in territorial conquest of the western part of the archipelago; their eyes were focused on the spice-producing Moluccas. Therefore, they established forts and trading stations on Ternate, Tidore, Ambon, and Borneo. They held no military outposts on mainland Southeast Asia, where there were powerful indigenous rulers. They were allowed trading posts, however, in Ayuthaya (Thailand), Cambodia, and on the Tenasserim coast (Myanmar).

Within a decade of their conquest of Malacca, the Portuguese were confronted with Spanish claims in Southeast Asia. Ferdinand Magellan, circumnavigating the globe, had arrived in the Spice Islands and the Philippines via the west in 1521, violating the Papal Bull of 1493 that had divided the world between the two Iberian powers along a line west of the Azores: east of the line to Portugal and west of it to Spain. (The pope had indeed assumed that the earth was flat.) In 1529, by the Treaty of Saragossa, Portugal and Spain agreed to reconcile their claims; the Spaniards gave up their positions in the Moluccas in exchange for the Portuguese undertaking to allow the Spanish conquest of the Philippines.

In the first decades of the sixteenth century, Malacca attracted considerable shipping, thanks to the effectiveness of the Portuguese navy in compelling non-Portuguese ships to touch the port and the continuation of the administration of Malacca along the old pre-Portuguese lines. Profits were extraordinarily high; pepper bought in the East fetched forty times its price in Europe. By 1550, the profits from trade amounted to four times Portugal's internal revenue. Until 1544, the Portuguese charged a reasonable tariff of 6 percent. Thereafter, the captain-governors of Malacca, most of them related to powerful nobility at court and overanxious to feather their own nests, arbitrarily charged port duties and forced private merchants to sell merchandise to them at discount prices. All such practices had the effect of injuring trade and creating anti-Portuguese feeling among the merchant community. The Portuguese had inherited the monopolistic aspirations of Srivijaya and Malacca, tapping the east-west flow of goods, particularly in spices. For most of the sixteenth century, they effectively dominated the Strait of Malacca and therefore the chief sea route from India to China.

A major weakness of the Portuguese policy was the linkage of religion with trade and politics. The uncouth, unruly, and uncultured Portuguese of the time could not have impressed the Southeast Asians as being the torchbearers of European civilization. Even a great missionary, Saint Francis Xavier, was so disgusted with their debauchery that he shook the dust of Malacca from his feet vowing never to return to the cesspool of vices again. The Portuguese habit of attacking Muslim shipping on the excuse of waging war against the "infidels" was regarded only as a flimsy excuse for piracy. Furthermore, their use of force in proselytization only created animosity in the minds of Southeast Asians, who had historically been receptive to peaceful penetration of religious influences. Consequently, conversion to Christianity was very marginal. Instead, by trying to force Christianity on the people of the region, the Portuguese inadvertently glamorized Islam as a weapon against Portuguese oppression.

The rapid spread of Islam in insular Southeast Asia in the sixteenth century could be counted among Portugal's indirect and, indeed, unintended cultural contributions to the region. The new converts to Islam preferred to trade with their religious brethren and worked to prevent trade from falling into Portuguese hands. Another factor in the decline of Portuguese power was their sheer shortage of manpower. A small country of a million people could not long stand the attrition among seamen caused by shipwreck, disease, and war. Furthermore, the extensive Portuguese empire was badly neglected by the Spaniards from 1580 to 1640 when the two crowns were combined. During that period, three other European powers arrived in Southeast Asia, and one of them, the Dutch, destroyed Portuguese power in the region. By the end of the seventeenth century, the Portuguese had lost all their territories in Southeast Asia except part of Timor and had only a shaky hold on Solor and eastern Flores.

THE DUTCH AND THE ENGLISH

By the end of the sixteenth century, two rival European merchant communities— the Dutch and the English—resolved to enter the spice trade directly. Beginning in 1595, several Dutch trading companies were formed, to be combined in 1602 into Vereenigde Oostandische Compagnie (VOC), the United East India Company. Paralleling the Dutch movement, 125 English merchants received a royal charter on December 31, 1600, for the East India Company, which began modestly by seeking to trade with India and Southeast Asia. To obviate the inevitable conflict, the governments of the two countries signed an agreement in Europe to share the Asian trade. The VOC representative in the East Indies, Governor-General Jan Pieterscoon Coen (1618–1623 and 1627–1629), was not prepared, however, to give up the Dutch drive toward monopoly. He ordered a massacre of the English on Ambon in 1623, which directly resulted in the East India Company's decision to abandon most of its positions and trade in the archipelago to the Dutch and to concentrate on India instead. During Coen's period, the VOC emerged well consolidated, with a strong basis for the Dutch commercial empire of the next three centuries. In the pursuit of monopoly, the Dutch combated the Portuguese outposts, which fell fairly rapidly. In 1641, the main Portuguese bastion, Malacca, was captured by the Dutch, who thereby secured control over both of the strategic straits in Southeast Asian waters—Malacca and Sunda.

The prime objective of the Dutch activity in Southeast Asia was trade rather than territory. Neither proselytization nor the material welfare of the indigenous people was among their concerns. Direct administrative responsibility was to be avoided at all costs unless the territory was of economic or strategic significance and was likely to fall under rival European domination. The Dutch avoided direct administrative responsibility until the middle of the eighteenth century, preferring to sign treaties placing indigenous rulers in charge of the local administration in exchange for agreement to supply spices and other commodities. Dynastic disputes as well as interstate feuds, however, hampered the flow of supplies and trade, necessitating Dutch intervention resulting in territorial acquisitions. Thus, the two principal Javanese states, Bantam in the west and Mataram in the center and east, were rivals for power on the island. They both resisted Dutch encroachments but could not combine against the alien power. Eventually, by the end of the seventeenth century, the VOC had installed its own candidates as rulers of the two states. By the 1770s, the VOC had acquired authority over all of Java.

A result of such gradual assumption of administrative control was the preservation of the old Indonesian political and administrative order. By and large, no bloody conflicts took place between the company and the indigenous rulers of Java, nor did any significant change occur in the traditional relationship between the ruler and the ruled. The VOC preferred this indirect and informal control because of the obvious savings in human and monetary costs of administration. Local rulers, doubling as principal traders, were allowed by the Dutch to remain in charge as long as they traded exclusively with the VOC. By the end of the seventeenth century, they were required under a system of forced deliveries called *leveringen* to send to the company's warehouses fixed amounts of produce at fixed prices. If a ruler was found colluding with any other European power, the Dutch did not hesitate to use force to discipline him or to oust him from power.

In the few areas like Ambon, the Bandas, and the Preanger region of west Java, which by the eighteenth century came under direct Dutch administration, the peasants were compelled to grow crops suitable for export. From the middle of the eighteenth century, coffee, sugar, and indigo crops became as important as spices. The size of the crop and the price of the produce were determined from time to time depending on the demand in the European markets. In order to avoid a glut of produce of certain commodities like nutmegs and cloves, the VOC confined the cultivation of these items to areas only under its direct administrative control. The Dutch fleet continually patrolled the other areas, particularly in the outer islands, and destroyed spice-bearing trees in forbidden areas.

Such an elaborately devised policy of internal regulation of production in the islands, whether by direct or indirect means, along with control of the straits of Malacca and Sunda, reinforced by what was distinctly the best navy in the area, enabled the Dutch to establish their preeminence in the archipelago's trade with Europe. At no time, however, were they able to establish a complete monopoly.[3] Within the archipelago itself, the inter-island trade remained as "peddler trade," to use the term made familiar by the Dutch scholar J. C. van Leur. Nor was the economy in nonexport crops and manufacture of handicrafts in the inland areas affected to any significant degree by the Dutch presence until the last quarter of the eighteenth century. Furthermore, the Dutch obsession with profits ruled out any major role that could conceivably alter the cultural, educational, or religious patterns of life of the bulk of the population. Whether in the coastal or inland areas, the majority of the people continued to live without any significant European impact.

Yet, in the territories directly under the VOC and in the areas where cash crops were cultivated for delivery into VOC warehouses, the lives of the common people were dramatically affected, though mostly to their detriment. After all, one of the primary objectives of the Dutch company was to establish an effective monopoly and, as a corollary, to maintain high prices for Eastern commodities in Europe and low prices in the East Indies. The results of such a policy were to divorce the peasant producers from participation in the external trade and to deprive them of any share in the profits of such trade. The enforced deliveries of produce at low and fixed prices was only another form of tribute that the colonial masters exacted from the traditional nobility and the helpless peasantry of the archipelago.

The Dutch trade provided no stimulus to the Indonesian economy. The pre-Dutch dichotomy of mercantile economy and agricultural-subsistence economy persisted even more acutely than before. On the other hand, the Dutch monopoly of trade displaced some indigenous elements involved in carriage and distribution of goods. Some trade lines were closed, and others monopolized by the Dutch. Consequently, many merchants served as collecting agents for the Dutch or became agriculturists. Many sailors took to the alternative of piracy, which became a serious problem in the seventeenth and eighteenth centuries. The rise of Bugis in Sulawesi (Celebes) and their loss of livelihood as peddlers and sailors followed the Dutch monopolistic practices in the archipelago.

THE FRENCH

Unlike the Dutch and the English, the French trading activity in Asia proved, at least in the short run, a big failure. One reason perhaps was that it was court-sponsored and its success fluctuated with the individual monarch and court intrigues. Second, like the Portuguese, the French combined religion and trade, missionaries more often hindering than helping the trade effort. A third factor that would jeopardize the French future for a considerable time was the conspiratorial role of a European adventurer, Constance Phaulkon, at the court of Ayuthaya.

French trade efforts beginning in 1601 were jeopardized by the Dutch. The French were far more successful in religious activities. In 1615, some Jesuits opened a mission at Fai Fo, south of Da Nang. Its most illustrious member was Alexandre de Rhodes, who, beginning from 1627, spent nearly four decades in missionary effort. His great contribution was to devise *quoc ngu,* a method of writing the Vietnamese language in roman that is widely used in Vietnam. Rhodes's motivation was to be able to reach the masses for conversion to Christianity. Some conversions did take place; by the end of the eighteenth century, French missionaries claimed over a quarter million converts in coastal Vietnam.

Missionaries were not always welcome in Vietnam. In 1662, reports of severe persecution of Catholics there compelled freshly arriving missionaries from France to stop in Ayuthaya instead. To their great delight, the Thai monarch Narai (1657–1688) offered them hospitality. The French quickly built a church and a seminary and made Ayuthaya their headquarters in Southeast Asia. Very soon, King Narai's kindly disposition made the French optimistic enough to hope for his conversion. If that happened, the missionaries knew that conversion of the bulk of his subjects would not be difficult.

Two factors led to the increase of French influence at Ayuthaya. The Thai monarch was concerned over Dutch demands for a complete monopoly of Thai external trade. Their threats to use violence to achieve their end could be silenced only with the assistance of another European power. The English refused to help; after Ambon, they had grown allergic to any confrontation with the Dutch. Would the French help? The second factor was the interest taken by Constance Phaulkon, a Greek adventurer, who had taken employment at the Thai court and risen to the powerful position of the superintendent of foreign trade. His hatred of the English, whom he had served for some time, and his own recent conversion to Catholicism had prompted him to favor the French. At his insistence, a Thai embassy visited the court of the Sun King, Louis XIV. Behind the scenes, Phaulkon laid before the French court a secret plan. According to it, French priests would arrive as laymen and take up important assignments in Ayuthaya as provincial governors and garrison commanders. At a suitable time, the priests would reveal themselves and play their role in the conversion of the king and the people. On the official plane, France agreed to send warships to the southern port of Songkhla to oust the Dutch. The French were promised trading concessions, some missionary privileges, cession of some islands off Mergui, and the right to extraterritoriality. When six French warships actually arrived with 636 soldiers under Marshal Desfarges, Phaulkon allowed them to garrison at Bangkok (instead of the far-off Songkhla) as well as Mergui, thereby effectively blocking trade routes both by sea and by land.

What Phaulkon had failed to anticipate was the reaction of the Thai nobility to the awesome accretion to his power and to the presence of French troops. In 1688, taking advantage of the absence of the king, who was ill and away from the capital, the antiforeign group at the court suddenly arrested Phaulkon and executed him in the public square. The Thais made sure that no foreigner or foreign power would attain a position such as Phaulkon or the French had enjoyed. Thereafter, until the end of the eighteenth century, the French influence was more or less confined to the Christian converts in Vietnam. There was no significant trading or territorial role for them in Southeast Asia until the middle of the nineteenth century.

THE SPANISH

Of all the European powers in Southeast Asia prior to the nineteenth century, the greatest impact was made by a people who made the least profit—the Spaniards. Having had a history of violence perpetrated on the hapless people of Latin America and, in the initial years of Spanish rule, on the Filipinos, the Spanish monarchs had a change of heart in regard to their country's role in the Philippines. They resolved early that religious conversion of the Filipinos was to be the only justification for holding the islands. Under the long Spanish rule (1571–1898), the Philippines became the only Asian country with a Christian majority population and with the highest degree of Western influence.

The Spanish arrived in Southeast Asia via the East. In 1521, Ferdinand Magellan lost his life on the small island of Mactan in a violent encounter with the local chief. In the postindependence era, the Filipinos erected a new marker to commemorate the event entitled "Lapulapu" adding this new inscription: "Here, on 27 April, 1521, Lapulapu and his men repulsed the Spanish invaders, killing their leader, Ferdinand Magellan. Thus Lapulapu became the first Filipino to have repelled European aggression."[4]

In 1565, the first Spanish settlement was established on the island of Cebu. Six years later, the Spanish conquered what was then a small town, Manila. The conquest arrested the further spread of Islam northward. Manila became the headquarters for Christianity and the base for Spanish expansion in the central and northern islands. Opposition came from several quarters, the toughest threat being posed by the southern islands of Mindanao and Sulu, populated and ruled by Filipino Muslims whom the Spanish called the Moros. It was not until the 1830s, when the Spanish employed the fast-moving *vintas* (speedy sailboats), that the Moros were defeated. Even so, there were at least one hundred rebellions in the newly conquered territories until finally the sultan of Sulu capitulated in 1878.

The Spaniards registered their greatest success in the field of religion. Unlike the other areas of Southeast Asia where Hinduism, Buddhism, and Islam held firm roots, the northern and central Philippines lacked a strong sacerdotal hierarchy. The long-standing Spanish and missionary propaganda that the Filipinos were culturally deprived was a product of their prejudice. Archaeological and linguistic researches have revealed plentiful evidence of cultural and perhaps political links with the Srivijaya and Majapahit empires as well as of general Indian influences in folklore, languages, and art. Such links were enduring but never so close as in the rest of insular Southeast Asia. At least two reasons can be readily adduced to explain why the Philippines remained "outside the region's mainstream of historical development."[5] First, the Philippines did not produce the spices and other commodities that attracted Arab, Persian, Chinese, Indian, and other merchants and seafarers. Second, the topography of the islands, with the surrounding deep, typhoon-prone seas, discouraged much traffic in the region. By and large, however, in contrast with the rest of Southeast Asia, the Philippines has no literary or historical annals and very few architectural and sculptural remains on the basis of which to reconstruct its political or cultural past.

When the Spanish arrived, Islam was well established in Mindanao and the Sulu archipelago. Elsewhere, belief in animistic spirits and the supreme being called Bathala predominated. Such beliefs continued even after the people in the central and northern Philippines were converted to Christianity. Thus, many Christian converts wore necklaces of charms (*anting anting*), marking a compromise between Christianity and the animistic folk beliefs. Many Filipinos still practice their traditional ancient rites, and they continue to believe in the spirits like *anitos* and *nunos*. The church had to compromise on all these practices to attract the indigenous people to Christianity because, unlike other colonial situations where converts stood to benefit materially, the Philippine converts had to pay *tributos* to the church and government for the protection they offered.

The influence of the church was extensive. Most villages had a priest who offered not only spiritual salvation but also looked after the church lands. The priests and the friars, though belonging to rival organizations, were unified on many points. They learned Tagalog and the many other Filipino languages and compiled grammars and dictionaries so that they could educate the people about Christianity. With very few exceptions, such as that of Tomas Pinpin, a Filipino who in 1610 was allowed to publish a book to help Tagalogs to speak Spanish, they were averse to imparting knowledge of the Spanish language or European literature for fear the indigenous people might get restive if they received sophisticated education. Consequently, the education was religious and anti-intellectual. Even so, the church was responsible for the establishment in 1611 of the oldest college in all of Southeast Asia, the College of Saint Thomas, which became a university in 1645. The church's role was dominant in Manila and the provincial capitals as well as in the countryside. Enjoying great influence at the Spanish court, the Vatican's nominee in Manila often upstaged the governor-general, whose time was divided between presiding over a rather limited bureaucracy that did not reach the village communities and conducting a perpetual war with the Moros. Besides, his tour of duty was short and could be further shortened if he imprudently persisted in his differences with the archbishop. The church's hold over the people was so complete that as late as 1859 a prominent British visitor, Sir John Bowring, was told: "The Governor-General is in Manila (far away); the King is in Spain (farther still); and God is in Heaven (farthest of all); but the priest is everywhere."[6]

Spanish policy in the Philippines was principally governed by considerations of religion. Having learned lessons from Central America, the government decreed in the eighteenth century that lay Spaniards live in cities only. There were to be no Central American–style *conquistadores,* no decimation of the population, and no extreme exploitation of labor. No mining or plantations were permitted. Consequently, there was little exploitation of the Filipino people; on the other hand, little change in agricultural methods, mining, or manufacturing was introduced in the islands.

The traditional Filipino social organization was hardly affected. The Filipinos identified themselves with the particular *barangay* (boat-load) that supposedly brought their ancestors from the Indonesian islands. Each *barangay* was headed by a *datu,* the same title by which village chiefs were known in Malaya. The *datus* elected a *gobernadorcillo* (little governor) to be the chief of a group of villages. The towns were headed by mayors, who along with the *gobernadorcillos* were responsible to the provincial governors. Thus, administration below the level of Spanish provincial governors was, in effect, indigenous and tradition-based.

Until well into the nineteenth century, the Philippines remained an economic backwater. Most people worked either for the friar estates or, until the eighteenth century, for the *encomiendas* (royal grants covering several villages), which were granted to Spanish individuals in the initial years of colonial rule as a reward on the same pattern as conquistadors in Latin America. The holders of these grants, called *encomenderos,* had the authority to collect tribute or labor from about six thousand families in return for Christianizing and protecting them from non-Christians. In many instances, the *encomenderos* assumed the powers traditionally exercised by Filipino village chiefs of administering justice at the local level. The friar estates were mostly given on lease to Filipino *mestizos* on a fifty-fifty basis. Only in the *pueblos* (village communities having at least 500 tribute-taxpayers) was there a common ownership of all residents. However, the system provided no great incentive to work hard because there were no remunerative markets for selling the surplus production.

The only exporting center was Manila, which was visited by an annual galleon from Acapulco. It did not carry any Filipino products but rather silks, porcelain, spices, and jewelry sold by Manilan Chinese merchants who imported these commodities from China. The famous Manila Galleon, the last of which sailed in 1811, paid an average of one million to three million pesos in silver in payment of these products from China, which accepted only silver or gold. It is not surprising that in the days of mercantilism, the Spanish limited Chinese trade severely and prohibited any Chinese import to Spain itself. A considerable portion of the Spanish payment to China was in the form of Mexican silver dollars, some of which found their way to Southeast Asia through China's trade with that region. In fact, the Mexican silver dollar remained the single most popular currency of exchange all over Southeast Asia for almost three centuries from the late sixteenth century. Yet trade itself had hardly any impact on the Filipino people or their economy.

6

Mainland Southeast Asia: The Consolidations of Myanmar, Thailand, and Vietnam

BURMESE TERRITORIALISM

After the disastrous fall of the Pagan kingdom at the hands of the Mongols in 1287, the majority Burmans were politically shattered. Not until the establishment of the Toungoo dynasty (1531–1732) did they retrieve their dominant position. After a brief period of political eclipse lasting two decades, they reestablished their power with the emergence of the last dynasty in Burmese history, the Alaungpaya, or Konbaung (1752–1885).

The Mons, who had never forgiven the Burmans for overrunning their state of Pegu in the eleventh century, declared themselves independent after the fall of Pagan in 1287. The Mons once again became restive in the sixteenth century after their freedom was liquidated by the Burmans, who reestablished their supremacy at Toungoo.

Toungoo Expansionism

Toungoo, a hill stockade in the valley of the Sittang River near Prome, had attracted Burman chiefs ever since the fall of Pagan. In the first quarter of the sixteenth century, the Toungoo ruler, Tabinshweti (1531–1550), and his successor, Bayinnaung (1550–1581), became the architects of the reunification of Myanmar and the restoration of Burman power.

Tabinshweti recognized that Mon cooperation was essential to the well-being of a reunified Myanmar. His coronation rites were Mon and Burman. The capital was moved to the Mon country. Tabinshweti wore a Mon headdress and cut his hair in the Mon fashion. Such gestures, however, failed to placate the Mon love for independence. Tabinshweti's dreams of expansion went beyond the Burmese borders eastward into Ayuthaya (Thailand), and in this again he needed Mon assistance because the best invasion route lay from the Mon country across the Three Pagodas Pass into Ayuthaya.

In the history of mainland Southeast Asia, the sixteenth and eighteenth centuries were notable for a series of wars between Myanmar and Ayuthaya. On the whole, the initiative was taken by Burmese kings, whose expansionist ambitions provided the principal motivation for the senseless bloodletting. Tabinshweti and Bayinnaung in the sixteenth century and Alaungpaya and Hsinbyushin in the eighteenth were all remarkable military leaders, extremely ambitious and aggressive. The urge for self-glorification was an irresistible element in their mental makeup. The existence of considerable surplus energy after the unification of Myanmar may also have been responsible for its spilling across its borders.

At least in the sixteenth century, the official Burmese justification for the attack on Ayuthaya was its refusal to part with some white elephants. White elephants—in reality, albinos—are highly regarded in the Hindu-Buddhist world as having magical qualities to produce rain-bearing clouds. According to a legend, Gautama's last incarnation immediately prior to his Buddhahood was as a white elephant. Possession of white elephants was a royal prerogative in traditional Southeast Asia, and a monarch could part with one of the prize beasts only at great peril to his position. Tabinshweti demanded that the king of Ayuthaya surrender some of the white elephants from the latter's stable.

The more significant reasons for the conflicts are provided by rival claims over the small state of Chiengmai. An economic explanation perhaps lies in the perennial need for labor in underpopulated Myanmar and Ayuthaya. Both could use large numbers of prisoners of war as slaves to cultivate land and help raise the royal revenues.

Tabinshweti was successful in the reunification of Myanmar, but twice failed in his attacks on Ayuthaya. The reverses his forces suffered demoralized him and encouraged the Mon minority to rebel against Burman rule. In 1550, he was killed by the Mons.

Bayinnaung, Tabinshweti's brother-in-law, adopted his dreams of expansion. After consolidating his rule over Myanmar, he conquered Chiengmai and marched into Lang Chan (Laos), which had challenged Burmese claims to Chiengmai. The Lao king, Settatirat, who had organized an anti-Burman alliance with the Shan states, was defeated in 1559. Bayinnaung then pressed his demand for two white elephants on King Chakrapat of Ayuthaya, who predictably refused to comply.

Myanmar's second invasion of Ayuthaya (1568–1569) resulted in the death of King Chakrapat and the occupation of his country for fifteen years. Thousands of Thais were taken prisoners of war. The Burmese occupation led to the Thai adoption of the Maha Sakarat era, which had begun in A.D. 78. It remained in use until 1887, when King Chulalongkorn adopted the Gregorian calendar. During the occupation, the Burmese also introduced their own law code, based on Manu's Code of Law, to Ayuthaya.

After Bayinnaung's death in 1581, however, the tide turned in favor of the Thais. The new Thai leader was Pra Naret (black prince). A hostage in Myanmar and married to Bayinnaung's sister, he was allowed to return to Ayuthaya. Not only did he expel the Burmese garrison but he invaded Myanmar itself and captured the southern Burmese ports of Moulmein and Tavoy. Pra Naret's failure to occupy Myanmar proper, however, showed that the military strength of the two countries was well balanced. Pra Naret, crowned King Nareseun in 1590, ruled until 1605.

During the seventeenth century, peace existed between Myanmar and Ayuthaya as the former abandoned its expansionist aims. The Burmese capital was moved to Ava in the north, and the kings assumed an isolationist policy. Both countries had problems with external powers: Myanmar with China and Ayuthaya with the Dutch and the French. In the last quarter of the seventeenth century, Ayuthaya also became an isolationist power because of its bitter experience with the machinations of the pro-French European adventurer Constance Phaulkon.

Konbaung Occupation of Ayuthaya

In 1752, the Burmans were piqued that the Mons had captured their capital of Ava. The leader of the new Burman resistance to Mon domination was Alaungpaya (embryo Buddha). Before long, Ava was retaken and the Mon forces were driven south. Alaungpaya managed to organize a vast army of dedicated and valiant Burmans, inspired by his dream of unified Myanmar. Within three years, Alaungpaya's forces had conquered central Myanmar and Pegu all the way to Dagon, which he renamed Rangoon, "the end of war"—a misnomer indeed.

Alaungpaya's wars in Lower Myanmar had resulted in depopulation of the province, with thousands of Mons fleeing into Ayuthaya. The Burmese leader felt compelled to attack Ayuthaya in 1760 to get the Mons back to repopulate their devastated country. The invasion of Ayuthaya met with stiff resistance. Alaungpaya was wounded while directing the siege of the Thai capital and died during the retreat of his troops to Myanmar.

Though Alaungpaya's leadership lasted a bare eight years, the energies he released among the Burmans and the hopes he raised of their destiny were such as to goad them into an orgy of conflict in quest of territorial expansion for the next several decades. It was a period of intense militarism for Myanmar, which continually warred with its neighbors. A number of great generals arose, and the rivalry among them led to an atmosphere of suspicion, intrigue, and wanton executions at the Burmese court.

Alaungpaya's second son, Hsinbyushin (1763–1776), led a three-pronged, well-planned attack on Ayuthaya through the Shan states and Laos. Ayuthaya was sacked and looted and many of its inhabitants were taken into slavery. The four-century-old beautiful city was so completely devastated that it never regained its importance. It was only the immediate need for the Burmese forces to withdraw in order to defend their homeland from Chinese attack that saved other Thai cities from further destruction. Hsinbyushin's brother, Bodawpaya (1781–1819), invaded Thailand on four different occasions between 1785 and 1802, but the strong Chakri dynasty that had emerged in Bangkok offered such staunch resistance that the Burmese decided they should seek territorial expansion in the west rather than the east. The consequent campaign in Arakan, Manipur, Kachar, and Assam brought the Burmese into conflict with the English East India Company, which by then had established itself firmly in power in nearby Bengal.

THE RISE OF A STRONG THAILAND

The Burmese attacks on Thailand served one constructive purpose: They aroused the Thai pride. A national consciousness manifested itself in the numerous centers of resistance all over the former state of Ayuthaya. The immediate consequence of the Burmese raids and retreat had been a fractionalization of Ayuthaya into five parts, each under a princely or military leader. Of these, at least one showed a vision extending beyond his domains. This was Phya Taksin, a general of half-Chinese descent, who led a series of wars against the Burmese foes. But the strain of providing leadership to diverse Thai factions proved too much for his nerves; from 1777, he showed signs of insanity. Some of his measures provoked rebellion against his authority. One such was ordering all monks to undergo an ordeal of sustained diving to prove their purity and moral standard. Many of those who surfaced or simply escaped the ordeal joined the rebels. Phya Taksin was made a prisoner, compelled to abdicate, and, as a mark of poetic justice, asked to become a monk.

Establishment of the Chakri Dynasty

The person who quickly ended the state of potential civil war was General Chakri, a confidant of Phya Taksin. The general restored order and assumed the royal title in 1782. The Chakri dynasty he established still reigns in Bangkok, which he made the capital. Later in his reign, he assumed the title Rama, the hero of *The Ramayana,* known for his valor, moral integrity, and justice. The succeeding monarchs numbered their reigns in reference to the dynasty's founder. Thus, the period since 1946, when the present king, Bhumibol Adulyadej, ascended the throne, is termed the tenth reign, his title being Rama IX.

Rama I's reign (1782–1809) was a period of consolidation and reconstruction. Rama I set for himself the task of restoring the moral standards of the bureaucracy and the monks, who had been corrupt. Considerable portions of the Buddhist canon of the Tripitaka (The Three Baskets) as well as of Thai civil law had been destroyed during the sack of Ayuthaya. In 1788, within six years of his ascending the throne, Rama I convened a Buddhist council of 250 monks and lay scholars, who worked for five months on the reconstruction of the Tripitaka. Several royal decrees were issued between 1784 and 1801 for the restoration of the monks' morals.

Flowering of Thai Literature

Thai tradition credits Rama I with initiating the famous *Phra Rajanibondh* (royal writings), most of them his own or written at his direction. The most notable of these was *Ramakien* (or *Ramakirti*), which differs significantly from its original inspiration, *The Ramayana*. It ran to some 3,000 pages in recently printed editions. Written primarily for the stage, it was composed in verses, with specific directions on how to set them to music.[1] *Ramakien* is a part of Thailand's national cultural treasure, read avidly and played as a *khon* (masked play).

Rama I's reign is also noted for a tremendous output of prose literature, in original and in translation. Thus, *Dalang* and *Inao* were adapted from Javanese tales of Panji, while *Unarut,* the story of Krishna's grandson, Aniruddha, was based on the *Mahabharata*. All three were adapted for dance-drama performances. Additionally, the Sri Lankan *Mahavamsa* was translated, as was also a collection of Persian tales, *Duodecagon,* then available in the Malay language, and a Chinese historical novel, *San Kuo Chih Yen-i* (*Sam Kok* in Thai). Dozens of other literary works belonging to Rama I's reign have been discovered by Thai scholars in the past few decades.[2]

VIETNAM'S UNIFICATION

Until the fifteenth century, the kingdom of Dai Viet was limited in territory more or less to the Tongking Delta. After a major defeat of Champa in 1471, the Vietnamese state extended south of the Annam range as far as Cap Varella (Hon Lon).

Pressures of population in the Tongking Delta, political ambitions of some Vietnamese princes and generals, and the lack of possibility of expansion northward resulted in Vietnamese movement southward. In 1527, the ruling Le, supported by Nguyen, suffered a major setback at the hands of a general, Mac Dang Dung, who seized power in Tongking. A mediation by China as Vietnam's overlord in 1540 brought about the first partition of the country. Mac was recognized as the ruler of Tongking, while Le and Nguyen made Hue their capital and sought their fortunes in what today is central Vietnam. The settlement was not as significant for its lasting value as much as for setting a precedent for Vietnam's partition. By 1592, a nobleman named Trinh overthrew the Mac regime in Tongking and usurped power in the name of the Le dynasty; Trinh managed to smuggle the nominal Le ruler from Hue to Hanoi. A wall from the Annam Mountains to the sea near Dong Hoi (very close to the seventeenth parallel, which marked the dividing line under the 1954 Geneva agreements) separated the territories under the control of Trinh and Nguyen families.

The Nguyen power grew rapidly in the south. First came the final extinction of the remnant of the Champa kingdom in 1720, its last king fleeing with large numbers of his people into present-day Cambodia, where their descendants still live. Thereafter, the Vietnamese extended their control in the Mekong Delta, then a part of the Khmer kingdom. No major battles took place for the conquest of these rich and fertile lands. Vietnamese control came about like ink spreading on a blotting paper. The Nguyen rulers encouraged their retired soldiers to establish colonies beyond the Vietnamese frontiers in Khmer areas. By the middle of the eighteenth century, virtually all the Khmer territories of present-day South Vietnam had become part of the Nguyen kingdom.

The Tayson Rebellion

The second half of the eighteenth century was a period of great social and political convulsions for Vietnam. Three brothers from the district of Tayson in central Vietnam—Nguyen Van Nhac, Nguyen Van Lu, and Nguyen Van Hue—raised the standard of revolt. They obtained control of all of Vietnam: Nhac was proclaimed emperor of Annam with Hue and Lu in charge of the Tongking and Mekong basins, respectively. In a sense, Vietnam was unified under the three brothers, though Vietnamese historians prefer to regard the Tayson revolt as a catalyst to the real unification brought about by Emperor Gia Long in 1802.

The Tayson success was helped by public disgust with the nepotistic, corrupt Trinh administration in Tongking and the belief that the Trinhs had lost the "mandate of heaven." Although the Taysons were hailed as deliverers in the north, they were regarded as unscrupulous usurpers in the south. They were accused of taking advantage of the tragedy in the Nguyen family when the king had died without leaving an adult heir. The teenage prince Nguyen Anh, driven into adversity, received sympathy and secret support from large numbers of people in the Ca Mau peninsula where he had taken refuge. Few shed tears for the debacle of the discredited Trinh family. In the public mind, the mandate to rule all of Vietnam had passed not to the Taysons but to the Nguyens.

Emperor Gia Long

Among the supporters of Nguyen Anh was a French missionary, Pigneau de Behaine, who regarded Vietnam as his second homeland. In 1787, he went to France—taking Nguyen Anh's son, Canh, with him—to the court of Louis XVI, seeking military assistance. Considering the domestic preoccupation and plight of the French monarch, it was a miracle that a Franco-Vietnamese treaty was signed. The treaty provided French military aid in exchange for a grant of monopoly of external trade and the cession of Puolo Condore Island and the port of Da Nang. The French government directed its colonial governor of Pondicherry (in south India) to provide the military assistance, an order he failed to carry out. De Behaine, however, raised 300 volunteers and funds in Pondicherry—enough to purchase several shiploads of arms. He arrived in Vietnam on June 19, 1789, barely a month before the fall of the Bastille.

The French aid was marginal to Nguyen Anh's success. Even before its arrival, he had captured Saigon in 1788; when he conquered Hue in 1801 and Hanoi a year later, there were only four Frenchmen in his army. The French helped in constructing improved forts, casting better and larger cannon, and creating a navy. Modernly, Vietnamese Communist historians have strongly criticized Nguyen Anh for accepting even this limited foreign assistance, comparing him with Ngo Dinh Diem and the French volunteers to the U.S. Military Advisory Group during the 1950s and early 1960s.[3]

In 1802, Nguyen Anh proclaimed himself emperor of Annam, taking the title of Gia Long. The title was a contraction of Gia Dinh, the name of the region around Saigon, and Thang Long, the name of the region around Hanoi. Gia Long is recognized as the first unifier of Vietnam.

Gia Long (1802–1820) was as remarkable a leader in peace as he was in war. He reorganized the entire country into three divisions and twenty-six provinces. The traditional center of Nguyen power, Hue, became the capital of the kingdom. The provinces were subdivided into districts, subdistricts, and villages.

Gia Long revived the imperial government as constituted by Le Thanh Ton in the fifteenth century, which was in turn based on the Chinese model. The emperor and six ministers in charge of public affairs, finance, rites, armed forces, justice, and public works constituted the Supreme Council. The civil service examination on Confucian lines was reinstituted, and a code of laws based on Chinese principles of jurisprudence was proclaimed.

Emperor Gia Long also devoted himself to the tasks of reconstruction of the country, ravaged by a four-decade civil war. The most urgent task was, indeed, to restore the age-old, intricate irrigation system of the Tongking Delta. Among his notable public works was the Mandarin Road (Route One) along the coast linking Saigon, Hue, and Hanoi, a distance of 1,300 miles, which could be covered on horseback in eighteen days. Fortifications dotted the strategic points along the entire route to maintain firm control over most of the country. Such remarkable work has, Communist criticism apart, earned for Gia Long the gratitude of the Vietnamese people as their country's unifier.

Part One Review

The history of Southeast Asia up to the end of the eighteenth century may be regarded as premodern, or traditional. European influence from the sixteenth to the eighteenth centuries was mostly coastal and commercial and therefore limited principally to some areas in the insular region. Most affected by European contact were the Philippines, particularly north and central, under Spanish control for two centuries and converted to Catholicism, though inadequately exposed to Western educational, cultural, or economic mores. Only those Indonesian islands or portions of them dealing with export crops—coffee, sugar, spices—came under Dutch influence and, after the middle of the eighteenth century, increasingly under alien political control. On the mainland, the dynamic of domestic politics was governed by traditional elements, scarcely influenced by Westerners, who rarely ventured beyond the capitals of the indigenous kingdoms. Most of the elements of the traditional Southeast Asian cultures—religion, literature, script, fine arts—continued down to the eighteenth century largely uninfluenced by the West.

Though the earliest kingdoms in Southeast Asia emerged along the Malay Peninsula, the ones that prospered longer arose on the eastern littoral in modern Cambodia and central Vietnam, which remained the center of power well past the thirteenth century. Funan's expansion by the third century from South Vietnam across Cambodia and Thailand to the upper Malay Peninsula was based on extensive maritime trade and intensive wet-rice cultivation. Chenla's defeat of Funan in the seventh century and the glorious rule of Angkor monarchs from the ninth century to the thirteenth were both achievements of the Khmer people, ancestors of modern-day Cambodians.

At the western end of mainland Southeast Asia, the Mons, cousins of the Khmers, held sway over maritime trade and enjoyed a cultural preeminence in Lower Myanmar, while the Burmans dominated the rest of the country, basing their power on the agricultural surpluses of the Kyaukse plain in Upper Myanmar. In the eleventh century, fascinated by Theravada Buddhism, which the Mons had followed for centuries thanks to their contacts with Sri Lanka, King Anawratha invaded Pegu (Lower Myanmar) and forcibly brought Buddhist scriptures as well as Mon scholars and artisans to Upper Myanmar. His unification of the country and adoption of Theravada Buddhism were to have long-term consequences for mainland Southeast Asia. Theravada Buddhism spread from Myanmar to Thailand, Cambodia, Laos, and South Vietnam in the succeeding three centuries.

In the insular region, Srivijaya (in Sumatra) and Sailendra (in Java) were rivals in the growing east-west trade during the prosperous T'ang dynasty in China. The Sailendras made the only effort in Southeast Asian history to bring both mainland and insular regions under a single political authority by attacking and occupying Chenla for a short period in the late eighth century. Srivijaya attempted to establish a monopoly of spices and resin trade in the archipelago and was successfully challenged by Rajendra Chola of south India in the eleventh century and by Majapahit of Java in the fourteenth century. Java also witnessed the rise and fall of dynasties, with power alternating between ruling houses in central and eastern parts of that fertile island. The Sailendras, Mataram, Singhasari, and Majapahit must be counted among the more illustrious dynasties of Java.

Until the thirteenth century, the entire region, with the exception of Vietnam and the Philippines, was deeply influenced by Indian culture. Although first introduced by Indian traders, the real initiative to import Indian ideas of kingship, court ritual, religion, literature, script, and fine arts came from the ruling classes of Southeast Asia. Vietnam, limited for the large part to Tongking Delta until the defeat of Champa in 1471, was ruled for the bulk of the first millennium, from 111 B.C. to A.D. 939, directly by China, which introduced Confucianism, Mahayana Buddhism, and other elements of Chinese culture to its Vietnamese subjects. Most of the major kingdoms in Southeast Asia, including Vietnam after it overthrew Chinese rule, sent periodic tributes to the Chinese court whenever China was politically strong.

Direct Indian influence on Southeast Asian cultures by import of Brahmans and artisans virtually ceased after the thirteenth century as the governance of India passed from Hindu to Muslim hands. Although Hinduism survived the onslaught of Islam (and later of Christian missionaries), it was on the defensive and not strong enough to provide intellectual or spiritual leadership to the peoples beyond the subcontinent. The major religion in mainland Southeast Asia from the thirteenth century was Theravada Buddhism, which had disappeared from India itself. Although the Southeast Asian centers of Buddhist learning and piety drew heavily from their counterparts in Sri Lanka throughout the second millennium, they were very much on their own from about the fourteenth century. In contrast with the period of Indian influence, there was a slowdown in construction activity in the entire region after the thirteenth century.

The advent of the Mongols to power in China had far-reaching consequences for Southeast Asia. The fall of the Thai state of Nan Chao in Yunnan accelerated the Thai exodus southward. Resistance on the part of some Southeast Asian monarchs to recognize the Mongols as suzerain authority invited retribution. Pagan fell; so did Singhasari in Java. Mongol armies were stymied in Dai Viet, Champa, and Myanmar as local resistance took the form of vicious guerrilla warfare lasting a couple of decades. The power equation on the mainland altered with the rise of the Thai kingdom of Ayuthaya, which expanded at the expense of Myanmar and from the weakened authority of the Khmer empire, whose capital fell to the Thais in 1431. Ayuthaya also became a maritime power rivaling Majapahit in Java and the newly established kingdom of Malacca in the Malay Peninsula.

Malacca remained the preeminent trade emporium of Southeast Asia throughout the fifteenth century. It also served as a focal point for the spread of Islam, which had been gradually introduced from coastal India by the newly converted traders from Gujarat and Coromandel as well as by the Sufi missionaries since the late thirteenth century. Islam flourished even more rapidly as a protective shield against the advancing Portuguese in the sixteenth century, in the process eclipsing the Hindu Majapahit power.

A major change on the mainland in the period from the sixteenth to the eighteenth century was a drive toward political consolidation in three centers of power: Myanmar, Thailand, and Vietnam. Correspondingly, there were greater interstate tensions and rivalries. The period was marked by Thai-Burmese wars, Thai-Vietnamese rivalry for domination over the prostrate Khmer kingdom, and tensions between Hanoi and Hue. By the end of the eighteenth century, strong monarchies had emerged and political consolidation had been achieved in all three states. Myanmar and Thailand seemed reconciled to each other's independent existence. Vietnam was unified as a single kingdom. One chief area of tension was Cambodia, where the Thais and the Vietnamese periodically fought for the loyalties of the hapless descendants of the once-powerful Khmer monarchy. In the nineteenth century, just before the Western drive for political domination of mainland Southeast Asia would fully manifest itself, each of the three mainland Southeast Asian states could boast a strong administration, a well-recognized hierarchical social order, territorial divisions, a bureaucratic system, and a self-sufficient economy.

Part Two

Colonial Interlude

With the exception of Thailand, Southeast Asia came under Western rule, most of it between 1860 and 1914, during the period of the so-called Economic Imperialism or New Imperialism. From the opening of the Suez Canal in 1869 until the outbreak of World War I, the map of Africa and Asia was dramatically redrawn. Although the term "scramble" is generally applied to the European rivalry in appropriating large chunks of territory in Africa and in carving out spheres of influence in China, the term is equally appropriate to describe the partition of Southeast Asia among Western powers in the same period.

Part II deals with the British acquisition of Burma and Malaya, Sarawak, North Borneo and Brunei; the French conquest of Laos, Cambodia, and Vietnam; and the Dutch extension of authority in the Indonesian archipelago. The American conquest of the Philippines at the turn of the twentieth century constituted a part of the same historical process of the New Imperialism, although it merely represented the transfer of control over those islands from one old colonial power to a new one. In all of Southeast Asia, only Thailand was able to retain its political independence, though not without having to surrender its claims to Laos in 1893 and to the provinces of Battambang and Siem Reap in Cambodia to France in 1904, and to the Malay states of Perlis, Kedah, Kelantan, and Terengannu to Great Britain in 1909.

What caused such dramatic change in the policy of Western powers that they shifted from their interest in trade to acquisition and administration of territory? How much was this change the result of the industrial revolution and the accompanying need for raw materials and guaranteed consumer markets? Or was it the product of the growth of monopoly capitalism, as the Marxist-Communist revolutionary V. I. Lenin, who explained the phenomenon of New Imperialism in Africa, would have us believe?

Historical sources for the period of Western trading activity as well as later territorial conquests and colonial administration are varied but principally European. They are predominantly the archives of the respective governments and of the trading companies concerned. Thus, the British East India Company's records provide the principal source of documentation for the early part of British activity in Lower Burma, the Malay Peninsula, Singapore, and Java. These records are the main sources for understanding the rivalry between Great Britain and the Netherlands for trade and strategic supremacy in the Indian archipelago until 1824 when the Anglo-Dutch treaty largely ended the competition by establishing a dividing line for future territorial ambitions. The line was drawn at the Strait of Malacca. Thereafter, the British East India Company focused on India, and the Dutch (their East India Company, or VOC as it was known, was dissolved in 1799) were left to expand in the Indonesian islands.

The European records also include accounts written by missionaries, individual traders, and travelers and books and memoirs of some colonial bureaucrats. The accounts by French missionaries are vitally important for the history of their court intrigues in Thailand in the 17th century and their aborted attempt to establish French ascendancy at the Thai court. The records also throw valuable light on French interaction with the Vietnamese monarchs and mandarins in the 19th century. Even more important are the missionary accounts of their activities in the Philippines, where they managed to convert the bulk of the population to the Catholic faith. Their accounts are singularly biased. Although admitting that the great majority of the Tagalogs and the Visayas were literate (far more than in contemporaneous Europe) and that the Tagalogs had written characters, the missionaries maintained the Filipinos had no written records, only oral tradition.[1] Recent research, however, has made clear that the bulk of the missionary writers did not adhere closely to the truth about Filipino culture. One must wonder if the conquistadores destroyed all existing records in the Philippines as they did in Mexico.

The documentation provided by such archives, however, is woefully inadequate in ignoring the non-European indigenous life and society. As a prescient, young Dutch scholar, J. C. van Leur, commented, the Dutch accounts were Eurocentric, full of observations made from "the deck of the ship, the ramparts of the fortress, the high gallery of the trading house."[2]

Such glaring bias has been partly rectified by modern postcolonial scholars, both of indigenous and European origin, in scholarly monographs on European economic activity in Southeast Asia, both for the pre-1800 period of trading as well as for the period of the New Imperialism.

7

The English and Dutch in the East Indies

With the French occupation of the Netherlands (1795–1814), the Dutch king, (Stadhouder) William V, fled to Britain, where he authorized his protectors to take over all the Dutch colonies everywhere. Britain asked the East India Company to occupy the Dutch possessions in the East. The company's occupation of Malacca in 1795 and Java itself in 1811 was at best reluctant. In 1814, by the Convention of London, Britain restored most of the colonies to William V to make Holland strong as a counterbalance to France.

ERA OF REFORMS

The period from 1800 to 1820 is notable in the history of the East Indies as an era of reform. Whether Dutch or British, the colonial reformers were imbued with humanitarian liberalism, a product of the late-eighteenth-century Enlightenment in England and on the Continent. In the economic sphere, the liberals shared Adam Smith's enthusiasm for abolition of monopolies and privileges and encouragement to entrepreneurship and free trade. However, such liberalism did not preclude an arrogant outlook. In fact, the reformers' attitudes toward colonial subjects were characterized by condescending, benevolent paternalism. Among them two men deserve a high place for their contributions to the East Indies. These were Hermann Daendels, governor of Java, 1808–1810, and Thomas Stamford Raffles, lieutenant-governor of Java, 1811–1816.

Hermann Daendels

Hermann Daendels was a Dutch lawyer before he joined the French army in 1793. He was an admirer of Napoleon Bonaparte, who conferred on him the rank of marshal. In January 1808, he was sent to Java with supreme powers to build defenses in the region against the British and to introduce liberal measures in the field of administration. His instructions to his subordinates were to "protect the common

man against all arbitrary treatment" and act toward him "more like a father study-
ing to promote the welfare of his family than a ruler governing his subjects." In a
bid to centralize administration, he divided the island of Java into nine units, each
under a revenue official directly under himself. Below these landdrosts were
salaried native regents, whose stature was thereby reduced in the eyes of their subjects. Daendels took effective measures to eliminate graft and corruption in the bureaucracy by appointing special inspectors who would pay the cultivators directly
for their products without rapacious intermediaries. Realizing the unfairness of the
Javanese being subject to Dutch law, he established new law courts that dispensed
justice according to *adat* (customary usage). The administration of justice according to *adat* remained a feature of subsequent Dutch rule in Java.

Daendels did not introduce any liberal measures in the economic sphere. His
instructions were to investigate the possibility of abolishing compulsory coffee cultivation and forced deliveries. Instead, he forced a threefold increase in coffee plantations and instituted a monopoly in rice trade to raise funds to finance the new
defense fortifications. A useful aspect of the latter was the construction of roads,
including an east-west road from Batavia to Surabaya.

Despite his well-intentioned policies, Daendels antagonized large sections of
Javanese society. The regents were incensed over their loss of status, the bureaucrats
over the loss of graft gains, and the peasants over increased coffee quotas and the

MAP 7.1 Western Expansion in Southeast Asia

high price of rice. His arbitrary methods earned him the dubious title "Tuwan Desar Guntur" (great thundering lord). The rising hostility toward him led to his recall in 1810.

Thomas Stamford Raffles

In June 1811, the British occupied Java. Daendels's fortifications on that island appeared to endanger the twin British interests in the East—security of India and that of the China trade route. Governor-General Minto led the successful invasion and left a young man, Thomas Stamford Raffles, who had just turned thirty, in complete charge of the defense and administration of the populous and fertile island.

Raffles had been in the Malay region since 1805, when he was posted to Penang as assistant secretary to the governor because of his knowledge of the Malay language, literature, customs, and history. The liberal Raffles believed that the Dutch rule in the East Indies was vicious and unjust and that the Javanese masses would be better off under the benign protection of the British. Further, he was convinced that the archipelago could be developed into a huge emporium for the distribution of British manufactures, provided drastic reforms were first instituted to revise the peasants' social and economic status.

Raffles's reforms were more far-reaching than those of Daendels. Like Daendels, he promoted direct rule, turning hereditary native chiefs into salaried bureaucracy, strictly under European supervision. The islands were divided on the Indian administrative pattern into districts, divisions, and villages.

The sharper contrast with Daendels was in the economic sphere, where Raffles's liberalism was substantially vindicated. A believer in free enterprise, Raffles decreed the complete abolition of the old forced delivery system, except coffee in the Preanger district. The Javanese peasants were given the freedom to cultivate and sell any crop of their choice. On the pattern of the *ryotwari* system in Madras, Raffles allowed land ownership by cultivators against an obligation to pay annual land rent, based on the fertility of the soil: one-half of the yield in cash for the best lands, one-fourth for the least cultivatable. The average was about two-fifths. The essence of the system was twofold: Government now dealt directly with the people, with the village as a unit of administration. Second, there would be a free play of market conditions for all products and, importantly, the peasants would have enough cash to buy consumer goods. As J. S. Furnivall rightly observed, Raffles's humanitarianism helped to liberate the masses from the oppression of their native rulers; his pragmatism acted to put money into the peasants' pockets so that they might buy English cottons. The British needed the tropical produce as much as the Dutch, but unlike the latter they had a line of cheaply manufactured goods, particularly textiles, to sell in exchange for raw materials from the colonies. To the British, in the long run trade was more profitable than tribute.

Raffles's economic policy has received much praise from most of his biographers. It must be noted, however, that his measures were neither comprehensive nor without some adverse consequences. Thus, the village headman, replacing the old regent, could be equally unscrupulous toward his fellow villagers. In the absence of official surveys, the allotment of land at the village level among peasants had to be left to the arbitrary will of the headman. Second, as the government preferred the payment of tax in cash, the cultivator sold rice at low prices or borrowed cash from moneylenders at exorbitant interest rates. Raffles did not abolish the compulsory cultivation of all crops. The coffee-producing districts of Preanger as well as the teak-bearing districts were retained under the old system of forced cultivation and deliveries because of revenue needs.

The judiciary also received Raffles's attention. His object was to simplify "the clumsy and unwieldy structure of the former courts." He set up separate systems for the indigenous and foreign populations. Thus, the three large ports of Batavia, Semarang, and Surabaya were each given a Court of Justice, a Court of Requests, and a Police Court. For the indigenous people, Raffles set up sixteen "land courts," one for each Residency, with the Resident as president and native officials as members to deal with petty claims and civil as well as minor criminal cases. Trial by jury was introduced for criminal cases, while the civil cases were conducted according to the old Dutch colonial law. Those involving the death penalty came under a Court of Justice (from one of the three ports) and five jurymen at least of the standing of a village headman. The death sentences required confirmation by the lieutenant governor. A Supreme Court in the capital heard all appeal cases.

There are contrary opinions on the merits of Raffles's judicial reforms. E. S. de Klerck praised Raffles's reorganization, insisting that "the system of judicature was found by the Dutch on their return to be so well regulated that reforms, if any, were restricted to matters that did not pertain to the existing conditions."[1] On the other hand, Bernard Vlekke considered the transplantation of "typical British institutions to absolutely foreign soil," particularly the jury system, a mistake and a failure. He pointed out that the jury system was "immediately abolished after the return of the Dutch authorities and was never regretted."[2] Another weakness of Raffles's reforms was that, unlike Daendels, he had ignored *adat,* the customary law of Java, and supplanted the traditional authority of the regents by the village headman, thus disregarding the accustomed native milieu in which disputes could be settled.

Raffles's regime was undoubtedly far more enlightened in its principles than any colonial rule up to that time in Southeast Asia. Unfortunately, he had little time and meager personnel and finances to implement his measures. The British government in India did not like the recurring deficits. Raffles was recalled to England. His aggressive personality had earned him many enemies, who complained about his wasteful expenditures and questionable dealings in land disposal. Raffles was recalled to explain his acts, but in the meanwhile, the territory for which he had labored so much had been returned to the Dutch. Both Calcutta and London favored the decision but for different reasons. Whereas Britain wanted to create a strong and financially stable Netherlands as a bulwark against French power on the continent of Europe, the Indian government found Java to be a drain on its budget.

Raffles's opposition to returning Java to the Dutch stemmed from his personal conviction that it would be detrimental to British political and commercial interests in the East. Second, he had not lost his faith in the doctrines of laissez-faire and free trade as being mutually beneficial to British enterprise and the Javanese masses. He could clearly foresee the dissipation of his cherished dreams and projects once the Dutch returned to Java. Third, Raffles had developed an emotional and intellectual attachment to Java—its monuments, history, and literature. He had ordered the first survey of the Borobodur complex and rendered assistance to the preservation of Java's heritage. He was a keen student of Javanese antiquities; in 1817, he published a classic work, *History of Java*. The return of Java to the Dutch was personally painful to the scholarly Raffles.

THE FOUNDING OF SINGAPORE

In March 1818, Raffles returned to Southeast Asia as lieutenant governor of Bencoolen, an unimportant trading post on the southwest coast of Sumatra. Meanwhile, the Dutch reclaimed all their possessions and signed monopoly trade treaties with local princes. Finding it difficult to compete with the British trading interests that had taken root during the Raffles era, the Dutch government prohibited British ships from trading in the archipelago except at Batavia. The Dutch actions infuriated Raffles, who used his able and persuasive pen to warn the East India Company directors of the danger of Dutch monopolistic practices to British trading interests. He therefore advocated establishment of a strategic port in the southern Malay waters that would challenge Dutch trade and supremacy.

Raffles's choice was Singapore, a small fishing village with a Malay community. He may have been aware of Singapore's potential because of his historical knowledge of the old kingdom of Tumasik on its site. With its excellent anchorage and well-protected harbor, Singapore indeed afforded the best site in the region. Lying at the southern tip of the Malay Peninsula, it commanded the shortest route between Europe and China. In those days when ships had to round the Cape of Good Hope, there was little to choose, in point of distance, between the straits of Sunda and of Malacca. For British ships calling on Sri Lanka or India on the way to China, Singapore meant a saving of 1,000 miles. Raffles's appreciation of Singapore's strategic significance was reflected in one of his letters:

> Our object is not territory but trade: a great commercial emporium and a fulcrum whence we may extend our influence politically as circumstances may hereafter require. . . . One free port in these seas must eventually destroy the spell of Dutch monopoly: and what Malta is in the West, that may Singapore be in the East.[3]

RESOLUTION OF ANGLO-DUTCH RIVALRY

Stamford Raffles signed a treaty on February 6, 1819, with a person he proclaimed the sultan of Johor and obtained from him the cession of Singapore to the East India Company. Both the appointment of the sultan and the treaty had doubtful legal value. The Dutch soon protested that their treaty of 1818 with the previous sultan had given them control over Rhio, which included Singapore. The governor-general of the East India Company in Calcutta was distressed that Raffles had involved the English in a legal and political conflict with the Dutch. At the same time, he did not want to withdraw from Singapore, both because he was not convinced of the Dutch rights to it and because, like Raffles, he was persuaded that its strategic importance was overwhelming.

The principal reason behind the British reluctance to relinquish claims to Singapore was the island's phenomenal success. At the time Raffles first arrived in Singapore, the island's population was around 500. By the end of the year, about ten times that number, mostly Chinese, were attracted by the many advantages offered by the new settlement: an excellent harbor, free trade, and the protection of the strongest maritime, military, and industrial power of the time. Many British firms dealing in shipping, trade, banking, and insurance and operating in India and Sri Lanka opened branches in Singapore. These firms were prohibited from participating directly in the trade between Britain and China because of the monopoly of such trade held by the East India Company. The merchants quickly discovered a legal loophole: Singapore could be used as an entrepôt for transshipment of goods from China bound for England, the legal position being that the goods were imported from Singapore and not from China. The company's monopoly was thus undermined; in 1833, it was abolished.

With the knowledge of such developments, the Dutch realized the impossibility of dislodging the British from Singapore. In 1824, the two countries signed the Treaty of London, which provided for a stable, peaceful relationship between them in Southeast Asia. The Netherlands ceded Malacca and recognized the British claim to Singapore, while the British agreed not to enter into any treaties with rulers in the "islands south of the Straits of Singapore." In essence, the treaty divided the archipelago into mutually exclusive spheres of influence. The British would remain thereafter the dominant European power in the Malay Peninsula. On the other hand, the Dutch were left free to build an empire in the East Indies (Indonesia). The treaty gave the Netherlands indirect British protection against other European interference in its goal of an empire in the archipelago.

RESTORATION OF DUTCH RULE AND THE DIPO NEGORO REVOLT

When the Netherlands's authority was reestablished in the East Indies in 1816, its financial position was weak. The old system of cultivating cash crops for export to Europe had fallen into disuse, thanks to Raffles's liberal policies. Besides, during Raffles's administration, most of the trade had passed into the hands of British entrepreneurs, while British mercantile shipping dominated the archipelago. Moreover, the official appointed by the Dutch king to administer Java from 1816 to 1820, Cornelis Elout, was himself a disciple of Adam Smith and a believer in liberalism, as was Raffles. He continued Raffles's land-rent system, which as previously noted favored the peasant more than the state. During this interim period up to 1820, most of Raffles's administrative and judicial arrangements (except the jury system) were also continued.

Such liberalism was an expensive proposition for King William V, who wanted to use profits from the colonies to mend financial fences in the Netherlands. A number of factors had led to further deterioration of the Dutch economy. Thus, in 1822, the price of coffee declined sharply, reducing the government's revenues from the Preanger plantations in Java. Worse, there were rebellions in Java as well as in Sulawesi, Borneo, and the Moluccas. The Dutch had lost their former prestige with the Indonesian people, and not unlike after World War II, their return was met with strong indigenous resistance. To put down the opposition, as well as to create conditions of law and order, the colony needed finances for a larger military and police force.

The most serious of the outbreaks was the Java War, or the Dipo Negoro revolt, 1825–1830. Dipo Negoro, a prince of the prestigious and powerful royal house of Jogjakarta, led the *jihad* (Muslim holy war) against the Dutch. The conflict began partly as a dynastic dispute. When Dipo Negoro's father, Sultan Amangku Buwono II, died in 1814, Stamford Raffles had recognized Dipo's half-brother, Djarot, as sultan in accordance with Javanese *adat* law (Djarot's mother was a higher-ranking queen than Dipo's). Recognizing Dipo Negoro's qualities of leadership, however, Raffles promised him succession if Djarot predeceased him. But when Djarot died in 1822, the Dutch authorities, possibly unaware of Raffles's promise, recognized the two-year-old son of Djarot as sultan. Dipo Negoro was appointed coguardian, but it was an arrangement that wounded him deeply.

The Javanese people's discontent was more deeply rooted than mere objection to foreign interference in a dynastic dispute. They were against the agrarian policy of Governor-General Van der Capellen. Javanese landowners in native states had been accustomed to leasing their lands to Chinese and Europeans, who exacted compulsory labor from the cultivators. In 1823, Van der Capellen invalidated all such leases and ordered the original landowners to refund the lease money to the lessees. The order hit Javanese landowners, who had already spent the money, and many of these chiefs joined Dipo Negoro in resisting the government. A second economic grievance was the collection of a toll by Chinese who had won contracts to collect a tax on goods carried across the boundaries between a native state and Dutch territory. An even more important factor that roused popular emotions was religion. The colonial government decided to construct a highway passing through Dipo Negoro's property, which included the site of a sacred tomb. Dipo, a devout Muslim, was unofficially regarded as the religious head by many Javanese. When he gave the call for a *jihad,* thousands joined him in a massacre of Chinese toll-farmers. The incident sparked a war with the Dutch authorities lasting five years. Lack of proper organization among Dipo's followers, however, eventually tilted the balance against him. In 1829, when two of his principal lieutenants crossed over to the Dutch side, Dipo agreed to negotiate. At the conference, the Dutch broke faith and arrested Dipo Negoro, banishing him to Sulawesi, where he died in 1855. The war proved costly as 15,000 government soldiers lost their lives, among them 8,000 Europeans. The number of Javanese killed in war and through succeeding famine and pestilence was estimated at 200,000.

The Java War resulted in a debt of the Dutch East Indies government of over 30 million florins, with an annual interest charge of over 2 million florins, both secured by the government in the Netherlands. The latter verged on bankruptcy with the costly revolt in Belgium against Holland's authority erupting in 1830 and brewing for the next decade. To add to these problems, the price of coffee slumped, reducing the government's revenues even further. The Dutch treasury was exhausted and with it dimmed any hope of liberalism in colonial policies.

THE CULTURE SYSTEM

It was to meet such a financial crisis that a new governor-general with profit-making ideas was sent to Java in 1830. Johannes Van den Bosch was not new to the East Indies. In the first decade of the century, he had served there in the army. In the post-Napoleonic era, he emerged as a writer on economic and political subjects; the "perverted liberalism" of Raffles and Daendels in Java was among his targets. In 1827, he visited the Dutch East Indies. On his return, he submitted to the Dutch government his ideas on how the colony could be administered profitably for the Netherlands. Van den Bosch assured the Dutch that the production of export crops could be stepped up to help the treasury to the extent of 20 million guilders annually.

Introduced in 1830, the *culturstelsel* (culture system) was implemented effectively for the next four decades, and in certain crops like coffee until 1917. The system was based on certain assumptions. First, the assumption was that the Javanese, however willing they might be, were too ignorant to make any progress unaided and without the guidance of the Dutch authorities. They "must be taught to work, and if they were unwilling out of ignorance, they must be ordered to work."[4] Second, a Javanese could achieve a satisfactory standard of living by working 120 days per year in agriculture. The person must not be allowed to spend the rest of the time in idling and indolence. Therefore, these people should be compelled to devote a part of their leisure time to the cultivation of export crops. In so doing, they would "learn" to work.[5]

Under the rules of the culture system, the Javanese peasant was required to devote one-fifth of his land or sixty-six working days in a year for the cultivation of cash crops for the government, under the supervision of the controllers. In practice, Van den Bosch "took whatever amount he pleased, even to one-half and even the whole."[6] The people did not question or complain, or if they did so, it was in the privacy of their homes. Under the culture system, they were subject to the control of their native chieftains just as their fathers and grandfathers had been before them. The Dutch used the old hierarchical relationship between the chiefs and the peasants to accomplish their ends. The obvious benefits of such an administration were to minimize governmental blame for the rigors of the exploitative system.

Van den Bosch restored to the various chieftains their previous status and power over the people. With Dutch support, the chieftains ruled as they pleased. J. S. Furnivall, an acknowledged authority on colonial administration, perceptively commented on the new "unstable equilibrium":

> The consolidation of Dutch rule tended still further to the weakening of native society. Under native rule authority was an expression of will and not of law, but at the same time it rested also on custom and consent; the strong man governed, but he governed by consent, even if consent was rooted in fear . . . the native prince or regent with Dutch power behind him was much stronger than he had ever been, much less dependent on consent, and far better able to act arbitrarily than former rulers who had depended solely on their force of will. Thus, under the Company, the center of gravity of the native social order was displaced and society was maintained in unstable equilibrium by the Dutch power acting from outside it.[7]

The native hierarchy, acting also as the new Dutch bureaucracy, used its position to take from the villager whatever it wished. Under the culture system, a certain percentage of crops was given to the native hierarchy as well as to government officials as an incentive to increase production. Given the several levels of the hierarchy, little if anything was left to the villager who had done all the work.

Of the cash crops, coffee was the most lucrative because it occupied the largest area. Preanger in western Java became virtually a vast state plantation, with intensive exploitation of land and labor. Van den Bosch built roads, by forced labor, to the mountain districts where the coffee was grown; storage facilities were constructed in the neighborhood of each coffee plantation. Each *kampong* (village) in the mountainous region was required to plant in four years 600 coffee trees per head of each family and to maintain a sufficient nursery of young trees to keep 600 trees per family head in full bearing. The Dutch controllers paid monthly visits to assure the government that this was being done.

By 1854, the Preanger district alone produced 243,554 piculs of coffee, and the rest of Java gave the government 843,310 piculs (one picul equals 133.33 pounds). The yield of coffee in 1854 was more than four times as great and about six times as valuable as that produced before the culture system. The actual profits were even greater because the government fixed a price on the yield much lower than the market price. For example, in 1833 it was fixed at about 21 guilders per picul, though the market price was 27.5.[8]

The cultivation of coffee did not interfere with subsistence agriculture. The same could not be said about indigo and sugar plantations, which required sacrifice of precious *sawahs* (rice paddies). The Dutch officials and Javanese regents alike compelled the villagers to allot the best parts of their land and often more than the legal one-fifth for cultivation of export crops. They also forced the peasant to attend first to the cash crops and then to rice cultivation. The result was a serious curtailment in the production of rice necessary for the peasants' sustenance. There were several famines in the 1840s in Java. The worst occurred in 1850 in the Residency of Semarang, where more than 300,000 perished because of starvation and the diseases that accompany famine. Many fled to adjacent provinces, which were hardly better provided. The cause of the famine was the preference given to tobacco crops over the rice crop.

As previously mentioned, the crop supervision and delivery of produce were left largely in the hands of traditional elements of social control. Some regents employed severe forms of corporal punishment. The lash was the favorite tool, but such tortures as hanging by the thumbs, tying the alleged culprit to an ant tree, or compelling the eating of horse feces were not rare. Nor were the Dutch authorities unaware of the practices, which were revealed by Edward Dekker, a Dutch official, who was disgusted with the culture system. The chiefs were handsomely rewarded for their cooperation in what was virtually an elaborate commercial machine for maximizing government profits. Obedience of the natives and deliveries of products at fixed prices were secured, while the government would only remotely be held accountable for the rigors of the system. The colonial power so successfully camouflaged its indirect control over the peasantry that Dekker, who wrote under the pseudonym Multatuli, described the administrative regulations as "nothing but the Javanese customs translated into statute terms."[9]

The beneficiaries of the culture system were the native regents, their subordinates at the district and village level, the middlemen or contractors in charge of delivery of the export crops, Dutch shipping interests, and, last but not least, the government of the Netherlands. In the early stages, the contractors were mainly Chinese, who also invested in the production of sugar. However, when Europeans realized that there were great profits involved in the enterprise, they too entered the system. The contractor and chiefs would deliver a crop to the Dutch trading companies, which would sell the products in the Netherlands. On the return trip, the trading companies would bring finished Dutch goods to be sold—at high prices—in Java. The trade helped the Dutch economy immensely.

The system as a whole performed a miracle for the Dutch economy. Van den Bosch's promise to his king of securing 20 million guilders in profit from the East Indies was shortly fulfilled. Between 1830 and 1877, a total profit of 837 million guilders was accrued to the Netherlands.[10]

Beyond this were the profits made by Dutch entrepreneurs in trade, shipping, and banking. The culture system thus succeeded phenomenally in its initial purpose: saving the Netherlands from bankruptcy. Indeed, it placed Holland on a sound economic footing and enabled it to finance its own industrial revolution. The originator of the system was amply rewarded: Van den Bosch was made a baron in 1836 and a count in 1839.

THE ILLUSION OF REFORM

The year 1848 was noted for liberal movements in many European countries, including the Netherlands. Constitutional changes of far-reaching consequences were adopted in Holland, some of them affecting control over and responsibility for the colonies. The most ardent advocate of colonial reform was Baron Van Hoevell, a former preacher in Java, who demanded for the East Indies greater freedom of the press, education, the abolition of slavery, and the protection of the natives against forced labor. The reluctance to apply liberal tenets to the East Indies may be explained by the economic background of the "liberal leadership," which came mostly from a prosperous merchant class that had benefited from the culture system. In fact, this class demanded a greater economic share and elimination of governmental control over the colonial economy. The resulting policy was to substitute Dutch private enterprise for the government in the exploitation of the colonies.

The revised constitution of 1848 gave the Dutch States General (the legislature) a voice in the colonial government. The king was required to submit an annual report on the colonies, although most members of the legislature knew very little about the East Indies. In any case, they were quite anxious to maintain the flow of profits and therefore hesitant to make changes. Thanks to Baron Van Hoevell's leadership, however, the States General passed in 1854 what was described as the "colonial constitution," which provided for the gradual abolition of the culture system and checking the evils inherent in its operation.

The orations of Baron Van Hoevell were supplemented in 1860 by the publication of *Max Havelaar* by Edward Douwes Dekker, or Multatuli. Dekker had condemned his superiors for overlooking the atrocities practiced by the Javanese regents and their subordinates. Because he resisted transfer to another district, he was dismissed. But *Max Havelaar* exposed the horrors of the culture system. It was an eye-opener for most Dutch, who had imagined all was well as long as profits kept pouring into the Netherlands and the taxes were kept low. Dekker appealed to his country for a change of policy. He declared: "Above the interests of the Fatherland stand those of Humanity."[11] *Max Havelaar* contributed greatly to the passing of liberal measures in the 1860s.

In 1864, a beginning was made to abolish the culture system; by 1870, all cash crops except coffee and sugar were removed from it. Yet these two commodities accounted for the bulk of the export crops. In 1890, sugar was exempted from the culture system; coffee was continued under the system in the Preanger districts until 1917.

These measures, however, were followed by legislation permitting increased participation of Dutch entrepreneurs in the East Indies. The Agrarian Act of 1870 opened the Indies for agricultural industry. Dutch subjects, whether residents of the Netherlands or the East Indies, as well as commercial corporations and non-natives were all now eligible to lease land. At the same time, the indigenous people were assured protection against abuses from their chiefs and from European lessees through a system of stricter supervision.

8

The British Role in the Malay States in the Nineteenth Century

British dominion over the Malay Peninsula was established primarily during the period 1874–1909. Until the last quarter of the nineteenth century, British interest in Southeast Asia itself was largely peripheral, serving the twin aims of bolstering the defenses of Britain's Indian empire and securing the trade route to China. For a half-century before 1874, the British Malay possessions were limited to the three ports of Penang, Singapore, and Malacca. These were organized as the Straits Settlements, with Singapore as center, and were under the administrative control of the Indian government in Calcutta until 1867. Thereafter, they were transferred to Colonial Office control in London with the status of a Crown colony.

INTERVENTION IN THE MALAY STATES

Throughout the half century from 1824, the British policy was to avoid intervention in the Malay states and extension of political control over them. The reasons for such an official policy were at least two. In the second and third quarters of the nineteenth century, Britain was generally reluctant to extend its empire. With an almost unchallenged control of the world's sea-lanes, the British national interest of trade was easily served. Further, Adam Smith's principles of free trade attracted many English liberals, who argued in favor of relaxed colonial rule and against any further annexations. It was only where trade was obstructed and diplomacy failed to correct the situation that British politicians would resort to force and annex a territory. From 1824, the agreement between the British and the Dutch on spheres of influence in the Malay archipelago made the China trade route secure for the British. The British policy during the "Little England Era" was, therefore, one of nonintervention in the Malay states.

The East India Company officials in Calcutta regarded the Straits Settlements as convenient ports of call on the trade route to China. No exclusive advantages accrued to the company in trading with the Straits Settlements because they were free ports. In 1833, when the company lost its monopoly of China trade, its interest in the Straits Settlements diminished further. It continued to govern them, but was certainly most unwilling to expend its resources in acquiring new administrative responsibilities in the interior of the Malay Peninsula. The reluctance of both the British government and the East India Company to acquire territories was such that they allowed even a private individual like James Brooke, who styled himself a rajah, to acquire for himself a kingdom in Sarawak in 1846. It remained with his family for a century, until the end of World War II.

The policy of nonintervention was maintained until 1873 despite the private and not-so-private views of the Straits Settlements officials and merchants, who continually advocated extension of British control over the Malay states. They were convinced that the Malay states contained great wealth and that they could sustain a far larger trade than had existed so far. Particularly attractive were prospects of investment in tin mining in Perak and Selangor. Chinese and European capital from Singapore and Penang financed most of the tin mining after 1850. The merchants argued that large-scale trade and steady returns on their capital could come about only if the interior states had political stability and reasonably good administrative standards.

Dynastic disputes and diffusion of power had always left the Malay states in weakened condition. In each state, power was divided among a number of minor chiefs, all more or less independent and jealous of each other. Piracy was rampant and river traffic insecure.

Further, the tin mining was carried on by Chinese labor, which was organized under Chinese captains, heading rival secret societies, who followed regulations established by their headquarters in China proper. A conflict in China would have its echo in Malay tin mines and in the Chinese community in the British-held Penang. To complicate the situation, the rival Chinese factions often supported rival claimants to the Malay throne in times of dynastic disputes. Due to a combination of these factors, the anarchic situation reached its worst level in Perak from 1871 to 1873. The sultan of Perak had died in 1871 and there were three claimants to the throne, supported by various Malay chiefs and different Chinese factions. The situation in Selangor around the same time was no less tense. The sultan of Selangor wanted to appoint his son-in-law, Tunku dia Oodin, who was the brother of the sultan of Perak, to a high position. He could not appoint him a district chief without displacing another chief. So, in 1868, he appointed him viceroy, leaving it to him to manipulate the power ambiguously implied in the title. The viceroy became the target of hostility. Turbulence in the Malay states did affect the peace of the nearby Straits Settlements, particularly Penang.

The Straits merchants agitated at first for the transfer of the Straits Settlements from the control of the Indian government to that of the Colonial Office in London. They believed their problems would thereby receive special attention and they would no longer be regarded merely as an appendage to India. After the Straits Settlements were transferred to Colonial Office control in 1867, the demand for British intervention in the Malay states increased greatly. Besides petitions and memoranda, the local press, largely financed by the commercial oligarchy, constantly called for intervention. In 1868, they established in London the Straits Settlements Association, a powerful lobbying agency; nine of its office bearers were members of Parliament. Their efforts must be counted among the important factors that altered the British policy of nonintervention in 1873.

Tin was indeed the most precious asset of nineteenth-century Malaya. In the third quarter of the century, there was a sudden increase in the world demand for tin. In the United States, the military needs of the Civil War, making of barrels to store oil, and roofing requirements of the frontiersmen all added to demand. The tinplate industry in Holland, France, and Germany competed with the British in getting U.S. orders. As the need for securing supplies of the tin metal became important, the pressures from the Straits merchants on the Colonial Office for intervention in Malaya stepped up.

Before 1860, the numerous British agency houses in Singapore had enjoyed a virtual monopoly over the trade in the archipelago. Several new factors contributed to increased European activity and competition, leading to the decline in the British share of the trade. New demands in Europe for raw materials and for markets for distribution of finished manufactures were accompanied by revolutionary changes in communications. The opening of the Suez Canal in 1869, the establishment of telegraph in Singapore in 1871, and the increasing use of steam-powered sea transport linked European ports directly with the Southeast Asian markets. British traders, unaccustomed to competition as yet, became restive as European rivals made important inroads into the tin trade and, worse, into Singapore's entrepôt business. Further, other colonial powers in Southeast Asia—the Dutch and the French—actively discriminated against British commerce. The British traders could do little to offset the growing European competition in free-trading Singapore, but they enjoyed certain advantages over their rivals in the Malay states, with whom they had long-standing contacts. Yet these contacts were infrequent, informal, and undependable. To exploit the advantages, it was necessary to establish a formal relationship that would guarantee preferential relationships through control over indigenous governments. The British government's policy of nonintervention in the Malay states, repeatedly enunciated in the second and third quarters of the nineteenth century, stood in the way of trading interests, which actively advocated in the late 1860s a vigorous course of action.

Notable among the Straits merchants were J. G. Davidson, a prominent businessman, secretary of the Singapore Chamber of Commerce, and legal adviser to Tunku dia Oodin, viceroy of Selangor; and W. H. M. Read, chairman of the Singapore branch of the Straits Settlements Association. Davidson held important tin-mining concessions on liberal terms in Selangor and was, with Read, a promoter of the Selangor Tin Mining Company. Read, Davidson, and their agent in London, Seymour Clarke (also Read's brother-in-law), were involved in a common project to lay a telegraph line from Burma through the Malay Peninsula and the East Indies to Australia. Read had secured concessions for this purpose from Thailand and all the Malay rulers concerned. But without the assurance of British protection, there was little prospect of selling the company's stock. Further, with British presence in the Malay states, there was every possibility of securing subsidies for the proposed telegraph line.

The interest of the Singapore traders in the extension of British authority over the Malay states is clearly evident. Finding the British government unresponsive to their pleas for intervention, they manipulated other channels of pressure. Thus, their hand was behind the Chinese merchants' petition dated March 28, 1873 (received in London on August 21, 1873), which in the opinion of C. Northcote Parkinson influenced a change of policy. The petition stated:

> Hitherto there has been a large trade with the Native States of the Malay Peninsula, but, owing to internal dissentions this has in some cases entirely ceased. Laroot, Perak, and Selangore have been and are in a state of such disturbance that all legitimate trade with them is at an end, and unless the British Government interferes to restore order and peace, these rich countries will be impoverished, and their inhabitants ruined.[1]

The British traders also raised the specter of a European power intervening in Selangor. On July 18, 1873, Seymour Clarke wrote to the Colonial Office that he had heard from "an old resident of Singapore" who had "intimate connections with many Native Chiefs" that the smaller states of the peninsula would seek protection of some European power and that, failing England, it would be Germany.[2] His basis was a letter from the viceroy of Selangor to the promoters of the Selangor Tin Mining Company, which included the Singapore merchants, Davidson and Read. Secretary of State Lord Kimberley reacted strongly to this letter.

The Chinese petition and the fear of foreign intervention, both manipulated by the British merchants in Singapore, were responsible for a change in British policy. On September 20, 1873, Lord Kimberley issued instructions to Governor-Designate Sir Andrew Clarke, asking him to "report" to him "whether there are . . . any steps which can properly be taken by the Colonial Government, to promote the restoration of peace and order, and to secure protection to trade and commerce with the Native Territories."[3]

Andrew Clarke (no relation to Seymour Clarke) proceeded to act. He presented a fait accompli without bothering to consult the Colonial Office by telegraph, although he did consult the leaders of the trading community. According to Read, in December 1873, at the end of a government house dinner, he asked the new governor if the latter would intervene in Perak. The governor replied: "I am ready at a moment's notice if I can get the key to the door." Read responded: "Give me a fortnight, and I will get it for you."[4] Read drew up a letter for the signature of Malay chiefs pleading British intervention. The signed letter was presented to the governor on January 9, 1874.

THE RESIDENT SYSTEM

Beginnings and Early Setbacks

Two days later, the governor summoned the Perak chiefs to meet him at Pangkor. There, despite the absence of the reigning sultan, who held the regalia, the chiefs were prevailed upon to sign an "engagement" recognizing the governor's candidate, Abdullah, as sultan. Among the main provisions were those that inaugurated the Resident system in Malaya. The sultan agreed to accept a British Resident, "whose advice must be asked and acted upon in all questions other than those touching Malay religion and custom." It was further stipulated that "the collection and control of all revenues and the general administration of the country be regulated under the advice" of these Residents.[5] The British agreed to protect the state against its internal and external enemies.

In the following month, Clarke turned to Selangor, where piracy had reached a new peak. The British blockaded the rivers of the state and overawed the sultan, who agreed to receive a Resident on the same pattern as Perak. The Singapore businessman J. G. Davidson was appointed the first Resident. Two months later, in April 1874, Clarke extended the Resident system in another state, Sunjei Ujong.

The British extension of empire in Malaya thus presented a combination of most of the factors indicated as being responsible for late-nineteenth-century imperialism in Southeast Asia. Different authorities have emphasized different factors: a turbulent frontier creating problems of law and order in the Straits Settlements;[6] fear of European intervention in the Malay states;[7] the personality of Governor Andrew Clarke;[8] the role of the British merchants in Singapore, who suffered from competition from European rivals in the post-Suez era;[9] and the British response to the petition of the Chinese merchants urging intervention.[10]

It should not be assumed that the Malay chiefs gladly welcomed the British intervention in their states. The new system involved loss of prestige for the sultan as well as for the chiefs, who also suffered heavy losses of their feudal dues apart from the river tolls they forcibly collected. Some years later, in 1877, thanks to the efforts of the then-Resident, Hugh Low, many of these chiefs were absorbed into the administration and allotted a percentage of revenue collections. But in the immediate aftermath of the Pangkor agreement, the chiefs' reaction was lacking in cooperation. Shortly after, it turned into open hostility. The sultan and chiefs of Perak had probably accepted the treaty without fully realizing "what they were asked to agree to; or if they did, had no intention of acting up to it."[11]

Neither for that matter did the British Residents in the Malay states have an exact understanding of what was expected of them. The British government, still reluctant to control the states, avoided spelling out the duties and responsibilities of the Residents or their relationship with the sultan. If the provisions of the Pangkor agreement were to be carried out, Residents would become controllers rather than advisers, as their advice had to be acted upon by the sultans. Clarke himself desired effective control over the native states and decided to camouflage it under the cloak of advice. All he should guard against was interference in the "Malay religion and custom," as specified in the agreement. Custom and tradition, however, played a greater role in the society and government of the Malays than in those of their white "advisers." Justice, tax collection, debt-slavery, and succession to the throne were all sanctified by custom and, therefore, in the Malay view, were beyond the pale of the Resident's advice. (Debt-slavery was a pernicious practice involving full and forced labor by debtors and their families in lieu of unpaid debts.)

The first Resident of Perak, J. W. W. Birch, assumed that the Settlement had authorized him to take complete charge of the Perak administration. Birch combined into himself a poor opinion of native caliber and the missionary zeal of Victorian times, a blend of humanitarianism and arrogance. Birch's new proposals for revenue collection and judicial administration ignored the prerogatives and the means of livelihood of the Malay chiefs. He reacted strongly against their customary rights to bear arms even for ceremonial purposes. More delicate was the issue of debt-slavery, a practice with socioeconomic implications, sanctioned by Malay custom and involving all important individuals, including the sultan. Determined to abolish the practice, Birch allowed his Residency to become a sanctuary for runaway slaves, most of them women, which persuaded the chiefs to imagine that the Resident was stealing their slaves to provide his police with mistresses.[12] Before his departure to India in May 1875, Governor Clarke counseled patience to Birch: "Debt-slavery is a bad thing; but until we are prepared to compensate in full and to show a better system to secure credit, let it for the present alone."[13] Birch was not dismayed by Clarke's parting advice; moderation was not among his virtues.

Meanwhile, Clarke's successor, Governor William Jervois, had come to the conclusion that the Malay states must be brought under closer British control. He proposed abandoning the advisory role and instead governing the states in the name of the sultans by British officers, to be called Queen's Commissioners and to have far greater powers than the Residents had over revenue collection, expenditure, and maintenance of law and order. Birch, who had threatened the sultan of Perak many times before, was to secure the sultan's consent to the new plan. If he did not agree, the throne was to be offered to another chief, Yusuf.

Anglo-Perak relations reached their lowest point in November 1875. In that month Birch was murdered. There is no doubt that the sultan had acquiesced in the ghastly act and that the chiefs had almost unanimously supported it. The British reacted with characteristic show of force. Troops were rushed from India and Hong Kong to fight the "Perak war." Three of the chiefs were captured and executed; the sultan was exiled to faraway Seychelles. The pliable Yusuf was made the new sultan. The Residents thereafter became the real rulers, even though their powers were never really defined.

Role of the Residents

What made the Resident system work was the lesson the Malays drew from the retribution of the Perak war and the personality of some of the early Residents, who used infinite tact and patience in dealing with the sultans and their subjects, combining firmness with friendliness and dignity with deference.[14] Among these were two of the best British civil servants, who with Governor Frederick Weld could rightly be described as the architects of modern Malaya: Sir Frank Swettenham, author of several books on Malaya and administrator in the region for over three decades; and Sir Hugh Low, who spent nearly half a century in various official positions in the Malay region.

There is no doubt that like most civil servants, Swettenham was exaggerating the risks of his office. It is true that the Residents had no legal basis for the vast powers they exercised. On the other hand, no native ruler had the courage to challenge the Resident's authority. In case of a real threat to British authority from the sultans, the might of the British empire would be used. The Resident system in Malaya was, like the chartered company rule, a device of indirect rule—a substitute for annexation and formal rule—and a means of power in the guise of protection to the sultans. As will be seen later, the extension of laws of the Straits Settlements to the Malay states, wherever deemed necessary by the colonial government, was a matter of mere formality.

CONTINUED EXPANSION AND BIRTH OF THE FMS

The second phase of British expansion in Malaya was initiated by Sir Frederick Weld, governor of the Straits Settlements from 1880 to 1887. Weld, typical of late-nineteenth-century empire-builders, considered it his highest duty to transplant British institutions among "backward peoples." Thus he wrote:

> Nothing that we have done has taught them [the Malays] to govern themselves; we are merely teaching them to co-operate with us in governing under our guidance. . . . Moreover, I doubt if Asiatics will ever learn to govern themselves; it is contrary to the genius of their race, of their history, of their religious system, that they should. Their desire is a mild, just and firm despotism.[15]

In Weld's opinion the states under the Resident system would provide such a striking contrast in administrative standards with those without Residents that the latter type of states would request British Residents. During his governorship, Weld used personal charm, authority, persuasion, cajolery, and threats in extending the Resident system to the remaining southern Malay states.

The Resident system was extended in 1888 to Pahang, a state on the east coast of the Malay Peninsula. Pahang was not valuable in itself, despite rumors of rich gold deposits. The trade with Pahang and further on through Pahang to northern Malay states and to Thailand, however, was fairly lucrative to Singapore merchants. In the early 1880s, Wan Ahmad, the new sultan of Pahang, was rumored to have sold two large mining concessions covering about 900 square miles to European concession-hunters. The news alarmed the British, who did not want any kind of European intervention in the area that could eventually pose a threat to British regional supremacy. The sale of concessions had also disregarded the existing rights of Malays and Chinese miners, some of whom were British subjects. In 1885, the British vainly attempted to put pressure on Sultan Ahmad to accept a British Resident. Two years later, under threat of putting Ahmad's rival on the throne, he agreed to receive a British officer and also to place the foreign relations of the state in British hands. The control over Pahang's foreign affairs should have dissipated fears of a European intervention in the area, but Governor Frederick Weld wanted some excuse to bring Pahang under closer British control. In 1888, the murder of a British subject of Chinese origin in Pahang provided the excuse. Weld sent his cousin's son, Sir Hugh Clifford, to twist the sultan's arm and get him to write a letter requesting appointment of a British Resident.

Governor Weld also succeeded in introducing the Resident system in a group of small states lying between Selangor and Johor. The only one in this group of Minangkabau states that had already accepted a British official prior to Weld's administration was Sunjei Ujong, to which Governor Andrew Clarke had posted an assistant Resident in 1874. During the 1890s, Weld intervened a number of times in the frequent disputes between rival states, each time successfully extending British influence as the price of the self-imposed mediation. Thus, in 1885, Jelebu and Sri Menanti had to accept a British collector of revenue; in 1887, it was Rembau's turn to do so. In 1889, all nine Minangkabau states, including Sunjei Ujong, joined to make a confederated state called Negri Sembilan, which received a common Resident whose advice would be accepted on all matters "except those touching Malay religion and custom."

By 1895, four Malay states had been brought under the Resident system: Perak, Selangor, Pahang, and Negri Sembilan. In that year, thanks to the efforts of Resident Frank Swettenham and Governor Cecil Smith, the four states were merged into a federation with a Resident-General whose headquarters would be Kuala Lumpur, eventually the capital of modern Malaysia.

Swettenham's famous memorandum of 1893 urging centralization of power and administrative uniformity in the four Malay states is a valuable document indicating the merits and demerits of the previous system. Swettenham opposed the existing system because the four states were drifting in matters of land legislation, fiscal policy, and justice. There was no justification, he pleaded, for their rigidly separate treatment in view of the commonness of religion and customs of the Malay people in all the states. The Residents had, in the past, been left largely to devise their own approaches and methods because the governor of the Straits Settlements was too busy to guide or control them. On the other hand, Swettenham argued against annexation and imposition of direct rule. He advocated indirect rule, preservation of indigenous institutions, and the supervision and guidance of British Residents "to steer them on the path of civilization and progress." Implicit was an attitude of condescending arrogance and paternalism, characteristic of Victorian humanitarians and Social Darwinists. Furthermore, it cannot be ignored that Swettenham had a vested interest in the preservation of the Resident system, of which he was a valued part. In 1895, with the creation of the federation, he became the first Resident-General of the Federated Malay States (FMS).

The FMS was a federation in name. In practice, the power was centralized in the hands of the Resident-General, who issued directives to Residents, who in turn went through the motions of advising the sultans. There were some redeeming features. Swettenham's plan provided for a federal structure and machinery for interstate consultations. The Resident-General could act in the states only through the Malay-dominated State Councils. To discuss the common problems of the federation, there were to be periodical meetings of all the Malay rulers and the Residents. Though unique in terms of bringing several Malay rulers together in a single assembly, their role was limited to being deliberative and advisory. The FMS hardly fitted any known federation anywhere in the world. There was no constitutional division of powers between the center and the units. As the FMS Secretariat continued to grow into its multifarious departments, members of the Malay civil service posted in the diverse states tended to take orders directly from the departmental heads in the federal capital of Kuala Lumpur. K. G. Tregonning has best summarized some other glaring defects of the so-called federation:

Swettenham, appointed Resident-General, fashioned within a few years a highly centralized administration which by depriving the states of most of their powers, and by centralizing that power in his own hands, made the word Federation ridiculous. . . . Strangely enough, neither in 1896 nor later was the Federal capital ever given any federal status. . . . No Malay ruler was made the symbol of the new state, and as a result, Swettenham created not a nation but an amalgamation.[16]

Pride and Paramountcy: Anglo-Burmese Relations in the Nineteenth Century

EARLY BRITISH VIEW OF MYANMAR

For most of the nineteenth century, the British view of Myanmar was that it was an extension of India—culturally, economically, and politically. With a major British base firmly established in the middle of the eighteenth century in the eastern part of India, the question of immediate security on India's eastern frontier engaged British attention. Thus far, British relations with Myanmar had not been very cordial. In 1753, taking advantage of the civil war in Myanmar between the forces of Alaungpaya (founder of the Konbaung dynasty) and the Mons, the East India Company had occupied the strategic island of Negrais. From there the British hoped to check French activity in the Bay of Bengal. Alaungpaya resented such interference, at first mildly, in a letter addressed to King George II. The British government's failure to reply and the knowledge gathered from Mon prisoners about British assistance to the Mon side in the Burmese civil war so provoked the Burmese monarch that he ordered a general massacre of the East India Company's officials on Negrais. The company, then involved with the French in a major military power game on the Indian subcontinent, swallowed its pride quietly, suffered the losses resulting from the Negrais episode, and left Myanmar undisturbed for at least three decades.

Toward the end of the nineteenth century, British interest in China trade was growing. In 1795, the first British official mission, led by Captain Michael Symes, was sent to Myanmar specifically to investigate the possibility of establishing trade communications between India and China through Myanmar. The Symes mission returned to India with permission to trade "without molestation" and with authority to depute a person "to reside at Rangoon to superintend mercantile affairs." Symes's report after his second visit to Myanmar in 1802 emphasized the extensive export from Myanmar to China of raw cotton, which could be valuable to the thriving textile industry of Britain. Even so, Burmese trade was not so important to the British as yet; keeping out French influence and imposing British paramountcy or political hegemony over Myanmar's kingdom in much the same fashion as in princely India were the primary concerns. Symes stressed both points in his report of 1802.[1]

Almost all through the nineteenth century, the British and Burmese clashed on one vital point. While the British persisted in their efforts to bring the Burmese kings down to the level of Indian princes in a subservient relationship, the proud Burmese kings did everything possible to retain their sovereign status.

THE FIRST ANGLO-BURMESE WAR, 1824–1826

In the official British view, the first Anglo-Burmese war broke out entirely because of Myanmar's aggressiveness and wanton pugnacity. The Burmese, who were restrained in the east by the rising power of the Chakri kings of Thailand, sought an outlet for their surplus energies in the west. It is possible, however, to argue that the Konbaung dynasty's ambition to reach the historical borders of the Myanmar empire coincided with large-scale British conquests in India, some of them on Myanmar's borders. The East India Company's officials instigated Myanmar's traditional tributary states like Arakan, Assam, and Manipur not to acknowledge Myanmar's suzerainty. It was probably a desire to discipline the vassal states that led to King Bodawpaya's (1781–1819) decision to annex Assam and his successor's march into Arakan.

Of the three Anglo-Burmese wars in the nineteenth century (1824–1826, 1852, and 1885), the first was the only one that fitted the description. The other two were occasions on which the British troops marched and few on the other side showed up. The first war proved costly to both sides. After the first year's successes in the Chittagong and Cachar areas, the Burmese lost heavily in Arakan and Tenasserim. After General Maha Bandula's death in April 1825, Myanmar's situation further deteriorated due to lack of military leadership. British troops then occupied Prome and were well on their way to the Myanmar capital when a cease-fire was ordered. Myanmar's fighting capacities, however, had convinced the British that any plan for the permanent occupation of the river valleys of Myanmar would not be an easy task. As it was, the British army had already paid a heavy price in what came to be described as the "most expensive and harassing war in India." The British lost about 15,000 troops, mostly Indian; of the 3,586 British troops in the first expedition, 3,115 were killed in Myanmar.

By the Treaty of Yandabo signed by the two sides in 1826, Myanmar ceded to the East India Company the two coastal provinces of Arakan and Tenasserim. It also agreed to pay an indemnity of one million pounds, payable in four installments within a period of two years. Myanmar believed that the two provinces ceded to the British were a kind of surety against the balance payment. It was a huge sum for the Burmese court to pay, considering that Myanmar had no flat currency and government revenues were collected in kind. The two countries also agreed to negotiate a commercial treaty, and Myanmar agreed to receive a British Resident at its court.

Toward the end of Bagyidaw's rule (1819–1837), Burmese hostility and ill feeling toward the British intensified. Myanmar accused the British of bad faith. At least partly, the situation was created by misinterpretation of the Resident's powers and of the provisions of the Yandabo treaty. The British equated the position of Resident at Myanmar's court with British Resident at the court of the Indian princes. A Resident was technically an adviser to an Indian prince; in reality, he was the all-powerful representative of British paramountcy. On the other hand, the Myanmar kings viewed the Resident as an envoy or plenipotentiary from one sovereign nation to another. Nevertheless, King Bagyidaw continued to maintain cordial relations with the East India Company in the hope that the latter would return the two seaboard provinces of Arakan and Tenasserim. In fact, the East India Company's files show such an intention on the part of the company. But as the 1830s unfolded, the British developed extensive rice cultivation in Arakan and built the port of Moulmein in Tenasserim for export of rice and timber. These achievements made them abandon any further thought of returning the two provinces to Myanmar. King Bagyidaw's pliant and patient ways had obviously not paid off, and the ultrasensitive, nationalist party at the court, headed by his brother Tharawaddy (1837–1846), decided to replace him. A palace revolution brought Tharawaddy to the throne in 1837.

Meanwhile, the British had been gradually pursuing their objective of opening an overland trade route to China. John Crawfurd, sent to Myanmar's capital in 1827 to negotiate a commercial treaty, estimated that the export of raw cotton to China accounted for between one-third and one-half of total exports. After the first Anglo-Burmese war, Myanmar was seen increasingly by the trading and manufacturing interests in Britain as the exclusive back door to a vast market in the interior of China.

But the East India Company was not as eager to push the exploration of overland China trade routes; there was enough scope for extension of trade within India itself. The company, however, approved some exploratory missions in the 1830s because of the persistence of the British Resident in Myanmar, Major Henry Burney (1830–1837), and the knowledge that the Burmese monarch was unlikely to create trouble as long as the carrot of retrocession of Tenasserim was dangled before him.

The political significance of these missions did not escape the Burmese or the Chinese. The governor of Yunnan cautioned the Burmese king in a letter:

> Everything that occurs in Elder Brother's Empire shall be made known to Younger Brother with respect to Younger Brother's Empire. It is not proper to allow the English after they have made war and peace has been settled to remain in the city. They are accustomed to act like the "Pipal tree" [which spreads extensively]. Let not Younger Brother therefore allow the English to remain in his country and if anything happens Elder Brother will attack, take and give.[2]

After 1837, the new king, Tharawaddy, was resolved to terminate all British explorations and to abrogate through inaction all the provisions of the humiliating Treaty of Yandabo. In 1840, the Residency was withdrawn because of complaints of ill treatment, thereby closing the only channel of peaceful communications between the British and Burmese governments.

THE SECOND ANGLO-BURMESE WAR, 1852

By the 1840s, Yangon had become an important trading center with numerous British firms in Calcutta having branches there. Their ostensible trade was in cotton piece goods and teak, but they also exported bullion, which was expressly prohibited under the Yandabo treaty of 1826. Alarmed at the efflux of the precious specie, the Burmese government took energetic measures to arrest the flow by searching ships, opening mail packets, and apprehending merchants and mariners suspected of smuggling. Those who were affected complained to the East India Company's officials in Calcutta of the "arrogant, arbitrary, and atrocious behaviour" of the Burmese governors of Rangoon.

Teak was another major source of conflict between the Burmese government and British merchants. Teak merchants had been looking for fresh fields for profitable investments and for new ways of evading government curbs, be they British or Burmese. In April 1841, Tenasserim Commissioner Edmund A. Blundell issued regulations to prevent further wasteful cutting of teak, and in the same year, King Tharawaddy proclaimed the inclusion of teak among royal monopolies, an act readily condemned by British merchants as violating the Anglo-Burmese commercial treaty. There was nothing in the Treaty of Yandabo or the Crawfurd convention of 1827 prohibiting royal monopolies. Besides, the Burmese king had traditionally been his country's chief trader with the privilege of declaring any commodity or natural resource in his kingdom a monopoly.

As Yangon's importance as a port augmented, so did the British mercantile pressures to bring Lower Myanmar under direct British authority. Complaint after complaint piled up at the governor-general's office in Calcutta about the handicaps, real and imagined, that British merchants experienced in Yangon.

Matters became worse in 1850 with the promotion of the collector of customs in Yangon, Maung Ok, as governor. Maung Ok needed money to rebuild Yangon, three-fourths of which had been devastated by fire in December 1850. In order to raise revenues, Maung Ok began a more careful collection of harbor and customs duties; fines were imposed for evasion or tardy payment of taxes. A merchant-captain, Potter, was not allowed to launch a newly built ship until he paid 16,000 rupees as tax. Fortunately for Maung Ok, Potter's protests did not provoke Calcutta enough to intervene in Lower Myanmar.

The following year, however, two incidents of alleged extortion of 9,000 rupees by Maung Ok from two British captains brought about British intervention. Governor-General Lord Dalhousie asked Commodore George Robert Lambert of the Royal Navy to investigate the matter. When Lambert arrived in Yangon on November 7, 1851, the foremost among the merchants complaining against Governor Maung Ok was the notorious May Flower Crisp, who had been caught several times before for illicit export of bullion.

Lambert did not bother to investigate the charges, most of which appeared to him "well-founded" and "proving" that the governor of Yangon was "unfit to be entrusted with the lives and property of British subjects." Lambert had already decided upon a war with Myanmar. Dalhousie was later to describe Lambert as a "combustible Commodore."[3] Within twenty-four hours of his arrival in the Yangon harbor, Lambert sent an ultimatum to the Burmese government and then sent a British ship up the Yangon River to demand a reply from the Burmese court.

Despite the serious differences of opinion between the government of India and Commodore Lambert, a war ensued. The British forces, much better equipped than a quarter century before, quickly occupied Yangon and Lower Myanmar up to Toungoo. There was almost no opposition on Myanmar's part. Governor-General Dalhousie unilaterally declared the annexation of Pegu (Lower Myanmar). The boundary between Lower and Upper Myanmar was fixed without waiting for a reply to the letter sent to the king of Myanmar. At the Burmese capital, a revolution was under way against King Pagan (1846–1852) and his supporters, who were advocating a hard line against the British. The leader of the opposition, Mindon Min, ascended the throne. Meanwhile, Captain Arthur Phayre, first British commissioner of Pegu, took advantage of the turbulent situation at Myanmar's court to advance the border by another fifty miles to include the teak forests of Toungoo province. Burmese teak was highly regarded by the British navy; Yangon teak merchants had coveted the rich teak forests of Toungoo for a long time. When Mindon's envoys arrived finally for negotiations on March 31, 1853, they were presented with a fait accompli, with little or no opportunity to modify the newly proposed boundary.

An Anglo-Burmese treaty concluding the second war was never finalized. Mindon maintained an extremely friendly attitude toward the British, partly because he hoped to get back the province of Pegu. Without it, Myanmar would be landlocked without an access to the outside world except through China. On the other hand, the British government desired a treaty that would recognize its status in Myanmar in the eyes of other countries. Governor-General Dalhousie was also keen to secure a formal commercial treaty in the absence of which British merchants might not trade with Upper Myanmar. The British also wanted formal rights of passage through Upper Myanmar for exploration of trade routes to western China. All British efforts to secure a formal treaty, however, proved futile. King Mindon would not risk his place in Burmese history by formally ceding a territory to an alien power. As for exploration of overland routes to China, the king would have suffered the most if Anglo-Chinese trade through Myanmar were to be encouraged. As noted earlier, the king was, after all, the principal trader of Myanmar, and the trade with China constituted a large chunk of that trade.

IMPROVEMENT IN ANGLO-BURMESE RELATIONS
British Exploration of China Trade Routes

Efforts to explore the China trade routes through Myanmar had been paralyzed since 1837. With the annexation of Lower Myanmar, enthusiasts for the exploration of China trade routes rallied once again, not in a joint effort but singly championing their favorite ideas. Two of these were old-timers—father and son—the Spryes. After five Chinese ports were opened for commercial intercourse to numerous Western powers in the 1840s, Captain R. S. M. Sprye campaigned even more vigorously for the exclusive opportunity of tapping the immense resources and markets of inland China. Sprye contrasted the short and direct route from

Yangon to southwest China with the much longer routes from the treaty ports across China, pointing out also that Yangon's relative proximity to Europe would entail considerable saving on ocean freight.

Sprye's propaganda regarding the overland railway route from Myanmar into China attracted the textile lobby in England. Trade with coastal China had not met the anticipations of Manchester, Lancashire, and other textile and industrial centers. English manufacturers and merchants now lent their support to Sprye's project in the hope that the opening of the interior markets through Myanmar for their country's exclusive exploitation would more than compensate for the losses in the seaboard trade with China.

In response to all this mercantile pressure, the government of India decided to send Phayre on his second mission to Mandalay in 1862. Phayre loved Myanmar and understood Burmese sensitivities. The treaty of 1862 was negotiated by him under cordial conditions. All transit goods to and from China passing through Burmese territory and using the port of Yangon were to pay a customs duty of 1 percent ad valorem to both the British and Myanmar governments. The lower customs duties would benefit the British overland trade with China inasmuch as they would enhance the competitiveness of English goods despite the costs of carriage from Yangon to the Chinese border. Certainly, they would be much cheaper than goods of European origin transported from the southeastern ports of China overland to southwest China. In addition, the treaty provided that the British and Burmese merchants would be allowed to travel in each other's country "without hindrance." These two provisions of the treaty virtually opened overland China trade to the British, who could travel to Bhamo and exchange goods with the Chinese traders there.

In 1866, Lord Cranbourne (later Lord Salisbury), who favored an active and aggressive policy to help trade and commerce, became the secretary of state for India. Cranbourne assured various chambers of commerce in England that he would step up pressure to secure better conditions of trade in Myanmar, facilities for exploration of trade routes to China, and establishment of a railroad link to the Chinese border. He was also determined to bring Upper Myanmar, in the manner of the Indian princely states, firmly under British paramountcy. He seemed to have been particularly concerned about French attempts to reach the interior markets of China. A month before he became the secretary of state, the Doudart de Lagree and Francis Garnier expedition had left Saigon to explore the Mekong route to China. Some intelligence had also reached Cranbourne that Mindon had permitted the Société des Missions Etrangères to work at Bhamo. British merchants expressed their fears that the French might spearhead penetration into Chinese markets from Indochina and Myanmar. These events marked the beginning of active Anglo-French rivalry for the interior markets of China. The situation also made the British apprehensive that their traditional enemy might gain an overriding influence in an area strategically vital for defense of their Indian empire. Cranbourne enunciated a policy at this point that remained valid for the remainder of the period of Myanmar's independence until 1885:

> It is of primary importance to allow no other European power to insert itself between British Burmah and China. Our influence in that country ought to be paramount.

The country itself is of no great importance, but an easy communication with the multitudes who inhabit Western China is an object of national importance. No influence superior to ours must be allowed to gain ground in Burmah.[4]

Mindon's Rule

In February 1867, Albert Fytche was appointed to succeed Phayre as commissioner of Lower Myanmar. Fytche ended the moderation that had marked Anglo-Burmese relations since Mindon's accession to the throne in 1852. Fytche's previous experience in Myanmar extended over two decades. He knew the Burmese differently from Phayre. He believed that the only way to deal with them was to treat them harshly.

Despite his long sojourn in Myanmar, Fytche had far less insight into the Burmese character and way of life than Phayre, but a great deal more self-assurance. He was proud of his own lineage; he was a descendant of the Elizabethan prospector Ralph Fitch, the first Englishman to set foot on Myanmar's soil. He also liked to tell everyone that he was the cousin of the poet laureate Tennyson. Fytche was disappointed at Phayre's deferential attitude and polite manners in dealing with King Mindon. He was furious at his failure in December 1866 in securing revision of the 1862 treaty. In that month, after his meeting with Cranbourne in London, he was determined to be the agent of the new secretary of state's "forward policy" in Myanmar.

Cranbourne and Fytche came to power at a time when Mindon's position was very shaky. A series of rebellions had broken out in Upper Myanmar during the 1866–1867 period. First was the Shan rebellion. Then, in a tragedy that shocked Mindon, two of his sons rebelled, killing Mindon's brother and heir apparent, Kanaung. This was followed by a rebellion of the regiments in favor of the son of the deceased crown prince.

The resulting chaos unnerved Mindon, who sorely needed arms to restore law and order. In that moment of desperation, he turned to the British for help, offering to discuss a revision of the commercial treaty. The price of British assistance was high. The high-handed Fytche successfully negotiated a treaty by which the king reluctantly agreed to abandon all his monopolies except rubies, earth-oil, and timber. Even Fytche concluded that the king had to retain those resources so as not to lose prestige with his people, who regarded the possession of forests, oil wells, and ruby mines as essential to the title and reputation of a Burmese king. Besides, as Fytche himself reported to Calcutta, the monopolies would not amount to more than 14 percent of the trade. The king agreed also to reduce all the frontier customs duties to 5 percent ad valorem. He granted certain rights of extraterritoriality, whereby the British political agent would have full jurisdiction over civil cases between British subjects at the capital, and those between British and Burmese subjects would be tried by a mixed court composed of the British political agent and a suitable Burmese of high rank.

The king made further concessions not officially incorporated in the treaty. A British Resident was to reside at Bhamo; a boat belonging to the Irrawaddy Flotilla Company would be permitted to navigate upriver to Bhamo once a week. Fytche ordered immediate and rapid exploration of the Bhamo route.

DETERIORATION IN ANGLO-BURMESE RELATIONS
British Paramountcy Versus Myanmar's Sovereignty

Mindon had, out of helplessness, agreed to the 1867 treaty, whose provisions were galling to Burmese pride. Moreover, he found that negotiations with the British for the import of arms needed to maintain law and order did not progress well because some local British officials themselves instigated the dissidents. In 1873, Mindon decided to send a delegation to London to clear the air by discussing the various outstanding issues directly with the British government. The delegation would also visit other European states, particularly France and Italy.

Myanmar's mission proved as much a failure in England as it was a success in France and Italy. The delegation was introduced to the British queen not by the foreign secretary but by the secretary of state for India, a deliberate move to demonstrate the Indian government's paramountcy over Myanmar. In contrast, the delegation was received warmly in Italy and France. It concluded a commercial treaty with Italy and approved a draft convention with France. As could be expected, rumors of an impending Franco-Burmese military alliance surfaced, making both British official and mercantile circles wary and nervous about possible French success in reaching the coveted markets of southwestern China.

The Indian government, however, planned an ambitious scheme, a two-way expedition between Bhamo and Shanghai to chart a route for future railroad construction. Colonel Horace Browne, a British official in Myanmar, was to lead a party from Bhamo to meet another led by a young member of the British consular service, Augustus Margary, overland from Shanghai. The Chinese government wrote to the provincial governors to ensure assistance to the mission; King Mindon provided a 250-man armed escort within Myanmar's borders. The mission ended in a tragedy. On his return journey, Margary was killed, possibly by Kakhyen tribals at Momein, a town on the headwaters of the Salween some distance within the Chinese border. The British capitalized on the incident to wrest more concessions from China. Myanmar was needlessly blamed for the tragic happening. Anglo-Burmese relations worsened. Governor-General Lord Northbrook ruled that no British representative thereafter would observe the Burmese protocol of removing the shoes before entering the Burmese monarch's court. The result was that there were no further meetings between Mindon and the British representatives in Mandalay. It was at such a low point of Anglo-Burmese relations that Myanmar's greatest monarch of the nineteenth century died in 1878.

Mindon was succeeded by one of his younger sons, Theebaw. An ambitious Burmese princess had given her daughter in marriage to Theebaw in the calculated hope that if she could manipulate his succession to the throne, the real power would rest in the mother's hands. Theebaw's long stay, prior to his marriage, at a Buddhist monastery as a scholarly recluse had apparently encouraged her to think that in the absence of any political experience he would be an ideal choice for a puppet monarch. Soon after accession to the throne, at the behest of his queen and her mother, Theebaw ordered about eighty persons, all those who could even remotely claim the throne, to be massacred. Protests from the British Resident Captain Shaw brought the rejoinder from a senior member of the Burmese Supreme Council, the Hluttaw, that this was an internal matter and that the steps taken were necessary to bring about law and order in a potentially explosive situation. In the following year, in June 1879, Shaw died. The Indian government decided at this time to withdraw the Residency altogether, once again eliminating the only agency for conducting a dialogue between the British and the Burmese.

Meanwhile, in mid-1882, power shifted at the Burmese court. The queen's protégé and adviser, Taingdar Mingyi, had succeeded in supplanting the influence of Kinwun Mingyi, who was known for his statesmanlike moderation. As the new court clique insisted on stiffer measures against the British, the negotiations then in progress at the Indian summer resort of Simla between Kinwun Mingyi and the Indian government were at once suspended. The anti-British group advocated abolition of the Treaty of Yandabo of 1826, acknowledgment of the king's sovereign right to declare any product a monopoly, and some restrictions on travel by British subjects within Myanmar. The two sides were clearly heading for a showdown. Once again, the old issue of Myanmar's insistence on its sovereign status basically conflicted with the British claim to paramountcy over Myanmar.

To reassert its sovereign status, Myanmar opened a fresh diplomatic offensive by sending an embassy to Europe, ostensibly for gathering the latest information on industrial and scientific development there and exploring the prospects of aid in introducing such innovations in Myanmar. There is no knowing if France had deliberately encouraged the Burmese in this diplomatic adventurism. In any case, it was not likely that the proud Burmese monarch would throw himself into French arms, as the British alleged; he was more likely trying to gain some diplomatic leverage against Britain, France's traditional enemy.

For the following two years, until Britain annexed Upper Myanmar, fact and rumor (sometimes deliberately combined by interested parties) produced the general feeling that well-laid French plans to gain control of Myanmar were in motion. The threat of control by Russia of India's northwest frontier had plagued British diplomats and strategists for most of the nineteenth century. In the 1880s, the possibility of French control of Myanmar was seen as endangering the security of India and trade with Myanmar. Further, Myanmar's strategic position on the route to the allegedly inexhaustible markets of western China was of no mean importance. The possibility existed that France was looking for all such gains and therefore wanted to attain a predominant position in peninsular Southeast Asia.

The Burmese mission spent over one year in Paris before a Franco-Burmese treaty was signed on January 15, 1885. Jules Ferry, an ardent imperialist, was at that time the French premier, who would not concede British claims to paramountcy over Myanmar. Thus, ten days before the Franco-Burmese commercial treaty was signed, Ferry told Viscount Lyons, the British ambassador to France, that Myanmar was also "a neighbour of French possessions" and that some "treaty arrangements with regard to the frontier" might be necessary.[5] The commercial treaty itself gave no specific concessions to France. It stipulated rights of residence, commerce, and the most-favored-nation treatment. Its principal gain for Myanmar was recognition of its equal sovereign status; the French government was to establish a consulate at Mandalay.

Rumors started getting thicker with the arrival in Mandalay of the French consul, Frederic Haas, in May 1885. It was believed by British official and commercial circles in Myanmar and Bengal that under the secret clauses of the Franco-Burmese treaty, France had obtained extensive concessions. A Franco-Burmese bank to be opened at Mandalay would give a loan of 25 million rupees to Upper Myanmar at 12.5 percent interest; the royal ruby mines would be turned over to the bank for security. France and Myanmar would jointly collect revenues from the monopoly on earth-oil and from trade and traffic on the Irrawaddy to pay the interest costs. The bank would also finance Myanmar's development projects, including a railroad from Mandalay to Tongking that would be used for transporting arms from French Indochina into Upper Myanmar. A French company would receive teak concessions; another would operate steamers in competition with the British-owned Irrawaddy Flotilla Company. French officials would run the posts and telegraph department. Charles Bernard, the British chief commissioner in Yangon, telegraphed to London that the French agents were trying to establish themselves strongly at Mandalay "with a view to joining hands at some future time with the French possessions on the upper reaches of the Red River."[6]

Some of these rumors were clearly fabricated by British officials and commercial interests. A Burmese scholar, Htin Aung, pointed out that closer examination would have revealed the impossibility of the grant by Myanmar of such far-reaching concessions:

> It was physically impossible to construct a railway from Mandalay to Tongking; . . . the ruby mines were such a requisite of the Burmese King that they would be given to a foreign company only if the monarchy had been destroyed; as the British controlled the lower region of the Irrawaddy, there could be no rival company without their consent; and the Burmese under Mindon had evolved a Morse code in their own language and had more recently issued their first postage stamps and were so proud of their achievement that they surely could not allow any foreigner to come and take the credit.[7]

Bombay-Burmah Trading Corporation Dispute

During that crucial year ending with the British annexation of Upper Myanmar in December 1885, the Rangoon [Yangon] Chamber of Commerce played a vital role. It had been foremost in denouncing Theebaw's massacres and restrictive trade policies and in advocating "the expediency of annexing Upper Burma."[8] Its chairman was S. G. Jones, manager of the powerful Bombay-Burmah Trading Corporation, which was the leading teak timber firm in Myanmar and Thailand. The chamber was also concerned about the fortunes of the largely British-owned rice industry. There had been a general decline in business as Myanmar's rice faced stiff competition from Saigon and Bangkok in European markets; several rice mills in Yangon were idle. News of further French success at Mandalay that would divert rice trade from British hands created panic in business circles. Under Jones's leadership, the chamber believed that if Upper Myanmar came under direct British control, there would be better scope for exploitation of teak forests. The demand for teak, used in building ship decks, railroad fish plates, and quality furniture, had been on the rise even during the European depression (1873–1896). Exports of the commodity had risen from an annual average of 85,000 tons during the period 1857–1860 to about 275,000 tons in 1883–1885.[9]

The Yangon merchants, who were looking for a cause célèbre, found a great opportunity in August 1885 when the Hluttaw delivered its judgment against the Bombay-Burmah Trading Corporation. The merchants alleged that the judgment was politically motivated insofar as the corporation was liable to be evicted to make room for a French syndicate that would take over the royal teak forests.

The Bombay-Burmah Trading Corporation had since 1862 been working the Ningyan teak forests, north of Toungoo within Upper Myanmar, under a lease contract with the Burmese king. Noting the rise in demand for teak and increase in world prices of teak, King Theebaw revised the lease terms in 1883, requiring lump sums to be paid by way of annual rental of the forests. The corporation accepted these revisions without demur because its profit margin was high; it did not ask for revision of the lease terms even after Upper Myanmar was annexed. In fact, it continued to work on those terms until 1899, when the leases expired. The easy terms did not, however, inhibit the corporation from attempting to manipulate the timber accounts by bribing local officials.

A case involving the corporation came before the Hluttaw, which according to Burmese tradition had the highest legislative, executive, and judicial authority, superseded only by the king. Some foresters who supplied logs to the corporation sued the latter for short payment. According to their past practice, the foresters had floated the logs down the Sittang to Toungoo, where the Bombay-Burmah Trading Corporation had a branch office. The foresters claimed payment for 89,800 logs as against 32,128 paid for by the corporation in the two years ending April 14, 1885. The Hluttaw examined the corporation's records at the Toungoo forest office and found a discrepancy of 57,955 logs for the period. By its judgment of August 12, 1885, the Hluttaw ordered the corporation to pay the foresters a sum of £33,333 in addition to a royalty of £36,661 to the king and a fine for underpayment of tax, which under the Burmese law was equal to the tax itself.

An advance copy of this judgment was obtained by the Bombay-Burmah Trading Corporation through some dubious means by its resourceful but unscrupulous agent at Mandalay, Chevalier Andreino. Andreino wore many hats. He was an agent of the Irrawaddy Flotilla Company, consul for Italy, and secret agent for the British government. Earlier, Andreino had also obtained a copy of a secret letter dated January 15, 1885, allegedly written by Premier Jules Ferry of France to the Burmese foreign minister, suggesting a Franco-Burmese military alliance. The seven-month-old letter, which later was proved a forgery and which was in any case no longer operative because Ferry had lost power in April 1885, was published by Andreino on the eve of the Hluttaw judgment in the Bombay-Burmah Trading Corporation dispute. Ferry's letter referred to the possibility of transporting arms to Myanmar through Tongking as soon as peace was restored in Tongking itself.[10]

A closer look at the situation could have dispelled any suspicion of Franco-Burmese collusion during 1884 and 1885. It should be noted that in 1884, Prince Myingun, who had been in British captivity since the revolt of 1866, had escaped from internment at Benares to the French colony of Chandernagore near Calcutta. Given Theebaw's fear of any surviving prince, the French could not have endeared themselves to him by treating Prince Myingun well and taking him to Saigon, from where they could always threaten to smuggle him to Upper Myanmar and put him on the throne. The British knew of such a possibility, and so did the

Burmese. Perhaps Premier Jules Ferry was using the fugitive prince as a lever to obtain some concessions from Theebaw, who would in that case have been friendly only to the British. It is highly unlikely that Theebaw would knowingly allow French influence to grow to a dangerous degree or that the Hluttaw judgment would be politically motivated to oust a British firm in favor of a French syndicate. As Htin Aung observed: "The rumours of French concessions, the alleged machinations of Haas and the bogus Ferry letter were the smoke bombs meant to create a screen to hide the true facts regarding the Bombay-Burmah case."[11] Besides, France officially denied existence of any noncommercial agreements with Myanmar and disowned actions of French Consul Haas at Mandalay if they contradicted the French government's assurance. In September 1885, after Ferry's fall, France proposed to Britain a scheme for division of influence in the Indochinese peninsula recognizing Myanmar's place within the British sphere of influence.

The secretary of state for India, Lord Randolph Churchill (Winston's father), however, precipitated British action in Upper Myanmar, preempting and even sabotaging the chance of any negotiations with France. It did not take much for Randolph Churchill to convince Salisbury and his cabinet colleagues that a live threat of French domination of Myanmar existed. On October 30, an ultimatum was sent to Upper Myanmar, whose terms were such that no one expected King Theebaw to accept them. It asked King Theebaw to settle the Bombay-Burmah Trading Corporation case in consultation with the viceroy's representative. Myanmar should conduct its foreign relations thereafter in accordance with the advice of the Indian government; it should afford facilities for opening up British trade with China. In a separate communication, the king was also apprised that the British representative to the court of Ava would thereafter see the king not only with his shoes on but also wearing a sword and that the British Resident would be provided with a guard of 1,000 soldiers and a steamer fitted with cannon. The ultimatum would expire on November 10.

Myanmar's reply of November 4, though couched in polite language, was firm on the question of sovereignty and the Hluttaw's legal jurisdiction. Myanmar agreed to have a permanent British Resident at Mandalay, but maintained that his intervention would not be necessary in the Bombay-Burmah Trading Corporation case. The case had been settled according to Burmese law and based on the company's forest records. An appeal would lie with the king of Myanmar. Foreign relations were an exclusive prerogative of a sovereign state, and friendly relations with France, Italy, and other states would be maintained.

Third Anglo-Burmese War and Myanmar's Annexation

The result was the British declaration of war against Myanmar in November 1885. It took only fifteen days and loss of ten lives for the British army to reach and take over the capital of Mandalay. The invaders showed scant regard for Burmese sensitivities or traditions. Soldiers wearing boots marched throughout the palace, shouting and singing bawdy songs and ordering royalty and nobility about. The king and his immediate family were given forty-five minutes to pack up; his request for a ceremonial march out of his capital on elephant was unceremoniously rejected. Instead, around dusk, in the twilight hour of the centuries-old Burmese monarchy, the royal family was taken in a bullock cart to a ship waiting to take them into exile to western India, while thousands of weeping Burmans, lined ten to twenty deep on either side of the road to the pier, witnessed the sad spectacle. That single day's acts of British callousness in Mandalay were to cost Britain dearly as intense hostility welled up in Burmese chests, enough to inspire thousands of them to take up arms and join the band of resisters. It took General Charles Crosthwaite 30,000 men and five years of a "pacification" campaign to contain the guerrilla warfare and establish full control over the country. The Burmese never forgave the British for the ignominies heaped on their king by the conquerors in their hour of triumph and Burmese defeat.

Upper Myanmar was annexed to the Indian empire. The British explained that they had been left with no other alternative because there was almost no surviving member of the royal family as Theebaw had killed them all. It was not the whole truth. The British still had in their captivity a Burmese prince, one of Mindon's sons who had taken asylum in 1866. But the Indian government's mind was already made up on the question of Myanmar's future. Even before the ultimatum had been served on King Theebaw, Viceroy Dufferin had telegraphed to his superior in London: "We are all agreed here that annexation is preferable to setting up another prince. If we are to tap China via Bhamo, we ought to have absolute control of the valley."[12] The secretary of state for India, Randolph Churchill, also favored annexation, "simple and direct." His enthusiasm for making Upper Myanmar "a New Year's present to the Queen" was unconcealed.

In sum, in the two decades before the third Anglo-Burmese war, two opposing concepts of power and objectives had produced a confrontation between Britain and Myanmar. The British doctrine of paramountcy in India was sought to be extended to those neighboring regions considered vital for the Indian empire's security. The treaties of 1862 and 1867 with King Mindon seemed to satisfy the British, at least for the time being. Subsequent attempts on the part of Mindon and Theebaw to reassert their sovereign status particularly in two sensitive areas—royal monopolies and relations with France—upset that delicate understanding underlying the fabric of "informal empire." British mercantile interests in overland trade with China and in the valuable teak trade constituted the irresistible force that regarded the Burmese king's sovereign status as an impediment and an affront to British commercial and imperial interests. Both the viceroy and the secretary of state for India concurred in thinking that formal rule over Myanmar was necessary from the point of security of Indian imperial and commercial interests.

10

The French in Vietnam and Cambodia

PERSECUTION OF CATHOLICS

Despite the long history of French presence in Vietnam going back to the beginning of the seventeenth century, major French territorial conquests had to await the second half of the nineteenth century. As noted in Chapter 5, successive French governments had demonstrated a consistent interest in proselytization, which had resulted by the end of the eighteenth century in about a quarter million Vietnamese converts, mostly in the coastal provinces. With the possible exception of Gia Long's personal relationship with Bishop Pigneau de Behaine, the missionaries (even during Gia Long's rule) did not enjoy the trust of the Vietnamese monarchs. De Behaine was posthumously made a duke of Vietnam, but his role in converting the young prince Canh (Gia Long's son) during his visit to France was neither forgotten nor forgiven. The numbers of Vietnamese Christians dwindled during Gia Long's rule by 60 percent.

Large-scale persecution of converts and missionaries probably occurred under Emperor Minh Mang (1820–1841) and Emperor Thieu Tri (1841–1847) and in the early part of Tu Duc's reign (1847–1883). The Chinese experience with foreigners (during the Anglo-Chinese war and its aftermath) and Christian missionaries (the Taiping rebellion) had done little to reassure the Vietnamese court. The close association of the missionaries with the rebellious governor of Gia Dinh (around Saigon), the eunuch Le Van Duyet, who attempted to prevent Minh Mang's succession to the throne in 1820, earned them the extreme wrath of the monarch.

The revolt posed a serious threat to Minh Mang because Thailand took advantage of it by sending troops to Gia Dinh. Recent research indicates that the real reasons for the revolt were not so much religious as political. Contrary to his father's policy of devolution of power, Minh Mang had attempted to control Tongking and Gia Dinh from Hue. The Gia Dinh rebellion was a protest against Minh

Mang's ambitions. The religious factor was of secondary importance. As an ardent Confucianist believing in ancestor worship, Minh Mang took serious note of the Roman Catholic missionaries preaching against the practice. In 1833, religion and politics were mixed in the activities of a French missionary, Father Marchand, who was suspected of instigating another rebellion in Gia Dinh led by Le Van Khoi. Minh Mang, a forceful personality in religion and war, led the troops to force the Thais out of the country and crushed the rebellion in Gia Dinh in both the 1820s and the 1830s.

It was no surprise, therefore, that Minh Mang's reign witnessed a series of proclamations to eliminate Catholic converts and their institutions. Minh Mang forbade in 1825 any further entry of missionaries into Vietnam. Eight years later, an extremely severe decree ordered churches to be demolished and made profession of the Catholic faith an offense punishable by death. Though the order was not literally applied, many Catholics, including priests, were killed. In 1836, the Vietnamese monarch closed his ports to European shipping.

The British success in "opening" China emboldened the French, who employed similar tactics in opening up Vietnam by using the excuse of religious persecution. In the 1840s, French merchant ships and navy, whose presence in the South China Sea had increased following the opening of five Chinese ports, intervened to secure the release of some French missionaries awaiting death sentences in Vietnamese prisons. Thus, in 1846, French ships blockaded Tourane (Da Nang) for two weeks and then bombarded the port, demanding the release of Monsignor Dominique Lefevre, who had been condemned to death by the Vietnamese government.

Figures of Catholic casualties of Vietnamese persecution as well as of French bombardment of Tourane have been grossly exaggerated. One must not lose sight of the fact that there was a great gap between the letter of the imperial edicts ordering persecution of Catholics and their implementation. Thus, even during Emperor Tu Duc's reign, when the persecution was supposedly at its worst, a Vietnamese Catholic, Nguyen Truong To (1827–1871), still served as a high official at the imperial court. He was able to go with a missionary to Europe, see the pope, bring home a hundred Western books, and advise Emperor Tu Duc to institute reforms in Vietnam based on his observations in Europe. The question of treatment of Catholics must be seen in the context of tensions at the imperial court, which regarded the Catholic activities as a threat to Vietnamese traditions and did not quite know how to deal with such a threat.

CONQUEST OF COCHIN CHINA

The French government of Napoleon III used the reports of persecution of Catholics as an opportunity for intervention in and acquisition of territory in South Vietnam. The new French imperialism of the time was widely based on a coalition of diverse interests of the church, traders, and manufacturers in search of new markets and was aided by the egotistic emperor's lust for colonies to augment national power and prestige. French business interests were not unaware of the exclusive advantages their position in South Vietnam could give for seeking access to the lucrative markets of interior China. Their aim seemed to be to establish a trading base in Saigon rivaling Singapore and Hong Kong particularly for funneling south China trade.[1]

In 1858, a joint Franco-Spanish expedition proceeded to Vietnam, ostensibly to save the missionaries. In that year, two priests—one French and one Spanish—had been killed in Vietnam. The Spanish quit after the Vietnamese government gave assurances of nonpersecution, but the French continued the fighting for three years until they secured a treaty from Emperor Tu Duc in 1862. The provisions of the treaty revealed the real French intentions: The Vietnamese emperor ceded three provinces in Gia Dinh region, including Saigon, which the French called Cochin China, and assured that no part of his kingdom would ever be alienated to any other power except France. He agreed to open three ports to France and to pay an indemnity of four million piastres in ten annual installments. Christianity would be tolerated in the future. More significantly, the treaty gave France the right to navigate the Mekong. Five years later, the French obtained the remaining provinces of Cochin China and established control over the entire Mekong Delta.

How does one explain French success in Cochin China? Most historians have based their analyses on French accounts, blaming the Vietnamese debacle on the inadequate and inefficient administration in the Mekong Delta. If this were so, it is difficult to comprehend how the Vietnamese court directed a war lasting three and one-half years against France, an enemy with far more sophisticated equipment than Vietnam. In fact, what made the Vietnamese emperor capitulate in 1862 was the need to divert his forces and attention simultaneously to North Vietnam to put down a rebellion there led by a descendant of the old Le dynasty. More plausible explanations have been provided by Bernard Fall and Le Thanh Khoi. Fall attributed the French success to the alienness of the Vietnamese in Cochin China, which they had "colonized" only recently and where they were "the least secure in their social structure and institutions." Hence, there was comparative lack of resistance among the non-Vietnamese population in South Vietnam to the French colonial penetration, which became increasingly difficult as it advanced northward.[2] Le Thanh Khoi, an eminent Vietnamese historian, held that the mandarins hid from the ruler, "isolated from his people by the high walls of the Forbidden City [the palace in Hue], national realities as well as the gravity of the crisis in foreign relations." In Le's opinion, it was their "blind pride as well as their narrowness of views which bears a large measure of responsibility for the fall of Vietnam."[3]

There is no doubt that along with Myanmar and Thailand, Vietnam was the most advanced administrative polity in Southeast Asia. The mandarinate recruited through the civil service examination system was still capable of governing the country. It continued to govern central and northern Vietnam for another two decades until the French progressively brought the rest of Vietnam under their control. What was basically wrong was the habit of the mandarins, who continued, like their counterparts in China of the nineteenth century, to look to Confucian classics of the past to find solutions for the challenges posed by the West. Under those circumstances, a national debacle at the hands of an aggressive Western power was only a matter of time.

PROTECTORATE OVER CAMBODIA

Undoubtedly, the most important provision of the 1862 treaty was France's right to navigate the Mekong, which was believed to originate in southwest China. Within four years of the treaty, the privately endowed Paris Geographical Society sponsored the exploration of the Mekong under the leadership of two naval officers, Francis Garnier and Doudart de Lagree. Significantly, the society's president was Chasseloup Laubat, head of the ministry of the Marine. The society itself was a front for business interests; in 1873, in cooperation with the Paris Chamber of Commerce, a Society for Commercial Geography was established, which sponsored and financed future explorations overseas. Francis Garnier, then a young naval officer, held grandiose visions of a French empire rivaling that of the British in the East. His consuming personal ambition was born of a sense of manifest destiny that he was the divine instrument for elevating France's prestige in the world.

In their exploration of the Mekong, the de Lagree–Garnier expedition, which left Saigon in June 1866, had soon to pass through Cambodia. Unfortunately, Cambodia had been in grave political trouble for quite some time, and its king had appealed to France for intervention, thus being the only mainland state specifically to request foreign protection.

For a half century before that desperate stage was reached, Cambodia had been struggling to retain its existence as a separate state. For over four centuries, since the fall of Angkor in 1431, the Khmer monarchs had been vassals of Thailand (Ayuthaya and Bangkok). Since the late seventeenth century, however, the Nguyen dynasty, based at Hue, had been impinging on Cambodia, gradually absorbing its territories in the Mekong Delta and demanding tribute and recognition as overlord. The frequent disputes in Cambodia for succession to the throne and the rival contenders' search for external support also contributed to Thai and Vietnamese interference in Cambodian affairs, often at the cost of Cambodian territory as the price of such aid. In general, the weak Khmer monarchs bowed to the Vietnamese and Thai courts, depending on whichever happened to be stronger at the moment.

The simultaneous consolidation of Thailand and Vietnam by the end of the eighteenth century under the Chakri and Nguyen dynasties, respectively, sounded trouble for Cambodia. In order to avoid an armed conflict between its two powerful neighbors on their own soil, the Khmer monarchs decided, from 1802, to send tribute both to Bangkok and Hue. But the eruption of a dynastic dispute in Phnom Penh in 1812 brought Thai and Vietnamese armies onto Cambodian soil in support of rival claimants—King Ang Chan and his brother Ang Duong. Fortunately for Cambodia, the Thai king, Rama II, did not want a bloody confrontation and withdrew his troops, occupying, however, the Cambodian provinces of Melouprey and Stung Treng as a price of withdrawal. His expectation that the Vietnamese would withdraw likewise did not materialize. Rama II's successor was not as tolerant. He invaded Cambodia in 1831, sending Ang Chan fleeing to Vietnam for assistance. Vietnamese armies of Emperor Minh Mang rushed to reinstate Ang Chan and were successful in scattering the Thai forces. But on Ang Chan's death in 1834, Vietnam practically incorporated Cambodia into its empire, placing

Princess Ang Mey on the Khmer throne as a puppet ruler. During this period, Cambodia became for all purposes a part of Vietnam.[4]

The years from 1841 to 1845 were the worst for the Cambodian people. Vietnamese occupation of the country was bitterly resisted by the Khmer people, who clandestinely installed the exiled pro-Thai Prince Ang Duong on the throne. Once again, the rival armies of Thailand and Vietnam fought on Cambodian soil, causing great misery to the people. It was probably then that the Cambodian proverb "When elephants fight, the ants in the grass die" originated. The Cambodians sought peace. The kingdom was placed under the joint suzerainty of its powerful neighbors. Thus, the practice that the Khmer monarchs had unilaterally devised in 1802 of acknowledging both Thailand and Vietnam as overlords was now confirmed by the rival parties.

In the process of placating its neighbors, Cambodia lost much territory to both of them. Concerned over the survival of his kingdom, Ang Duong wrote to Napoleon III in 1853 seeking intervention and assistance, little realizing at the time that France also had territorial designs in Southeast Asia. By the time of his death in 1860, this had become a reality, with French forces pitted against Vietnamese in Cochin China.

With the conquest of Cochin China in 1862, France claimed to have succeeded Vietnam as overlord of Cambodia. In the following year, the French offered to establish a protectorate over Cambodia, a proposal readily accepted by King Norodom, who had succeeded his father, Ang Duong. A Franco-Khmer treaty was drawn up on August 11, 1863.

There was one major legal hurdle before the treaty could be valid. Norodom had not been formally crowned; the royal insignia was in Bangkok and the Thai monarch insisted on the coronation of his vassal king at his own hands. However, Norodom's efforts to go to Bangkok were blocked by French gunboats. During the ensuing negotiations between France and Thailand, the Thais revealed a previous secret treaty between Bangkok and Phnom Penh confirming Thailand's suzerain rights and acknowledging the Cambodian monarch's status as Thai viceroy of Cambodia. The Thais used the document to wrest the best terms under the circumstances from France. By the ensuing Franco-Thai treaty of 1867, Thailand gave up all claims to suzerainty over Cambodia in return for French recognition of Thai sovereignty over the western Cambodian provinces of Battambang and Siem Reap, which had been in Thai hands since the end of the eighteenth century.

GARNIER'S TONGKING ADVENTURE

The de Lagree–Garnier expedition had reported on the unsuitability of the Mekong as a commercial artery into south China. The frequent waterfalls and gorges in northeast Cambodia and Laos impeded navigation on the Mekong. De Lagree lost his life in the upper reaches of the river. Garnier managed to proceed to Yunnan and return to Saigon via Hankow. He had discovered while in Yunnan that the bulk of the south China trade in silk, tea, and textiles passed through Tongking. Garnier argued in favor of exploration of the Red River route.

The serious domestic crisis in which France was engulfed following disastrous defeat by Prussia arrested all plans for exploration in Vietnam for some time. By 1873, however, a chorus of mercantile agitators in Paris and Saigon demanded that France strengthen its hold on Indochina and precipitate access to the markets of interior China before the other European powers did. Three principal actors of the drama to be enacted momentarily in that year in Tongking were Admiral Marie-Jules Dupre, governor of Cochin China; Francis Garnier; and a French adventurer-trader, Jean Dupuis.

Dupuis had been in the East since 1858. An extremely able but unscrupulous man, he had established an official arms procurement agency for the Chinese government. Dupuis's interests soon extended to trafficking in minerals and salt between Yunnan and Tongking, violating the monopolistic interest of Vietnamese mandarins in those items. In 1868, Dupuis discussed with Francis Garnier in Hankow the possibility of opening the Red River route, and while in Paris in 1872, he also met Admiral Dupre and apprised him of his future plans.

Meanwhile, a series of disturbances had broken out in the almost inaccessible mountainous terrain on either side of the Sino-Vietnamese border. Hordes of fugitive Chinese bandits and rebels moved across the border, preying on the produce and property of Vietnam's Montagnard population. Two of the largest, best-organized bandit armies were the notorious Black Flags and Yellow Flags, who soon vied with each other for control of the trade of the upper Red River Valley. The situation was exploited by Jean Dupuis for illicit trade in salt, minerals, and gunrunning. In addition to some covert support from French officials, Dupuis had a well-trained and well-armed force of 150 men.

Dupuis's force clashed with local mandarins in Hanoi in May 1873, and they refused to allow the Frenchman to proceed upstream with a cargo of salt and arms. Dupuis's response was to occupy a section of Hanoi and to appeal to Governor Dupre to mediate with Vietnamese authorities. Ironically, Emperor Tu Duc also appealed to Dupre to order Dupuis out of Hanoi. This was, indeed, a heaven-sent opportunity for Dupre, who wanted an excuse to fish in Tongking's troubled waters. He decided to send a "mediation force" of two gunboats and a hundred men, including sixty marines, under Francis Garnier.

Once in Hanoi at the head of a picked group of forty men, Garnier threw to the winds the assurances given to Emperor Tu Duc to evict Dupuis from Tongking. Instead, he joined hands with Dupuis and, on November 16, unilaterally declared the Red River open to international trade and revised the customs tariffs to make them more advantageous to foreigners. Five days later, in a brash and bold action, Garnier stormed the citadel of Hanoi. Within three weeks, he brought lower Tongking, including Haiphong and Ninh Binh, under his control. The spectacular success was just too easy to last long. The mandarins, whose pride, position, and profit were hurt by Garnier's actions, used the Black Flags then roaming and raiding in the Tongking countryside to attack Garnier. On December 21, during a hot chase of the Black Flags, Garnier lost his life.

There is no knowing whether the entire episode stemmed from the rash initiative of the men on the spot—Garnier and Dupre—acting according to their own whims or whether it was a carefully planned covert maneuver of the French government, which could always denounce the action in the event of failure. The news of Garnier's death shocked Saigon and Paris. France officially disclaimed Garnier's action, ordered Dupuis to leave Tongking, and drew up a treaty essentially conciliatory toward Tu Duc. Even so, Garnier's objectives had at least partly been attained. The Red River and three ports of Tongking were declared open to foreign commerce, and a French consul and garrison were allowed to be stationed in each of them. The death of Garnier, however, was a serious setback to further French expansion for at least a decade.

FRANCE COMPLETES VIETNAM CONQUEST

Despite the Garnier episode, and France's preoccupation with domestic affairs, certain groups continued to press for expansion in Southeast Asia. By 1881, the imperialist advocates found a most vocal and powerful proponent in the new premier, Jules Ferry. "There needs to be no hesitation," he wrote, "in affirming that colonies in the present state of the world is the best affair of business, in which the capital of an old and wealthy country can engage."[5] He justified his own efforts for the conquest of the Tongking Delta with yet another reason:

> It is not a question of tomorrow but of the future of fifty or a hundred years; of that which will be the inheritance of our children, the bread of our workers. It is not a question of conquering China, but it is necessary to be at the portal of this region to undertake the pacific conquest of it.[6]

The treaty of 1873 provided France the excuse for the next move. The French alleged that the Vietnamese mandarins had severely obstructed a French expedition of 400 men led by Henri Riviere to clear the Red River Valley of the piratical Black Flags. In 1883 and 1884, under immense pressure, Vietnam signed new treaties agreeing to become a French protectorate, to surrender administrative responsibility for the Tongking province to France, and to accept French Residents at Hanoi and Hue. At the same time, in utter helplessness, the emperor of Vietnam appealed to his overlord, the emperor of China, for assistance in resisting further French encroachments.

On March 28, 1885, French forces were badly beaten by Chinese troops at the Sino-Vietnamese border post of Langson. The incident immediately led to Ferry's fall. France, however, retaliated by attacking Keelung in Taiwan, occupying the Pescadores Islands, blockading the port of Foochow, and destroying the Chinese navy there. In the end, the poorly equipped Chinese armed forces could not hold ground before the sophisticated French weaponry. The Treaty of Tientsin of June 9, 1885, recognized the French protectorate over Annam (as the French called central Vietnam) and Tongking, conceded preference to France over all European powers in Yunnan, and granted it the right to construct a railway paralleling the Red River Valley from Hanoi to Kunming. The treaty marked the extinction of the nearly two-millennia-old subordinate relationship of Vietnam to China.

11

Thailand Remains Independent

Thailand distinguished itself from other Southeast Asian states in the nineteenth century as being the only kingdom that survived the aggressive thrust of the New Imperialism. Among the significant factors that helped Thailand preserve its independent identity were its geographical location, its able diplomacy, and its policy of modernization. Although some credit for Thailand's independent status may rightly be given to the Anglo-French desire to avoid a common frontier and, therefore, to keep Thailand as a buffer state, a considerable share of the credit is owed to the policies of two remarkable Thai monarchs: Rama IV, or Mongkut (1851–1868), and Rama V, or Chulalongkorn (1868–1910). Together, they brought about a fair measure of modernization, revolutionary in the context of Thailand of those times. They successfully used diplomacy, playing the British against the French and losing some of the Thai territories to both, but preserving the core of the kingdom where the ethnic Thais lived.

MONGKUT, 1851–1868

Mongkut, who ascended the Thai throne as Rama IV at the age of 47, was perhaps the most qualified Asian monarch of his time. In his youth, he was trained in the traditional arts proper for a potential successor to the reigning monarch. When his father died in 1824, however, Mongkut's half-brother seized the throne and ruled as Rama III.

Mongkut, then only nineteen, decided discreetly to withdraw into a monastery. For the next quarter century, he led the ascetic and disciplined life of a monk. The experience proved valuable and, in some respects, unique for a monarch destined to be the most liberal and enlightened Thai ruler up to that time. The democratic character and organization of the Buddhist monasteries, where the monks

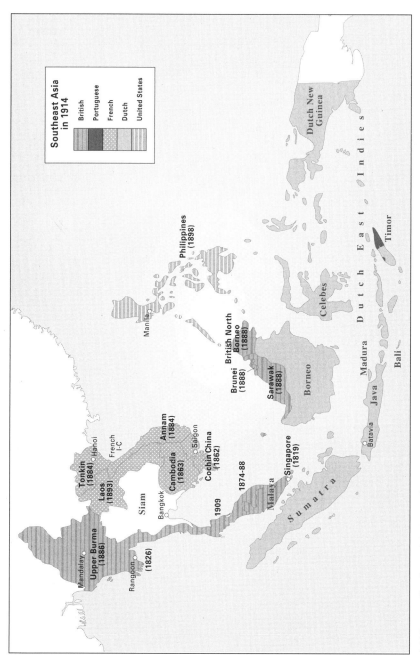

MAP 11.1 Southeast Asia in 1914

came from all classes and backgrounds, instilled in Mongkut a new outlook that enabled him to view himself as an ordinary human being. As a monk, Mongkut also had the opportunity to travel extensively in the countryside. During this period, he made contact with Western missionaries—French, English, and American—from whom he learned Latin and English, humanities, mathematics, and astronomy. More significantly, he was able to keep himself informed of events in Europe and Asia, as well as of the relative political, economic, and military strengths of the West and the East. Such knowledge of the changing times must have been extremely important in his later decision to open his country to European contacts and commerce.

During this period of monastic life, Mongkut perceived clearly that if a great country like China, after its defeat in 1842, was compelled to bow to Western pressures and end its isolation, a weak Thailand would not be able to keep the foreigners out for long, and thus important changes in the old ways of Thai society and government would have to be instituted to accommodate the West. At the same time, Mongkut did not want his country's glorious cultural traditions to be swept away by the tide of Western civilization. As a matter of fact, he himself had made significant contributions to the tradition. He had earned a great reputation for his scholarship in the sacred scriptures in Pali and for founding a reformed Buddhist sect called the Dhammayutika.

Mongkut was a complex and even contradictory personality—at least he has been made to appear so, thanks to the contrasting colors in which he has been portrayed by his various biographers. Many contemporary U.S. missionaries commented on his dual personality: "irregular and inconsistent; shrewd and arbitrary; magnanimous but suspicious and easily offended; alternately generous and niggardly, kind and vindictive; a great humanitarian at one turn and petty beyond belief at another."[1] Some part of his seemingly contradictory nature can perhaps be explained by Mongkut's desire to strike a balance between the opposing forces of tradition and modernity; between authoritarianism and liberalism in government; and between the status quo of feudal privilege and the new order to be created through progressive change.

Eager not to give the Western countries any excuse for intervening in Thailand's domestic affairs, King Mongkut altered court customs to enable easy contact with foreigners. Thus, he exempted foreigners from the practice of crawling on all fours while approaching the "august feet" of the monarch; they were allowed to assume any position deemed respectful in their country. He signed treaties of commerce and friendship with foreign countries and launched his country on a program of modernization, particularly in those areas where the Thais came into contact with Westerners. Such reforms, therefore, dealt with trade and transportation, communications, and currency.

ANGLO-THAI TREATY, 1855

The first major breakthrough came in 1855 with the conclusion of a treaty with the British envoy, Sir John Bowring. The treaty, signed in an atmosphere of mutual cordiality, set a pattern for treaties with many other European countries. Its principal features included three points common to the "unequal treaties" signed by China with foreign powers in the 1840s: the most-favored-nation clause, tariff control, and the right of extraterritoriality.

According to the Anglo-Thai Treaty of 1855, the rate of customs duty on British imports was limited to 3 percent, with the exception of opium, which could be imported duty-free but subject to certain restrictions of quantity. Export duties were to be clearly defined and not left to the arbitrary will of the customs official. Second, British subjects were permitted to own land in and around Bangkok. More important, they were to be governed by the extraterritoriality system, according to which they were not subject to Thai laws and courts but were to be tried for any civil and criminal offense by the British consul according to the British legal system. The third important aspect of these treaties was the interlocking most-favored-nation clause, which automatically granted to the treaty-signing country any concessions made to any other power. The Anglo-Thai Treaty of 1855 became the pattern for similar treaties with the United States and France (1856) and Belgium, Italy, Norway, and Sweden (1868), thus throwing Thailand open to foreign enterprise. Mongkut believed that treaties with as many countries as possible would help prevent any one country from becoming paramount.

Such treaties would not have necessarily ushered Thailand into the modern era. Mongkut made a conscious decision to modernize his country. He stepped up the construction of roads and canals and introduced shipbuilding. Facilities for the study of foreign languages were opened; princes and high officials were encouraged to learn them. The printing press was introduced. From 1861, flat coins were minted. Mongkut also laid foundations for systems of education, health, and public welfare. Since the country lacked competent personnel to direct these efforts at modernization, the king employed a number of European advisers, who became, in effect, heads of government departments. Here again, in order to offset the predominance of the British advisers, Mongkut appointed a number of Danes, Italians, French, and Americans.

Although Thailand had treaty relations with and employed advisers from different countries, Britain was considerably ahead of all other foreign states in influencing Thai economy and government. By virtue of its possessions in Myanmar and Malaya, Great Britain was the immediate neighbor of Thailand and was far more powerful politically, militarily, and economically than France, the other colonial power adjacent to Thailand. Further, the French appeared more aggressive in their expansionist designs at the cost of Thailand's eastern vassals. The Thais hoped to use the stronger British against the rival French and minimize the losses. Moreover, Britain seemed more interested in securing economic benefits through commerce, shipping, and investment than in territorial acquisitions.

Several British firms opened branches in Bangkok, and British shipping handled the bulk of the trade. British investments were the largest, principally in tin and timber. More Thai students were sent to Britain for education than to any other country. The preponderance of British-educated Thai officials further ensured British influence in Thai bureaucracy and government.

CHULALONGKORN, 1868–1910

Mongkut's reforms, important as they were, only scratched the surface of a society bound by tradition and obscurantism. His background as a monk, his study of the classics and scriptures, and his courtiers' opposition to changes tended to inhibit the pace of reforms. Yet he was the innovator, the path-setter, and the pioneer in advocating changes. His son Chulalongkorn, who ascended the throne as Rama V and ruled for four decades, plunged headlong into the rationalization of administration and the Westernization of society and government to a revolutionary degree.

Chulalongkorn's early training was a great factor in his outlook toward modernization. He received a Western education first from an English governess at the palace, Anna Leonowens, and later from an English tutor, Robert Morant. His own upbringing convinced Chulalongkorn of the need to educate other princes, many of whom were sent during his reign to England for schooling. Upon their return, they figured among his agents for change. During his own minority (the government was under a regency until 1873), Chulalongkorn visited Java and India, where he acquainted himself with Dutch and British administrative methods.

The range of reforms undertaken by the young king was very impressive and embraced many aspects of human activity. Through a series of decrees, he regulated debt-slavery, controlled the sale of opium, widened the role of witnesses in litigation, streamlined court procedures in the interests of efficacious disposal of cases, and provided for more accurate records of taxation and ownership. His very first decree, issued at the time of his coronation in 1873, abolished the practice of prostration in the royal presence. In the following year, the first step toward the complete abolition of slavery (achieved in 1905) was taken. The king also abolished the compulsory services of the Prai and Sui classes in the army and police force. Instead, the recruitment in the army was thrown open to all. The pace of introduction of technological innovations was stepped up. In 1875, the telegraph was established; in 1893, construction on the first railroad began. Educational facilities were increased, though these were designed for children from affluent families.

The major field of reform was the administration, which was gradually but completely overhauled. The numerous defects of the previous system dating from the fifteenth century contributed to the erosion of the central government's authority, overlapping zones of jurisdiction, and fusion of the military, civil, and judiciary functions—all leading to confusion, corruption, and severe decline in revenues. The principal features of the reorganization under Chulalongkorn were the gradual extension of the central government's authority into the provinces, districts, and villages and reorganization of governmental activity into a set of functional departments with a clear division of duties and responsibilities. By 1887, with the help of British advisers, the administration of finance was streamlined with procedures established for budgeting, accounting, and auditing. In 1892, Prince Damrong, who was educated in England and had familiarized himself with the British administration in Myanmar, took charge of the Ministry of the Interior and assumed direct responsibility for provincial administration. The kingdom was divided into eighteen zones, each under a high commissioner responsible to the Ministry of the Interior. The zones were further subdivided into provinces, villages, and hamlets. Some amount of local self-government was introduced, allowing each hamlet of about twenty families to be represented by an elder who would participate in the election of the village headman. In the same year, the Ministry of Justice was created to coordinate the judicial functions previously performed by a host of governmental agencies. Under the aegis of the ministry, presided over by the Oxford-educated Prince Rajaburidirekrit, later called the "father of modern law," a system of central, provincial, and regional courts was established. Then with the help of French jurists, Thai laws were revised and codified; in 1908, the penal code was published. All these efforts were directed toward creating confidence among Western nations in the Thai legal system and, therefore, warranting the abolition of the extraterritorial rights of foreigners. A number of Belgian lawyers and judges were imported. In order to eliminate such dependence in the future, a law school was established in 1897 to train Thai lawyers and potential judges.

Most of the administrative reorganization could not have been accomplished without the help of foreign advisers; there were 549 foreigners during Chulalongkorn's reign, surpassing the number employed by Mongkut. The principal adviser was an eminent lawyer, Rolin Jaequemins, who had served formerly as minister of the interior in Belgium. As before, the British advisers outnumbered those of other nationalities and were principally used in police administration and finance. Germans were employed to advise on postal service and railway administrations, and the French were used in the Department of Justice. Unlike during Mongkut's time, all the ministries and most of the departments were headed by Thais; the role of the Europeans was advisory.

Chulalongkorn also instituted some changes at the highest levels of government. A Council of State and a Privy Council were established to advise the king on matters of high policy. The counselors, mostly drawn from among the princes and nobility, were appointed by the king. The councils' functions were consultative. Chulalongkorn opposed the introduction of parliamentary institutions on the specious plea that they would be ineffective as a check on royal authority because he held it by the love of his people. He created the two councils and gave them Western names, principally to create the impression of Westernization rather than with any desire to broaden the base of government.

Though these wide-ranging reforms were forward-looking, marking a break in several areas with the Thai traditional administrative, social, and judicial structures, they were far from bringing the country in line with modernization in the West or in Japan. In effect, the monarchy had strengthened its base of power by providing education and appointments to younger members of the royalty and nobility and making them dependent for their material and career advancement on the goodwill of the monarch. In the course of time, the effect of some of the reforms would reach the countryside, as improved communications and a larger number of college-educated officials would serve as agents of modernization. The judicial system also would help people in the country, as its efficiency and relatively low cost would encourage greater use of the courts. As Thailand moved into the twentieth century, its complexion clearly showed significant changes, but they were not revolutionary enough to affect the country's power structure. The government remained, until the revolution of 1932, largely the preserve of the aristocrat as in previous centuries.

FOREIGN RELATIONS UNDER CHULALONGKORN

During Chulalongkorn's reign, pressures from Britain, and more particularly from France, increased. By 1885, Britain had acquired the whole of Myanmar, and its position in the southern Malay Peninsula was that of a paramount power. Yet Britain did not seem eager to extend its control over the other Malay states close to Thailand's borders. The French empire extended by 1885 to Vietnam and Cambodia. It soon became apparent that the French were interested in establishing a protectorate over Laos, on which, in the French view, Vietnam had better claims than Thailand.

France also claimed the territories on the left bank of the Mekong River, using the excuse that these territories once belonged to Vietnam and Cambodia. If France succeeded in obtaining this territory, Anglo-French contact would extend along an eighty-mile frontier. Recognizing this potential source of conflict, representatives from both powers agreed in 1893 that a buffer state was needed. In 1896, the two powers issued in London a declaration guaranteeing the integrity and neutralization of the Menam Basin. Neither power would seek exclusive advantages in this heartland nor send any armed forces there without the other's consent. The agreement thus removed Thailand's fears of ultimate annihilation. After this, Franco-Thai relations improved. In the early twentieth century, France recognized Thailand's right to jurisdiction over Asiatic French subjects. There were, however, further losses for Thailand in 1904, when it agreed to cede to France the two Cambodian provinces of Battambang and Siem Reap.

Anglo-Thai relations never reached the low point marked by Franco-Thai relations. However, there were at least three points of possible friction between Thailand and Britain. A number of British merchants and adventurers had sought concessions in northern Malay states, which were vassals of Thailand. On the other hand, Thailand entertained proposals by France and Russia to construct a canal across the Isthmus of Kra, which would certainly reduce if not destroy the commercial importance of Singapore, thereby affecting Britain. To keep out other European powers, the British secured in 1897 an agreement from the Thais not to cede any rights or concessions south of the eleventh parallel to any power other than Britain. Another point at issue between Britain and Thailand was in regard to jurisdiction over British Asiatic subjects resident in Thailand. The application of extraterritorial rights to them had created sanctuaries for certain Asiatic minorities in Thailand. In 1909, an Anglo-Thai agreement replaced the jurisdiction of the British consuls in Thailand with binational courts presided over by British and Thai judges. The agreement also granted a loan for the construction of a railway in the southern part of the country. In return, Britain obtained suzerain rights over the four northern Malay states of Kelantan, Trengganu, Kedah, and Perlis.

Thailand thus survived the period of New Imperialism at the expense of territories in Laos, Cambodia, and Malaya. Mongkut and Chulalongkorn used these peripheral areas as diplomatic leverage in protecting the core of their kingdom, where ethnic Thais lived. Thailand was undoubtedly the most fortunate of the Southeast Asian states in having these two statesmanlike rulers, who played the diplomatic game well and introduced timely reforms on the domestic front, well calculated to preserve Thailand's identity and independence. It must be agreed, however, that they were considerably helped in their endeavor by the geographical accident of their kingdom's location between two rival empires desirous of avoiding a common frontier. It was the combination of these factors that enabled Thailand to exist as the only independent country in Southeast Asia in the age of imperialism.

Part Two Review

By the beginning of World War I, all of Southeast Asia, with the exception of Thailand, had come under Western colonial rule. Even Thailand lost some of its territories—four northern Malay states to the British in 1909, Laos in 1893, and Battambang and Siem Reap provinces in western Cambodia in 1904 to the French. These areas were vassal states of Thailand and sent periodic tribute to it. Their loss still left the core of Thailand, whose ethnic Thai population predominated, independent of Western rule.

Most of the territories in Southeast Asia were acquired by the Western powers during the nineteenth century, more than 70 percent between 1860 and 1914, roughly corresponding to the era of "economic imperialism" during which the African continent was partitioned and spheres of influence were carved out in China among European powers. Thus, the British conquered Myanmar in three stages: 1826, 1852, and 1885. Also to come under British control were Singapore in 1819, Malacca in 1824, and the nine Malay states and Brunei between 1874 and 1914; Sarawak in 1846 under a private British individual, Rajah Brooke; and North Borneo in 1888 under a British corporation, the North Borneo Company. The French extended their control, direct or indirect, over Cochin China in 1862, Tongking in 1873, Annam in 1885, Laos in 1893, and Battambang and Siem Reap in 1904. The Dutch received Java back from the British in 1816, but had to fight several wars to complete the conquest of the East Indies by 1914, when the last of them, Bali, fell. Imperialistic fever seemed to have affected even a republican power like the United States during this period, and the United States replaced Spain in the Philippines as colonial master at the turn of the century. The fifth Western "power" in Southeast Asia was Portugal, which had lost all its possessions well before the nineteenth century but had clung to half the island of Timor as its only colony in Southeast Asia.

The economic needs of the industrial revolution in Europe provide only a partial but vital explanation of such a dramatic and phenomenal expansion of territorial authority in Southeast Asia. Diplomatic rivalry among European powers, particularly between the old enemies across the English Channel—Britain and France—was a potent factor in expansion. So also was the prospect of lucrative trade in the interior of China, which provoked a British quest of a trade route through Upper Myanmar and similar French efforts along the Mekong and Red rivers. British desires to protect the flanks of its valuable Indian empire and to secure the strategic trade route between India and China through the Strait of Malacca were also factors. So also was the personal ambition of some of the over-zealous proconsuls, both British and French, responsible for expanding the colonial domains without permission of their superiors in Europe.

The large-scale expansion was rationalized by all but the Dutch, who were honest enough to admit the colonial exploitation for the benefit of the mother country. The British called it "the white man's burden," the French "la mission civilisatrice," the Americans "the manifest destiny." All of them introduced far-reaching changes in most walks of life, including administration, education, economy, transport, and communications, affecting not only the top classes but also large numbers of the masses, the impact of which has survived the end of colonial rule itself. The British ruled Myanmar and the Straits Settlements directly, exercising degrees of indirect rule over their Malay territories; the French treated Cochin China as a direct colony, others as protectorates. The Dutch too retained the fiction of indirect rule over certain parts where the chiefs and sultans were left with fictional authority. In the Philippines, the United States behaved almost like a caretaker government fairly soon after the occupation, declaring its intentions and introducing reforms to lead the colony to self-government.

The impact of colonial rule on the people varied from unashamedly exploitative to the benign and benevolent. It generated forces of industrialization, urbanization, modernization, intellectual ferment, and political ambition that inspired at least a small elite in each colony to abandon part of the traditional trappings and step into the modern age. The colonial coin had nationalism stamped on its reverse side. That is the theme of Part Three.

Part Three

Nationalist Response

This section deals with the reaction of the colonial people to the respective alien regime and their demand for independence. Foreign rulers, however, considered such a reaction completely unwarranted, because they believed—or at least they asserted—that their exertions so far from home were mostly, if not entirely, for the good of the subject people, to bring them into modernity through Western education, communications, and public health. The French proudly proclaimed their "mission civilisatrice," or civilizing mission, through the two stages of association and assimilation; the British often acted as if they were only philanthropically carrying the "white man's burden"; and the Americans believed they were fulfilling their "manifest destiny." Only the Dutch seemed honest enough to admit that the wealth siphoned off from their colony was used to fuel the industrial revolution at home.

The colonial landscape had indeed changed, both physically and intellectually. Vietnam was divided into three parts, each called a *pais* (country/nation), which together with Laos and Cambodia the French called "French Indochina." That the partition of Vietnam divided a people who had shared a common language, religion, or culture for centuries, did not bother the French. Of course, some commentators have wondered if partition was intentionally pursued as part of the French "divide and rule" policy (just as the British did in India) as a means of jeopardizing the people's urge for unity or smothering their common cry for decolonization or independence.

Administrative variations in French, British, and Dutch possessions were often accompanied by economic variation depending on what each region had of value to the colonial power in terms of raw materials or potential consumers of finished goods. Railroads and other communications connected the plantations and mines with the ports and not necessarily with old clusters of population. New industry, mines, and plantations were owned by corporations and individuals from the ruling country, as were the banks, insurance, and freight companies. A new class of indigenous people became collaborators as they helped the colonial masters in their administration at lower and intermediate levels as well as in their economic activities. Colonial empires linked the colonies with the respective colonial powers, often requiring complicated shipping arrangements for products from one colony;

for example, goods shipped from Saigon to Rangoon, had to make the circuitous and expensive journey to France and then on to Britain and finally back to Rangoon in British ships. Barriers were thus established also in other areas such as education and thought.

In some countries, most notably Vietnam, there was a nexus for a time between nationalists and communists. Both of these large groups were opposed to imperialism and to French rule in Vietnam, Laos, and Cambodia. Soon after World War I, Lenin published his famous *Theses on Imperialism and Nationalism* stressing the need for nationalists and communists in the colonial world to pull together against the imperialists all over Asia and Africa. Such an alliance of forces would be on a tactical level, but the strategic goal would be to create a classless society and the dictatorship of the proletariat following the Soviet model. The rise of Popular Front politics in France in the 1930s made it incumbent on the nationalists and communists in Vietnam to work together in that decade. In fact, throughout the Vietnamese fight against the French and later against the United States, the forces of nationalism were by far the stronger stimulant than the communists, although the latter were superior in organization and consistent dedication by the membership. The ideological dimension of communism barely affected the rural peasantry, who constituted the overwhelming bulk of the population. The Communist Party's top leadership exploited the rural people, presenting their economic problems and solutions in ordinary terms comprehensible to them and not in Marxist jargon.

The lines between nationalism and communism were deliberately blurred and exploited to galvanize opposition to the foreign occupation of the country. In the end, the Communist Party of Vietnam emerged as victors and rulers, but communism as an ideology did not triumph. By 1986, the Communist Party of Vietnam adopted the Chinese model of market capitalism combined with the party's political monopoly. However, the Communist Party of Vietnam did not see eye to eye with its Chinese counterpart, and the two countries even went to war with each other in the late 1970s.

12

Nationalist Movements in Southeast Asia: General

Nationalism was undoubtedly the single most potent, dynamic, emotive element that altered the political configuration of Asia and Africa in the twentieth century. Recent nationalism has been in most cases a response to imperialism and the political and economic exploitation of the governed. In a certain sense, nationalist revolutions were the creation of Western colonial powers themselves. In fact, the political borders of some of the new nations of Southeast Asia were the product of the colonial era and have no history of a common political administration previously. This applies to Indonesia, the Philippines, Singapore, and Malaysia, and to a smaller extent, Laos.

It is difficult to provide a definition of nationalism that could be acceptable to all scholars and would meet the circumstances of all countries around the globe. Depending on personal preferences and predilections, different scholars have emphasized different criteria to describe a nation-state. Without doubt, a conscious sentiment of kinship is the bedrock of nationalism, fostered by common characteristics such as language, territory, religion, race, and heritage. Beyond this, sociologists have stressed common cultural and psychological traits or the group consciousness engendered by literature, arts, and institutions. The commonality of these factors is not always a necessary prerequisite of nationalism. Witness, for example, Switzerland with four languages, Canada and Belgium with two, and the United States, a "nation of immigrants" with a medley of languages, religions, and races; the geographical distance between outlying Hawaii and Alaska and the mainland; and the historical roots and heritages of different ethnic communities. Yet modern nationalism based on a commonality of some or all of these characteristics was bred in Europe since the late eighteenth century, flowering in the nineteenth, and degenerating in the twentieth. It may be said that nationalism was one of Europe's exports to the colonial world. Although it is true that the Western-educated political elites of Asia, Africa, and Latin America learned their first lessons in Europe or European-style academic institutions in their own countries, the actual form of nationalism varies from country to country depending on its social milieu, cultural ethos, and the historical march of events. Two additional factors, not necessarily present in European experience yet extremely important in the development of nationalist movements in Asia and Africa, have been the nexus of communism, by definition an international movement, and nationalism. The other factor was a common hostility toward a colonial rule imposed by a distant and discriminating people.

Was nationalism an entirely new force among Southeast Asian peoples? Vietnamese history is replete with examples of large-scale movements to overthrow Chinese rule at various times; the Chams, the Burmese, and the Vietnamese resisted through decades-long guerrilla movements attempts to establish Mongol supremacy over their countries. The "nationalist" sentiment was also evident in the numerous intraregional wars between the Burmese and the Thais, the Mons and the Burmans, the Chams and the Vietnamese, and the Khmers and the Javanese. Indeed, the withdrawal of Western colonial powers from Southeast Asia after World War II and later from Vietnam have rekindled the fires of historical nationalist rivalries among the states of the region. The memory of such historical resistance and rivalries is a potent factor in fostering nationalism, but such premodern movements must be distinguished from the twentieth-century phenomena largely by their aims and goals. The mass participation in the nationalist movements of the twentieth century was triggered largely by aspirations of economic equity, social justice, and a widely based government with public participation. All these factors were missing among the goals of the earlier revolts, which were led by feudal elements. In the modern period, guarantees of political, economic, and social freedom for the common citizen have formed the essential planks of the political manifestos of the nationalist leaders and their political parties.

The economic dislocation and distress caused by Western rule were, indeed, very important factors responsible for the growth of nationalism. With the exception of Malaya (and perhaps Laos and Cambodia, which did not undergo major economic changes), the infusion of Western capital, communications, and technology had the effect of actually lowering the economic well-being of the people. Western laws, educational institutions, money economy, immigration policies, and technological development all helped not only to undermine the traditional structure and values of the rural society but also to disrupt its economy and way of life. In the urban areas, the growing unemployment among the educated served as grist to the nationalist movement's propaganda mill. Nationalist leaders continually harped on the theme of colonial economic exploitation, which could be ended only by overthrowing alien rule and ushering in independence and indigenous control of economic institutions. Nationalist governments would further curb the immigration of Chinese and Indians and redress the balance in favor of "the sons of the soil" through purposeful policies directed to that end.

Perhaps the most potent factor creating nationalist consciousness among Southeast Asian elites was education. As the Dutch scholar W. F. Wertheim asserted, "Western education had the effect of dynamite upon the colonial status system."[1] Education opened the minds of the youth to political ideas of the West, including self-government and the fundamental freedoms of press, assembly, and speech. It also brought knowledge of revolutions elsewhere in Western experience, notably the French and American revolutions and the tumultuous movements in mid-nineteenth-century Europe that replaced autocracy with individual rights. Western education also imported Western philosophies and ideologies of all kinds, including Marxist. Those among the Southeast Asians who were privileged to take higher education in Europe got the opportunity to exchange ideas with fellow colonials from other countries at various international gatherings of the League of Oppressed Peoples and the League Against Imperialism and for National Independence. They experienced insults and ignominies in the Social Darwinist and racially discriminatory environment of Europe during the late-nineteenth and the first decades of the twentieth centuries. They discussed economic and political exploitation of their countries at the hands of diverse colonial powers and planned common strategies for eventual independence of their countries. Upon returning home after completion of studies, they often faced the prospect of unemployment or underemployment, which they blamed—often with justification—on the colonial policies that preferred to employ nationals of the ruling race. It was no accident that most of the leadership in nationalist movements had a background of Western education and training.

Western rule ironically had the effect of also helping the revival of a glorious historical past for most Southeast Asians. Largely due to Western efforts, archaeological excavations were undertaken, historical antiquities unearthed, temples restored, and arts studied. The effect of all these endeavors—most notably those of Thomas Stamford Raffles in Malaya and Java, of L'École Française d'Extreme Orient (founded in Hanoi in 1898), and of the Burma Research Society (founded by J. S. Furnivall in 1909)—was to infuse nationalists with a legitimate pride in their country's past and with hope for a bright future. The nationalists reminded their fellow citizens that if they could have such glorious chapters in their history, they could equally mold their own future through self-government.

Knowledge of epoch-making events in neighboring countries in Asia also promoted a nationalist feeling among the Southeast Asian peoples. Thus, the Boxer Rebellion in 1899 against Western presence and domination of China found echoes of sympathy everywhere in Asia. The shining example of Japan's military victory over Russia in 1905 inspired Asian nationalists tremendously. Not only was the myth of European invincibility nurtured by colonialists and missionaries thereby destroyed, but it also held the hope that, given an opportunity, Asians could build up their country's military and economic strength to a highly advanced level. Such sentiments were expressed in the autobiography of almost every prominent Asian nationalist of that time. A few years later—in 1911—came the successful overthrow of the decadent Manchu dynasty in China and the proclamation of the Chinese republic. The event was hailed as a people's revolution against autocracy. Chinese leaders, particularly Sun Yat-sen and his Kuomintang (KMT) party, profoundly influenced nationalists all over Southeast Asia, notably in Vietnam. Last but not least was the awareness of the nationalist struggle in nearby India, where the Indian National Congress since 1885, and more especially after Mahatma Gandhi's entry into Indian politics during World War I, led India's teeming millions from one stage of protest against British rule to another, scoring progressive victories in the field of representative and responsible government. Many Southeast Asian nationalists attended the annual sessions of the Indian National Congress, and many others visited India to consult with Gandhi and Nehru. Further, Indian and Chinese immigrants brought information about struggles against imperialism in their countries, thereby providing greater impetus to growing Southeast Asian nationalist sentiment. It should be noted that although resentment against these immigrants and their success in the economic field occasionally fostered grassroots cultural xenophobia, the Southeast Asian leaders held their Indian and Chinese counterparts in high regard. The success of the nationalist struggle in India had a ripple effect in Southeast Asia—and Africa—in the succeeding decades.

If events in neighboring countries influenced Southeast Asian nationalists, so did some of the happenings on the global stage, particularly the two world wars. In his Fourteen Points address, President Woodrow Wilson had given prime importance to the right of small nations to exist and to determine their own future. Most nationalists and many of the more than one million army personnel returning from the battlefields of World War I believed in the rhetoric. Among those Asians who hoped and pleaded for self-determination outside the Versailles peace conference was the placard-carrying Ho Chi Minh. That the doctrine of self-determination was to be applied only to East European nations brought about a disillusionment that led many a nationalist, including Ho Chi Minh, to the Marxist fold. During World War II, Japan's slogan of "Asia for the Asiatics" initially won millions of sympathizers all over Asia. The incredible defeat of the Western colonial powers all over Southeast Asia completely destroyed the myth of Western supremacy, as was painfully realized by the bureaucrats and military officials who returned to their former colonies after World War II. The Japanese occupation served as both a catalyst and an inspiration to Southeast Asian nationalist movements. Japan set up nationalist governments in Myanmar and Indonesia, supported the establishment in Southeast Asia of the Indian National Army, and promoted a government in exile under the former president of the Indian National Congress, Subhas Chandra Bose. Such moves had the positive effect of strengthening nationalism among the people and self-confidence in leaders who headed their national governments during the period. Though experience was soon to reveal to the Southeast Asians the true nature of Japanese intentions and of their self-serving "Co-Prosperity Sphere," the occupation period gave the leaders, particularly in Myanmar and Indonesia, valuable administrative experience that would serve as an asset in the postindependence era.

13

The Filipino Urge for Freedom from Spanish and U.S. Rule

END OF THE SPANISH ERA

The Filipinos carry the distinction of being the first people in Asia to successfully launch an anticolonial nationalist movement for independence. This was despite the numerous handicaps that hampered their quest for unity. Very loyal to their immediate community, they identified themselves by the particular boatload (*barangay*) that brought their ancestors from the Indonesian islands possibly in the early centuries of the Christian era. Dispersed over several thousand islands, large and small, and without the benefit of a common language or a strong historical tradition, it was comparatively easier for the Spaniards to rule the population. The Filipinos' submissive attitude was partly the result of the friars' constantly telling them how intellectually inferior they were; it was also due to a lack of national consciousness among the Filipinos, whose loyalties rarely transcended the *barangay* group or the *pueblo* (township) level.

Early Revolts Against the Spaniards

Even so, the first three centuries of Spanish rule brought at least thirty revolts, major and minor. These were marked by opposition to colonial injustice, racial discrimination in appointments to clerical positions, and agrarian exploitation by the friars.[1] Some of the uprisings covered large segments of the population and territory. Such were the revolts in Bohol in 1744 and in Pangasinan and the Ilokos in the 1760s.

The Bohol revolt began as a protest against the refusal of a friar to give a church burial to a Filipino constable who died before receiving the sacraments. Francisco Dagahoy, the brother of the dead man and an influential headman, led an antifriar movement, killing friars and taking over their lands. His following numbered thousands, keeping the colonial government troops engaged for decades of fighting. The independent state that Dagahoy established survived in certain regions long after his death until 1829.

The Pangasinan revolt led by Juan de la Cruz Polaris, the revolt of the Ilokos led by Diego Silang, and numerous other revolts against Spanish rule followed the British occupation of Manila in 1762 during the Seven Years' War. They were the first purely politically motivated movements and were sparked by the explosion of the myth of Spanish invincibility. Their supporters' demands included dismissal of provincial governors and appointment of local persons to important civilian positions. Both Silang and Polaris established independent governments, but both men were captured and killed. Silang's indomitable wife, Gabriela, held out for several months after her husband's death. Though these were strictly regional movements, the three revolts served as inspiration for the nationalist movements of the late nineteenth century.

Changes in Spanish Policy

Major changes in economic policy first became manifest in the last quarter of the eighteenth century. The policy of prohibition of commercial plantations and mining was abandoned; instead the cultivation of cash crops such as tobacco, indigo, hemp, and sugar was actively encouraged. Manila was opened to foreign shipping. The result of these changes was the rise of a new, prosperous, Filipino, export-oriented, agricultural elite—the *ilustrados*—that would have important consequences for the emergence of the nationalist leadership in the second half of the nineteenth century.

The introduction of free trade policies in 1834 brought seamen and traders from Europe and the United States in increasing contact with the new entrepreneurial class in the Philippines. Export of agricultural commodities like hemp, tobacco, and sugar boomed. The opening of the Suez Canal in 1869 gave the Filipino trade with Europe a stimulus as never before. The Spanish authorities were compelled by these developments to modernize the ports and communications. The upshot of all these happenings for the nationalist movement was the increasing contact with foreign traders, foreign goods, foreign books, and foreign ideas. The younger members of the families of prosperous landowners and entrepreneurs absorbed these materials and prepared themselves to go abroad for higher education and also to see things for themselves.

Contributing to the formation of such an elite was the liberal phase in colonial policy from 1855 to 1872, coinciding with the period of revolutionary changes in Spain itself. The Educational Code of 1863 decreed compulsory and free primary education with at least one school in every *pueblo* in the Philippines. Spanish language and literature were taught. Institutions of higher learning, including normal schools for training of teachers, and an agricultural college were opened. In the new environment, debating societies and libraries, newspapers, and periodicals flourished. In 1871, the Spanish Republic proclaimed in 1868 was ended. With that, a reactionary governor-general was sent to the Philippines. He repressed the Filipino nationalists and completely reversed the previous liberal policy. By 1872, when open discussion in educational and other forums was muted, large numbers of young people had become aware of the outside world and scores had left for higher education in Europe, mainly in Spain, England, France, and Germany.

Rizal Lights the Torch of Freedom

Among these young people abroad, certainly the most scholarly and articulate, intense yet moderate, was José Rizal, whose memory is invoked by numerous monuments and institutions throughout the Philippines. A multitalented individual, Rizal was an ophthalmic surgeon, poet, novelist, journalist, and linguist, who carried on correspondence in six different languages. Born of well-respected middle-class Catholic parents in the farming town of Calamba, dominated like most other Philippine towns by Dominican friars, young José soon became aware that his fellow citizens were economically oppressed by Dominican friars, smothered by religious bigotry, and neglected by the Spanish administration. His writings, before he left for Spain at the age of eighteen, included a poem—"To the Philippine Youth"—in which he exhorted them to work for the glory of their motherland, the Philippines. The poem roused the ire of his Jesuit and friar educators, who were incensed at his advocacy of a motherland other than Spain.[2]

During their visits to other European countries, Rizal and other Filipino students became aware of the high degree of individual freedoms elsewhere. They also became aware of the relatively low place Spain occupied in the European community of nations. On a personal level, their self-confidence and self-esteem rose because of the ease with which they could compete with Europeans in the universities. They were thereafter determined to raise the spirit of the common people in their own country and restore their dignity and pride, which had for so long been stifled by Spanish rulers and friars.

Neither Rizal nor his Filipino fellow students were advocates of revolution; their aim was reform. They knew that the Philippines was not ready to stand by itself and that, like it or not, Spanish rule would continue for quite some time. Writing in the magazine *La Solidaridad,* established by a small group of patriotic Filipinos and liberal Spanish who called themselves the Propaganda Movement, Rizal called attention to the injustices committed by the Spanish authorities, the enemies of progress. In his famous novel *Noli Me Tangere,* first published in 1887, Rizal attacked the "friarocracy" and the defective education it imparted because it recognized in the Filipinos only the "imitative and atrophied virtues of the lower animals." The hero of the novel did not advocate rebellion, but appealed to the government to correct the abuses. Two years later, Rizal pleaded: "We struggle for greater justice, for liberty, for the sacred rights of mankind, asking nothing for ourselves, sacrificing all for the common good. . . . We are not revolutionaries; we desire no blood, we have no hatred."[3] Rizal asked for freedom of the press and representation for the Filipinos in the Spanish Cortes (legislative assembly).

At the behest of the friars, the colonial government of the Philippines banned Rizal's writings. The ban led to a much greater readership among the Filipinos than would have been the case had the books been allowed to be circulated freely. After the publication of *Noli Me Tangere,* Rizal returned home to the Dominican friar estate of Calamba, whose abuses he had described in the novel. He then prepared a detailed report citing grievances of the people in the Calamba estate and sent it to the governor-general. Thereupon, Rizal's family, relatives, and friends became the hapless victims of the friars' persecution. Emilio Terrero, helpless in the face of the powerful "friarocracy," advised Rizal to leave the country. Back in Europe, Rizal became disillusioned and bitter; his changed attitude was evidenced in his second novel, *El Filibusterismo,* published in 1891, in which the hero, Simoun, incites violence and advocates total freedom for the Filipinos. Yet Rizal knew that the Filipinos were not ready for a revolution. In mid-1892, he returned to the Philippines and established the Liga Filipina, a civic association aimed at uniting the whole archipelago into one compact, vigorous, and homogeneous body. Its program included defense against all violence and injustice; encouragement of education, commerce, and agriculture; and a study of reforms. It did not call for armed insurrection against Spain.

Only two days after the league was founded, José Rizal was arrested and deported to remote Dapitan at the northwestern tip of Mindanao. With that, the moderate leadership was replaced by a militant organization, the Katipunan. A plebeian secret organization led by a plebeian, self-educated man, Andres Bonifacio, the Katipunan's objective was to unite the people into a nation without any social barriers. The Katipunan (literally meaning "highest and most respectable society of the sons of the people") held before the masses a new vision:

> The greatest man is not the King, nor he with high bridged nose, nor white skin, nor the priest who represents God, but he is really noble who, born in the forest possesses no language save his native tongue. . . . This man is a patriot who knows how to defend his country.
>
> When the country is radiant with the light of the liberty and we are all united as brothers, then the pains of the past shall be rewarded.[4]

In pursuit of these ideals, the Katipunan urged the end of Spanish rule, which it felt could be brought about only through violent means. Without Rizal's consent or knowledge, he was designated honorary president of the society, a move designed to ensure popular support. When the Katipunan began an armed revolt in August 1896, Rizal was accused of sedition, tried, and ordered to be executed on December 30. The event shocked the nation. The long, patriotic, emotion-filled poem "Ultimos Adios," which he had authored on the eve of his execution and smuggled out of his cell, continued to inspire and move Filipinos.

Rizal had succeeded in creating a national consciousness among the people. Among his many contributions was the translation of a little-known history of the Philippines before the advent of the Spanish rule, written by Antonio de Morga in Spanish in 1609. Rizal had discovered a copy in Europe. This publication refuted the friars' oft-repeated thesis that Spaniards had organized the islands for the first time and brought civilization and provided the Filipinos with a common historical heritage. The revolutionary movement that followed Rizal's death and the large-scale support it received from all parts of the country left no doubt that the Filipinos had attained nationhood. Rizal's life and writings served to restore dignity, self-respect, pride, and patriotism among Filipinos, who regard him as a symbol of their national unity and the most learned and respected member of the Malay race.

Rizal's martyrdom continued to blaze the path of the nationalist movement. Yet it was markedly different from the nonviolent direction that Rizal would have preferred. Further, the leadership of the movement could not match Rizal's intellect or his strength of character. Nevertheless, the leaders were all intensely patriotic and eager to end the hated Spanish rule and usher in freedom and independence for their country.

The leadership of the Katipunan was soon divided. Bonifacio's ill-trained, illiterate forces had not succeeded in attaining any of their military objectives. His leadership was challenged by Emilio Aguinaldo, a young schoolteacher, born in a middle-class family of part-Chinese ancestry. Aguinaldo had proved himself a better organizer and had won several major battles in the province of Cavite, a few miles south of Manila. In March 1897, an assembly of the revolutionaries proclaimed the Philippines a republic and elected Aguinaldo its president, which prompted Bonifacio to establish a rival revolutionary government. Within two months, on orders of Aguinaldo or of the Council of War, Bonifacio and his brothers were summarily tried and executed. The struggle against the Spanish authorities continued but did not register much advance; on the other hand, the colonial power could not crush the movement. Only one in ten of Aguinaldo's men had a gun; it was next to impossible for them to capture the well-fortified cities. The colonial army could not eliminate Aguinaldo's rural strongholds either. The situation was a blow to Spanish pride. An end to stalemate was sought by a peace pact signed at Biacnabato between Aguinaldo's republic and the Spanish authorities. Spain agreed to pay a certain amount in return for Aguinaldo's agreement to turn in all arms and leave the country along with thirty-three other leaders. There were verbal assurances given to Aguinaldo that Spain would grant representation to the Filipinos in the bureaucracy and that the press would be free. The Spanish government also agreed to pay a sum of money to the families of those who had suffered privations during the conflict. In fact, the government paid only half of the contracted amount to Aguinaldo before he left with other leaders of the movement for exile in Hong Kong, and it did not implement any of the promised reforms.

U.S. INTERVENTION

The United States Terminates Filipino Independence

If the Spanish authorities imagined that the revolutionary movement had been bought out, they were mistaken. Truce was only a part of Aguinaldo's strategy. He used the money to buy arms and the stay in Hong Kong to establish contacts for external help for his movement. By a fortuitous set of circumstances, he was approached by the U.S. consul and later by Commodore George Dewey. The United States had just entered into a major conflict with Spain in the Caribbean, ostensibly to help the Cubans but in reality to protect U.S. interests there. On the strategic level, it was deemed important to eliminate any possibility of the Spanish fleet in the Pacific joining the one in the Caribbean. It was realized after the conflict that the Spanish fleet in the Philippines was in such bad shape that it had to be towed into position for the battle. Despite Dewey's later disclaimers, it can well be believed that he promised Aguinaldo assistance to liquidate the Spanish rule and reestablish his republic. Aguinaldo and his followers sailed to the Philippines on a U.S. ship accompanied by U.S. Assistant Consul Edwin Wildman. Within a fortnight of his landing at Cavite, Aguinaldo organized a remarkable resistance movement with the aid of arms bought in Hong Kong and those supplied by the United States.

Meanwhile, Dewey had laid siege to Manila. Aguinaldo's men, who had surrounded Manila, were awaiting Dewey's mutually understood signal to enter the city. That signal never came; Dewey had other plans. What happened at Manila Bay was not a battle—it was a transaction. Dewey secured the surrender of Manila from the Spaniards under the terms of a secret treaty between the United States and Spain. It provided for payment of $20 million by the United States; each country agreed to assume the war-damage claims of its nationals; and Spain was granted trade rights with the Philippines for ten years on a par with the United States. The attack on Manila was merely a mock assault by which Spain was allowed to offer token resistance to salvage its honor.

Reasons for U.S. Intervention

Why did the United States take over the Philippines? A noted U.S. historian, Richard Hofstadter, observed: "The taking of the Philippine Islands from Spain in 1899 marked a major historical departure for the American people. It was a breach in their traditions and a shock to their established values."[5] What made the United States adopt the New Imperialism and liquidate the freedom of the Filipinos, who had proclaimed themselves a republic?

Among the strongest advocates of expansionism in the United States were John Fiske, who authored the essay entitled "Manifest Destiny" in 1885,[6] and Social Darwinists, who propounded that Anglo-Saxons had been divinely commissioned to rule over others. However, not all expansionists were Social Darwinists. For example, Alfred Thayer Mahan believed in sea power as the most important factor in the making or breaking of nations. He argued that U.S. maritime strength coupled with the growing productivity of U.S. farms and factories would compel a search for foreign markets and colonial expansion. In this he came close to the anti-imperialist, economist, and social activist J. A. Hobson, who wrote: "American imperialism was the natural product of the economic pressure of a sudden advance of capitalism which could not find occupation at home and needed foreign markets for goods and for investments."[7]

Mahan also maintained that by its frontage on the Pacific, the United States should not only defend but extend the blessings of its Western civilization to the region. The basic ideas of all these men—Darwin, Fiske, and Mahan—were in circulation at the beginning of the 1890s. They all contributed to the intellectual climate in the United States, particularly influencing some of the key political leaders of the time such as Henry Cabot Lodge and Theodore Roosevelt.

There was also the economic factor. The depression of 1893 and the restrictive tariff policies of European countries led U.S. business to fear the prospect of shrinking markets. Events in China in the last decade of the century made imminent the partition of that country among some European nations, notably Britain, France, Germany, and Russia. A report prepared by the New York Chamber of Commerce bluntly stated that in the face of the prospect that European spheres of influence in China might become permanent territorial acquisitions, the only course by which the United States could protect its interests appeared to be active participation in politics of the Far East that might be "hastened and materialized through our possible occupation of the Philippine Islands." The *New York Commercial* pointed out that countries closely adjacent to the Philippines contained 850 million people, "who annually purchased over one billion dollars worth of goods, mostly articles grown or manufactured in the United States," adding: "With the Philippines as a three-quarter way house forming a superb trading station, the bulk of this trade should come to this country."[8] Henry Cabot Lodge best represented the views of fellow expansionists when he later defended U.S. action in the Philippines in the U.S. Senate: "Duty and interest alike, duty of the highest kind and interest of the highest and best kind, impose upon us the retention of the Philippines, the development of the islands and the expansion of our Eastern commerce."[9]

Thus, a combination of economic and noneconomic factors led the U.S. venture into the New Imperialism. Naval strategy, urgings of "manifest destiny," and the warmongering headlines of William Randolph Hearst's newspapers also played a role. The personality factor was no less important. Roosevelt, Lodge, and Dewey were significant believers in the "duty of the highest kind." It was no coincidence that the English imperialist poet Rudyard Kipling chose the occasion to write the well-known poem "The White Man's Burden" and send it to Theodore Roosevelt, urging him to end the nonwhite Iberian powers' "under the law" rule in the Philippines and take over the "burden" of administration. For the Filipinos, both the Spanish and U.S. regimes represented the white man's rule and a "brown man's burden" that should be excised as soon as possible.

The Filipino Resistance Continues

The realization that the United States had duped them led the Filipinos to take several steps. Aguinaldo's forces quickly registered several victories in many parts of the country. The republic he had proclaimed in 1897 was revived; the revolutionary capital was established at Malolos in Bulacan province, and a constituent assembly was called to draft a constitution. The constitution of January 1899 provided for a government of three separate branches—legislative, executive, and judiciary—separation of church and state, and a bill of rights. Resolutions protesting the U.S. annexation and favoring the continued struggle for freedom were passed all over the Philippines.

The conflict between the numerically greater but poorly equipped Filipinos and the militarily superior Americans brought no great credit to the latter. The United States had expected the confrontation to be brief. Its prolongation brought frustration and consequent employment of more drastic, inhumane measures against a civilian population supporting the revolutionary guerrillas. In a statement reminiscent of some rhetoric during the later Vietnam War, the general in charge of the campaign in central Luzon said: "It may be necessary to kill half the Filipinos in order that the remaining half may be advanced to a higher plane of life than their present semi-barbarous state affords."[10]

During 1901 and 1902, the war evolved into senseless, wanton carnage with massive slaughter. The U.S. military command practically adopted the *reconcentrado* policy familiar in the Spanish-American War in Cuba, ordering the entire population of Marinduque Island into five concentration camps, for example. Those outside the camps were branded enemies. Their villages and crops were burned by U.S. troops. In Samar, General Jacob F. Smith told his troops: "Kill and burn, kill and burn, and the more you burn, the more you please me. This is no time to take prisoners." When asked about the children, he replied, "Kill everything over ten."[11] In Batangas, under General Franklin Bell's *reconcentrado* policy, at least 100,000 Filipinos lost their lives. In coastal Visayan, U.S. shelling of villages resulted in thousands of Filipino casualties.

In March 1901, Aguinaldo was finally captured by Captain Frederick Funston, but Filipino resistance continued unabated. A year later, in April, Filipino General Miguel Malvar was compelled to surrender only when General Adna Romanza Chaffee threatened to cut off food supplies to an estimated 300,000 Filipinos held in concentration camps. Although the war was declared officially to have ended in 1902, resistance to U.S. takeover continued to plague the new administrators to the point that William Taft, the first governor, found it necessary to introduce in 1904 an identification card system for all Filipinos in the hope of isolating the "bandits." In the following January, he declared a general state of insurrection, and in March, the *reconcentrado* was again resorted to in Laguna and Rizal. It was only a year later that the back of Filipino resistance was truly broken. It is impossible to calculate what the U.S. venture cost the Filipinos. General Bell estimated before a Senate committee that 600,000 Filipinos died of disease in concentration camps or on the battlefields of Luzon alone. Perhaps more than a million—one-seventh of the total population—were killed before the country was completely "pacified."

THE U.S. ERA

Initial Policies

In the first decade of U.S. rule in the Philippines, policy was determined by at least three different factors: divisions within the United States over the question of annexation of the Philippines; some awareness of the intensity and maturity of Philippine nationalism; and the Spanish colonial heritage. The United States, committed in theory to individual and national freedom, found it difficult to accept its status as an imperial power and therefore advanced various arguments, moral and material, to rationalize it. Large numbers of U.S. citizens protested their government's imperialist adventure, some urging immediate freedom and others statehood for the Philippines. Mark Twain warned that the United States would lose its vitality and abandon its age-old promises of freedom and liberty if it ruled distant and alien peoples.[12] A single-vote majority by which the proposal to annex was passed by the U.S. Senate indicated that the imperialist fervor was not all-pervasive. President William McKinley lamely defended the annexation on four grounds: that the territory could not be given back to Spain because that would be "cowardly and dishonorable"; that France or Germany would grab it if the United States abandoned it; that it could not be left to the Filipinos who were "unfit for self-government"; therefore, that there was nothing left for the United States to do "but to take them all, and to educate the Filipinos, and uplift and civilize and Christianize them."[13]

The three-year war with the Filipino nationalists between 1899 and 1902 convinced the United States of the intense patriotic fervor among the Filipinos and the support enjoyed by their leaders. The five-member commission sent by the United States under the chairmanship of President Jacob G. Schurman of Cornell University in 1899 reported unanimously that all Filipinos desired complete independence, though the commission was doubtful if they were capable of self-government. Such an assessment reflected more the delusions of racial superiority and the big-brother attitude of the United States rather than an objective study of the situation, because within only a few years, numerous Filipinos who were placed in responsible positions in their country's administration proved very capable indeed.

It was partly the recrudescence of nationalist violence that brought forth the U.S. assurance guaranteeing individual rights and self-government as soon as possible. Reforms demanded by the nationalists prior to the outbreak of hostilities with Spain were now taken up by the United States. In July 1901, a new five-member commission under the chairmanship of Judge (later President) William H. Taft replaced the military rule with civilian governors in most areas except in a few nationalistic strongholds, which still refused to acquiesce in U.S. rule. A year later, the United States declared a state of peace and general amnesty. The Taft Commission acted as a legislative and executive body at the national level, and Filipino participation was allowed at the municipal and provincial levels through elected officials. The commission also proclaimed the rule of law and the separation of church and state and granted freedom of press and of assembly. The Filipinos were practically given all the guarantees of the U.S. Bill of Rights with the exception of trial by jury and the right to carry arms.

The U.S. colonial regime had to take into account the heritage of more than three centuries of Spanish rule over most of the Philippines. Thus, the United States decided to retain the Spanish civil law. The Filipinos were further assured that their customs and traditions (which included Spanish traditions) would be fully protected. On the other hand, certain much-despised features of the Spanish period, particularly in the field of landholdings, were eliminated. Thus, the Organic Act of 1902, providing for separation of church and state, declared that friar lands constituted public property and would thereafter be available for sale to the public. Many large estates from the Spanish period still remained, despite the new laws attempting to protect the small farmer. Innovation in judicial administration included the establishment of a Supreme Court and introduction of habeas corpus and civil marriage. The jury system, the time-honored Anglo-Saxon institution and a mainstay of the U.S. judicial system, was not introduced for fear it might be "abused."

Politically, the Filipinos advanced more rapidly than most other colonies of any other Western power. In general, the progress toward freedom was greater during Democratic than Republican administrations. In 1907, the Philippines were given further political reforms, including the election of a legislative assembly of eighty members having substantial voice in determining domestic legislation even in financial and land tenure matters. The new leadership of the Filipinos consisted of lawyer-politicians. Two persons dominated the political platform: Sergio Osmena, perennial Speaker of the Assembly and leader of the Nationalist Party until 1922; and Manuel Quezon, the majority floor leader of the 1907 Assembly, president of the Philippine Senate in 1922, the first president of the Commonwealth of the Philippines in 1935, and regarded as the father of Philippine independence—the "most dynamic, peerless and dominating leader of the Filipino people in their peaceful struggle for political emancipation."[14] From the birth of the Assembly in 1907, these leaders expressed their dissatisfaction over the slowness in sharing power. Until 1913, the Assembly had little power, most of it being with the governor-general and the Taft Commission, the latter doubling also as the cabinet and the upper house of the legislature. Every piece of legislation had to be approved by both houses, which therefore gave Americans in the upper house virtual veto authority over all legislation.

Constitutional Liberalization

The victory of the Democratic party in the U.S. presidential elections of 1912 augured well for the Filipinization process. President Wilson could not have chosen a better person for the implementation of the new liberal policy than Governor-General Francis Burton Harrison (1913–1921). He was partly instrumental for the passing in 1916 of the Jones Act, which became the cornerstone of Philippine constitutional development. The act prepared ground for full political autonomy with very few discretionary powers left to the governor-general and the president of the United States. The law created a constitution modeled upon that of the United States, providing for separation of powers among the governor-general, a bicameral legislature, and a supreme court. The electorate was to consist of all literate males. The House was to have 84 elected members in addition to the 9 appointed by the governor-general, and the Senate had 24 members, of which 22 were to be elected and 2 appointed by the governor-general to represent non-Christian areas. Filipinization was encouraged and enforced, resulting in the reduction of U.S. bureaucrats and teachers from 2,600 in 1913 to 614 in 1921. By 1916, Filipinos were serving as chiefs of 30 bureaus.

The Republican administrations of Harding, Coolidge, and Hoover in the United States marked setbacks for the Filipino march to independence. Under Governors-General Leonard Wood and Cameron Forbes, Filipino aspirations were repressed, and the nationalist movement was smothered. Wood was stiff-necked and arrogant but was a competent official who promptly restored to his office the powers wrested from it by Filipino political leaders during Harrison's time. In contrast to the latter, Wood, who had served before in the Philippines as a provincial governor in 1903, did not believe Filipinos were ready for independence, and he favored retention of the Philippines for an indefinite time under U.S. control. Throughout his administration, tension and hostility existed between him and Manuel L. Quezon, who as president of the Senate was a widely respected leader of his people. A dozen Filipino "independence missions," some of them led by Manuel Roxas and Quezon, traveled to Washington between 1919 and 1934 with the emphatic demand for independence. The conflict between the U.S. administration and Filipino political leaders eased considerably with Wood's sudden death in August 1927. Subsequent governors-general were more tactful in dealing with Filipino elected officials and the Filipino people's aspirations.

In the early 1930s, the situation changed dramatically, with support for Philippine independence coming from unexpected quarters. Hit by the Great Depression, U.S. economic interest groups that only a few years before would have vehemently opposed Philippine independence now joined hands with Democratic liberals in lobbying for it. The sugar and tobacco interests wanted to end the free trade that allowed the competitive Philippine products a free entry into U.S. markets. The cottonseed oil interests did not want Philippine coconut oil used in the making of soap, and the dairy interests wanted the coconut oil to be so expensive as to make oleomargarine costly enough to drive consumers to using butter again. Organized labor joined the farming lobby not because it loved farming interests but out of disdain for the influx of cheap Filipino labor, which could enter the United States at will because the Oriental Exclusion Act of 1924 did not apply to them. Election of a Democratic Congress in 1930 and of a Democratic president in 1932 made the passage of the Tydings-McDuffie Act in March 1934 even easier.

The act created the Commonwealth of the Philippines and provided for the grant of complete independence in 1946. It also authorized the Philippine legislature to call a convention to draft a constitution. Foreign relations, tariff, and coinage were to be under U.S. control during the transitional ten-year period. The act also provided quotas for import into the United States of Philippine sugar and coconut oil. An export tax of 5 percent was to be levied on all items shipped to the United States from January 1, 1941, to be gradually raised to 25 percent by 1946.

Japan and the Philippines

The progressive noninvolvement on the part of the United States in the internal affairs of the Philippines in the late 1930s gave Japan an opportunity to augment its influence there. By World War II, Japanese interest in Philippine lumber, hemp, and copra was substantial. In minerals—iron, manganese, and copper—the Japanese controlled the maximum of 35 percent of the shares permitted by law.

Manuel Quezon either ignored or underestimated the nature of Japanese expansionism, emphasizing instead the Japanese contributions to the Philippine economy. He urged the Filipinos to adopt Japanese industriousness and technology. In his view, the increasing Japanese influence in the Philippines would only prove a blessing in the long run.

When Japanese troops landed in French Indochina, the United States promptly responded in July 1941 by freezing Japanese assets, ordering an oil embargo, and putting General Douglas MacArthur in command of the expanding U.S. military forces in the Philippines. The Japanese were already talking of the Philippines as a "pistol aimed at Japan's heart"; the United States was now, most conspicuously, loading the pistol.

Within a few days of the attack on Pearl Harbor on December 7, 1941, Japan attacked the Philippines. Although General MacArthur managed to remain in Bataan for several weeks thereafter, stubbornly resisting the Japanese threat, the situation worsened quickly enough for him to flee to Australia on March 17, 1942. President Quezon also fled the country, set up a government in exile in Washington, and impatiently awaited the ouster of the Japanese and the opportunity to reestablish a "true" Filipino government. Meanwhile, substantial numbers of Philippine guerrillas resisted the Japanese in many areas for the next three years, even as they maintained a radio coast watch for MacArthur's intelligence and the return of U.S. troops.

Meanwhile, the Japanese established a puppet government in the Philippines in the hope of persuading the people to abandon their guerrilla activities through Japanese rhetoric that championed Asian brotherhood. The Japanese failed to win over the Filipinos and decided in October 1943 to confer upon them the "honor of independence." The gesture failed to have much effect on the Filipinos, who continued to harass the Japanese through guerrilla operations.

In October 1944, the liberation of the Philippines began with MacArthur's forces retaking Leyte. MacArthur's task was considerably lightened by Filipino guerrillas, who controlled by then vast portions of northern Luzon and virtually all of Mindanao. Even before the war ended, the government of the Commonwealth of the Philippines had been reestablished not under Quezon, who had died two months before the liberation of Leyte, but under Vice President Sergio Osmena. Full independence was granted to the Philippines on July 4, 1946, making that country the first colony in Asia to be freed of Western rule.

U.S. Economic and Social Impact

Trade. U.S. economic policies worked at cross-purposes: Some were supportive of Philippine independence and economic self-reliance; others emphasized increasing dependence of the colony on the United States. Several shifts in the tariff policy between 1899 and 1934 reflected one consistency, though—a U.S. interest in protecting or promoting its own trade and industry. While U.S. exporters wanted the colony to be treated as an integral part of the United States, U.S. sugar and tobacco interests wanted to inhibit imports of Philippine products through application of tariff laws on a par with all foreign countries. As a critic observed: "Philippines was foreign to the United States for domestic purposes, but domestic for foreign purposes."[15] U.S.-Filipino trade relations may usefully be examined in the following time periods: 1898–1909, an era of preferential trade; 1909–1913, qualified free trade; 1913–1934, mutual free trade.

During the first period, the United States was inhibited by the Spanish-American Treaty of Paris disallowing for a period of ten years, until 1909, any tariff regulations that would favor U.S. ships or goods over their Spanish counterparts. British, Swiss, and German traders soon demanded and received the same privileges as the Spanish. The result was that U.S. traders could not make any significant dent in the trade because of the well-established European merchants. Thus, between 1901 and 1909, Britain controlled 90 percent of Philippine imports of cotton goods, the largest item in the import trade. Only two years after such treaty inhibitions were removed, U.S. cotton manufacturers were able to outsell the British.

With the passage of the Payne-Aldrich Tariff Act of 1909, the situation changed. All U.S. products, except rice, were now allowed free entry into the Philippines, and Philippine products, with the exception of rice and limited quotas of sugar and tobacco, were permitted to be imported into the United States free of customs duties. Goods from other countries were subject to stiff tariff rates, even as the United States was simultaneously championing an "open door" policy in China.[16]

U.S.-Filipino trade relations were liberalized with the adoption of the Underwood Tariff Bill in 1913 removing all quota restrictions on Philippine imports into the United States. A classic colonial economy developed, making the Philippines an important source of agricultural exports like sugar, hemp, coconut products, and tobacco and a heavy importer of manufactured goods. Before the Payne-Aldrich Act, U.S. exports had increased from $1.5 million in 1899 to $5 million in 1908. Under the mutual free trade conditions, trade expanded phenomenally, boosting U.S. exports to $92.5 million in 1929; Philippine imports into the United States increased from $32 million in 1908 to $164.5 million in 1929, which accounted for 83 percent of all Philippine exports.

Such policies on the part of the colonial power failed to benefit more than a minority of Filipinos who were involved in the production and export of agricultural crops. Most of these came from the old gentry families, who had lands during the Spanish period and whose children had received higher education. The U.S. administration tried in vain to limit the landholdings by individuals to 355 acres and by corporations to 2,530 acres. Homesteading was provided, but general ignorance and paperwork proved too complicated for many peasants to take advantage of it. In the entire period of U.S. rule, only 35,000 homestead applicants received patents to their lands, whereas the number of tenant farmers increased by 700,000. Thus, traditional relationships between Filipino peasants earning a marginal subsistence and a landlord class living in a luxurious style persisted through the U.S. era. The deformed character of the Philippine economy did not help the growth of a healthy middle class and kept the peasants in a depressed economic condition, which became the root of major difficulties confronting the postindependence tasks of economic reconstruction.

Conversely, some deliberate measures prevented the recrudescence of the exploitative patterns found in the other colonies of Southeast Asia. Thus, the new land and corporation laws forced U.S. sugar and pineapple enterprises to limit themselves to smaller plots, unlike the French development of large sugar and rubber estates in Vietnam and eastern Cambodia. Again, thanks to the active opposition of the War Department, plans to split off Mindanao and Sulu islands for rubber plantations, as occurred in Sumatra and Malaya, did not materialize. Nor did the administration permit the massive importation of alien labor as the British did in Myanmar and Malaya. Further, government opium concessions were not established in the Philippines, thereby avoiding the kind of social decay this practice had brought to parts of Indonesia, French Indochina, and Malaya.

Investment. In general, U.S. capital was shy about entering the Philippine investment market, largely because of the possibilities of the grant of early independence to the colony. By 1940, only $140 million were invested in the Philippines; the Philippine market absorbed less than 0.2 percent of the U.S. gross national product. Most U.S. investment was made by large corporations in the plantations of sugarcane, tobacco, and hemp. The import of U.S. manufactures was detrimental to the indigenous handicrafts industry. The colonial government gave only minimum encouragement to light consumer goods industries and power production. In the field of transportation, Britain controlled the carrying trade to the extent of 60 to 70 percent. Attempts by U.S. shippers, especially railroad magnate James Hill, to get the Congress to exclude British shipping in the Philippines were blocked by the U.S. cordage industry on the East Coast, which imported hemp from the Philippines via London at half the U.S. freight rates. U.S. rail construction also suffered from British competition; the British-owned Manila-Degupan railroad commanded the best route on Luzon. In 1906, Morgan bankers bought out the British company's interest, but new U.S. railroad investment was not forthcoming until the government guaranteed a 4 percent annual return. Of the original plans to build 1,233 miles of U.S. track, only 866 miles had been constructed by 1954.

Social Welfare. In contrast to its economic policies, the United States had truly outstanding achievements in health and education in the Philippines, surpassing the work of any other colonial power. The 1,000 dispensaries and 40 hospitals established provided medical care to the needy, rich and poor alike. Epidemics of cholera and smallpox, which previously claimed a large number of lives, were overcome through wide-scale programs of immunization carried out by the Department of Public Health. Infant mortality was cut drastically, and life expectancy rose from 14 years in 1900 to 40 years in 1940.

Educational reform was certainly the greatest achievement of U.S. rule. In 1901, the Taft Commission imported 600 U.S. primary teachers, who helped establish an admirable system of universal free and secular education at the primary level. By 1922, expenditure on education had risen to nearly 50 percent of government expenditure. Filipino teachers were trained rapidly; by 1927, most of the first-wave U.S. teachers had been repatriated. Free public education at the *barrio* (farming village) level became a reality, bringing a larger proportion of population than in any Asian country other than Japan into high schools and universities. Public education raised the level of literacy to nearly 50 percent by World War II. The expanding use of English provided a common medium of communication among a growing number in the myriad islands. U.S. education policies also helped to stimulate social change in the Philippines. If the Philippines can boast today of the largest educational system—school, college, and university—in all of Southeast Asia, the credit goes substantially to the programs initiated during the U.S. colonial regime.

14

The Nationalist Movements: Indonesia

PRIYAYI AND *SANTRI* FRUSTRATIONS

The Indonesian nationalist movement truly began in the first decades of the twentieth century. Indonesian nationalists have hailed earlier revolts such as the Java War of 1825–1830, the struggles in western Sumatra in the 1820s and 1830s, and the resistance to the imposition of the Dutch rule in Atjeh later in the nineteenth century, as the precursors of the nationalist movement. None of these agitations, however, had nationwide organization or appeal.

The Indonesian nationalist movement was initiated and led by the twin elites of the islands, the *priyayi* and the *santri*. The *priyayi,* particularly its upper levels, belonged to the landed aristocracy in interior Java, whose circumstances of birth entitled them to positions of regents and district and subdistrict heads, almost the same traditional elite as in the pre-Dutch times. The *santri,* on the other hand, came from the coastal and commercial community, well exposed traditionally to external influences, including those of reformist Islam.

In 1893, the Dutch opened two types of primary schools, the First-Class Native Schools, meant for the children of the *priyayi,* and the Second-Class Native Schools, giving a rudimentary education to the others. The first Agricultural Secondary School was started in 1903, the Veterinary School in 1907, and the Law School in 1908. Graduates of these schools and those who dropped out after three or four years of study, as well as those who returned from higher studies in the Netherlands, formed a new class of professionals and semiprofessionals, the core of a new elite of the Indonesian society. In 1905, the government introduced the policy of substitution of Indonesians for Europeans in civil service, but with a difference in the conditions of service.

There was discrimination based on color, whereby even within the same categories of government employment, the Indonesians were given a lower salary than their Dutch or Eurasian colleagues. In the educational institutions, the Indonesians had to pay substantial tuition fees, which were waived for Dutch and Eurasian (mixed Dutch and Indonesian parentage) children unless their parents earned more than 1,200 guilders a year. In the beginning, an educational diploma meant security of employment, but very soon the lesser *priyayi* were to realize that the avenues to bureaucratic employment or teaching positions were inadequate.

Members of the *santri* class were even more discontented. They had hoped that the liberal economic provisions of the Ethical Policy initiated in 1900 would open better business opportunities for them. Instead, the Dutch companies and overseas Chinese continued their grip on the economy. The Chinese dominated the economy in almost every sector except shipping, banking, petroleum, and other capital-intensive economic enterprises. They almost monopolized the sale and distribution of batik textiles, a traditional stronghold of Javanese and Sumatran small businesses. The processing of rice, coconut, tapioca, and kapok was also in Chinese hands. With their greater capital, business experience, and wider contacts all over the oriental business world, the Chinese traders were difficult for the Indonesians to compete with. The economic distress in the indigenous community provided a potent impetus to Indonesian nationalism.

NATIONALIST ORGANIZATIONS

The beginnings of the Indonesian nationalist movement can be traced to some new educational institutions started by the *priyayi* class in the early twentieth century. Education helped to revive traditional consciousness and made the people aware of the subordinate positions to which they had been relegated by their colonial masters. Anti-Dutch sentiment and nationalism were subtly fostered by these organizations, which remained officially nonpolitical because of fear of Dutch repression. Their anti-Dutch feeling did not necessarily mean opposition to Westernization, however. On the contrary, they believed that Western education would open for the people sure avenues of individual and national progress.

In 1902, Raden Adjeng Kartini, daughter of the regent of Japara in Java, founded a school for the daughters of Javanese officials. Although she died at the early age of twenty-four in 1904, her inspiration was responsible for the numerous Kartini schools for girls all over Java. Many of the products of the Kartini schools later joined a new organization called the Boedi Utomo (high endeavor). Founded in 1908 by Kartini's associate, Dr. Waidin Sudira Usada, the Boedi Utomo soon claimed over 10,000 members. Among its supporters were many Javanese aristocratic families, civil servants, students, and intellectuals, drawn principally from the *priyayi* class. The movement soon gained wide recognition for its advocacy of a desirable blend of Westernization with Javanese tradition. Although the Kartini schools and the Boedi Utomo were laudable organizations, their scope was more or less limited to the island of Java. They appealed only to the upper *priyayi* class; their objectives were limited to education and cultural revival.

The Sarekat Islam

The first organization with mass appeal dealing with broad political and economic issues was the Sarekat Islam (Islamic association), founded in 1912. Its focus of activity was economic and, therefore, anti-Chinese. The Islamic appeal of Sarekat Islam provided a common link, a welding force binding the divergent communities together. Some of them had been concerned over the aggressive efforts of the Christian missionaries who had of late stepped up their proselytizing activities. The membership of the Sarekat was principally drawn from the *santri* and the lower *priyayi* classes. Educationally, the members were above the general level of Indonesians, with the most exposure to the West and from mostly middle-class families. Because of the flexible nature of Islam in Indonesia and more specifically because of the influence of modernist Islamic doctrine, religion could play a significant role as a vehicle for Indonesian nationalism and the people's social and political aspirations.

The Sarekat was led by the charismatic Umar Sayed Tjokroaminoto, known as the "*ratu adil*" (righteous prince), who would lead people to abiding happiness. Peasants flocked by the thousands to touch him, kiss his feet, and hear him speak. For two decades, Tjokroaminoto's residence remained the rendezvous of social and political activists, among them a young man named Sukarno, who lived in Tjokroaminoto's house for several years and married his daughter.

The Sarekat Islam's initial objectives were modest. These were to promote among Indonesians a commercial spirit and a feeling for the "true religion of Islam." Its activities included protection of Indonesian merchants against the Chinese and defense of Islam against the proselytizing efforts of the missionaries. Its national status was justified by a membership all over Indonesia of approximately two million by 1919. The heterogeneous nature of the organization soon brought conflict within it over the long-range goals of the party and the methods to achieve them.

Most Sarekat members agreed on a number of issues, such as the need for modernization, self-government, and socialism. The differences were on the acceptable level of radicalism and how rapidly the socialist programs should be adopted. Capitalism was considered "sinful," largely because it was European and Chinese, responsible for Indonesia's miseries. Besides, socialism seemed to suit the Indonesian temperament of a group spirit (*gotong rojong*), the traditional outlook favoring mutual cooperation as against Western individualism.

Partly in response to the Sarekat's demands, the colonial government agreed to introduce some administrative and constitutional reforms. In 1903, Indonesians had been allowed some modest participation in the local and regional councils. Then in 1918, the People's Council, or Volksraad, was inaugurated. One-half of its members were appointed by the governor-general in his discretionary authority, while the other half were elected by local councils. The Volksraad's powers were advisory: The governor-general even needed permission from The Hague to accept its advice. No wonder Indonesian nationalists felt completely frustrated with the pace and content of political reforms.

The most radical of the socialist groups within the Sarekat fold was the Indies Social Democratic Association (ISDA), founded in 1914 by the future leader of the Dutch Communist party, Henrik Sneevliet. Its Indonesian leaders included Semaun and Tan Malaka, who insisted that the Sarekat come out openly as a political organization with a radical and revolutionary program for the overthrow of Dutch rule and the establishment of a socialist state. In 1920, they broke away to form the Partai Kommunis Indonesia (PKI), or Communist Party of Indonesia. The PKI detested Sarekat's emphasis on religion and preference for evolutionary rather than revolutionary means to attain independence. In 1921, the Sarekat Islam prohibited its members from joining any other political organization. The die was cast. The Communists were expelled from the Sarekat.

The PKI and the "Revolution" of 1926

The rift in the Sarekat Islam helped the PKI. Many young members of the Sarekat, impatient but hitherto not Marxist, turned to the PKI as the only radical vehicle for their energies and aspirations. By 1923, the PKI claimed some 50,000 members and a significant control of the trade union movement. Its success was partly owed to the Dutch decision in 1921 to balance the budget without hurting Dutch economic interests. Consequently, the government discharged considerable numbers of lower staff and stopped payment of cost-of-living bonuses. Tax levels for Indonesians were raised: Indonesians with an average income of 225 guilders per year now paid 10 percent in taxes, while the Dutch paid that percentile only after they reached 9,000 guilders. Understandably, the PKI had a substantial following among urban workers, educated youth without jobs, and middle-income persons burdened with taxes. A later survey of 1,000 PKI internees showed a literacy rate of 76.1 percent, compared with the general literacy rate of 5 percent. Ten percent of the men had long periods of unemployment despite their diplomas from Dutch native schools.[1] The PKI successfully exploited the economic frustrations of the Western-educated, middle-class youth and the urban workers in forging a radical movement in the 1920s.

In 1923, the PKI organized a railroad strike that successfully paralyzed most economic activity on the island of Java. Inspired by the success, Semaun, Alimin Prawirodirdjo, Musso, and Tan Malaka amalgamated twenty-two trade unions into a Communist-dominated federation. It soon became the operational channel for the revolutionary aims of the PKI, organizing between 1923 and 1926 numerous strikes, lockouts, and demonstrations. In 1926, the PKI considered the situation ripe for revolution and for overthrow of the colonial government. In November 1926, the Communists proclaimed a republic and announced that PKI members would be exempted from the payment of taxes. Although the PKI uprisings were spectacular and fairly widespread, they were largely limited to city workers. The call for a revolution was certainly premature, and the Dutch government had little difficulty in crushing the movement. The PKI was banned and about 13,000 of its members were arrested and thrown into prisons or exiled for long periods of time to the concentration camps in New Guinea. The PKI suffered so badly it did not raise its head for the remainder of the Dutch rule.

What were the reasons for the PKI's collapse? Most Communist ideologues have attributed the disaster to the party's refusal to conform to the Communist International's "Theses and Statutes." These had specifically enjoined Communist parties in all colonial countries to establish "temporary relations and even unions with the revolutionary movements." Political extremism, conceit, and ambition to monopolize the leadership of the nationalist movement contributed to the PKI's decision to scoff at the Comintern's suggested policy of forging a "united front" on the tactical level. Its secession from the Sarekat Islam was suicidal. The PKI's main point of dissension with the Sarekat had been the latter's religious bias. Little did the PKI realize that the moderate central leadership of the Sarekat was closer to the bulk of the religious-minded Indonesians than the atheist Communists could ever hope to be. Moreover, the series of labor strikes had led to the arrest and detention of many prominent PKI leaders, leaving mostly the second-level echelons to lead the abortive revolt of 1926–1927.

The PKI revolution could not involve the masses of peasants. Its leadership, coming for the most part from the *priyayi,* had traditionally looked down upon the toiling peasants. Even the lower ranks of the PKI were educated far above the level of an average Indonesian and had a certain aversion toward the inarticulate, untutored peasant. The party's work in the agrarian sector of the society had been negligible, and the Communists' refusal to give religion any place in life had only helped to alienate them further from the peasants. Consequently, the PKI's call for a nationwide revolution failed to evoke a sufficient response in the countryside.[2]

The PNI and Sukarno

Meanwhile, the Sarekat Islam avoided overt political activity for fear of repression. Instead, it paid attention to education and economic questions. During the same period, a movement that began in 1921 prospered—the Taman Siswa (garden of pupils), aimed at a school system blending Indonesian with Western culture. Though their activities were overtly nonpolitical, the schools fostered a national consciousness and helped to create a cadre of educated youth who would join the nationalist movement in later days. Such a program aimed at slow progress did not satisfy many, particularly the young educated Indonesians returning from Holland. Many of them were members of the leftist Indonesian Union, organized in Holland in 1922. They were joined by Sukarno, a young engineer with a gift for political rhetoric. He established the Perserikatan Nasional Indonesia (PNI), or Indonesian Nationalist Party, on June 4, 1927. It soon brought all non-Communist nationalist elements under its fold in a noncooperation movement on the lines of the Indian National Congress. In 1928, the PNI adopted the red and white flag, Bahasa Indonesia (the Indonesian language), and the anthem "Indonesia Raya" (Greater Indonesia) as the symbols of national unity.

The Dutch government quickly moved to liquidate the threat it recognized in the PNI's growing strength. In 1930, Sukarno and other PNI leaders were jailed and the PNI was outlawed. In 1932, Mohammad Hatta and Sutan Sjahrir returned from their university education in Holland, where Hatta had been the president of the Indonesian Union. On their arrival in Java, they found the PNI leaderless and split into factions. Along with Sukarno, who was then out of prison, they brought all the splinter groups together into a mass organization called the Partai Indonesia (Partindo). In 1933, they were all arrested. None of the three leaders was freed until the advent of the Japanese in 1942. Sjahrir's book *Out of Exile* is a sad commentary on the harsh prison conditions to which the leaders were subjected.

TOWARD FREEDOM

Constitutional Reforms?

Meanwhile, the Dutch authorities made some marginal constitutional concessions aimed at placating the moderate opinion among the nationalists while ruthlessly repressing the extremists. Thus, legislation in 1925 raised the Volksraad's membership from 48 to 60 (30 Indonesians, 26 Dutch, and 5 "Asiatics"). The elected Indonesian members formed a minority in the new council. The Volksraad's powers were limited to criticism of the government. It could not initiate any legislation, and a legislative proposal rejected by it could, after a lapse of six months, be decreed law by the Dutch crown. The act of 1925 also provided for partly elected councils with a non-European majority at the provincial level. The implementation of the provincial part of the act was so slow that it was not completed until the beginning of World War II.

The repressive policy of the government had kept the "extremists," both Communist and non-Communist, in prisons or in exile. The nationalistic sentiment, however, was so high and intense that even the moderate Volksraad called for an imperial conference to discuss ways and means for the introduction of self-government. This was in 1936. In July 1941, the Dutch government, then in exile in England, promised to convene such a conference at the conclusion of the war. To use Gandhi's phrase when he reacted to similar British promises in 1942 to grant self-government to India at the end of the war, the Dutch promise was like a "post-dated check on a crashing bank." The promise was not honestly made. After the war, the Dutch returned to Indonesia with no genuine desire to relinquish control over the islands.

Japan and the Nationalist Movement

When the Japanese troops arrived in Indonesia in 1942, they did not make any concessions to nationalist demands for independence. Japan's immediate policy was to encourage religious groups and repress the political ones. Thus, they tried to suppress the revived Sarekat Islam as well as the various groups of the PNI. The MIAI—Madjlisul Islamil a'laa Indonesia (Great Islamic Council of Indonesia), also known as the Islamic Federation—was used to help recruitment of a local army and to secure food supplies. Within a year, even the MIAI was exasperated. Japanese arrogance requiring all "colonials" to bow toward Tokyo and recognize the divinity of the Japanese emperor was most repugnant to some of the devout MIAI followers, whose religion required bowing in the opposite direction, toward Mecca, and denouncing any divinity in a human being. Further, the harsh treatment and brutalities inflicted on the peasant masses alienated the Japanese from the MIAI. The federation's refusal to cooperate prompted the Japanese to seek other political alternatives.

Noting the people's considerable experience and ability to conduct a campaign of noncooperation, the Japanese felt it prudent to concede some of their political demands in order to secure cooperation in the economic field. They therefore appealed to Sukarno for help, feeling that since they had freed him from exile, he might cooperate. A puppet political body called the Putera was formed. Sukarno, Hatta, Sjahrir, and Amir Sjarifuddin agreed that they should exploit the freedom they had been offered to promote the nationalist cause in a guarded fashion by having Sukarno and Hatta head the government and feign to aid the Japanese, while Sjahrir and Sjarifuddin would organize an underground movement to hamper the Japanese war effort and to train people in resistance and sabotage operations.

Within a year, the Japanese authorities suspected the loyalty of the Putera and abolished it. Yet they continued to use Sukarno and Hatta as leaders of government to exploit even the minimum of cooperation they could get from the people. Sukarno's government gained valuable administrative experience while giving minimum assistance to the Japanese. The Indonesian army of more than a million troops, officially organized to help the Japanese, used the opportunity for officer training and showed its mettle in the fight against the Dutch in the Indonesian revolution of 1945–1949. Public rallies were organized supposedly to support the Japanese cause but really to promote the spirit of nationalism. On the eve of Japan's surrender, the Independence Preparatory Committee was formed.

Only three months earlier, in an extemporaneous speech, Sukarno had presented to the people the famous Pancasila, or Five Postulates: nationalism, internationalism, the principle of consent, social justice, and belief in God. Nationalism involved the establishment of one national state based on the entity of one Indonesian soil from the tip of Sumatra to Irian, a means of promoting unity through diversity. Internationalism would seek to establish a family of nations, with each one recognizing its respective nationalism. Though details were left to be worked out, Sukarno's plan recognized the importance of the principles of consent, representation, and consultation to the strength of the Indonesian state. The principle of social justice underlined a political-economic democracy in which all people would prosper. Finally, Sukarno emphasized the right of every Indonesian to believe in his or her own particular God, which amounted to secularism.

The Indonesian Revolution, 1945–1949

In the summer of 1945, with impending defeat in sight, the Japanese tried to make a gift of independence to the Indonesians. But Sukarno's government did not want it as a gift from the Japanese—both because of Indonesian hostility toward them and because of the possible difficulties it might create in getting recognition from Western countries. Instead, the Indonesians declared themselves a republic.

The Republic of Indonesia encountered a host of problems during the period 1945–1949, some of them stemming from disunity among the nationalist ranks. There were those who scorned any compromise with the groups that had collaborated with the Japanese. The Islamic Masjumi party denounced the Marxist-oriented socialism. The PNI was split into several groups. The greatest challenge to the republic came from the Communists, who attempted to overthrow the government by kidnapping members of the cabinet in June 1946. Two years later, another Communist revolt took place. Both revolts were effectively suppressed by the republic, which was also fighting the Dutch forces intermittently from late 1945 to 1949.

In the period of transition—amid the trials and tribulations, the differences and divisions in the nationalist ranks—there was one cementing force to hold the infant Indonesian republic together. This was the common opposition of most

Indonesians to the restoration of Dutch rule. When British troops on behalf of the Allies landed in Java in September 1945, they released nearly 200,000 Dutch prisoners of war. The Indonesians were prepared to negotiate details of Dutch interests in Indonesia provided the Netherlands first recognized the Republic of Indonesia. To appease Dutch sensitivities, Sukarno even stepped down in favor of Sutan Sjahrir as head of government, but on the question of demand of recognition of the republic, the nationalists would brook no compromise.

In terms of political reform, the Dutch resurrected from their war-time closet Queen Wilhelmina's offer of 1942, which in D.G.E. Hall's words was "already half-a-century out of date."[3] Indonesian nationalism had taken tremendous strides since then, and the Dutch seemed to be incredibly ignorant of the republic's real strength in most of the archipelago. The islands were soon divided, between those under complete republican control and those the Dutch had occupied with the help of Allied troops. There were interminable negotiations finally leading to the Linggadjati agreement signed at Batavia on March 25, 1947. The areas under the control of the republic—Java, Madura, Sumatra, Borneo, and the "Great East"—were to be component parts of a projected United States of Indonesia (USI) as part of a larger Netherlands-Indonesian-Surinam-Curacao union, the last two in South America. Defense, foreign relations, and finance were to be under the union. The USI would be an independent member of the United Nations. The Dutch wanted to remain the sole sovereign power throughout the archipelago—a view that was galling to Indonesian nationalist pride. Soon both sides were accusing each other of breach of agreement.

Within three months of the ratification of the Linggadjati agreement, the Dutch launched what was euphemistically called the "police action," a vicious attack on the territories held by the Republic of Indonesia. A shocked world brought pressure on the Dutch primarily through the United Nations agencies. A cease-fire resolution was adopted by the Security Council on August 1, 1947. It also established a Committee of Good Offices, consisting of the United States, Belgium, and Australia, to talk to the two parties. An agreement emerged in January 1948 on board the U.S.S. *Renville* proposing plebiscites in various islands of the archipelago to decide whether the inhabitants preferred to join the Indonesian republic or to have Dutch sovereignty continue. Meanwhile, clashes between the Dutch and Indonesian forces continued on a small scale, escalating into another "police action" in December 1948. This time the world reaction was sharper. Prime Minister Jawaharlal Nehru of India convened the Asian Conference on Indonesia in New Delhi in January 1949, denied the Dutch aircraft and shipping refueling facilities, and successfully persuaded Pakistan, Sri Lanka, Myanmar, Saudi Arabia, and Iraq to apply similar sanctions. Nehru's speech reflected the Asian wrath as well as its solidarity and support:

> We meet today because the freedom of a sister country of ours has been imperilled and dying colonialism of the past has raised its head again and challenged all forces that are struggling to build up a new structure of the world. That challenge has a deeper significance than might appear on the surface, for it is a challenge to a newly awakened Asia which has so long suffered under various forms of colonialism.[4]

At the conference's urging, the Security Council ordered an immediate cease-fire, release of political prisoners, and the reestablishment of the republican government in Jogjakarta. The United States also brought tremendous pressure on the Netherlands government, which yielded to the tide of world opinion, finally agreeing to transfer sovereignty to Indonesian hands on December 27, 1949. Indonesian nationalism had, at last, fully triumphed over an obstinate colonialism.

15

The Nationalist Movements: Myanmar

ECONOMIC DISCONTENT

The British rule introduced numerous economic changes, hardly any of which benefited the Myanmar people. Large tracts of land were brought under rice cultivation and exports mounted phenomenally, but they benefited the Indian moneylenders and British companies involved in processing, shipping, and exporting of the grain. Crops and lands were mortgaged by the Burmese peasants to the south Indian moneylenders, the Chettyars, who charged exorbitant rates of interest, up to 50 percent, and through foreclosures came to own one-fourth of the entire arable land by World War II. The alienation of land, not allowed by Burmese tradition, was blamed by the Burmese on the pernicious Anglo-Saxon law. Tremendous insecurity and restlessness pervaded the peasants, who moved from village to village, ready to listen to political leaders who identified the influx of Indian moneylenders and labor with British imperialism. It was in the rice-producing delta of Lower Myanmar that nationalism was most rife.

What was true of rice was also true of the extractive industries such as oil, zinc, lead, wolfram, and tin. The Burmese did not benefit economically from the exploitation of mines or teak forests. Railroads laced the country, and shipping clogged its ports. Yet both capital and labor were largely alien, mostly British and Indian, who did not share their profits with the indigenous Burmese.

The British administration destroyed the old system. It removed the traditional headmen because they had led the resistance movement after 1885 and replaced them with salaried ones. In the second decade of the twentieth century, many villages were grouped together under a circle head, thus reducing the number of village headmen. Numbers apart, the new headmen failed to inspire the kind of trust and loyalty among the peasantry that the *myothugyi-* (district chief) based circle system did in the pre-British era. The Burmese felt alienated also because of the British distrust and policy of not associating the Burmese with the administration in significant numbers. Instead, the British preferred Indians and minority tribals, particularly the Karens, many of whom had embraced Christianity. The higher levels of society found the status of Myanmar as an Indian province (until its separation in 1937) offensive to their pride in Myanmar as an ancient kingdom with its own glorious traditions.

NATIONALIST ORGANIZATIONS

The most important single factor disruptive of Burmese society had been the British neglect of the Buddhist *sangha* (association). Traditionally, the monks had played a crucial educational and cultural role helping social cohesion. The opening of government and missionary schools competed directly with the Buddhist schools. The cultural inroads made by the West were opposed by the Buddhist monasteries, which became centers of resentful opposition to the West.

Not surprisingly, the Myanmar nationalist movement began with the establishment of the Young Men's Buddhist Association (YMBA) in 1906. Originally patterned after the Young Men's Christian Association (YMCA), the YMBA established schools conforming to the governmental curriculum requirements but also giving lessons in Buddhist scriptures to counter the Christian missionary schools, which offered Bible lessons. The YMBA schools soon became centers of the community's social life and national awareness. They resorted to religious organizations as a politically safe way to promote nationalistic sentiments. Buddhism provided a common platform for those who deeply resented the colonial government's neglect of and injury to their faith. Numerous political parties of later times were led by former YMBA volunteers.

Although Myanmar was a province of India, it was treated differently in regard to political reforms. Thus, the liberal Montagu-Chelmsford reforms of 1919, which provided for an elected majority in the central legislature and a part-Indian executive at the provincial level, were not applied to Myanmar. Around the same time, the University of Rangoon Act was passed, but unlike its Indian counterparts, the new university was not given autonomous status. This double affront produced great agitation. The YMBA, at the time renamed the General Council of Buddhist Associations (GCBA) and led largely by European-educated youth, protested along Gandhian lines against the discrimination and demanded the same reforms as in India. Students protested all over the country the denial of autonomy to the university. By the time the British responded in 1921 by extending dyarchy to Myanmar, the GCBA had stepped up its demands. Significantly, the students demanded control over land legislation and immigration. They boycotted the elections to the new councils and refused the executive positions in the new cabinet, which were filled by Karens, Indians, Chinese, and British, making a mockery of the Montagu-Chelmsford reforms.

The depression of the 1930s hit the Burmese rice industry severely and further aggravated the economic and political tensions among the people. Prices dipped to one-third of prior levels, while property foreclosures, unemployment, and the crime rate soared. Not understanding the forces of worldwide economic phenomena, the

Burmese became suspicious of the British government and Indian moneylenders, the latter becoming the special target of the wrath of Burmese tenant-farmers and agricultural workers. The suspicion of British intention was such that when in 1929 a commission, headed by Sir John Simon and appointed to review the constitutional demands of Indian nationalists, recommended the separation of Myanmar (in response to past Burmese demands), the recommendation was regarded as an "imperial plot" to rule Myanmar indefinitely. Despite Burmese protests, the British passed the Government of India Act of 1935 separating Myanmar from India. The act gave provincial autonomy to Myanmar, with "reserved" powers to the British governor.

Meanwhile, a serious peasant rebellion had broken out in Lower Myanmar, where a former Buddhist *pongyi* (monk), Saya San, proclaimed himself the king. A former leader of the GCBA, Saya San used the traditional, mystical symbolism to restore a Buddhist monarchy and to reach the peasant masses. His peasant army roamed the countryside, killing British forestry officials and Indian laborers. The rebellion was effectively crushed by the police and militia units; Saya San was executed after a lengthy trial in 1937. Saya San's revolt was the last attempt to reverse the tide of modernization and restore the Burmese monarchy and traditional way of life.

The constitutional agitation of the 1930s produced a number of political parties, all of them supporting land reform and opposing Indian immigration and moneylenders. The most important were the Sinyetha and Thakin parties. The Sinyetha (poor man's) party was founded by Dr. Ba Maw, who became minister of education in 1932 and the first prime minister under the 1935 act in 1937. Sinyetha advocated tax reductions, protection of farmers from moneylenders, and compulsory education.

A more important party was the Thakin (master), an offshoot of an organization started by Rangoon University students in 1929 called the Dohbama Asiayone (We Burmans Association). The party attracted students, teachers, and other intellectuals. The Thakin party urged the Burmese to be masters of their own country. Previously, it was the British practice in Myanmar to demand use of the term "Thakin" when the Burmese servants addressed them. Now, the term was used at the University of Rangoon by students in speaking to each other to emphasize their equality with the British and to signify that they were their own masters. The Thakin party stood for the revival of Burmese-Buddhist cultural tradition. It sternly opposed the British educational system, which devised a curriculum suited to produce members of the subordinate civil service. The party was well organized, with young leaders, mostly Myanmar-educated, who had wide contacts among the depression-ridden peasantry. The party had several study groups, mostly leftist. The socialism most of them advocated, however, was not inspired so much by Marxism as by the Buddhist precepts of equity and justice and by opposition to non-Burmese hold over Myanmar's economy. Like all other Burmese parties, the Thakins hated the Indian community in Myanmar, but it had tremendous regard for the Indian National Congress and its leaders. In 1939, the Thakins joined the Indian leaders in withholding cooperation in the British war effort and were imprisoned by the British.

JAPAN WOOS BURMESE NATIONALISTS

During World War II, the Thakins were divided into three groups. Those committed to communism included Thakin Soe and Thein Pe; the Communist party was formally established in 1943. The bulk of the Thakins, including Aung San, embraced democratic socialism. The third group consisted of U Ba Swe, U Nu, and others who disfavored factionalism. In 1940, a Japanese agent, Colonel Suzuki Keiji, contacted the Thakins to offer military help if they would agree to side with the Japanese in the impending war. The Communists in the group rejected the offer. So did Aung San, who preferred then to ask for assistance from the Chinese Communist party and secretly left for Shanghai. Disguised as a Chinese crewman with a letter of introduction from the Communist party of India, he was waylaid in Amoy by the Japanese, who offered to train Aung San's famous "thirty heroes" on the island of Hainan. These would later invade Myanmar and form the nucleus of the Burma Independence Army, later called Burma National Army (BNA), with Aung San as its commander. Despite the Japanese help in training his men, Aung San remained opposed to Japanese fascism.

When the Japanese drove the British out of Myanmar, most Burmese, who had been fascinated by the Japanese slogan "Asia for the Asiatics," expected immediate independence. On August 1, 1943, the Japanese military administration was disbanded and Myanmar's independence proclaimed with Dr. Ba Maw as head of government. In exchange, Myanmar declared war on the Allies and pledged support and cooperation in the building of the Greater East Asia Co-Prosperity Sphere. The warmth the Burmese held for the Japanese soon dissipated because of the callous disregard the Japanese military showed toward Burmese susceptibilities. Acts such as face-slapping of the village notables, forced labor, mandatory and uncompensated requisitions for cattle and rice, and, strangely enough for fellow Buddhists, the use of pagodas as latrines and the burning of Buddhist scriptures, earned undying Burmese hatred for the Japanese. On the economic front, the exploitative ways of the greedy Japanese war contractors raised apprehensions in Burmese minds as to what could be expected in the Co-Prosperity Sphere that would follow in the event of Japanese success in the war.

AFPFL LEADS MYANMAR TO FREEDOM

The Japanese experience was a great disillusionment for the Burmese nationalists. By early 1944, the people, the government, and the armed forces were all demoralized and depressed. The underground resistance of a small band of Communists under Thakin Soe was now joined by groups of Thakin nationalists to oppose the Japanese. They made contact with British Force 136, which had been specifically created to organize and assist resistance movements. Meanwhile, Aung San and his associates had held secret talks with Thakin Soe for cooperation in guerrilla operations against the Japanese. By August 1944, all these groups came under the common aegis of the newly founded Anti-Fascist People's Freedom League (AFPFL). Than Tun, a longtime Communist leader, became its secretary-general and Aung San became president.

The AFPFL's manifesto, clandestinely published and circulated, promised to establish a "people's government" with a constitution approved by all people of Myanmar to include freedom of thought, speech, the press, assembly, and religion and the outlawing of discrimination on grounds of race, religion, sex, or minority status. Its immediate plan was to use guerrilla operations to obstruct the Japanese war effort by cutting its supply lines.

The AFPFL-led revolt came on March 27, 1945. The BNA engaged the Japanese in the Upper Myanmar plain around Meiktila, supplementing the effort of the British invasion forces in reoccupying Myanmar. By now, the AFPFL was enlarged to include virtually all nationalist elements. As the Japanese withdrawal began on May 7, 1945, the AFPFL extended its control over Myanmar.

After the war, the British insisted on the need for a transitional period of their rule in order to be able to restore the country's economy, communications, and administrative system, which had grievously suffered during the war. Indeed, the river transport as well as the railroad had become unserviceable, and the docks were badly damaged. The Indian trading class and most of the Indian civil service officials, doctors, and lawyers had left for India either during the anti-Indian riots of 1938 or after the outbreak of war. Despite such chaotic conditions, the Myanmar people wanted the British to quit immediately. The AFPFL, with its broad base of nationalist political representation and under the uncompromising leadership of Aung San, demanded immediate and complete independence.

Events in nearby India accelerated the pace of independence in Myanmar. Assessing the postwar situation and the virulent nationalist movement in India, the postwar Labor government in Britain decided to withdraw from the subcontinent. Paralleling the stages of withdrawal of power in India, the British requested Aung San to form a Council of Ministers in October 1946. In January 1947, Britain announced elections to the Constituent Assembly. The AFPFL was returned almost unanimously in April, trouncing all opposition, particularly Communist. The Burmese happiness over these events soured in July, however, when Aung San and six associates were killed at the instance of U Saw, a defector from the AFPFL who wanted a more revolutionary program but had himself none to offer. He had expected to blame the heinous murders on the British government and to goad the people into a general revolt from which he hoped to emerge as the supreme leader. U Saw was tried and executed. The AFPFL, now under the pious U Nu, led the Burmese to complete independence from Britain on January 4, 1948. Myanmar became a republic with U Nu the first premier and the Shan chief Sao Shwe Thaik as president. Significantly for Anglo-Burmese relations, the new Union of Burma decided to sever all ties with Britain, except normal diplomatic relations, by choosing not to join the British Commonwealth of Nations.

16

Thailand's Constitutional Revolution

THAILAND, 1910–1932

The momentum to modernization and centrally well-regulated administration given by Chulalongkorn lasted for more than a decade after his death. By the late 1920s, rumblings among the commoner official class as well as in the army ranks against the autocratic and nepotistic monarchy were increasingly evident, eventually leading to the revolution of 1932.

Two of Chulalongkorn's sons succeeded him: Maha Vajiravudh (Rama VI) from 1910 to 1925 and Prajadhipok (Rama VII) from 1925 to 1935. Both were educated abroad, Westernized, and, to a deplorable extent, alienated from the cultural and political interests of their people. Rama VI was profligate, nonconformist, and whimsical, with strange notions of Westernization. He introduced monogamy and urged the women to adopt Western hairdo and dress. He made primary education compulsory and in 1917 established the famous Chulalongkorn University, named after his father. But he also introduced a public school on the British pattern and the Wild Tiger Scout Movement, whose activities were at best infantile and unproductive. His Anglicization was external and ill-suited to the traditions of Thai aristocracy. A clubhouse, a rugby football team, and colorful uniforms for his bodyguards completed his Westernization. The inordinate importance and privileges granted by him to the scout movement roused the envy and anger of high officers in the army and the navy. Two unsuccessful attempts were made on his life in 1912 and 1917, but these did not deter him from his strange ways and policies. Rama VI died in 1925 without a male heir, leaving the throne to his younger brother, his father's seventy-sixth child.

Rama VI's rule was, however, notable for some of Thailand's achievements in the external field, thanks to World War I and the opportunistic diplomacy of the veteran Prince Dewawongse. With the intention of pleasing the British but also with an eye on potential booty in the form of German shipping and German interests in Thai railways, Dewawongse declared war on Germany. In 1919, Thailand became the only Southeast Asian member of the League of Nations. Three years later, thanks to Thai diplomatic efforts, the United States became the first of the treaty powers to abandon the rights to extraterritoriality. In this, Thailand was ably assisted by Francis B. Sayre, President Wilson's son-in-law, who served Thailand as Foreign Office adviser from 1920 to 1927. Between 1924 and 1930, all the other treaty powers agreed to end the unequal provisions of previous treaties and sign new ones.

Rama VII, or Prajadhipok, was a well-intentioned reformist and a modernizer but unconcerned about the impact of his policies on his people. In 1927, Prajadhipok revived and enlarged the Privy Council and the Supreme Council of State, both of which he intended to turn eventually into a bicameral parliament. The aristocracy's pressures, however, made him appoint the five most important princes to the Council of State, which then proceeded to appoint and promote a number of other princes to high official positions and exempt them all from the application of the provisions of the Civil Service Law of 1928. Such actions invited charges of nepotism from the commoner educated class, which though small had expected a greater role in the now-enlarged democratic institutions of the country. Prajadhipok's measures reversed the process by which educated professional commoners had been absorbed and advanced in high civil service positions in the country. Many of Prajadhipok's other reforms were of benefit to the country. Prajadhipok built an airport, improved public health facilities, promoted Thai banking, and lent patronage to arts and learning through the new National Library and Museum as well as the Royal Institute of Literature, Architecture, and Fine Arts. Yet these measures failed to evoke popular acclaim because of discontent of the educated class over lack of opportunity in public service and public life.

THE REVOLUTION OF 1932

The immediate cause of the revolution of 1932 was provided by Thailand's depression, necessitating budgetary cuts in the salaries and promotions of junior civil service and military officers. The country had chosen to remain on the gold standard after most countries had abandoned it. This resulted in Thai rice being expensive in the world markets. The revenues from exports of rice and teak timber dwindled to the point of extinction. The discontent brought young army officials, unemployed foreign-educated youth, and some older moderates together to stage a bloodless coup on June 24, 1932.

Since the end of the absolute monarchy in 1932, Thailand has withstood thirteen revolutions and eight constitutions. The period is marked by government by decree alternating with experiments in constitutional rule. Military officials played a crucial role for most of the time until 1973; in the four decades between the revolution and 1973, civilian prime ministers ruled for a mere four years. The immediate leadership of the movement and of the government alternated in the first few years of the revolution between two young leaders representing the small Western-educated middle class: Pridi Phanamyong (Pradit Manuthum), leftist professor of law at Thammasat University, and Phibun Songkhram, an army colonel with ultranationalist military supporters. The gains between 1932 and 1935 included the establishment of a limited constitutional monarchy on the British pattern and the abdication of King Prajadhipok in 1935 in favor of his ten-year-old son Ananda, then in school in Switzerland.

Among the first postrevolution prime ministers was Pridi, whose legal expertise and desire to retain power in the hands of his People's party inspired the first constitution, which remained theoretically in force until 1946. There was to be an Assembly of 156 members, half appointed by the king, which in practice meant by the ruling party, and partly elected by the people indirectly through local- and district-level electors. The cabinet was to be responsible to the Assembly, which could be dissolved by the king, who was obliged to call fresh elections within three months of such a dissolution. The princely class was not eligible to hold legislative or executive positions, but could serve in diplomatic service or in an advisory capacity. The king's powers were limited; he had power to veto a piece of legislation once, but it would become law if the Assembly approved it again. In effect, the new government was elitist, certainly not democratic enough to include the grass roots; it was traditional enough to co-opt and continue the nobility in permanent civil service positions. Thailand's several constitutions have maintained certain common features, including separation of powers, rights and duties of the citizens, and the cabinet's submission of policies to and subservience to the parliament. These borrowed elements of Western democratic principles did not mean the rigid observance of such practices in the actual functioning of the government.

Pridi's effectiveness soon ended when he revealed his leftist inclinations in mid-1933 by unveiling an economic plan aimed at governmental takeover of major industrial and commercial activities. The reaction was twofold: a split in the People's party and a royalist countercoup. The latter was effectively crushed by the army, whose nominee, Phraya Phahon, replaced Pridi as prime minister and continued to hold that office until December 1938.

Except for the brief period of Pridi's rule, the Thai elite in the postrevolution era did not differ radically from its predecessor. Except for the princes, who came under a cloud for some time at least, the aristocratic elite that had dominated the higher bureaucracy was now enlarged to accommodate the victors of the revolution. Fortunately for Thailand, the country did not need much new reform in landholding. The peasantry was relatively contented and was happy to leave the redistribution of political power in Bangkok and the provincial capitals to be sorted out by the enlarged elite. But on one issue, the common people could not have agreed more. This was the government's policy of diminishing the disparities between the people and the affluent Chinese.

The Thai policies of the second half of the 1930s were marked by ultranationalism, religious revivalism, and militarism. Nationalism took the form of an anti-Chinese movement, a revival of the campaign of the late 1920s when large-scale immigration of the Chinese had evoked hostility among the Thais. The new immigration had a substantially higher proportion of females than ever before, which had the effect of reducing the pace of assimilation. The victorious emergence of the Kuomintang (KMT) party in China had led to a new assertiveness among the overseas Chinese. Anticipating the KMT's initiative in seeking a special legal status for the overseas Chinese, Thailand had unilaterally ended the existing extraterritorial privileges of the Chinese in 1930. The new nationalist fervor following the revolution of 1932 showed itself in the form of an anti-Chinese movement, leading to closure of Chinese language schools and newspapers, restricting Chinese immigration to an annual quota of 10,000, and deporting illegal aliens. The government also proceeded to reserve certain occupations for ethnic Thais, who were also made exclusively eligible for special governmental assistance in business. Nationalism worked also against the powerful British timber firms, whose leases of teak forests were renewed on less favorable terms than before. Further, Thais showed "religious nationalism," treating Christians as aliens and encouraging them to convert to Buddhism. Externally, the Thais demanded surrender of the Cambodian provinces of Siem Reap and Battambang, which had been ceded to the French by the Thais in 1904. In June 1939, the country changed its name from Siam to the more nationalistic Thailand, the Land of the Free.

THAILAND AND THE JAPANESE

Meanwhile, the ascendancy of militant nationalism had brought about the direct rule of the army in December 1938 with Phibun Songkhram as prime minister. Of late, the army had become an admirer of the Japanese military establishment and its successes in China and disdainful of the Western countries, which seemed to capitulate to German and Japanese pressures. When World War II broke out, Thailand declared war on France and demanded the western Cambodian provinces of Battambang and Siem Reap, which it finally secured through Japanese intervention. When Japanese forces landed in Thailand, the Phibun government did the bidding of the Japanese military hierarchy, providing transit rights and essential supplies. In return, Japan rewarded Thailand with additional territories in Laos, northern Malaya, and the Shan region of Myanmar.

Despite a treaty of friendship and cooperation with Japan that allowed Thailand greater internal autonomy than enjoyed by most other Southeast Asian countries, there was no love lost between the two Asian allies. The prime consideration of Thai leadership was the preservation of the country's independence. As Phibun Songkhram told his chief of staff in 1942: "Which side do you think will be defeated in this war? That side is our enemy."[1] During this period, the Thai ambassadors in London and Washington promoted resistance to Japan; in fact, the Thai ambassador to the United States, Seni Pramoj, on his own authority decided not to inform Washington formally that his country had declared war against the United States in January 1942. In Thailand proper, Pridi Phanamyong, whose official position was that of regent to the young monarch, secretly organized the resistance movement called the Free Thai movement, which was assisted by the OSS (U.S. Office of Strategic Services) and British Force 136, a guerrilla-intelligence unit operating from Sri Lanka and with the OSS through Yunnan. The Free Thai movement received substantial public support because of discontent over martial law, scarce supply of food, high prices, and the domination of their economy by huge Japanese combines. The Chinese community in Thailand also helped the resistance movement because community assets had been frozen by the government under

Japanese pressure. Besides, there were the hardships caused by Japanese military demands of food, labor, and materials for construction of barracks and bases throughout the country.

As the tide of Japan's fortunes turned in mid-1944, the Thai National Assembly compelled Phibun Songkhram to resign in favor of a civilian government headed by Khuang Aphaiwong, with Pridi unofficially manipulating the wheels of power. The ruling clique was quick to do penance for its past mistakes and used the good offices of Pridi to negotiate secretly with the Allies for the best terms possible and to win its way back into their good graces. Phibun was briefly detained in Thailand and later jailed in Japan as a war criminal by the Allies, but was eventually allowed to return to his country in 1947. Meanwhile, the new Thai government agreed to give up its newly acquired territories of the western Cambodian provinces, four northern Malay states, and two Shan states in Myanmar. The new Thailand also established an amicable relationship with the KMT in China, promised most-favored-nation status to the United States, and in a move to please Russia (then an Allied power) agreed even to legalize the Communist party of Thailand.

17

The Nationalist Movements: Vietnam

THE SOCIAL SYSTEM UNDER FRENCH RULE

Vietnamese nationalism was nurtured in the cradle of the country's history of resistance to Chinese domination. Direct Chinese rule from 111 B.C. to A.D. 939 and again from 1407 to 1428 was punctuated by numerous uprisings and the final ouster of the northern invaders. However, hatred of Chinese rule did not preclude a willing absorption of some of the traits of the culture of China, the Chinese civil and moral law, the Confucian glorification of bureaucracy, the civil service examination system, and finally, the institution of an emperor, whose primary duties included establishing harmony between earth and heaven. More important, it should be noted that the Sinicization of Vietnam affected mainly the upper classes of society, whereas the villagers were left to themselves. The peasants clung to the Vietnamese habits of chewing betel nut and worshiping hosts of village genies, spirits of their ancestors, and mountains and rivers. They rejoiced in the ceremonies and festivals that predated the advent of Chinese culture. In that sense, Chinese domination had never posed much threat to the traditional modes of Vietnamese rural social behavior as the French administration did, particularly toward the end of the nineteenth century.

The French administration in Vietnam destroyed the peasants' traditional civilization, which had persisted with nominal external interference for two thousand years. Each Vietnamese village was a bamboo-fenced, practically autonomous social entity, governed by a council of village notables, who collected taxes on behalf of the central government, determined the agrarian chores, and distributed the rice product among the peasants. They also dispensed justice. The imperial government interfered only for purposes of census or recruitment of soldiers in times of war. As the folk saying had it, "The laws of the emperor are less than the customs of the village." The French broke the village autonomy and its corporate character, substituted elections for cooperation of council members, instituted regular registration of births and deaths (resulting in more accurate tax polls than hitherto), and exercised tighter control over fiscal matters. The elections themselves returned Western-educated individuals who lacked the traditional following or influence among the peasants. The traditional notables joined the ranks of the opposition. The system was so discredited that the French themselves abandoned it in 1941. Moreover, the French sought to create a new type of Vietnamese, a prototype of a French gentleman who was given large land concessions and who would willingly accept French beliefs, standards of behavior, and values.[1] At the same time, French education created a new type of elite, which would eventually provide leadership for the nationalist movement. Many of these leaders had "the mind of a sceptic who would accept nothing which he could not verify from his own experience or by his own thinking."[2]

EARLY RESISTANCE AGAINST FRENCH RULE

Opposition to French rule began almost as soon as the French had occupied Cochin China in 1862. It was led by all types of people, including peasants and fishermen, who were not prepared to abandon their time-honored culture for that of people separated from them "by thousands of mountains and seas."[3] The resistance movement grew to revolutionary proportions after the French conquest of Annam in 1885. The so-called pacification program, like its British counterpart in Myanmar, was most intense until 1895, but it extended in Vietnam to 1913. In a particularly vicious campaign from 1909 to 1913, the French hounded the resistance leaders and murdered them one by one. The peasantry harbored and supported the leaders of the resistance movement, known as Can Vuong (aid the king), which included the scholar-gentry, the Vietnamese mandarin class. In the decades before 1900, the mandarins appeared to believe that the French occupation of their lands might spell loss of political control but not a cultural or spiritual loss. By 1900, however, a new generation of maturing mandarins grew apprehensive that the educational and cultural impact of French culture had become pervasive. They were haunted by the image of *mat nuoc* (losing one's country), not merely in political terms but more seriously in the sense of their future survival as Vietnamese. Mandarins thus fell into three groups: those who had collaborated with the colonial masters, those who withdrew to the villages in a sort of passive noncooperation, and those who struggled desperately through participation in the resistance movement to bring new meaning and ethnic salvation (*cuu quoc*) to the populace.[4]

Two major events in Asia influenced the direction of the Vietnamese opposition to French rule. One was Japan's spectacular rise as an industrially and militarily strong nation, and the other was China's reform movement and overthrow of the decadent Ch'ing monarchy. Two Vietnamese anticolonialist leaders, Phan Boi Chau (1867–1940) and Phan Chau Trinh (1871–1926), were directly influenced by these happenings in eastern Asia. Born into a mandarin family, Phan Boi Chau passed the regional examination in 1900 and had by 1902 acquainted himself with the writings of the Chinese reformer Liang Ch'i-ch'ao. In that year, Phan Boi Chau published a book, *Ryukyu's Bitter Tears,* superficially dealing with the loss of sovereignty of the Ryukyu Islands to the Japanese but in reality alluding to the Vietnamese loss of freedom at the hands of the French. Two years later, Phan Boi Chau and a number of his pupils and associates launched the Duy Tan Hoi (Reformation Society). This organization, standing for revolutionary monarchism, secured the support of Prince Cuong De and decided to secure outside assistance to achieve its nationalist ends. In 1905, Phan Boi Chau secretly went to Japan, where he met the Chinese scholar Liang and through him the top Japanese leaders, who promised liberal scholarships to Vietnamese students but no military assistance to overthrow French rule. Shortly thereafter, Phan published his *History of the Loss of Vietnam,* which quickly went into five editions in China and which clandestinely circulated all over Vietnam. Soon there were scores of Vietnamese students enrolled in Japanese institutions, including the military academy.

For Phan Chau Trinh, however, monarchy as an institution had become outdated. He was a firm believer in democracy and an advocate of a Western-style republican constitution. He led a tax resistance movement in 1908 and was arrested and later deported to France, where he was in exile and for periods of time in French prisons until 1925. A few months after his release, he managed to reach Saigon, where he perceived that politics had changed so much during his long absence that he could not take part in the nationalist movement even if he wanted to.

THE NATIONALIST MOVEMENT PROPER

In the second decade of the twentieth century, the purpose and leadership of the nationalist movement underwent gradual changes. The effects of French education had begun to show. Many young individuals from well-to-do families with the benefit of higher education in Vietnam and France became nationalist leaders. Many of the more than 100,000 Vietnamese who saw wartime service in France joined the nationalists in making modest demands for participation in the councils and for a larger number of positions in civil service. Nearer home, a large group of Vietnamese youth had crossed over into China after the Chinese revolution of 1911. In 1913, they established the Association for the Restoration of Vietnam and instigated a number of small uprisings in Tongking and Cochin China.

In the 1920s, many underground secret organizations sprang up—Marxist and non-Marxist alike. The most prominent was the VNQDD (Viet Nam Quoc Dan Dang, or the Vietnamese Nationalist Party), founded in 1927. Organizationally modeled on the Chinese Kuomintang (KMT), it adopted Sun Yat-sen's principles of nationalism, democracy, and the people's livelihood.

Ho Chi Minh (the name being one of his numerous aliases) was born in 1890 into a modest mandarin family. He left Vietnam as a cabin boy on a merchant vessel and after many odd jobs in England and France established his reputation as a good pamphleteer in leftist circles in Paris. He appeared in 1919 outside the Versailles Conference with a petition asking for the right of self-determination for his country. Active in the French Socialist party, he attended its congress in 1920, voting with the majority that decided to form the French Communist party. In 1923, he visited Moscow as the party's delegate to the Peasant International. He quickly gained attention of the Soviet hierarchy and in 1924 was sent to Canton, ostensibly as a translator to assist Mikhael Borodin, adviser to the KMT, but really to organize the Communist movement in Vietnam. A year later, he formed the Association of Vietnamese Revolutionary Youth, or the Thanh Nien. Over a period of two years, Ho trained about 250 men in Marxist techniques, got some of them enrolled in Whampoa Military Academy in China, and sent some others to Russia for studies in Marxism. In 1930, Ho fused the three prominent Communist groups in Vietnam into a single party and significantly named it Indochina Communist party (ICP), although there were few Communists then in Laos and Cambodia. By 1931, the ICP claimed 1,500 members besides 100,000 peasants affiliated in peasant organizations.

The Uprisings of 1930–1931

In 1930, the VNQDD decided that it was time for a nationwide revolt, although the timing of the revolt was perhaps forced by the Communists. On February 9, 1929, a French settler, Rene Bazin, was killed by a Vietnamese youth, possibly at Communist instigation. The French authorities suspected the VNQDD's hand in the death and reacted quickly by imprisoning several VNQDD supporters and ordering a thorough, secret investigation of the VNQDD's underground activities. Afraid of French retaliatory action that could destroy the VNQDD, its leader, Nguyen Thai Hoc, ordered a nationwide insurrection on February 10, 1930, later postponed to February 15. The military garrison at Yen Bay was not aware of the change in date, and the troops consequently led their own uprising on February 10 by killing their French officers. The VNQDD expected the Yen Bay uprising to spark a general revolution. There were sporadic peasant uprisings in some provinces but not a nationwide movement. Besides, the French police had been alerted. They easily suppressed the disturbances and conclusively destroyed the effectiveness of the VNQDD, many of whose members fled northward to China. Many others were arrested and executed. The French destruction of the VNQDD accounted for the lack of strong and effective non-Communist leadership among the Vietnamese nationalist ranks in the post-1930 period.

Undeterred by the VNQDD failure and, in fact, to offset the VNQDD's relative popularity among the masses, the ICP decided to exploit the prevalent peasant unrest brought on by successive crop failures. Strikes in plantations and factories were organized beginning May Day, 1930, and soviets were established in the provinces of Nghe An and Ha Tinh. The ICP met the same fate as the VNQDD at the hands of the French police. Hundreds were killed, many more arrested. Ho Chi Minh was arrested in Hong Kong by the British police on June 30 of the following year.

The two uprisings—the VNQDD's and the ICP's—had a tremendous impact on the Vietnamese. It also affected public opinion in France, leading to some slight change in colonial policy. In September 1932, Prince Bao Dai was brought back from France to head a reformed monarchy. That was an opportunity for moderate nationalists such as Ngo Dinh Diem, Bao Dai's new minister of the interior and chief of the reform commissions, to push the reformist movement ahead. It was a short-lived hope. Realizing that the French did not mean to give Bao Dai any substantial power, Diem resigned in frustration in September 1933.

The VNQDD apparatus had been crushed by the French repression, but the ICP was soon able to reassemble its party machinery, thanks to its superior organization and party discipline. It benefited from the politics of detente (1936–1939) in France when the Popular Front government decided to release all political prisoners, including Communists. The ICP took advantage of the political situation to organize a broad Democratic National Front under the leadership of Pham Van Dong and Vo Nguyen Giap. With the outbreak of war, the Popular Front government fell in France, the honeymoon with Communists ended, and the ICP was banned. Most of its cadres went underground, though some fled to China.

The Viet Minh and the DRV

During World War II, a general accord between the Vichy government and Japan in August 1940 provided for the continuation of French sovereignty and administration in Indochina in return for placing the military facilities and economic resources of the colony at Japan's disposal. The Allies, including the Soviet Union and Nationalist China, were engaged in a common struggle against the Japanese, a situation making for strange political bedfellows. Ho Chi Minh was released from a Chinese prison at Chiang Kai-shek's orders to enable him to lead a resistance movement in Vietnam against the Japanese-dominated Vichy government. Military and other supplies would be made available to him among others by the U.S. Office of Strategic Services.

Meanwhile, the ICP's central committee met in southern China in May 1941 and decided to subordinate its plans for agrarian reform and class revolution to the immediate goal of independence and freedom for all Vietnamese. A new organization, the Viet Minh (Viet Nam Doc Lap Dong Minh Hoi, or the Vietnam Independence League), was launched to bring all the political groups together to pursue the goal. A military force was organized under the leadership of Vo Nguyen Giap. By September 1944, the Viet Minh had an army of 5,000 men and the three mountainous provinces of Cao Bang, Lang Son, and Bac Kan under its control. Ho Chi Minh could clearly see that the day of his country's independence was not too distant. From the jungles of northern Vietnam, he wrote in the same month:

> Zero hour is near. Germany is almost beaten, and her defeat will lead to Japan's. Then the Americans and the Chinese will move into Indochina while the Gaullists rise against the Japs. The latter may well topple the French Fascists prior to this and set up a military Government. . . . Indochina will reduce to anarchy. We shall not need even to seize power, for there will be no power. . . . Our impending uprising will be carried out in highly favorable conditions, without parallel in the history of our country.[5]

When Japan surrendered to the Allies on August 14, 1945, the Viet Minh emerged from the sidelines to the center of politics. A national congress of the Viet Minh met at once and elected a National Liberation Committee, which was like a provisional government, headed by Ho Chi Minh. A ten-point plan approved by the congress was to seize power, gain independence for the Democratic Republic of Vietnam (DRV), develop the army, abolish inequitable taxes, promulgate democratic rights, redistribute communal lands, and maintain good relations with the

Allies. There was no mention of major agrarian reform or nationalization of any kind of property. It was a nationalist, not a Communist, program. On August 26, after the Viet Minh took over Hanoi, Bao Dai abdicated (handing over the sword and seal as signs of sovereignty) in favor of the provisional government, thus providing the new administration with legitimacy. A week later, on September 2, 1945, a crowd of a half million in Hanoi heard Ho Chi Minh proclaim the birth of the DRV. On that occasion, Ho Chi Minh read out his Declaration of Independence, which ironically contained passages lifted directly from the American version. It was a Communist victory inasmuch as ten of the fifteen members in the new cabinet were Communists.

The DRV was not recognized by any country. The Allies, meeting at Potsdam, had decided to establish the status quo ante and to that end asked Nationalist China to occupy Vietnam north of the sixteenth parallel and Britain south of it. The Chinese forces arrived in North Vietnam in early September, while the British troops under General Douglas Gracey landed in Saigon on September 12. Gracey immediately released the French from prison but, contrary to instructions, gave them arms. Liberated France was, ironically, planning to reassert its colonial rights in Indochina despite an impassioned appeal to General Charles de Gaulle from Emperor Bao Dai:

> You would understand better if you could see what is happening here, if you could feel the desire for independence which is in everyone's heart and which no human force can any longer restrain. Even if you come to reestablish a French administration here, it will no longer be obeyed: each village will be a nest of resistance, each former collaborator an enemy and your officials and colonists will themselves ask to leave this atmosphere which they will be unable to breathe.[6]

The Viet Minh forces would have easily established themselves in North Vietnam but for the presence of the Chinese troops and the members of the VNQDD and the Dong Minh Hoi (Nationalist party), a group sponsored by China to collect anti-Japanese intelligence in the Tongking region during the war. By September 16, Hanoi was divided, with the central and southeast suburbs under Viet Minh control, while the pro-Chinese nationalists held the northeastern parts. Soon the pro-Chinese nationalists held several provinces. In South Vietnam, the Viet Minh acted as the Committee of the South. After the French takeover there, the Viet Minh continued the pressure on the government through guerrilla warfare, but its advances were not spectacular. Ho Chi Minh therefore took several measures. First, on November 11, 1945, to the surprise of the non-Communists, he announced the dissolution of the ICP. Second, he offered the VNQDD seventy seats in the upcoming free elections to the National Assembly in January 1946. Power was ostensibly shared in a new cabinet composed of the Viet Minh, the VNQDD, and others. On March 6, Ho Chi Minh signed an agreement with the French, allowing the latter to send troops to Hanoi to replace the Chinese in exchange for French recognition of the DRV as a "free state having its own government, its own parliament and its own finances, and forming part of the Indochinese Federation and the French Union." France also agreed to sponsor a referendum to determine whether Cochin China should join the union and if French troops should gradually be withdrawn from all of Vietnam.

Why did Ho Chi Minh agree to the return of the French to Hanoi? It was principally to get rid of the Chinese troops, who had rampaged the countryside in a campaign of loot, plunder, and rape. Second, with their withdrawal, the power of the VNQDD could be easily broken. Third, he felt it would be easier to oust a distant power like France than the closer, traditionally dominant China. On this matter, Ho is reported to have remarked to a friend, in his customary earthy fashion: "It is better to sniff the French dung for a while than to eat China's all our lives."[7]

THE FIRST INDOCHINA WAR

Meanwhile, the French attempted to strengthen their military and political position. Having no desire to give up its sovereignty, France hesitated, hedged, and finally reneged on most of the assurances. Finally, on November 23, the French cruiser *Suffren* bombarded the Vietnamese quarter of Haiphong, killing over 6,000 in a matter of hours. That became a signal for the outbreak of general hostilities between the Viet Minh and France. The DRV leadership and its army of 40,000 trained troops took to the countryside of Tongking. The First Indochina War (1946–1954) had broken out all over Vietnam, North and South, and the French had to face the Viet Minh at once on scores of fronts.

The French intransigence had led to the popularity of the Viet Minh, although its Communist nature was known to many Vietnamese nationalists. Having officially dissolved the party in November 1946, the Communists maintained that they were first and last nationalists. The devotion and dedication of the Viet Minh cadres to the cause of independence and their ascetic way of life had won over large segments of the population. As Milton Osborne observed, they had at least two advantages:

> Convinced of the value of their own cause, they worked with a population which, after decades of disorientation, was pre-disposed to change. The old values which had been personified in the Emperor at Hue, and through him in the traditional mandarinate, had been shattered. The French had once represented unassailable power, but the impression of invincibility had passed. Into this situation came men of their own race and culture who were prepared to work with the peasants and who promised at the same time the alleviation of problems which had pressed upon the rural population for generations.[8]

In March 1949, France announced the birth of the Republic of Vietnam as an associated state within the French union, along with Laos and Cambodia. It made very little difference in practice because the major instruments of power were firmly under French control. The new state was recognized by Great Britain and the United States. The Soviet Union and China reacted by recognizing the DRV, bringing the Cold War to Indochina.

It is difficult to clear the maze of propaganda and identify the real reasons for the Viet Minh's military success and successive French defeats. Both sides made blunders costing heavy casualties, with the French generals not knowing how to fight a nonconventional guerrilla war and the Viet Minh forces lacking experience of pitched battles. By 1952–1953, however, the baby-faced former teacher of history, General Giap, had learned to campaign cautiously. Large amounts of ammunition and weapons had come across the northern borders to strengthen his supply position. In early 1954, he accepted the challenge of a conventional warfare at Dien Bien Phu. By that time, the French forces were thoroughly demoralized, particularly by the public opinion at home, which overwhelmingly pressed for ending the "dirty war." Cabinets fell rapidly until Pierre Mendes-France, who became premier on June 17, 1954, vowed to resign his office if a settlement on Indochina were not reached by July 20, 1954.

The last French commander, Henri Navarre, regarded control of the valley of Dien Bien Phu, close to the Laotian border, strategically important. Besides, a major defeat of Giap's forces there would be crippling to the Viet Minh's military effort. The French general had underestimated the Viet Minh's physical ability to transport large cannon and position them in the surrounding hills, besieging the French troops. In April and early May 1954, the use of nuclear weapons seemed to U.S. Secretary of State John Foster Dulles the only way to save the beleaguered French garrison from total extermination by the Viet Minh. But the United States would act only jointly with Great Britain; the latter firmly refused to go along and thereby open the prospect of a third world war, as the action probably would have brought massive Soviet retaliation. The situation enabled General Giap to register his greatest triumph at Dien Bien Phu on May 7, the eve of the Geneva conference on Indochina.

The Geneva settlement of 1954 temporarily divided Vietnam along the seventeenth parallel into two zones, with the question of reunification to be decided by a Vietnam-wide election in 1956. The Viet Minh accepted the settlement most reluctantly under pressure from its Communist allies, the Soviet Union and China, who were at the time espousing a global policy of peaceful coexistence. China could have had a special reason of its own: historically, its policy was not to encourage political consolidation among its neighboring countries. The Viet Minh urged a division at least along the fourteenth parallel and called for the proposed elections to take place within six months. If negotiations are to some a continuation of war by other means, to the Vietnamese Communists they represented a big power game that had snatched a sure political victory from their hands. The Geneva conference sounded the death-knell of French colonialism in Southeast Asia but without assuring freedom to Vietnam as one nation and without guaranteeing continued peace to an already war-weary land.

18

The Nationalist Movements: Malaya, Cambodia, and Laos

In contrast to Vietnam, Myanmar, and Indonesia, there was no concerted nation-wide opposition to colonial rule in British Malaya or the French protectorates of Cambodia and Laos. In all three areas, the colonial authorities had preserved the traditional monarchy, in fact with greater pomp and security than existed before. Except for a few members of the royal family and the nobility who went abroad, there was no opportunity for higher education. No institutions of higher learning existed in any of the three countries until well after World War II, and there was little national consciousness or awareness of individual rights. The indigenous elite was left to hold the prestigious but powerless positions in the administrative hierarchy, and the key positions were staffed by the colonizers. Furthermore, the Chinese and Indians in Malaya and the Chinese and Vietnamese in Laos and Cambodia were used by the colonial powers in the ancillary services in administration and economy. Thus, even if there was some amount of frustration among the educated elite, it was not enough to foster a nationalist movement until at least the outbreak of World War II.

MALAYA AND SINGAPORE
Prewar Malaya
Although the immense investment in tin and rubber in the Malay states was primarily for the investor's profit, it did not exploit the Malay population as such. The agricultural rights of the indigenous Malays, the "sons of the soil," were protected by law, and the business-oriented Chinese immigrants and their descendants were given plenty of scope to enrich themselves in export-oriented activity. The Indian minority, mostly engaged in rubber plantations, was not as ambitious and rapacious as its counterpart in Myanmar. In fact, the British boasted that

Malaya's pluralist society and its booming colonial economy made it the show-piece of the empire.

Most authors who pictured such a blissful situation in prewar Malaya ignored a segment of the Chinese population, which had been turning to communism. Involved in industries hit by the depression, many Chinese lost their livelihood and became squatters on government land. More than any other overseas Chinese community, the Malay Chinese took sides in the intensifying struggle between Communists and Nationalists in their mother country. Consequently, when the Japanese occupied Malaya, they faced the toughest local opposition anywhere from the Malay Chinese, whom they treated most harshly. Bands of them, notably with a background of suffering during the depression and squatter experience, joined the Communist guerrillas in an anti-Japanese resistance movement called the Malayan People's Anti-Japanese Army. In 1943, the Allies smuggled a special group called Force 136 into the Malay jungles to train and equip the Malay Chinese guerrillas. After the war, British efforts to disarm them were only partly successful, which left a core of several thousand to launch an armed anti-British struggle in 1948.

Birth of UMNO

Shortly after the war, reaction to a new British policy created a strong Malay nationalist movement. In October 1945, a Malay Union was proposed by Harold MacMichael, a British diplomat, involving the surrender by all nine Malay sultans of their sovereignty, thus changing the political status of the Malay states to a colony. A common citizenship for Malays, Chinese, and Indians was created for all those born in any of the Malay states and the Straits Settlements (except Singapore) or who had lived there for at least the previous ten years. The laws no longer needed ratification by the sultans but were to be signed by the governor-general of the Malay Union, which included the nine Malay states, Malacca, and Penang. The British move was interpreted to mean taking power away from the Malays. The massive protest movement, initiated by Onn bin Jafar, a district officer in Johor state, resulted in May 1946 in the establishment of the United Malay National Organization (UMNO), whose main objective was to acquire power. Subsequent British-Malay negotiations led to the abrogation of the Union of Malaya, retrocession of sovereignty to Malay states, and the integration of the states and the Straits Settlements (except Singapore) into a new Federation of Malaya from February 1, 1948, with citizenship rights restricted only to Malays. The short-lived MacMichael plan had served as a catalyst to foster Malay nationalism.

Emergency in Malaya: 1948–1960

By this time, Britain had withdrawn from the Indian subcontinent and Myanmar. There was, therefore, decreasing incentive to hold on to the Malay Peninsula, where British control had partly served the significantly strategic purpose of the defense of the Indian empire. The advent of independence to Malaya was delayed by more than a decade (1948–1960) because of the declared state of emergency. In June 1948, the Malayan Communist party (MCP), consisting overwhelmingly of the ethnic Chinese and under the leadership of Chen Ping, began an insurgency, attacking miners, planters, and officials irrespective of their ethnic origin. The MCP's strategy was to destroy the British economic base, occupy certain areas, and raise an army, which would then lead the masses in a countrywide revolution. The Communists were partly successful in achieving the first stage of the three-part revolutionary plan and were able to rule over some territories for a while. The third stage could not materialize because of an almost complete apathy on the part of the Malay population.

The MCP may have been inspired to launch the revolt by the Communists on mainland China. Indeed, there was the local issue: The new Federation of Malaya had imperiled the legal status of the Chinese community. Although it is correct to say that the bulk of the guerrillas were Chinese, it would not be proper to say that all Malay Chinese favored the revolt. At no time did the guerrillas number more than eight to ten thousand, nor could they claim support of more than 15 to 20 percent of the total population. Their principal support came from the squatters, numbering about a half million Chinese. Yet they succeeded in creating terror among the people and in badly hurting the Malay economy.

The British success in crushing the insurgency, in sharp contrast with the French and later U.S. failures in Vietnam, was owed to several factors. The most important of these was that, unlike in Vietnam, the guerrillas in Malaya were easily distinguishable from the rest of the population. Second, the British quickly recognized the existence of a political problem, namely, the need to associate the Chinese community with any new constitutional or political setup in the country. They encouraged the formation in February 1949 of the Malayan Chinese Association (MCA) as an alternative organization for the Chinese to channel their political aspirations. Under the able leadership of the wealthy industrialist and veteran politician Tan Cheng Lok, the divergent Chinese communities were brought together for the first time. Tan forged collaboration with the UMNO in a common call for *merdeka,* independence for Malaya. Third, the insurgents received a negligible amount of external assistance in the form of arms or advice. Lieutenant-General Harold Briggs, appointed director of emergency operations in March 1950, identified the Chinese squatter communities as the principal sources of recruitment, supply, and information. The "Briggs Plan" was to establish 600 large fenced resettlement areas, or "new villages," for the squatters, with educational and health facilities and security provided through police and home guard units. The new villages served as channels of intelligence for the government; refusal to give information could invite punitive curfews for the entire community. About 10,000 Chinese, whose cooperation was impossible to secure, were deported to China. Briggs thus hoped to provide "complete security within the populated areas in order to instill local authorities with confidence."[1] Last, General Gerald Templer, British high commissioner in Malaya (January 1952–April 1954), ably combined the military effort with socioeconomic programs. Police and intelligence activities were well coordinated. By 1954, the brunt of the insurgency had been broken, although the state of emergency was continued until July 1, 1960. Not all the guerrillas had been eliminated, though; some groups numbering about two thousand were known to be operating in the late 1980s on the Thai-Malay border.

Independence for Malaya and Singapore

All through the emergency period of 1948–1960, the British showed their clear intent of quitting the colony and handing over power to the indigenous people. This was extremely important in securing the support of the Malay population in the task of crushing the insurgency. In 1955, elections were held to both the Malay Federal Assembly and the Singapore Legislative Council. In Malaya, the MCI (Malay, Chinese, Indian) Alliance party won 51 out of 52 seats. In Singapore, a moderate left-wing leader of the Labor Front, David Marshall, won only 10 seats and therefore formed a coalition with the Malay Union Alliance (8 seats) to garner a majority of 18 in a house of 32. In Malaya, the victory of Abdul Rahman as the leader of the legislature was clear-cut. It gave him tremendous political leverage during the negotiations he held with the British for complete independence. The British did not hesitate this time; they agreed to hand over power by August 31, 1957, to the MCI.

In Singapore, David Marshall's government was not as fortunate. The Chinese riots in Singapore, which led to the closure of the city's schools in 1956, gave the British a temporary excuse to procrastinate on the issue of further self-government for the colony. Thereupon, Marshall resigned. His successor, Lim Yew Hock, a highly respected leader of the Chinese community, was able to negotiate with the British government in the following year a new constitution under which Singapore would have internal self-government, while defense and foreign affairs would be controlled by an Internal Security Council with British and Malay Federation representatives sitting on it. In the elections held in 1960, the People's Action Party (PAP) emerged victorious, with the brilliant barrister Lee Kuan Yew forming the government. Complete independence came to Singapore in 1963 but as a part (along with Sarawak and Sabah) of the new Federation of Malaysia. Two years later, when Singapore was removed from the Malaysian Federation, it declared itself an independent state.

CAMBODIA

Free Khmer Movement

The nationalist movements in Cambodia and Laos gained momentum in the last months of World War II. At Japan's urging, on March 11, 1945, King Norodom Sihanouk proclaimed Cambodia's independence; a month later, King Sisavang Vong declared Laos independent. Perhaps because of Sihanouk's pro-French proclivities, the Japanese were not too sure of him. They therefore supported the Free Khmer movement led by Son Ngoc Thanh, who was then one of the two best-known commoners, the other being the celebrated Pali scholar Pach Chhoeun.

Of Khmer-Vietnamese descent, Son Ngoc Thanh was born in South Vietnam and educated in Paris. On his return, he joined the National Library in Phnom Penh. He also founded the first Khmer-language newspaper, *Nagaravatta* (City News), in 1936 and along with Pach Chhoeun took a leading interest in the affairs of the Buddhist Institute of Phnom Penh. By 1942, the institute had become the hotbed of the Cambodian nationalist movement, organizing demonstrations and distributing political literature. The French authorities jailed Pach Chhoeun in the Vietnamese concentration camp of Poulo Condore, but Son Ngoc Thanh managed to escape to Japan with the connivance of Japanese military officials in Cambodia.

When the Japanese took over the direct administration of Cambodia in March 1945, Son Ngoc Thanh returned to organize the Khmer Issarak (Free Khmer) movement of nearly 2,000 armed volunteers and joined with the Viet Minh to oppose the return of the French. Recognizing Son's importance and partly to buy off the movement, King Norodom Sihanouk, who still fitted the image of a Francophile playboy-monarch, appointed him his foreign minister. Two months later, on the eve of Japan's surrender, Son Ngoc Thanh practically staged a coup, compelling the king to appoint him premier. It was a short-lived success for Son. The arrival of the Allied troops in October 1945 sealed his political fate, as returning French General Jacques Philippe Leclerc, with active assistance of the king, arrested Son and sentenced him to twenty years hard labor on the charge of threatening the security of the state. Later, bowing to public opinion, the French commuted his sentence to house arrest. Son withdrew to Thailand for a while and, with the help of the Thai government, established a provisional government of Cambodia in exile. He also built the Free Khmer movement in cooperation with Pach Chhoeun.

Meanwhile, the French attempted to create a facade of self-government for Cambodia. Thus, on January 7, 1946, a modus vivendi declared Cambodia "an autonomous state within the French Union." Although the Khmers had relative independence of action in strictly local affairs, the new arrangements left all the major departments to the French-controlled Indochina federation. Such a state of conditions soon became intolerable not only to the opposition Democrat party but also—happily enough for the Khmers—to their young monarch, Norodom Sihanouk.

Sihanouk's Crusade

It is not easy to pinpoint the time when Norodom Sihanouk underwent a metamorphosis and became a hardworking leader, but over the next two decades he assimilated the mystique of divine kingship, party leadership, and even world statesmanship. On November 8, 1949, France granted Cambodia a larger measure of internal autonomy, though still retaining foreign relations, defense, police, and judiciary matters under its control. Such halfhearted measures failed to satisfy the Khmer nationalist aspirations. In October 1951, Son Ngoc Thanh returned to Phnom Penh to campaign against Cambodia's continuance in the French union. The king tried to repress the dissidents, including Son Ngoc Thanh, who fled the capital in March 1952. Three months later, the king in an unpopular move dismissed the cabinet composed of Democrat party leaders and demanded from the National Assembly autocratic powers to govern the country for three years.

Suddenly, in January 1953, the mercurial Sihanouk startled the world by his "Crusade for Independence." He visited Paris, Washington, and New York and then declared he would remain in exile in Bangkok and later in western Cambodia until his country was granted complete independence, including immediate authority over the armed forces. The crusade was effective. It received sympathy in most places, including the United States. Beginning July 3, 1953, a number of agreements were signed recognizing the de facto independence of Cambodia and consenting to transfer authority over the police, judiciary, and army by November 7. Two days later, the king returned a triumphant, nationalist hero to Phnom Penh; it was his birthday, November 9, 1953, which came to be celebrated thereafter, until Sihanouk's fall in 1970, as Cambodia's Independence Day.

LAOS

Beginnings of the Laotian Independence Movement

As in Cambodia, there was little anti-French sentiment in Laos. On March 9, 1945, when the French government was finally deposed by the Japanese, the latter urged the Laotians to declare their independence. But Prime Minister Savang Vatthana, also the crown prince of Laos, refused to do so, as it would involve the formal abrogation of Laos's status as a protectorate of France. The Japanese therefore turned to Prince Phetsarath, the oldest of the three brothers of the viceregal branch of the royal house, to replace Savang Vatthana as prime minister. When the French senior Resident sought to return to Laos toward the end of the year, Phetsarath made it clear he would not be allowed to resume his powers. He was not supported by his king, Sisavang Vong, who declared that Laos's status as a protectorate was still valid and informed Phetsarath that his titles had been revoked. It was at this point that a challenge to the French and to the king's authority took shape.

The king's action led to the Laotian declaration of independence. The event triggered the formation of the Lao Issarak (Free Lao) movement, which nominated a provisional government to be headed by Phetsarath's brothers, Souvanna Phouma and Souphannouvong (later known as the Red Prince). The king's continued refusal to nullify the protectorate led to the provisional assembly's vote to depose the monarch and sever ties with France. The Lao Issarak included virtually all the Western-educated elite of the country, many of them from the Lao royalty and nobility.

By late 1945, the French had entered the country from the south. They decimated the Lao Issarak units and succeeded in capturing Vientiane, the administrative capital of the country, on March 25, 1946, and the royal capital of Luang Prabang a month later. The king was restored to the throne, and the Lao Issarak leadership was forced to flee into exile in Thailand.

Birth of the Pathet Lao

It is important to bear in mind that the Lao Issarak was not at that point Communist or even Communist-dominated. Phetsarath remained the nominal head of the government in exile, with Souvanna Phouma as deputy prime minister and Souphannouvong in charge of the small Lao Issarak army. From his exile, Souvanna Phouma, who had always advocated a moderate position in politics, attempted to negotiate with the French authorities. But French intransigence divided the ranks of Lao nationalists, and by 1949, the split was complete.

Souphannouvong had established firm contacts with the Viet Minh. In August 1950, he suddenly appeared in North Vietnam and announced the creation of a guerrilla organization called the Pathet Lao (land of the Lao).

Meanwhile, in 1949, France had granted limited autonomy to all the three states of Indochina. The French concessions led directly to the dissolution of the Lao Issarak on October 24, 1949, and the return to Laos of all its leadership, with the exception of Prince Phetsarath. In 1951, Souvanna Phouma became the head of the Laotian government, which was still controlled by the French though to a lessened extent because of their preoccupation with the war in nearby Vietnam. Such constitutional concessions did not, however, satisfy the Pathet Lao, which had come increasingly under the influence of Vietnamese Communists. In 1952, the Laotian Communist party was formed. Its cadres, trained by the Viet Minh, were almost in control of two northeastern provinces, Phong Saly and Sam Neua, at the time of the Geneva conference of 1954.

Laos Becomes Independent

The fates of Laos and Vietnam were intertwined from 1953 onward, and a solution of the more important of the two struggles was expected to apply to the other. Toward the end of the First Indochina War (1946–1954), the Viet Minh forces had entered Laos and used it as a staging area. The last crucial battle was fought close to the Laotian border, at Dien Bien Phu. At Geneva, France's decision to withdraw from Vietnam automatically brought complete independence to Laos. The Geneva agreements did not recognize the Pathet Lao's territorial claims, but did acknowledge its special position in the two northern provinces. The Pathet Lao forces were required to regroup in those two provinces, which were to be integrated into the rest of the kingdom. What was parenthetically expected was an internal settlement by which the Pathet Lao would be dissolved and its members allowed to participate in the government.

Part Three Review

Colonial Southeast Asia did not accept alien rule passively. There were resistance movements in Myanmar and Vietnam and virulent nationalist movements in Myanmar, Vietnam, and Indonesia. The Philippines was a special case in being the oldest colony and pioneer in the nationalist movements in Asia. The movement there began to mature even before countries like Myanmar and Vietnam had passed fully under the colonial orbit. It proclaimed itself a republic by 1897, but in accepting U.S. assistance in order to drive out the Spaniards, it got cheated in the process. Its resistance to establishment of U.S. rule was incomparably more virulent than its later movement for independence from the United States because of the latter's willingness to concede reforms leading to self-government.

The one exception to this process was, indeed, Thailand, which had retained its independent status, thanks to the enlightened, modernizing policies of Kings Mongkut and Chulalongkorn. Chulalongkorn's period of rule almost coincided with the Meiji era in Japan, another Asian country that managed to avoid foreign domination. Thailand's geographical location (not lying on the trade route between China and Southeast Asia), the Anglo-French desire to avoid a common imperial frontier in Southeast Asia, and the Thai ability to play the two European powers against each other were important contributing factors.

Nationalism in Myanmar, Vietnam, and Indonesia was partly a reaction to colonial policies of discrimination and political and economic exploitation but also a result of Western education. It was significantly influenced by events in neighboring countries—Japan's victory over Russia, Sun Yat-sen's revolution in China, and Gandhi-Nehru leadership of the Indian nationalist struggle against the mighty British empire. The Bolshevik Revolution and the establishment of Communist parties under Comintern direction provided, at first, a rival but later in some cases a complementary force to nationalist groups. In some countries, notably Cambodia, Laos, Malaya, and Singapore, anti-imperialist reaction was very slow in manifesting itself, not surfacing until almost after World War II. Cambodia and Laos experienced benign neglect and lack of economic exploitation under the French, whereas Malaya and Singapore had been, with justification, paraded by the British as a showcase of benevolent foreign rule.

The two world wars fostered the development of nationalism in a variety of ways. Japan's occupation of Southeast Asia served as a catalyst. The shroud of Western supremacy and invincibility had been irretrievably shattered. Under Japanese aegis, nationalist governments were set up in Myanmar, Indonesia, and the Philippines. In the interregnum between Japanese withdrawal from Southeast Asia and the reimposition of Western colonial authority, valuable time and opportunity became available to the nationalists (including Communists) to declare republics in Vietnam and Indonesia.

Although the Philippines was the first to gain independence in 1946, the event that precipitated momentum for decolonization and freedom in Asia and Africa was the British decision to transfer power on the Indian subcontinent to India and Pakistan in August 1947. Myanmar became independent in the following year, and the decision to withdraw from Malaya was delayed largely because of the Communist insurgency there. The Dutch intransigence was met with stiff indigenous opposition of the fledgling republic and international diplomatic pressures, notably from India and the United States, resulting in 1949 in formal transfer of power to the Indonesian republic.

French reluctance to release its hold over its colonies ignited the French-Indochina War in 1946. The predominant Communist leadership of the Viet Minh colored the complexion of the movement and made it a part of the expanding Cold War between the superpowers, which rallied their support after 1949 indirectly to the two sides. The emergence of the People's Republic of China in the same year establishing a common Communist frontier enabled direct assistance to flow to the Viet Minh, whose successes frustrated a succession of French generals in Vietnam. The final showdown came in May 1954 at the battle of Dien Bien Phu, where the French defeat on the eve of the Geneva conference conclusively sealed the fate of colonial rule in French Indochina. The Geneva agreements brought independence to Cambodia, Laos, and Vietnam, but temporarily partitioned the latter, ushering in an uneasy peace that was to prove a portent of one of the most gruesome, tragic wars in modern history.

Thus, by the mid-1950s, almost all of the countries of Southeast Asia had benefited from the "winds of change," having won freedom or been promised it. The colonial interlude had ended, and the era of independence had dawned, bringing in its wake a different set of problems—the subject of Part Four.

Part Four

Fruits of Freedom

This fourth and final section describes how the Southeast Asian countries regard themselves not only as sovereign states but also as members of the United Nations and other world bodies, such as the World Health Organization (WHO), the World Bank (WB), the International Monetary Fund (IMF), and, in many cases, the World Trade Organization (WTO). Most of them also belong to regional organizations such as the Association of Southeast Asian Nations (ASEAN) and the Asian Development Bank (ADB). Membership in such multinational organizations is a realization for individual states that they belong to a larger entity—that they share a commonality on economic, communications, and defense issues as well as on health and environmental concerns. For example, tsunamis and cyclones do not recognize political borders. Nor can the spread of epidemics such as the avian influenza be contained without regional, multinational measures. Noteworthy of this phenomenon is the development of ASEAN, which was born in 1967 with only five pro-Western states—Malaysia, Singapore, Philippines, Thailand, and Indonesia. ASEAN grew by 2007 to include the remaining five states of Southeast Asia regardless of their political inclination.

RETREAT OF COLONIAL POWERS

The process of decolonization and attainment of independence spread over several decades. The first of the former colonies to gain independence was the Philippines, which under the inspiring leadership of José Rizal proclaimed its nationalism. The Filipinos overthrew the Spanish regime and declared themselves a republic in 1897 when the United Sates intervened on the pretext of helping the Filipinos against Spain. Instead, the United States appropriated the country as a U.S. colony but promised the Filipinos they would be fully independent ten years after passage of the Tydings-McDuffie Act in 1934. Fulfillment of this promise was delayed until 1946, however, by the exigencies of World War II.

Elsewhere in Southeast Asia, the British decision to pull out of the Indian subcontinent in 1947 brought Burma (now Myanmar) independence in the following year. The Dutch were forced out of Indonesia in 1949, but the withdrawal of British power in Malaya and Singapore was delayed by over a decade because of a

Communist-led insurgency in Malaya. The French withdrew from its colonies of Vietnam, Laos, and Cambodia in 1954 after being defeated in the First Indochina War and as a result of the Geneva agreements on Indochina. These divided Vietnam along the seventeenth parallel, with the North being governed by Communists and the South by a U.S.-backed anti-Communist government. Vietnam became part of the global Cold War between communism and anticommunism, a political stalemate that led eventually to terrible, prolonged war between poorly clad and equipped Vietnamese guerrillas and the highly militarized United States. The superpower's defeat and withdrawal from Vietnam was followed by the unification of Vietnam and its emergence as a single state under the control of the country's Communist party. Finally, the Portuguese withdrawal from its small colony of East Timor was capitalized on by the Jakarta government, which occupied and "integrated" it into Indonesia in 1976. A fierce struggle and United Nations assistance finally brought independence to East Timor in 2002. With that, the process of decolonization was completed in Southeast Asia.

Freedom from colonial rule has not brought the same level of freedom to all people. Withdrawal of foreign authority did not bring democratic rule everywhere. The military has been dominant in Indonesia, Thailand, and Myanmar for varying periods of time, holding unbridled power in Myanmar since 1962. The Communist parties of Laos and Vietnam have dominated the governments there without allowing other groups to run for political positions. Cambodians suffered horrifying experiences during 1975 and 1977 when the Communist government under the Khmer Rouge unleashed a genocide in which an estimated two million people lost their lives. Singapore has been ruled by the same party since its inception as a separate state in 1965. Indonesia, the most populous country of Southeast Asia, was under authoritarian rule first under its charismatic nationalist hero, Sukarno, from 1949 to 1965, who then was replaced by General Suharto until his ouster in 1999. The Philippines endured the dictatorship of Ferdinand Marcos for two decades until the People's Power Revolution terminated it in 1986.

ETHNIC MINORITIES

The issue of ethnic minorities became significant in almost every state in Southeast Asia and assumed increasing importance after withdrawal of the colonial powers and efforts by different communities to assert themselves in the political and economic spheres. Some of the minorities demanded special rights, some autonomy, and some complete independence. Thus, several minorities in Myanmar, notably the Karens, Shans, and Mons, carried on violent movements against the government of the "Union of Burma." Muslims in southern Thailand demanded autonomy, if not independence, as did the Muslim minority in the southern Philippines and the Sulu Archipelago. Acheh in western Sumatra engaged in armed rebellion against the Indonesian government demanding independence but, after being battered by the 2004 tsunami, settled for autonomy. Similar but less violent movements affected relations between Maluku, Papua, and the central government, but these groups also settled for autonomy a half decade into the twenty-first century. The separation of Singapore from Malaysia and its emergence as a separate state was based on the Malaysian leader Tunku Abdul Rahman's concern that in a Malaysia-Singapore combined state, the high numbers of Chinese might upset the balance against the Malays and consequently their political aspirations. Even after the separation of Singapore, Malaysia had to maintain a balance among the three principal communities: Malays, Chinese, and Indians. The vicious racial riots of 1969 underlined the crucial ethnic balance, and the main ruling party, the UMNO, scrupulously sought the cooperation of the Malayan Chinese Association (MCA) and the Malayan Indian Congress (MIC).

There are two minorities in some countries of Southeast Asia that came from outside the region, principally during the colonial period. These were the Indians and the overseas Chinese. The Indians were brought by the British to Myanmar, Malaysia, and Singapore, and the French brought Indians largely from their tiny Indian colonies to Vietnam. Of the overseas Chinese, 80 percent live in Southeast Asia, principally in Indonesia (7.2 million), Thailand (5.8 million), Malaysia (5.2 million), Singapore (2 million), Myanmar (1.5 million), Philippines, and Vietnam (800,000 each).

The colonial powers showed a marked preference for Indians and Chinese, who were, contrary to foreigners' opinion of them in their home countries of India and China, regarded as industrious, dependable, and particularly adept at managing money. During the colonial period, the overseas Chinese became the envy especially of the indigenous majorities in Malaysia, Vietnam, and Indonesia. Indeed, there was tremendous disparity in financial and professional standing between the indigenous people and the Chinese minority that led, after independence, to discriminatory policies against the Chinese, notably in Malaysia, Indonesia, and Vietnam. The Chinese minority in almost all countries of Southeast Asia owned businesses, banks, insurance companies, and freight lines, to mention only a few sectors. They were ahead of the indigenous people in gaining admission to institutions of higher learning and in becoming established in professions.

In clearly anti-Chinese measures, the postindependence Malaysian governments favored the *Bumiputras,* the "sons of the soil," by granting them business licenses, giving them liberal bank loans, and extending them preference in many other ways. When the military-led Suharto government went after the PKI (Communist party of Indonesia) for its leadership role in the 1965 rebellion, killing six generals, the Chinese were made the scapegoat, on the ground that the PKI membership included a large number of Chinese. When the South Vietnamese government launched an anticorruption drive, it was basically against the Chinese business community in Saigon's twin city, Cholon. The hatred against the Chinese surfaced soon after the Vietnamese Communists established their authority over all of Vietnam and no longer needed Chinese military assistance. The Chinese government sent ships for those Vietnamese Chinese who wanted to migrate to China, and larger numbers of Chinese left as "boat people," choosing the risks of boat journeys in pirate-infested seas over harsh discriminatory treatment at the hands of the Vietnamese police and army.

19

Independent
Philippines

POSTWAR DEVELOPMENTS TO 1965

The New Constitution

For a quarter century after attaining complete independence on July 4, 1946, the Philippines functioned as a working democracy, with elections held on a regular basis. Two major parties, the Liberals and the Nationalists, dominated the political scene. The fact that there were six presidents drawn from the two rival parties and that none of them was reelected showed that the electoral process had been given a reasonably fair trial. The political parties were dominated by a small oligarchy, largely drawn from the landholding class; this group controlled appointments, distributed the spoils of office among relatives and friends, and exploited the unlimited opportunities for corruption and self-gratification through control of licenses, leases, and foreign exchange permits. Political opportunism, including wholesale defection of large numbers of elected representatives from one party to another, was not uncommon and was even deemed respectable. Despite its Western trappings, Filipino democracy was truly indigenous, understood and enjoyed by its people, until Ferdinand Marcos clamped down on individual freedoms in the 1972–1973 period.

Although the inspiration for the constitution of the Philippines was the U.S. version, it provided for a unitary government. Power was centralized in the office of the president, elected quadrennially by direct suffrage. The constitution provided for separation of powers among the executive, legislative, and judiciary branches. The legislature had two houses: a Senate with 24 members, one-third elected every two years for a period of six years, and a House of Representatives, the lower chamber with a maximum of 120 members, elected every four years. A system of courts headed by the Supreme Court reasserted its four-decade-old tradition of independence and integrity. A Bill of Rights gave Filipino citizens full freedom of the press, association, religious pursuit, and movement. The country's government held sovereignty and jurisdiction over all the islands except the military and naval bases granted to the United States.

The Huk Rebellion

The first major challenge to the authority of the new government came from the Hukbalahap rebellion. The Japanese occupation of the Philippines (1942–1945) proved a catalyst for the formation of the Hukbalahap. The discontent among farmers caused by exactions of food grains by Japanese troops and by inflation was exploited by the Communists, who organized the Hukong Bayan Laban Sa Hapon (People's Anti-Japanese Army) movement, or the Hukbalahap, in 1942. The group was helped in the countryside by some of the Filipino troops who had refused to surrender to Japan. The leader of the movement was Luis Taruc; its base of operations was central Luzon. In fact, the Huks killed fewer Japanese than they did Filipino landlords, which has made some critics hold that their anti-Japanese activities were little more than a cover for their Communist activity.

The motivation for joining the Huks ran from the noble to the base.[1] A number of guerrilla peasants used the movement to settle old grudges and feuds, not only against the landlords but generally against all oppressive elements in the society. Membership in the movement included party cadres, students, and unemployed youth; many professional bandits used the opportunity to plunder the countryside in the name of the movement. During World War II, the Huks controlled the province of Luzon, seizing large estates, killing their owners, and redistributing the land to the people. They instigated agricultural reform and succeeded in undermining the prewar social structure of the community to a certain extent. When the war ended and the Japanese surrendered, the movement did not disband.

Roxas and Quirino

It was this peculiar situation that largely accounted for U.S. support of Manuel Roxas in the presidential elections of April 1946. Roxas was a collaborator, a cabinet minister in the Japanese-sponsored Laurel government. Even so, his anti-Communist credentials endeared him to the Filipino landlord class, the church, the civil service, and importantly, to the U.S. army brass, business interests, and State Department. The Liberal party won the election. The Roxas government nullified the election of six Democratic Alliance candidates from central Luzon, including the Huk leader, Taruc, and charged them with fraud and terrorism during the elections. The Roxas regime received considerable moral and material support from the United States, including more than a half billion dollars for war-damage claims and general rehabilitation. Instead of rehabilitating the war-affected people, however, Filipino officials rehabilitated their own pocketbooks. Since the Huks were denied any peaceful means of political participation, they returned to the mountains and resumed the guerrilla movement. The Huks were able to muster greater support from the peasants and others who, according to William Pomeroy, an ex-GI who stayed in the Philippines after the war and joined the Huks, were largely non-Communist.[2] They were revolting against genuine socioeconomic problems. For example, the rice cultivators were still paying more than one-half of their crop to the absentee landlords despite the passage of the Rice Share Tenancy Act that guaranteed the cultivators 70 percent of the crop. Implementation of the laws was lacking, and those frustrated with the governmental machinery were resorting to violence under the leadership of the Huks.

Both Manuel Roxas, who died in 1948, and his successor in office, Elpidio Quirino (1949–1953), introduced land reform and new plans for the country's industrialization in order to improve the common people's economic conditions. The Quirino government received a great boost for its economic plans in November 1950, when the United States granted a loan of a quarter billion dollars over a five-year period. No benefits, however, accrued to the average person. Instead, the government's land reform, tax reform, and minimum-wage laws were exploited by the very elements who were backing the government—big landlords and Filipino and U.S. entrepreneurs. Frustration mounted and the Huks benefited. The Huks changed their name to Hukong Mapagpalaya Ng Bayan (People's Army of Liberation), now aimed at the overthrow of the government. Its immediate targets were the U.S. advisers who had been brought in by Quirino to help in the working of almost all departments of the government. The Huks pointed to these advisers as evidence of the continuation of U.S. imperialism.

The Magsaysay Revolution

The anti-Huk campaign succeeded dramatically in the early 1950s with the appointment of a former guerrilla captain, trucking operator, and congressman, Ramon Magsaysay, as the country's new defense minister. In his drive, dubbed by his admirers "the Magsaysay Revolution," he used methods that would later serve as a model for counterinsurgency warfare elsewhere. Magsaysay rightly perceived that the majority of the Huk guerrillas were not Communists; their success was largely attributable to the public's loss of confidence in or indifference toward the government. Accordingly, he organized a campaign on two fronts: He gave the army a dynamic leadership in destroying Huk pockets; at the same time, he initiated imaginative plans for winning over many of the active Huk guerrillas, who he realized had been driven to rebellion by the harsh realities of economic misery. Magsaysay promised social welfare legislation, expeditious and better justice, and education and general services at the village level. Any Huk surrendering to the government was offered amnesty, twenty-five acres of land, and a house. Magsaysay's policy of identification with the common people and his combination of force and friendship in dealing with the Huks destroyed the movement by 1951, reducing it to a few hard-core remnants in the mountains of central Luzon.

Magsaysay endeared himself to the people by carrying his campaign to the village level, offering radical land reform and laws to remove social ills. True to his campaign promise, he had the Agriculture Tenancy Act passed, which granted greater security to tenant-farmers and offered them more land, loans at low rates, and technical advice on better production and distribution of agricultural products. He appointed an assistant for community development and created an agrarian court, on the pattern of courts of industrial relations, for speedy justice for peasants. Magsaysay's open approach to government won him immense popularity as he established a Complaints and Action Committee to investigate the grievances of average citizens. An ambitious economic program was proposed to industrialize the country, to create jobs, and to keep prices within bounds. Magsaysay's frequent forays into the rural areas and his personal attention to people in the *barrios* made him the most-loved government leader in Filipino history. Unfortunately for the country, this unique public figure, who had brought peace by defeating and winning over the Huks and who had set a new tone of morality and efficiency in government, thereby raising the people's aspirations for a brighter future, died in a plane crash against a mountain near Cebu in March 1957. Thereafter, under both Carlos Garcia (1957–1960) and Diosdado Macapagal (1961–1965), politics assumed primacy, and the programs for the peasants and the poor initiated by the government went unimplemented.

THE MARCOS REGIME

The Early Years

Ferdinand Marcos, "the politician who had never suffered an election defeat," was elected president in 1965; he later became the only president to be reelected. Young and handsome, Marcos's personal appeal was enhanced by his beautiful wife, Imelda, daughter of the late Speaker of the House, Daniel Romualdez of Visayan. President of the Liberal Senate during Macapagal's administration, Marcos defected to the Nationalist party to be elected president in 1965 on a platform of land reform and economic development. His first administration was marked by some improvement in the economy helped by the use of miracle rice, (IR-8), developed by the International Rice Institute of Luzon in 1967–1968. The country suddenly became an exporter of rice, though on a modest scale. The new strain of rice, however, required sophisticated equipment and heavy economic inputs far beyond the small farmer's means, leaving this new field of prosperity to larger landowners. Prices soared by more than 50 percent amid reports of widespread corruption and rumors of vast accumulation of wealth by the Marcos family. In 1971, the Senate elections were marred by two hundred deaths and several hundred casualties, among them a few candidates. The election results were a rude shock to Marcos, whose opponents won six of the eight Senate seats; his vice president had already deserted him to join the opposition Liberal party. A year later, in July 1972, the report of the constitutional convention, which had been meeting for a year, proposed a shift to a parliamentary system of government. Whatever the system of government, Marcos perceived a major threat to himself in the popular, dynamic, and brilliant Senator Benigno Aquino. Son of a former senator, young Aquino knew politics well. In his early twenties, he had been the mayor of his town and thereafter the governor of Tarlac. At thirty-five he became a senator, the minimum age under the constitution for that office. If the presidential system were to continue, he was most likely to succeed Marcos, who would be disqualified from running for office after his two terms. As popular feelings were running high for Aquino, Marcos acted swiftly to freeze the political process.

Martial Law and Consolidation of Autocracy

On September 23, 1972, Marcos proclaimed martial law. He jailed thousands of his political opponents, including Benigno Aquino, shut down newspapers, and established governmental control over radio and television. Within months, he dismissed an estimated 150,000 civil servants and judges to "reform" the government. All individual freedoms were suppressed; strikes were banned. Significantly, Marcos had consulted the armed forces in all his acts, thus giving the military a political role for the first time in Filipino history.

After 1972, the government progressively became the preserve of the Marcos family, their relatives, friends, and sycophants. Imelda was appointed governor of Manila in 1975. Her unofficial position as a cabinet member was regularized in June 1978 with her appointment to head the Ministry of Ecology and Human Settlements. She represented her husband at numerous international meetings and conducted delicate negotiations, for example, at the Islamic Conference at Tripoli concerning the Moro revolt and diplomatic and trade discussions with Beijing. Their daughter, Imee, became a leader of the officially sponsored Youth Movement (Kabataang Barangay), while their son, Ferdinand Jr., was appointed presidential assistant in early 1979.

Meanwhile, the constitutional convention had been ordered to write a new "basic law" for the "New Society." Though the new constitution of 1973 provided for a parliamentary system of government, Marcos did not hold elections. Instead, he chose to rule through a series of referenda. These extended his term of office, allowing him concurrently to hold the office of president and prime minister and to create a National Assembly (Batasang Pambansa). Neither he nor his cabinet could be dismissed by the Assembly, nor could his decrees be invalidated by it. On the other hand, the term of the Assembly was not specified, leaving it entirely at the mercy of Marcos.

The elections to the National Assembly in April 1978 were fought between Lakas Ng Bayan, or LABAN, a coalition of opposition parties, and the New Society Movement, or Kilusang Bagong Lipunan (KBL), consisting primarily of officials and formed by Marcos himself. As could be expected, widespread fraudulent practices ensured that the election results would favor Marcos. Immediately after the elections, Marcos arrested hundreds of his opponents, proving that the elections were held only to burnish his international image.

The opposition to Marcos's rule was not limited to nonviolent movements. The most potent uprisings were led by the Communists and the Moros. The Communist New People's Army (NPA) soon became several thousand strong. In late 1977, the government captured its top leader, Jose Maria Sison. In 1978, it claimed to have killed 6 and captured 15 of the 26 members of the party politburo. The Moro National Liberation Movement spread in late 1978 from southern Mindanao to the Palawan Islands. It had the unofficial backing of the Malaysian government of Sabah and, for a while, of Libya. The Philippine government had vainly tried to enlist the assistance of a number of Muslim countries—Saudi Arabia, Indonesia, Algeria, and Egypt—to mediate between the government and the Moro National Liberation Front (MNLF). Finally, in 1976, a dramatic initiative on the part of Imelda Marcos led to her five-hour meeting and discussion of the Moro question with Libya's Muammar Gadaffi in his tent at the Organization of Islamic Conference (OIC) meeting held at Tripoli. The Tripoli Agreement signed between the Philippine government and the MNLF promised autonomy to thirteen provinces in the southern Philippines, including Mindanao, Palawan, Basilan, Sulu, and Tawi-Tawi, following a "constitutional process." However, a plebiscite held by the Marcos government that was not accepted by the MNLF showed only four provinces voting in favor of the Autonomous Region in Muslim Mindanao. The MNLF thereupon unilaterally invalidated the Tripoli Agreement and resumed its antigovernment revolt. By 1980, the movement had cost about 50,000 lives and created nearly a half million refugees.

For the next eight years until his downfall, Marcos ruled dictatorially through referenda and constitutional amendments. In April 1981, Marcos secured overwhelming approval for a constitutional amendment that would allow him a renewable six-year term of office. The presidential elections would be direct instead of by the members of the National Assembly. On the basis of the new amendment, he was elected president in June with 88 percent of the vote, made possible by massive fraud and because of the boycott of elections by the United Nationalist Democratic Organization (UNIDO). Benigno Aquino, who had spent eight years in prison and was "on parole" in the United States for medical treatment since May 1980, was ineligible to run for the presidency because he was two years below the new constitutional age requirement of 50. After the elections, Marcos named Finance Minister Cesar E. A. Virata as prime minister. He also appointed his own cousin, Fabian C. Ver, as chief of staff of the armed forces. An executive committee of the cabinet was created to assist the president in routine governmental affairs. It would succeed the president collectively in case of his death, disability, or resignation. In July of the following year, Imelda Marcos was nominated a member of the executive committee and daughter Imee appointed an "observer member." For a while, Marcos and his cronies appeared well set for a full term of six years.

The lifting of martial law in January 1981 witnessed heightened opposition activity. UNIDO, a "grand coalition" of twelve opposition groups, was put together under Salvador Laurel (son of a former president) as president and the exiled Benigno Aquino as one of the vice presidents. In May 1982, UNIDO prepared a unity charter with a five-point program: eliminating dictatorship and restoring the people's sovereignty; establishing human rights and social justice; emphasizing economic development and social reconstruction; eradicating graft and corruption; and maintaining friendly relations with all countries. The opposition's effort was to impress the people that its goal was not a negative one of overthrowing Marcos but a positive one of restoration of democracy and an active program for the people's amelioration.

Meanwhile, the Marcos administration succeeded in antagonizing several segments of the public, notably the press, labor, and above all, the church. The more his policies became reprehensible to these groups, the more UNIDO's strength grew. In early 1982, the government created a special force of 1,000 troops to patrol Manila. The government intelligence agencies had learned that a nationwide strike and a large number of bombings and political assassinations were planned by the labor unions. In a week's time, the special police force had killed 41 persons in downtown Manila and arrested labor leaders.

Despite the lifting of martial law, the press had remained subject to limitations because of several existing laws. As Marcos became increasingly sensitive to criticism, he came down heavily on the press. Thus, the editor of *Panorama,* the Sunday supplement to the largest newspaper, *Bulletin Today,* was pressured to resign because he commented on Marcos's June 1981 election as being "marked by suspicions of connivance, corruption and dishonest counting." In the following months, a number of journalists who had exposed governmental corruption were shot dead by unknown gunmen. In December 1982, two leading opposition papers, *WE Forum* and *Malaya,* were closed, as was the weekly *Philippine Times* in September 1983. Their editors were arrested and charged with subversion and alleged involvement in a conspiracy against the government through political propaganda. Such atrocious measures rallied the 250-strong Philippine National Press Club unanimously to condemn the government's actions.

Marcos and the Church

The lifting of martial law in January 1981 was timed for the visit of Pope John Paul to the Philippines in February. The pope refrained from any comment on the domestic conditions, but made a strong plea for the safeguarding of human rights, which was a reference to the detention of hundreds of persons without trial and to their torture in prisons. In June 1981, Cardinal Jaime Sin openly charged the government with mounting a deliberately orchestrated campaign to throttle the freedom of the church to speak up on matters of Catholic morality. The government had been alleging for quite some time that some priests and nuns had joined the Communist NPA. Cardinal Sin conceded the point, but explained that some priests who had become Marxists did so after listening continuously to "the despair of the people."

In mid-1982, the military raided a number of church institutions at the instructions of the government. All of them were charged with having links to Communist organizations. The action brought vehement protests from both Protestant and Catholic Church officials. On July 20, 1982, Cardinal Sin asserted that Marcos had lost the respect of the people because he had failed in his sixteen years of rule to solve the nation's problems. The cardinal urged the president to resign in favor of the new leadership, meaning UNIDO, to stem the advance of communism. At Sin's suggestion, a direct dialogue between the church and the military was held in January 1983. Dissatisfied with the outcome, all the bishops assembled—both pro-Marcos and anti-Marcos—unanimously drafted a pastoral letter, to be read in churches on the first day of Lent in February 1983, criticizing the government and the military and expressing the church's misgivings about curtailment of freedom of expression and attempts to discredit the church. Sin sent a message to all Catholic bishops in the United States to exert their influence to stop arms supplies to the Philippines because they helped an authoritarian state "based on the shifting sands of personal ambition and brute power." With that, the church, led by the blunt, sharp-tongued, influential prelate, had at last declared war on the Marcos administration.

THREATS TO MARCOS'S REGIME

Benigno Aquino's Assassination

On August 21, 1983, the civilized world was shocked to learn that Benigno Aquino was shot to death at Manila airport as he was stepping down from a Taiwanese airliner. While two Japanese journalists on board the plane witnessed soldiers fire at Aquino's head, the Philippines government identified Ronaldo Galman y Dawang, a Communist, as the assassin. He was killed instantly by three of the fifteen soldiers sent to "escort" Aquino.

The assassination shook the nation as two million people filed past the dead leader's body. It galvanized the opposition parties, the church, and the general public as never before. Aquino's LABAN announced plans to launch a civil disobedience campaign along Gandhian lines. The tragedy provoked a national and international reaction of outrage on a massive scale. Protest demonstrations became more frequent, with demands from large segments of the public for Marcos's resignation. The commission appointed by him to investigate the murder resigned on September 30, 1983, because of lack of official cooperation, and another committee was appointed under a former appeals court judge, Corazon Juliano Agrava.

Despite the partial boycott and government efforts to rig the elections, the opposition improved its position in the National Assembly elections in May 1984 substantially, from 16 to 61 seats. Among the defeated were 4 cabinet ministers and 16 out of the 21 KBL candidates in Manila, a dramatic setback for Imelda Marcos as the governor of Manila. The public had, in a sense, also demonstrated its preference for UNIDO's nonviolent approach over the leftist opposition's recourse to violence.

The Agrava commission investigating the Aquino assassination unanimously repudiated any Communist involvement in the slaying, instead holding by a 4–1 vote that 25 military men and 1 civilian, including Chief of Staff General Fabian Ver, were responsible for the murder. Under tremendous pressure, Marcos agreed to suspend Ver and have charges filed against the 26. The trial dragged on for seven months, but it was clear by August 1985 that all 26 would be acquitted by the panel of three judges, all Marcos appointees. The verdict was expected, yet it shocked the nation as a mockery of justice further compounded by Marcos's reinstatement of Ver as chief of staff.

Meanwhile, the economy was in ruins. Marcos's gross mismanagement of it was marked by large-scale corruption, profligate spending on hotels, monuments, and palaces, and siphoning off of government funds by the Marcos family into bank accounts overseas. The budget deficits mounted during the Marcos regime from 16.4 million pesos in 1965 to 7.946 billion pesos in 1985. They were financed with foreign loans that soared from $600 million in 1965 to $25.6 billion in 1985. After the Aquino assassination, the foreign exchange situation deteriorated rapidly because of the massive flight of capital out of the country due to the critical political situation. The inflation was, in some years, as high as 50 percent, and the peso had to be devalued three times in four years. The country's credibility to meet its international financial obligations became questionable. The government manipulated the figures of foreign exchange reserves in order to secure an

International Monetary Fund (IMF) loan, meanwhile seeking and getting a postponement of interest payments three times, quarter by quarter.

The Communists and the Moro Revolts

Politically, the situation worsened also because of the progress made by the NPA. In January 1985, Defense Minister Juan Ponce Enrile revealed that the NPA had been growing annually at the rate of 23 percent since 1981 and in the province of Negros by 37 percent. Official reports placed NPA strength at 20,000, possibly an underestimate, with substantial numbers of supporters and sympathizers among the local population in the countryside. The NPA had already set up its own government in parts of Mindanao and Negros. In 1985, it demonstrated its daring by successfully stripping two armories in Isabela and Negros Occidental. The Communists also showed their political clout in the urban areas by organizing major protests against the Bataan nuclear plant and a major strike and huge rallies on May 1, the Labor Day holiday. Demonstrations held to support the national strikes provoked police shootings in a number of places throughout the country, and the funerals of the victims of the shootings provided occasions for even larger sympathy demonstrations. All these were visual manifestations of the growing strength of the Communists among urban white-collar workers, intellectuals, and students.

Also in mid-1985, the Moros revived their struggle, taking advantage of the general turbulent situation elsewhere in the country. The conflict had abated since 1980 because of the government's increased allotment for development in Mindanao and the general amnesty granted to those guerrillas who surrendered voluntarily. Peace talks had been tried in Indonesia between the government representatives and the MNLF but had failed because of the lack of cooperation of Nur Misuari, chairman of the MNLF, who was in the Middle East in self-imposed exile. During his visit to Saudi Arabia in 1982, Marcos had sought Saudi cooperation in persuading Misuari to drop his demand for a separate state, offering to hold elections in the southern provinces for representation in the National Assembly and to concede a certain amount of autonomy. The revival of the Moro movement did not pose as much of a threat to the government as did the NPA because of serious splits among the MNLF leadership. While the extremists under Nur Misuari continued to demand complete secession, the faction called the Moro Islamic Liberation Front, led by the fundamentalist Hassim Salamat, was willing to settle for autonomy. There were reports in mid-1985 of a possible or projected collaboration between the MNLF and the NPA, discounted by some as being impossible because of the deeply religious nature of the Muslim cause and the disparity in objectives.

Reports of the Communist gains, the acquittal of Fabian Ver, and the extensive holdings of the Marcos family, including real estate in the United States, brought a reversal in U.S. policy toward the situation in the Philippines. President Reagan, who had supported Marcos solidly as an ally, now stated that it was a case of either Marcos or the Communists. The need for immediate political, economic, and military reforms was stressed. Perhaps it was too late to expect changes under Marcos. Rumors of a U.S.-supported coup against Marcos were in the air, although they were officially denied as such by the U.S. ambassador to the Philippines, Stephen Bosworth. Because he needed to prove his credentials, Marcos finally ordered presidential elections to be held in February 1986, a year before they were due.

The EDSA Revolution—The People's Power

The historic presidential elections of February 1986 were fought between Ferdinand Marcos and Corazon Aquino, a grieving housewife who had been catapulted into the political maelstrom by the events following her husband's assassination. After some initial wrangling, UNIDO's president, Salvador Laurel, withdrew his bid for the presidency, agreeing instead to be the running mate of Corazon Aquino, who had by then emerged as the national symbol of opposition to the authoritarian excesses of Ferdinand Marcos. It was like a gigantic contest between the forces of good and evil, dictatorship and democracy, oligarchy and people's power. Aquino's candidacy reflected the new Filipino resurgence unwilling to put up any longer with a tyrannical rule.

The elections were widely criticized for chicanery, deception, and fraud on a large scale. The National Movement for Free Elections (NAMFREL) charged that the mail carriers and water-meter readers had supplied the government with addresses of households that displayed pro-Aquino stickers and that such homes were rigorously removed from the registration rolls. It also alleged that at least 3.3 million Filipinos had been prevented from voting. NAMFREL's vote count disagreed with the official count; NAMFREL declared Corazon Aquino to be far ahead of Marcos. The Roman Catholic Bishops Conference of the Philippines declared that the polls were "unparalleled in the fraudulence of their conduct." The National Assembly's declaration on February 16 that Marcos had won the election compounded the fraud, provoking public protest that Marcos had stolen the election. Corazon Aquino condemned the announcement as "a conspiracy to cheat the people," proclaimed herself president of the Philippines, and announced a nonviolent, active resistance campaign "if the goliath refuses to yield." She met with ambassadors from fourteen European nations and Japan and urged their governments not to recognize the Marcos regime.

The international reaction was almost unanimously in favor of Aquino. The European Parliament, in an unprecedented action, condemned the election as a massive fraud. The co-chairman of the U.S. Senate delegation sent to observe the election, Republican Senator Richard Lugar, blandly declared that it was "fatally flawed." President Reagan, who had earlier supported Marcos, changed his stance completely, declaring on February 15 that "wide-spread fraud and violence" had been "perpetrated largely by the ruling party" and that the credibility of the elections was in question. To mollify the United States, Marcos announced the retirement of the controversial Fabian Ver and his replacement by General Fidel Ramos as acting chief of staff. On February 19, the U.S. Senate by an 85–9 vote resolved that the Philippines election "could not be considered a fair reflection of the will" of the people.

The real turning point in the stalemate came on February 22, when Defense Minister Juan Enrile and acting Chief of Staff Fidel Ramos quit their posts to protest the rigged election. They took over the Defense Ministry headquarters at Camp Aguinaldo and pledged support to Aquino. Their call for Marcos to resign was supported by Cardinal Jaime Sin on a private radio station asking people to pour into the streets. Within twenty-four hours, over a million Filipinos formed a human barrier between Camp Aguinaldo and Camp Crame, the headquarters of Ramos's police constabulary, physically pushing back the loyalist troops and their equipment, including tanks. What followed in the next forty-eight hours was a drama without parallel in the history of the downfall of dictators and assertion of the will of the people. The United States warned Marcos against "prolonging the life of the present regime by violence"; it offered him and his entourage a safe haven in the United States in exchange for a peaceful transition to a new government under Corazon Aquino. With the unceremonious flight of Marcos, his family, and cronies, Filipino "people's power" had accomplished a spectacular, bloodless revolution. It was dubbed the EDSA Revolution, EDSA being the acronym for the highway between Camp Aguinaldo and Camp Crame.

THE AQUINO (1986–1992) AND RAMOS (1992–1998) ADMINISTRATIONS' RESTORATION OF DEMOCRACY

Considering the varied threats to the exercise of power, it was a miracle that the Corazon Aquino administration lasted its full term. It survived challenges from her own erstwhile supporters such as her first defense minister, Juan Enrile, and vice-president, Salvador Laurel; several cabinet reshuffles; and at least five attempts by factions in the military to overthrow her. Aquino's only major constant supporter turned out to be Fidel Ramos, who, ironically, in his capacity as the head of the Philippine Constabulary, had helped her foe, Marcos, in the enforcement of his declaration of martial law in 1972. After switching his support to Aquino during the EDSA Revolution in February 1986, Ramos held the position of Chief of Staff of the Armed Forces until 1988, when he was named secretary of defense. He adroitly foiled five coup attempts against Aquino, won her admiration and eventually her endorsement for his successful bid for the office of the president of the Philippines in May 1992.

The People's Power Revolution had heightened people's expectations of the government in terms of not only restoration of democracy and individual rights but also amelioration of the country's social and economic ills. Although Aquino admirably succeeded in restoring the democratic edifice, she failed to alter traditional political practices and transfer genuine power to the people. She conducted elections fairly and freely under new liberal constitutions, but her proposed plans for decentralization of authority through the creation of "people's councils" failed to materialize. Power continued to be exercised by most of the same families that had traditionally controlled the political machine through personal control and corruption.

Despite such negative assessment, it must be conceded that within weeks of her assumption of power, President Aquino breathed new life into Filipino politics. She dissolved the KBL-led corrupt National Assembly, abolished the post of prime minister, and deleted the emergency powers of the president. The 1973 constitution was abrogated; instead, the Freedom Constitution was adopted on March 26, 1986. A key proclamation announced her aims to include reorganization of the government, restoration of democracy, protection of basic human rights, revival of the economy, recovery of the illegal plunder by Marcos and company, an end to corruption, and reaffirmation of civilian control over the military. A commission was appointed to write a new constitution to be submitted to a popular referendum so that a new legislature could be elected by the first anniversary of the proclamation.

On October 12, 1986, the 50-member constitutional commission approved a new constitution by an overwhelming majority (44 yes, 2 no, 4 absent). It proposed a six-year presidential term, limited to one term of office. The president was forbidden to impose martial law for longer than 60 days without the approval of the legislature. The latter would be bicameral—a 250-member House of Representatives and a 24-member Senate—and the judiciary would be independent. A national referendum held on February 2, 1987, in which 87 percent of the country's nearly 25 million registered voters participated, gave an overwhelming 76.4 percent endorsement to the proposed constitution and Aquino's leadership.

Among the principal opponents of the new constitutional draft was Aquino's first defense minister, Juan Ponce Enrile, who had played a key role in bringing her to power. Within a few months of her presidency, differences between Aquino and Enrile came to the fore. Enrile severely deprecated Aquino's "soft" policy toward the New People's Army. He asserted that Aquino, who had been elected under the constitution of 1973, had forfeited the public mandate by proclaiming the Freedom Constitution, which had, according to him, created a revolutionary government. He now demanded that she seek a fresh election instead of accepting a six-year term of office under the newly proposed constitution. Allegations of Enrile's involvement in a coup against Aquino led to his dismissal on November 23, 1986. Thereafter, he became the leader of the newly created Grand Alliance for Democracy (GAD), a conservative grouping of seven parties that included supporters and opponents of former President Ferdinand Marcos.

Another dissident was Vice President Salvador Laurel, leader of UNIDO, a partner in the ruling coalition. UNIDO resolved to field its own candidates in the forthcoming congressional elections in May 1987. Despite UNIDO and GAD opposition, Aquino's coalition won handsomely, 22 out of 24 Senate seats. Enrile won a Senate seat with the smallest number of votes of all the successful candidates. His winning margin was so narrow that he was not confirmed until August. Aquino's coalition also won over 150 out of 200 elected seats in the House, among them 6 by her own relatives.

DISSIDENT CHALLENGES

To the two old challenges to the Philippine state—Communist insurgents and Muslim secessionists—was added a third early in the Aquino administration: rightist rebels within the military establishment. They opposed her socioeconomic reforms in general and negotiations for peace with the Communists in particular on grounds that she had no electoral mandate to carry out such activities. Both Corazon Aquino and her successor, Ferdinand Ramos, made it a central plank of their policies to negotiate with all three groups of rebels under the auspices of the

National Unification Commission, with the twin aims of strengthening the nation and ushering in a long-awaited peace.

Communists

Within weeks of assuming the presidency, Aquino took a number of measures to end the seventeen-year-old insurgency led by the Communist-dominated National Democratic Front (NDF). In March 1986, she had ordered the release of Jose Maria Sison, former chairman of the outlawed Communist party of the Philippines, and Bernabe Buscayno, the organizer of the NPA. In August, talks were opened between the government and the NDF leaders, who were issued safe-conduct passes by the military. Aquino's earnestness and sincerity were manifested in her travel to the island of Panay for talks in mid-October with regional NPA leaders. The negotiations were interrupted in September because of the arrest of an NDF leader, Rodolfo Salas, who did not have a safe-conduct pass, and again in November owing to the murder of prominent labor leader Rolando Olalia. The talks were aborted on January 30, 1987, even before the end of the 100-day truce between the two sides. On February 28, Aquino announced a new plan with a view to encourage Communist guerrillas to surrender their weapons in return for an unconditional amnesty, an employment training program, and cash incentives: $450 for each M-16 rifle and $275 for each Kalashnikov AK-47. Expected to cost $50 million, the program was to last six months and to include rehabilitation centers throughout the country.

Despite strenuous efforts on the part of the Aquino and Ramos administrations, a comprehensive settlement with the NDF proved elusive. A serious hurdle was a major factional split within the Communist rank and file. The Manila Rizal Regional Committee (MRRC) and its counterparts in the Mindanao and the Visayas, together responsible for three-fifths of Communist party membership, emphasized an urban struggle as opposed to the Maoist mainstream, pro-Sison faction's continued endorsement of a protracted, rural-based movement. The government continued to recognize the Sison-led faction as NDF and refused to negotiate with the breakaway faction despite its larger numbers. Negotiations with the pro-Sison NDF conducted in the Netherlands stalled mainly on questions such as agrarian reform, repayment of international debts, and official participation in the General Agreement on Tariffs and Trade (GATT).

From the late 1980s there was a marked decline in the mass support base of the Communist movement in the Philippines. Apart from the factionalization in leadership, the movement suffered from the collapse of communism in the Soviet Union and Eastern Europe and its general decline worldwide. The NPA's ranks decreased from about 26,000 in 1985 to less than 5,000 in 1995, partly also because of the "weariness of the movement's mass base over the 27-year-old insurgency."[3] In 1999, following the ratification of the Visiting Forces Agreement with the United States, including the programs for the modernization of the Philippines armed forces, the CPP protested vociferously about the growing U.S. influence in the government. The NPA, whose strength, allegedly augmented to 10,000, had mounted several attacks against isolated police and army posts. In April 2001, talks began between the Philippines government and the CPP in Norway amid continuing reports of NPA attacks on various government facilities. The U.S. presence in the form of 650 U.S. soldiers (including 160 Special Forces) at the beginning of 2002 in pursuit of the Abu Sayyaf Group (ASG) further angered the CPP.

Muslim Insurgents

Negotiations were also opened with the Muslim secessionists. They had been fighting a war of attrition since the 1970s, demanding a separate state for nearly five million Muslims in the southern Philippines. On September 5, 1986, Aquino flew to the island of Jolo for talks with Nur Misuari, president of the MNLF, the largest of the guerrilla factions, the other two being the Bangsa Moro National Liberation Front (BMNLF) and the Muslim Islamic Liberation Front (MILF). Misuari had just returned to the Philippines at the invitation of President Aquino from his ten-year self-imposed exile in the Middle East. A resumption of the talks, this time in Jeddah, Saudi Arabia, between Misuari and the president's brother, Agapito "Butz" Aquino, resulted in an agreement on January 17, 1987, modifying the Muslim demand from independence to full autonomy. A plebiscite in 1989 created the Autonomous Region in Muslim Mindanao (ARMM), consisting of the four provinces of Tawi-Tawi, Sulu, Maguindanao, and Lanao del Sur. (In 2001, it was expanded to include Basilan and Marawai City.) However, the MNLF reneged and did not endorse the ARMM.

Under the Ramos administration, attempts to conciliate all dissidents were accentuated. An amnesty program favoring all groups of rebels applied also to MNLF. The latter also showed signs of weariness and suffered from factionalization. By mid-1995, the Moro revolt had engaged one-third of the country's armed forces, with fatalities rising to an estimated 120,000 soldiers, insurgents, and civilians. Pressure from the OIC (Organization of Islamic Conference), some of whose member states over the previous quarter century had been providers of money and material for the MNLF revolt, made the MNLF move to the negotiating table. A dramatic breakthrough was announced by both parties in July 1996. The Southern Philippines Council for Peace and Development under Misuari's chairmanship would be created. On September 30, 1997, Misuari was inaugurated as governor of ARMM. The Philippine government also agreed to integrate some 7,000 MNLF soldiers out of an estimated 30,000 into the country's armed forces.

The ARMM was not supported by the more radical Moro Islamic Liberation Front, which had broken from the MNLF in the early 1990s because it insisted on a government run strictly according to the Sharia law. There ensured several unsuccessful negotiations between the MNLF and the MILF as well as between the government and the MILF for bringing the MILF into the ARMM. In August 2000, during a period of breakdown of such talks, the government seized the MILF headquarters and many of its jihadi training camps. After a series of bombing incidents in early 2001 in several cities, a cease-fire was agreed upon by the government and the MILF in August. The infusion of 650 U.S. soldiers, including some Special Forces, in Mindanao in January 2002 to help Manila capture the ASG affected MILF's activities as well. The MILF continued to hold out with its estimated fighter strength of about 15,000.

Effective as a leader of insurgents, Misuari proved, by all accounts, a disaster as an administrator. He obliged anybody from the MNLF by providing a position in the bulging bureaucracy. The administration became unwieldy and thoroughly inefficient. Even his MNLF followers were critical of his authoritarianism and failure to implement programs for the welfare of the disadvantaged. In April 2001, he was removed as chairman of the MNLF. Instead, a committee of fifteen was created; one member of the committee, Parouk Hussin, replaced Misuari as governor of ARMM. As a result, the MNLF was further factionalized. Incensed that Manila refused to support his group, Misuari raised the banner of uprising on the island of Jolo in November 2001. The revolt failed, and Misuari fled to the Malaysian province of Sabah, where he was arrested and ordered to be repatriated to the Philippines.

In addition to the MILF, the ARMM was opposed by the radical ASG, which in the 1990s had drawn worldwide attention by undertaking wanton acts of terrorism. Its possible roles in the 1993 bombing of the World Trade Center in New York, the June 1994 kidnapping of seventy Christians, the December 1994 bombing of a Philippine 747 airplane, the January 1995 attempt to assassinate the visiting pope, and a dastardly attack on Ipil township and the killing of more than 100 people later that year made ASG the most feared terrorist group in the Philippines. In 2000, ASG kidnapped a group of European tourists from Sipadan, Malaysia, who were released gradually as ransom money, estimated to total US$20 million, came in from different parts of the world, including Islamic states. Even though the Philippines government's stepped-up campaign against the ASG resulted in the capture of several training camps, the ASG kidnapped twenty tourists from a Palawan Island beach resort in May 2001. These included an American missionary couple—Martin and Gracia Burnham—and a Filipina nurse, Deborah Yap. Although most of the hostages were subsequently released, at least two Filipinos and one American were killed while the Burnhams and Yap continued to be held. In May 2002, a report circulated that ASG would release the Burnhams against a $300,000 ransom; the U.S. ambassador, Frank Ricciardone, responded by announcing a $5 million reward for information leading to the capture of five prominent ASG leaders.

On June 7, 2002, in a dastardly encounter, Martin Burnham and Deborah Yap were killed; Gracia Burnham was wounded, then later rescued by government forces. In a stepped-up campaign, the government claimed in late June that the most prominent ASG leader, Aby Sabaya, was killed. By September the government further claimed its forces had killed forty-seven ASG rebels.

As if to show it still counted as a force, the ASG two months later, on August 20, 2002, abducted six Christians belonging to the Jehovah's Witnesses on Jolo Island. Two days later they beheaded two male hostages, leaving their decapitated heads with notes calling for an Islamic holy war. There was no trace of the remaining four hostages. The dastardly act, committed in the post–September 11 period, brought an offer from the U.S. Defense Department to help the Philippine armed forces to combat Islamic terrorism.

The arrival of a U.S. contingent of 300 crack troops, including seventy Special Forces, touched a sensitive nationalist chord among the Filipinos, who protested vehemently against any combat role for the aliens. In late February 2003, differences arose between Manila and Washington over the role of the U.S. forces in the Philippines. The consequence was that President Macapagal-Arroyo limited the American role to training and surveillance. On February 28, she ordered the military to liquidate the ASG within ninety days.

The Honasan Revolt

President Aquino's efforts to bring peace and harmony by conciliating the Communists and the Muslims were labeled as appeasement both by the rightists belonging to the armed forces and by those who supported the return of Ferdinand Marcos to power in the Philippines. Of the five attempted coups during 1986 and 1987 against the Aquino administration, the most serious threat was posed by one led by Colonel Gregorio "Gringo" Honasan on August 27, 1987. At age thirty-nine, Honasan had built up an impressive academic and military record including a commendation for bravery against Muslim separatists in Mindanao. In February 1986, he became Juan Ponce Enrile's security chief. After Enrile's dismissal in November of that year, he was posted to Fort Magsaysay, from where he launched his coup against Aquino for her "softness" toward the NPA and the MNLF. He called for fresh presidential elections because, in his view, Aquino did not have a mandate to deal with the rebels, whether Communist or Muslim.

The military rebels captured Camp Aguinaldo, the army headquarters in northern Manila, as well as administrative offices, banks, and radio and television stations. An important leader of the revolt was Colonel Tito Legaspi, a close associate of Enrile. Enrile was absent at the emergency session of both houses of Congress on August 28, which were meeting to declare their support and loyalty to Aquino. According to the government, 1,350 members of the armed forces, including 50 officers, had participated in the revolt, which cost the lives of 53 rebels, loyalists, and civilians. Honasan was captured on December 9; he escaped from jail, however, in 1988. Three generals and 17 officers who were dismissed from service, along with 21 others, were formally charged.

Taking advantage of the strains between the government and the military seen during the Honasan revolt, the Communists stepped up their own attacks against the government between August and October 1987. This included cutting off the lines of rail and road communication in the narrow Bicol Peninsula, southeast of Manila, and capturing several army bases in the provinces of Luzon and Quezon.

The Honasan revolt and the Communist activity in its wake shook the confidence of the Aquino administration. On September 9, she called for resignation of the entire cabinet in order to reshuffle it. Four important ministers were dropped: Salvador Laurel, foreign secretary (who retained his position as vice president); Joker Arroyo, executive secretary; Teodoro Locsin, presidential counselor; and Jaime Ongpin, finance secretary. Significantly, Aquino depended increasingly thereafter on Fidel Ramos, the only major figure steadfastly supporting her position. She became politically more cautious than before, abandoning whatever little economic and other reforms she had launched and veering more toward the traditional political patterns with which the Filipino elite had been familiar for decades.

GOVERNMENT AND THE MARCOSES

There seemed to be only one popular plank in Aquino's policies still persisting, namely, her relentless drive against the Marcoses and her efforts to recover the huge amounts of money, variously estimated between $5 billion and $20 billion, allegedly siphoned off and sent abroad by Marcos. By August 22, 1987, the deadline laid down in the constitution, the government had filed 35 cases seeking civil damages of over $90 billion against Ferdinand Marcos, Imelda Marcos, Benjamin Romualdez (Imelda's brother), Eduardo Cojuangco (Imelda's cousin), Juan Enrile, General Fabian Ver (former chief of staff), and a number of others who were allegedly involved in graft and corruption during the Marcos regime. There were also cases filed in U.S. courts. On October 21, 1988, a U.S. grand jury indicted Ferdinand and Imelda Marcos under the Racketeer Influenced and Corrupt Organizations Act on charges of illegally transferring into the United States over $100 million in funds reportedly embezzled from the Philippines government or extorted through "bribes, kickbacks and gratuities."

Relentless efforts on the part of the Philippine government under Aquino and Ramos, through legal battles in U.S. and Philippine courts and diplomatic intercessions with the government and relevant banks in the United States and Switzerland, met with some success during 1995. In August of that year, a Swiss court approved the transfer of US$500 million from Marcos's frozen accounts to the Philippine government The Swiss banks, however, made the actual transfer conditional upon a criminal conviction of Imelda Marcos by a Filipino court. On another front, a U.S. court in January 1995 decreed payment of US$766 million by the Marcos estate as compensation damages to about 10,000 Filipino dissidents who claimed to have been tortured during the Marcos regime.

Despite all such measures detrimental to the Marcos family's reputation, there were still significant pockets of popular support for the former president's widow in the Philippines. In May 1995, Imelda won a landslide victory in her election to the House of Representatives. Though her election was at first invalidated by the Election Commission on grounds of nonfulfillment of residency requirements, the Philippine Supreme Court, by a majority decision in September 1995, upheld it. It was nevertheless inconclusive evidence of the Marcos family's political appeal to the people because in senatorial elections held simultaneously, Marcos's son, Ferdinand (known as Bong Bong), lost his bid for a senatorial seat. Soon thereafter, in July, he was convicted of tax evasion and sentenced to nine years' imprisonment. Also, the midterm elections of May 1995 gave an overwhelming victory to Ferdinand Ramos both in the Senate and the House of Representatives, defeating most of Imelda's nominees and thereby proving that the Marcos family's political influence on the national level had been reduced at best to being marginal and inconsequential.

Meanwhile, secret negotiations were held between the Marcoses and the Aquino administration on terms and conditions on which the former president and his wife could return to the Philippines. In May 1988, the government officially refused Ferdinand Marcos's request to visit his country to attend his mother's funeral. In September 1989, he died in Honolulu. Thereafter, the focus changed to bringing his body home for burial in the Philippines. In October 1991, Imelda Marcos was allowed to return to the country, but it was not until September 7, 1993, a year after Aquino's term of office ended, that the body of Ferdinand Marcos (which had been preserved in a refrigerated crypt in Hawaii) was allowed to be brought to the country of his birth. Although denied full state honors, his funeral was attended by thousands before the body was finally laid to rest in a mausoleum in Batac in his native Ilocos Norte.

THE RAMOS, ESTRADA, AND MACAPAGAL-ARROYO ADMINISTRATIONS

Fidel Ramos, elected in 1992 as president, basically continued the policies of Aquino, whose administration he had served loyally; many of her policies were acknowledged by most observers as his. The country saw new levels of stability and economic improvement. His most important accomplishments came in the relationships with dissidents, Communists, and Islamic militants in the south. He legitimized the Communist party of the Philippines, and the numbers for the New People's Army's were estimated to be around 1,000 (down from more than 10,000 in the late 1980s). The agreement with the MNLF in 1965 produced peace in the south, with Nur Misuari agreeing to serve as governor of the ARMM.

The 1986 constitution provided for a single six-year term for the president; elections for president and vice president were held separately, meaning the two highest offices could be held by persons from two different political parties. Resisting pressures to amend the constitution so he could run for a second term, Ramos backed a favorite. Instead, the people gave a landslide victory (in fact, the highest majority ever in the country's history) to Joseph "Erap" Estrada, idolized by the masses as a popular film star. He ran a campaign on behalf of the teeming millions of poor, promising them an economic miracle. A new party, the Struggle of the Filipino Masses (LaMMP), was established to support his candidacy. Estrada's ten-point platform included drastic reductions in government expenditures, eradication of corruption, reduction of inflation, lowering of interest rates, increasing foreign investment, and currency stabilization. Vice President Gloria Macapagal-Arroyo belonged to Lakas-NUCD, a conservative grouping favored by business as well as large sections of the middle class, including Christian Democrats.

Within two years of his administration, in a scenario reminiscent of the People's Power Revolution of 1986 that brought down the mighty Marcos, the people demonstrated against Estrada's massive corruption. On November 13, 2000, he was impeached by the House of Representatives on charges of accepting bribes totaling millions of dollars from illegal gambling operations. However, his trial by the Senate, which began in December, ended in a farce the following month as the Senate voted 11–10 to preserve the secrecy of the bank account in which a large portion of Estrada's ill-gotten gains had been deposited. By that time, however, the people had voted him out of power, with several hundred thousand demonstrating against the excesses and demanding his removal. The armed forces withdrew their support. On January 20, he was forced to step down; three months later, in April 2001, he was sent to prison on charges of economic plunder.

Estrada was succeeded by Vice President Gloria Macapagal-Arroyo, the daughter of former president Diosdado Macapagal, who was trained in the United States as an economist. Instead of appointing politicians to her cabinet, she relied on experts from the private sector to pull the country out of the economic morass that her predecessor had created in such a short period. This was also necessary to attract the foreign investment that had fled the country during Estrada's tenure.

In September 2001, within a fortnight of the terrorist attacks in New York, President Macapagal-Arroyo journeyed to Washington to restate her unquestioned support of the Bush administration in its fight against international terrorism. Washington had already managed to convince Manila of the financial links between Al-Qaeda and the ASG, notorious for their kidnapping activities over the years. By January 2002, the United States sent 650 soldiers (including 160 Special Forces) to train the Philippines military in its efforts to capture ASG bases. Although several groups (including the Communists, Muslims, and those who had vociferously agitated against the U.S. bases only a decade previously) were angered by her wooing of the United States, her contribution to the security and stability of her country was laudable.

Estrada's Shadow

The deposed Estrada continued to cast his shadow on the Macapagal-Arroyo administration and through two major elections in the Philippines. Estrada's trial dragged on for six years, from October 2001 until June 15, 2007, and involved a number of important individuals, many of whom proved to be only fair-weather friends, ready to testify against him. Estrada's opponents had contacted Luis "Chavit" Singson, who was involved in illegal gambling (called *jueteng*) and had used his money to become governor of Ilocos Sur. In exchange for a promise not to press charges against him, Chavit blew the whistle on his former "business partner" Estrada, declaring that he had personally given Estrada 400 million pesos (over US$8 million) as a bribe for allowing him to operate his gambling facilities. He also alleged that Estrada had given a government price subsidy of 180 million pesos (about $3.75 million) to the tobacco farmers cooperative. Those revelations became the basis of the impeachment of the president by the House of Representatives on November 13, 2000. A special impeachment court, created with Chief Justice Hilario Davide Jr. as presiding officer, considered the articles of impeachment drawn up by the House.

The month of January 2001 proved dramatic and consequential for politics in the Philippines. First came evidence that Estrada had powerful friends in the impeachment court, which voted on January 16, with the narrowest majority, 11–10, that a crucial envelope containing details of a bank account in the name of Estrada's assumed name, Valerde, would not be opened. On the evening of the same day, anti-Estrada protesters swarmed around the historic EDSA shrine marking the site where the People's Power Revolution, which had successfully overthrown the dictatorial President Marcos, had taken place in 1986. As the numbers of protesters swelled in the ensuing days, the army declared it could not stand still and that it had decided to transfer its allegiance from President Estrada to Vice President Macapagal-Arroyo. That was a signal to the Supreme Court, which declared on January 20, 2001 (coincidentally the day President George W. Bush was sworn in as U.S. president), that the seat of presidency of the Philippines had fallen vacant. An hour later, the Chief Justice of the Supreme Court administered the oath of office to Gloria Macapagal-Arroyo as the fourteenth president of the Philippines.

The entire development from the time people began assembling at the EDSA shrine has been termed the Second People's Power Revolution. Estrada, who was bundled out of the presidential palace, however, continued until 2007 to regard the development as illegal and maintained he was still legally the president of the country. So did at least one Supreme Court Justice, Cecilia Munoz Palma, who held that EDSA 2 violated the Constitution of 1987, in which case one would have to say that EDSA 1, the First People's Power Revolution overthrowing Marcos, also would be unlawful.

Such challenges prompted Estrada's supporters to stage their own EDSA. On May 1, pro-Estrada supporters, calling themselves the United Opposition movement and naming Estrada its "chairman emeritus," rallied at the EDSA shrine and thereafter marched on the presidential palace, demanding freedom for Estrada. There was violence; the government called the continued protest a state of rebellion, which it put down effectively with the help of the military. Estrada's supporters called their own movement EDSA 3.

On September 12, 2007, the special graft court, presided over by Justice Teresita De Castro, found the former President, Joseph Ejercito Estrada, guilty of plunder and sentenced him to "*Reclusion perpetua*" (lifelong isolation). Under the 262-page judgment, Estrada forfeited 542.701 million pesos, the balances in his name plus interest; 189 million pesos, which represented balances and interest in the name of Jose Velarde (the fictitious name supposedly used by Estrada); and his mansion in New Manila. Estrada's son, Senator Jinggoy, was acquitted. In order to close the divisions among the people on this issue, President Macapagal-Arroyo signed a proclamation declaring the day of the judgment, September 12, 2007, "a National Day of Prayer for Peace and Reconciliation of Our Nation." Within a year, she declared September 12 a "National Day of Prayer, Reparation, and Consecration for the Nation." The following month, on October 22, the seventy-year-old Estrada appealed for a "full, free and unconditional pardon," citing his mother's illness as the reason. He committed not to "seek public office." Three days later, on October 25, President Macapagal-Arroyo granted executive clemency, restoring to Estrada his "civil and political rights." Although there was much acrimony among Estrada's family and friends, there was not much strength in the movement to restore him to his former position. For all purposes, a curtain had been drawn on the scandal and the man.

Gloria Macapagal-Arroyo's Problems

The public admiration for Gloria Macapagal-Arroyo following EDSA 2, which removed President Estrada from power and brought her into the presidency, did not last long. Within two years, in 2003, she faced a major military revolt, and the general elections in the following year brought a variety of charges against her, including corruption and electoral manipulation. She achieved the dubious distinction of being proposed for impeachment by the House of Representatives four times in each of the years 2005–2008.

Gloria Macapagal-Arroyo is well educated, her strong point being her knowledge of economics, in which she held a doctorate from the University of the Philippines. She came to know the United States fairly well as a student in Washington D.C.'s Georgetown University's Walsh School of Foreign Service (Bill Clinton was her classmate). She taught economics at a number of academic institutions, including the University of the Philippines, and was chairperson of the Department of

Economics at Assumption College. During her presidency, the Philippines economy rose at the fastest pace in three decades; in 2007, the GDP grew at 7 percent. The inflation rate averaged the lowest in two decades at 2.5 percent; the Philippines currency, the peso, was valued in 2007 at 20 percent higher than before.

As a daughter of a well-known former president, Diosdado Macapagal, Gloria Macapagal was accustomed to power. At age forty, she joined government as an assistant secretary in the Aquino administration. In 1992, she entered public life when she was elected to a three-year term in the Senate as the thirteenth top vote-getting candidate. (Under the new 1987 constitution, the top twelve senatorial candidates would win a six-year term, and the next twelve would get a three-year term.) In 1998, she was elected vice president of the country but not on the same party ticket as that of Estrada, who appointed her to a cabinet position as secretary of social welfare and development (under the 1987 constitution, a vice president could also hold a cabinet position). As Estrada was accused of corruption, Gloria Macapagal-Arroyo stayed away from the beleaguered president by resigning the cabinet position in October 2000. That action helped her to be nominated president when Estrada was forced to resign by EDSA 2. Among her influential supporters at that time were two former presidents: Fidel Ramos and Corazon Aquino.

The Elections of 2004

By the time of the presidential election of 2004, a substantial amount of the goodwill generated by Gloria Macapagal-Arroyo at the start of her presidency in 2001 had evaporated. Her candidacy itself was a surprise to many, who were impressed in December 2002 when she announced she would not seek a new term. She changed her position less than a year later in the name of "a higher cause to change the society."

Macapagal-Arroyo's opposing candidates in that election included Estrada's friend and fellow actor, Fernando Poe Jr. Despite what seemed like an uphill contest, she won the election with over one million more votes than Poe scored. Soon after, there were widespread allegations that she had indulged in electoral rigging. The charge would plague her for years. In mid-2005, the National Bureau of Investigation disclosed the existence of audio tapes of wiretapped conversations between Macapagal-Arroyo and an official of the Elections Commission in which the president had asked the bureaucrat to secure a majority in her favor of one million votes. In August 2006, Antonio Rasalan and Clinton Colcol testified that the election returns presented to the lower house of the Congress were, in fact, manufactured. The feeling that Gloria Macapagal-Arroyo had rigged the election was never abandoned by many people, and at times they formed the majority of the Philippines electorate.

Other charges were included in the charge sheets for the 2005–2008 impeachment proceedings. They fell broadly into charges of gross corruption and of misuse of power against the press and opposition politicians, and there were allegations of "extrajudicial killings." Several economic scandals were unraveled. Among them was the awarding of contracts for construction and purchase of telecommunications equipment for the National Broadband Network, a trilateral project among China, Vietnam, and the Philippines. The individuals who were alleged to have benefited from large bribes included President Macapagal-Arroyo; her husband, Mike; Benjamin Abalos, chairman of the former Elections Commission, which was supposed to have manipulated the elections in 2004 in Arroyo's favor; and a host of prominent politicians including Speaker of the House Jose de Venecia Jr. Other major economic scandals in which bribes passed hands were the Northrail project, the Mount Diwalwal project, the fertilizer-fund scam, and the swine scam under the Rural Credit Guarantee Corporation.

Even more serious charges were that during the Macapagal-Arroyo administration, there had been several extrajudicial killings, particularly of people belonging to leftist groups and political entities such as BAYAN, Bayan Muna, and Anakpawis. More than twenty journalists were either killed or simply disappeared. In addition, a large number of persons were arrested in the name of terrorism and held without trial. An independent commission, however, appointed in August 2006 under former Supreme Court Justice Jose Melo, denied the existence of an official policy to eradicate antigovernment persons, instead holding the Armed Forces of the Philippines responsible for the excesses that had occurred.

FOREIGN RELATIONS

"Special Relationship" with the United States

How great was the U.S. responsibility for the initial socioeconomic problems of the newly independent Philippines? Filipino nationalists and other critics of the United States have rightly pointed out that U.S. policy was more liberal toward a defeated Japan than to its own former colony. The terms of independence for the Philippines extended its economic dependence on the United States to such an extent that even U.S. High Commissioner Paul V. McNutt was prompted to comment that it was more than that of any state of the Union. The continuation of preferential tariffs protected U.S. economic interests and helped the small Filipino landholding class involved in exporting agricultural products, thus leaving the old patterns of colonial economy virtually unchanged. The United States passed the Philippines Trade Act in 1946, providing for reciprocal free trade until 1954 and annually raising customs duties thereafter by 5 percent until July 1973, when the full rates would become applicable. Despite the free trade provision, seven of the most important exports were subject to quota restrictions. The act also gave U.S. businesses access and right to exploit natural resources and operate utilities on a par with Filipinos. Further, the Filipino peso was tied to the dollar. Its convertibility into dollars and transfer of funds from the Philippines to the United States could not be restricted without the agreement of the president of the United States. All this had been achieved through the U.S.-sponsored amendment—the Parity Amendment—to the Philippine Constitution, which had sought to limit the exploitation of the islands' natural resources to Filipinos and to corporations in which the foreign capital was no more than 40 percent. But the Filipinos were left with little choice, as U.S. grants and loans for reconstruction and rehabilitation were made contingent upon Filipino agreement to amend their constitution of 1935.

The economic relationship was somewhat improved in favor of the Filipinos by the Laurel-Langley Agreement, effective January 1, 1956, whereby the peso was liberated from U.S. control and the parity provisions for exploitation of natural resources and operation of public utilities were made reciprocal. In reality, such reciprocity had little meaning, because there was little chance that Filipino capital would be invested in the United States. Besides, the new agreement granted an additional parity to the U.S. entrepreneurs, permitting them to compete in business on the same terms as Filipino citizens. Such a special relationship, giving practical advantages to the former colonial power, was justifiably resented by Filipino nationalists.

U.S.-Filipino military agreements also confirmed the critics' view that the Filipinos were compelled to play the undignified role of an American dependency. In March 1947, the United States was granted for a period of 99 years a number of naval and military bases over which the Philippines government would have no sovereign jurisdiction. Of the nearly two dozen bases thus granted, the United States used only two: the 132,000-acre Clark Air Force Base, the largest U.S. military installation outside the United States; and Subic Bay, the largest U.S. ship-repair and refueling facility in the Pacific. U.S. military presence on Filipino soil legally beyond the pale of the Philippines government was galling to a proud and newly independent people.

The bases became an irritant in more than one way. U.S. army personnel on base and off on official duty were exempt from Filipino law. U.S. troops repeatedly fired at alleged Filipino pilferers on base property. The use of the bases was theoretically subject to mutual consultations, but the United States disregarded the provision, using Clark Air Force Base as a "logistical center" during the Vietnam War. Filipino youths, intellectuals, and leftists particularly resented the alleged storage of nuclear weapons at the bases and in the nuclear-powered naval vessels that docked at Subic Naval Base. On the other hand, the bases provided security to the Philippines and were an important source of economic gain to the Filipinos working there. In 1966, in the beginning of the Marcos administration, new agreements limited the U.S. concessions to twenty-five years, temporarily assuaging Filipino feelings. Intermittent negotiations over a decade finally produced a major accord on January 6, 1979. Filipino sovereignty over the bases was recognized, as was the right to appoint Filipino commanders. The area of Clark Air Force Base and of Subic Bay Naval Base was reduced. The United States was allowed "unhampered use of operational areas" within these limitations in exchange for a package of a half billion dollars of credits and an equal amount in military and economic assistance. These terms were subject to a five-year review.

The special relationship with the United States became a perpetual target of criticism, internally and externally. Besides the military bases, the Philippines almost invariably sided with the United States in international affairs. It sent troops to Korea and 1,200-man "civil action teams" to South Vietnam. Along with Thailand, it joined the U.S.-sponsored SEATO. Throughout the Vietnam conflict, when the United States found little sympathy in Asian countries, the Philippines stood as an ally alongside its former colonial master, thereby inviting the charge from some fellow members of the Afro-Asian bloc of being subservient to U.S. neocolonialism.

The U.S. image was also increasingly tarnished by Washington's steadfast support of the hated Marcos martial-law regime from 1972 to its end. Filipino feelings toward the United States were tempered when under U.S. pressure, Marcos announced elections to the presidency in February 1986. The popular appreciation of U.S. condemnation of those elections and support to the People's Power Revolution in its final stages was, however, diminished by revolting revelations of the comfortable style in which the exiled Marcoses lived in the United States, closer to the billions they had stolen from the Filipino people and siphoned to U.S. and Swiss banks.

With the agreement on U.S. leases of military bases on Philippine soil due to expire in September 1991, talks between the two sides commenced in May 1990. A ten-year agreement providing compensation for the use of the bases to the extent of US$393 million during 1992 and $203 million thereafter annually up to 2001 was finally reached by mid-1991—subject, however, to ratification by a two-thirds majority vote of the Philippines Senate.

The question of renewal of lease rights to the United States divided the ranks of the government, nongovernmental political leaders, and the people at large in the Philippines. The Philippine Chamber of Commerce and Industry and the prestigious Makati Business Club agitated against the rejection of the treaty, pointing out that the action might invite U.S. retaliation including denial of access to markets of the United States and some of its allies as well as withdrawal of foreign investment. The Philippines Center for Research and Communications pointed out that the withdrawal of bases would spell an economic loss of 2.5 to 3 percent of the GNP from 1992 to 1994. Apart from about 30,000 jobs directly related to the bases, there would be a loss of about 250,000 jobs because of the indirect impact on the economy. Such a decision would be particularly unwise at that time because of the prevailing deep economic recession, and the acute need for funds for the rehabilitation of people affected by the volcanic eruption of Mount Pinatubo, which had also added to the ranks of the jobless by 650,000. An additional argument against the withdrawal of the bases was provided by the top brass of the Philippines military establishment, who warned that such an action would help the growth of the Communist movement in the country.

All these arguments weighed on President Aquino, who reversed her own pre-election stand against the renewal of the treaty. It was one of the few points on which Vice President Salvador Laurel and Miriam Defensor Santiago agreed with her. Opinion polls conducted in September 1991 by the Social Weather Station Survey in Metro Manila also indicated a sharp increase in public opinion favoring U.S. retention of the bases. However, the strongest opposition to the treaty ratification came from some crucial political leaders who were members of the Senate. They were among those who had rallied on a common platform in 1985 to oppose Marcos and his pro-U.S. and pro-bases policies. Their votes were responsible for the rejection by the Philippines Senate on September 16, 1991, of the proposed Philippines-U.S. Treaty of Friendship, Cooperation, and Security, which would include extension of U.S. rights to the bases. It should be noted that even before the Senate action, Clark Air Force Base had been closed because of the devastating damage done to it by the volcanic eruption of Mount Pinatubo in June 1991. Around the same time, the United States unilaterally returned to the Philippines smaller military facilities, including Camp John Hay at Baguio. After the Senate vote, the United States prepared itself for the return to the Philippines of its only major base in the country, namely, Subic Naval Base. With that action, a nearly hundred-year-old chapter of a close and special relationship between the two countries ended.

After some years of a "correct but cool" relationship, the United States and the Philippines negotiated in 1996 the Visiting Forces Agreement, although it took until May 1999 for the Philippines Senate to get over the bitterness created during the controversial closure of U.S. bases and ratify the VFA. The new agreement, which would provide for training of the Philippines armed forces as well as joint exercises had one offensive clause, a bitter reminder of colonial days. It gave the United States jurisdiction over U.S. personnel in the Philippines for any of their criminal acts. The bitter pill was swallowed by the Filipinos because of their recent vulnerability to Chinese attacks in the Spratly Islands, claimed by both countries. Considering the new closeness between the United States and China, it seemed advantageous to restore the old relationship the Filipino armed forces had had with the Pentagon. The first major exercise under the VFA, named Exercise Balikatan, took place on Palawan Island not far from the northern Spratly Islands in February 2000. A year after the VFA went into effect, the United States agreed to assist the Philippines in its plans to modernize its armed forces.

Following the September 11 terrorist attacks in New York and in light of the alleged links between the Abu Sayyaf Group and Al-Qaeda, President Macapagal-Arroyo offered unconditional support to the U.S. fight against international terrorism. The move elicited mixed reactions among her compatriots—nationalists, the NPA, and Muslims in the south. Four months later, in addition to military aid, the United States sent 650 soldiers, including 160 Special Forces, to train the Philippines military in hostage-rescue tactics and assist their efforts to eliminate the ASG redoubts in the mountains of Basilan Island. The FBI maintained that part of the millions of dollars paid in ransom to Abu Sayyaf in recent years had been transferred to Al-Qaeda. Such measures, which restored the status of the Philippines as the closest U.S. ally in the region, invited extensive criticism among Filipinos, as well as among ASEAN members, that the United States was using the alleged link to Al-Qaeda as a "convenient pretext" to mark its presence in the South China Sea.

Relations with Other Countries

Partly to establish its identity as an independent nation and partly to enhance its security, the Philippines took a lead in establishing various regional organizations. Manila was the site of the founding of the eight-nation SEATO (Southeast Asia Treaty Organization) in 1954. The Philippines also took the initiative in forming ASA (Association of Southeast Asia) in 1961 and, with Malaysia and Indonesia, the Maphilindo in 1963. It joined the ASEAN (Association of Southeast Asian Nations), where its role has been prominent, constructive, and fruitful. The Philippines also worked actively in the pro-U.S. and now defunct ASPAC (Asian and Pacific Council), founded in 1966 in Seoul to include Malaysia, South Vietnam, South Korea, Taiwan, Japan, Australia, and New Zealand. Manila has also provided a forum for many international conferences and has served as the headquarters since 1966 of the Asian Development Bank. The institution of the Ramon Magsaysay award to prominent social workers in Asia has also helped to project a favorable Filipino image in the region.

In an effort to move away from the preponderant dependence on the United States, the Philippines government diversified its foreign relations in the mid-1960s. In particular, it took steps to improve its relations with neighboring Japan and China. Previously, Filipino-Japanese relations were clouded by resentment against the atrocities during the Japanese occupation. The Japanese reparations of $800 million remained unused by the Philippines government for a decade for fear of Japanese business invading the Filipino market. In the mid-1960s, new trade and tax facilities were granted to Japan, augmenting exports of Philippines timber, hemp, and copra products in exchange for Japanese consumer goods. The treaty's formal ratification could not, however, be accomplished until December 1973 because of strong opposition from the Philippines Congress, which was muted after the proclamation of martial law. By that time, Philippines trade with Japan had outpaced that with the United States, and Japanese investments threatened the U.S. position as the leading foreign investor. By the late 1970s, the Japanese preponderance in the Filipino economy had already become a major target of official criticism. By a revised Treaty of Friendship, Trade, and Navigation of May 10, 1979, Japan finally agreed to correct the trade imbalance.

As one of the leading anti-Communist states, the Philippines found it difficult to normalize relations with China and other Communist nations. The constraints included the existence of Maoist Communist insurgency in the Philippines and the desire to continue the commercial and cultural ties with Taiwan. The first major policy change was signified by the visit of Imelda Marcos to Beijing in September 1974. In the following year, in the aftermath of the fall of Saigon, Ferdinand Marcos visited Beijing in June 1975 and announced the normalization of relations. On its part, Beijing helped the process. In the joint communiqué at the end of the Marcos visit, China condemned interference by one country in the affairs of another, thereby assuring no material assistance to the Filipino Communists. Sino-Filipino relationships improved dramatically thereafter. During the third visit of Imelda Marcos to Beijing in July 1979, several agreements were signed: an eight-year bilateral trade agreement amounting to $2 billion whereby China would supply the Philippines with refined petroleum products, coal, light machinery, ships, steel, silk, and foodstuffs in return for raw sugar, copper concentrates, coconut oil, wood products, chrome ore, and chemicals. China also agreed to supply the Philippines with a minimum of 1.2 million tons of crude oil per year. The agreements also provided an air link between Manila and Beijing and for the Philippines to build tourist hotels in China.

The Philippines was not the only ASEAN country to notice a new aggressive posture on the part of China in the 1990s toward Southeast Asia. Manila was particularly concerned with China's projection of power in the South China Sea, notably on Mischief Reef (located in the Spratly Islands), claimed by the Philippines as falling within its territorial jurisdiction. China augmented its fortifications on several other islands in the Spratly group. As China built up its blue-water capabilities and improved its air force projection capability, the Philippines became increasingly apprehensive over China's plans to seize some of the Spratly Islands by force, which was the main reason for Manila to renew its close military relationship with the Pentagon. There were armed confrontations between Chinese and Filipino forces in 1995 and 1997, and there have been continuing tensions since then.

The Spratly Islands are also claimed by Malaysia, which has allegedly completed permanent structures, including a helicopter landing site, radar, and a pier on Investigator Shoal. In October 1999, there were incidents of Malaysian and Philippines aircraft chasing each other in the region.

The Sabah Dispute and Relations with Malaysia

No account of Filipino foreign policy would be complete without the mention of the only major dispute that the Philippines had with a Southeast Asian country. This was with Malaysia over Sabah (North Borneo), which was included in the Federation of Malaysia in 1963. Before its "lease" or "cession" in 1878 by the Sulu sultan to Baron von Overbeck, then the Austrian consul at Hong Kong, and its subsequent sale to the British North Borneo Company, the territory had been claimed by the sultans of Brunei and Sulu. It was taken over in 1946 by Britain, which claimed the right to hand it over to the Federation of Malaysia. Copies of the 1878 treaty in Spanish, Moro, and English gave rise to conflicting interpretations: The Moro term *padjuk* and the Spanish *arrendamiento* suggested lease, while the words *cede* and *grant* in the London copy belied any temporary arrangement. The Philippines government maintained that the sultan of Sulu was independent of Spanish authority, that he had only "leased" the territory, and therefore the British North Borneo Company's transfer of it to the British government in 1946 was illegal. Since Sulu is a part of the Philippines, the latter argued, Sabah was *ipso facto* Filipino territory.

Myanmar: Toward Integration and Democracy

THE UNION OF BURMA (MYANMAR)

The leadership of independent Myanmar was drawn from a somewhat limited elite, mostly English-educated, who loved democratic forms of government and preferred socialist as opposed to Communist socioeconomic goals. The country's constitution gave the state authority to restrict if not confiscate private property (including that belonging to foreigners) and to nationalize natural resources, transport, financial institutions, and any other economic activity, including export of the country's principal product—rice. The constitution, modeled after the British parliamentary system but providing for a federal "union" of the several ethnic groups, had two houses of legislature. The Chamber of Nationalities consisted of 125 members representing the various segments of the population, more or less in proportion to their numbers. The Chamber of Deputies, the lower house, of 250 members was elected from territorial constituencies irrespective of their ethnic composition. The executive branch was to be headed by the prime minister with a titular president elected by the legislature by rotation from the various ethnic groups. Thus every effort was made consciously to provide for a balanced polity that would alleviate the historical fears and apprehension of the minorities. To emphasize the new nation's sovereignty, the Union of Burma (Myanmar) chose to remain outside the British Commonwealth of Nations.

CIVILIAN GOVERNMENT UNDER U NU

Threats to National Integration

In the first decade of independence, Myanmar was dominated by the Socialist party under U Nu's leadership within the AFPFL (Anti-Fascist People's Freedom League), a wartime freedom-front coalition. The AFPFL leadership had already suffered a grievous blow in the internecine assassination of its wartime leader,

Aung San, and six of his top governmental associates on July 19, 1947. Worse challenges came soon after the British quit and independence arrived. In March 1948, a Communist insurrection took place led by Than Tun. The area of intense activity was central Myanmar, including the strategic oil fields. The Communists also tried unsuccessfully to organize a general strike in Yangon and other urban centers. U Nu's government, actively assisted with arms and other supplies from India and Great Britain, was able to suppress the 25,000-member Communist force largely because of the general antipathy of the people for communism. The AFPFL took determined steps to infiltrate the All Burma Peasants Union and to purge its Communist leadership. Further, the Trade Union Congress of Burma was rid of Thein Pe's Marxist control in favor of the AFPFL's U Ba Swe. In 1953, the government officially banned the Burma Communist party (BCP). Thereafter, only a handful of Communists under the leadership of Than Tun continued to carry on the antigovernment struggle in the Pegu-Yoma mountain strongholds. Later, they retreated to the northeastern Shan region, closer to the source of their assistance from across the border in China.

Throughout the twelve years of his premiership, U Nu's principal problem was that of welding Myanmar into a nation. During the British days, the non-Burman minorities of Chins, Kachins, Shans, and Karens, occupying the largely hilly and relatively infertile half of the country's geographic area, had been administered separately as "excluded areas." With the advent of independence, minorities feared the traditional tendency of the Burman majority, constituting 75 percent of the population and occupying the best lands in Pegu and central Myanmar, to dominate the politics of the country. Some of the minorities, particularly the largely Christian Karens, were incited by some foreign missionaries to rise against the Burman, Buddhist-led government and demand a separate state. Beginning in 1948, the Karen National Defense Organization, having in its ranks some of the best British-trained soldiers in Myanmar, rose up in rebellion, demanding an independent state that would include the Irrawaddy Delta. Early Karen military victories during 1948 and 1949 included seizure of important towns like Moulmein, Bassein, and Prome; at one time, the Karens threatened to take the country's capital. Doubting the abilities and possibly the loyalty of the army commander, General Smith Dun, himself a Karen, the government replaced him with General Ne Win. The Karen movement was temporarily contained through military action; of note is the fact that at that time the Chin and Kachin regiments were foremost in suppressing the Karen rebels.

Socioeconomic Measures

U Nu early perceived the need to seek a nonmilitary solution of the ethnic discontent. He believed that social and economic reform would be the best measure to alleviate frustrations among all segments of the society, including the ethnic minorities. His own reputation for personal honesty, integrity, devotion to Buddhism, and overt determination to end the widespread corruption won him considerable support among the rural as well as the urban population. As a cohesive measure, U Nu sponsored a Buddhist religious revival, giving extensive patronage to pagoda building and restoration, holding examinations in Buddhist scriptures, and awarding prizes to monks for their scriptural versatility. Myanmar was foremost in the worldwide celebrations in 1956 to commemorate the 2,500-year anniversary of the Buddha, hosting an international gathering of Buddhist scholars. During U Nu's premiership, Buddhism came closest to being the state religion, despite the lack of such a provision in the country's constitution.

In August 1952, U Nu launched a four-year economic plan to convert Myanmar into a *pyidawtha* (land of happiness). The plan included welfare measures for improvement in education, public health, subsidized housing, reclamation, irrigation, easy credit, and elimination of old debts. Nine million acres of land were reallocated to new tenants, and better tenancy laws enacted for all peasants. The emphasis was on rural projects instead of industry, on private enterprise instead of nationalization. Bowing to popular wishes, U Nu had allowed the simple, austere, and humane aspects of Buddhism to override his own initial enthusiasm for semi-doctrinaire socialism. Unfortunately for Myanmar, most of the well-conceived economic schemes went awry because of a variety of factors. The global price of rice slumped by 25 percent in 1955 and 1956. The cost of suppressing ethnic revolts and the salaries of government workers added to the financial burden. Moreover, the large-scale efflux of Indians, who had been made to feel unwanted in Myanmar for a long time, deprived the government of the much-needed technical personnel to implement the administrative and economic programs of the *pyidawtha*. By 1956, the plan was in shambles.

U Nu's Failure

Until the elections of 1956, U Nu's authority met little political challenge. Outwardly, the ruling AFPFL still appeared invulnerable, winning an overwhelming 183 out of the 250 seats in the Chamber of Deputies. Its principal opposition, the NUF (National Union Front), got only 48 seats, but with one-third of the national vote. The core of the NUF was the Burma Workers and Peasants party, a vehicle of extremist elements, including the Communists, who operated undercover within the NUF because the party had been officially banned in 1953. The NUF was popular in central Myanmar, enjoyed some support in all regions of the country, and claimed able leadership, including the charismatic Aung Than, brother of the late Aung San. The NUF's impressive gains were more a reflection of the public's ire against high prices and unsalable stocks of rice than a preference for its socioeconomic programs. The elections made the NUF's political potential evident, posing a serious challenge for the first time to AFPFL leadership. To make matters worse for U Nu, the AFPFL was seriously factionalized, the principal groups being the All Burma Peasants Organization (ABPO) under Thakin Tin and the Trade Union Council (TUC) under U Ba Swe and Kyaw Nyein. U Nu's overtures to both the NUF and the conservative elements, perhaps made for reasons of political expediency, cost him support in his own party. In 1958, the split in the AFPFL was complete, giving the Communists an opportunity to fish in troubled waters by staging violent outbreaks in many parts of the country. The Communists even helped some ethnic dissident groups—Kachins and Shans—to revive their demand for separate states. The combined effect of AFPFL factionalism, Communist uprisings, and secessionist movements was such as to create the most serious threat to the integrity and security of the state. At this point the military, which had always been subordinate to the civilian government and had enjoyed a national reputation for efficiency, honesty, and political neutrality, was called in by U Nu to assume temporary control under the "emergency" clauses of the constitution. The army's intervention was appreciated by the people because of the quick restoration of law and order, but its continuation in power beyond the statutory period of six months brought some strong public disapproval.

In 1960, the political process received a reprieve as General Ne Win ordered national elections leading to the formation of a representative government. The military was no longer apolitical, however, having tasted power and authority during the period of "caretaker" government for two years. It had also gained valuable administrative experience in various branches of government. After civilian rule was restored in 1960, the military continued to wield political influence. In March 1962, Ne Win, on his own, imposed military rule on the country.

The interregnum between the two periods of military rule was not used by the AFPFL to close its ranks. In a bid to enlist support from various quarters, U Nu made vital concessions in 1961 by getting the legislature to amend the constitution making Buddhism the state religion. Worse, U Nu practically conceded the Shan demand for a quasi-autonomous state, thereby spurring similar demands from other ethnic minorities. In early 1962, he actually started negotiations with the leadership of the various groups seeking ethnic autonomy, endangering, in the army's view, the integrity of the Union of Burma. Though U Nu was still very popular, General Ne Win seized the government on March 2, 1962, this time more decisively than before. The political process was stymied, the legislature dissolved, and large numbers of dissenting politicians, including U Nu, were interned. The freedoms of speech, assembly, and press were allowed, provided that they were not directed against the government.

MILITARY GOVERNMENT UNDER NE WIN

For the next quarter century, until 1988, Ne Win and his Burma Socialist Program party (BSPP) remained at the helm of affairs in Myanmar. The country was given a new constitution in 1974, and some elections at the national, district, and village levels were held, but since the BSPP was the only political party permitted to function and it was dominated by the military, these trappings of democracy were more of a farce than a genuine exercise in popular representation.

As a leader, Ne Win carefully cultivated an image of a successor to Aung San, the father of independent Myanmar. He was a member of the nationalist movement dating back to the University of Rangoon student activism of the 1930s and a member of the "thirty heroes" group, organized during World War II by Aung San. Ne Win shared his leader's secular and socialist ideals. He had been the country's commander in chief since 1948, had a brief stint as a member of U Nu's cabinet in 1950, and then was prime minister from 1958 to 1960. In March 1962, he emerged as the chairman of the seventeen-member Revolutionary Council, all of them drawn from the armed forces.

Ne Win's Socialistic Measures

Soon after its birth in July 1962, the BSPP recruited members at all levels—national, state, district, subdistrict, and village—and formed the Peasants and Workers Council on the Soviet model. The party's policies, officially entitled "The Burmese Way of Socialism," were an assortment of ill-conceived and ill-implemented programs, which led the country down the road to bankruptcy by the end of the 1960s. Because the intelligentsia refused to cooperate with the blatantly militaristic regime, the BSPP came increasingly under the influence of left-wing or Communist army commanders and Marxist theoreticians. They advocated an economy geared to the welfare of the peasants and workers by eliminating the profit motive and the alien (Indian and Chinese) middlemen and establishing state-controlled cooperatives in all sectors of the economy.

Accordingly, the Ne Win government ordered nationalization of almost every economic activity, large and small, including the retail trade. Indians and Chinese, who had been active in the Burmese economy as shopkeepers, moneylenders, importers, and exporters, were expelled and their property confiscated. Banks and insurance companies were also nationalized and assets of British-owned trading companies liquidated. The paucity of business and management skills among the Burmese made replacements impossible. There were shortages all around, including rice, which was rationed in a country known in the previous century for being a leading exporter of rice to the rest of the world. The scandalous inability of the public sector to manage the distribution of consumer goods through the "people's stores" created a vicious and lucrative black market with articles of common use smuggled from East Pakistan (now Bangladesh) and India. The policy of isolation from the rest of the world cost Myanmar heavily as the import-export trade and foreign investment virtually ground to a halt.

From 1964, Myanmar reverted to its historical isolation, practically shutting itself off from the rest of the world. Even diplomats were required to seek official permission to move outside the capital city. Burmese nationals had to obtain prior permission for seeing foreigners or writing to them and were obliged to report to the government everything that transpired in their meetings or correspondence. Most foreign agencies except diplomatic missions were expelled or asked to withdraw from the country. The only significant exceptions to all this were diplomats and technical advisers from China. The official justification for these strictures was that Myanmar wanted no outside interference in its efforts to integrate the diverse ethnic communities and to build up its economy through indigenization and nationalization. Except for periods of temporary relaxation, the country remained, by and large, closed to the outside world.

Efforts Toward Political Liberalism

Earlier, in 1967, the government released several hundred political prisoners, including U Nu. In 1968, Ne Win appointed thirty-three of the top civilian leaders to the newly created Internal Unity Advisory Board. The board's report of May 1969, very likely drafted by U Nu and supported by eighteen members, recommended reversion to constitutional government by reconvening the remnant of the 1962 parliament, restoring the judiciary, and reappointing U Nu premier. The parliament would then appoint Ne Win as president, who would then call a national convention to draft a new constitution.

The rejection of the report by Ne Win's Revolutionary Council was to be expected. In protest, in June 1969, U Nu left the country on the pretext of making a pilgrimage to India and from there going to Thailand to participate in a Buddhist ceremony. He used the opportunity to visit London and the United Nations, where he denounced the Revolutionary Council and announced the formation of a rival government on the Thai border. Despite such efforts, the anti–Ne Win movement failed to pick up any momentum because the authoritarian regime ruthlessly repressed any dissent or criticism of the government.

In the 1970s, the BSPP showed a new vitality in seeking the political, economic, and social transformation of Myanmar. In the political sphere, having failed to enlist the cooperation of U Nu and other politicians, Ne Win presented a new constitution in 1974 to the people, who approved it with 90 percent of the vote. The constitution stipulated a unitary state in place of the old federal polity. Along with a new citizenship act, it aimed at dismantling the traditional quasi-autonomous relationship that had existed between the central government and the multiethnic society in Myanmar for nearly a millennium.

Both the promulgation of the constitution in 1974 and the adoption of the citizenship act in 1982 were preceded by a public discussion for several years. According to government count, the citizenship bill, initiated in 1976, drew suggestions from 1.9 million persons involved in diverse meetings. The three classes of citizenships were citizens, associate citizens, and naturalized citizens. Citizens included all ethnic groups residing in Myanmar before 1823, just before the first Anglo-Burmese war, thus excluding the Indians. The complex regulations were intended to keep communities from the Indian subcontinent and the Chinese out of the BSPP and the People's Assembly (the Pyithu Hluttaw). Only citizens were eligible to sit on policymaking bodies and take charge of government departments. Anybody's citizenship status could be reclassified or revoked by the "Central Body," consisting of ministers of home affairs, defense, and foreign affairs, in effect three of the important military members of the cabinet.

Economic Revival

On the economic front, the progress in the 1970s was spectacular. In 1972, the BSPP's central committee approved a twenty-year plan to be implemented through five four-year plans, projected to make Myanmar an industrialized, socialist state. The third plan was particularly successful. Completed by March 1982, it overfulfilled its target of 6.6 percent annual growth largely because of progress in agriculture. Thus, in place of a projected annual growth of 5.8 percent with an investment of 13.6 percent of public funds, agriculture grew at 8.6 percent with a public investment of only 9.18 percent. Myanmar did not fare equally well in its fourth four-year plan (1982–1986).

Among the reasons for such spectacular success was Myanmar's "green revolution," attributable to the Whole Township Special High-Yield Paddy Production

Program. By 1982, 78 townships were developed. Political persuasion, administrative coercion, and peasant mobilization were important. More significant were the use of fertilizers, better credit facilities, and above all, new strains of paddy seed that raised the paddy yield from 36.8 baskets (one basket equals 46 pounds) per acre in 1976–1977 to 67.98 baskets for the high-yield varieties in 1981–1982. It enabled rice exports in that year to reach 905,000 tons, the highest since the army's takeover in 1962, though well below the 1.67 million tons in 1961–1962 or 3.12 million in 1940–1941.

The forestry, mining, and oil exploration sector did not fare equally well. After spectacular increases in 1978–1980, production of teak and hardwood lagged. Similarly, crude oil production also slackened after initial successes, largely because of poor management. Myanmar's hope after 1981 was the three new onshore oilfields, estimated to have a potential of 3 billion barrels. A major natural gas reservoir also was discovered in the Gulf of Martaban.

Apart from domestic sources, Myanmar financed its development plans through external assistance, which Myanmar resumed accepting in large doses in 1975. Most of the assistance came from the West and Japan and from international financial agencies like the World Bank (WB), the Asian Development Bank, and the United Nations Development Program. In 1975, the country's external debt was only $300 million; it rose to $1.78 billion by 1981–1982. The debt-service ratio rose alarmingly fast to 40 percent in 1984, twice what is considered an acceptable norm.

Efforts Toward Integration

On the social level, the principal effort after independence was to bring about better cohesion through integration of the diverse ethnic units. At various times throughout the 1960s, government troops were engaged in fighting the Karen National Union (KNU), the Kachin Independence Organization (KIO), the Shan United Revolutionary Army, the Arakan Liberation party, and other ethnic movements. The constitution of 1974 that established a unitary government in effect did not recognize the diversity of Myanmar, which led to the formation in 1975 of the NDF, a coalition of all the ethnic movements. In 1980, one of them—the KIO—left the NDF and allied with the BCP in a common fight against the Ne Win government.

In 1980, the government announced a general amnesty aimed at bringing all dissidents—individuals as well as insurgent movements—back into the mainstream of Burmese society. Ne Win met with the leaders of the KIO and their ally, the BCP, in 1981. Both sets of negotiations failed because of the groups' separate demands to recognize the territories under their respective control as autonomous regions. The BCP even wanted inclusion of its armed forces as a military unit under the State Defense Council with at least one or two BCP representatives on that body. The Karens under their leader, General Bo Mya, reiterated their resolve to fight for an independent state. So did the Shans, who held extensive territory in eastern Myanmar, including control of a part of the lucrative opium trade of the Golden Triangle (an opium-growing area in eastern Myanmar, northern Thailand, and northern Laos), and they vowed to continue their struggle for complete independence.

In mid-1982, the NDF held its first congress secretly. It claimed to be a "third force," grouping together all the ethnically based movements opposing both the government and the BCP, regarding the latter as a tool of foreign interests. The NDF reportedly resolved to send token contingents to join the Karen National Liberation Army (KNLA). After 1983, the government troops engaged the NDF troops under the KNLA in every dry season, in March 1984 destroying the KNLA headquarters at Maw Pokay and sending masses of Karen refugees into Thailand. While the government was unable to crush the insurgent movements, the BCP cleverly adopted the strategy of extending its influence among the ethnic groups. It specially developed a closer relationship with the Kachins and the Shans, to use the Shan drug traffic as a source of revenues to offset the lack of assistance from the People's Republic of China.

End of the Ne Win Era

In mid-1988, Myanmar passed through its most tumultuous phase since the country's independence. A mostly nonviolent people's movement, as in the Philippines, succeeded in overthrowing the autocratic regime of Ne Win, who had controlled the Burmese government for slightly over a quarter century. Unlike in the Philippines, however, there was no highly organized church in Myanmar to support the popular upsurge, nor was there accumulation of ill-gotten wealth by Ne Win of the vulgar magnitude of Ferdinand Marcos.

Because of the violently repressive nature of the Ne Win regime, public discontent over government policies had not been as evident. Whenever groups of people protested in different cities, Ne Win's right-hand man, Sein Lwin, who was also the BSPP's secretary-general and in command of the security forces, quickly and ruthlessly clamped down on the demonstrators, winning from the people the hated sobriquet "the butcher." Some of the protests were directed against runaway inflation as high as 100 percent a year. The government found itself helpless in the face of a black market that thrived on extensive illegal imports from across the country's borders, notably from India and Thailand. The unofficial parallel economy controlled 60 percent of the country's currency, which fetched 45 kyats to a U.S. dollar as against the official exchange rate of 6.29 kyats. The government's credibility was lost in September 1987 when it decided to invalidate all 25-, 35-, and 75-kyat notes, which virtually wiped out savings of the middle class. In reaction to such policies, masses of people, often wearing masks, took to the streets in opposition to the government.

In March 1988, large-scale protests were put down by Sein Lwin's riot police killing 300 protesters, raping some female demonstrators, and torturing political prisoners. Continued public outcry led to Ne Win's decision to call the party (BSPP) congress on July 23, a year ahead of schedule, at which he dramatically took blame for public discontent and rioting and offered to resign. He also proposed a national referendum on whether the country should have a multiparty system. His stunned colleagues accepted the resignation but not his proposal for a referendum, which could have eliminated their privileged and lucrative political, military, and economic positions built over a quarter century.

Ne Win's moves did not usher in any liberal programs. Sein Lwin's succession to Ne Win as chairman of the BSPP implied continuation of the repressive regime. Some even suspected that Ne Win manipulated the government from behind the scenes. The famous Shwedagon Pagoda in Yangon as well as pagodas in sixteen other cities now became the rallying points for hundreds of thousands of protesters, some of whom made liberal use of Molotov cocktails against Sein Lwin's forces. Large numbers of Buddhist monks joined the protesters; there were reports of government troops and security forces also defecting to join the ranks of opponents of the regime. On August 8, only seventeen days after assuming power, Sein Lwin resigned.

Thereupon, the BSPP elected Dr. Maung Maung, the attorney general, as party chairman, and the People's Assembly elected him chairman of the State Council and president of the country. Although he quickly revoked martial law and ordered the release of nearly 3,000 dissidents, he was unacceptable to students and other demonstrators. On August 29, the leading dissidents—among them former prime minister U Nu, former president U Mahn Win Maung, and former chief of staff and defense minister General Thura Tin U—formed the Democracy and Peace (Interim) League (DPIL). U Nu announced on September 9 the formation of a provisional government with himself as prime minister, claiming continuation of the administration that was pushed aside in 1962 by the military coup engineered by General Ne Win. Three days later, agitating students from all universities combined to form the All Burma Students Organization. On September 28, the DPIL registered itself as a political party under the name of National League for Democracy (NLD).

Among the leaders of the popular protests were Aung Gyi and Daw Aung San Suu Kyi. Aung Gyi was the number-two man in the 17-member Revolutionary Council of Ne Win in 1962. He was jailed in the following year for resigning from the government because of differences with Ne Win. Released from prison, he had become a businessman. Following the tumultuous events of March 1988, he wrote a series of letters critical of the government's economic policies and human rights record. Even more dramatic for the protesters was the return to the country of Aung San Suu Kyi, daughter of the legendary Aung San, who had been assassinated in January 1947. She was married to British scholar Professor Michael Aris, an expert in Tibetan and Himalayan Studies, and had been living in England.

CHANGE OF GUARD UNDER THE STATE LAW
AND ORDER RESTORATION COUNCIL

Reacting to U Nu's establishment of a rival government, the armed forces led by General Saw Maung dismissed President Maung Maung on September 24 and announced the formation of a new government in the name of a body that would eventually be called the State Law and Order Restoration Council (SLORC). Saw Maung became chairman of the council, which included eight of Burma's nine regional commanders, other high-ranking military officers, and, of importance, Brigadier-General Khin Nyunt, director of Defense Services Intelligence. Despite the official changes, authority remained, at least for the next two years, in the hands of General Ne Win. Transfer of power to the SLORC signified merely a change of guard with repression renewed and democracy denied even more than before.

SLORC Versus Aung San Suu Kyi

After 1990, Aung San Suu Kyi and the military were in a seemingly intractable confrontation as she emerged as the symbol of Myanmar's struggle for democracy and the greatest threat to the military's claim to power. The national elections held on May 27, 1990, gave an overwhelming popular mandate to the NLD, which secured 392 out of 485 seats. Suu Kyi had been barred from running on the grounds that she was married to a foreigner. In fact, she had been placed under house arrest since July 20, 1989, and denied any contact with the outside world, including her own family. The NLD's demand to form a National Assembly was, however, dismissed out of hand by the SLORC, which now maintained that the revolution of 1988 was a "clever plot" by the Communists to capture power and that such a threat still persisted. On July 29, 1990, the SLORC officially declared that it ruled not by constitution but by martial law, that its legitimacy came not from the people but from the United Nations and from the governments around the globe that recognized it as the government of Myanmar. It proclaimed its intention to rule until a government was formed under a new constitution.

Thereafter, the SLORC brutally suppressed all dissent, annulling the representative status of elected NLD candidates and imprisoning a large number of NLD leaders. It smothered dissent through the use of arbitrary arrest, imprisonment, and torture of political prisoners. Many died in prison; countless others went into exile, notably to Thailand. Political parties were declared deregistered; students were kept under strict vigilance. Many elected leaders fled to Karen strongholds, joining them and other minorities, students, and dissident monks who had formed the Democratic Alliance of Burma (DAB) in 1988. The elected leaders now proclaimed the National Coalition Government of the Union of Burma (NCGUB), indicating reversion to the U Nu government's (1948–1962) policies of associating the country's ethnic minorities with the political process.

The international community reacted sharply to human rights abuses by the SLORC, but no state recognized NCGUB. The United States declared suspension of all aid; Japan would limit its aid only to unfinished projects. Senator Daniel Patrick Moynihan of the United States secured the Senate's approval of a motion requiring the president to report semiannually on the state of human rights and progress in democracy in Myanmar. If the findings were unsatisfactory, the resolution empowered the president to apply economic sanctions against Myanmar. The United Nations Human Rights Commission (UNHRC) in Geneva sent a special rapporteur to Myanmar. The persistent negative reports from the UNHRC, Amnesty International, and Asia Watch failed to make the military junta in Myanmar rectify the human rights situation. In October 1991, Suu Kyi was awarded the Nobel Peace Prize in recognition of her nonviolent campaign for democracy. The SLORC junta declared that if she left the country to receive the prize, she would not be allowed to return. On December 10, 1991, her son Alexander received the prize "in the name of all the people of Myanmar." The award awakened the world community to the utterly unacceptable human rights conditions in Myanmar.

The sharp international reaction to the SLORC's brutal treatment of dissidents of all kinds—students, monks, tribal and religious minorities, and, most significant, a Nobel Peace Prize winner—had some effect on the military junta. The government feared that the UN General Assembly meeting of 1992 might resolve to unseat the SLORC representative from that world body. On April 23, 1992, the SLORC announced major changes calculated to impress the international community. First, General Saw Maung, who had earlier given up his position as minister of foreign affairs and defense, was removed from his position as head of the SLORC. Authority passed on to General Than Shwe, deputy chairman of the SLORC, and to Khin Nyunt, head of the Directorate of Defense Intelligence Services and first secretary of the SLORC. Second, a large number of political prisoners, including the eighty-five-year-old U Nu, NLD Secretary Chit Khaing, and Ma Theingi, Suu Kyi's personal secretary, were released by the end of September. Third, permission was given for immediate family members to visit Suu Kyi. Accordingly, her husband and two sons visited her in May 1992. Fourth, the government announced the suspension of fighting against all minorities. On April 28, 1992, in response to mediatory efforts by an emissary of the UN secretary-general, Myanmar and Bangladesh signed an agreement whereby the Rohingya Muslims would be allowed to return to their homes provided they could show evidence of previous residency in Myanmar. Fifth, martial law, in operation since July 1990, was declared ended on September 26, 1992. Even so, Suu Kyi as well as some other important NLD figures, such as former general Tin Oo and former colonel Kyi Maung, continued to be under detention. In fact, Amnesty International charged in the aftermath of these "liberal" measures that over 1,500 political prisoners still remained incarcerated in Myanmar. Sixth, colleges and universities were allowed to reopen after August 24, and the curfew was lifted after September 10. Last, the government promised to hold a political convention in eight months to formulate principles for drafting a new constitution. Accordingly, the junta opened a dialogue with the NLD but without results. The eight-month deadline passed without any progress toward holding the promised convention.

Delegates to the constitution-drafting convention, which first met in January 1993, were nominated by the SLORC from each division, state, and district so that all important minorities would be represented. Importantly, a number of military officers selected to represent the *tatmadaw* (military elite) were appointed to the convention, which met only sporadically. By April 1995, when it adjourned for six months, the convention had merely approved some "guidelines." One such guideline provided for a crucial role in Myanmar's polity for the military, which alone was believed capable of enforcing discipline and bringing all communities together. Another "guideline" was to debar citizens who were married to foreigners from being elected to the proposed bicameral legislature. This was an obvious move to prevent Suu Kyi, who was married to a British citizen, from participating in Myanmar's public life.

Suddenly and quite unexpectedly, on July 10, 1995, the SLORC released Suu Kyi from house arrest, perhaps in the belief that she had been rendered incapable of significant political opposition to the SLORC. After all, most of her NLD associates were behind bars (a few had been released from prisons over the years), in exile, or involved in running the clandestine National Coalition government established by NLD in the jungles. The government had so far allowed the NLD to operate legally but only under the leadership of Aung Shwe, a former military leader who had assumed chairmanship of the party. All Suu Kyi could do to maintain contact with the people and mobilize them to restore democracy was to address several thousands of them, who devotedly attended her weekend meetings in front of her house. The popularity of those appearances forced the legal NLD to reappoint her as secretary-general of the party, a post from which she had been ousted by government action in April 1991. Reacting through its electoral commission, the government now invalidated her reappointment by citing a 1991 law that required governmental consent for changes in party leadership. At the same time, the SLORC invited the NLD to attend the 702-member national convention that would reconvene on November 28.

Meanwhile, the NLD-led National Coalition government, which claimed legitimacy by virtue of its electoral victory in 1990, and the multiethnic DAB met in their jungle headquarters and drafted a constitution of their own, proposing a federation of eight states, a bicameral legislature, division of powers between the federation and the states, and guarantees to all citizens of their human and political rights.

Suu Kyi reacted to the governmental moves aimed at ensuring her nonparticipation in public life by repeatedly appealing to the government to discuss the democratic reforms with the NLD. Frustrated with the government's ignoring her requests, she announced that the NLD would boycott the national convention because "the party cannot in all honour support a national convention which is not heading for what the people want, which is not in any way desirous of bringing about national reconciliation, multi-party democracy or a constitution that will be acceptable to all the people of our country."[1] The government retaliated by expelling the NLD from the convention, launching a multimedia campaign denouncing Suu Kyi as a traitor, getting some NLD members to defect, and even inciting some of Suu Kyi's neighbors to complain to the government about the noise caused by weekend meetings.

Suu Kyi thereupon called for a meeting of the Parliament elected in 1990, refuting the SLORC's contention that the term of those elected then had expired. At her weekend meetings, she asked foreigners to desist from investing in Myanmar. She set the stage for the next confrontation with the SLORC by announcing her party's convention to be held on the front lawn of her house in May 1996. The government responded brutally by arresting some 256 NLD members, including 232 representatives elected during the 1990 general elections.

Nevertheless, at least four NLD annual meetings did take place at Suu Kyi's residence, including the attendance of a handful of delegates who were not in prison. During the same period, Suu Kyi made several attempts to travel outside Yangon to meet with various NLD chapters. In September 2000, she spent more than a week in her car until government security used force to bring her back to Yangon. A few weeks subsequently, she was not allowed to travel by railroad to Mandalay and was placed under house arrest again. The government's callous disregard for fundamental humanitarian considerations was underscored when it denied the request of Suu Kyi's ill husband, Michael Aris, to visit her in Yangon before he died of cancer on March 27, 1999.

After 1997, those in the higher echelons of government dreaded the month of November, which became notable for major reshufflings in government. Thus, in November 1997, the government was renamed the State Peace and Development Council (SPDC), with four of the most senior members of the defunct SLORC and an additional general forming its core. In November 1998, a third deputy prime minister, Lieutenant General Tin Hia, was added, and the foreign minister, Ohn Kyaw, was replaced by Win Aung. In November 2001, Secretary III, Lieutenant General Win Myint, and Deputy Prime Minister and Military Affairs Minister Lieutenant General Tin Hia were removed on corruption charges. Several other senior generals who held cabinet positions were retired; two powerful bureaucrats were suspended and placed under investigation for unacceptably high levels of corruption. One leader, Than Shwe, despite his ill health, seemed most durable; it was feared that his departure from government would trigger an intraparty struggle for power among several generals, most notably between two bitter rivals, Army Commander General Maung Aye and intelligence czar Lieutenant General Khin Nyunt. The occasion was used to abolish the positions they held, making a triumvirate of Than Shwe and longtime rivals General Maung Aye and Lieutenant General Khin Nyunt. Ten of the twelve military commanders on the SPDC were removed, further strengthening the authority of this trio.

SLORC Versus Ethnic Minorities

Although the SLORC's commitment to restoration of democracy was doubtful, its political and military moves toward integration of the nation's numerous ethnic communities into the "Union of Myanmar" proved very successful. Beginning with a broad and vigorous offensive in late 1991 against various rebel forces, the SLORC was able to sign pacts of peace, amity, and constructive cooperation with all of them between 1992 and 1996. Such ethnic struggles, extending over four decades, had seriously eroded the national spirit. Some of the rebels had openly aimed at total independence, among them the Karens, Mons, and Shans. The last were led by a notorious drug warlord, the half-Chinese Khun Sa, who commanded his well-equipped Mong Tai Army (MTA) of over 10,000 in the northeastern highlands and financed the operations through extensive production and trade in opium with a value in Myanmar in 1994 of around US$100 million but a street value as heroin in the United States of ten to twenty times as much. In January 1996, the U.S. government offered a reward of US$2 million for information leading to the arrest and conviction of Khun Sa, who had been indicted in the United States in 1989 on drug trafficking charges.

Initially, in 1992, the junta's aggressive drive against diverse ethnic minorities sent hordes of refugees, notably Karens, into Thailand and over 200,000 Muslims from Arakan into neighboring Bangladesh. Thailand retaliated by attacking Myanmar with its fighter bombers, and Bangladesh engaged Myanmar forces in border action and raised the matter at the United Nations. Myanmar's neighbors were soon impressed, however, with the SLORC's spectacular success in signing amity pacts in 1992–1993 with all but the Karens and the Shans, promising local autonomy as well as significant participation in the country's political process. A series of military campaigns against the KNU forces finally resulted in January 1995 in the subjugation of their two-decades-old headquarters at Manerplaw in the steep, in-hospitable, mountainous terrain on the Thai border. Thereafter, the SLORC's forces were able to "corner" the redoubtable Khun Sa by a combination of concilia-tion and military superiority. In November 1995, Khun Sa announced his "retire-ment" as MTA's commander-in-chief, and the SLORC paid the price of an amnesty for him and his troops and a guarantee against extradition to the United States. At the same time, remnants of Khun Sa's MTA refused to lay down their arms, contin-uing with the drug trade and challenging Myanmar's military government.

Although the SLORC was serious about liquidating the separatist ethnic movement, it was half-hearted in its efforts to eliminate drug trafficking. In fact, from 1988, when the SPDC and, later, the SLORC assumed office, the production of opium and heroin doubled as the government co-opted certain ethnic groups who continued their dominance in the production and transshipment of drugs.

One such group was a well-organized economic enterprise run by the 20,000-strong United Wa State Army (UWSA) on the border with Thailand. After signing a pact in 1989 with the SPDC, the UWSA shifted its focus from narcotics to the production and trafficking of methamphetamine tablets (with sales in Thailand tripling from 200 million tablets in 1999 to about 600 million in 2001). The UWSA settled some 25,000 ethnic Wa, as well as ethnic Chinese brought from the Myanmar-China border, to Thailand's Chiang Rai province, and stationed about half of the UWSA troops there for the protection of settlers as well as for the smooth conduct of drug trafficking. The Chinese government actually assisted the Wa operation because it inhibited the growth of poppy cultivation in the area, but the SLORC looks at the ethnic Wa settlement and the presence of UWSA troops on the Myanmar-Thai border as a buffer between the SLORC and the anti-SLORC Shan insurgents, who are ethnically Thai and had often sought sanctuary in Thailand in the past.

FOREIGN POLICY

Foreign Policy Under Ne Win

Of all the countries in Southeast Asia, Myanmar has been the most assiduous practitioner of nonalignment in international relations. From 1962 until the mid-1970s, isolationism was added to nonalignment. The foreign policy was main-tained on a very low key, taking the greatest pains not to invite acrimony from either of the superpowers or from either party in the Sino-Soviet conflict. Myan-mar refused to condemn the U.S. activity in South Vietnam, but it also spurned invitations to join any of the pro-Western organizations of the region, including ASEAN, even after the latter veered away from its earlier anti-Communist stance.

The prime concern of Myanmar's foreign policy since independence has been maintaining cordial relations with its major neighbors, China and India. Relations with India have always been cordial and friendly; India has never posed a threat to Myanmar's security. Both countries together and independently followed a com-mon policy of neutrality and nonalignment. The personal rapport between Nehru and U Nu was followed by cordial relations between successive Indian prime min-isters and Ne Win. The virtual confiscation by the Burmese government of properties and valuables belonging to Indians was not allowed to spoil India-Myanmar relations. Implementation of the Indo-Myanmar agreement for boundary demarcation proceeded smoothly all through the 1960s. In 1971, temporary tension between the two countries occasioned by Yangon's moral support for China and Pakistan in the East Pakistan crisis subsided with Myanmar's prompt recognition of Bangladesh in 1972.

On the other hand, relations with China had their ups and downs. Myanmar was the first country to recognize the People's Republic of China, India being the second. Despite such a warm gesture, China continued to brand U Nu, along with Nehru and Sukarno, as stooges of Western imperialism. Beijing also gave clandestine support to Burmese Communists. Part of the reason for the unfriendly Sino-Burmese relations was the presence of some KMT forces in the northeastern parts of the country. However, taking advantage of the peaceful coexistence phase of Beijing's foreign policy, U Nu in 1956 initiated negotiations to demarcate the 1,360-mile border with China and sign a treaty in 1960. It was reinforced by another treaty of friendship and mutual nonaggression in January 1961. After Ne Win's takeover in 1962 and the increase of Marxist influence in his government, relations with China became closer than with any other country. Ne Win visited Beijing several times, far more than he did Moscow or Washington. China extended loans for several new irrigation works and industrial plants to be built with the help of Chinese technicians. China also agreed to purchase Burmese rice on a barter basis. Until the mid-1970s, however, China supported the BCP's insurgency on the specious plea that it was a matter between the Communist parties of the two countries, which should not affect the official state relationship between governments.

Sino-Burmese relations took a turn in the mid-1960s when Ne Win refused to be persuaded by the visiting Chinese President Liu Shao-chi and Foreign Minister Chen Yi to condemn the U.S. role in Vietnam. During the Cultural Revolution, the Chinese embassy's most blatant interference in the Burmese school system and open support of Burmese Communist rebellion brought a sharp reaction from the Ne Win government. Pro-Beijing activists were arrested and several hundred Chinese technicians expelled. During this period, 1967–1970, Myanmar briefly drew closer to the Soviet Union and the East European countries than ever before. But it also improved its relations with the United States, even accepting limited economic and military aid.

In the aftermath of China's Cultural Revolution, Sino-Burmese relations improved. Diplomatic relations were restored in October 1970, and Ne Win visited China in August 1971. In the process, Soviet influence was not reduced. In mid-1971, Soviet Union President Nikolay Podgorny signed an economic assistance agreement during his visit to Yangon. Thereafter, Myanmar maintained an even-handed policy with the two Communist giants, taking particular care not to offend but also not to get too close to either. The BCP's stepped-up insurgency operations in the Shan areas, supported as before by Beijing, soured Sino-Burmese relations once more. Myanmar's appeals to Deng Xiaoping and top Chinese leaders to condemn the BCP resulted in reduction of direct Chinese help to the insurgents. Moscow and Hanoi were sympathetic to the Ne Win government's efforts to maintain its integrity and, in fact, wooed Yangon against Beijing. Given Myanmar's geographical position and the country's success in following a policy of neutrality, it was logical for the Ne Win government to use its diplomatic leverage in the Communist world to improve its relations with China rather than offend it.

Foreign Policy Under SLORC

Foreign policy since the revolt of 1988 and the establishment of the SLORC has been markedly different from the previous quarter century in several respects. Following China's example, the SLORC abandoned Myanmar's socialist policies and significantly liberalized its previously restrictive policies in regard to foreign trade and investment. The government invited massive foreign capital needed to improve the country's infrastructure—roads, ports, airports, and telecommunications. Privatization and globalization became the new slogans.

As noted earlier, Myanmar has been more responsive, particularly since April 1992, to international criticism of its treatment of political prisoners, including Nobel Laureate Suu Kyi and her NLD associates, who had received an overwhelming public mandate in the elections of 1990. The United States was joined by Western European countries and Japan in withholding foreign aid, linking its continuation with Myanmar's substantial improvement of its human rights record and steps toward restoration of democracy. The United States condemned Myanmar in the same manner as it had Iraq, Libya, and Iran for its atrocious human rights record and led those in the United Nations who through annual resolutions condemned Myanmar for its treatment of political prisoners and minorities. Although Myanmar continued to reject UN resolutions, it allowed visits by UN officials, including Yozo Yokota, special rapporteur of the Commission on Human Rights, whose report became the core of the debate on the fifth consecutive annual UN resolution in late 1995.

Western allies in Southeast Asia, however, sounded a different note. Thus, the ASEAN countries, most of which had their own human rights problems, declared their preference to have a "constructive dialogue" in private with the government of Myanmar while officially exploiting the new trade and investment opportunities. The exception to this generally cordial relationship with ASEAN member-states was criticism by Indonesia and Malaysia of Myanmar's handling of Arakanese Muslims.

Along with relaxation of political controls and lifting of martial law announced between April and September 1992, Myanmar broke out of its self-imposed isolation in a bid to again become a full member of the international community. Thus, it rejoined the Non-Aligned Movement (NAM), from which it had resigned in 1978 because it had then felt that the organization had veered too close to the Soviet Union for China's comfort.

From 1988 until Myanmar's admission to ASEAN, China was its only political and economic window to the world. In turn, Myanmar provided China a gateway to the warm waters of the Indian Ocean and a "strategic bridge" to South Asia and Southeast Asia. China's military aid to Myanmar from 1988 (exceeding $1 billion) helped the Myanmar government establish internal supremacy over dissident ethnic minorities. China served as Myanmar's economic model in the age of liberalization; it became Myanmar's principal trading partner and the leading foreign investor, with visible Chinese impacts on the infrastructure in Mandalay. Yunnan in South China became "the front door" to Myanmar, with the five new ports constructed in the 1990s with Chinese aid along Myanmar's coast, servicing southern China's export-import needs. China also invested significantly in major irrigation projects and the building of a new large bridge over the Hlaing River in the capital city of Yangon. As John Badgley reported, "road construction in the north, private investment in north-central towns and cities, and consumer products of every sort all reflect the embrace of the classic big brother-cum-enemy."[2]

With its admission to ASEAN, Myanmar took a second look at its relationship with its big brother to the north, particularly the impact on local ethnic Chinese in Myanmar, notably along the Chinese border and in the city of Mandalay, whose Chinese population represented almost one-third of the total. After 1998, China-Myanmar trade and Myanmar's purchases of Chinese military hardware declined appreciably. In 1999, Yangon bravely declined China's offer of $100 million in military credits, choosing instead to buy from European sources.

Myanmar's relations with neighboring Thailand have seen ups and downs. The factors complicating the relationship include Myanmar's drives against its rebellious minorities, some of whom—notably the Karens (70,000 Karen refugees in 1995) and the Shans—have sought refuge across the border; cultivation of opium in the Golden Triangle and its traffic across mutual borders; exploitation by rogue timber merchants of the unstable situation created by the Shan and Karen rebellions in order to smuggle hundreds of thousands of teak logs across into Thailand; and the impact of all such illicit cultivation and trade on the financing of these revolts.

Despite such negative factors, Myanmar-Thailand economic relations have improved significantly. Thai cooperation has helped foreign investment in Myanmar: In February 1995, three oil companies—Total (France), Unocal (United States), and PTT, a subsidiary of Thailand's Petroleum Authority—signed an agreement to build a gas pipeline from the Gulf of Martaban to Thailand. Thailand also financed construction of the "friendship bridge" over the Moei River, linking Myawaddy and Mae Sot. Of even greater significance than economic cooperation was Thailand's active role in bringing Myanmar closer to ASEAN. Thus, as host of the July 1994 ASEAN foreign ministers' meeting, Thailand invited Myanmar to attend. The following July, at the ASEAN foreign ministers' meeting in Brunei, Myanmar was able to sign the 1976 Treaty of Amity and Cooperation. And in December 1995, despite domestic opposition, the Thai government invited Myanmar's Than Shwe to attend the meeting of heads of government of ASEAN in Bangkok, at which Myanmar signed the ASEAN agreement on the region as a nuclear weapons–free zone.

MYANMAR IN THE NEW MILLENNIUM

It appeared, at first, in the new millennium that the military government had softened its policy. Not only was the NLD leader, Aung San Suu Kyi, free to move about, but her NLD party also was allowed to open offices throughout the country.

Beginning in mid-2003, however, the policy reverted to draconian ways. Aung San Suu Kyi's convoy was attacked by a mob in northern Myanmar, and suspicion fell on the military. Using her security as a pretext, the government once again placed her under house arrest on May 31, 2003, treatment that was still in place in late 2008. All NLD offices were ordered closed by the government.

In addition, there was a major shake-up at the top levels of government that held consequences for democracy and human rights in Myanmar. Prime Minister Khin Nyunt, who was also the military intelligence chief and regarded internationally as somewhat of a liberal, was removed from office by the junta. He was replaced by Lieutenant General Soe Win, a professed hard-liner. Khin Nyunt had been in the midst of promoting a seven-point road map to democracy leading eventually to popular elections. His deals with the ethnic minorities were now regarded as ominous harbingers of autonomous regions in the Union of Burma. Khin Nyunt's removal spelled an even more authoritarian regime under the junta chief, General Than Shwe.

The continued detention of the Nobel Peace Prize winner Aung San Suu Kyi has stirred criticism all over the world, including from other winners of the prize. Among them, Vaclav Havel, former president of the Czech Republic, and South Africa's Bishop Desmond Tutu urged national reconciliation in a well-publicized report of mid-2005, "Threat to the Peace: A Call for the United Nations Security Council to Act in Burma." Submitted under article 39 of the UN Charter, the report asked for urgent and binding action under chapter 7 of the Charter. UN Secretary General Kofi Annan appealed to Prime Minister General Than Shwe to release Suu Kyi; so did the leaders of ASEAN, all in vain. In December 2005, the UN Security Council agreed by consensus to hold informal consultations on the situation in Myanmar. China and Russia opposed the measure, but since the demand was for an "informal" consultation, their opposition did not amount to a veto. In January 2007, however, when a formal resolution condemning Myanmar came before the Security Council, China and Russia vetoed it. Furthermore, ASEAN, which had closer ties with Myanmar, informally asked its government not to chair the ASEAN meetings in 2006 as was scheduled.

New Constitution

As planned by the army top brass, a new army-drafted constitution was approved by the National Convention (boycotted by, among others, Suu Kyi's NLD) through a referendum, with a dubious 92.4 percent vote. It was the first national vote since the general elections in 1990, which was of little significance since the convention delegates were all handpicked for their support of the regime. The convention had been deliberating intermittently for fourteen long years. It was no wonder the new constitution gave the military a quota of 25 percent seats in the national legislature. Ironically, it provided for the end of the five-decade military rule with the holding of general elections and the formation of a civilian government in 2010. This outcome seemed unlikely, given the military regime's consistent resistance to democracy. Foreigners and those with foreign spouses were barred from running for office, effectively banning participation by Aung San Suu Kyi and her sons (half Burmese and half British).

Relations with the United States

The United States has consistently and vociferously stood by the 1990 electoral results of Aung San Suu Kyi and her NLD party and demanded that she be released and allowed to form a government based on those results. It has applied economic sanctions against Myanmar and has successfully persuaded European countries to follow suit. As a part of such sanctions, the United States banned all imports from Myanmar under the Burmese Freedom and Democracy Act of 2003. In November 2006, President Bush attended the Asia-Pacific Economic Cooperation Forum summit meeting in Hanoi and pleaded with attendees to exert political and economic pressure on the military government of Myanmar to relent.

All these moves have met with the approval of Aung San Suu Kyi and the Free Burma activists, who successfully boycotted all products, principally clothing and shoes, manufactured by U.S. and European companies in collaboration with companies owned by the Myanmar government or by the military. After the United States and the European Union imposed sanctions in 2003, most Western companies, with the significant exception of some oil companies, withdrew from Myanmar. Two major oil companies, Total S.A. (France) and Chevron (United States), continued their operations of the Yadana natural gas pipeline from Myanmar to Thailand.

The Myanmar regime has had considerable relief, however, from its immediate neighbors—China and India. China is disinclined to oppose the Myanmar government for strategic reasons, including its need for imports of oil from Myanmar. In April 2006, China announced plans to build a pipeline from the Myanmar deep-water port of Sittwe to carry China's oil imports from the Middle East to Yunnan. The route would save China time and cost, since it has been transporting the Middle Eastern oil via the much longer route through the straits of Malacca and the South China Sea. Myanmar's neighbor to the west, India, which had already changed its policy toward the nondemocratic regime in the late 1990s, has reinforced its new stance by signing agreements to buy oil from Myanmar.

21

Thailand: Independence at Any Price

At the end of World War II, Thailand had to adjust to the victorious Allies. In the domestic sphere, however, there were few adjustments because the power elite remained substantially unchanged. Unlike its neighbors about to overthrow or in the process of discarding the Western colonial regimes, Thailand had been an independent country and had already experienced a major political revolution in 1932. Since then, the political changes in Thailand had been more or less along the same continuum, with power shared by an elite of military, bureaucracy, and a small segment of middle-class, educated, professional politicians.

CHAOS UNDER CIVILIAN RULE

Immediately after Japan's defeat, the man most acceptable to the Allies, Seni Pramoj, was rushed from his wartime position of "Free Thai" ambassador to the United States to take over as prime minister under the general direction of the senior statesman, Pridi Phanamyong. The Allies negotiated a postwar settlement with Seni. The Thais surrendered the territories acquired during the war and agreed, in general, to establish a status quo ante as a price for admission to the international community. Internally, Seni and Pridi introduced a new constitution, more liberal than ever before, providing for a bicameral legislature with a fully elected lower house, whose members would elect the Senate. Elections were accordingly held, and by March 1946 a parliamentary democracy was restored.

In the three turbulent years after World War II ended, Thailand experimented with the parliamentary system, producing nine administrations in rapid succession. Indeed, such government turnovers meant little for the masses because it was essentially a rearrangement of a narrow elite of about five thousand struggling for reallocation of the spoils of office. Yet in the short run, the atmosphere of freedom provided under the new constitution and the opportunity to make pecuniary gains promoted the formation of political parties, whose aim seemed to be to get into power by any means, fair or foul. In March 1946, the Constitution Front and the Cooperation party coalesced to back Pridi. Within three months, the mysterious death of the young King Ananda in his bed on June 9 brought about the fall of Pridi's government. Thereafter, until the coup of April 1948, factionalism ruled Thailand, making the political and economic conditions the despair of its people. The only group that had the potential of ending the rampant corruption, administrative ineptness, and general chaos seemed to be the army.

QUARTER CENTURY OF MILITARY RULE

Phibun Songkhram, 1948–1957

By 1947, the astute Phibun Songkhram, the ex-collaborator with the Japanese, had perceived the Thai desire for political stability. The army was already very restive. In November 1947, a coup group was formed, but it did not openly take over. Instead, it backed the faltering government of Khuang Aphaiwong and forced Pridi to flee into exile, alleging his complicity in the king's death in 1946. The incident had provided an excuse to Pridi's enemies, though a jury had ruled that the death could have been caused by accident or suicide.

The situation gave Phibun the opportunity to stage a coup on April 6, 1948, and assume the position of prime minister. Thus, after a brief period of civilian rule, Thailand reverted to a government run by the military. It appeared then and for a long time thereafter that Thailand could be ruled only by its armed forces. For nearly a quarter century after Phibun's coup, Thailand enjoyed a good measure of stability largely because of four factors: monarchy as a unifying symbol; an apolitical, pliant, collaborating bureaucracy running the administration; a fairly well-disciplined, cohesive military elite; and last, a consistently pro-U.S. and anti-Chinese foreign policy. The army rule received the support of young King Bhumibol Adulyadej.

One of the most crucial yet undefinable factors in Thai politics and society is the role of the monarch. Although limited in power since the revolution of 1932, the king has extensive influence, encompassing all segments of society and all regions of the country. A patron and leader of Buddhism, he is revered as the "Lord of Life," as a divine or semidivine entity in keeping with the age-old Hindu-Buddhist traditions of Southeast Asia. King Bhumibol Adulyadej and Queen Sirikit have consistently risen in the public's esteem for their extensive travels throughout the length and breadth of the country and their genuine concern for the common people. In fact, the government has frequently used the royal couple as symbols of national unity. Though the king did not interfere actively in politics before 1973, his several interventions after that—in 1973, in the early 1980s to thwart coups against the government, and in May 1992—were appreciated by the Thai public for lending stability to the country in times of crisis. Moreover, his national eminence is considered too important a factor to be ignored by politicians planning any major social or economic program. He is certainly far more influential than, for instance, the British monarch in the exercise of the right to advise, warn, and moderate the policies of successive governments.

During the decade 1948–1957, government was controlled by a military triumvirate consisting of Phibun Songkhram, Phao Sriyanon, and Sarit Thanarat. Domestically, Phibun won public acclaim by moving against the Chinese community, whose numbers had increased considerably because of the large-scale immigration permitted after the establishment of friendly relations with the Kuomintang (KMT) in 1945. Phibun slashed the annual immigration quota for the Chinese from 10,000 to a mere 200. He also reduced the KMT's influence by closing its consulates and ordering a stricter supervision of the Chinese language schools and newspapers. After the People's Republic of China was established, Thailand feared large-scale subversive activities through Beijing's support of local Chinese and of the Thai Communist party. Therefore, Phibun launched a twofold program. He tightened the naturalization laws and levied a prohibitively high alien registration fee, both measures being directed against the Chinese. In 1952, he banned the Communist party. At the same time, the government encouraged greater assimilation between the Thais and the Chinese through marriage. This helped both communities. The Thai political elite, which had prestige and power but lacked financial strength, could compensate for it by marrying into rich Chinese families, while the latter could take advantage of the "Thai connection" to more easily secure business licenses and other economic privileges.

Fear of communism, the Chinese, and, after 1954, the North Vietnamese, dominated Thai foreign policy all through the 1950s. China's aid to the Meo tribesmen in northern Thailand, its ability to strike at Thailand through the narrow corridor of Laos, and the Communist Pathet Lao's and North Vietnam's support of the insurgency among the tribal population of northeast Thailand did, indeed, justify Thai fears. Therefore, the U.S. policy of containment of Communist China and North Vietnam suited Thailand's apprehension of their domination of Southeast Asia. Instead of taking more imaginative measures to integrate the northern, northeastern, and southern population through economic advancement and increased political participation, Thailand came to depend increasingly on U.S. financial and military assistance to win its battle against domestic dissidents. The juxtaposition of Thai domestic and external needs was responsible for the country's enthusiastic participation in SEATO and the signing of a mutual security pact with the United States. In fact, Thailand became the foremost U.S. ally in the pursuit of the latter's foreign policy goals in the 1950s and 1960s in Southeast Asia.

Sarit-Thanom Rule, 1957–1973

By the mid-1950s, Phibun was being increasingly challenged by Sarit Thanarat. In the hope of rallying public support in his own favor, Phibun ordered elections in February 1957. His party won an overwhelming majority in the National Assembly, but the victory had been secured by intimidating the voters and rigging the ballot. Chief of Police Phao sided with Phibun and cooperated in the massive irregularities. Sarit openly condemned the illegalities of the elections and was backed by college and university students, among others, who had hoped for the restoration of true democracy. Thereupon, Phibun moved to hit Sarit economically. He decreed that all military and cabinet officials must sever their ties with commercial and industrial undertakings, a move calculated to hurt Sarit Thanarat, who held substantial interest in numerous companies, including the lucrative lottery enterprise in Bangkok.

On September 16, 1957, Sarit Thanarat retaliated with a bloodless coup d'état. He forced Phibun first to leave for Cambodia and later to Japan in exile; Phao fled to Switzerland, closer to the money he had siphoned off to his numbered accounts there for several years. There were few tears shed for Phibun, though he had played such a distinguished, heroic role in the revolution of 1932. He had thoroughly discredited himself during the decade immediately prior to his ouster in 1957 through a corrupt, self-serving administration. Sarit's rule was marked by regressive measures, such as abandonment of the legislature and the constitution, and there was a marked shift in the development policy. Corruption reached new heights, with more U.S. aid being appropriated by Sarit and his men for their own profit. Sarit headed the government for six years and on his death in 1963 was succeeded by his nominee, Marshal Thanom Kittikachorn.

The Sarit-Thanom period brought Thailand even closer to the United States. Thailand received more than $1 billion in economic and military aid, besides the unaccounted millions spent by U.S. armed forces from Vietnam spending their R & R (rest and recuperation) leaves in Bangkok. The bilateral relations were officially strengthened by the Rusk-Thanat Assistance Agreement of 1962, signed by U.S. Secretary of State Dean Rusk and Thailand's Foreign Minister Thanat Khoman, and the Military Contingency Plan of 1964. During the Vietnam conflict, Thailand proved crucial to the U.S. war effort in many ways. Thailand allowed the United States to build some sophisticated bases in the country, notably at Udorn and Sattahip, and use them for making bombing raids over Vietnam. Besides, some 50,000 U.S. troops were stationed on Thai soil, and Thais were asked to show their solidarity with the United States by dispatching combat personnel—about 12,000—to Vietnam and several thousand to Laotian battlefields. Thailand had thus taken grave risks in assisting the United States during the Vietnam War and earned the hatred not only of China and North Vietnam but also of the numerous countries in the Third World opposed to the U.S. war effort in Vietnam.

Such close involvement with the United States cost Thailand domestically, in terms of both an internal insurgency instigated by China and North Vietnam as well as a general upsurge of nationalism opposed to the presence of foreign troops on Thai soil. Thus, on January 1, 1965, China retaliated by establishing a Thai Independence Movement and a Thai Patriotic Front whose goal was to overthrow the Bangkok government. China also stepped up its program of constructing roads in Laos close to the Thai borders. At the same time, North Vietnam activated its own program for training anti-Thai tribal groups in northeast Thailand.

IMPACT OF CHANGES IN U.S. POLICY

President Johnson's announcement of March 31, 1968, that the United States would seek a negotiated settlement with Hanoi brought the first fissures in Thai government over its future role as a pro-U.S. power in the region. On the one hand, several members of the government, including the prime minister, believed in retaining strong U.S. ties and suggested a broader military alliance along with South Korea, South Vietnam, and the Philippines for stronger opposition to communism. On the other hand, Foreign Minister Thanat Khoman urged his cabinet colleagues to increase their options because he himself was convinced the United States would soon withdraw from the region. Beginning in mid-1969, the United States was asked to reduce its troop levels in Thailand. Efforts to move closer to Communist countries were slowly initiated. A trade agreement was concluded in December 1970 with the Soviet Union, and a special committee was established to study relations with China. In the following year, Thailand joined the other ASEAN members in endorsing the Malaysian proposal to declare all of Southeast Asia a zone of peace, freedom, and neutrality.

Despite all such precautionary moves, the Thais were, like the Japanese, caught completely unaware by the sudden announcement in July 1971 of President Nixon's projected visit to Beijing and the radical alterations in U.S. foreign policy that it signified. Two years earlier, in 1969, a new constitution had been adopted by the Thanom government and a legislature elected. For a brief period, though still under the army's domination, the Thai people had tasted the atmosphere of freedom, and politicians had demonstrated an unusual boldness in criticizing the government. U.S. policy changes toward China promoted a new national debate along two additional dimensions.

First, there was vehement criticism of the United States for initiating such momentous changes without prior consultation with an ally like Thailand. Then, there were people openly critical of the military leaders for their lack of imagination, initiative, and flexibility in revamping Thai relations with China. After China's admission to the United Nations in October 1971, some opposition leaders congratulated Beijing and sought permission to visit China. The open discussion in the legislature and the press was too much for the military. In November 1971, Thanom Kittikachorn reacted by dismissing Thanat Khoman, abrogating the two-year-old constitution, dissolving the National Assembly, instituting press censorship, abridging personal freedoms, and reverting to the previous form of rule by a tight military clique.

STUDENT REVOLT BRINGS CIVILIAN RULE

The Thanom government had been unaware of the seething opposition to the reimposition of army rule. The initiative was taken by university students. The movement was triggered on October 6, 1973, by the arrest of twelve students handing out leaflets demanding a constitution, thereby violating the official ban on political activities. To protest this action, thousands of students and other civilians poured into the streets. Police opened fire and soon army tanks rolled, killing a hundred persons on a single day, October 14, 1973. At this point, the king, in one of his rarest political interventions, ordered Thanom Kittikachorn and Prapas Charusathien, deputy prime minister, out of the country and invited an extremely well-regarded individual, Sanya Thammasak, formerly chief justice of the Supreme Court and adviser to the king, to become prime minister. Sanya was then the rector of Thammasat University and as such enjoyed the confidence of the students.

With that, a quarter century of almost uninterrupted army rule came to an end. In the euphoric atmosphere of the time, students rejoiced over the "power to the people," expecting the new government to perform wonders through a clean, honest administration dedicated to the well-being of the common people instead of merely serving the interests of the bureaucratic-military elite.

The experiment in constitutional democracy lasted for a brief three years, during which time there were four governments, one of them lasting barely a week. Immense frustration and factionalism beset the student groups as well as other nontraditional political groups, as legislators and constitutional experts dragged their feet for nearly a year working on a new constitution. Though Sanya Thammasak was sympathetic to the students, he was more at home among the traditional elite and brooked no radical reform. The students therefore chose to work outside the governmental structure through the NSCT (National Student Center of Thailand), going in thousands to villages to explain the meaning of the new "revolution." Many of them were leftist, a few clandestine Communists; both types took up popular issues like land tenure, high urban rents, and the pervasive corruption.

In the February 1975 elections, forty-two different political parties fielded candidates. No party secured a majority. The minority government formed by Seni Pramoj lasted only eight days. In order to keep up the parliamentary system of government, three rightist groups coalesced to form the middle-of-the-road Social Action party (SAP), with Seni's younger and far more capable brother, Kukrit Pramoj, as prime minister. For the next year, Kukrit's intellect, wit, and political skills were put to the sorest test ever as he was buffeted by leftist student leaders and the reemerging rightists.

The rightists—military and bureaucratic—saw their traditional power position obviously threatened by the students' radical postures and programs and reasserted their strength through two new organizations: Nawapon (new resolve) and the Red Gaurs (rightist equivalent of the Red Guards in China). The Nawapon operated at the national, provincial, and district levels with the clandestine collaboration of bureaucrats and army and police officials, including the anti-Communist Internal Security Operations Command. Its motto was to save the nation, religion, and king, the three acknowledged pillars of Thai society, from total ruin by student Communists. By now, the students were themselves divided along ideological lines, the rightists among them joining the Red Gaurs and provoking violence for which the leftists would be blamed. The Red Gaurs were certainly behind the assassination of a score of leaders of the Farmers Federation of Thailand in mid-1975, vandalism of Prime Minister Kukrit's residence in August, destruction of property at the Thammasat University campus (the unofficial headquarters of the leftist and centrist student movement), and the assassination of the young, brilliant, and dynamic secretary-general of the Socialist party, the Cornell-trained Dr. Boonsanong Bunyothayan, who had previously taught at Thammasat University. By early 1976, the Nawapon and the Red Gaurs had accomplished their mission of creating an atmosphere of fear, uncertainty, and complete chaos in the country.

The elections of April 4, 1976, the most violent ever, routed the leftists, defeated Kukrit Pramoj, and returned traditionalists-conservatives in large numbers, bringing in a shaky, diffident government under Seni Pramoj. Clearly, the rightist groups—with covert financial and other support from elements of the army, police, and civil service—had succeeded through the use of violence in scaring the people and making them wish for a return to stability, law, and order.

ABOUT-FACE IN FOREIGN RELATIONS

After almost a quarter century of staunch pro-U.S. policy, the Thai leaders, and even more so the Thai people, perceived the need for a radical change to suit the new balance of power in Southeast Asia. In the early 1970s, the traditional Thai genius was asserting itself to adjust to a changed international environment. As the decade progressed, it became increasingly clear to the Thais that the United States would be less important as a dependable regional power and that Thailand would have to reckon with China and North Vietnam as the most dominant factors. The adjustment was brought about with customary Thai finesse, the diplomatic bamboo bending and bowing without breaking under the political strain and stress. In 1972, Thailand officially initiated a dialogue with China by sending a table tennis team in September and following it with a trade mission in October. Earlier, the Thais had attempted since 1970 to open communication with Hanoi on an issue that did not impinge on the Democratic Republic of Vietnam's relations with the United States. This was the question of repatriation of some seventy thousand Vietnamese refugees long resident in northeast Thailand.

After the overthrow of the military regime in October 1973, the entire U.S.-Thai relationship came to be questioned. Some raised emotive, nationalistic questions that the presence of foreign troops degraded the Thai nation; others pragmatically argued that the Thai-U.S. alliance should be discarded because it had nothing more to offer Thailand in the new international environment. Although the latter provided a respectable, intellectual basis for argument, growing Thai nationalism gave the anti-alliance movement its muscle.[1]

The demand for removal of U.S. troops from Thai soil became more vociferous after the arrival of a former CIA official, William Kintner, as the new U.S. ambassador in early 1974 and the revelation of a letter to the prime minister from a CIA agent posing as a leader of the insurgency. Large-scale anti-U.S. demonstrations followed, and the Thai government officially asked the United States not to interfere in Thai domestic affairs. Two months later, U.S. withdrawal from Thailand began with reductions in B-52 bombers. After the populist Kukrit Pramoj became prime minister in March 1975, the United States was given twelve months in which to complete the withdrawal of all its armed forces and equipment from Thailand. U.S. pleas in early 1976 to permit a limited presence went unheeded; the only concession made was to move the deadline to July. The public position on the subject was so clear and emphatic that even the rightist government of Seni Pramoj, installed after Kukrit's defeat in the April 1976 elections, would not dare to give an extension to the U.S. armed forces in Thailand. By July 20, 1976, evacuation of U.S. troops and equipment was completed.

Kukrit Pramoj's prime ministership was also noted for the final steps leading to establishment of diplomatic relations with Beijing in July 1975 and the liberalization of citizenship regulations in favor of the Chinese in Thailand. On August 9,

1976, three weeks after the U.S. troop withdrawal was complete—a Vietnamese precondition for the establishment of diplomatic ties—Hanoi and Bangkok announced the recognition of each other's government.

MILITARY RULE UNDER DEMOCRATIC GARB

Democracy—restored by the student movement as a form of government in October 1973—lasted until the coup of February 1991 brought the army back to power again. Direct control of government by the armed forces, however, remained only for a brief period of eighteen months. In May 1992, a mass movement, this time supported by much larger numbers not merely of students but also of middle class and professional people, ended the army rule. In the absence of a clear majority of any single political party in the legislature, coalition governments have ruled the country ever since with opportunistic alliances among numerous fractious political parties, in the process damaging and diluting democracy itself.

For the most part since the cataclysmic events of October 1973, Thailand has remained outwardly a democracy, dominated at least until September 1992 by men drawn from the armed forces. The political spectrum has been, in general, heavily weighted in favor of the right. Most rightist parties have been founded or dominated by high military officers, active or retired, who have managed to keep for themselves the most important positions in the cabinet. The coalition governments between 1980 and February 1991 were led by army men: from 1980 to 1988 by Prem Tinsulanond and thereafter until the coup of 1991 by Chatichai Choonhavan.

A former commander in chief, Prem Tinsulanond was generally acceptable both to the army and to the political parties. Prem had established his reputation for combating the Communist guerrilla movement during the period 1974–1977 in the northeast not only by actively fighting but more importantly by winning over the peasantry. In September 1978, he became army commander in chief and was appointed concurrently defense minister in Kriangsak's cabinet in May 1979. He was known for being opposed to corruption and had kept himself out of political intrigue. Throughout his premiership, he remained nonpartisan and in fact did not join any political party. A source of great strength and support for the prime minister was the king, who intervened at least twice in his behalf, once to get his military position extended by one year beyond the mandated age of retirement and, more significant, on another occasion by helping to defuse a coup against him led by the "Young Turks" in April 1981.

Despite Prem Tinsulanond's ability to conciliate and mediate diverse interest groups within the military as well as among the political parties and his personal commitment to democratic norms, Thailand was far from being a congenial democracy. On the other hand, the military was too factionalized and politicized to abandon the democratic framework and rule by itself. Rival power figures surfaced within the military. Thus, former Prime Minister General Kriangsak Chamanan, whom Prem replaced in 1980, established his own National Democrat party in 1981, but was arrested in 1985 for helping the coup against Prem. General Arthit Kamlang-Ek, who had staunchly supported Prem and had "saved" him in the 1981 coup, showed independent ambitions after 1984. His "retirement" from the office of the commander in chief by Prem in 1986 was well timed for the elections to the House of Representatives.

The parliamentary elections of July 24, 1988, also failed to give a clear majority to any single party. A tired Prem refused to accept the invitation of several parties once again to form a coalition government. Thereupon, the leader of the largest party in the House, Chatichai Choonhavan of the conservative, probusiness Chart Thai (CT) or Thai Nation party, became prime minister. Chatichai, a retired major-general, was the son of Field Marshal Pin Choonhavan, a deputy prime minister in the 1950s. After several ambassadorial appointments, Chatichai had become an entrepreneur, rapidly assuming the position of a prominent industrialist and founder of the CT party in 1974. He was a supporter of Prem Tinsulanond and held the position of deputy prime minister in his coalition cabinet.

Chatichai's prime ministership, in marked contrast to that of Prem Tinsulanond, damaged the military's position in the country's politics, perhaps irreparably. His regime was widely known to be the most corrupt among a people whose threshold of tolerance for corruption has been high. Many deals had been struck and projects undertaken by the government with businessmen who were members of the most dominant element in the ruling coalition. Members of the prime minister's Advisory Council behaved haughtily and provoked confrontations, contrary to Thai culture. The bureaucracy, a steady and respected component of the Thai governmental structure, which had traditionally enjoyed semi-independence even during the authoritarian military regimes, was grossly bypassed by Chatichai's aides on several occasions.

What led to the overthrow of Chatichai's government, however, was the military's resentment caused by the treatment meted out by the government to Chavalit Yongchaiyudh, who after his retirement as army commander in March 1990 had joined the government as deputy prime minister and defense minister. After only seventy-four days in office, he had resigned from the government because, in his view, the prime minister had not defended him against attacks by a cabinet minister, the vitriol-tongued former police captain, Chalerm Yoobamrung. The episode strengthened the military's complaint that the government had not shown enough respect to its leader and was intolerably insensitive to its interests. Out of the government, Chavalit established a new party, the New Aspiration party (NAP), which openly accused the government of rampant corruption. The military leaders also accused Chalerm of eavesdropping on the military communications network.

Another major bone of contention between the army leadership and the government was the reinstatement and promotion of Manoon Roopkachorn, a former "Young Turk" leader who had been instrumental in the rise of General Kriangsak to power. The Young Turks were members of Class 7 of the Chulachomklao Military Academy, opposed to the military leadership of the 1980s drawn from Class 5. Manoon was among those who had engineered the unsuccessful coup attempts in 1981 and 1985 and who had fled to Germany after each coup attempt. He was also allegedly involved in the 1982 plot to assassinate the queen. In late 1990, he was reinstated and promoted as major-general and given a crucial position in the defense ministry, which was also headed by Prime Minister Chatichai. In January 1992, the government transferred the head of the Central Bureau of Investigation, a Class 5 graduate and close associate of the top military commanders. It seemed as if the Chatichai government was favoring Class 7 over Class 5 military leaders.

THE COUP OF FEBRUARY 1991

The six-man junta that toppled the Chatichai government on February 23, 1991, called itself the National Peace Keeping Council (NPKC). It seized all power, but unlike in the previous coups, the NPKC did not ban political parties. Nor did it impose censorship on the press and the media, although they were urged to exercise self-restraint. General Sunthorn Kongsompong, supreme commander of the armed forces, became chairman of the NPKC, but it was well known that General Suchinda Kraprayoon, deputy chairman of the NPKC, was the real center of power. For reasons of general acceptability, however, the junta appointed a civilian government under Anand Punyarachun as prime minister.

The appointment of the much-respected Anand Punyarachun helped to win the support not only of the general population but also of the international community. He was well reputed for his experience in diplomacy, having served previously as a permanent secretary in the Foreign Office and as ambassador to the United States and to the United Nations. Because of accusations that he was a Communist sympathizer, he had resigned from government service in 1977. Thereafter, he joined the private sector, eventually becoming chairman of a major industrial group, Saha Union. He was well known to the leader of the coup, General Suchinda Kraprayoon, who had served in the capacity of military attaché in Washington under Anand. As prime minister, Anand enlisted some of the best-known civil servants and businessmen in his cabinet. The key portfolios of Interior and Defense, however, were reserved for the military.

Within a year of the coup, a constitution was adopted and general elections to the House of Representatives were announced for March 22, 1992. The constitution left vague whether the prime minister and members of the cabinet would have to be drawn from among elected representatives. The fully nominated 270-member Senate continued to enjoy vital powers, including the right to vote on no-confidence motions against the government. Constitutional amendments would need a majority of a joint meeting of the two legislative houses. In the event of a divided House, whose membership was 360, and a united Senate, the latter could still prevail over the wishes of the elected representatives. The Senate speaker would preside over the joint meeting of the two houses. Apart from these special features, the Senate would have only the power to delay but not to deny legislation. The constitution was approved on December 7, but only after the king intervened, subtly suggesting that it be passed.

In the elections to the House of Representatives announced for March 1992, all parties except the long-banned Communist party of Thailand were allowed fairly free play. As planned, the NPKC, established in advance of the elections, and a new party, Samakkitham, ostensibly under the leadership of a former air force officer, aimed at forming a government. Despite the fact that CT had suffered the most in the 1991 coup, it decided to support the NPKC after the elections. In particular, it supported the then army chief and deputy NPKC leader, General Suchinda Kraprayoon, for the prime ministership. The Samakkitham, CT, and SAP were the principal promilitary parties. Their opponents—the prodemocracy side—consisted of the Democrats; the NAP led by General Chavalit Yongchaiyudh; the Palang Dharma (PD) led by the former governor of Bangkok, Chamlong Srimuang; and the Solidarity party (SP).

As in the past, the elections of March 1992 did not yield a majority for any single party: Samakkitham won 79 seats, CT 74, and NAP 72. The prodemocracy parties, by then dubbed the "angels," protesting against the new constitution because it would merely facilitate the continuation of military rule under democratic garb, insisted that the new prime minister must be an elected member of the Parliament.

THE REVOLT OF MAY 1992 AND ITS AFTERMATH

Despite the clear statement by the "angels," the promilitary parties nominated Suchinda, who was not an elected member of the Parliament, to lead the government as prime minister. Thereupon, the "angels" planned a protest under the leadership of Chamlong Srimuang, whose reputation for honest and austere living was well established among the people. The angels demanded Suchinda's resignation and approval of an amendment that an incumbent of the prime minister's office must be an elected member of the Parliament. The protest was the largest ever, attracting 500,000 people, largely middle class and professionals. It was met by brutal military force on May 19, resulting in heavy casualties: nearly 100 killed and many times more injured. The military-led government arrested many protesters, including Chamlong Srimuang.

Those repressive acts sealed the military's active and direct role in Thai politics. There were daily mass protests in a month-long confrontation between the promilitary and prodemocracy sides, attracting worldwide publicity. Finally, the king himself intervened and used his moral authority to "instruct" Suchinda and Chamlong on live television to reconcile their differences in the interests of the nation. Suchinda stepped down from the prime ministership and announced retirement from politics.

In a desperate move, the promilitary parties passed a constitutional amendment requiring the prime minister to be an elected member of the Parliament and nominated a CT leader, Somboon Rahong, for the post. The Thai people, however, protested the action of the promilitary parties to hang on to power. To avoid chaos, the speaker of the House of Representatives nominated former prime minister Anand Punyarachun to lead the government, dissolve the House, and hold fresh elections.

The new elections held on September 13, 1992, gave the five prodemocracy angel parties a slender majority—185 out of 360—with the Democrats winning 79 and NAP 51 seats. They nominated Chuan Leekpai of the Democrat party for prime minister. Theirs was a feeble government, however, dependent on the support of the small prodemocracy parties and faced with the formidable opposition of promilitary parties that had 144 House seats held by CT and Chart Pattana (CP), or National Development party.

It was a credit to Chuan's long experience in the Parliament and his consummate political skills that his government lasted three years, during which the promilitary parties tried every trick in the political book to tempt some NAP and SAP members to defect. There were serious fissures in the coalition, also, because of differences between the Democrats and the NAP. The latter opposed the government-proposed constitutional amendment to introduce elections to local administrative bodies, which were viewed by some NAP leaders as pocket constituencies.

By 1994, the politics of defection, party-hopping, and rank opportunism had a field day as Chatichai Choonhavan, the former premier and now leader of the promilitary CP, declared a merger of SAP with his own party in September in a bid to topple Chuan's government. However, on December 8, when Chuan's political partner NAP with its 51 seats pulled the rug out from under the coalition government, Chatichai and his CP's 60 seats allied with Chuan to retain the government's majority in the House of Representatives. The still-shaky government finally collapsed on May 19, 1995, when an important coalition partner, the PD party of Chamlong Srimuang (which held 46 seats in the House) withdrew shortly before a scheduled vote of no-confidence. Thereupon, Chuan dissolved the House and announced a snap election on July 2, a year before the official four-year term of the House would have ended.

Just before the elections of July 1995, a new political alignment, representing an opportunistic mixture of prodemocracy and promilitary parties under the leadership of the promilitary CT (the other parties being NAP, SAP, PD, Prachakorn Thai, and Muan Chon), presented a joint program to the people. After the elections, this new six-party alliance, with the addition of a seventh party, the Nam Thai, became the ruling coalition. It held 233 seats in the 391-seat House of Representatives. As the leader of the largest vote-winning party, Banharn Silpa-Archa of the CT became the prime minister.

From the beginning, the CT-led coalition came under severe criticism from the media for its corruption and ineffectiveness, so much so that even the king joined the chorus, albeit in a subtle manner. With that, the government's fate was sealed; new elections were announced for November 1996, much earlier than scheduled.

The November 1996 elections resulted in a coalition government under Prime Minister Chavalit. In the 393-member House of Representatives, the New Aspiration party held 125 seats, with the Democrat party a close second with 123 seats. CT came in fourth with only 38 seats. Chavalit, however, resigned a year later in November 1997, the victim of the Southeast Asian currency crisis. A new coalition was put together by the former prime minister, Democrat party leader Chuan Leekpai. Although he accepted the $17.1 billion IMF's bailout recovery program for Thailand and was praised by the IMF for providing a stable and effective government, he was criticized at home for toeing the IMF's line. Although he survived three votes of no-confidence in the House of Representatives, the last in December 1999, he became widely unpopular because of unacceptable levels of unemployment, sporadic recovery, and widespread misery in the countryside, all of which affected his party's fortunes in the elections of January 2001.

In the elections held in January 2001, the Democrat party lost badly to the nascent Thai Rak Thai party (TRT; Thais Love Thais party) led by the billionaire Thakin Shinawatra. It secured 248 seats (3 short of an absolute majority) to the Democrat party's 128. The Thai Nation party came in third with 41 seats, and the New Aspiration party won only 36 seats. For the first time, the elections were held on both constituency and party-list bases. Four hundred representatives were elected from individual territorial constituencies, and 100 came from political party lists on the basis of proportion to the election results. The elections led to charges of massive vote-buying, resulting in many reelections in numerous constituencies and delaying the final composition of the National Assembly.

The Thailand Farmers Bank estimated that 24 billion bahts (US$555 million) were spent in purchasing the votes in the countryside, which dominates the National Assembly. The new prime minister faced the National Counter-Corruption Commission on charges of amassing wealth by ill-gotten means and concealing the assets from public scrutiny. In June 2001, the Constitutional Court acquitted him by the narrowest of margins (8–7) on dubious legal grounds, with many in the media and the public questioning the integrity of the judges involved.

The spectacular success of the TRT revolutionized Thai politics in both style and substance: The old pattern of weak coalition governments yielded to a strong, well-focused government, which prompted smaller parties to join it, thereby raising hopes that a two-party system might be in the making.

THE SHINAWATRA PHENOMENON

The decade following the end of military rule in 1992 was marked by regular elections in Thailand, though power was limited to the upper classes, the urban centers, and business leaders. People in rural areas, who accounted for over 75 percent of the population, and the urban poor played barely any role in the Thai democracy. All that changed dramatically with the rise of a Thai billionaire, Thaksin Shinawatra, from his lower-middle-class, northern Thai small-town background, to soaring riches, thanks to his business acumen in electronics, cell phone, and cable television enterprises. In the late 1990s, he showed a penchant for politics, establishing the Thai Rak Thai (Thais Love Thais), or TRT party, challenging the Democrat party in the general elections of January 2001. The TRT won a spectacular 296 out of 480 seats in *Sapha Phuthaen Ratsadon* (the lower house of the Parliament), giving its leader, Thaksin Shinawatra, the position of prime minister. Thaksin portrayed himself as the voice of the poor, particularly the *ban nok* (countryside people), who had so far been largely ignored in Thai politics. In the February 2005 elections, Thaksin won a landslide victory, the TRT improving its record to 374 seats and giving the populist Thaksin an authority that truly became the envy of the established elite politicians, the military, and, above all, the monarch.

In justification of his claim of leadership of the poor, the Thaksin administration proclaimed a number of pro-poor schemes involving hundreds of billions of *bahts* (1 US$ = about 40 *bahts*). The schemes included a health program, a development fund for each village, and a debt-suspension plan; in February 2005, Thaksin declared that by 2009, "there will be no poor people." No one in Thailand's entire history had vowed to do so much for the miserable poor. At the same time, in order to raise Thailand's competitiveness in the international sphere, Thaksin promoted globalization. His measures included signing trade agreements with large economies such as the United States, China, India, Japan, and Australia; privatization of state enterprises; economic restructuring; and improvement of the economic infrastructure.

Thaksin met severe opposition to his policies from both the left and the right. His pro-poor schemes were opposed by the urban middle-class and established business families, who regarded his policies to woo the dispossessed an abuse of democracy. On the other hand, the leftist activists and the intellectuals resisted his globalization policies. By late 2004, the charges against Thaksin included cronyism in helping his family, relatives, and fellow businessmen; and promotions in the military of favorites, notably his class fellows in the police cadet corps. Thaksin was accused of undermining all the institutions established under the 1997 constitution, including the National Counter-Corruption Commission and the Election Commission. His greatest failure was in the country's three southern provinces, where a virulent antigovernment movement had mushroomed into a major separatist insurgency in late 2004 thanks to Thaksin's strong-headed countermeasures.

INSURGENCY IN THE SOUTH

The Buddhist Thais and Muslim Malays had lived in relative peace for almost a century since the Thai kingdom had absorbed the territories of the Sultanate of Pattani in 1902 and had the acquisition and the international border recognized by a dominant Western power in 1909 with the signing of the Anglo-Siamese Treaty. The territory was divided into three provinces of Thailand: Narathiwat, Pattani, and Yala. Today, their predominantly Muslim population of 1.5 million constitutes the most backward, underdeveloped region of Thailand, suffering from governmental neglect and disregard. The people have periodically raised the standard of rebellion regarding Thailand as "foreign colonizer of a Muslim homeland."[2]

The demands of the armed movements in the three provinces have ranged from provincial autonomy, joining Malaysia, or full independence. One such armed rebellion took place in the 1960s; by the 1970s, it seemed to have petered out. The new millennium has witnessed a far more virulent form, claiming several hundred lives, both Muslim and Thai, the latter being mostly low and mid-level bureaucrats, teachers, monks, judges, policemen, and other security personnel. Several groups claim to speak for the Muslim population of the three provinces, among them the Pattani United Liberation Organization (PULO), Mujaheddin Islam of Pattani (MIP), and Barisan Revolusi Nasional (BRN) with BERSATU as an alleged umbrella organization.

Traditionally, the insurgency operations have adopted guerrilla warfare, conducted mostly on foot in the rugged jungles. The insurgency beginning in January 2004 involved some 8,000 to 10,000 men, many of them using motorcycles, mounted with automatic rifles, as attack vehicles. Their tactic of detonating bombs in public places, sometimes by suicide bombers, showed similarities with operations of some international terrorist organizations, notably Al-Qaeda. There were dozens of attacks on state facilities, such as police booths/stations, schools, and health clinics. The incidence of attacks reached a peak in March–April 2004 when 36 government buildings were burned down and a bomb exploded in a bar in a town in Narathiwat province. On March 31, 10 armed rebels stole 1.4 million tons of ammonium nitrate (which could be used in the making of bombs), 50 sticks of dynamite, and 2 detonators in Yala province. On April 30, when the insurgents attacked 11 police bases, 112 people were killed. In the first four months of 2004, over 60 policemen lost their lives.

The government's reaction was severe. Martial law was proclaimed in the three southern provinces, 1,000 Muslim schools were ordered closed, and an undisclosed number of persons were arrested and imprisoned. Prime Minister Shinawatra was insensitive and complacent at first, ridiculing the insurgency as the work of some "drug-crazed bandits" and, later, acknowledging that they must be well-trained Islamic militants and blaming the rebellion on the dominant northern Malaysian political organization, Partai Se Malaysia. He accused the Malaysian government of fomenting the problem and proposed a fence be constructed all along the Thai-Malaysian border. He also blamed the disturbances in the South on the madrassa-type schools, called *ponohs,* in the three rebellious provinces, where some of the teachers were allegedly insurgency leaders. There was no effort to understand the state of poverty, underdevelopment, or neglect in the three provinces. Some of Shinawatra's ill-thought statements and policies may well have contributed to strengthening ethnic southern Malay nationalism.

THE TAK BAI TRAGEDY

The disruption in southern Thailand attracted the attention of international human rights organizations, including the United Nations, in October 2004. The police had arrested six young Muslims, who were suspected of regularly stealing weapons from military depots in the vicinity and distributing them among rebel Muslims in the area. A large crowd estimated at several thousand assembled outside the police station of Tak Bai. Thai security forces fired on the crowd, killing six. About 1,300 persons were detained and taken away by military trucks. Of these, 78 suffocated when they were stacked atop each other in the back of the trucks. The tragedy sparked riots in the Tak Bai region. The incident drew international attention and became the subject of numerous articles in the Thai and Malay press.

In advance of a special joint session of the two houses of the Parliament (the first since 1992) on March 30, 2005, and its expected criticism of his policies, Prime Minister Thaksin Shinawatra took a number of measures to conciliate the South. On March 29, he announced the appointment of a 48-member National Reconciliation Commission under the chairmanship of former prime minister Anand Panyarachun (1991–1992). He had recently won laurels for serving on a panel that had proposed reforms for the United Nations. On March 31, Shinawatra apologized to the joint parliamentary session, accepting responsibility for the excesses in the South and offering to withdraw heavily armed troops from the region.

On the day the joint parliamentary session met, the cabinet approved compensation totaling 28.4 million bahts (about US$710,000) for families of 85 persons who lost their lives in the Tak Bai tragedy in October 2004. These measures were taken in anticipation of the beginning of the trial of eight teachers in Islamic schools in the South, who were accused of treason and described as leaders of the insurgency. The measures did not appease the rebels, however, who on July 14 and 15, 2005, carried out a well-coordinated series of attacks in Yala. About 60 insurgents, with bombs, guns, and Molotov cocktails, attacked a power station, hotels, restaurants, a cinema, and a number of small shops, killing two policemen and a number of civilians in that provincial city.

During the fifteen-month military rule beginning September 2006, the administration of Prime Minister Surayud Chulanont adopted a more conciliatory approach than before toward the South. As a part of his peace initiative, he retrieved the recommendations made by the Shinawatra-appointed (but ignored) National Reconciliation Commission. Surayud offered to hold talks with the insurgents, even proposing a pre-talks amnesty for low-ranking rebels as an inducement.

ECONOMY

Among the ASEAN countries, Thailand was one of three that enjoyed a booming economy in the 1990s, with annual growth rates of more than 8 percent. This brought unprecedented prosperity to a large segment of the population until the 1997 Southeast Asian currency crisis. One of the victims was the government of Prime Minister Chavalit. Under the leadership of his successor, Chuan Leekpai, the country was pulled out of the catastrophe (marked by 9 percent economic contraction in 1998 and zero growth in 1999), thanks to massive financial assistance ($17.1 billion) from the International Monetary Fund. The adoption of the IMF recovery plan, however, brought charges of a sellout to foreigners, which contributed partly to the prime minister's defeat in the elections of January 2001. In addition to the external factor of the currency crisis, there were internal problems of oversupply in the construction sector and lax regulation of the banking industry, replete with corrupt practices and accounting irregularities. The IMF plan and the subsequent legislative and administrative actions addressed some of these problems in the Thai economy. Two years of steady economic recovery and governmental austerity led to an increase in the value of the baht. Thailand once again became the world's largest rice exporter and developed electronics as a new field of export. The September 11 terrorist attacks in the United States and the consequent global economic decline once again threw the Thai economy into disarray, affecting the country's financial infrastructure, the lucrative international tourism, and tourism-related employment.

Drug syndicates have been a persistent problem affecting the economy, law and order, and politics in Thailand. For a long time, the syndicates have involved several members of Parliament, a retired general, and a former prime minister. Thanks to international (mostly U.S.) pressure, opium production and heroin manufacturing have been significantly reduced, but Bangkok and southern Thai ports still function as major transshipment centers, notably to the West Coast of the United States but also elsewhere, for narcotics from the Golden Triangle (now limited to Myanmar and Laos). In this pernicious trade, Thailand serves as a source of finance and money-laundering, with consequences for domestic law and order and the black-market economy. In addition to local crime syndicates, those of foreign origin, notably the Japanese Yakuza and Hong Kong–based triads, are attempting to make inroads into politics. Unfortunately, Thais are the world's largest consumers of methamphetamine tablets, which are produced across the western border in Myanmar.

THE ANTI-THAKSIN COUP AND PROLONGED CRISIS

The anti-Thaksin forces mobilized after the TRT's victory in the February 2005 elections. The economy was severely affected by several factors over which Thaksin had no control: the soaring international oil price; the tsunami in December 2004 followed by floods in the east and the northeast in 2005; and the avian flu affecting tourism, a principal economic earner. Massive protests in the streets led by opposition leaders received covert support from the military. Various groups coalesced into the PAD (People's Alliance for Democracy), openly scorning the government's pro–*ban nok* (countryside) policies. The PAD's leader was Sondhi Limtongkul, a media tycoon, who had fallen out with his former close associate, Thaksin Shinawatra. The PAD petitioned the king to dismiss what was, indeed, a democratically elected government and to appoint a "royal prime minister." Among their charges was the tax-free sale of the Shinawatra family's telecommunications empire for about US$2 billion to a Singapore government–controlled corporation. The transaction was also held to be contrary to Thailand's national interest. The PAD's demand was that Thaksin step down immediately and that an amendment to the constitution be approved barring him from returning to power. In response, Thaksin dissolved the Parliament and called for fresh elections on April 2, 2006. Conservative elements concluded that it was time for the king and the military to intervene.

The military staged a coup on September 19, 2006, declared the abolition of the constitution of 1997, banned all political activity, and established the Council for Democratic Reform (CDR) headed by General Sonthi Boonyaratglin within the framework of a constitutional monarchy. The Thai Rak Thai (TRT) party was banned. The CDR ordered the drafting of a new constitution under which new elections would be held within twelve months. Three months before the coup, Prem Tinsulanond, former commander in chief and prime minister and at the time chairman of the King's Privy Council, had ominously told the graduating class of the Royal Military Academy in July 2006 that the military "served the king and the country, not any particular government."[3]

In the end, the elections were held on December 23, 2007. Though the TRT was banned, a new party that included most of its membership replaced it in the name of the People's Power party (PPP). Its two main rivals would be the Democratic party (DP) and the Thai Nation party (TNP). No single party obtained a majority of seats in the Parliament or a majority of the votes cast. The PPP won the highest number of seats, 199 out of 400 with 36.63 percent of the vote; the DP won 132; and TNP only 33. Under the parallel voting system that allowed for proportional representation, 80 additional seats were allotted in the Parliament: The PPP received 34, the DP 33, and the TNP only 4.

THE SAMAK REGIME

The PPP formed a six-party coalition government with Samak Sundaravej, a strong Thaksin supporter, as the prime minister. Samak held a law degree and had been an experienced politician since he was thirty years old, when he became a member of the Democrat party. Later, he served as minister for the interior in a military government. Still later, he established his own party, Prachakorn Thai, but joined Thaksin Shinawatra's government as one of the deputy prime ministers. He also served as governor of Bangkok for four years. In the elections of 2007, his newly established PPP platform was a replica of Shinawatra's TRT program promising more facilities to the rural population, including education and health services, and championing a better economy for the country overall. Soon after the elections of 2007, Samak was dubbed Thaksin's puppet.

The anti-Thaksin forces led by the People's Alliance for Democracy (PAD) joined hands by June 2008 to make Samak the target of their street protests. He was accused of corruption and for helping his brother-in-law Thaksin, who had taken refuge in Great Britain and against whom court cases were pending in Thailand. On August 26, thousands of protesters outside the Government House vowed to stay there until their demand was met that the prime minister step down. Two weeks later, Samak was forced to resign not because of the PAD-led demonstrations but because of a court verdict disqualifying him from holding the position of prime minister. Samak, a former television chef, had recently participated in a television cooking show and accepted fees for his performance. On October 21, the court held his television participation was a conflict of interest and a violation of the Constitution. Samak was banned from participating in politics for five years.

Despite the PPP's resolution to renominate Samak for the prime minister's position, the constitutional ban on his participation in politics was respected by the Parliament, and Somchai Wongsawat was appointed the new prime minister. He too was a Thaksin crony. The army did not intervene; neither did the king. By late November, the PAD-orchestrated crisis paralyzed activity at the two airports, including the newly opened Suwarnabhumi International Airport, where about 300,000 passengers were stranded. This event brought the crisis international attention and reflected poorly on Thailand for lost tourist revenues. The PAD's seizure of the airports cost Thailand 3 billion bahts (about US$100 million) a day. Britain declared that it had frozen Thaksin's assets and revoked his visa.

The crisis was "resolved" by another decision of the Constitutional Court. It held on December 2 that the PPP and two other parties in the ruling coalition were guilty of voter fraud in the December 2007 elections. The leaders of the parties involved were banned from participation in the country's politics for five years, which left Somchai Wongsawat no alternative but to resign his prime ministership. The crisis was over, and the airport siege ended. On December 14, a new coalition in the Parliament elected Abhisit Vejjajiva, the DAP leader and an Oxford graduate, as prime minister. Over the previous two years, he had shown tremendous ability to keep all the traditional sectors of power pleased: the elite, the military, and the monarch. The Thaksin era had ended.

22

Indonesia:
Unity amid
Diversity

THE SUKARNO ERA

Problems of Freedom

After achieving full independence in 1949, the Indonesians experienced tremendous difficulties in creating and operating viable political systems. Whereas the Filipinos, Burmese, and Malaysians had considerable experience with representative institutions during the colonial era, the Indonesians had very little. Before World War II, the Dutch held the majority of seats in the colony's legislature, though they constituted less than 1 percent of the population. Under Dutch rule, political institutions did not develop in an atmosphere of individual freedom.

During Indonesia's formative years, 1949–1955, there was great instability of government and very little prospect for a smooth functioning of the party system. There were five cabinets in six years. In the first elections to the National Assembly in 1955, sixteen parties captured one or more seats. Of these, four emerged as "national" parties, but none with a majority mandate to form a government. The PNI (Partai Nasional Indonesia, or Indonesian Nationalist party) and the Masjumi (Council of Indonesian Muslim Associations) each secured about 22 percent of the seats; the Nahdatul Islam and the PKI (Partai Kommunis Indonesia, or Indonesian Communist party) secured 16 percent each.

Matching the chaotic political situation was the rapid decline in the new nation's economy. Inflation soared in the years 1949–1955, doubling the prices in the rural areas and even more in the cities. The threat of nationalization of industries and trade scared foreign investors, including the overseas Chinese who had financial connections in Singapore and Hong Kong. The salvation of the peasantry was the rich, fertile, volcanic soil of Java, which seemed to hold unlimited potential for feeding its burgeoning population.

"Guided" Democracy

The political plurality precluded the formation of an effective government, thereby giving President Sukarno scope for playing a major role in the governance of the country. In a self-proclaimed effort to "save" the country from political ruin, he turned the government on February 21, 1957, over to a national advisory council on which various functional and political elements like peasants and workers and nationalist, Communist, and military leaders were represented. Sukarno himself became the chairman of the council. The objections of the Masjumi and the Nahdatul Ulama—as well as of noted politicians like Dr. Hatta—were brusquely set aside. Sukarno quickly introduced his new concept of "guided democracy," a government by mutual consensus rather than majority rule, in effect replacing normal democratic practices and processes with a personal dictatorship.

In 1958, there were rebellions in various parts of the country, notably in Sumatra, where the regional military commanders and civilian leaders overestimated the degree of public discontent over Sukarno's rule. In July 1959, Sukarno reinstated the 1945 constitution, which gave wider executive and legislative powers to the president. He declared several political parties illegal, including Masjumi on grounds it had supported some "rebel" leaders. At the same time, he forged a National Front, mobilizing the masses in support of his policies. He also suspended the parliament because, he said, the political parties no longer represented the people. Instead, he appointed a "cooperative parliament." Differences of opinion could be expressed, but there was to be no formal voting on issues; all decisions were to be made by traditional Indonesian means like *mushawara* (deliberation) and *gotong rojong* (consensus).

Instead of cleansing the administration and striving for the economic well-being of the people, Sukarno concentrated on projecting Indonesia and himself, though not necessarily in that order, dramatically onto the international stage. Such measures helped to divert the people's attention from their pressing daily wants, to weld them into a national front, and to convince them to stand behind their president in fighting the nation's foes, real and imaginary. Sukarno talked incessantly of Indonesia as the leader of the Newly Emerging Forces (NEF), playing host at such events as the Asian Games and the Games of the Newly Emerging Forces (GANEFO). Huge sums of money were diverted to the erection of prestigious monuments and to rebuilding the capital, Jakarta. The country's debt soared; inflation skyrocketed; production and exports suffered. Corruption among bureaucrats as well as army officials swelled to intolerable proportions—particularly in the government agencies dealing with licensing, police, and taxes. Petty government officials held second jobs, many of them often driving pedicabs. The frustration in the urban centers among the educated and unemployed youth was tapped by the PKI, which by the early 1960s claimed a membership of three million, the largest Communist party in Asia outside of China.

Foreign Policy

From the mid-1950s, external affairs took primacy over domestic matters to such an extent that by the early 1960s, they determined the course and contours of domestic politics, leading to the chain of cataclysmic events that ended with Sukarno's removal from the presidency. In the first decade of Indonesian independence, Sukarno had followed Nehru's lead in adopting a policy of nonalignment in international affairs, which would enable Indonesia to decide various issues on their merits irrespective of the superpowers. Indonesia was in the vanguard of countries opposing colonialism, offering moral and diplomatic support to struggles for freedom in areas of remnant colonial rule in Asia and Africa. Such a policy also served Indonesian national interest. Thus, in December 1954, Sukarno secured from the meeting of the Colombo Powers (India, Pakistan, Sri Lanka, Myanmar, and Indonesia) in Bogor, Indonesia, support for his claims to Dutch New Guinea, or as the Indonesians called it, West Irian. The following year, in April 1955, Indonesia took tremendous pride in its selection to play host to the twenty-nine-nation Asian-African conference at Bandung, the first such bicontinental meeting of newly freed peoples.

From the beginning, Indonesia was most interested in friendly relations with the People's Republic of China despite the fact that its leaders denied the validity of the "third path" (nonalignment) and branded Sukarno and Hatta, along with Nehru and U Nu, "lackeys of Western imperialism." Indonesian leaders felt that physical distance from China ruled out a direct security threat from that direction. Taking advantage of China's new policy of peaceful coexistence beginning in 1954, Sukarno opened negotiations with China on a Dual Nationality Citizenship Treaty to resolve the status of more than 1.5 million economically dominant Chinese in Indonesia. A treaty was eventually concluded and ratified in 1960 whereby many Indonesian Chinese accepted Indonesian citizenship.

West Irian. Bandung lifted Sukarno's spirits, giving him tremendous self-confidence and what proved in time to be an insatiable ambition to play a larger role on the international stage. He became more stubborn and overreaching in his demands and strident and overtly arrogant in his denunciations of Western leaders, whom he branded "neo-colonialists." He was justified in demanding Dutch withdrawal from West Irian, although the manner of his confrontation policies prompted even the Colombo Powers to suggest moderation. To some extent, Sukarno was goaded into such a position by the intransigence of the Netherlands, which had left the question of West Irian unresolved at the time of Indonesian independence in 1949. The Dutch had toyed with the idea of carving out a separate homeland there for Indonesian Eurasians and probably planned to develop its petroleum potential for their own benefit. They argued that the ethnically distinct Papuans of West Irian had never been ruled by the Indonesian Malays in the past and did not wish to join the Indonesian republic. On the other hand, the Indonesian government maintained that the republic was coterminous with the Dutch East Indies and that the country's freedom could only be complete with the merger of West Irian. A joint

Indonesian-Dutch commission in 1950 had presented in a lengthy report contradictory evidence of the Papuan people supporting either side.

In the 1950s, Indonesia persuaded the United Nations to compel the Netherlands to resume the stalemated negotiations. Failing and frustrated, Indonesia unilaterally abrogated the Netherlands-Indonesian union, the various economic agreements, and its financial obligations to the Netherlands. Sukarno launched a new anti-Dutch campaign. He banned Dutch language publications, closed the offices of the KLM airline, disallowed remittances by Dutch expatriates, confiscated Dutch property, and terminated nonconsular functions of the Dutch mission in Jakarta. During this phase of hostility in Indonesian-Dutch relations, the Dutch were supported by Great Britain, France, Australia, and New Zealand, but the United States abstained on the issue partly because of Dutch membership in NATO and partly because of Secretary of State John Foster Dulles's general displeasure with the policies of all nonaligned countries, including Indonesia. On the other hand, Indonesia received diplomatic support from all Asian and African member-states of the United Nations, excluding Taiwan, Turkey, South Africa, and Israel but including the Asian members of SEATO and the Middle East Defense Organization. More significant for future Indonesian politics was the diplomatic, economic, and military assistance from the Soviet Union and China. Eventually, Indonesia decided to use force, landing one thousand Indonesian volunteers by ship and parachute in March 1962 in West Irian. World attention was drawn to the issue because of the intervention of UN Secretary-General U Thant. The mediatory role played by him and by veteran U.S. diplomat Ellsworth Bunker resulted in an agreement stipulating UN administration of West Irian from October 1962 to May 1963 before handing over control to the Indonesian government.

"Crush Malaysia" Campaign. The successful resolution of the West Irian dispute encouraged Sukarno to embark on further international adventurism as he changed his position from tacit acceptance of the impending formation of the Federation of Malaysia to all-out opposition in August 1963. Sukarno's change of attitude may have been brought about by the PKI and its frustration over the failure of a revolt in Brunei. In December 1962, a guerrilla revolt in Brunei broke out under the leadership of A. M. Azahari, a Labuanese of Arab descent. The reasons for the PKI's support of the Azahari-led revolt were not clear. Perhaps the PKI was fishing in troubled Malaysian waters to get hold of the independence movements in British Borneo territories. Perhaps it wanted its cadres to profit from participation in the guerrilla movement, an experience that could conceivably help at some future date in Indonesia itself.

When by early 1963 the Azahari-led revolt ended in a fiasco, the PKI was frustrated, and Sukarno launched a vicious campaign to "crush Malaysia." He condemned the new federation as a British creation designed to continue Britain's control over Malay tin and rubber and Brunei's oil resources. He branded it as neocolonialism of the Old Established Forces, posing a threat to the Newly Emerging Forces represented by Indonesia. In the anti-Malaysia confrontation, all three elements of the Indonesian polity—Sukarno, the PKI, and the army—were interested.

The army was concerned that Singapore's pro-Beijing Chinese would dominate the Federation of Malaysia, indirectly enhancing China's influence in the region so close to Indonesia. Indonesia took a number of anti-Malaysian measures. In mid-1964, Indonesian guerrillas entered Sarawak and North Borneo and attacked the Malay coast. Diplomatic and trade relations with Malaysia were snapped, although the trade embargo was ineffective because of extensive smuggling.

The confrontational politics alienated Indonesia from many fellow Asian and African nations. Since the late 1950s, Indonesia had attempted to persuade the nations of Africa, Asia, and Latin America to band together as Newly Emerging Forces in a confrontation with the surviving elements of the Old Established Forces of "decadent capitalism" and "imperialism." In this, Sukarno did get some support, particularly from Ghana's Nkrumah and Cambodia's Sihanouk, but not from others, including his old friend Nehru, who openly asserted at the conference of nonaligned nations at Belgrade in 1961 that colonialism was a dead issue. In the early 1960s, some of Indonesia's neighbors became apprehensive of Sukarno's ambitions and the implications of his militant chauvinism for their own security. First came West Irian, then Malaysia. They wondered which country would be next on his list if he succeeded in having his way against Malaysia. While Sukarno's stock undoubtedly went up internally, the chances of his acceptability as Southeast Asia's regional leader were progressively whittled down by his vitriolic, irresponsible, saber-rattling behavior against the duly constituted legal state of Malaysia. When Indonesia withdrew from the United Nations over the Malaysia issue, few tears were shed by other Asian countries. By mid-1965, Indonesia's image had suffered grievously, and the country was isolated by most of the non-Communist world.

Tilt Toward Communism. One of the principal consequences of the confrontational politics was Indonesia's growing dependence on Communists—internally and externally. Sukarno received support from the Soviet Union for West Irian and for his concept of confrontation between Newly Emerging Forces and Old Established Forces. Moscow willingly stepped into the role of a military and economic ally, selling massive quantities of arms on easy credit terms as well as offering economic aid on a lavish scale, amounting by 1965 to over $2 billion. The Soviet assistance was designed not only to obliterate Western influence in Indonesia but also to counter potential Chinese domination of the most populous country in Southeast Asia. While the Soviet Union was the leading foreign donor, China used its foreign aid shipments clandestinely to smuggle small arms to the PKI, for example, through shipments of construction materials meant for a sports stadium. Funds were also made available to the PKI through some Indonesian-Chinese businessmen. PKI Secretary Aidit himself was loath to choose sides in the Sino-Soviet conflict. Despite his pleas to the party membership to remain neutral in the dispute so that they could act together in the domestic struggle to attain power, the PKI's rank and file was attracted more to Beijing than to Moscow because of China's common Asian bonds and even more because of its radical stance within the Communist camp and leadership of the liberation movements in the Third World. Around the time of the coup in September 1965, China's influence over the PKI was at its peak.

THE GESTAPU AFFAIR

Until 1960–1961, Sukarno's power had rested upon his consummate skill in playing the army against the PKI, with the nationalist centrist force represented by Sukarno himself. His latest moves in favor of the Communists, domestically and internationally, upset the army leadership, although it did not take the initiative to seize power. It is alleged that on the night of September 30, 1965, the Communists, possibly to preempt the army or perhaps fearing Sukarno's sudden death due to his kidney and heart ailments, attempted a coup of their own by rounding up six leading generals, taking them to Halim Air Force Base, and brutally killing them. There is no clear evidence that Sukarno himself had any knowledge of the impending PKI coup, although the participants claimed they were acting on Sukarno's behalf. Sukarno himself did not blame the murders on the Communists. General Nasution, who escaped by jumping over the back wall of his house, and Major General Suharto, who was left out because of his known neutralist views, quickly mobilized the counterattack, curbing Sukarno's authority and setting the stage for a nationwide massacre of Communists. Perhaps as many as a half million people, mostly of Chinese origin, were killed, while several hundred thousand suspected Communists and their sympathizers were thrown behind bars. In the mass witch-hunt, many took advantage to settle age-old scores, particularly against the Chinese community, which had amassed fortunes through diverse economic enterprises while Indonesians had been left to languish in misery. D. N. Aidit and the two other members of the PKI triumvirate—M. H. Lukman and Njoto—were killed. The ease with which the PKI's power was broken raised doubts about its real strength, the more so because most Western observers had believed a PKI victory was imminent. Sukarno still commanded such respect in the country that it was hard for the new leadership to remove him formally and completely from the presidency. This was gradually but finally accomplished by March 1967. Sukarno died in 1970.

THE SUHARTO ERA

The New Order

In his house-cleaning operations from 1965 to 1968, Suharto had the solid support of a majority of the people, who were shocked by revelations of Sukarno's excesses. Suharto revived the parliament of 1955, giving the various parties, except the PKI and the Masjumi (which had backed the 1958 rebellions), the same representation that they then enjoyed. The armed services were given an increased representation, from 43 to 75 seats. As president, Suharto relied heavily on three individuals: Hamengku Buwono, sultan of Jogjakarta, who became deputy prime minister and in charge of several economic portfolios; Adam Malik as foreign minister; and Dr. Bambang Sumitro, an eminent economist, who joined Suharto's cabinet in June 1969 as minister of trade. The three men were the leaders of the Orde Baru—the New Order.

Certainly the greatest challenge that Suharto faced was that of pulling the country out of the economic morass and bankruptcy into which Sukarno had led it through his profligate spending measures. The new government's efforts to deal with rampant inflation, escalating unemployment, and lack of capital were hampered by the huge foreign debt of nearly $1.7 billion. Thanks to the negotiations ably conducted by Malik, an agreement (later to serve as a prototype in dealings with the Soviet Union and East European countries) was reached in 1970 with Western creditor countries whereby arrears of interest were canceled and loans were rescheduled and made payable in thirty equal annual installments. In 1973, the massive price hike declared by the Organization of Petroleum Exporting Countries (of which Indonesia is a member) suddenly brought in windfall revenues. The new agreements with the United States and Japan made an additional $600 million available to the government, enabling the resumption of many economic projects, including the Assahan Dam project and the modernization of port facilities in western Java.

Part of the credit for the economic recovery was owed to foreign policy. Suharto quickly ended the wasteful confrontation with Malaysia; instead he sought economic and political cooperation with it. In 1966, he joined in the establishment of the largely pro-Western ASEAN. In the early 1970s, Indonesia joined Malaysia and Singapore in rejecting the Japanese position that the Strait of Malacca be considered an international maritime highway free from any nation's sovereign jurisdiction.

As expected, Suharto reversed Sukarno's foreign policy and befriended the United States, Britain, Australia, and Japan. Relations with Communist China remained hostile; Indonesia voted against China's admission to the United Nations because of China's continued support of Indonesian Communist guerrillas operating in parts of the country. Indonesia also attempted to play a peacekeeping mediatory role in neighboring areas. Thus, it convened a conference on the Cambodian situation, and in 1972 it accepted membership in the new International Control Commission to supervise the ceasefire in Vietnam. Its role as arbitrator was somewhat tarnished, however, by its training program for the officers of the Lon Nol regime during the early 1970s. Despite its pro-West moves, however, Indonesia did not abandon its membership in the nonaligned movement nor its right to take a position in international affairs on the merits of each case.

The Elections of 1971

In 1971, for the first time in sixteen years, national elections were held. The government itself organized a party of functional groups, Sekber Golkar, putting up candidates from economic and professional groups such as civil servants, trade unions, students, businessmen, professionals, and farmers. Besides Sekber Golkar, nine other parties participated in the elections. Among the important opposition parties were the Nahdatul Ulama, an orthodox organization of Muslim *ulama* (teachers); the PNI; and the liberal Permusi Muslim party. Government officials were encouraged to campaign for the Golkar candidates and to speak favorably of official performance. On the other hand, the opposition was forbidden to criticize the president or the government's preelectoral acts.

Despite the controlled conditions in which the elections were held, the Golkar won 236 seats (65 percent) with 63 percent of the total vote, a performance that brought some credibility to the elections. The Nahdatul won 60 seats, the Permusi 23, and the PNI 20, while the remaining 21 were shared by six other parties.

Disillusionment with the New Order

Two years later, in 1973, in keeping with Suharto's promise of 1968, the People's Consultative Assembly was convened. The assembly was a kind of supreme parliament consisting of the members of the House of Representatives and an equal number of special functional delegates from different regions of the country. The Congress reelected Suharto to a second term as president. Control of the government, however, continued to rest in the hands of Suharto and the top military brass, whose authority was now somewhat legitimized through the national elections.

The New Order did not succeed for long in endearing itself politically to the bulk of Indonesians. In 1973, the 9 opposition parties were steamrolled into 2 parties—the 4 Islamic parties joining the Unity Development party (PPP) and the remaining 5 merging into the Indonesian Democracy party (PDI). The parliament was not free to discuss sensitive issues likely to embarrass the government. The democratic process was thus stymied, leading to eruption of student resentment beginning in 1974 and the increase in popularity of Islamic parties.

Interference with the political process was only one aspect of the general discontent. Disillusionment over the government's economic policies, growing dependence on foreign investment, aid, and trade (particularly Japanese), widespread corruption reaching all the way to President Suharto and members of his family, and the widening gap between the urban and rural population fueled opposition to Suharto's government. If the Sekber Golkar initially received support of students and the intellectual elite, it was because so many of them genuinely believed in crystallization of political parties as opposed to the tremendous waste of public energy involved in a plethora of parties. By 1973–1974, they came to realize that the Sekber Golkar was only a tool of the military and its henchmen for monopolizing power for their own selfish ends.

Two major setbacks for the New Order in the mid-1970s were the Pertamina crisis and the suppression of a liberation movement in East Timor. Pertamina, the state-owned oil corporation under the management of a top general, Ibnu Sutowo, was found to be grossly mismanaged. It amassed a huge debt of $10.5 billion, reneged on tanker obligations, and aborted Indonesia's opportunity to improve its economy through oil revenues.

The Timor situation did not discredit the government as much as was expected. Revolution in Portugal in 1974 opened the prospect of liberating East Timor. Indonesia had refrained from any action against the Portuguese colony because of its own declaration that its territorial claims were coterminous with the former Dutch empire in Southeast Asia. The Suharto government did not want to take any action for fear of arousing memories of Sukarno's expansionism among both Southeast Asian neighbors and Western aid donor countries. It rather expected that with some clandestine aid some local East Timorese party would overthrow the Portuguese rule and appeal for merger with Indonesia. To its shock, the ultraleftist Front for the Independence of East Timor (Fretilin) party managed to get control of the colony in August and in November 1975 proclaimed its independence. The anti-Communist government of Indonesia was both embarrassed and outraged. It quickly sent in "volunteers" before the Fretilin had time to settle down. East Timor was occupied by Indonesian forces and formally integrated into the Indonesian republic in July 1976. In the process, an estimated 100,000 (16 percent of the population) Timorese perished, and half that number were imprisoned.

The May 1977 parliamentary elections, which were preceded by forty-five days of individual freedoms, witnessed a vicious, vitriolic, and violent campaign during which both students and Islamic groups strongly opposed the Golkar party. Although the Golkar won handsomely with 62 percent of the vote as against the Islamic PPP's 29 percent and the secular PDI's 8 percent, the government was most concerned with the tremendous tensions generated by the PPP's virulent propaganda for Islam.

Perhaps to combat the Islamic wave, President Suharto embarked on an intensive program of emphasizing the Pancasila (five principles) doctrine enshrined in the 1945 constitution: belief in one god, humanitarianism, national unity, consensual democracy, and social justice. In the late 1970s, Pancasila was equated by Suharto's government with traditional indigenous values of social harmony, political consensus, and culturally neutral norms of behavior in a plural society.

Beginning in 1978, the government took steps to impart ideological training in Pancasila at all levels. Anyone opposed to Pancasila was branded either a Communist or an Islamic extremist. In 1983, the People's Consultative Assembly adopted a resolution making Pancasila the sole official ideological principle to be accepted as such by all political parties. The reaction of the Islamic parties, political leaders, and *ulamas* was vicious and violent. They inspired thousands of Muslim youth to riot in north Jakarta's Tanjung Priok dock areas on September 12, 1984; twenty-eight lives were lost. In the following year, the government was authorized to close down any associations that failed to contribute to the development of a Pancasila society.

Widespread Dissent

The Tanjung Priok riots were not incited entirely by Islamic extremists—they were to a considerable extent a reflection of the socioeconomic problems of the large urban slums. Numerous newspapers and periodicals that commented on them were later banned. The public resentment was against the nexus between the military and the Chinese business community, which seemed to be the only two groups benefiting the most from the government's economic policies.

The first such major expression of dissent came in the form of a petition of May 13, 1980, signed by fifty prominent political figures and presented to the Parliament. It was a statement of criticism and concern. The signatories included two former prime ministers of the 1950s, a leader of the Sumatra rebellion of 1958, the secretary-general of ASEAN, and the celebrated former defense minister, General Abdul H. Nasution. The petition was also supported by student groups. The petitioners accused Suharto of a tendency to view all criticism of him and his policies as being subversive. They criticized Suharto for dividing the nation and encouraging the armed forces to take sides in the forthcoming parliamentary elections. They further deprecated his policy of politicizing Indonesia's state ideology, Pancasila, and using it as a weapon against the opposition. In 1981, there were more petitions. One signed by sixty-one dissidents, again including General Nasution, asserted that the government had failed to implement a truly democratic system free of military intervention in the political process. Such petitioning groups became the conscience of the nation in the 1980s.

The excesses of the security forces against the youth involved in the Tanjung Priok riots provoked one group to produce a White Paper. Signed by General Hartono Dharsono, former secretary-general of the ASEAN, and twenty-one others (including sixteen members of the "petition of fifty"), it questioned the official account of the riots and called for an independent investigation of the affair. In a swift reprisal, the government arrested Dharsono as well as several signatories who had formerly held high government positions. There were trumped-up charges against Dharsono including inciting militant Muslims to violence such as the bomb attacks in Jakarta in October 1984. After an extended trial, Dharsono was sentenced in January 1986 to ten years of imprisonment, an indication that the government would accept no opposition no matter how distinguished the individual.

The Downfall of Suharto

By 1996, Suharto had been at the helm of affairs for three decades, a decade longer than Sukarno's tenure before him. He had been elected president six times by the People's Consultative Assembly. In 1983, the assembly bestowed upon him the title of "Father of Development" in recognition of his endeavors for economic development of the country.

Speculation about his successor dominated the gossip mills of Jakarta. Two types were mentioned: from the military, or a relative of the president. The succession was eventually determined by a popular movement against him, reminiscent of the anti-Marcos opposition wave in the Philippines in the 1980s.

Among the principal causes of popular discontent were Suharto's record of corruption and cronyism and his bowing-down to the IMF's bailout package after the economic disaster that affected all of Southeast Asia, including Indonesia, in the aftermath of the currency and economic crisis of 1997–1998. The value of Indonesian currency plummeted more than 70 percent. The consequent economic contraction worsened the disaffection, already widespread, among the masses, causing a series of riots in Jakarta and other principal cities. Instead of responding with ameliorating measures, the government's answer was more violence. The middle and lower classes increasingly demanded a more open political environment and an equitable slice of the economic pie.

By May 1998, repeated incidents of violence and unrest among the masses, as well as huge rallies by student protesters, led to a determination within the armed forces that President Suharto had become a liability. This view was reinforced after six students were shot to death by security forces on May 12, 1998. The combined opposition scheduled a rally for May 21 that was expected to attract 1 million protesters. The choice in the military was whether to crush the public unrest with violence (which would, in all likelihood, fuel more violence and bloodshed) or to replace Suharto with a leader acceptable to the public. The military, led by General Wiranto, prudently chose the latter alternative. On May 20, the army took over Jakarta, bringing in 40,000 troops, tanks, and attack dogs. Suharto concurred with the army's decision, but not before his own Golkar party joined the opposition in demanding his resignation or face a recall by a special session of the People's Consultative Assembly. U.S. Secretary of State Madeleine Albright publicly appealed to him to quit office. In succeeding days, Suharto agreed to a number of opposition and student demands, including political reform, naming a new cabinet and promising to hold fresh elections in which he would not be a candidate. But it was too late. On May 20, 1998, the wily, durable general who had presided over Indonesia's fortunes for thirty-two years peacefully stepped down and allowed for a smooth transition, following the constitutional provision governing succession. Vice President B. J. Habibie was sworn in as the new president. To his credit, Habibie promised to hold national elections as soon as possible.

Thus ended the rule of an army general who was regarded in the mid-1960s as Indonesia's savior. He had successfully crushed a leftist coup in 1965 and, the following year, taken control of the government from the nation's founder, President Sukarno, who had increasingly come under the influence of the largest Communist party outside the Soviet Union and China. Unfortunately for the aspirations of his compatriots, Suharto gave in to corruption and cronyism, promoting relatives and favorites to posts in the government and the armed forces and amassing a personal fortune estimated by *Time* magazine at US$15 billion (and estimated by President Abdurrahman Wahid at three times that amount). By throwing away the opportunity presented by the oil boom of the 1970s, he failed to gain the economic betterment of the miserable masses. He carved out segments of the economy and neatly allocated them among members of his immediate family. Suharto also used the military to crush political dissent and muzzle the media; he founded a political party and promoted a political system that would enable him to win seven five-year terms as president.

In the same manner as in the Philippines, the new government (first under President Wahid and later under President Megawati Sukarnoputri) tried to retrieve some of the wealth presumably stashed away by Suharto and his family. In May 2000, Suharto was placed under house arrest and charged with stealing some US$571 million in state funds during his presidency. A report by an independent commission of physicians stated that the seventy-nine-year-old Suharto was physically and mentally unfit to stand trial because of dementia and memory loss; this led to a reprieve from the proceedings for Suharto but not for his son, Hutomo "Tommy" Mandala Putra, who was sentenced in October 2000 to eighteen months in prison for corruption. He became a fugitive from justice for more than a year before he was captured in late 2001 and charged with a new offense: the murder of the judge who had sentenced him in October 2000.

Indonesia After Suharto

The parliamentary elections of June 1999 were the first genuinely free, democratically held elections in more than four decades. The campaign was short, but it was bereft of the restrictions that had marked Suharto's repressive regime. As many as 48 political parties entered the fray, and more than 90 percent of the populace went to the polls to cast votes on June 7 for 462 members of the 500-member House of Representatives (the DPR). Under the constitution, 38 seats were reserved for the armed forces. Most of the votes were garnered by five prominent parties; the Indonesian Democratic party of Struggle (the PDI-P) of the opposition leader, Megawati Sukarnoputri, daughter of the late President Sukarno (still considered the father of the nation), won the plurality. The government-sponsored Golkar party, drawing support principally from the outer islands, came in second.

The constitution stipulated that the election of the president and the vice president be carried out by a vote of the People's Consultative Assembly (the MPR). The electoral college consisted of the 500 members of the DPR, 135 appointed members from each of the twenty-seven provinces, and sixty-five members appointed by the National Election Commission to represent various community groups. In October 1999, the MPR elected Abdurrahman Wahid, a respected, nearly blind Muslim cleric and leader of the country's largest Islamic organization, the 30-million-member Nahdatul Ulama (NU), as president and Megawati Sukarnoputri as vice president. In keeping with the Indonesian tradition to seek compromise and consensus, the MPR also elected leaders of two other parties, Golkar and the Partai Aman Nasional (PAN), to the chairmanships of the MPR and DPR, respectively.

President Wahid's administration proved a disaster for the people, who had expected political reforms and economic betterment with the removal of the dictator Suharto. Wahid began well, with intentions to bring all the people together, forming a National Union Cabinet (or "rainbow coalition") that included representatives of all the major political parties, the government bureaucracy, and the military. However, it produced an unworkable government, providing instead a forum for internecine rivalry and competing corrupt interests. Wahid proved thoroughly indecisive, erratic, and intolerant of opinions contrary to his own. To make matters worse, he went on several foreign tours. And contrary to his initial impulses to work out a consensus on most matters, he became increasingly dictatorial. The parliament, the press, and the people accused him of arbitrarily reshuffling his cabinet, not sharing his authority with the vice president; submitting even more than Suharto to the IMF in the regulation of the economy; not responding adequately to the separatist demands in Acheh and Irian Jaya; and failing to contain the violence in the Moluccas. The country seemed dangerously close to falling apart.

In February 2001, the parliament censured President Wahid and failed to receive any response in the prescribed three-month period; it censured him again that May. Wahid's inadequate response led to a special meeting of the MPR on July 21, 2001, to impeach him. Wahid's response was to block the MPR's action by declaring a state of emergency. He fired the chief of police, suspended the Golkar party, and ordered the closure of the parliament building. None of these orders was honored by any government agency, including the police and the military. The Supreme Court ruled that none of Wahid's decrees had legal validity. An emergency session of the MPR voted unanimously (591-0) on July 23, 2001, for the president's impeachment and for the elevation of Vice President Megawati Sukarnoputri to president. To promote unity, the MPR elected Hamzah Haz, the leader of the moderate Islamist United Development party who opposed Megawati for the vice-presidency in 1999, as the new vice president.

Separatist Movements and Devolution of Powers

The biggest political challenge facing Indonesian governments since the country's independence from Dutch rule has been a persistent demand for devolution of powers from the center to the outlying provinces. The central government's insufficient responses became even more evident in the 1990s with the success of the East Timorese in attracting international attention and wresting independence from Indonesia. The most significant of these separatist movements have been at the two extremities of the archipelago: in Acheh in northwestern Sumatra, and in Papua (formerly West Irian, or West New Guinea). The economic woes in the post-1997 currency crisis, and the release of pent-up political aspirations, brutally suppressed during the long Suharto regime, accentuated the demands for autonomy, if not outright independence, in Acheh and Papua.

The Acheh freedom movement, begun in 1976, is spearheaded by the Acheh Sumatra National Liberation Front (ASNLF; commonly known as GAM). Rich in natural resources, notably oil and natural gas, Acheh has complained for decades that the revenues accruing from the numerous megacompanies exploiting these resources have not been used to benefit the people of the province. Efforts by the military to put down dissidents resulted in growing unrest and the recruitment of more guerrillas to carry out protracted warfare; according to human rights activists, by May 2000 the toll was at least 5,000 lives over the previous decade.

The first major positive response to the Achehnese came from President Wahid, who assured them in late 1999 that, short of independence, which could trigger disintegration of the country itself, all their demands, including an equitable share of the revenues from oil and natural gas, would be granted. Accordingly, on May 12, 2000, Zaini Abdullah, health minister of the separatist GAM, and Hassan Wirajuda, Indonesia's permanent representative to the United Nations, signed an agreement near Geneva for a three-month ceasefire effective June 2, after which negotiations for autonomy would take place. On July 19, 2001, the DPR approved a bill granting wide-ranging local autonomy to Acheh, which would include 70 percent of oil and gas revenues and the establishment of courts that would follow the Sharia law for Muslims in the province (non-Muslims would be governed by secular Indonesian laws). The DPR also granted Acheh the right to have its own flag but required that it be flown at the same height, and next to, the national flag. The provisions of the Acheh Autonomy Bill, scheduled to come into effect in 2002, were more extensive than those granted to Indonesia's other provinces. The United States, the United Kingdom, Australia, and Japan lauded Jakarta's efforts and condemned any threats to the integration of the Indonesian republic.

But even this major devolution of authority failed to satisfy a core group in the GAM, which continued the guerrilla war with about 2,000 armed fighters. Their activities led to economic disruption in the province; in March 2001, the giant ExxonMobil corporation closed its operations at its Arun natural gas fields. With the government providing better security and launching a major campaign against the guerrillas, the facility reopened in July. Meeting in Stockholm in July 2002, the GAM reiterated its demand for complete independence; it renamed itself the State of Acheh. Headquartered in exile in Stockholm with Tgk Malik Mahmud as prime minister, it claimed to be the only legitimate government of Acheh. It also claimed to have an alternative administration in place whereby local military commanders established a council of elders to dispense justice to the people. Negotiations between the government and GAM representatives, facilitated by the Henry Dunant Centre for Humanitarian Dialogue (HDCHD), a Geneva-based group of facilitators, resulted in an agreement on December 9, 2002. It provided for a ceasefire monitored by 150 international observers, largely from Thailand and the Philippines under the auspices of the HDCHD. A joint security committee of the two sides would implement demilitarization and secure the surrender of rebel weapons. The agreement stipulated free and fair elections in Acheh leading to a substantially autonomous government that would retain 70 percent of the revenues from Acheh's large oil and gas revenues.

As for Papua, the movement for independence was much weaker, with only about 200 armed guerrilla fighters. When Indonesia became independent of Dutch colonial rule in 1949, the territory of West New Guinea, known to the local population as Papua, was retained by the Netherlands. In 1961, the people adopted a declaration of independence to establish Papua as a separate state. After a transitional UN administration, West New Guinea was brought under the Indonesian government in 1963. In 1969, a poll held under questionable circumstances confirmed its permanent incorporation into the Republic of Indonesia as a new province; in 1973, the province was renamed Irian Jaya (Victorious Irian). With Eastern New Guinea acquiring its independence in 1975 as Papua New Guinea, the people of Irian Jaya also cherished similar aspirations for an independent state.

With only about 500 members and 200 fighters in the jungle redoubts, and a fractionalized leadership, the Free Papua Movement (Organisasi Papua Merdeka, or OPM) was not a major threat to the government. The factions advocated autonomy, independence, or a merger with Papua New Guinea. Just as in Acheh, the major complaint was inattention to the province's needs and the appropriation of the rich resource base of Papua without creating educational facilities that would make locals eligible for jobs in the public and private sectors. The province, rich in gas, oil, copper, and gold, has been identified by the U.S. multinational Freeport McMoran Inc. as holding the world's largest gold and copper mine at Grasberg. In March 1996, the people of the Papuan towns of Timika and Tembagapura, near the PT Freeport Indonesia mining concessions (with an estimated annual profit of US$2 billion), rioted, demanding that some of the revenues from the mining corporation be spent for the welfare of tribal communities. The council of the local tribe, the Amungme, also accused the PT Freeport Indonesia of ecoterrorism and human rights violations. Meanwhile, the OPM managed to draw international attention with the kidnapping, in 1996, of a group of European scientists and, in 2001, of several South Korean forestry consultants.

The OPM's Theys Eluay, the "Great Leader of the Papuan People," had originally been with the Indonesian government in signing the Act of Free Choice in 1969 and later was a member of the provincial parliament as the leader of Suharto's Golkar party. Disappointed in the central government's unwillingness to stand by the Papuan aspirations for economic and social betterment, he quit the Golkar and on December 1, 1999, raised the banner for independence. In June 2000, the second Papua National Congress, the political arm of the freedom movement representing 245 tribal groups, meeting in the capital, Jayapura, elected him president of the Papua Presidium Council, a body that advocated working with Jakarta for the greater good of Papua. On November 10, 2001, he was mysteriously murdered while returning from a dinner with the commander of the Indonesian Special

Forces in Jayapura. Investigations did not prove the identity of the perpetrators of the crime; they could have been from the hard core of the OPM, lower-ranking members of the Indonesian military, or business interests.

The post-Suharto governments responded to the Papuan demands. In late 1998, a ceasefire agreement was signed with one of the OPM factions. In an effort to articulate its demands, the Papuan People's Congress, at the session of May 31–June 4, 2000, in Jayapura (Port Numbay), attended by some 4,000 people, adopted a five-point resolution. Partly in response to it, the Indonesian parliament passed a bill in October 2001 granting Irian Jaya autonomy similar to that of Acheh. Irian Jaya would get 80 percent of the revenues from fishing and forestry and 70 percent from gas, oil, and mining. Irian Jaya's provincial legislature would have the right to appoint the governor of the province, which would be renamed Papua in deference to the wishes of the people. The Papuans would also be able to fly their own flag, the Morning Star, along with the Indonesian flag. Significantly, President Megawati preceded the passing of the autonomy bill by apologizing to the people of Irian Jaya for the repressive policies of the central government in the past. The implementation of the autonomy measures commenced, albeit at a slow pace, at the beginning of 2002.

FOREIGN RELATIONS

There has been a growing feeling among the Indonesian leadership that the country deserves a major role as a regional power based on its size, population of over 200 million, geostrategic importance, and natural resources. There has been vocal demand for a respectful, international recognition of the spectacular achievements of the New Order in contrast to the failures of the Sukarno era. The demand has also been based on claims of internal political stability, consistent economic growth, and economic liberalization. Indonesia has sought large-scale international aid and foreign investment as well as greater export opportunities for its nonoil products to the Western world. In all these areas, Indonesia achieved impressive targets until 1991. At that time its repression of independence-seeking people of East Timor and its treatment of political prisoners provoked international ire that led to a halt of aid and a linkage of trade, sale of armaments, and good relations with the Indonesian government's improvement in human rights and its settlement of the Timor issue to the satisfaction of its people.

Role in the Cambodian Question

As a mark of its independent foreign policy, Indonesia followed a "dual track" policy in regard to the Cambodian question. The first track was to hold bilateral dialogue with Vietnam for a more realistic approach to Cambodia, independent of and somewhat different from that of the ASEAN. The second track was marked by adherence to ASEAN's policy whenever possible. During 1984 and 1985, Indonesian and Vietnamese defense and foreign ministers exchanged visits. There were also other important visits: A delegation from Jakarta's well-known Center for Strategic and International Studies attended a seminar in Hanoi on peace and stability in Southeast Asia, as did members of the National Defense Institute of

Indonesia. It was following a meeting between the foreign ministers of Indonesia and Vietnam in August 1985 that Vietnam first announced it would withdraw all its troops from Cambodia by 1990. (In fact, it pulled out by September 1989.) In mid-1988, Indonesia provided a forum for the Vietnam-backed government in Phnom Penh to meet with leaders of the three factions of the coalition opposing that government. Indonesia's continuing role as a mediator in the Cambodian conflict was rewarded by its co-chairmanship, along with France, of the 19-nation Paris Peace Conference on Cambodia, which eventually resulted in the peace agreements of October 1991.

Relations with Major Powers

Another mark of Indonesia's independent policy was to establish equidistance between the two superpowers, altering its image of being completely pro-U.S. It put the United States on notice that Indonesia could not be taken for granted and that the United States should not exploit the China connection at the expense of ASEAN, particularly Indonesia. In 1984, Foreign Minister Mochtar Kusumaatmadja visited Moscow, the highest Indonesian official to do so in a decade. Large delegations from the Indonesian Chamber of Commerce and Industry (ICCI), as well as Economic and Finance Minister Ali Wardhana, visited Moscow and East European capitals. Constraints on trade with Communist countries imposed in 1967 were removed. In October 1985, a protocol on trade between Indonesia and the Soviet Union was signed during the visit of Soviet Deputy Prime Minister Yakov Ryabow, the highest Soviet official to visit since 1965.

Indonesia also tried to improve relations with China to balance those with the Soviet Union. The relations between the two countries had been severed since 1967 because of China's role in helping the PKI in the Gestapu affair of 1965. For the first decade and a half after 1967, Indonesia made the restoration of relations with China conditional upon an official apology by the latter in addition to a clear disavowal that it would not, in the future, assist Communist parties in Southeast Asia in toppling the existing governments in the region. Sino-Indonesian relations improved significantly after 1985. In that year, the Bandung conference's thirtieth anniversary celebration gave Indonesia an opportunity to invite Chinese Foreign Minister Wu Xueqian, the first distinguished Chinese visitor in eighteen years. Some discussions on the resumption of direct trade did take place during the visit. Following Wu's visit, Suharto's half-brother, Probosutadjo, visited China in his capacity of deputy chairman of the ICCI and discussed further details. These were incorporated in an agreement of July 5, 1985, in Singapore between the ICCI and the China Council for the Promotion of International Trade whereby China agreed to buy $200 million of Indonesian nonoil items like plywood, coffee, and spices, thus helping Indonesia to reduce its trade deficit with China.

A breakthrough in Sino-Indonesian relations occurred at the funeral of Emperor Hirohito in February 1989, when President Suharto had talks with China's foreign minister, Qian Qichen, and agreed that the respective missions of China and Indonesia at the United Nations begin discussions on normalization of relations. The relations were formally restored to normalcy in August 1990 during the visit of the Indonesian foreign minister, Ali Alatas, to Beijing. China did not apologize; nor did it make a direct statement disavowing assistance to Communist parties to topple governments in Southeast Asia. Instead, the Chinese Communist party's secretary-general, Jiang Zemin, generally stated that no country should interfere in the internal affairs of another country, and the Chinese premier, Li Peng, told an Indonesian journalist it would be impossible for China to have relations with the PKI because China had no idea whether the PKI existed at all! As a part of the normalization agreement, Indonesia committed itself to pay $80 million to China in cash and commodities to settle debts incurred during the Sukarno regime. In turn, China agreed to offer citizenship to about 350,000 Chinese settled in Indonesia. Those who declined the offer would be granted permanent residency rights by the Indonesian government. Normalization was quickly followed by the visit of Chinese Premier Li Peng to Indonesia and of President Suharto to China in November 1990. Since then, Indonesia-China relations have been cordial, and there have been several high-level visits. Presidents Wahid and Megawati both visited Beijing, the latter's visit marked by the Chinese pledge of US$400 million in loans to Indonesia.

The East Timor Problem

Indonesia's relations with most Western powers and Australia suffered grievously because of its human rights record in East Timor. Australia and the United States took the lead in bringing such atrocities to the attention of the United Nations and the world. In 1991, following the massacre at Dili, the United States canceled Indonesia's participation in the International Military Education and Training (IMET) program. Limited participation was restored in 1996. In 1997, the U.S. Congress condemned Indonesia for gross violations of human rights in East Timor. Indonesia reacted strongly, canceling an order for nine additional F-16 fighters. The Leahy amendment in Congress prohibited funding the IMET program and suspended sales of military equipment on government accounts. The Leahy amendment also demanded satisfaction on several points: improved security between the two halves of Timor; disarmament of the pro-Indonesian militia forces and an end to armed incursions in East Timor; proper trial and just punishment for those convicted of killing three UN staffers; and the trial and punishment of senior military officers responsible for the violence in East Timor. Although U.S.-Indonesia relations improved with the emergence of East Timor as an independent state, normalcy in the military relationship was far from restored. In the post–September 11 scenario, there was at first some misunderstanding between Indonesia and the United States; the former, being a Muslim country, was seen as not aggressive enough in confronting the Islamic militants. However, President Megawati's visit to Washington that same month cleared the air, as she unreservedly offered cooperation and assistance in the common fight against international terrorism. In early 2002, the United States agreed to fund a program to upgrade the capabilities of the Indonesian police and the National Intelligence Agency. However, the United States is not likely to restore the full military relationship until military officers and civilians are tried and punished for their roles in the violence in East Timor.

Indonesia's relations with the United States improved in the wake of September 11 and its own declared resolve to root out terrorism. Washington appreciated

Jakarta's stand, describing it as a "voice of moderation in the Islamic world." Consequently, the Pentagon's ties with the Indonesian Armed Forces (TNI), which had been substantially loosened after the 1992 massacre in East Timor and almost completely severed after the TNI's atrocities in 1999 following the referendum in East Timor in favor of independence, were almost restored. The resumption in May 2005 of the sale of U.S. nonlethal equipment to Indonesia was followed in November by lifting the embargo on weapon sales.

SETTLEMENT OF THE SEPARATIST MOVEMENTS
Acheh

By the beginning of the new millennium, both sides in the Acheh conflict—the Indonesian government and the Free Acheh Movement (GAM)—were weary. The conflict lasting a quarter century had, by that time, claimed over 12,000 lives. With mediation assistance from the Henry Dunant Centre and after nearly two years of talks, an agreement to end the rebellion was signed on December 9, 2002. A ceasefire was to be in place, to be monitored by 150 observers largely drawn from Thailand and the Philippines. The rebels would also surrender their weapons within two months and prepare themselves for elections in 2004 based on Acheh's autonomy. The province's fiscal autonomy would be based on Acheh retaining 70 percent of its revenues from its considerable oil and gas reserves. The implementation of the agreement began in earnest but was stalled because the GAM declared it had not abandoned its demand for complete independence. Violence too was resumed on both sides, with President Megawati Sukarnoputri imposing martial law on Acheh province and increasing TNI attacks and heavy aerial bombardments. The government feared that the GAM controlled the countryside and its own army controlled the cities, at least during the day. It announced its readiness to move some 200,000 civilians away from the known guerrilla positions, a kind of strategic hamlets program, which, in the end, was not implemented.

The only silver lining of the December 2004 tsunami was the political settlement of the three-decades-old rebellion in northern Sumatra, the Free Acheh Movement (GAM). In August 2005, the Achehnese signed a peace agreement with the national government by which the GAM agreed to accept autonomous self-government instead of its previous demand for complete independence. Nine leaders of that movement returned to the country in April 2006 after thirty years of exile in Sweden. Young and middle-aged men returned as old people to their homes, ostensibly to see how the peace agreement was being implemented by the Jakarta government and to see for themselves how the survivors of the tsunami disaster were recovering financially and psychologically.

The military aspects of the agreement were quickly implemented and in good faith. By September, GAM's 3,000 guerrilla fighters had been demobilized, and 25 percent of its 840 kinds of weapons surrendered to the government. On its part, the federal government had withdrawn significant numbers of the Indonesian Armed Forces (TNI) paramilitary police from Acheh. The peace agreement stipulated that by December 31, 2005, the national troops in Acheh would need to be reduced to a maximum of 14,700 and the national police strength to 9,100 from the combined total of 57,000 at the time of signing the agreement. Likewise, within days and weeks of the agreement, most of the GAM rebels had been released from prisons.

In July 2006, the national legislature unanimously approved a law granting autonomy to Acheh, which would be allowed control of 70 percent of the revenue from Acheh's oil and gas production. Additionally, Acheh would get 2 percent from the national budget for twenty years for economic reconstruction. The political autonomy included—significantly for the overtly Islamic province—the ability to formally adopt the Islamic Sharia law.

A major concession made by the federal government was to allow GAM, a local party, to run for the provincial elections. Under Indonesia's constitution, only national parties were permitted to contest elections, and every such party was required to maintain an office in the nation's capital, Jakarta. This was to promote unity in the sprawling country. Special legislation passed by the federal legislature in mid-2006 made an exception in favor of GAM.

The talks between GAM and the Indonesian government were resumed, this time facilitated by Finland, which provided a venue for the negotiations in its capital of Helsinki. The former president of Finland, Martti Ahtisaari, skillfully moderated. It was during the fifth round of talks in July 2005 that the real breakthrough came when President Yudhoyono agreed to allow GAM to be transformed into a political party and to participate in provincial elections in 2006. That was a major concession, because the constitution disallowed local parties. Every political party was required to maintain an office in the capital of the country and have branches in at least half of the total of 33 provinces. With that concession, the GAM agreed to abandon its demand for complete independence and agree to provincial autonomy.

As a follow-up to the peace agreement, President Yudhoyono ended the emergency in Acheh effective May 18, 2006, restoring full civilian rule to the autonomous province.

West Papua

In November 2001, the proindependence Papuan leader, Theys Eluay, who was the chairman of the Papua Presidium Council, was abducted and killed by the TNI.

In January 2002, a special law was passed granting autonomy to the province of West Papua (the former Irian Jaya), which was renamed Papua. The autonomy included retention by Papua of 70 percent of the provincial revenues mainly from minerals and forestry.

The special measure did not appease the separatist Free Papua Movement (OPM), which was still not satisfied with the government's investigation into the death of their late leader, Theys Eluay. OPM supporters also resented the continued presence of the Indonesian Armed Forces in Papua. Another source of conflict was the U.S. mining company Freeport McMoran Inc., which claimed to have paid as much as $20 million to the TNI as protection money between 1998 and 2004 and had opted to discontinue the payments. In August 2001, a convoy of vehicles including a jeep carrying three teachers, two of them American, working for Freeport McMoran, was ambushed. Among the dead were the two American teachers. The TNI and the OPM accused each other of the dastardly act. FBI investigators were involved, and in early 2006, an OPM member, Anthonius Wamang, was arrested in the United States and handed over to the Indonesian authorities. At the same time, seven TNI members—four officers and three soldiers—were convicted by a court martial in April and awarded short sentences that left international human rights groups even more critical than before. The OPM itself was far from satisfied with the judicial aspect of the case. Its followers used the anniversary of the murder of Theys Eluay to raise the Papuan flag and demand independence.

YUDHOYONO'S PRESIDENCY, 2004–

The elections of 2004 were the first to provide for direct voting for the president and the vice president. This provision had been secured during the administration of Megawati Sukarnoputri in August 2002 through the People's Consultative Assembly, the highest body in the nation.

Although Yudhoyono was elected with an overwhelming 61 percent vote during the second round against his rival, Megawati Sukarnoputri, his party did not have even a simple majority in the National Assembly (DPR). His program was to boost the economy, to rehabilitate the victims of the tsunami, actively to combat corruption, and to resolve the separatist movements in Acheh, Papua, and Maluku. However, his dependence on other parties to get his policies approved by the legislature compelled him to dilute his platform. His cabinet virtually became a coalition of several parties, such as the National Mandate party (PAN), the United Development party (PPP), the Justice and Prosperity party (PKS), and the Crescent Star party (PBB). He even included two members of the opposition Golkar party in his cabinet, one of whom was Finance Minister Aburizal Bakrie of the Golkar party, for whose sake he had to forgo his plans to appoint to the post Mulyani Indrawati, the well-known liberal, pro-West former IMF official.

Since the election of Yudhoyono Susilo Bambang as president in 2004, Indonesians have felt the presence of a government that can assure them of relative stability, peace, and order. The previous five years since Suharto's thirty-three-year political domination ended in 1999 had been a tale of chaos and disorder marking new lows of corruption and nepotism.

Yudhoyono was no stranger to politics and administration. His career had been a healthy mix of military and civilian positions. Trained as an economist with a doctorate in agricultural economics from Bogor Agricultural University in October 2004, and recipient in 1991 of a master's degree in management from Webster University in the United States, Yudhoyono spent twenty-six years as an army man, serving in various capacities until his early retirement in 1999 as a lieutenant general; he was made an honorary general in 2000. Yudhoyono had better exposure to the external world than any of his predecessors in the president's office, with two terms of training in the United States and a year's stint in Bosnia as the chief military observer of the UN Peacekeeping Force in 1995–1996. Even while in the armed forces, Yudhoyono showed his intellectual inclination by co-writing a book entitled *The Challenges of Development.* For his doctorate, he completed a thesis on "The Rural and Agricultural Development as an Effort to Alleviate Poverty and

Unemployment [in Indonesia]," which would later become the basis of part of his economic policy as president.

After early retirement from the armed forces, Yudhoyono's reputation as a reformer brought him into the cabinet of President Abdurrahman Wahid as minister for mines and energy in 1999; a year later he took the crucial position of coordinating minister of politics and security. He was liked not only for his efficiency but also because he held the view that the armed forces should not have a "dual function"—that the military should have no political mission.

In 2001, when Wahid was replaced as president by Megawati Sukarnoputri, Yudhoyono ran unsuccessfully for vice president. However, Megawati reappointed him as coordinating minister of politics and security. As Megawati learned more about proposals from the various parties to have Yudhoyono run for president in 2004, she consulted him less on crucial issues facing the government. In September 2001, Yudhoyono had already formed his own political party, the Partai Demokrat (PD). On September 20, 2004, he was elected president in the country's first direct election for that post. In the runoff election, he scored 60.87 percent of the vote.

Yudhoyono's policy has been to bring about unity among diverse groups of Indonesians. Although two other parties joined his PD party to form a coalition, Yudhoyono reached out to other parties, notably the Golkar, and included their members in his cabinet, which he called significantly the "United Indonesia" cabinet. To bring his countrymen together, he negotiated agreements to end the rebel movements in Acheh, Papua, and Maluku.

The tsunami of December 2004 provided an opportunity for Indonesians to set aside their differences and unite to alleviate the suffering of those affected and to work toward rehabilitation. It was also an early test of the will and efficiency of the Yudhoyono administration and was his best moment in crisis management. Within six months of the disaster, his administration had committed and spent US$1.2 billion.

Yudhoyono's strong point is economic matters. During his electoral campaign, he widely circulated a booklet entitled "Vision for Change," in which he promised to focus on four "pillars": prosperity, peace, justice, and democracy. He has been able to attract considerable foreign direct investment aiming at an average annual growth of 7 percent. Within a year of his presidency, Indonesia had reached that goal, the first time since 1996. In 2005, he outlined his "triple-track strategy." In his view, the first track was to achieve sustainable growth through a combination of strong exports and increased investment, both domestic and foreign. The second track was to stimulate the performance of the economic sectors to create employment. The third track was to promote the development of the rural economy and agriculture to alleviate poverty.[1] It is too early to assess the results of his administration's efforts, but certainly the will is not lacking.

23

East Timor:
Birth of a Nation

On May 20, 2002, a new nation was born in Southeast Asia. East Timor (which had been under colonial Portuguese rule for more than 450 years, under Indonesia for two decades, and administered by the United Nations for three years) emerged as an independent state: the Democratic Republic of Timor Lorosae. In the wake of Portuguese withdrawal in 1974–1975, Indonesian armed forces occupied it, while the Revolutionary Front for an Independent East Timor (Fretilin) declared its independence. Fretilin, joined by others, carried on a struggle against Indonesian domination that attracted much international attention, culminating in UN intervention. In 1996, the two leading East Timorese, Jose Ramos-Horta and Bishop Carlos Filipe Xinenes Belo, who brought Indonesian atrocities to the world's attention, were awarded the Nobel Prize for Peace. With the independence of East Timor, the last vestige of Western colonialism in Southeast Asia, which had begun in the second decade of the sixteenth century, at last disappeared.

By the Treaty of Lisbon of 1859 between Portugal and the Netherlands, the Portuguese ceded the western portion of Timor to the Dutch. Long before that, the Portuguese had lost all their Southeast Asian possessions to the far more powerful Dutch. As the only Portuguese outpost in Southeast Asia, East Timor was grossly neglected by its colonial masters. The only major change brought about by the Portuguese in almost five centuries of rule was the conversion of East Timor's population to Catholicism, beginning with the first settlement by Catholic friars in Occussi in 1556 (the UN census of 2001 found that 98 percent of Timorese were Catholic). In the long fight between the Dutch and the Portuguese, the indigenous Timorese kingdoms were extinguished. During World War II, the Japanese occupied East Timor; the Dutch possessions, including West Timor, were ruled by an Indonesian puppet government under Japan's domination. After the restoration of East Timor to the Portuguese at the end of the war, neglect under Portuguese colonial rule continued; the handful of Portuguese officials sent there by the dictator, Oliveira Salazar, regarded the posting as banishment.

In 1974, after dictatorship was ended in Portugal and Lisbon began taking steps to wind up its overseas empire, the East Timorese were granted the right to form political parties. East Timor was given three options: full independence, autonomy within the Portuguese rule, or integration with neighboring Indonesia. Of the five political parties that immediately emerged, the most important was the leftist Fretilin, which demanded complete independence. The Timorese Democratic Union (the Uniao Democratica Timorense, or UDT) stood for autonomy within Portugal. One major party, the Popular Association for a Democratic Timor, and two smaller ones (the Sons of the Mountain Warriors and the Timor Labor Party) stood for integration with Indonesia.

INDONESIA AND EAST TIMOR

President Suharto of Indonesia did not want an independent state on the border. It could emerge as a Communist state, with Fretilin spreading its own brand of socialism and democratic rights among other Indonesian islands. Suharto pushed for the integration of the former Portuguese colony into Indonesia. His generals launched a policy of destabilization in East Timor, training thousands of East Timorese to fight against Fretilin forces and organizing covert operations against the guerrilla movement. With Jakarta's encouragement, the pro-Indonesian groups among the East Timorese adopted the Balibo Declaration of November 30, 1975, which was immediately ratified by the Indonesian parliament. The declaration provided Indonesian troops the pretext to invade East Timor on the grounds that it should be integrated into Indonesia. Indonesia launched a full-scale military invasion of East Timor, a move that prompted Fretilin to declare East Timor independent of Portugal on November 28, 1975. Indonesia formally integrated East Timor as its twenty-seventh province in 1976 and succeeded in gaining recognition of its action by some Western powers (including the United States and Australia, which had strong military and economic ties with the Indonesian government).

After its incorporation into Indonesia in 1976, East Timor was closed to the outside world for thirteen years. During that period, according to numerous human rights groups, notably the London-based Amnesty International and U.S.-based Asia Watch, about 200,000 Timorese were killed or died of starvation. On December 27, 1988, East Timor was accorded open-territory status following a military report that the independence movement there (i.e., Fretilin) was no longer a security problem. The action was taken not only to placate critics of Indonesia's human rights record but also to secure UN recognition of Indonesia's annexation of East Timor.

The East Timor situation attracted global attention when on November 12, 1991, Indonesian troops opened fire on pro-independence demonstrators at the Santa Cruz cemetery in Dili, the capital of East Timor, killing about 50 and wounding twice that many. The international media reported torture at the hands of police and the army of another 300–400 political dissenters arrested on this occasion. The estimated 3,500 demonstrators had marched peacefully to the cemetery to commemorate a student killed in clashes with the police on October 28. A week after the Dili incident, President Suharto appointed an inquiry commission headed by Chief Justice Jaelani with representatives from the home, external affairs, and justice ministries as well as the Supreme Court, parliament, and the armed forces.

Meanwhile, Indonesian troops continued to consolidate the government's grip on East Timor and to contain the independence movement there. In November 1992, they captured Jose Alexandre Gusmao (also known as "Xanana"), the head of Fretilin, which had led the guerrilla campaign for independence since 1975. More than 1,000 Fretilin members surrendered or were captured following their leader's arrest, leaving the movement for independence virtually decimated. After a three-month trial in Dili for sedition, Gusmao was sentenced to life imprisonment the following May. Because of an international outcry, led by Amnesty International and Asia Watch, President Suharto in August reduced the sentence to twenty years. Reports of the military's brutal treatment of Fretilin prisoners remained a concern to international human rights activists.

INTERNATIONAL REACTION

The international reaction to such gross violations of human rights was swift and decisive. Portugal used its position as chair of the European Community during the first half of 1992 to withhold aid to Indonesia. The European Parliament called for an immediate and independent inquiry and proposed an arms embargo on Indonesia. Portugal also raised the question in the European Community (EC) in order to make the long-awaited EC-ASEAN trade pact conditional on Indonesia's improvement of its human rights record in East Timor. Portugal also attempted to stop the new international aid consortium, meeting in Paris, from granting $4.94 billion in development assistance to Indonesia. Additionally, Portugal introduced an EC-sponsored resolution in the UN Human Rights Commission condemning Indonesian acts in East Timor. Many other countries also reacted strongly. Canada, Denmark, and the Netherlands suspended aid to Indonesia. The U.S. House of Representatives voted a $2.9 million cut in military training assistance. The United States, Australia, and Japan warned that they would review their aid commitments to Indonesia if the findings of the inquiry commission appointed by President Suharto were little more than a "whitewash." In July 1993, the United States vetoed a plan by Jordan to sell to Indonesia some U.S.-made F-5 fighters. In September, the U.S. Senate Foreign Relations Committee approved an amendment to foreign aid legislation requiring the administration to review the human rights situation in East Timor before resuming arms sales to Indonesia.

The saga of Fretilin fighters who waged guerrilla warfare against Indonesian forces from their redoubts in the mountains, and reports of large-scale deaths due to disease and lack of medical facilities among the East Timorese, who were relocated by Indonesian authorities as part of their counterguerrilla tactics from their cooler highland homes to the strategic hamlets along the northern hotter coastline, moved the international conscience. Over the next two decades, Indonesian forces were able to decimate the Fretilin forces, but not their spirit, reinforced by clandestine but consistent supplies of funds, food, and weapons from the common people.

A number of international human rights agencies became involved in recording and publicizing the atrocities, notably the notorious Santa Cruz massacre in which nearly 300 civilians were killed at the local cemetery in November 1991. The incident is regarded by observers as the turning point in the international perception of the Indonesian regime in East Timor.

With the change of government in Jakarta (i.e., the removal of Suharto and the installation of the liberal Habibie as president), the situation changed dramatically. In January 1999, Habibie proposed extensive autonomy for the East Timorese. Following talks between Indonesia, Portugal, and the United Nations, Habibie proposed a ballot vote. The poll, on August 30, 1999, attracted 98.5 percent of East Timor's registered voters, who rejected the proposal by 78.5 percent. The clear verdict (i.e., against autonomy and in favor of independence) was not appreciated by the Indonesian militia in West Timor, which went on a rampage of violence and brutality aided by Indonesia's regular military. The two-decade conflict in East Timor had also resulted in nearly 250,000 people fleeing to West Timor, where they lived in makeshift camps. The Indonesian authorities saw the writing on the wall and cooperated within limits. Members of the Indonesian militia operating in West Timor complained of abandonment by Jakarta.

This time, international reaction was swift and decisive. The International Force in East Timor handed over the control of the territory to the UN Transitional Administration of East Timor (UNTAET), which had been organized after the Cambodian model, in November 1999. On July 15, 2000, UNTAET and the National Council of the Timorese Resistance (CNRT) agreed to form a coalition government with cabinet positions shared equally between UN officials and East Timorese. The arrangement continued under the overall control of a UN-appointed administrator until independence for East Timor came on May 20, 2002.

ELECTIONS AND THE NEW GOVERNMENT

UNTAET included 6,200 troops, 126 military observers, 1,500 police officers, and a secretariat of bureaucrats, entrusted with the task of training the Timorese; by June 2000 it began a policy of Timorization, giving educated East Timorese and local leaders a role in the new government. Meanwhile, the first congress held by the CNRT (August 2000) approved Portuguese as the official language and Tetum as the national language. On August 30, 2001, under the UNTAET, an election was held for the Consultative Assembly of eighty-eight members, which included thirteen members elected from each of East Timor's districts and seventy-five elected by proportional representation. The elections, contested by twelve political parties, installed twenty-four women and handed Fretilin fifty-five seats, three short of the two-thirds required to pass any legislation. The Consultative Assembly also serves as the national legislature. In the new government, the Fretilin held six of the ten ministries. The Consultative Assembly's responsibilities included the framing of a constitution that outlined, among other things, the form of government following independence.

On March 21, 2002, the Consultative Assembly approved a constitution, which adopted a republican system of government for the new state. It provided for the direct election of the president, who would be the head of state; the prime minister would be selected by the national parliament to head the government. Under the new constitution, the East Timorese elected resistance leader Jose Alexandre "Xanana" Gusmao as the country's first president with 83 percent of the votes cast. Under him and a newly created body called the Commission for Reception, Truth, and Reconciliation, the process of uniting all East Timorese, including the repatriated refugees from West Timor, was launched for a term of two years. All prisoners except those charged with major crimes were given the option of asking for forgiveness or facing trial. On May 20, 2002, the country's administration by the United Nations ended; East Timor declared its complete independence to coincide with the anniversary of the founding of Fretilin.

Under three years of UN administration, a program of financial assistance by a group of international donor countries was begun for East Timor along lines similar to that for Cambodia. The UN High Commissioner for Refugees assisted in the repatriation and partial rehabilitation of about 250,000 East Timorese who had fled to West Timor in the previous quarter century. The economic situation was so bad that in 2001 an estimated 80 percent of young people were without employment. East Timor's dependence on international handouts should end, however, with the exploration for oil and natural gas in the Timor Gap between East Timor and Australia. The agreements signed in June 2001 between the United Nations and Australia, and ratified in May 2002 by the new government of East Timor, assigned 90 percent of oil and gas royalties to East Timor and 10 percent to Australia; this was expected to bring an estimated US$7 billion to East Timor over two decades.

Disturbances and International Intervention Again

The harmonious relationship among the Timorese leaders, which had marked the birth of the new nation, did not last beyond a few years. In April 2006, Prime Minister Mari Alkatiri, a member of the minority Muslim community, without consulting with President Gusmao, dismissed 594 members of the armed forces, effectively reducing the latter by one-third. They were principally ethnic Loromonu from the west of the country, who had gone on strike to protest the discrimination by senior officers from the ethnic Lorosae from the east. Minister of the Interior Rogerio Lobato was accused of supplying arms to an illegal militia formed to fight the enemies of Alkatiri. The political and military developments sparked ethnic riots. The dismissed soldiers retained their weapons as they fled to the hills around the capital city of Dili. Apart from the supporters of Alkatiri and Gusmao engaging in conflict, the disturbances were taken advantage of by miscreants including armed gangs of unemployed young men. Thirty-seven persons died and 155,000 persons, most from Dili, fled their homes. In one dire incident on May 26, the military shot at unarmed police, killing ten and injuring twice that number. On the same day, a mob burned down Lobato's home, killing six members of his family. Alkatiri stepped down June 26 from the position of prime minister; he was replaced by Ramos Horta. The situation approximated a civil war.

The riots brought international intervention. In fact, the government of President Gusmao heaved a sigh of relief when 3,000 Australian troops landed in East Timor and relative peace and order were reestablished. Smaller contingents from New Zealand, Malaysia, and Portugal also arrived. On August 25, the UN Security Council authorized the establishment of a new and expanded mission named the UN Integrated Mission in Timor-Leste (UNMIT) to replace the UN Office in Timor-Leste (UNOTIL). Its mandate was for six months (later extended to February 26, 2008); it would have 1,608 police (increased in February 2007 by another 140), 34 military staff, and some liaison personnel. Its duties would include not only maintaining law and order but also preparing the country for the presidential and parliamentary elections in 2007. External economic assistance arrived notably from the United Nations and from Australia.

The situation brought into the open acute differences between Alkatiri and Gusmao, the latter strongly supported by Nobel Prize–winning Foreign Minister Ramos Horta. The divisions between Alkatiri and Gusmao, which had so far been suppressed because of the latter's legendary popularity, also came out in the open. Fretilin now made clear that it did not support Alkatiri either; its membership weighed in favor of Jose Luis Guterres, Timor-Leste's ambassador to the United Nations, for the position of prime minister.

Elections of 2007

The divisive situation in the country was reflected in the 2007 presidential and parliamentary elections. Ramos Horta, Gusmao's chosen candidate, who was running as an independent, failed to top the list of candidates, none of whom met the required minimum of 50 percent to be elected president. In the second round held on May 9 between Ramos Horta and the Fretilin's candidate, Francisco Guterres, Horta won to become the second president of Timor-Leste. Meanwhile, on April 30, Gusmao and Horta founded a new party, the National Congress of Reconstruction of Timor (CNRT), which would contest the general elections to the parliament scheduled for June 30.

Those elections also did not return a majority for any of the fourteen political parties contesting the 65 seats. Although Fretilin, led by the former prime minister, Mari Alkatiri, won 21 seats as being the largest group in the national legislature, Gusmao's CNRT, which won only 18 seats, was able to cobble together a coalition with the Social Democratic party (SDP) (11 seats) and the Democratic party (PD) (8 seats). In August, the new president, Ramos Horta, appointed his friend and political ally, the former President Gusmao, to become the country's prime minister. The leftist Fretilin and the Church-supported CNRT were then ranged against each other.

Gusmao's appointment as prime minister was opposed by the revolutionary Fretilin, which staged riots in Dili and the eastern towns of Baucau and Viquesque. The rioting mobs burned down over 300 houses, rendering thousands homeless. The situation was brought under control by UN police and Australian peacekeepers. The report of Atul Khare, the UN's representative, pointedly identified the Fretilin as the source of the continued violent protests.

TREATY WITH AUSTRALIA ON THE BOUNDARY

One major factor boosting the survival and prosperity of the new state was a border treaty with Australia that had tremendous economic implications. On January 12, 2006, East Timor signed a treaty with Australia on the maritime boundary between the two countries, which had been a bone of contention because of the major economic consequences it had for the poorest nation of Southeast Asia. Australia had wanted to preserve the boundary agreed with Indonesia in 1972, which was 150 kilometers (about 100 miles) from East Timor, effectively keeping the Greater Sunrise gas field, arguably the largest hydrocarbon reserve in the Timor Sea, under Australian control. On the other hand, East Timor had argued in favor of customary maritime law that would draw the line exactly between the two disputants, a little less than 300 kilometers (about 200 miles) from the Timorese coastline, which would place almost all the proven gas and oil reserves within the new nation's control. That would assure it an annual revenue of about US$10 billion, a sum that would certainly mitigate its dire poverty and make possible its entry into the modern world. It was President Gusmao's insistence on customary maritime law that had prevented an agreement with Australia thus far, and the pressures were mounting on the Canberra government from the companies that had invested in the gas field and had stopped operating since the end of 2004. In January 2006, the two countries agreed on a fifty-year moratorium on the border issue, agreeing in the meantime to share the revenues from the gas field on a fifty-fifty basis. It was a victory for the new Southeast Asian nation.

24

Malaysia, Singapore, and Brunei

MALAYSIA: THE ANGLOPHILE PHASE
Lifting the State of Emergency

Although Malaya became independent in 1957, the British lingered on until 1960 when officially the state of emergency was ended. The new government was headed by Tunku Abdul Rahman (1957–1970), who came from a princely family and was a pro-Western, pronouncedly anti-Communist Anglophile. He wanted very much to redress the imbalance of the British days when the ethnic Malays had lagged far behind the Chinese community in education, economy, and civil service. As prime minister, his policy would be to integrate the Chinese community into the national mainstream by containing the Communist guerrilla movement (mostly consisting of ethnic Chinese) and to give special attention to the Malays, the *Bumiputras* (sons of the soil), to make up for past neglect.

The ethnic Malays were not directly exploited by the colonial rulers. They had been left to their traditional means of livelihood and way of life, and they had benefited little from Malaya's new prosperity based on tin and rubber. On the other hand, the Malay rulers and nobility had been well looked after by the British. Their status had been retained and their pay and perquisites enhanced beyond their wildest imagination. They were, for the most part, British-educated and Anglophiles. In contrast, the Chinese community, descendants of the nineteenth-century tin-mining laborers, had advanced markedly in commerce, education, and civil service. They centered in urban areas, whereas the Malays lived mostly in the countryside and occupied themselves in agriculture and fishing. On the economic and educational ladder, the Indians, who had also immigrated as rubber plantation labor, occupied the middle position.

To contain the Communist threat and to integrate the Chinese community, the government offered a general amnesty to all insurgents and free transportation to those who wished to migrate to Communist China. Prime Minister Abdul

Rahman served notice that his government desired peace but not at the cost of appeasement. The Communist party was outlawed. By 1960, with the assistance of British troops, the Communist insurrection had been suppressed, and most of the guerrillas had surrendered, though a handful continued to operate on the Thai-Malay border.

Although the prime minister had thus successfully contained the Communists, he was far from successful in integrating the bulk of the Chinese community. Numbering 36 percent of the population, as against Malays of 53 percent and Indians of 11 percent, the Chinese could not grasp the secondary role to which they were relegated by the new constitution and regulations. Thus, the state would be headed by one of the nine Malay sultans, elected among themselves and called *yang-di-pertuan* (paramount ruler). Malay was to be the official language. The citizenship laws excluded 41 percent of the Chinese population. The constitution (article 153) specifically allowed the *yang-di-pertuan* to authorize quotas for civil service positions, scholarships, and licenses for the Malays.

Birth of Malaysia

At that point, negotiations were under way for granting independence to Singapore and perhaps to Sarawak and North Borneo. The prime minister hoped that the last two would merge with the Malay federation so that the overall percentage of ethnic Chinese would be reduced, but the leaders of the Chinese community favored the merger of Singapore with the proposed Federation of Malaysia, which would have the opposite effect because of Singapore's overwhelmingly Chinese population (75 percent). The Chinese also argued in favor of Singapore's merger on grounds of mutual economic benefit for Malaya and Singapore because they constituted a single economic unit. Singapore handled a substantial part of Malaya's exports and imports; an economic barrier along the Straits of Johor could ruin Singapore. The two were also militarily interdependent. Curiously, the People's Action party (PAP) of Lee Kuan Yew, the future founder of Singapore as a separate state, supported the merger in the strongest terms.

The Malays were not enthusiastic about a merger with Singapore for several reasons. First, Singapore's 1.2 million Chinese would upset the racial balance in the federation. Second, all left-wing parties in Singapore, including PAP, were regarded with a great deal of apprehension by the leaders of Malaya's Alliance party (AP). After all, Singapore had supplied a large number of recruits to the Communist guerrilla movement in Malaya during the recently ended state of emergency. Moreover, Singapore had in the previous century and a half dominated the politics and economics of the entire peninsula to the relative neglect of Kuala Lumpur. The Malays were keen on boosting the new political eminence of Kuala Lumpur in any political arrangement. However, Prime Minister Abdul Rahman saw economic advantages of a merger with Singapore and wanted Sarawak and Sabah (North Borneo), which had not yet been granted independence, to be included in the proposed Federation of Malaysia. The Borneo population was not Malay but, to be sure, it was not Chinese. Being fellow Muslims, they could be depended on to provide the crucial numerical balance that would help to keep the Chinese in a minority status in the enlarged federation. In the end, the prime minister's plan met with the approval of the British, who granted independence to the Borneo territories and persuaded them, along with Singapore, to join the Federation of Malaysia, which was formed on August 31, 1963. The new federation consisted of fourteen states—the nine Malay princely states, plus Malacca, Penang (and Province Wellesley), Singapore, Sarawak, and Sabah (North Borneo)—with Kuala Lumpur as capital. This was a blow to Chinese aspirations and could have given the Alliance a major setback had it not been for the Indonesian "Confrontation" policy. The danger to the security of Malaysia that the policy posed helped unify the Malays and Chinese. The results were clearly seen in the Alliance victory of 1964, which was much more spectacular than its performance five years earlier.

Singapore's membership in the Federation of Malaysia proved short-lived. The new political setup could perhaps have survived the communal differences, but it could not contain the egos of the two rival leaders—Abdul Rahman and Lee Kuan Yew. Lee was a brilliant barrister, very ambitious and abrasive. He headed the local government of Singapore as its prime minister. His aim was to bring all non-Malays, including those of Sabah and Sarawak, under his leadership and use the leverage to wrest control of the government from Abdul Rahman. British efforts to mediate between the two were regarded by the Malays as favoring Singapore. Before the British or other Commonwealth leaders could interfere any further, the prime minister took the sudden initiative to throw Singapore out of the Federation of Malaysia in August 1965. In the remnant federation, the Malays would constitute 56 percent as against 34 percent Chinese and 9 percent Indian (see Table 24.1).

Racial Riots of 1969

Abdul Rahman's daring act of ousting Singapore assured Malay leadership of the federation, but contributed to exacerbation of the fears and apprehensions of the Chinese community. Even before this, the Chinese and Indian minorities had been feeling that the privileges given to the Bumiputras under the constitution were being grossly abused by the government to discriminate against the non-Malays in an effort to keep them permanently subservient.

Originally, the concessions were made because of the relative educational and economic backwardness of the Malays. The pursuit of a discriminatory policy against the non-Malays bred a feeling of acute resentment by the mid-1960s among the Chinese, who pointed out that there were poor and less privileged people among them too. Tensions between the Malays and the Chinese manifested themselves in the worst form ever in the fiercely fought elections of 1969, which unseated large numbers of Alliance members of the National Assembly, particularly

TABLE 24.1 Principal Ethnic Communities of Malaysia, 1963 (in thousands)

	Malays	Chinese	Indians	Others
Fed. of Malaya	3,461	2,552	773	123
Singapore	227	1,231	138	38
Sarawak	129	229	2	384
N. Borneo	25	105	1	322
Total	3,842	4,117	914	867

those representing the urban centers, where the Chinese were concentrated. The explosive riots that followed the elections shredded the fabric of social harmony, taking a toll of more than 2,000 lives, mostly Chinese. This had grave implications for the survival of democracy itself as the government ordered suspension of all political activities in the country with a declaration of a new state of emergency. Politics has never been the same in Malaysia since.

The end of the 1960s marked major changes in Malaysia's policies, domestic and foreign. There were at least three new factors responsible for the alterations: the racial riots, the British decision to withdraw their forces from the east of Suez, and a change in leadership at the top caused by the resignation of Abdul Rahman in 1970 and the rise of his deputy, Abdul Razak, to the prime ministership (1970–1976).

Following the riots, parliamentary government was suspended for twenty-one months. The time was used by the Alliance party to reach a political understanding with the United People's party of Sarawak; together, they would have the two-thirds majority to push through constitutional amendments. During the suspension period, the Alliance adopted a new national platform called Rukunegara, consisting of five principles: belief in God, loyalty to king and nation, upholding the constitution, rule of law, and good ethics. It was a combination of Thailand's Three Pillars and the Pancasila of Indonesia. Rukunegara eventually assumed the status of state ideology. It has been further developed to include respect for a pluralistic (*Negara*) or multiracial (*bangsa*) and multireligious society (*agama*). These principles constitute the ideology of the UMNO (United Malay National Organization), the ruling coalition. In February 1971, the parliament passed the Constitutional Amendments and Sedition Act forbidding public discussion of issues having a racial bearing. The act muted the resentment of the Chinese and Indians to the Malay domination of politics and enabled the government to favor the Bumiputras without the risk of opposition.

FOREIGN POLICY
Multilateral Defense Arrangements

The leadership of Abdul Razak as prime minister from 1970 until his death in January 1976 marked the end of openly Anglophile and anti-Communist policies. Partly this was a difference in personalities. Even as deputy prime minister, Razak had actively promoted the idea of a more nonaligned posture in foreign policy. Since independence, Malaya (and later Malaysia) had depended on the Anglo-Malayan Defense Agreement (AMDA), under which Great Britain would join Malaya in dealing with external aggression. In 1959, Australia and New Zealand had associated themselves with the AMDA. The British military assistance was crucial both in dealing with the domestic Communist insurgency up to 1960 and later with Indonesia during the "Confrontation" policy in the mid-1960s. It was because of the AMDA that Malaysia could resist membership in SEATO or in a bilateral defense pact with the United States.

The British government's announcement in January 1968 that it would withdraw its forces from the east of Suez by March 1971 compelled Malaysia to reconsider its security arrangement. In fact, soon after the end of the Confrontation with

Indonesia in 1966, Malaysia had begun to reduce its dependence on British ties so as to prove that it was "an Asian country and not a creation or protege of Britain."[1] During the 1968–1970 period, there was ambivalence in foreign policy as Abdul Rahman spoke of the desirability of nonalignment and the neutralization of Southeast Asia in the same breath that he mentioned a British-related defense pact and diplomatic support of the U.S. position in Vietnam. Eventually, Malaysia was able to work out new defense arrangements with Britain, Australia, New Zealand, and Singapore in a five-power amalgam in November 1971. There would be a sizable British naval and air force presence in the area, with only a single battalion of British troops stationed in Singapore. The agreement provided for consultation among the five partners, all of them members of the Commonwealth of Nations, in the event of external aggression against Malaysia or Singapore. Although the Malaysian government remained skeptical of actual commitment of the three non-regional powers to the country's security, it saw the benefit of a "mechanism through which it could pressure its allies for assistance and felt that it might give a potential aggressor reason to pause."[2] The arrangement lasted nominally for more than a decade and a half. Britain and Australia withdrew their forces by the mid-1970s. In 1988, Australia removed its last squadron of Mirage fighter aircraft from Malaysia, and New Zealand pulled out its 740-strong infantry battalion and a helicopter unit from Singapore in 1989.

Proposal for Neutralization of Southeast Asia

Concurrently with the efforts to work out a five-power defense agreement, Malaysia initiated and pursued a proposal for neutralization of the entire region. It was a proposal of which Malaysia was immensely proud, as it was seen as one that could usher in long-term peace in a troubled region of the world. First conceived by Tun Ismail, Malaysia's home minister in the Abdul Rahman cabinet in January 1968, it received a great boost when Razak became prime minister in September 1970 and made Ismail his deputy. The Malaysian proposal was threefold, designed to meet the three aspects of security: external, internal, and intraregional. It included the following proposals:

(1) All the Southeast Asian countries should agree on ending alliances with external powers and elimination of foreign military bases. The neutralization of the region should be guaranteed by all the major powers including the People's Republic of China.

(2) All the Southeast Asian nations should sign treaties of non-aggression with each other.

(3) All the Southeast Asian nations should declare a policy of non-intervention in one another's internal affairs.[3]

The idea of neutralization of one or more countries of the region was not entirely new. A plan as detailed as Malaysia's was novel. The Vietnam conflict and the British decision to withdraw from the east of Suez made it more meaningful. No formal request was made to the three powers concerned—the United States, the Soviet Union, and China—to guarantee the security of the Southeast Asian nations in the event of neutralization of that region. Malaysia insisted that before doing so, there must be agreements among all the Southeast Asian states to disallow foreign troops on their soil and to respect each other's borders. In November 1971, the proposal made major headway by receiving the endorsement of ASEAN.

Relations with Other Countries

Just as Malaysia was the first among Southeast Asian countries to perceive the need for neutralization, it also led the other pro-West states in recognizing the Communist countries. Malaysian leaders have repeatedly stated that there is no contradiction between a policy of friendship with Communist countries and commitment to oppose internal communism. Diplomatic relations with the Soviet Union were established in 1967. In 1971, trade missions were exchanged with China. However, in order to reduce contacts between China and the Malaysian Chinese, arrangements were made to channel the trade through the largely Malay-staffed state trading corporation, Pernas. Malaysia's efforts to normalize relations with China were, however, delayed until 1974 because of a 1971 understanding among all ASEAN nations to inform each other of talks with China and the consequent restraints from Indonesia and Singapore, which opposed normalization. After 1974, Sino-Malaysian relations were strengthened by a number of high-level exchange visits. Thus, China's Vice Premier Deng Xiaoping visited Malaysia in 1978, and Prime Minister Datuk Hussein bin Onn reciprocated in the following year. In 1981, Chinese Premier Zhao Ziyang visited Malaysia and tried to smooth relations, particularly on the issue of China's help to the Malayan Communist party (MCP). In 1984, Chinese Foreign Minister Wu Xueqian stated in Kuala Lumpur that China was not helping the MCP materially but that it would not end its "moral support."

Malaysian relations with the ASEAN member states improved markedly over the years. The bilateral talks at the ASEAN meetings led finally to the Philippines agreeing in 1977 to end the dispute over Sabah in exchange for Malaysia's implicit agreement not to help the Moro rebels with arms. Cooperation between Malaysia and Thailand in dealing with insurgencies in the common border areas was reinforced by a formal agreement in March 1977. Thailand all along denied refuge to remnants of the MCP insurgency—about 400 guerrillas operating under Chin Peng's leadership. The two governments held joint operations using regular security forces instead of police to suppress Communist insurgencies in the border region. In the early 1980s, Malaysia estimated guerrillas in southern Thailand at 2,000. In 1985, it announced plans to build a sixteen-mile-long concrete wall along a section of the Malaysia-Thai border to prevent infiltration by Communists, at a cost of about $18 million.

Malaysian forces similarly operated in the early 1970s jointly with their Indonesian counterparts against Communists on their common border in Borneo. Relations with Indonesia improved across the board dramatically after the end of Confrontation policies in 1966.

Malaysia endorsed Indonesia's foreign policy in almost every aspect except in the degree of hostility toward China. More notably, as a country concerned with the control of the Strait of Malacca, Malaysia agreed with Indonesia that the strait was a part of territorial waters and not an international waterway. In February 1982, Malaysia became the first country formally to recognize Indonesia's "archipelagic principle," whereby Indonesia's territorial seas enclosing its 13,000 islands were delineated by straight baselines drawn from the outermost points of the outer islands. Under a maritime treaty of 1982 relating to parts of the South China Sea separating peninsular Malaysia from Sabah and Sarawak, Malaysia recognized Indonesia's sovereignty and exclusive economic rights. In turn, Indonesia recognized Malaysia's traditional fishing rights, rights of free sea and air passage between the two parts of Malaysia, and rights to lay submarine cables and pipelines.

MALAYSIA: THE SELF-ASSERTIVE PHASE

Bumiputra, Barisan Nasional, and Ethnic Accommodation

After the racial riots of 1969, the question of giving concessions in education, industry, and civil service to Bumiputras was more relentlessly pursued. At the same time, it was realized even more than before that ethnic compromise and accommodation were at the center of Malaysian politics. Before the elections of 1974, a broader front was formed of eleven parties (there were three additions and one expulsion by 1988) called the Barisan Nasional, or National Front. The Chinese and the Indian communities were still represented as in the old Alliance by the Malay Chinese Association and the Malay Indian Congress. The Gerakan (Gerakan Rakyat Malaysia) and the People's Progressive party helped the Barisan in blunting the more partisan attitudes of the Democratic Action party (DAP), consisting of moderate left-wing Chinese committed to multiracialism in Malay politics but at the same time championing the cause of non-Malays. Because of the need to retain the trust of the MCA within the Barisan, the government was compelled to moderate its Bumiputra policies.

Within the Barisan, the United Malay National Organization (UMNO) was the most important element, with great strength in the rural areas where the bulk of the Malays lived. All the prime ministers were leaders of the UMNO, the prime minister and deputy prime minister by tradition being the president and vice president, respectively, of the UMNO. Another convention was that the deputy prime minister would succeed the prime minister in office after the incumbent's retirement or death. The Barisan itself was so strong that it (and its predecessor, the Alliance) were repeatedly elected by a clear majority, more than two-thirds until the elections of March 2008. There was no effective opposition to it, no successful vote of no-confidence against the ruling party, and never a military coup. Such conditions were secured partly by curbs on freedom during the electoral campaigns, which became progressively shorter with every election. There were also antisedition laws in effect, a ban on discussion of ethnic issues, and significant curbs on the press and government control of the other media. In 1978, the excuse for banning public rallies was expectation of trouble from the MCP's plans to celebrate the thirtieth anniversary of its armed struggle. In 1982, outdoor public meetings were banned on grounds that they would create security problems, and indoor meetings attended by invitation only (*ceremah*) were subject to police permission. Neither the state-owned broadcast media nor the press gave much coverage to the opposition. The print media were controlled by the Printing and Presses Act, requiring obtaining and annually renewing a publishing license.

In late 2007, a few months before the general elections in March 2008, the opposition parties stepped up their demands, asking for real freedom of speech. Their reaction to the government's Malaysian Communications and Multimedia Commission's directive to all privately owned television and radio stations was to limit severely the exposure to opposition party leaders. However, the opposition was better organized than before as a coalition of political parties and nongovernmental organizations (NGOs) from all over the federation emerged as BERSIHH. Their agitation was indicative of the widespread anti-Barisan, specifically anti-UMNO feeling, which led to severe electoral setbacks for the UMNO in March 2008.

In the 1980s, the Barisan became more and more authoritarian and pro-Malay because of two kinds of pressures: the Islamic fundamentalists and the DAP's open partisanship of Chinese interests. In the aftermath of the 1969 riots, the government introduced the New Economic Policy aimed at reducing the disparities between different ethnic communities through an increase in the proportion of the corporate wealth owned by the Bumiputras to 30 percent by 1990. The goal was to be achieved by reducing the level of foreign ownership to 30 percent, the remaining 40 percent to be owned by Chinese and Indians. The policy had to be somewhat relaxed in the mid-1980s because of a severe economic recession. The government found it necessary to attract foreign capital. After rapid rates of economic growth averaging 7 percent per annum during the early 1980s, deterioration set in during 1985 with the fall in prices of Malaysia's commodity exports, bringing the growth rate down to 2 percent. By 1987, there was a modest recovery at 4.7 percent. In order to pursue its policy of increasing Bumiputra ownership, the government decreed that Bank Negara (central bank) must make 20 percent of its loans to Bumiputra businesses. In early 1988, the government created a $500 million (Malay dollar; approximately US$250 million) Enterprise Rehabilitation Fund to help banks out of bad loans made to Bumiputras.

THE MAHATHIR ERA

In July 1981, because of Prime Minister Hussein bin Onn's illness and resignation, Dr. Mahathir bin Mohamed was elected president of the UMNO and prime minister, with his close friend and colleague Musa Hitam as deputy prime minister. In popular parlance, the two became known as the M & M administration, or the 2-M government. Dr. Mahathir was the first nonlawyer (he is a medical graduate) prime minister; he was educated locally, a product of the postindependence period, had not held any post under the British, and was not involved in any negotiations leading to independence. He was no Anglophile. On the contrary, more than any other Malay politician, he consciously moved Malaysia away from Britain and the Commonwealth of Nations. A committed Bumiputra, he was in the early stages of his political career a right-wing UMNO member holding parochial views about the government's role in helping the indigenous people. His book *The Malay Dilemma,* in which he argued for the Bumiputra vis-à-vis the Chinese, was regarded by the latter as being too chauvinistic and was banned by the government in 1970 as being capable of arousing racial tensions. Dr. Mahathir was himself suspended from the UMNO for a period of time for holding such uncompromising views.

In 1978, the Bumiputra Investment Foundation was created with a paid-in capital of 200 million ringgits, or Malay dollars; it was headed by Dr. Mahathir, then deputy prime minister and minister of trade and industry. Its subsidiary, the Permodalan (National Equity Corporation), received a boost in early 1981 with the transfer to it of 552 million government-held shares in a number of leading companies worth about 1.5 billion Malay dollars (1 U.S. dollar equaled about 2.30 Malay dollars in 1981). In April 1981, a National Unit Trust Scheme (Amanah Saham Nasional) linked to Permodalan was launched. Its units of 10 Malay dollars each were easily accessible to the common people, who could also borrow funds from the Bumiputra banks to make the purchases.

The next major step of the government to reduce foreign holdings in the country were the controversial "dawn raids" through the London Stock Exchange. For instance, blocks of shares of the Guthrie Corporation were purchased in a mere three hours to raise the Permodalan's holdings from 24.88 to 50.41 percent, a transaction costing 72 million pounds, and further offers were made to buy out all shareholders. The Guthrie Corporation held 190,000 acres of rubber plantations in Malaysia. A major reason for the government action was indeed to penalize the company, which had allowed the MCA's Multi-Purpose Holdings (MPH), a vehicle for promoting Chinese interests in direct response to UMNO's policies favoring the Bumiputras, to buy 73 percent of the shares in Guthrie Berhad in Singapore. The government set the Guthrie pattern to acquire control over other plantation companies, marking the end of British control over major Malaysian plantations and making Permodalan one of the largest plantation owners in the world.

"Look East" Policy

The dawn raids brought reprisals from the British government, which intervened to change the London Stock Exchange operating rules on the pretext of protecting interests of small investors. A number of other issues led to deterioration in Anglo-Malaysian relations. One of these was the British government's decision in late 1979 to raise the fees of overseas students, making them also ineligible for fellowships and scholarships, a decision that hit Malaysia severely because of the large contingent of students that traditionally attended British institutions of higher learning. Consequently, there was a phenomenal increase in Malaysian students attending U.S. universities in the 1980s. The Mahathir government downgraded its relationship even with the Commonwealth, declaring its international priorities in 1981 as ASEAN, the Organization of Islamic Conference, the nonaligned movement, and thereafter, the Commonwealth. He issued directives to the various government agencies to have a definite preference for non-British sources for official purchases. There was no formal boycott of British goods, but the privileged position of the British in Malaysia was ended. Not even the April 1985 visit by Prime Minister Margaret Thatcher to Malaysia mollified Mahathir, who in fact used the occasion to criticize the Commonwealth by saying that its ideals of sharing wealth had been grossly neglected and that it was a creation of the past with very little relevance to the present.

The downgrading of relations with Britain was also a part of a new "Look East" policy. Mahathir openly called for rejection of residual Western political and economic influence and its replacement by a development strategy in which Japan and South Korea would provide more relevant examples for Malaysia. Mahathir's criticism of the West became increasingly strident in the 1980s and the 1990s, encompassing diverse aspects from economics and environment to ethics. Articulate in English, he projected himself as a spokesman for the Third World, a champion of poor nations, and hero of the South. He encouraged building regional economic strength through the ASEAN Free Trade Area (AFTA). In 1988, at a meeting of the Group of Fifteen in Kuala Lumpur, he proposed schemes to circumvent financial institutions and the "inequitable economic order" under the control of the United States and European Union by establishing the South Investment Trade and Technology Data Exchange Center to help form networks among the companies of the developing countries to help each other.

Noting that other countries of other regions had formed protectionist blocs such as the European Union and North American Free Trade Agreement (NAFTA), Mahathir proposed in late 1991 the establishment of an East Asian Economic Caucus (EAEC) that would include China, Japan, South Korea, Taiwan, and ASEAN but would exclude the United States and Australia. Contrary to his expectations, the idea did not receive adequate support of some of his ASEAN colleagues, who disagreed with his anti-West rhetoric. More importantly, not wanting to hurt U.S. sensitivities, Japan did not show any enthusiasm. Peeved over the lack of success of his EAEC idea, Mahathir refused to attend the U.S.-sponsored APEC meeting in Seattle in October 1993. He also modified his EAEC proposal so as to accommodate it within the ASEAN framework by calling a meeting of ASEAN plus three countries—China, South Korea, and Japan—for an informal dialogue, thereby bringing together nine Asian economies in a common forum. Mahathir attended the second meeting of APEC at the behest of the Indonesian president in Bogor, Indonesia, in November 1994. There he articulated the apprehensions of Malaysia and other developing countries over the pace of economic liberalization. He appealed for liberalization commensurate with the needs of development. His concerns were vindicated at the third meeting of APEC in Osaka in November 1995 when all the attendees except Singapore supported the Malaysian position.

In 1988–1989, the Malaysian government came under severe criticism by Western agencies, notably Amnesty International, for detention of political dissenters without trial. In 1991, the U.S. Congress suspended a military training program for Malaysia because in that year Malaysia pushed back Vietnamese boat people, predominantly of Chinese origin. Mahathir accused the West of insensitivity to Malaysian concerns about the effect on the country's ethnic balance of an influx of largely ethnic Chinese boat people.

In the 1990s, the Malaysian prime minister went on the offensive by attacking Western perceptions of democracy, human rights, and environmental policies. In June 1992, Mahathir played a prominent role at the Earth Summit in Rio de Janeiro, condemning the ecological depredation of the South by the North. At that forum, Malaysia joined Brazil in drafting the UN-sponsored resolution linking the environment and development. Mahathir's forceful and articulate exposition of the need to foster sustainable development in the South was most appreciated by the Third World nations. It positively contributed to the summit's resolutions on the subject. Mahathir also condemned the Western-dominated International Labor Organization (ILO), alleging that its policies were basically directed toward eroding the comparative advantage of developing countries over their Western counterparts in low-cost production.

Mahathir's anti-West pronouncements, however, should not be construed to mean a complete reversal of Malaysia's pro-West foreign policy of the previous two decades. Indeed, Mahathir was accused by his critics of blowing hot and cold in the same breath in his relations with Western nations. Thus, Mahathir continued to rely heavily on the U.S. market for Malaysian products. In 1992, 25 percent of the country's exports of manufactures went to the United States; only 8 percent went to Japan. Mahathir's government continued aggressively to attract Western capital to Malaysia. Significantly, during the 1990–1991 Gulf crisis, Malaysia consistently voted in the United Nations with the Western powers against Iraq.

On a global nonpartisan level, Malaysia sent peacekeeping forces to Cambodia, Somalia, and Bosnia. Malaysia represented a moderating element on the Bosnia question in the OIC. In September 1995, Kuala Lumpur hosted a meeting of foreign and defense ministers of the OIC troop-contributing countries to organize military assistance to Bosnia to redress the latter's weakness vis-à-vis Serbian forces. That meeting and Malaysia's strong stand in the UN may have influenced the United States to adopt a more decisive approach toward Bosnia, shortly culminating in the Paris Peace treaty in December 1995. On another front, Malaysia's consistent espousal of nuclear disarmament finally resulted in the signing by the ASEAN Summit of the Southeast Asian Nuclear Weapons–Free Zone Treaty in November 1995.

Mahathir Emerges Supreme

Like most countries with a Muslim majority, Malaysia felt the wave of Islamic fundamentalism in the wake of the movement in Iran. The PAS (Partai Islam Se Malaysia), at first a partner in the Barisan, emerged as the leader of the "Islamic challenge" particularly in Kelantan, where it held a majority in the state legislature. Its objective was to overthrow the secular, democratic state and instead set up an Islamic state. The ruling Barisan could not afford to be completely Islamic because of its partnership with MCA and MIC representing the Chinese and Indian communities. The Barisan was committed to preserving the racial balance established by the founders of the country and confirmed in the aftermath of the racial riots of 1969. Even so, the government was compelled to counter the fundamentalist PAS propaganda by itself advancing the interests of Muslim Malays. Thus, Mahathir made a pilgrimage to Mecca in 1981 and paid several visits to Arab states to show Muslim solidarity. He also announced plans for an Islamic university. The extremely conservative program of PAS had little appeal in the southern states and urban centers. The party won five seats in the national legislature in the 1978 and 1982 elections, but managed to get only one in the 1986 elections, in which its electoral platform called for banning liquor, gambling, and popular music and depriving women of the vote. In 1990, it improved its strength to seven seats by joining hands with a breakaway UMNO grouping, Semangat '46, led by former UMNO leader Razaleigh Hamzah.

The PAS's stronghold lies in the northern Malay states. In addition to Kelantan, it won a majority of seats in the Terengganu legislature in 1999 and formed the government there. In 1999, the PAS organization, together with a coalition called Barisan Alternatif, managed to secure 42 seats in the national legislature at the expense of the UMNO. In the general elections in 2004, however, the PAS lost Terengganu to the Barisan, though retaining its majority in Kelantan.

From 1986, the Mahathir government had to face two additional challenges: factionalism within the UMNO and the growing popularity of the DAP within the Chinese community. In February of that year the Mahathir–Musa Hitam partnership broke up, posing a challenge to Mahathir's party leadership in April 1987. Mahathir was accused of high-handed arrogance, violation of party traditions, economic blundering, and personal corruption. In the end, Mahathir's presidency of UMNO was confirmed by a very narrow margin of 761 votes to 718 secured by his rival, Razaleigh Hamzah, who was supported by Musa Hitam. The split within the UMNO was the first in the party's history. As a punitive measure, Mahathir removed three and secured the resignation of two other cabinet members. Although both sides had championed the economic interests of the Bumiputras, Mahathir was deemed to have given in too much to Islamic fundamentalists and acted against the minority interests. Mahathir's repressive actions in October 1987, when he imprisoned 106 dissenters of all kinds under the Internal Security Act (detention without charges or trial) and closed down the *Star,* an English-language daily of which the UMNO's elder statesman, former Prime Minister Tunku Abdul Rahman, was the chairman and frequent columnist, alienated Mahathir from a large number of UMNO members. Of the detainees, fifty-five were released by December 26, 1988, thirty-three were served with detention orders of two years, eight were placed under house arrest, two were banished from their district, and the remaining eight were kept under investigation. Of those detained for two years was the secretary-general of the DAP, Lim Kit Siang.

The intraparty differences reached crisis proportions in early 1988, leading to the UMNO breaking into two separate parties. Eleven UMNO members, all supporters of Razaleigh, had filed a court case seeking to invalidate the party leadership elections of April 1987. The High Court's decision of February 4, 1988, declaring the UMNO itself illegal because it had not registered 30 of its branches, sent shock waves throughout Malaysia. Large numbers of UMNO members, including Tunku Abdul Rahman, demanded Mahathir's resignation. Razaleigh and Musa Hitam now joined hands openly to form what came to be called UMNO's Team B to oppose Mahathir's Team A. With the court's verdict, the original UMNO was "deregistered" as a party. The court decreed that the UMNO's massive portfolio of real estate and corporate holdings and other financial assets could be claimed by whichever political entity could enroll more than 50 percent of the original UMNO membership of about 1.4 million.

Mahathir took up the challenge both by building up UMNO Baru (New UMNO) and crippling his opposition. Complaining of declining loyalty and inadequate national pride, Mahathir launched the Semarak (Loyalty with the People Movement), in support of which he held huge rallies in all the states to boost his own image and the political base of his party, even by the use of state funds. He indulged in several populist measures in the name of national unity, including construction of a 250-foot monument, Menara Semarak, and the hoisting of a huge national flag—335 by 235 feet—in Kuala Lumpur during the National Day celebrations on August 31, 1988. By that date, the UMNO Baru claimed to have registered 931,361 applications for membership, more than the number needed to claim the assets of the defunct UMNO. The epithet "Baru" was now deemed unnecessary; Mahathir's party became the successor of the old UMNO.

Meanwhile, Mahathir's opponents from the defunct UMNO, Musa Hitam and Razaleigh Hamzah, were joined by two former prime ministers, Abdul Rahman and Hussein Onn, in forming the UMNO Malaysia. It was, however, not allowed by the relevant government officials to be registered as a political party. The leaders of the UMNO Malaysia harked back to the "Spirit of 1946," when all Malays were united under the common banner of a single Malay national organization. Despite the Mahathir administration's efforts to prevent the opposition from holding rallies or gaining access to television and press, it thrived by using the underground electronic media, which came to be popularly called TV4 in contrast to the UMNO Baru–controlled broadcast station, TV3. Not until May 1989, however, was the opposition's party, then called Semangat '46, able to register itself as a political party. By that time, Mahathir had made important inroads into Razaleigh's ranks and secured the defection of some members; most important was the defection of Musa Hitam, who was readmitted to the UMNO in February 1989. His acceptance of an appointment as Malaysia's ambassador to the United Nations, far away from the center of domestic politics, undoubtedly brought delight and relief to the prime minister.

Under the circumstances, Mahathir felt ready for general elections, which he called prematurely for October 21, 1990, one year before their due date and with only ten days allowed for campaigning. For the first time since independence, the opposition front, named the Gagasan Rakyat (People's Might), included Malays. It was led by Razaleigh Hamzah, whose own party, Semangat '46, agreed with the right-wing PAS not to put up candidates against each other. Although the opposition front found it hard to get its message to the people, thanks to government control of the media and the need for police permission to hold public meetings, the election itself was fair and free. Mahathir's strength was reduced from 133 to 127, though he still retained in the 180-seat parliament the two-thirds majority needed to effect any constitutional changes. The opposition front improved its position from 37 to 53, the PAS moving up from 1 to 7 seats, and Semangat '46 moved down from 12 to 8. The ruling Barisan Nasional, of which Mahathir's UMNO was a member, won in all states except Kelantan and Sabah.

By the mid-1990s, Mahathir had successfully surmounted all major domestic challenges to his leadership. The ninth general elections for the national parliament as well as all eleven state assemblies held in April 1995 gave his Barisan Nasional (BN) a landslide victory with the largest plurality of votes since the country's independence, winning 162 out of the 192 parliamentary seats with 65.4 percent of the total vote. The elections were fair and free. In the state assembly elections, the BN was the leading coalition in all states except Kelantan, but unlike the previous election in which the BN did not secure a single seat in Kelantan, in April 1995 the BN won 8 seats in its state assembly and 2 of Kelantan's parliamentary seats. Once again, Islamic fundamentalism showed its strength in Kelantan as the coalition of the Islamic party, PAS, and Semangat '46 formed the government there. The DAP, representing the Chinese community's interests, nationally went from 20 seats in 1990 to 9 in 1995 and in its stronghold in Penang from 13 to 1.

The last general election under Mahathir's leadership of the UMNO and Barisan was held in November 1999. Although the BN as a whole fared extremely well with three-fourths of the seats in the national legislature, the UMNO's strength was reduced from 94 to 72. The Barisan Alternatif coalition of the PAS and Semangat '46 formed a strong opposition, winning 42 seats. A major reason for the UMNO's decline was Mahathir's treatment of his one-time deputy prime minister and close friend, Anwar Ibrahim (discussed in a later section).

Malaysian Economic Miracle

The dramatic emergence of Malaysia since the late 1980s as a rapidly growing economy in the midst of largely stagnant recession-plagued Western economies has impressed most international observers. The country has attracted large amounts of foreign investment from Japan, the United States, Singapore, and the European Union (in that order) despite its prime minister's strident criticism of the West and the West's displeasure over his record on human rights and environmental policies. For eight consecutive years since 1987, the Malaysian economy registered a growth of over 8 percent; in 1995, the real gross domestic product (GDP) grew by 9.6 percent, the highest among all ASEAN nations. Since the mid-1980s the ASEAN region has been one of the fastest growing in the world.

Since the late 1980s certain definite divergences in Malaysia's economy have contributed to its spectacular growth and are reflective of its maturity and self-confidence. In 1990, Prime Minister Mahathir gave the country a thirty-year mega-strategic plan, called Wawasan (Vision) 2020, for transforming Malaysia by the year 2020 into a fully developed society not only in the economic sense but also in the political, moral, social, and psychological areas.

The changes in Malaysia's economic policies were spectacular and far-reaching. First, Malaysia moved from its "assembler" status to a manufacturing one chiefly employing low- and medium-level technologies, providing in the process supply links to multinational corporations and thereby developing technical skills and additional jobs. The country has attained full employment and needed foreign labor of nearly a million workers by 1994. At the same time, the manufacturing sector, though foreign owned, has been deepened and diversified; it has gone from being primarily concentrated in electrical and electronic industries, textiles, and rubber products to include chemicals, metals, transport, and machine goods industries. The economy has expanded through both increased domestic demand as well as energetic exports. The share of manufactures in the country's exports has consequently continued to increase.

A segment of the economy that has seen a dramatic increase is tourism. In the first half of 2004, more than 9 million people, a significant number from the Middle East, visited Malaysia. Tourism contributed US$4.8 billion to the Malaysian economy, responsible for over 6 percent of the country's GDP in 2003.

Second, the traditional policy of governmental assistance to Bumiputras has been replaced by market incentives. The old policy of maintaining UMNO and governmental linkages with business in order to "bring up the Malays" was abandoned by the early 1990s. It was now felt that the Malays were finally ready to be on their own in the business world on a level of competitiveness with others. The new slogans of the ruling party included Malay self-reliance.

Third, there has been an emphasis on development of infrastructure, particularly in the areas of power, communications, and telecommunications. A prime project in power generation is the Bakun Dam in Sarawak, estimated to cost US$6 billion and expected to produce 2,400 megawatts of power, having the world's longest submarine cable of over 405 miles. The Malaysian government has also launched large projects for construction of roads and development of ports and for building a new international airport at Sepang.

Anwar Ibrahim Saga

In early 1998, in the wake of the Southeast Asian currency crisis, which severely affected Malaysia, Deputy Prime Minister and Finance Minister Anwar Ibrahim, who had been regarded as Prime Minister Mahathir's close confidante and presumed heir apparent, adopted economic reforms along lines suggested by the IMF, which involved consolidation and mergers of banks and other financial institutions (and which were contrary to the currency controls proposed by Mahathir). Thus, there was some surprise when 30,000–40,000 Anwar supporters thronged the streets of Kuala Lumpur in September. Perceiving the events as a threat and a challenge from Anwar to his leadership, Mahathir quickly responded by removing Anwar from his official positions as well as from the UMNO.

Mass protests in favor of Anwar followed for weeks, further aggravated by Mahathir's arrest of Anwar on the dubious charge of homosexual behavior and corruption, which totally lacked credibility in domestic as well as diplomatic circles. The Anwar saga gained momentum as the movement, now called Reformasi, prompted thousands of his followers to take to the streets in demonstrations and clash with police. The movement received international publicity when the visiting U.S. vice president, Al Gore, expressed support and sympathy for the Reformasi and requested a fair trial for Anwar. News of police brutality attracted further sympathy when Anwar appeared in the court with a black eye and bruises on his neck and arms, evidently the work of police handlers. In April 1999, Anwar was sentenced to six years in prison for corruption; the court proceedings on other charges continued. The public interest in his case faded for a while until September; there were allegations carried in the press that Anwar was being poisoned in jail. Legal challenges to Mahathir's refusal to appear in court as a witness dragged out the trial until August 8, 2000; Anwar was sentenced to nine years in prison for sodomizing his chauffeur. Anwar's adopted brother, Suka Darmawan, who was accused of the same crime, was sentenced to six years in prison and four strokes of a cane. Anwar was exempted from caning because of the existing law exempting persons over fifty from such punishment. Anwar was declared disqualified to run for any public office for an additional five years. The general belief that the charges were trumped up was reflected in Anwar's bold statement in the court in July 2000: "The prime minister was a maestro in the orchestration of the scheme. . . . There were adequate motives to get me dismissed and charged and convicted." The Anwar saga tarnished Mahathir's image internationally. Internally, opponents of his administration, including detractors within the UMNO, used Anwar's testimony against the administration's corruption to question his leadership.

The reelection of Mahathir in November 1999 did not bode well for Anwar, though Mahathir's UMNO suffered a backlash from the public over his ill treatment of Anwar. The entire drama evoked public support for a new party, the National Justice party (Parti Keadilan Nasional, or PKN), which was established in April 1999 by Anwar's wife, Wan Azizah Wan Ismail, who won the parliamentary seat held by her husband in the November elections. Although the Reformasi movement no longer posed a major challenge to Mahathir, he exhibited nervousness. Thus, in February 2002, when Anwar's appeal was taken up by the Malaysian Supreme Court, and Anwar himself appeared before a panel of three federal court judges headed by the chief justice, Mahathir ordered a clampdown on several PKN leaders. In general, Mahathir's treatment of his former close colleague and his wife's party, PKN, showed a high-handedness born of political insecurity and a readiness to resort to any means to secure his desire to remain in power. Mahathir's retirement from the position of prime minister in October 2003, however, did not end the Anwar saga.

Challenges to Mahathir's Leadership

The 1999 elections reinforced several challenges to Mahathir's leadership. First, there was a backlash over Mahathir's ill treatment of his one-time close friend and colleague, Anwar Ibrahim. Second, his party, the UMNO, suffered electoral reverses in many areas to an Islamic fundamentalist party—the Pan-Malaysian Islamic party—in the provinces of Kelantan, Terengganu, and Kedah. Nationally, the UMNO won only seventy-one seats compared to ninety-four in 1995. Third, the undercurrent of disappointment within the UMNO ranks became a groundswell as several openly criticized Mahathir at a rally of more than 3,000 members in Kuala Lumpur in February 2001. The main charges were cronyism and authoritarianism, that his government lacked transparency, and that he had misused the Bumiputra policy to benefit rich Malay businessmen. To distance himself from the prime minister's policies, his finance minister and mentor of two decades, Daim Zainuddin, resigned in June 2001. Another point of friction within the UMNO was how far the state should be Islamicized; Mahathir's faction favored the UMNO policy since 1957 of promoting a secular government, whereas a small but vocal section advocated a more Islamicized state. Bowing to the challenges, Mahathir declared in mid-2002 his intention to quit as prime minister in October 2003, well before the 2004 national elections, leaving enough time for the UMNO to choose someone who would lead the party in the election campaign.

In keeping with the previous practice, the UMNO chose the party's vice president, Ahmed Badawi, as Mahathir's successor as prime minister. Badawi promptly pledged to follow Mahathir's policies, though it would soon be clear that in both style and substance, he would walk a different path from the one of audacious, confrontational tactics for which Mahathir was known both domestically and internationally.

Within less than a year, Mahathir's ire against Badawi became a public issue. In the general elections of 2004, the BN under Badawi's leadership scored a landslide victory with a 92 percent majority in the national legislature. It recaptured the state of Terengganu, which it had lost in the previous elections of 1999 under Mahathir.

By 2006, the rift between Badawi and Mahathir was in the open, as the former prime minister accused his successor of incompetence and "stabbing him in the back," particularly by abandoning some of his pet projects including the replacement of the causeway linking Singapore to the Malay Peninsula.[4] In March 2006, Badawi's government unveiled the Ninth Malaysian Plan, 2006–2010, which while retaining Mahathir's famous "Vision 2020" as the goal and the slogan, showed substantial departures. The government now projected a focus on people rather than on the grandiose infrastructure projects of the Mahathir regime. It planned to develop technological skills among people to increase their competitiveness to meet the challenges of globalization. In fact, Badawi's government took several measures, including negotiating agreements with a host of countries such as the United States and Japan to promote globalization. Contrary to Mahathir's restrictive policies, Badawi made possible the foreign ownership of banks. Badawi was not throwing all of Mahathir's policies out the window, although Mahathir's annoyance at what Badawi did change created that impression.

Not only was Mahathir's famous "Vision 2020" retained as the nation's goal, but Badawi actively pursued Mahathir's basic policy of affirmative action seeking to help Malay Bumiputras attain the goal of owning 30 percent equity in the corporate sector by 2020. In fact, the policy of affirmative action had moved off center stage during Mahathir's time in the late 1990s. Badawi revived that policy actively declaring that his government would, by 2010, make it possible for the Bumiputras to hold 20 to 25 percent equity in the corporate sector so that the government and his party coalition could meet the promised goal of 30 percent by 2020. In 2004, Badawi's government claimed that the Malays were already holding 18 percent of the equity in the corporate sector.

Critics of the Bumiputra policy in the age of globalization have pointed out that the Malaysian goal of global competitiveness would be hard to achieve if the country's official policy was also to protect the Bumiputra regardless of merit. Besides, if the Malaysian pluralistic polity was to hold together, any official effort to discriminate among major ethnic groupings could destabilize the delicate balance that had kept racial tension at bay since 1969. As Colum Murphy opined, "Malaysia can't expect to be competitive in external markets if it is protectionist in the domestic market."[5]

The discord in the BN, whose partners included the MCA and the MIC, had its roots in Badawi's Bumiputra policy. Although his first general election had brought him a landslide victory, the March 2008 election cut the BN's majority in the national legislature to a record low, far below the two-thirds majority it had previously enjoyed. Moreover, the BN lost five out of twelve state legislatures and governments; they would be controlled by the opposition parties.

SINGAPORE'S SUCCESS STORY
Lee's Leadership

Since its ouster from the Federation of Malaysia in 1965, Singapore has functioned as a separate state. There are four factors that are crucial to the understanding of Singapore: its size and strategic location, its proximity to the Malayan mainland, the predominantly Chinese component of its population, and its traditional free-port status.

The state of Singapore consists of one large island and several small satellites. It is deficient in food and drinking water, for which it is dependent on the Malayan mainland. Though a part of the Malay world, between Malaysia and Indonesia, its population is predominantly Chinese (75 percent), the only Chinese-majority state outside the People's Republic of China. Singapore's leadership has not wanted the island state's image as a Chinese state in a region where the overseas Chinese are a prime target of jealousy, hatred, and hostility.

At the time of Singapore's independence, the Chinese community was divided between those who wanted to emphasize English-language education and economic links with the Western world and others who were eager to cast off colonial ties and use Chinese as a medium of instruction and cultural development. The latter group was responsible for the founding of Nanyang University in 1955. These divisions within the Chinese community corresponded with the 1961 split in the People's Action party (PAP) whereby the leftist elements moved out to form the Barisan Socialis (Socialist Front). The split left the PAP overwhelmingly English-educated, anti-Communist, and wedded to parliamentary government, though ideologically socialist-oriented.

Singapore's supreme political leader since 1959 has been Lee Kuan Yew, himself of Chinese origin. Although he formally retired as prime minister on November 26, 1990, he continued as a senior minister in the cabinet until he was given the status of Mentor Minister. Indeed, very little of importance is accomplished by the Singapore government without consultation with its guru, the Confucian mentor Lee Kuan Yew. Under his direction, Singapore's Communists were suppressed and stronger ties built with fellow Southeast Asian states. Lee Kuan Yew repeatedly emphasized the plural character of Singapore's society (Malay 14 percent, Indians 9 percent). Internally, the government has, through a number of studious measures, striven to change the state's Chinese image, notably through some organic changes in the curriculum of Nanyang University and its integration into the National University of Singapore. In 1975, a cabinet minister was given the task of re-organizing Nanyang University and supervising the introduction of English there as a medium of instruction. Joint classes in numerous courses at the two universities helped in building bridges between the two factions of the Chinese community. More and more Singaporean Chinese have rallied around the banner of the state's cosmopolitan character, not so much because of the state's cultural and educational policies but because of its dynamic economy. Its crucial ties with trade and finance centers in the Western world and Japan have been helped by an English-language education.

Singapore is practically a single-party state. The PAP consistently held all the seats in the legislature until 1981, when the Workers party's J. B. Jeyaretnam won a seat; in 1984, he and the Singapore Democratic party's Chiang See Tong won in the election. The lack of opposition in the legislature was made up by the PAP often designating some of its members as the opposition so that the government could benefit by criticism of its policies. In early 1990, the constitution was amended to create six nonconstituency members of parliament, allowing the six highest-losing candidates to be members of parliament provided they had secured at least 10 percent of the votes in their respective constituencies, perhaps the only democracy in the world to have such a provision in its constitution.

At the same time, the election of a lone member of the opposition in 1981 and two of them in December 1984 shook the PAP, which scored only 62.9 percent of the vote in 1984 as against 75.5 percent in 1980. The PAP promptly embarked on a campaign to strengthen its relationship with the community and to reestablish governmental responsiveness in a variety of ways. It also showed its paranoia in reacting to the court acquittal of J. B. Jeyaretnam in 1984 of fraud charges involving his inability to account for a few hundred dollars in contributions to his party. The government pressed for a retrial and gained conviction of Jeyaretnam in September 1986; he was given a jail sentence of one month and a fine of 5,000 Singapore dollars. Jeyaretnam lost his seat in parliament because of a law that required anyone fined more than 2,000 Singapore dollars to vacate his seat. It also made him ineligible to run for parliament until 1991. Additionally, Jeyaretnam was forbidden to practice as a lawyer. In October 1988, the Judicial Committee of the U.K. Privy Council, to which he had appealed, ruled that he had been disgraced for offenses of which he was not guilty and reinstated him as a lawyer. Promptly, the parliament of Singapore legislated in January 1989, disallowing those who had been disbarred after disciplinary proceedings from appealing to the Privy Council. In May, a presidential pardon was officially declined to Jeyaretnam. Further, the government announced that general elections to parliament would be held as early as August 1991, two years before they were due and three months before the ban on Jeyaretnam was due to expire, which, indeed, prevented him from contesting them. Such governmental moves prompted all the opposition groups to arrive at an electoral understanding to avoid three-cornered contests with the PAP.

In the 1991 elections, the opposition contested only 40 out of a total of 81 parliamentary seats. The strategy was to take into account the public's perception that the ruling party maintained governmental stability. That is, by contesting less than a majority of the seats, the opposition could ensure that citizens would vote based on the merits of the candidates rather than on fears of a new party taking over. The strategy paid off: The opposition garnered an unprecedented 39 percent of the vote and 4 seats in parliament.

Despite the continued ascendancy of the ruling People's Action party, there was concern and nervousness among the party leadership about PAP's future. Though PAP won 81 out of 83 seats in parliament in the January 1997 elections, there was concern that the share of the vote was 65 percent, below its previous record. The concern was hardly warranted: The opposition Workers party and Singapore People's party obtained just one seat each. Following the general economic decline in Southeast Asia in 1997–1998, there was concern whether PAP's popularity may have suffered a decline. In 1999, the presidential elections did not prove anything, because the only candidate for the position was the PAP's S. R. Nathan. In order to be certain of electoral success, PAP took advantage of the dramatic rebound growth rate of 9.9 percent in 2000, and the fearful prospect of an economic recession in the second half of 2001, to announce parliamentary elections a year ahead of time in November 2001. Earlier in the year, the government announced significant tax breaks, amounting to US$1.1 billion, in the 2001–2002 budget. In the 2001 elections, PAP improved its position winning 82 out of the 83 seats. Even the combined opposition has very little chance of dislodging it from power in the foreseeable future. And the people seem to be understandably reluctant to rock the economic boat that has continued the streak of prosperity for four decades.

Other recent concerns have been self-renewal of political leadership and the moral quality of the population, especially the youth. In 1982, the government introduced religious courses in the schools because of increasing materialism and erosion of moral values. Although such courses are available in all religions, the great emphasis on Confucian ethics has led to accusations of encouraging Chinese chauvinism and of building a Confucian state. The government believes in providing its citizens with Confucian "immune systems" to counter the massive impact of Western values brought about by global electronic communications. It wants to promote the institutions of family and "patriarchy" and to encourage Mandarin Chinese and hard work ethics instead of welfare handouts except in housing, education, and health. In order to boost the institution of patriarchy, 1994 legislation made adult offspring legally responsible for the maintenance of their parents, denied medical benefits to families of female civil servants, and disallowed subsidized housing to unmarried mothers.

The program of self-renewal of political leadership progressed in the 1980s. In the cabinet of January 1, 1985, only three out of twelve ministers, including Lee himself, belonged to the old guard. Two ministers in their mid-fifties were considered to be the "bridging generation." The second-echelon leaders held important portfolios: Goh Chok Tong and Ong Teng Cheong were appointed first and second deputy prime ministers, while Dr. Tony Tan, S. Dhanabalan, and Dr. Ahmad Mattar continued in positions of great trust. Lee's son, Brigadier General Lee Hsien Loong, was inducted into politics in 1985. Educated at Cambridge, England, and at Harvard, his late entry into politics did not inhibit his rapid rise. He was named to the twelve-member executive committee of the ruling PAP, and in 1985 appointed as minister of state for trade and industry and minister of state for defense. In 1991, he was elevated to deputy prime minister in the cabinet headed by Lee's successor, Goh Chok Tong.

In the Singapore constitution, which is patterned on the Westminster model, the president resembles the British monarch in being the head of state with little power, with the prime minister exercising real power as the head of government. In 1991, a constitutional change introduced the election of the president by a popular vote; the first president so elected in 1993 was Ong Teng Cheong, a former second deputy prime minister who was "kicked upstairs" as president. Since his retirement at the end of his six-year term in August 1999, no president has been elected as such, since there is only a single candidate for the prestigious but powerless office and therefore there has been no need felt to hold a ballot. In 2005, when the office fell vacant, the Presidential Elections Committee appointed by the government processed all candidates and found only one candidate eligible for the office and declared S. R. Nathan unanimously "elected" president.

In August 2003, at the end of a long spell of 13 years as prime minister, Goh Chok Tong declared he would step down in favor of Lee Hsien Loong, son of the senior minister and "real" authority in Singapore, Lee Kuan Yew. The junior Lee had already been prominent as deputy prime minister, finance minister, and head of the central bank in his role as chairman of the Monetary Authority of Singapore. Goh retired in the middle of his term, declaring his intention to give Lee Hsien Loong enough time to prepare for the general elections. A year later on August 12, 2004, Lee Hsien Loong was sworn in as prime minister, continuing to hold the finance portfolio as well. Goh then was made senior minister (the position previously held by Lee Kuan Yew) and the prime minister's father, Lee Kuan Yew, then age eighty, was appointed the minister mentor. Goh was also appointed chairman of the Monetary Authority of Singapore. In the general elections of May 2006, Prime Minister Lee Hsien Loong led his party, the PAP, to victory, winning 82 out of 84 parliament seats, though the overall vote was lower than in 2001 by 8.7 percent. Though the opposition put up 47 candidates and scored more than a third of the entire vote, it won only two seats—Low Thia Khiang of the Workers Party (WP) and Chiang See Tong of the Singapore Democratic Alliance (SDA) being the winners.

Significantly for Singapore, the cabinet ministers are reviewed fairly often, in the same manner as are corporate heads. They are evaluated for their performance and, if found inadequate, are removed from office. The appointments to the cabinet are made on the basis of the individual's cerebral qualities, in the manner of a Confucian scholar or a Hindu Brahman. As Michael D. Barr observed:

> Scholars not only lead the Administrative Service, but also the military's officer corps, as well as the executive ranks of statutory boards and government-linked companies (GLCs). Movement between these four groups is fluid, with even the military officers routinely doing stints in the civilian service. Together with their political masters, most of whom are also scholars, they make up the software for the entity commonly known as "Singapore Inc."—a labyrinth of GLCs, statutory boards and ministries that own or manage around 60% of Singapore's economy.[6]

It is no wonder then that Singapore's cabinet ministers, unlike politicians in most countries, are paid highly, their salaries being competitive with the corporate sector and sufficient to lead them to eschew bribes. In April 2007, the prime minister and the cabinet gave themselves a 60 percent salary increase. The prime minister's salary was raised to 3.1 million Singapore dollars (about US$2 million), five times the annual compensation for the U.S. president. The other ministers would earn an average of Singapore 1.9 million. The increases did not go without a public outcry despite the government's efforts to justify them and, more significant, to suppress public discussion of them. Thus, in the week of the salary-increase announcement, the opposition Singapore Democratic party planned a discussion forum at which prestigious individuals, including several members of the European Parliament and a Filipina congresswoman, would participate, the government reacted by simply banning the event. However, the public opposition had some effect: The prime minister announced he would donate to charity the amount of his salary increase, 600,000 Singapore dollars.

Spectacular Economic Success

In the past four decades, Singapore has achieved phenomenal success in the economic field. Singapore's economy has been rated the second most competitive in the world. In the 1960s, its gross national product (GNP) averaged 10 percent, accelerating to 14.3 percent in the 1970s, slowing to around 5 percent in the early 1980s, and rising to 9–10 percent by 1995. The economy's dependence on the international market, particularly American, was demonstrated not only in the currency and economic crisis that hit the Southeast Asian region but also in the manner the recession in the United States has affected its economy since 2001. The destination of a quarter of Singapore's nonoil exports is the United States, mostly high-tech electronic goods. Since the crisis of 1997, Singapore has lost considerable foreign direct investment (FDI), as much as one-third, more than any country in the region.

On the whole, however, Singapore's economy has been sound and its inflation and unemployment rates have been modest, with an increasing number of women in the work force and about 10 percent of labor imported, mostly from Indonesia, the Philippines and IT workers from India. Singapore's success has been built on the state's free-port status and fairly liberal policies permitting large-scale foreign investment. The ruling People's Action party was originally a socialist party. Although Lee claimed to be a socialist, he took care not to antagonize the interests of capitalists, local and foreign, who are the essential anchor of Singapore's prosperity and survival as a separate state. Since the late 1960s, the state's economy has shifted its character from the entrepôt trade to manufacturing and financial and banking services.

Since the late 1980s when the economy resumed its robust growth, Singapore has focused on development of computer software. Universities have focused on the development of the island state's intellectual capital. Given Singapore's sophisticated infrastructure of telecommunications and well-developed human resources, it is poised to be one of the world's foremost centers for information and knowledge-based industries, as well as for financial services.

Lee's consummate skills were demonstrated in the way he took his party over the years from its anticapitalist posture to supporting capitalism. While Prime Minister Margaret Thatcher applauded it as "an example of free market economic success," it was also praised by the Keynesian economist John Kenneth Galbraith for its positive, productive state interventionism.[7] Lee's planning and efficient implementation of social welfare projects are evident notably in the government-subsidized housing development that provides accommodation to 75 percent of the population. The government is the exclusive provider of economic and social services: utilities, telephone, and telegraph; ports and airports; radio and television; medical and health services; education at the primary, secondary, and tertiary levels; and the successful Singapore Airlines. Except for the welfare agencies, all of the government enterprises make profits; if they do not, the management is changed or the enterprise closed down. Interestingly, 90 percent of the union membership belongs to the ruling party's National Trades Union Congress, which is headed by a government minister and run by bureaucrats. Consequently, there are no strikes or any major disturbances in the smooth running of trade and industry.

According to the World Bank, Singapore's per capita income is among the top ten in the world. The Organization for Economic Cooperation and Development includes it in the category of developed countries. *Fortune* magazine has rated it the top global city for business. And the Heritage Foundation's 1996 Index of Economic Freedom, covering 142 countries, rated Singapore second. In the 1960s, Singapore was probably one of the world's dirtiest cities; today it is arguably the cleanest. The island state's airline has been successively rated the best, its port the busiest and most profitable in the world.

Despite the prosperity or perhaps because of it, Singapore feels uncertain of its continued prosperous condition, particularly because of its linkages with European and North American economies that periodically unpredictably go into recession. In the beginning of 1992, when the GNP dropped to 5.8 percent, Prime Minister Goh warned that Singapore's "competitiveness" must be maintained to ensure a high standard of living and that double-digit growth as in the previous decades should not be taken for granted. Both he and Senior Minister Lee Kuan Yew came up with new ideas to assure Singapore's place "ahead of the pack." One such idea was to "go regional," to emphasize trade and investment in neighboring countries such as Myanmar, Vietnam, Indonesia, India, and China where wages were still low and where it would be "prudent to become owners of high-yielding assets." Singapore had already launched the Suzhou Industrial Township Project in China in the 1980s, which it took up in earnest in 1994. (It withdrew from the project in 1999 because of unacceptable cost increases.) In the early 1990s, Singapore began to build industrial parks and resorts on Bantam Island, Indonesia, and entered into collaborative projects in Bangalore, India. To promote such economic ties, Prime Minister Goh and Senior Minister Lee each visited twelve countries in 1994, most in Asia. Goh concentrated on economic agreements and joint ventures in South and Southeast Asia, and Lee focused on China. Singapore also gave its expertise to Vietnam for its infrastructural projects, to Cambodia for development of its seaport airport development, and to China for assistance in telecommunications, tourism, and hotel management. Singapore also offered China its banking and oil-refining facilities.

It is such successful policies that have taken the wind out of Communist sails. It has been suggested that if the rest of non-Communist Southeast Asia were to adopt Singapore's model combination of capitalism and social welfare schemes, there would be little scope for communism to succeed. Yet Singapore's example is not easy to duplicate. The island state's unique geographical position, its century-old tradition as a free port, and its size have been used imaginatively by Lee Kuan

Yew and his associates to make it the uniquely successful brand of state-sponsored capitalism.

Foreign Policy

Singapore is an important member of the ASEAN and has shared with Indonesia its view of China's long-range threat to the region. However, relations with China markedly improved in the wake of the visit of Deng Xiaoping in 1978 to Singapore and his open-door policy and serious interest in free enterprise and joint ventures. On October 3, 1990, after Indonesia overcame its anger about China's assistance to the PKI in the Gestapu affair, Indonesia decided to restore diplomatic relations with Beijing. Singapore has always been concerned that China might try to subvert the loyalties of Singapore's majority Chinese population. However, Singapore found it hard to miss the economic opportunities in China opened by Deng Xiaoping's liberal policies. The two countries entered into numerous agreements whereby Singapore's expertise would be used for the Chinese drive for modernization. During a visit to China, Lee Kuan Yew clarified that the bottom line for Singapore in any business deal was profit or loss, not sentiment or ideology. In 1994, Singapore agreed to build a Singapore-style industrial city in Suzhou; however, Singapore backed out of the project in 1999 because the costs had escalated to more than US$400 million, foreclosing any real long-term profitability.

The most important country for Singapore in foreign relations is Malaysia, with whom it has a special and symbiotic relationship. In August 1995, the two neighbors signed the Straits of Johor Boundary Agreement precisely delimiting the maritime boundary between Malaysia and Singapore. Since then further efforts have improved coordination between the marine police of the two states. In 1998, a second causeway linked Singapore with Johor. Any instability in Malaysia (and Indonesia) is perceived by Singapore to constitute an external threat to its own well-being as a state. Singapore's security concerns have included its dependence on Malaysia for water supplies; the revival of ethnic tensions between Malays and Chinese as in the ethnic riots of 1969; the possibility of Islamic or ultranationalist political forces ascendant in northern Malaysia spreading south, closer to the Singapore border; and the rise of Islamic terrorism in the predominantly Muslim Malaysia.

Malaysia provides a hinterland producing rubber, tin, palm oil, and timber, which are reexported through Singapore. Although Malaysia is a leading trade partner of Singapore after the United States, Japan, Saudi Arabia, and Hong Kong, the leading investor in Malaysia after Japan is Singapore, mostly in food processing, transport equipment, textiles, and garments. The two states have agreed upon a number of cooperative projects. Of note are projects to meet 30 to 50 percent of Singapore's energy needs by 1990 through piping liquefied gas extracted off the Terengganu coast. In 1988, Malaysia agreed to increase its water sales from Johor to Singapore in exchange for the latter buying 150 million cubic feet of gas per day. In 2002, Malaysia proposed an upward revision of water rates. In 1998, a second causeway linking Singapore and Johor was opened.

Singapore's relations with the United States, consistently cordial since the 1960s, became even closer after August 1989, when Singapore offered to accommodate some of the U.S. military facilities then in the Philippines if the leases for the bases there were not renewed. Ever since the U.S. withdrawal from Vietnam, Singapore has supported U.S. military presence in the region as a positive factor promoting regional stability. Singapore already had long-standing links with the United States but never a formal agreement on the purchase of arms and training or for the use of its port facilities by the U.S. Navy. In November 1990, a formal agreement between the two countries was signed in Tokyo by Lee Kuan Yew and Vice President Dan Quayle whereby U.S. naval units would use the Sembawang dockyard for repairs and the U.S. Air Force would use Paya Lebar airport "several times a year" for training missions. The cautionary language of the agreement whereby no permanent military base was ceded to the United States was in deference to the opposition by Malaysia and Indonesia that such an action would jeopardize the ASEAN goal of establishing a zone of peace, freedom, and neutrality (ZOPFAN) for the region.

The United States is the main supplier of defense equipment to Singapore, including F-16 fighter planes. Since 1988, Singapore Air Force personnel have been receiving training in the United States on leased aircraft. Since signing a treaty in 1990, about 100 Singapore Air Force personnel are regularly trained at Luke Air Force base in Arizona. In January 1998, Singapore and the United States entered into a new agreement that would allow U.S. naval units—including aircraft carriers and submarines—to use Singapore's planned new naval facility for visits and maintenance repair beginning in 2000. In strict legal terms, Singapore's Changi naval facility is equally open for use by any country, including China, on a commercial basis. Defense experts doubt whether Singapore would allow American use of the facilities in Singapore in case of an open Sino-U.S. conflict over Taiwan. On its part, Beijing strongly condemned the visit to Singapore of the U.S.S. *Kitty Hawk* in March 2001.

There were strains on the Singapore-U.S. relationship, however, on two counts in the mid-1990s arising out of the differing perceptions of civil rights and freedom of the press in the two countries. The first was the case of an American citizen, eighteen-year-old Michael Fay, who was convicted by a Singapore court and sentenced to four months' imprisonment, a substantial fine, and six lashes by a rattan cane. The charge was a ten-day vandalism spree that included spray painting cars and stealing Singapore flags and traffic signs. Fay agreed he had committed those acts of vandalism. The judgment received tremendous publicity in the U.S. media, which criticized the severity of the punishment and invited reaction of high officials. President Clinton himself appealed to the Singapore government thrice for clemency in the case.

While U.S. polls revealed that many Americans favored some kind of punishment as a deterrent, a Singapore poll showed support of 80 percent for the court decision. Singapore officials rejected U.S. criticism, arguing that the island state's tough laws prevented it from "falling prey to the fate of cities like New York where even police cars are not spared the acts of vandals." On May 5, 1994, Michael Fay was given a slightly reduced punishment in deference to U.S. requests: He was given four mild strokes instead of the stipulated six.

The second problem came in 1995, when two cases—a contempt of court complaint and a libel suit—were filed against the U.S.-owned *International Herald*

Tribune for two stories it published. One was an article written by Christopher Lingle, a visiting fellow at the National University of Singapore, on October 7, 1994, alleging, without naming Singapore as such, that some Asian government had used a compliant judiciary to bankrupt opposition politicians through court actions. Another article in the same paper alleged nepotism. Without mentioning names, it suggested that Lee Hsien Loong's appointment as Singapore's deputy prime minister had taken place only because he was the son of the architect of modern Singapore, Lee Kuan Yew. The issue was aggravated by a U.S. State Department statement that "freedom of expression is a universal right of people," which was interpreted in Singapore to mean extension of the U.S. Constitution's First Amendment provisions worldwide and, therefore, infringement upon the sovereignty of other countries. A Singapore court found all five defendants, including Professor Lingle and the Asian editor and publisher of the *International Herald Tribune,* guilty of contempt of court. Each defendant was fined, Professor Lingle to the extent of US$10,000, and ordered to pay costs. Both cases involving human rights tarnished Singapore's image in the United States.

Singapore's relations with the United States improved dramatically in the aftermath of September 11 because of the perception of a common enemy—international Islamic terrorism. Singapore became an active member of the U.S.-led war on terrorism when in December 2001 and January 2002 two vicious plots came to light suggesting Al-Qaeda would attack Western strategic, economic, and diplomatic establishments. The United States claimed to unravel one of these plots based on the CIA's recovery of videotapes and handwritten notes in Arabic from the rubble of the house of an Al-Qaeda leader, Mohammad Islam (a Singaporean of Pakistani descent), in Afghanistan. In contrast, Singapore's Internal Security Department (ISD) claimed that the revelations were based on its intelligence network in several ASEAN countries. Either way, it was revealed that Al-Qaeda had plotted a bombing attack on U.S. warships, airplanes, military personnel, and offices of major American companies in Singapore. Other targets included U.S., British, Israeli, and Australian diplomatic establishments. Also revealed was an elaborate infrastructure operated by Al-Qaeda, with plans for terrorist acts in several ASEAN countries. In a wide-ranging operation, Singapore authorities enabled the arrest of 13 suspects in Singapore, 23 in Malaysia, and 4 in the Philippines.

Despite its size, Singapore's economic standing, technological superiority, excellent management abilities, and political stability have thrust upon it a leadership role among the countries of the ASEAN and the Pacific. In 1992, the newly formed APEC forum decided to locate its permanent secretariat in Singapore. In 1993, Singapore served as the venue for the Fourth ASEAN Heads of State meeting and for a meeting of the foreign ministers of the ASEAN and twelve other Pacific Rim "dialogue partners" to discuss regional security. In the same year, Singapore also hosted the ASEAN Economic Ministers meeting that resolved to integrate the regional markets, reduce tariffs below 5 percent, and accelerate the establishment of the AFTA before the year 2008. Singapore was also chosen to host the first meeting of the new World Trade Organization (WTO) in December 1996. With its enhanced international role, Singapore established a Volunteers Overseas Program beginning with Vietnam and Indonesia. It already had some international experience in peacekeeping because of its involvement with the UN Transitional Authority in Cambodia (UNTAC) during 1992. In the mid-1990s, Singapore made a bid for an elected nonpermanent seat in the UN Security Council in 2001.

BRUNEI: A NEW STATE
The Birth of Brunei

On January 1, 1984, little Brunei, a British protectorate since 1888, became an independent state. With an area of 2,226 square miles and population of about 328,000 (the World Health Organization's 2000 estimate), including Malaysians, Filipinos, and Thais, it is a ministate like Singapore and extremely wealthy, thanks to its oil and natural gas reserves. The territory can be described as an enclave within the Malaysian state of Sarawak, divided into two parcels separated by Sarawak's territory of Limbang. Its population is roughly two-thirds Malay and one-fourth Chinese and the rest a mixture of several tribals. Yet it refused to be a part of the Federation of Malaysia in 1963 and struggled successfully to retain its independent identity.

Historically, Brunei was the focal point of a large kingdom covering North Borneo and, at the height of its power in the sixteenth century, portions of the Philippines. It did not attract European traders or colonialists because it had no agricultural or mineral resources. In 1839, James Brooke, the first of the White Rajahs, set sail from Singapore and captured part of the present Sarawak. He involved himself in palace politics and extended his domains northward, completing the conquest of Sarawak in 1846. Later in the century, in 1878, the sultan of Sulu leased (according to Spanish and Filipino interpretations) or sold (according to British and Malaysian versions) North Borneo (Sabah) to Baron von Overbeck, who sold it in 1888 to a chartered company, the British North Borneo Company. It did not prevent Rajah Brooke from swallowing Limbang in 1890 and dividing whatever remained of the Brunei kingdom into two areas. In 1906, the British introduced the Resident system in Brunei on the pattern of the federated Malay states, indirectly administering it and offering it security from external enemies.

The discovery of rich oil fields in 1929 changed the economy of the little protectorate and its political and strategic significance. After World War II, when the Brooke group and the British North Borneo Company ceded Sarawak and Sabah, respectively, to the British administration in Malaya, Brunei remained a protectorate. In 1959, the British granted it internal self-government with defense and foreign policy remaining in British hands. The state's economy was dominated by Brunei Shell Petroleum (BSP), a British-Dutch company sharing profits with the sultan on a fifty-fifty basis. Although oil prices were not very high until 1973, the oil revenues and returns on British investment were important enough for Britain to maintain a crack Gurkha battalion for the security of oil installations in Seria.

Though inadequate, Brunei's defense is largely in British hands. In 1996, Britain and Brunei signed a memorandum of understanding, the terms of which were not disclosed. In March 1997, Britain deployed 1,800 Royal Marines to Brunei for bilateral exercises. About sixty British aviators are on loan to the small

Royal Brunei Air Force. In 2001, Britain agreed to deliver three offshore patrol vessels to the Royal Brunei Navy. Brunei has increasingly turned to Singapore for joint defenses.

With the winds of independence and representative government blowing hard in the entire Malay region, there were pressures on the sultan of Brunei to liberalize the political process. At the same time, there were pressures for Brunei, along with Sarawak and Sabah, to merge in the projected Federation of Malaysia. In the early 1960s, the most popular and powerful mass-based group to emerge in Brunei was the Partai Rakyat Brunei (PRB), led by A. M. Azahari, a Labuanese of Arab descent. Neither the PRB nor the sultan wanted a merger with Malaysia. That is where their agreement ended. The PRB favored unilateral, immediate independence, but the sultan was most reluctant to rush into independence and sever the valuable British link. Azahari received help from the Philippines, which at this time disputed Malaysia's claim over Sabah. He also received substantial assistance from the North Kalimantan (Borneo) National Army, in turn aided by the PKI. Together the PRB and the PKI briefly seized the BSP facilities at Seria in 1962. The revolt was quickly quelled by the sultan with the help of British regiments. Azahari fled to Indonesia, some other PRB leaders went into exile in Malaysia, and several others were killed or jailed. The entire episode made the sultan totally suspicious of his neighbors' intentions. He was now completely averse to the merger with Malaysia and drew closer to the British than before. The democratic process was ended, the PRB was banned, and a state of emergency was declared, renewable every two years.

The British decision in 1968 to pull its forces from east of Suez by 1971 affected Brunei. A British-Brunei treaty signed in 1971 provided for a limited British military presence, with a British-officered, thousand-strong Gurkha battalion paid by Brunei. Further negotiations led to the agreement of 1979, marking a transition of five years to full independence by the end of 1983. It was also provided that the Gurkha battalion would be withdrawn by September 1983.

In 1967, the sultan abdicated in favor of his son, Sir Muda Hassanlal Bolkiah (whose full name and title is Paduka Seri Baginda Sultan Haji Hassanlal Bolkiah Mu'izzaddin Waddaulah), who then became the twenty-ninth sultan. Even after independence, he retained British officers to lead the two Royal Brunei Armed Forces battalions, originally raised in 1961. Additionally, he established a third battalion and raised a reserve unit of retired Gurkhas to guard the palace and government installations. Despite British reluctance, he managed in last-minute negotiations to retain the Gurkha battalion beyond the scheduled September 1983 withdrawal. The new agreement, to be reviewed every five years, allowed the British command to continue.

The government of Brunei is a benevolent autocracy, an oligarchy, that has much in common with the ruling style of Saudi Arabia or of the Middle Eastern sheikdoms. The sultan himself is the prime minister, and several members of his family hold ministerial and other positions. There are very few outside the royal family holding important positions in government. The aim seems to be to keep the subjects so contented that they would not bother about politics. There is free schooling, medical aid, and no income tax in the small state, which had one of the highest per capita incomes in the world in 1990: B$29,400, or about US$18,490. The sultan is ranked among the top three or four richest persons in the world.

A major blow to the Brunei oligarchy came with the 1998 collapse of the four-year-old Amedeo Group, the nation's leading investment and construction enterprise, largely because of the profligate spending of the sultan's flamboyant brother, Prince Jefri, who was a member of Amedeo's board. The amount was placed at between US$25 billion and US$40 billion. The cost of 2,000 cars and seventeen aircraft purchased by Prince Jefri accounted for US$2.7 billion; the prince had bought several hotels (the Plaza Athenee in Paris, the New York Palace, the Dorchester in London, and the Bel-Air in Los Angeles) on his personal account. There was no accounting of cash totaling several billions.

Apart from the huge financial loss, the scandal was a blow to the national pride, hurting the country's ability "to make it on its own." The sultan took steps to refurbish the country's image and Amedeo's finances, placing the affairs of the group in the hands of the accounting firm Arthur Anderson as caretaker. The government sued Prince Jefri and his associates for mismanagement of state funds. The out-of-court settlement worked out by the sultan himself in March 2000 included Prince Jefri's agreement to return the ill-gotten assets to the government. However, much damage was done by the trial and the media publicity, which tarnished the royals' image and their extraordinarily affluent lifestyle. In the following year, auctions raised about US$6 billion from the sale of some of the prince's assets, including some real estate and his luxury yacht. He had been ordered by the Chief Justice to transfer some more specified assets to the Brunei Investment Authority. In May 2006, the prince lost an attempt to overturn the order through the Brunei Court of Appeal. He could no longer retain two of his hotels, three of his residences, valuable diamond jewelry, and an undisclosed amount of cash.

Among the crucial levers of control are the citizenship requirements. Most of the Chinese, numbering about 50,000, are among the more educated and entrepreneurial. As in many other parts of the British empire, the British had guaranteed legal protection to the minorities. In 1961, nonindigenous people were subject to a citizenship language test in the Malay language. As of September 1984, only 10 percent of the Chinese were eligible for citizenship. At that point, the sultan raised the residency requirement to 30 years, 25 of which must be continuous (previously 25 and 20 years, respectively). The language test was made so strict that candidates were asked to identify in the Malay language unusual jungle plants that would be known to few of the indigenous residents. Such restrictions rendered more than forty thousand Chinese stateless with only identification papers in place of passports. In May 2006, the sultan relaxed the rules for citizenship particularly for those foreigners with significant investment in Brunei, or married to Brunei women, but in all cases, requiring an understanding of local culture and ability to read and write in Malay. Effective May 15, foreign nationals who had contributed to Brunei growth by investing at least a half million Brunei dollars (US$1 equaled 1.5672 Brunei dollars) qualified for citizenship. In the alternative, those who through their professional expertise were deemed valuable for Brunei also qualified for citizenship.

The reigning oligarchy centered on the sultan, however, realized that some kind of an outlet for the people's political views must be provided as a safety valve.

In September 1985, the government approved the launching of the Brunei National Democratic party (BNDP), renamed Brunei Solidarity National party (BSNP) in 1994. Its official links and patronage were clear. Its principal office-bearers, founding chairman, and president were related to Brunei's royal family. Even so, the BNDP made certain demands that were difficult for the sultan to concede: holding general elections, abrogating the 1962 emergency regulations, increasing salaries of lower and middle levels of bureaucracy, and augmenting the state's share in BSP from the present 50 percent to 70 percent, of which 10 percent is to be allocated to the people of Brunei.

No major political liberalization has yet occurred at the national level, but some small steps toward people's participation at lower levels have been taken. In 1994, local elections for village chiefs were introduced, and in the following year the government appointed a committee to advise on the suitability of reviving the 1959 constitution under which limited elections had been held. On National Day, February 23, 1995, the BNDP was suddenly revived, seemingly with the unofficial blessing of the government. Renamed the Brunei Solidarity National party (BSNP), the party's inaugural assembly of fifty members elected as its president Haji Latif Chuchu, who had been jailed under the Internal Security Act for three years from 1988 to 1990 for criticizing Brunei's lack of civil liberties. The assembly also elected other officers and promptly proceeded to enroll members and hold a number of public meetings. The last person detained under the dreaded Internal Security Act was released in 1996.

In May 2005, the sultan reshuffled his cabinet, for the first time in seventeen years, placing some young persons in responsible positions. Crown Prince Haji al-Muhtadee Billah Bolkiah, who was thirty-one, was promoted from his position as deputy minister to senior minister in the prime minister's office. The crown prince's position was thereby strengthened as heir to the throne. Significantly, Pehin Dato Haji Abdul Aziz, the education minister, was removed because of his overemphasis on religious education at the expense of study of science and technology. Also for the first time, the sultan appointed two out of ten deputy ministers from the private sector and appointed one non-Muslim to the cabinet. Such changes were expected to be harbingers of more adjustments to come.

Economy and Foreign Relations

No state in the family of nations could have started economically as well as Brunei. The BSP project pumps about 1.7 million barrels of oil per day, with an estimated reserve to last another thirty years. The gas from offshore wells is pumped to the world's largest liquefaction plant at Lumut, jointly owned by the Brunei government, Shell, and Mitsubishi. More than 5 million tons of liquid natural gas (LNG) is exported annually to Japan. Brunei's imports are also mainly from Japan, with Singapore following closely behind.

Soon after its independence, Brunei was admitted as the sixth member of the ASEAN. It also joined the United Nations, the Islamic Conference Organization, and the Commonwealth of Nations. The most important membership was that in ASEAN because of fears of aggrandizement of its neighbors, particularly Malaysia and Indonesia. As they are fellow members of ASEAN, Brunei can expect disputes with such neighbors to be resolved through the consultative machinery of the organization.

Among all its neighbors, Brunei feels closest to Singapore, though its population and leadership are Chinese. It shares a kinship in size and wealth with that island state, and they share a vulnerability to pressure from their much larger neighbor states. Brunei's International Investment Advisory Board has Singaporean consultants; Brunei has investments in Singapore. The currency is pegged to the Singapore dollar. Brunei's civil service workers and military personnel receive their training in Singapore and Malaysia. Singapore's infantry and artillery battalions are regularly rotated through Brunei for jungle training in the Temburong district. Brunei looks up to Singapore for defense cooperation, particularly air defense. In November 1995, the two states held the first joint air defense exercises in Singapore.

Brunei's defense absorbs almost one-third of its annual expenditure, the highest percentage among all the ASEAN states. Yet its real defenses lie in its good relations with its neighbors and in its willingness to liberalize the political process.

Aware of such concerns, Brunei has attempted to diversify its economy and introduce more social programs. In 1999, the Brunei Darussalam Economic Council drafted a strategic economic plan, which, if implemented, would go a long way toward reducing the country's overwhelming dependence on oil and gas for survival. The social welfare programs, if imaginatively conceived, may address issues of concern to its young population (nearly 50 percent are below the age of twenty-one). Though schooling is free from age five to sixteen, there are few avenues of employment outside government, which currently employs more than 75 percent of Brunei's workforce. As the Brunei youth become educated, particularly abroad, the demand for political participation is bound to increase. If not properly and adequately responded to, it may turn violent. As a rich infant, Brunei must learn to walk wisely.

25

Nationalism and Communism in Vietnam, Cambodia, and Laos

THE CONFLICT IN VIETNAM

With the exception of Cambodia, there is hardly a country in the world that could claim to have suffered as much as Vietnam in the post–World War II period. Continual conflict, with only a brief period of peace following the Geneva settlement of 1954, has marked its recent history. Millions of Vietnamese children grew to adulthood carrying memories of bloodshed, terror, bombing, dislocation—man's inhumanity to man. Vietnam occupied the front page of newspapers and figured prominently in other media consistently for years, more than any other single country. The long undeclared war there in which the United States was involved divided public opinion all over the globe, affecting human values, national economies, presidential prospects, and military strategies. The spectacle of a Third World people with far less sophisticated weaponry than their opponents and with no use of aircraft immobilizing the most advanced, militarily best equipped nation in human history questioned the very basis of strategic defense in the modern world. Hopes were that the end of the conflict in 1975 and the reunification of Vietnam a year later would usher in an era of peace and reconstruction to that war-ravaged country. Instead, Vietnam's occupation of Cambodia in late 1978 and China's "punitive" action in Vietnam in early 1979 revived tensions in the region for a decade.

These events also highlighted the political interdependence of the three Indochinese states—Vietnam, Laos, and Cambodia. The emergence of Communist regimes in all three countries in the same year was no coincidence. The Pathet Lao and a segment of the Khmer Rouge had both received assistance from Hanoi, perhaps with the latter's expectation that they would seek guidance and direction after coming to power. Was the Vietnamese decade-long occupation of Cambodia an implementation of a plan to create an Indochinese federation or part of a plan to dominate the entire Southeast Asian region? If Southeast Asian nations lived for a quarter century in the shadow of China, they have in the last two decades been apprehensive of the rising power of Vietnam. It is perhaps to "contain" Vietnam that its arch enemy, the ASEAN, admitted it as a member in July 1995.

Roots of the Conflict

The success of the Geneva agreements that ended the First Indochina War (1946–1954) was dependent on a number of conditions. The single most important provision of the Geneva settlement was the Vietnam-wide elections in July 1956 leading to the reunification of the country. Behind the scenes were the major powers—Great Britain and the Soviet Union as co-chairmen of the Geneva conference; the Soviet Union and China as major Communist powers ensuring Hanoi's compliance with the agreements; and the United States, which had joined South Vietnam in not endorsing the Geneva declaration. The United States asserted, however, at Geneva that it would not use force to disturb the settlement and that it would continue to seek to achieve unity of all nations divided against their will. U.S. actions in the next two years completely belied such assurances and were primarily responsible for the unfortunate events of the next two decades in Vietnam.

U.S. policy toward Vietnam was principally governed by the doctrine of containment of communism almost consistently from the early 1950s to at least the end of the following decade. Within two months of Geneva, the efforts of U.S. Secretary of State John Foster Dulles resulted in the Manila pact on September 8, creating the Southeast Asia Treaty Organization (SEATO). Its name belied its membership. It included only three Asian members—Pakistan, Thailand, and the Philippines—to complement the United States, the United Kingdom, France, Australia, and New Zealand. The major nonaligned powers of South and Southeast Asia—India, Myanmar, and Indonesia—opposed the pact. SEATO did not include Laos, Cambodia, and South Vietnam because this would have openly violated the Geneva agreements. SEATO's Article IV included these areas as "protocol" countries to be defended by SEATO powers in the event of subversion or open attack by Communists. Thus, while the Soviet Union, China, and nonaligned countries like India, Indonesia, and Cambodia laid faith in the efficacy of the Geneva settlement to maintain peace in the former French Indochina, the SEATO powers, more particularly the United States, trusted SEATO's military strength to serve as a deterrent against any attempt by Communists to change the political map of the region. Later, in the 1960s, when the Second Indochina War (1964–1975) broke out, the U.S. involvement in it was based on the relevant articles of the SEATO pact as well as on the bilateral agreement between the United States and the government of South Vietnam.

Diem Family Rules South Vietnam

While the Geneva conference was in session, the French appointed the U.S.-supported Ngo Dinh Diem as prime minister of the "State of Vietnam." With the temporary partition of the country in July 1954, Diem faced enormous challenges to his authority. He found South Vietnam virtually under the control of three religio-military sects: the Cao Dai, the Hoa Hao—both with private armies estimated at fifty thousand men each—and the Binh Xuyen, which operated gambling houses, narcotics dens, night clubs, and brothels and controlled the city police in Saigon. With what must be regarded as admirable ability, Diem was successful in the first six months of his administration in crushing the sects and eliminating all extralegal challenges to the government's authority. His handling of the problem of rehabilitation of nearly a million refugees, mostly Catholics from North Vietnam, won Diem international acclaim, notably in the United States. Through a referendum held on October 23, 1955, which he rigged, he secured an embarrassing 99 percent vote in his favor against Emperor Bao Dai. Three days later, he proclaimed South Vietnam a republic with himself as president. Recognized by the United States and thirty-five other countries of the Western bloc, the "Republic of Vietnam" became by late 1955, for all purposes, an independent member of the international community.

The United States supported Diem as an intense anti-French, anti-Communist, nationalist leader with a legendary record of honesty and integrity and paraded him as a nationalist alternative to Communist Ho Chi Minh. But Diem had been for too long out of touch with the people's aspirations. Further, his style of government was paternalistic and aloof like that of the outdated mandarins. He withdrew increasingly within the walls of the Forbidden Palace, depending for information and guidance on a close coterie of sycophants and even more on members of his extended family.

Diem did not have the aura of prestige, sacrifice, and struggle against colonialism to match Ho Chi Minh's reputation. In contrast to the gentle-looking (despite his ruthlessness), ascetic (though atheist), simply clad (fatigues and rubber sandals) Ho Chi Minh, Diem always dressed nattily in shark-skin and Irish linen suits and, as a fervent Catholic with a monastic background, appeared more a sectarian than a national leader. Both men were bachelors. That is where the comparison ended. Lack of family ties was an asset to the avuncular Ho Chi Minh (he was called Uncle Ho); the nation became his family. Diem's strong ties with his extended family became his greatest liability. He distributed powerful positions among his family: Diem's brother, Nhu, and his vitriolic-tongued wife, Madame Nhu, became the president's closest advisers. Nhu kept himself intoxicated, perhaps without Diem's knowledge, on drugs and shared with his president-brother an abstract philosophy of "personalism," which was unintelligible to everyone, perhaps including themselves. Madame Nhu, a recent convert from Buddhism to the Catholic religion, became an ardent champion of her new faith and of puritanism in public life. Having a magnetic hold on the president, she was single-handedly responsible for alienating large sections of the predominantly Buddhist population through her ill-advised pronouncements on religious as well as secular matters. Diem's elder brother was, in his capacity of archbishop of Hue, the highest Catholic official in the land; another brother virtually ruled central Vietnam as a personal fiefdom; yet another brother served the government as ambassador to Great Britain. The increasing involvement of all these members of the president's family in governmental affairs was in direct proportion to the growing isolation of the president from his people.

Communist Rule in North Vietnam

The first two years after the Geneva conference were very hard for North Vietnam as well. A number of factors led to considerable discontent among the people. First, the Democratic Republic of Vietnam (DRV) could not do much to fulfill the promised redistribution of land in the already congested and overfragmented Red River Delta. Imminent famine conditions could not be relieved by imports of grain because of lack of foreign exchange. At the instance of the United States, the French managers had removed the U.S.-made installations from the coal mines that had been North Vietnam's principal earners of foreign exchange. The DRV's crash program of building roads and railroads leading to China by using forced labor on a massive scale also increased the discontent. All these factors combined with the most potent of them—the religious factor—helped to swell the flood of refugees from the North to the South. Most of these were Catholics, who had been told in their parishes that God had moved south, where the government was headed by one of their Catholic brethren. At least one million people migrated from the North to the South during 1954–1955. In 1956, the land reform campaign was resumed. Many Communist party cadres "used the land reform campaign as a weapon against their old enemies or to gain material advantages for themselves."[1] The land reform campaign became a major terror campaign according to the critics of the DRV, taking a toll of perhaps as many as half a million lives. The figures may have been exaggerated by willful mistranslation or misinterpretation of North Vietnamese documents by interested parties, as was later suggested by D. Gareth Porter's studies,[2] though the fact of large-scale peasant discontent and repression is incontestable.

In terms of political stability, however, North Vietnam contrasted sharply with South Vietnam. The government was headed by a legendary nationalist hero, Ho Chi Minh, who as a one-time Bolshevik also commanded respect in the Communist world. Ho's cabinet comrades as well as the common cadres were known for their dedication to the country's achievement of socioeconomic goals. Their firm commitment to the reunification of the country further endeared them to the majority of the people both in the North and in the South. As President Eisenhower later observed, 80 percent of the Vietnamese people would have voted for Ho Chi Minh in mid-1956.[3]

Diem's Oppressive Policies

After the suppression of the sects, Diem could have liberalized politics and turned to the much-needed alleviation of social and economic problems. Instead, he unleashed in 1957 a "mopping up campaign,"[4] using emergency powers and vague definitions of espionage and treason to carry out arbitrary arrests of Communists and non-Communists alike. His principal sources of power at that time were the United States, members of his extended family, and Catholics. The latter constituted a 10 percent minority and were largely refugees from the North, who were hated by most of the southern Buddhist population because of their religion and northern origin. Dissident nationalists were soon branded Communist traitors and censorship was imposed on the press, more severe than during the worst times of French colonial rule. By 1957, Diem's state had become a "quasi-police state."[5]

It must be noted that Diem did introduce some land reform. But his policies were ill-conceived and ill-implemented. Thus, he sought to rehabilitate refugees and the landless poor by expropriating and redistributing landholdings in excess of the permitted 247 acres. Even so, only 20 percent of the rice land would have been available for redistribution to small farmers. In reality, only 10 percent of all tenant farmers benefited. As much as 47 percent of the land remained concentrated in the hands of 2 percent of the landowners; 15 percent of the landlords owned 75 percent of all the land. The few farmers who benefited from the program were more often than not northern Catholic refugees, which invited the charge of favoritism and thereby further deepened peasant alienation in South Vietnam. There were even widespread allegations that the Diem family had enriched itself by manipulating land transfers.

In June 1956, the Diem government replaced village notables with its own appointees. To add insult to injury, most of the new appointees were "outsiders"—northern Catholic refugees. Peasant discontent was also fanned by official measures for enhancing rural security. Between April 1957 and late 1961, inspired by Malaya's example during the state of emergency there (1948–1960), the president's brother, Ngo Dinh Nhu, launched a strategic hamlet program. The program's gains did not offset its social and economic costs. Only 2 percent of the population was involved, but it absorbed over 50 percent of U.S. aid marked for agriculture during that period.

By 1960, Diem had alienated all major sections of the South Vietnamese population. The intellectual elite was rendered politically mute, labor unions impotent, Buddhists distrustful, and Montagnards suspicious, while loyal opposition in the form of organized parties was stifled out of existence. Diem's policies virtually assured that opposition to him would have to be extralegal.

Opposition to Diem's Rule

To what extent was the opposition in South Vietnam to Diem's rule an indigenously inspired movement and what was the degree of Hanoi's involvement in it? A few dates are significant in this respect. Until July 1956, Hanoi had hoped that the reunification of the country would be accomplished through elections. Thereafter, until early 1959, North Vietnam was compelled by considerations of Sino-Soviet global policies of peaceful coexistence to refrain from resorting to a violent alternative for achieving the country's reunification. The first rumblings of the Sino-Soviet dispute in 1959 may have led to certain decisions in Hanoi in regard to the South.

Thus, in May 1959, at the fifteenth plenum of the central committee of the Lao Dong party, the North Vietnamese leaders resolved to create a unified Vietnam through all "appropriate means." In December 1960, the National Liberation Front (NLF) was established in South Vietnam. In the official view of the government of South Vietnam and the United States, the NLF was entirely guided by Hanoi and its leader, Ho Chi Minh. As Douglas Pike commented: "The creation of the NLF was an accomplishment of such skill, precision and refinement that when one thinks of who the master planner must have been, only one name comes: Vietnam's organizational genius, Ho Chi Minh."[6]

Even if the movement received organizational and material assistance from the North, its initial stimulus undoubtedly came from the South. There was, indeed, a core of Communist cadres at its center. When the Viet Minh regroupment was carried out in terms of the Geneva accords during 1954–1955, a force of five to ten thousand cadres was left in the South. As George McTurnan Kahin and John Lewis observed:

> The insurrection is Southern rooted; it arose at Southern initiative in response to Southern demands. The Liberation Front gave political articulation and leadership to the widespread reaction against the harshness and heavy-handedness of Diem's Government. It gained drive under the stimulus of Southern Viet Minh veterans. . . . Contrary to U.S. policy assumptions, all available evidence shows that the revival of the civil war in the South . . . was undertaken by Southerners at their own—not Hanoi's—initiative.[7]

As the movement in the South gained momentum, the DRV assisted the NLF in military training, arms supplies, and later, manpower. All these forms of assistance were stepped up after 1964 in direct correlation to U.S. commitment of troops, money, and supplies. Equally, the United States claimed that its increased involvement was a direct response to the level of insurgency in the South, which it alleged was entirely inspired, directed, manned, and supported by the North.

Ironically, Diem's downfall was brought about by non-Communist elements in South Vietnam. The most serious challenge to his rule was posed in the spring and summer of 1963 by religious malcontents. The movement, led by Buddhist monks and nuns, drew its strength not from the abstractions of Communist ideology, which could only be antithetical to Buddhism, but from the wave of social discontent silently sweeping the population.

Traditionally, the Vietnamese had not perceived religion and politics as separate entities. According to Paul Mus, a French scholar of Asian religions who was raised in Vietnam, Buddhism had always stressed "a morality that lay beyond loyalty in existing authorities."[8] The Buddhist *bonzes* (monks) had provided in the past an intellectual and moral leadership to oppose an oppressive regime.

During French rule, the Buddhist monks had remained largely apolitical. They had been allowed internal autonomy in the running of the monasteries and freedom to celebrate the numerous Buddhist holidays. Unlike the Catholics, the Buddhists did not have a well-organized "church" hierarchy. With Diem's overly pro-Catholic policies, however, the Buddhists felt threatened enough to organize themselves into the General Buddhist Association in 1955. In 1963, in direct response to the religious crisis, the Unified Buddhist Church was created. It did not take sides in the ongoing conflict in South Vietnam until the government blatantly acted against the Buddhists.

On May 7, Ngo Dinh Thuc, Diem's brother and Archbishop of Central Vietnam, forbade the display of Buddhist flags in Hue to commemorate the birth of the Buddha and banned the general festivities as well. As a result, 3,000 Buddhists stormed a radio station and demanded that they be allowed to broadcast a program in honor of the Buddha. What they received in response was tear gas and shooting in which nine people lost their lives.

To protest the government's action, the Buddhists launched a series of self-immolations, beginning with Thich Quang Duc, a venerable monk, who poured gasoline over himself and set himself afire in the full view of the public. Such acts of supreme sacrifice had brought in the past masses of people together as equals against a common tyranny. Madame Nhu publicly ridiculed the sacrifices as a "barbecue of bonzes," while her husband, Ngo Dinh Nhu, ordered the police to raid the pagodas. The press and television coverage brought the magnitude of the government's injustice and callousness to an international audience.

The Buddhist crisis exposed the excesses of Diem's rule to the world. It also changed the official U.S. view of the merits of his administration. So far, the United States had been totally impervious to Vietnamese opposition to Diem, viewing the conflict exclusively as an extension of the clash between the forces of freedom and Communist totalitarianism. The problem was perceived as being military, not political. Even in late 1961 the United States characterized the conflict in South Vietnam in terms of aggression by North Vietnam,[9] claiming it therefore justified expenditure on military build-up rather than on social welfare.

The U.S. military commitment to Vietnam was increased sharply thereafter. During the Kennedy administration, the number of U.S. military "advisers" rose from several hundred to 16,500. From mid-1963, U.S. support of Diem rapidly declined because of his intransigence toward the Buddhist majority. He and his brothers wanted U.S. aid, equipment, and troops but no U.S. advice on how to handle the Buddhist question, which they regarded as a purely domestic matter.[10] Consequently, the United States did not discourage the generals who decided to overthrow the government and assassinate President Diem and his brother Nhu on November 1, 1963.

The liquidation of the Diem regime did not solve any of South Vietnam's basic problems. The political instability worsened with several generals jockeying for power. All of them were pro-U.S. and dependent upon it to keep them in power. With the exception of General Duong Van (Big) Minh, who was inclined to establish a "neutral" government with NLF participation, they were all thoroughly anti-Communist, believing that the conflict was first and last a Communist conspiracy hatched in Hanoi. Throughout the decade from Diem's assassination to the withdrawal of U.S. forces from Vietnam, the United States continued to give priority to the pursuit of the war effort, only half-heartedly insisting after 1966 on democratic trappings like elections and believing that major socioeconomic reforms would have to await a successful conclusion of the war.

The Buddhist crisis, Diem's assassination, and the succeeding series of military regimes involving coups and countercoups gave the NLF a tremendous opportunity to augment its strength. In April 1964, the U.S. Department of Defense estimated that the South Vietnamese government controlled only 34 percent of the villages as against the NLF's control of 42 percent, with the loyalties of the remaining villages still being contested. Both Washington and Saigon continued to believe that Hanoi effectively controlled the NLF and regulated the level of antigovernment activity in the South. Indeed, the United States was looking for a pretext to invade the North; the excuse was provided by the Gulf of Tongking incident.

U.S. INTERVENTION

The Tongking Incident and Escalation of the War

It can be very dangerous for a country to allow foreign policy to become an issue in an election. In 1964, President Lyndon Johnson did not want to look too "soft" on Communism when his rival, Barry Goldwater, was advocating a policy of military escalation against North Vietnam, including limited use of nuclear weapons. In July 1964, the U.S.S. *Maddox* was engaged in espionage in the Gulf of Tongking, ten miles off the North Vietnamese coast.[11] Claiming a twelve-mile maritime boundary, North Vietnam's naval craft attacked the *Maddox* on August 2. Two days later, Johnson informed the American people that the U.S.S. *Maddox* (and the U.S.S. *Turner Joy* sent to join it) had been wantonly attacked by North Vietnamese torpedo boats and that the United States had retaliated by bombing North Vietnamese strategic targets. The U.S. Congress proceeded without much debate (the vote in the House was 416–0 and in the Senate 88–2) to authorize the president to take "all necessary measures to repel any armed attacks against the Forces of the United States, and to prevent further aggression,"[12] a blanket authority that was in the ensuing years to involve the country deeply in the quagmire of the worst war in its history. The Congress was not adequately informed. As the Pentagon Papers revealed later in 1968, Captain John Herrick of the *Maddox* had informed Washington that there was no direct visual evidence of any North Vietnamese torpedo attack and that the sonar operators may have mistaken "freak atmospheric conditions" for torpedos.[13] Neither was Defense Secretary McNamara convinced that such an attack had occurred at all.

Nonetheless, with such sweeping congressional authority and a national consensus behind him, Johnson exercised no restraint in escalating the war. After the NLF's attack on the U.S. air base at Pleiku on February 7, 1965, bombing of North Vietnamese targets was undertaken on a regular basis as part of Operation Rolling Thunder. The operation's objectives were to reduce the flow of men and supplies to the South, to raise morale of the South Vietnamese army, and to raise the price the DRV would have to pay for continued aid to the "Viet Cong." (This derogatory term was first used by President Diem to describe Vietnamese Communists. He also identified the NLF with the Viet Cong, thus denying the NLF its claim of a broader base.) The bombing, however, had very little effect on the progress of the war[14] and soon became almost an end in itself. North Vietnam offered very few bombing targets of real strategic value since its economy was largely agrarian, most of its sophisticated military equipment coming from Soviet and Chinese sources. For one-third of the year, the two monsoon seasons produced poor weather conditions that obscured the landscape and inhibited the efficacy of strategic bombing. Moreover, the NLF's dependence on North Vietnamese supplies was not absolute; most of the NLF's ammunition was obtained by capturing South Vietnamese and U.S. arms depots.

By spring 1967, U.S. forces in South Vietnam had reached a staggering half a million. U.S. estimates of Viet Cong at that time were 250,000. The U.S. military strategy was to "search and destroy" the enemy in the South through a variety of means, including bombing, chemical warfare, psychological warfare, and counter-insurgency operations. The criterion of success was not how much territory was conquered or brought under control but how many Viet Cong were killed. Consequently, unit commanders were compelled to justify previous requests for aerial support by manipulating figures of enemy casualties even if they were not matched by counts of dead bodies or captured weapons. Discrepancies in the body count were explained by the Viet Cong practice of not leaving dead bodies behind. Accounting for weapons was manipulated by counting caches previously captured but not reported.

Impact of the U.S.-Assisted War

The inevitable consequence of such a policy coupled with the growing U.S. military presence was the militarization of South Vietnamese society. The dominance of the armed forces, numbering one million Vietnamese and a half million U.S. troops, was evident everywhere. The opportunities available to military officials for graft and corruption in a U.S.-funded war were unlimited and had debilitating effects on the society. Black-marketing of essential goods, smuggling, pilferage from military bases, and foreign exchange racketeering became rampant; a class of nouveau riche emerged that completely undermined a social system in which bureaucrat-intellectuals and monks had commanded general respect.

The effects of the war on the common people were disastrous. In the countryside, many youths either volunteered or were forced by the NLF to join it. Others were drafted by the ARVN (Army of the Republic of Vietnam). Still others escaped NLF recruitment or deserted the ARVN by discreetly disappearing into the burgeoning population of Saigon-Cholon. Agriculture suffered because of the paucity of workers, bombing raids, defoliation, and the general lack of incentive. Tempted by the lures of city life, or simply due to economic necessity, young girls migrated to Saigon or to the periphery of U.S. military bases to become prostitutes. According to a 1975 World Health Organization estimate, Saigon alone had about 400,000 prostitutes. Small boys, in thousands, touted themselves as pimps or homosexual objects. The city's population expanded from the prewar 2 million to over 7 million, placing an unbearable strain on its infrastructure. According to figures released for the first time by the Vietnamese government in 1995, over 3 million Vietnamese lost their lives during the war.

United States Decides to Disengage

The realization of the futility of the war in Vietnam came to a number of high U.S. government officials as early as 1967, though they were then in the minority. Defense Secretary McNamara and his successor, Clark Clifford, both disagreed with President Johnson in regard to the rationale of the war.

The discordant voices in the U.S. administration had been preceded by a nationwide student concern. By 1968, an election year, the anti–Vietnam War protest movement had widened to include most of the intellectuals and had created a severe rift in the Democratic party's ranks. The recession, growing unemployment, and the declining dollar boosted public clamor to end the "dirty war."

On the night of January 31, 1968, the lunar new year, or Tet, the NLF attacked every important city, town, and military base in South Vietnam. The U.S. embassy in Saigon was also attacked; two U.S. guards were killed. Most cities and towns had to be abandoned by the NLF after being held briefly. Only Hue remained in NLF hands for a month. There the NLF wantonly killed 3,000 civilians, mostly Catholics. Some of the battles between the NLF and the South Vietnamese government and U.S. forces during the so-called Tet Offensive were the fiercest of the war, causing heavy losses on both sides. In Washington, a major debate ensued on the potential costs of continuing the war on the assumption that only a quarter of North Vietnam's forces were involved in the Tet Offensive. The U.S. resolved to disengage from Vietnam "with honor." Johnson decided not to seek office again, and Richard Nixon was elected to the presidency on a platform of disengagement.

For the next four years until the signing of the Paris Accords in January 1973, the United States followed the "Two Tracks Plan"[15] of Henry Kissinger, Nixon's national security adviser and later U.S. secretary of state. While the United States and the DRV would negotiate a military settlement of the war, the Saigon government would seek a political solution with the NLF. U.S. forces would be gradually withdrawn; the war would be "Vietnamized." In May 1969, President Nixon promulgated a new doctrine limiting any U.S. role in future Vietnam-type situations. U.S. response to aggression that did not involve one of the nuclear powers would thereafter be "to provide elements of military strength and economic resources approximate to our size and our interests," and to regard the "defense and progress of other countries" as "first their responsibility and second, a regional responsibility."[16] The new policy was also based on rapprochement with China; Washington's interest in leaving Vietnam divided fitted into the traditional Chinese policy of weakening its neighbors.

The U.S. plan to withdraw with honor was not achieved without further bloodshed. There was more saturation bombing of Vietnam—North and South—than ever before, mining of the Haiphong harbor, escalation of the "clandestine war" in Laos, and an overt invasion of Cambodia. The implications of the extension of the war were grave.

THE CONFLICT SPREADS TO CAMBODIA AND LAOS

Cambodia Under Sihanouk

Until 1969–1970, Cambodia was successful in preserving its independence despite the fires of war raging around it. This was largely due to the leadership of Norodom Sihanouk. Wielding untrammeled power and unparalleled popularity, the cherubic-faced, dynamic prince amazed foreign observers by his flamboyant style of diplomacy that saved his small country from serious entanglement in the nearby holocaust. His popularity was partly based on the traditional Khmer reverence for their monarchs.

Within a year of the Geneva conference, Sihanouk had set his house in good order. On March 2, 1955, he surprised everyone by abdicating in favor of his father to be free to participate in politics. In the following month, he organized his own party, the Sangkum Ryaster Niyum, or Popular Socialist Community. The Sangkum won all the National Assembly seats with 82 percent of the vote in the elections held on September 11, 1955. Until his ouster in 1970, Sihanouk was domestically supreme, whether formally in office or not.

Cambodia's foreign policy during the Sihanouk era could be summarized in one phrase: the struggle for survival as an independent state. Wedged between traditional foes on either side, Vietnam and Thailand, independent Cambodia was fearful and apprehensive of their aggressive intentions. From 1955, Sihanouk followed neutrality in foreign policy.

Describing neutrality as a "dictate of necessity,"[17] Sihanouk alternated between pro-West and pro-Communist policies until the mid-1960s. At this point, he felt that the North Vietnamese and NLF represented the winning side in the Vietnam conflict and, therefore, potential neighbors of Cambodia. Consequently, friendship with China and the Vietnamese Communists became the anchor of Cambodia's foreign policy. Sihanouk admitted, however, that he was apprehensive of the Vietnamese traditional expansionist tendencies. He was also aware that Communists, whether Chinese or Vietnamese, would regard a feudal prince like him as a logical target for political liquidation. Besides, friendship with China could be used as a lever against the Vietnamese, who were historically suspicious of their northern neighbors.

Vietnam Conflict and Cambodian Neutrality

Since Cambodia's principal concern was to safeguard its national integrity, it frowned upon violations of its frontiers by Communists and non-Communists alike. In the late 1960s, the Communist use of eastern Cambodia increased. U.S. bombing of North Vietnam led to increased use of the Ho Chi Minh Trail that passed through southeast Laos and extended to northeast Cambodia. The Communists also used the new port of Sihanoukville to bring in supplies and equipment from North Vietnam and China and transport them to the underground storage facilities in eastern Cambodia. Realizing that the Communists could not be ousted, Sihanouk urged them to exercise self-restraint.

The Communists abandoned such restraint toward the end of 1968. In the sanctuaries, the Communists allegedly established an almost complete administration. U.S. intelligence claimed that the headquarters of the guerrilla movement, the Central Office for South Vietnam (COSVN), was based in the Cambodian sanctuaries.

Of immediate concern for Sihanouk's government was the increase in the activities of the Khmer Rouge, as the Cambodian Communists were called. When the Khmer Rouge was disbanded in 1954, about 5,000 of its members, later labeled "Hanoi Khmers," withdrew to North Vietnam. A smaller number that stayed behind were decimated by Sihanouk's government, but they were reinforced by younger men like Ieng Sary, Khieu Samphan, Hou Yuon, and Saloth Sar (later known as Pol Pot).[18] They were fiercely anti-Hanoi and independent of the ICP (Indochina Communist party). The new Khmer Rouge neither forgot nor forgave the Viet Minh for their abandonment of the Cambodian Communist cause in 1954 at the Geneva conference on Indochina. At that time, the Viet Minh had accepted an independent Cambodia without any role for the Khmer Rouge in that country. In the late 1960s, contrary to Hanoi's wishes, the Khmer Rouge conducted guerrilla operations against Sihanouk's government.[19]

During 1969, Sihanouk condemned Hanoi's and the NLF's efforts to "Vietnamize" the Cambodian province of Ratanakiri, and he moved closer to the United States. Sihanouk also appointed the anti-Communist General Lon Nol as prime minister, although there were differences between the two on how to deal with the Communist threat. Sihanouk stressed the use of diplomacy and his leverage in Moscow and Beijing, while Lon Nol preferred increasing use of the armed forces and assistance from the United States. Indicative of the domestic pressures was the appointment of Prince Sirik Matak to assist Lon Nol. Sirik belonged to the rival dynastic line, the Sisowaths, and favored closer relations with the United States. In January 1970, Sihanouk went abroad, ostensibly for medical treatment but really to try diplomatic channels to bring pressure on Hanoi to desist from aiding the Khmer Rouge.

Sihanouk's Ouster and U.S. Invasion of Cambodia

In Sihanouk's absence, the anti-Communist movement gained momentum. In March, mobs sacked the embassies of North Vietnam and the NLF in Phnom Penh. While Sihanouk was on his way home via Moscow, he learned on March 17 of a Lon Nol–Sirik Matak–led coup deposing him. He proceeded to Beijing, accepted asylum, and headed the government in exile until after the fall of the Lon Nol government in 1975. The coup delivered the prince, who was still immensely popular in Cambodia, to the Communists.

Despite the warnings of responsible senators like Mike Mansfield that any U.S. interference in Cambodia would lead to a general Indochina war, the United States sent military assistance to Lon Nol. Washington used its new leverage with him to invade Cambodia to capture the COSVN. The U.S. action fueled a civil war in Cambodia, which had so far been an oasis of peace in the midst of the holocaust in neighboring Laos and Vietnam. But the military value of the adventure was very limited. Large caches of ammunition were found but not the COSVN itself.

Laos Becomes a Cockpit of International Rivalry

Laos emerged from the Geneva conference of 1954 independent, sovereign, and undivided. Under the agreements, the Pathet Lao forces were to regroup in Phong Saly and Sam Neua, which were then under their control. The Pathet Lao army units would be disbanded or integrated into the Laotian National Army, while the members of the Pathet Lao organization would be free to participate in the political process. There were high hopes for a national reconciliation because of the good relations between the neutralist Prime Minister Souvanna Phouma and his half brother, the Pathet Lao leader Souphannouvong. In November 1957, a National

Union government was inaugurated with Souvanna Phouma as premier and Souphannouvong as a member of the cabinet. They both vowed to keep Laos neutral and nonaligned.

The victory of the leftists in the supplementary elections of May 1958 alarmed the pro-West elements as well as neutralists like Souvanna Phouma. With help from the United States, the radical rightists formed the Committee for the Defense of National Interests (CDNI). The rightist movement led to Souvanna Phouma's resignation; his successor, Phoui Sananikone, immediately infused four more CDNI members into the cabinet and six months later another three. Several more rightist moves followed. Thus, all the Pathet Lao deputies were placed under house arrest; neutralist Souvanna Phouma was sent off to Paris as ambassador. The rightist government attempted to compel the integration of the two Pathet Lao battalions. One of them escaped to North Vietnam and the other managed to desert after its integration. Thereupon, the government placed Souphannouvong and his lieutenants in Vientiane's maximum security prison.

Politics in any country can be unpredictable. But between 1959 and 1962, little Laos went through several governmental changes. On May 24, 1960, "Red Prince" Souphannouvong and seven other Pathet Lao leaders escaped from prison. On August 9, while the entire cabinet was attending the customary prolonged funeral ceremonies of the king in the royal capital of Luang Prabang, an unimpressive commander of a paratroop battalion, twenty-six-year old Kong Le, staged a coup in the administrative capital of Vientiane and announced a neutralist government under Souvanna Phouma as premier. Full-scale hostilities followed between the rightists and the neutralists, who were forced to retreat from Vientiane northward, where they joined the Pathet Lao. Souvanna Phouma vainly tried to negotiate formation of a coalition government to include the CDNI and Pathet Lao. By October, U.S. aid to the Souvanna Phouma government was suspended because of his refusal to break off negotiations with the Pathet Lao. Thailand was asked to declare a blockade of Laos, while the CIA helped the flow of supplies to a rightist government established at Savannakhet under Prince Boun Oum as premier in January 1961. While Souvanna Phouma turned to the Soviet Union for help (it airlifted all kinds of supplies through Hanoi), the Boun Oum troops were fully dependent on U.S. assistance.

For the next eighteen months, the prolonged crisis in Laos attracted tremendous international attention and brought the conviction to both the major external powers involved that a military solution was not possible. A new conference was convened at Geneva. A protocol signed in mid-1962 called for a broad-based government representing all factions.

Accordingly, a troika-type government was installed in Laos under the less controversial Souvanna Phouma as premier. It was then hoped that at least the international weariness would ensure peace and stability to the troubled nation. This was not to be. During the Second Indochina War, Laos would be used as a part of the "Ho Chi Minh Trail," which passed from North Vietnam across southeast Laos and northeast Cambodia, to move troops and supplies to the NLF in South Vietnam.

END OF THE CONFLICT

The Paris Accords and the Communist Victory

The Paris accords finally signed by the four parties concerned—the DRV, the Provisional Revolutionary Government (PRG), the government of South Vietnam, and the United States—on January 27, 1973, provided for withdrawal of all U.S. troops, the return of prisoners of war, and a cease-fire in place without demarcation lines. A democratic solution for the South was envisaged. A Council of Reconciliation and Concord was to be established for organizing elections in the South, after which a coalition government of Thieu, the PRG, and neutralists would be established. Reunification of Vietnam could be considered through subsequent consultations between the North and the South. It was rumored that as a price of the agreement, the United States had offered to pay $3.2 billion toward the reconstruction of the DRV.

The accords brought the Nobel Peace Prize jointly to Le Duc Tho, chief North Vietnamese negotiator (who did not accept it), and Henry Kissinger—but no peace to Vietnam, Laos, or Cambodia. The withdrawal of U.S. forces left the South exposed to an invasion by the North.

Following the peace accords, all three Vietnamese parties—the PRG, DRV, and Thieu—broke faith. Thieu asked for immediate withdrawal of DRV troops as a prerequisite to elections. Neither the DRV nor the PRG had ever acknowledged the troops' presence in the South. Thieu would not allow the PRG candidates freedom of movement for campaigning. War was resumed by the end of the year, although military operations were low-key on all sides throughout 1974. Then, on March 25, 1975, the DRV suddenly launched the final offensive. The DRV's decision was predicated on the military weakness of the Thieu government caused by reduced U.S. aid and the perception that the Ford administration would be incapable of any retaliation because of the post-Watergate U.S. political environment and the lack of will to fight in Vietnam. The gamble paid off. Thieu's order to his army in the central highlands to make a "tactical retreat" produced disastrous disarray and dismal defeat on April 30. The DRV and PRG troops took over Saigon and South Vietnam. In recognition of Ho Chi Minh's contribution to the movement, Saigon was renamed Ho Chi Minh City.

Meanwhile in Cambodia, the Khmer Rouge had continued its guerrilla operations against the Lon Nol regime. The Khmer Rouge ranks were not united. In the early 1970s, an estimated 5,000 Hanoi Khmers entered eastern Cambodia from their exile in North Vietnam. After the Paris accords, conflict developed between the Hanoi Khmers and the Khmer Rouge in which large numbers of the former were killed. The Khmer Rouge refused to heed Hanoi's pleas to lay down arms as stipulated in the Paris peace accords. Even though Hanoi cut off all further military assistance, the Khmer Rouge continued with the offensive, bringing down the Lon Nol regime a fortnight before Hanoi's march into Saigon. The new regime changed the country's name from Cambodia to Kampuchea, calling itself the government of the Democratic Republic of Kampuchea (DRK).

Reasons for U.S. Failure in Vietnam

The U.S. defeat in Vietnam can be attributed primarily to a wrong diagnosis of the reasons for the struggle. The conflict was not as much pro-Communist as it was anti-Diem and later anti-Thieu because of their failure to initiate and implement the much-needed political and socioeconomic reforms. The movement began with South Vietnamese initiative and was primarily manned and supported by Southerners and not by Hanoi. There was indeed a widespread urge to unify the country, but the conflict had to have a political not a military solution. Most of the American aid was military. As for economic aid, as much as 40 percent was swallowed by corrupt contractors, high administrators, generals, business intermediaries, and government officials. The common people suffered from the inflation caused by infusion of aid on such a large scale.

The impact of infusion of U.S. military power was even worse: The specter of alien forces revived anticolonial nationalist sentiments. Thus, the Second Indochina War was as much directed against the U.S. presence as was the first against French rule. After all, it was because of U.S. support that corrupt, self-serving, discredited military dictatorships had survived in South Vietnam for a decade—and in Cambodia for half a decade—contributing to the social and moral decay, creating spiraling inflation, and causing devastation of the countryside. The NLF's ranks swelled after 1964 to include large numbers of non-Communist university students and faculty and professionals who seemed, like their forerunners in the late nineteenth century, to be gripped by the fear of "losing their country." The United States failed in the early years to insist on socioeconomic reforms or liberalization of the political process. Saigon's policies failed to create a public stake in the country's government. The failures of the Diem regime were basic; the momentum lost during that time was never regained. The postponement of sociopolitical reforms until the end of the military conflict and the characterization of that conflict in Communist versus anti-Communist terms were fatal.

Vietnam and Cambodia Under Communism

POLITICAL REORGANIZATION OF VIETNAM

The Government

After the conquest of South Vietnam in April 1975, the Communist and NLF organizations in the South were either dissolved or integrated with the appropriate North Vietnamese governmental or party agencies. The NLF was integrated with the National United Front.

The PRG did not take over the administration in the South. Instead, in the transitional period, Military Management Committees were constituted in certain areas, including Saigon, while the People's Revolutionary Committees were established at the district and village levels. The PRG was formally dissolved after the National Assembly elections and formation of the new government in mid-1976. In the various top-level government and party posts, there was a preponderance of Northerners, to the consternation of NLF and PRG members.

The reunification process was formally launched in November 1975 with a Consultative Conference on National Reunification in Saigon. A formal program for the reunification, already a fait accompli, was drawn up. General elections to the National Assembly were accordingly held on April 25, 1976. At the first session of the National Assembly, a national government replacing the PRG and the DRV was announced and the country renamed the Socialist Republic of Vietnam (SRV). Hanoi became the capital, and Saigon was renamed Ho Chi Minh City.

Technically, the whole country from 1975 to 1980 was governed by the DRV's constitution of 1959. Under it, the National Assembly elected the president (a nominal head of government), vice president, and a Council of Ministers headed by the prime minister. The council was, however, subject to the direction of the Assembly's standing committee, which also supervised the Supreme People's Court. Truong Chinh became the chairman of that powerful committee. Thus, there was no separation of powers between the legislative, executive, and judicial branches of the government.

The Party, the Constitution, and the Leadership

The SRV gave itself two constitutions, the first in December 1980 and the second in 1992. The first was patterned on the 1977 constitution of the Soviet Union. It gave more authority to a new body, the Council of State, which had both legislative and executive functions. Parallel to it but subordinate in powers was the Council of Ministers, mostly an administrative body. The Council of State was composed of a chairman, several vice-chairmen, a secretary-general, and members, all elected by the National Assembly. It constituted a presidium, or collective presidency. It had wide planning and policy-making functions, including the power to declare war, proclaim mobilization or a state of siege, ratify treaties, supervise the work of the Council of Ministers and of the Supreme People's Court, and make certain kinds of laws when the Assembly was not in session. A National Assembly was elected under the 1980 constitution in April 1981. It in turn elected a Council of State with Truong Chinh as chairman. Its four vice-chairmen included Nguyen Huu Tho, formerly chairman of the NLF, and Xuan Thy, former foreign minister of the DRV. Pham Van Dong, the DRV's prime minister since 1955, became the chairman of the Council of Ministers.

The Vietnamese Communist party (VCP) guided and directed the government, which therefore was no more than an agency for the implementation of the party's policies. The VCP also led the society through its mass organizations of peasants, workers, youth, women, and so on. The party functioned at four levels: central, provincial, district, and village. At the apex was the Politburo (political bureau). Elected by the party's central committee, it had 13 full members and one alternate member and was in charge of implementing policies laid down by the central committee, which had 124 full members and 49 alternate members. There was also a party Secretariat of 10 members under the powerful secretary-general. Numerous departments, more or less corresponding to the state's agencies, worked under the control of the Secretariat.

The 1992 constitution retained the leadership role of the party, leaving the routine administration to an executive branch headed by the prime minister. The Council of State and the Collective Presidency of the 1980 constitution were abolished. Instead, the National Assembly, with its standing committee and permanent committees, would have authority over defense and finance, including budget. The office of president was revived, giving it a largely ceremonial role of head of state and chief commander of the armed forces. The president was empowered to ask the National Assembly to review policies and appointments. Le Duc Anh, then seventy-two, known for his conservatism, was appointed president; the liberal reformist Vo Van Kiet was elected prime minister, and the southerner Madame Nguyen Thi Minh, formerly of the PRG, was named vice president.

The strength of the National Assembly was reduced from 500 to 400 to make it a more efficient deliberative body. The 1992 constitution differed from its predecessor also on the economic front, institutionalizing the market-oriented policies adopted by the country since 1987. It also deleted references to the country's wars against its old enemies: France, the United States, and China. Instead, it emphasized a policy favoring good relations with all nations, irrespective of their ideology.

The VCP's highest "legislative" body is the party congress. No meeting of the congress had been held since 1960 because of the exigencies of the war. Since the establishment of the SRV, ten congresses have been held, the last in 2006. The last Congress was held in April 2006. Thanks for pointing out. These are large conclaves of more than a thousand delegates representing a party membership of nearly two million in 2001. Delegations from fraternal Communist parties usually attend such congress meetings, sometimes using the occasion to present medals and honors from their countries to Vietnamese leaders.

The Communist leadership of Vietnam is largely a gerontocracy despite several major reshuffles. The average age of the Politburo members in 1992 was over 70. All of them were educated in the 1920s or 1930s in Vietnam or in south China and spent their youth in the mountainous jungles of North Vietnam during World War II and the First Indochina War and some of them in the Vietnam War. They all belong to the generation of veteran revolutionaries, but have little knowledge of modern economy, technology, or methods of management.

The Communist leadership of Vietnam was divided in the 1960s among the pro-Chinese and pro-Soviet factions. The conditions of war compelled the party leadership to hold the middle position. After the war ended in 1975, the pro-Soviet faction won and until 1991 retained its ascendancy. After 1975, Le Duan, the party's general secretary, and Le Duc Tho, who at the Paris talks had negotiated the withdrawal of the United States, emerged as the main leaders. They ruthlessly removed members of the old guard opposed to their authority, particularly if they were pro-China. Some like Truong Chinh, a pro-China hard-liner, moderated their stand in order to retain power. Until 1985, four categories could bring dismissal from the party: advocates of a softer approach toward China and the Khmer Rouge; critics of the management of the economy in the South; corrupt and inefficient members; and the opponents of Le Duan. Among those removed was Vo Nguyen Giap—architect of the Vietnamese Red Army, hero of Dien Bien Phu, and defense minister from 1954 until February 1980—who was "retired" for his failure to modernize the armed forces and for his faulty assessment of China's capabilities in its invasion of Vietnam in February 1979. Those who were favored included the heroes of the 1975 offensive against South Vietnam, the march into Cambodia in late 1978, and the 1979 war with China. Thus, Giap was replaced by Van Tien Dung, the mastermind of the Saigon offensive of 1975, in the post of defense minister. Pham Hung, one of the principal Communist leaders of the long conflict in South Vietnam, was made minister of the interior in 1980. Le Trong Tan (died December 1986), a general trained in the USSR and East Germany and crucial to the South Vietnam offensive, took over as chief of the general staff. Le Duc Anh, military commander of the Vietnamese forces in Cambodia, became a member of the Politburo in 1982. He later became minister of national defense, a position he held until the party's Seventh Congress in June 1991.

The Sixth Congress, held in December 1986, witnessed the most dramatic political change in the party's history. For quite some time, discontent had been brewing in the party over the unsatisfactory economic performance as well as the lack of progress in military operations in Cambodia. The changes in 1986–1987 came after a year of unprecedented, intense self-criticism by the established leadership of the party. Le Duan's death in July 1986 favored the fortunes of the economic reformers and younger officials, who succeeded in pushing out the old guard. They argued that in the altered context of Mikhail Gorbachev's conciliatory policy toward China, the Cambodian question would have to be resolved on the political plane rather than on the military, particularly because China had cited it as one of the three preconditions for normalizing relations with the Soviet Union. Three senior leaders of the party were compelled to resign from the Politburo: Secretary-General Truong Chinh, Prime Minister Pham Van Dong, and Le Duc Tho. A governmental shake-up in June 1987 ended the long career of Pham Van Dong as premier (since 1955) and Truong Chinh as chairman of the Council of State. The new premier, Pham Hung, died nine months later, in March 1988, and was succeeded by Do Muoi. Vo Chi Cong, the minister of agriculture, who had allowed farmers to sell excess produce in a free market, became the chairman of the Council of State. Nguyen Van Linh was raised to the most powerful position of secretary-general, a position he held until the Seventh Congress in 1991.

Nguyen Van Linh, not exactly young at seventy-one, had been Hanoi's representative in South Vietnam around the time of the takeover of Saigon. He had been identified with liberal economic measures in the South, which included abolition of rationing, extra payment to workers for higher productivity, and establishment of import-export companies. He had met strong resistance within the Politburo, and been removed from that body in 1982, but returned to it in 1985. Along with Vo Chi Cong and Vo Van Kiet, the latter the chairman of the State Planning Commission, he had been actively campaigning in favor of liberalizing the economy in both the North and the South. The Sixth Congress in December 1986 was a triumph for the group of economic reformers.

Further progress toward political and economic reform was somewhat stymied by the dramatic developments leading to the collapse of communism in Eastern Europe and the Soviet Union. The Seventh Congress in mid-1991 marked a further triumph for the liberals. In August, the National Assembly elected Vo Van Kiet, a southerner with strong reformist credentials, as premier to succeed Do Muoi, who had been elected secretary-general of the party to replace the ailing Nguyen Van Linh. Among the important changes were the resignation of Vo Nguyen Giap as vice-premier, the replacement of Foreign Minister Nguyen Co Thach with Nguyen Manh Cam, and the appointment of General Bui Thien Ngo as interior minister and of General Doan Khue as defense minister replacing Le Duc Anh.

ECONOMIC RECONSTRUCTION OF VIETNAM
Problems of Reunification

The reconstruction of Vietnam since 1975 has not been an easy task. The Communist leadership did not show itself as adept in peace and reconstruction as in war and privation. The dismal economic situation in Vietnam since the end of the war was, in some substantial measure, also attributable to the particular conditions in the previous decade. The socioeconomic legacy of a long, brutal war, the special character of the U.S.-subsidized, capitalist-oriented economy of South Vietnam, a succession of natural calamities like drought and floods between 1976 and 1978, war with China and occupation of Cambodia, nonrealization of anticipated foreign assistance—all these may be advanced as factors responsible for lack of success of plans to stabilize the economy and fulfill the expectations of a people whose primary needs had been denied for decades. The leadership was divided between those who stood for ideological purity and would brook no delay in the transformation of the South Vietnamese economy to socialism and the pragmatists and moderates who saw no alternative to making concessions and offering capitalistic incentives, particularly to boost production in the South. Consequently, the economic policies vacillated from liberalism in 1975–1976 to rigidity during 1976–1979, only to retreat again to some liberalism in the form of limited private trade and incentives to boost production in agriculture and manufacturing.

The impact of the long war on the economy of North Vietnam and the society and economy in South Vietnam was deep and disastrous. A United Nations mission visiting Vietnam in 1976 reported that the entire North Vietnamese economic infrastructure had been destroyed. Railroads were inoperable for several-mile stretches as most of the bridges on the Hanoi–Lang Son and Hanoi–Vinh lines had been blown up. Tongking's dike system, over two millennia old, had suffered grievously as 183 dams and canal areas and 884 water installations had been damaged. Twenty-nine of the 30 provincial capitals were damaged and 9 of them completely destroyed. Thousands of villages were damaged and several dozen completely devastated.

The greatest loss in the South was caused to its ecological balance. Under the U.S. military's "food denial program," which was an excuse for defoliation (foliage helped hide Vietnamese guerrillas and obstructed U.S. aircraft landing), millions of acres had been sprayed with herbicides. The ruinous impact of the removal of the jungle canopy—on rainfall, soil erosion, and consequently on the productive abilities of the land—was incalculable.[1] A non-Communist Vietnamese scholar estimated that South Vietnam's timber supply for three decades had been destroyed and that it would take "anywhere from five years for the fruit trees to a century or so for the rare timber trees to become productive again."[2]

In the South, the problems of reconstruction were on all levels: economic, social, political, and ideological. As Huynh Kim Khanh summarized them:

> The legacy of the U.S.-Thieu regime was an economic and social malaise of unknown proportion: an economy that was on the verge of bankruptcy; a threatening famine in the northern provinces of Central Vietnam; more than three million unemployed people, excluding an army of a half-million prostitutes about to be out of work; six to seven million refugees who had been forced by wartime activities to flee their native villages into the cities, etc.[3]

The new government inherited an economy in which more than 50 percent of the GNP was generated by a service sector almost completely dependent upon a U.S.-funded war and in which imports were twelve times the exports. The industry was 85 percent dependent on foreign countries for raw materials and 100 percent dependent on foreign machines and fuel. Moreover, fleeing officials and bankers had stolen most of the country's foreign exchange reserves. The new government also had to do something about an estimated 1.1 million ARVN troops and an additional 1 million persons including police (125,000), militia (500,000), and civil service officials (350,000), only some of whom could be relied upon for their loyalties to the Communist regime. Given the ideological context, reconstruction in the South included not only rehabilitation but relocation and "reeducation" of several million individuals. Also to be relocated were a large number of handicapped from an estimated 2.2 million war casualties, some of whom could not be expected to contribute at full strength to the rebuilding of the economy.

Five-Year Plans

The new Vietnam aimed at a "triple revolution"—collectivization and nationalization of industry and agriculture; ideological transformation; and scientific and technological revolution. It seemed pragmatic and not bound by ideological purity, as it welcomed outside investment of finance and technology. To prove its legitimacy, Vietnam enthusiastically joined the International Monetary Fund, unlike most Communist countries. However, efforts to attract capital from non-Communist countries did not succeed because Hanoi refused to honor the former South Vietnamese government's debt obligations and because immediately after the takeover of Saigon it nationalized all foreign enterprises.

In December 1976, Vietnam adopted an ambitious second five-year plan. It was termed second in relation to the first five-year plan for the DRV during 1961–1966. That plan was abandoned halfway into it because of the exigencies of the Vietnam War. Of the projected outlay of 30 billion dongs, or about $10–12 billion, more than half was expected to come from outside donors. The Soviet Union promised $2.7 billion and East European countries $700 million. China was expected to contribute $600 million. Vietnam also expected the United States to fulfill a "promise" made at the time of the Paris peace accords to give Vietnam $3.2 billion in reconstruction aid. By the forcible capture of South Vietnam in April 1975, the North Vietnamese had, in the U.S. view, violated those accords and absolved the United States of the alleged "promise." Vietnam, however, continued to hope that some U.S. assistance would be forthcoming, particularly after the advent of the Carter administration and as a reward for efforts to investigate the whereabouts of U.S. soldiers missing in action (MIAs). The U.S. aid never materialized. Assistance from socialist countries also dropped below expectations or, as in China's case, altogether dried up.

The plan combined major agricultural and industrial projects involving large-scale demographic changes. Out of the total planned expenditure, about $3 billion were marked for agriculture, $3.5 billion for industry, and an equal amount for transportation and services. The country would, after feeding its population, have a surplus of 3 million tons of rice for export.

Most of the agricultural development was to be achieved in the South by reclaiming about 6.4 million acres of land, mostly in the Mekong Delta. Large-scale collectivization of agriculture was envisaged through the creation of 250 giant agrofarm collectives, one in each district of South Vietnam, each employing about 100,000 persons. By 1978, before the march into Cambodia, the Hanoi government claimed to have established 137 such collectives, which reportedly released some 4 million people who were then settled in the New Economic Zones (NEZs) in both parts of the country. Additionally, half the population of the Saigon-Cholon and Gia-Dinh area and people from the densely populated Red River Delta were relocated in the NEZs, particularly on the country's border with hostile Cambodia. The economic plan thus involved demographic relocation on a gigantic scale, not unlike what the Soviet Union and China did after their respective revolutions. The Vietnamese government also announced plans to remove in the following two decades about 10 million people from the country's overcrowded areas to the mountainous zones in the north and west bordering all three of the country's neighbors.

The concept of organizing the territory into New Economic Zones was not new; it had been earlier adopted in North Vietnam in 1970 with the creation of 23 NEZs in 14 provinces. In the South, however, the motives for the establishment of the NEZs were not purely socioeconomic. They were primarily aimed at population control—they facilitated the work of the internal security police and the strategic purpose of peopling the underpopulated regions along the country's borders. As economic units, the NEZs would develop centers of light industry, helping to produce articles of consumption not only for the domestic population but also for export. In previously sparsely populated regions, the NEZs would be used for bringing new areas under cultivation.

Vietnam's wars with Cambodia and China in 1978–1979 cost Vietnam dearly. The occupation of Cambodia by Vietnamese forces and the state of preparedness on the Sino-Vietnamese border limited the funds available for developmental programs. In 1979, the party decided to decentralize the industries as part of the national defense strategy, and from the following year, the government formally increased the defense expenditure to absorb almost half of the nation's budget.

There were other reasons for the failure of the second five-year plan. Paucity of funds—internal and external—was one factor. The government's lack of appreciation of the socioeconomic structure of pre-1975 South Vietnam and the forced pace of changes was another. Many loyalists of the former anti-Communist regime were accused of sabotaging the state plans. Moreover, there was widespread corruption among the party cadres and officials who lined their pockets at the cost of the state. Last, three successive years of bad weather, floods, and drought severely affected agriculture. The country depended on external assistance, predominantly from the Soviet Union, not only for grain but also for fertilizers and fuel.

Economic Liberalization

Facing the failure of the second five-year economic plan, the party's central committee decided in September 1979 to decelerate the collectivization and cooperativization of agriculture in South Vietnam. Family farms that were run efficiently were to be left alone. All control stations established to check the movement of goods between rural areas and urban centers—which had virtually become bureaucratic bottlenecks and hunting grounds for pilferers, profiteers, bribe-takers, and black-marketeers—were to be abolished. It was acknowledged that there were severe problems in the public-sector undertakings: poor management skills, inadequate technological know-how, and insufficient worker enthusiasm. The party therefore resolved to rescind the orders nationalizing private business and trade and restore small-scale enterprises and retail trade to the private sector. Additionally, the party unhesitatingly adopted the capitalist practice of increasing productivity through economic incentives both in agriculture and manufacturing. During 1980–1981, the party further resolved to decentralize management from the central to the local level, clearly defining the rights of major industrial and economic establishments to make their own decisions in most matters including wage schemes, bonuses, and worker welfare.

By the beginning of 1984, Vo Van Kiet, Chairman of the State Commission for Planning, was able to report an upward trend in the economy, with major accomplishments in agriculture and industry. The agricultural production would be enough to meet domestic needs with a small surplus for export; industrial production marked a 25 percent increase over that of 1978. Such accomplishments were primarily the result of the product contract system, under which incentives were offered individual families on collective farms by allowing them to sell any surpluses grown in excess of fixed production to be handed over to their collectives. A free market flourished along with the government's rationing system.

The reactions of the party hierarchy to such achievements were mixed. The party noted the existence of large-scale corruption among officials and cadres, who rewarded themselves with monetary benefits which the others received from the incentives and bonus system. It was apprehensive of the creeping capitalism and its cultural manifestations particularly in Ho Chi Minh City, which had impeded the socialist transformation of Nam Bo (South Vietnam). The Fifth Party Congress in 1982 therefore resolved to complete the transition to socialist forms of ownership in the South by the end of 1985. That would never happen.

The economic situation in Vietnam worsened in the mid-1980s with large-scale unemployment, triple digit inflation, resistance to collectivization in the countryside particularly in the south and diplomatic isolation caused by continued occupation of Cambodia. Therefore, the Sixth Congress, held in December 1986, adopted radical measures, practically reversing the process of transforming the country into a socialist society and, in effect, resolving to apply the liberal measures of the South to the North as well. The package of reforms known as *doi moi* adopted economic pragmatism in approving an export-oriented economy, welcoming direct foreign investment and decollectivization of agriculture and abandoning central economic planning altogether as a strategy for economic development. The existing cash incentives to peasants and workers were increased. Rice farmers were allowed to earn up to 40 percent profits over production costs, and the more productive among the industrial workers were rewarded with bonuses and piece-rate wages. Tax exemptions were provided for new and expanded industries and for handicraft industries producing goods solely for export. To relieve hardship among the middle class, the government legalized moonlighting by government employees. There were to be no subsidies hereafter for the State-Owned Enterprises (SOEs). The government would allow wholly owned foreign companies in all sectors except defense. There were guarantees offered against nationalization of foreign property at least for twenty years.

Spectacular Progress

By 1992, the economy had turned the corner, registering a GDP growth of 5.3 percent, which further accelerated to keep pace with the best among ASEAN members. In 1994 and 1995, GDP grew annually at 8.8 percent and 9.5 percent, respectively. Thus, the annual increase in industrial output was around 14–15 percent, in agriculture around 4.5–5 percent. Exports went up from $2.5 billion in 1992 to $5.3 billion in 1995; imports (of which nonconsumer goods accounted for 88 percent) increased from $2.3 billion in 1992 to $7.5 billion in 1995. For the first time in three decades, Vietnam resumed its role as a leading rice exporter, behind only Thailand and the United States since 1993.

The Seventh Congress, held in June 1991, witnessed fierce debates on the cataclysmic changes that had taken place in the Communist world in the late 1980s and on the pace of political and economic reform in Vietnam. The liberals in the government favored turning state enterprises into shareholding companies; the conservative diehards in the party fiercely opposed such a dilution of socialism. As a result, only a small number of state enterprises could be privatized. The liberal position was hamstrung by financial stringency caused by massive reduction of aid and concessional trade from Russia. The situation was not helped by the continuing U.S. trade embargo. The United States had also successfully pressured the International Monetary Fund since 1985 into denying credit to Vietnam.

The Vietnamese economy suffered a devastating blow with the Southeast Asian currency crisis of 1997. Foreign direct investment (FDI), never too happy with Vietnam's rampant corruption and bureaucratic deadlocks, fled the country: 70 percent of FDI came from ASEAN states, which received 60 percent of Vietnamese exports. FDI plummeted by 60 percent in 1998 and by 64 percent the following year. By the end of 1999, the Vietnamese operations of three-quarters of all foreign companies were in the red. Exports dwindled, and the Vietnamese dong became overvalued. By 2000, the trade deficit exceeded US$1 billion; 45 percent of the 6,000 State-Owned Enterprises (SOEs) were losing money. To add to the government's woes, the IMF and the World Bank withheld loans of about US$500 million in 1999 and US$700 million in 2000, demanding that Vietnam adopt a "more comprehensive approach" to economic reform. In general, liberals in government were not able to cope with the 1997 economic crisis because of the rigidity demanded by conservative diehards in the VCP.

The growing economic crisis strengthened the opposition to promote cooperation with the capitalist world, facilitate FDI, and encourage Vietnam becoming part of the global marketplace. Party conservatives argued that the West would continue to exploit countries like Vietnam in order to keep them perpetually underdeveloped. In the process, the gap between rich and poor nations would widen. They also maintained that Western attempts to promote privatization and economic competition were designed to weaken the authority of the state and that of the VCP. The consequence was the Politburo's rejection of a draft bilateral trade agreement with the United States whereby the Vietnamese trade tariff would be reduced drastically from 40 to 3 percent, which, according to a World Bank study, would increase exports to the United States by $800 million in the first year of the agreement. In the end, however, conservative General Secretary Le Kha Phieu had to give in to the potential benefits of the U.S. bilateral trade agreement and signed it in July 2000.

VIETNAM-CHINA RELATIONS

The end of the war in South Vietnam and the reunification of Vietnam did not make China happy. Traditionally, China has regarded the emergence of strong states on its borders as a threat to its security. It was further distressed to note Hanoi's ambitions to dominate Laos and Cambodia and to assist fraternal Communist parties in the rest of Southeast Asia, which China regarded as an area for its own political influence. After the end of the Vietnam War, the Chinese leaders insisted that Hanoi join them in condemning the Soviet Union for hegemonism. Hanoi's refusal to toe Beijing's line in regard to Cambodia as well as in its relationship with the Soviet Union finally led to open warfare between China and Vietnam in early 1979. Other contributing factors to the steady deterioration in Sino-Vietnamese relations included the dispute over the offshore islands and Vietnam's new policy toward people of ethnic Chinese origin.

The overseas Chinese in Vietnam were as much hated by the local people as they were elsewhere in Southeast Asia (except Singapore) because of their superior economic standing. After the Communist victory in Saigon, the Chinese were grouped along with intellectuals, devout Buddhists, and Catholics as enemies of socialism, and many of them moved to the NEZs, particularly in the border province of Tay Ninh. There, the Chinese would serve additionally as a buffer between Vietnam and Cambodia.

In March 1978, the government initiated overt action against the Chinese community. Cholon, the mostly Chinese-inhabited twin city of Ho Chi Minh City, was raided and Chinese assets frozen. The Chinese were officially reclassified as an ethnic minority and the special category status they had thus far enjoyed was abolished. The change was to indicate the government's firm resolve to integrate them along with the other ethnic minorities into the national community. The policy caused a hue and cry among the Chinese, leading to an exodus. Of note was the flight of a substantial number of Chinese from North Vietnam across the land border into China, indicating that the feeling of insecurity permeated the Chinese community all over Vietnam.

It may be assumed that the persecution of the Vietnamese Chinese would not ordinarily have moved Beijing: Of the 1.5 million Vietnamese Chinese, 90 percent lived in the South, had amassed fortunes, and generally supported the capitalist way of life. The indignation of the Chinese government can be explained only in political terms as an attempt to find an additional excuse to attack Vietnam. It was evident in the half-hearted manner in which China tried to evacuate the Vietnamese Chinese. Thus, the two ships China sent to Ho Chi Minh City and Haiphong to evacuate the refugees remained off the coast for six valuable weeks while an acceptable evacuation procedure was negotiated with Vietnamese officials. Also, China accepted across the land borders only those refugees who could produce exit visas issued by Vietnam along with repatriation certificates from the Chinese embassy in Hanoi. Such strict adherence to documentation clearly showed that the Chinese government's concern for Vietnamese Chinese was not genuine.

VIETNAM AND CAMBODIA

Disputes with Cambodia

In Cambodia, tensions continued to exist between the two factions of the Khmer Rouge: the Khmer Viet Minh (Pol Pot, Khieu Samphan, Ieng Sary) and the Hanoi Khmers (Chea Sim, Heng Samrin). Additionally, there was a third group consisting of moderates like Prince Sihanouk, who was made head of state, and other non-Communists, who were intensely nationalistic, suspicious of Vietnamese expansionism, and advocates of rapprochement with the United States.

The Khmer Viet Minh, led by Pol Pot, dominated. In an action that perhaps had no precedent in human history, the DRK emptied the cities and towns, compelling former civil service officials, teachers, and monks to work with their hands in agriculture. The regime demonetized the currency, shut down all major establishments, and closed the country to the whole world. These programs (rather, pogroms) were carried out in the most brutal, insensate manner, dislocating, decimating, and alienating the bulk of the population. Estimates of those killed vary, but probably more than a million people lost their lives. The horrors of the Pol Pot regime made any aggression by an external power to terminate the horrible conditions in Cambodia look relatively benign in comparison.[4]

One of the principal goals of the DRK was to make the Vietnamese vacate the decade-old sanctuaries in eastern Cambodia. Therefore, to put pressure on the Vietnamese, Cambodia attacked the border provinces in April 1977, particularly the NEZs in Tay Ninh. Further, it allied itself with Vietnam's enemy, China, in what Vietnam called a bid to "encircle" it.

Cambodia was wary of Vietnam for several other reasons. Thus, in May 1976, Vietnam questioned the entire maritime boundary with Cambodia that had been "settled" by the Brevie Line in 1939 during French rule. It claimed some islands in the Gulf of Thailand. Suspicions of Vietnam's intentions were roused by its alleged support to some Hanoi Khmers who attempted a coup in September 1976. Cambodia also alleged a Vietnamese plan to integrate it into a Vietnamese-dominated Indochina federation.

Vietnam's Occupation of Cambodia

In mid-1978, Vietnam made clear its choice between Moscow and Beijing. On June 29, it joined the Moscow-dominated COMECON, the Communist equivalent of the Common Market, and on November 3 signed with Moscow a comprehensive twenty-five year treaty of friendship and mutual assistance. China retaliated on July 3, 1978, by terminating all its economic, military, and technical assistance to Vietnam and withdrawing Chinese experts. Beijing also alleged that the USSR and Vietnam had a plan to "encircle" China and labeled Vietnam the "Cuba of Asia," a satellite of the Soviet Union helping the latter to achieve its strategic aims in Asia.

Having armed itself with the November treaty with the Soviet Union, Hanoi was ready to invade Cambodia. It helped establish the Kampuchean United Front for National Salvation (KUFNS) under Hanoi Khmers like Heng Samrin and Chea Sim and some exiled Cambodian intellectuals and monks. An important component of the new party was a section of the Khmer Krom, the Cambodian minority of over half a million in South Vietnam.

Unlike the NLF in South Vietnam, the KUFNS did not inspire popular support in Cambodia because of its subservience to Vietnam. It was clearly a Vietnamese smoke screen created on the eve of their invasion to legitimize it in world opinion. The superior Vietnamese forces, numbering about 160,000, took only seventeen days to dislodge the Pol Pot group and replace it with one under Heng Samrin. The new government called itself the People's Republic of Kampuchea (PRK), as opposed to the fugitive DRK.

Pol Pot and his cohorts fled to western Cambodia. For a while, China was able to continue making military and economic aid supplies to the anti–Phnom Penh guerrillas, thanks to the airstrip at Siem Reap, passages through Laos and Thailand, and smuggling along the 450-mile Cambodian coastline. The Laotian corridor was soon plugged by the pro-Vietnam government, which also expelled Chinese technical and military personnel from the country. With such handicaps, the Pol Pot group was obliged to join hands with other foes of the Heng Samrin regime, including Sihanouk moderates and Khmer Serei who ironically had been pushed either across the Thai border or into the hideouts of the Cardamom Mountains by the Pol Pot regime in 1975.

Vietnamese overthrow of the Beijing-backed Pol Pot regime was a great blow to China. In February 1979, China attacked Vietnam and kept the pressure on for a month before unilaterally withdrawing its forces. China's public posture was that it was "teaching a lesson" to Vietnam for its action in Cambodia and treatment of the ethnic Chinese. On neither count did Hanoi seem to have learned the lesson. Vietnam did not withdraw its forces from Cambodia. Further, Vietnam stepped up its persecution of the ethnic Chinese, causing a mass exodus in the first half of 1979.

In a sense, both Hanoi and Beijing came out losers in the two clashes. The tensions on the Sino-Vietnamese border continued. There were serious clashes between the troops of the two countries in the 1980s coinciding with Vietnam's dry-season offensive in Cambodia. Vietnam's military and political domination over the rest of Indochina was achieved at tremendous costs to its own economy, security, and international image. For a decade, the country's military and diplomatic dependence on the Soviet Union and East European countries became as complete as its isolation from the rest of the Third World. Moreover, its chances of getting developmental assistance from the United States, Western Europe, and Japan evaporated. Hanoi's action drastically diminished its credibility among ASEAN states as a nation committed to carving a zone of peace in Southeast Asia.

Vietnam and the Soviet Union

Over the next decade, Vietnam had to pay a heavy price for Soviet assistance, military and economic. It had to grant the Soviet Union port facilities at Cam Ranh Bay, which remained thereafter until the collapse of the Soviet Union its most important strategic base, the only one between Vladivostok and East Africa. Its value to the Soviet Union was inestimable particularly because of its proximity to the largest overseas U.S. naval base in the nearby Philippines.

The Soviet Union's economic assistance was overwhelming to Vietnam's economic plans. It was crucial for the success of Vietnam's five-year plans. The Soviet Union's military assistance enabled Vietnam to augment its military forces from 600,000 in 1975 to 1.1 million in 1978–1979 and to keep up a military presence of about 160,000 troops in Cambodia and 40,000–50,000 in Laos. The costs of maintaining the fourth largest army in the world would have been impossible for Vietnam but for Soviet assistance, which was estimated at between $1 billion and $1.5 billion annually from 1979 to 1983. Thereafter, until 1987, the military component of assistance was reduced in favor of the economic. At the same time, agreements for Vietnamese repayments included not only raw materials but also Vietnamese "guest workers" in the Soviet Union, perhaps as many as 50,000 persons, part of whose wages were used to offset the Vietnamese debt burden to the Soviet Union.

Such major concessions were galling to the self-esteem of Vietnam, which prided itself on the sacrifices involved in the long struggle of liberation against another superpower. By the mid-1980s, a readjustment of relations with major powers as well as neighbors was deemed prudent and vital. Therefore, the Sixth Party Congress in December 1986 voted in favor of improvement of relations with China; better economic ties with the West, the ASEAN, and Japan; and above all, a negotiated political settlement of the Cambodian problem.

The political and economic collapse of the socialist systems in Eastern Europe and the Soviet Union in the late 1980s further underlined the need for completely redirecting Vietnam's international relations. Real changes had to wait, however, until the ideological debate among Vietnamese leaders—divided between the conservatives and the liberals over the issues of political reform, a market-oriented economy, resolution of the Cambodian imbroglio, and closer ties with Western and pro-Western countries—was resolved. This was accomplished a little before the Seventh Congress of the VCP in June 1991. As a consequence, there were drastic changes in Vietnam's relations with Russia, China, ASEAN, and the United States.

Economic Liberalization and Foreign Policy

The most important single decision of the VCP and the government was *doi moi*, or renovation through liberalization of the economy: giving market incentives to individuals, compelling state enterprises to compete in the marketplace, closing down economically inefficient units, and reforming the banking, legal, and taxation systems so as to attract massive foreign investment. It would be crucial to have resumption of foreign loans and grants. Since the late 1980s, Vietnam's goal has been to become an Asian Tiger like the other ASEAN and northeast Asian states around it. A key to the achievement of such objectives was, indeed, normalization of relations with the United States. In fact, since the late 1980s, the Vietnamese foreign policy has served as an adjunct of its economic policy.

With the U.S. decision on July 2, 1993, not to vote against clearing of past Vietnamese debts, foreign aid and soft loans from the IMF and the WB resumed their flow. France and Japan at once agreed to lend $50 million each to Vietnam, with some other countries contributing smaller amounts to retire Vietnam's old international debt of $140 million. In November, a meeting of twenty-three donor states and international agencies in Paris pledged $1.86 billion in loans to Vietnam for 1994, three-fifths from individual governments and two-fifths from the IMF, WB, and the Asian Development Bank. Of the governments, Japan, Australia, France, Great Britain, and South Korea pledged more than 50 percent of the aid, which was earmarked for rebuilding roads, revamping education, and implementing other infrastructural projects. Japan had already resumed aid to Vietnam in November 1992 (suspended after the Vietnamese occupation of Cambodia in 1979); it now offered the largest amount of all donors, $555 million—90 percent in soft loans and the balance in grants and technical aid. And France, which also had resumed its aid to Vietnam in 1992 by giving it $36 million, doubled it for 1993. In November 1994, the second donors' conference in Paris, attended by eighteen countries and fifteen international agencies (with the United States as a noncontributing observer), pledged $2 billion in support of the Vietnamese government's "medium-term economic stabilization and structural reform program."

The lifting of the U.S. embargo in February 1994 opened the door to American trade and investment in Vietnam. The decision encouraged Western European nations, Australia, New Zealand, Japan, South Korea, Taiwan, and ASEAN states to augment their business relations with Vietnam. FDI flowed into Vietnam, peaking in 1996 when FDI stood at US$8.3 billion. In the aftermath of the 1997 Southeast Asian currency crisis, FDI in Vietnam dwindled to a meager US$1.5 billion in 1999; in 2000 it fell by another 55 percent. With the passage of the amended Law on Foreign Investment in August 2000, which liberalized the conditions for FDI and allowed the repatriation of profits, FDI increased to US$2.4 billion by the end of the year. The trend continued with an increase of 7 percent during 2001. The Ministry of Planning and Investment projected FDI of US$11 billion by 2005. Although the currency crisis of 1997 affected the Vietnamese economy, including the flow of FDI, the real reasons for the drop in FDI included rampant corruption, bureaucratic hurdles, the practice of invalidating contracts if some other party offers better terms, and the lack of physical infrastructure.

Normalization of U.S.-Vietnam Relations

In July 1990, the United States announced the first major shift in relations with Vietnam, as a consequence of which Vietnam's foreign minister, Nguyen Co Thach, and U.S. Secretary of State James Baker met in New York on September 29, 1990. This was the first such high-level meeting between the two countries in seventeen years. The meeting was officially described by the United States as a "step in the direction of normalization of relations."

Relations with the United States improved markedly in the aftermath of the VCP's Seventh Congress. A major landmark in the new relationship was the U.S. proposal of April 1991 for a four-stage solution, involving Vietnam and Cambodia and leading to full resumption of diplomatic ties between the United States and Vietnam:

1. Discussions on normalization of relations would take place at the time of signing the diplomatic settlement of the Cambodian conflict; simultaneously, the United States would approve visits by U.S. business leaders and veterans' groups to Vietnam.
2. With the establishment of a U.S. transitional presence in Cambodia, the United States would partially lift its trade embargo against Vietnam and Cambodia; the second phase would also require increased accounting for U.S. MIAs.
3. The third phase would begin after the UN process in Cambodia had lasted at least six months and would include the establishment of U.S. and Vietnamese diplomatic offices in Hanoi and Washington, respectively, a full lifting of the U.S. trade embargo against Vietnam, and an easing of U.S. opposition to international bank lending to Vietnam; this phase would also involve further substantial progress in accounting for U.S. MIAs.
4. The final phase would follow UN-supervised elections in Cambodia and would include full normalization of U.S. diplomatic and economic relations with Vietnam and Cambodia as well as support for international bank lending.

A number of positive measures included the visit of a U.S. business delegation led by Warren Williams, president of the U.S. Chamber of Commerce, to Vietnam in December 1991. Williams was assured by Hanoi that it would reserve for the United States a stake in one of the country's major offshore oil fields. In January 1992 the first U.S. aid to Vietnam came in the form of relief assistance to Vietnamese typhoon victims. Three months later, Washington lifted its trade embargo on commercial sales of medicine and agricultural supplies to meet basic human needs of the Vietnamese people. The United States also ended restrictions on the activities of U.S. nongovernmental and nonprofit organizations carrying out humanitarian work in Vietnam. Simultaneously, Hanoi released all remaining South Vietnamese detained in "reeducation" camps since 1975.

The MIA Question

The improvement in U.S.-Vietnam relations was suddenly arrested in April 1993 when an Australian researcher at Harvard University disclosed a document he found in the Russian archives that presumably contradicted the information on MIAs previously supplied to the United States by the Hanoi government. The document quoted Vietnamese general Tran Van Quang's speech to the VCP's Politburo on September 12, 1972, stating that North Vietnam was holding 1,205 U.S. servicemen, a much higher figure than the 368 given by North Vietnamese officials in December 1970. During General Vessey's visit to Vietnam in April 1993, the Vietnamese government, notably General Tran, produced evidence to show that no such Politburo meeting had taken place. Vessey closed the controversy by stating that a number of figures cited in the document were inconsistent with U.S. records as well as the internal records of the then North Vietnamese government. However, the controversy—taking place as it did so soon after the publication of the U.S. Senate's Final Report on prisoners of war (POWs) and MIAs—had the effect of delaying the progress toward normalization of relations.

There was substantial progress made on the MIA question in the early 1990s because of Hanoi's cooperation. In March 1992, Vietnam had agreed with the United States on a five-point program to accelerate the accounting of the MIAs in accordance with, in Hanoi's words, "the policy of reconciliation and restitution." Accordingly, Vietnam opened its museum archives to U.S. researchers, accelerated live-sighting investigations, and broadcast a nationwide appeal to the Vietnamese people to turn over any remains of U.S. soldiers. The U.S. Senate Select Committee on POW/MIA Affairs, which had been meeting for 15 months since late 1991, held 23 public hearings, heard sworn testimony from nearly 200 witnesses, reviewed more than one million pages of previously classified documents, and issued its Final Report of 585 pages in January 1993. The report concluded that there was no compelling evidence that "any American POWs were still being held in Indochina." It stated that out of the 2,264 U.S. servicemen officially listed as MIAs in Indochina, 1,095 were known to have been killed but their bodies had never been recovered. Of the remaining, only 305 (196 in Vietnam) could have survived for a brief period. The United States had concluded that 61 of them had died before 1973. The report added that the United States was spending at least $100 million annually to resolve the issue. After an agreement to open a U.S. Liaison Office in Hanoi was signed on January 27, 1995, a special section in that office began assisting families and friends of the MIAs in their efforts to "ascertain the status of their loved ones."

Normalization at Last

The most significant step toward normalization of relations was taken in February 1994, when the United States announced that it was lifting the embargo on trade with Vietnam, which had been in force with North Vietnam since 1964 and with all of Vietnam since 1975.

At that point, American trade and investment interests were well poised to exploit the new opportunities in Vietnam. Thus, a survey by the U.S.-ASEAN Council of more than 110 American companies had identified $2.6 billion in potential sales to Vietnam by 1995 and over $8 billion by 1998. At least eight U.S. oil companies were involved unofficially in offshore oil exploration in Vietnam. The U.S. Chamber of Commerce in Hong Kong reported in early 1995 that more than 150 American companies associated with it were already carrying on business in Vietnam. Even so, the U.S. unofficial participation in Vietnam did not extend to more than 34 out of nearly 1,000 projects.

Meanwhile, there were pressures on the U.S. administration from several sides in favor of an expeditious normalization of relations with Vietnam that would include full diplomatic relations. The arguments in favor of opening a U.S. embassy in Hanoi were several. First, it would help Americans to influence the reform process under way in Vietnam both in the economic and political spheres; second, it would offer U.S. companies a fair share of the enormous trade and investment opportunities that other countries had been able to exploit in the wake of Vietnam's liberalization policies; third, it would enable U.S. military attachés to assess Vietnam and China's strategic plans in the Tongking Gulf and the South China Sea.

With substantial progress made on the MIA question thanks to Hanoi's cooperation, the last major hurdle in the normalization of relations was removed in January 1995. Six months later, on July 11, 1995, President Clinton announced normalization of relations with Vietnam, a country that had waged a war and had left deep scars in the American psyche. The president said that normalization would further U.S. interests "in working for a free and peaceful Vietnam in a stable and peaceful Asia." And although the administration denied it, there was much truth in the statement by Senator John McCain (a former POW) that the recognition would "serve as a strategic counterweight to Chinese military power in Asia."[5]

Thereafter, U.S.-Vietnam relations continued to improve: Douglas "Pete" Peterson, a former Air Force pilot who had been shot down and imprisoned in the Hanoi Hilton, was named the first U.S. ambassador to Vietnam in 1997. In August 1999, U.S. Consul General Charles Ray inaugurated a new U.S. consulate building in Ho Chi Minh City.

The development of a close U.S.-Vietnam relationship, however, was stymied by Vietnam's questionable record on human rights. Business activities, including U.S. investment in Vietnam, were inhibited by rampant corruption, bureaucratic hurdles, and the realities of low profits. The United States also pushed for political reform, that is, toward a pluralistic system against the VCP's monopoly of power.

President Clinton Visits Vietnam

History was made when the first executive-level meeting between the two former foes—Vietnam and the United States—took place in November 2000 with the arrival of President Bill Clinton, the first U.S. president to visit Hanoi and the first to visit Ho Chi Minh City (formerly Saigon) since President Richard Nixon's brief stopover there in 1969. Clinton was accompanied by a trade mission organized by the U.S.-Vietnam Trade Council consisting of thirty U.S. companies, including Boeing, General Motors, Lucent Technologies, Oracle, Coca-Cola, Nike, Motorola, Citigroup, Federal Express, and United Parcel Service. The mission's objectives were to explore further business opportunities, remove bureaucratic obstacles, and terminate the discriminatory pricing system that made foreign firms pay much more for basic services than domestic counterparts.

THE VIETNAMESE ECONOMY IN THE NEW MILLENNIUM

In the more than two decades since the beginning of the liberalization program, *doi moi* (renewal) in 1986, the Vietnamese economy has attained the distinction of growing at the fastest rate of any ASEAN country's. In the new millennium, it has averaged 7.5 percent annual growth, a little lower than China's and India's, but Vietnam's growth has been decidedly more effective than either of theirs in cutting poverty. In the process, collectivization of agriculture was abandoned, and farmers were permitted to own their own land and settle prices of their produce by market forces. Corporatism has been officially encouraged in the same manner as in neighboring Communist China. In 2000, a stock exchange was created, and five years later, in March 2005, Vietnam opened an over-the-counter exchange, the Hanoi Securities Trading Center, whose principal aim was the rapid transformation of State-Owned Enterprises (SOEs) into corporate-structured, private equity firms. Six months later, the government raised the limit on stock ownership by non-Vietnamese from 30 to 49 percent.

The process of globalization and integration into the global economy has been consistently followed. A bilateral trade agreement (BTA) with the United States became a reality on July 13, 2000, giving Vietnamese goods "normal trade relations" (NTR) status. However, there have been major disputes over textile and catfish exports to the United States, and the U.S. Congress has consistently linked non-humanitarian aid to Vietnamese attitudes on human rights. After a twelve-year negotiating effort, Vietnam succeeded in becoming a member of the World Trade Organization (WTO) on November 7, 2006. Membership gives Vietnam inestimable opportunities for expansion of trade but also brings with it the responsibility for undertaking legal and financial reforms of the country's economy so that it becomes more open for participation by foreigners. Significantly, WTO membership eliminated textile quotas for Vietnam imposed under the Multifiber Arrangement (MFA) of 1974, which put restrictions on the amount of textiles developing countries could export to developed countries. Notable in the development of Vietnamese foreign trade was the declaration by China and the ASEAN countries in November 2004 to create the world's largest free trade zone by 2010. Vietnam will, indeed, be a part of it.

Foreign direct investment (FDI) has been extremely significant for Vietnam's development, starved as the country was of foreign exchange and capital for a long period. From the beginning of *doi moi* to 2004, Vietnam had received FDI commitments of $46 billion, of which only about 58 percent was made available. The quantum of FDI was hampered by Vietnam's legal framework, corruption, noncooperating and insufficiently motivated bureaucracy, and lack of a commercial banking infrastructure suitable for foreign investment. Since 2004, the government has facilitated the flow of FDI by liberalizing the bank structure particularly in regard to foreign banks. Predictions were for the country to receive an additional $18 billion by 2010. In addition, another $15 billion would come by way of official development assistance (ODA) from international donors, including the World Bank, International Monetary Fund, Asian Development Bank, and foreign states, notably, Japan.

The government's aim of reaching 9 percent growth in 2007 and 2008 was hampered by excessive inflation, which jumped by 14.1 percent in early 2008 and largely accounted for the increase in fuel and foodstuffs by 22 percent. A country once known to the outside world for its fleeing boat people and starving citizens has been transformed into one of the largest exporters of food produce in the world, including rice.

On the one hand, the International Monetary Fund reprimands Vietnam for spending funds saved from tax reforms on public projects and on development of infrastructure, arguing that excessive public spending results in excessive inflation. In contrast, the World Bank encourages the government in the opposite direction, urging it to build megaprojects such as electricity plants to provide a steady supply to industrial projects and even to construct more luxury hotels to promote more FDI.

The main guidelines for the country's economic activity come from the ten-year Economic Plan approved by the Vietnamese Communist party in 2001. The apparent aim is for the country's economy, by 2020, to be predominantly manufacturing-based, technology-led, and export-oriented. Immediately after the plan was unveiled, Vietnam achieved a growth rate of 6 to 7 percent despite the global recession, making the country the second-fastest-growing economy behind only China. A savings drive in the same period registered a 500 percent increase, and official investment figures tripled.

To run a market economy with management suitable for a planned economy is difficult. Among the principal handicaps to growth are rampant corruption, absence of property rights legislation, and inefficient regulation of markets. Notwithstanding some economic activity under the plan, credit was very limited because Vietnamese state-owned commercial banks principally lent funds to the SOEs, whose default rate was very high. In September 2005, as part of the liberalization process, Vietnam privatized all five state-owned banks. The multinationals and companies in which FDI was invested found it hard to manage credit because of the limited activity allowed foreign banks. At the time, foreign banks could hold only minority stock in local banks; for example, Standard Chartered held 15 percent in Asia Commercial Bank, and HSBC Holdings held 13 percent of the Hanoi-based Vietnam Techcombank. In early 2008, Vietnam permitted, for the first time, large foreign banks to open "wholly owned units" in the country. With the new policy in place, HSBC Holdings made Ho Chi Minh City the base of its operations, and Standard Chartered Bank did likewise in Hanoi.

Vietnam's main exports in 2007 amounted to $48.7 billion, derived from crude oil, rice, coffee, tea, fish, clothing, and shoes. Main export destinations were the United States, Japan, China, Australia, Singapore, Germany, and the United Kingdom, in that order. Crude oil represented roughly a quarter of total exports, but that share is likely to decline given that reserves are limited, estimated at 270–500 million tons, and that peak output was reached in 2004 at 403,300 barrels per day. Oil exports could have been much higher in value if the oil could have been refined. As it was, refining capacity was severely limited to 800 barrels a day at the country's single facility at Cat Hai near Ho Chi Minh City.

Vietnam's main imports in 2007 were machinery and equipment, refined petroleum, raw cotton, cement, and motorcycles. These amounted to $52.238 billion, coming mainly from China, Taiwan, Singapore, Japan, South Korea, Thailand, and Malaysia, in that order.

Vietnam is still predominantly an agricultural country with over 75 percent of the population living in the countryside, principally subsisting on agriculture. The ten-year plan begun in 2001 has seen a significant rise in the industrial and manufacturing sector, accounting for a little over 40 percent of the GDP, though employing only about 11 percent of the labor force. Of the new industrial activity, including manufacture and retail, almost one-third of the whole is mainly in and around Ho Chi Minh City.

VIETNAM AND CHINA AFTER THE WITHDRAWAL FROM CAMBODIA

Along with normalizing relations with the United States, Vietnam focused on improving its relations with China. Vietnam's withdrawal from Cambodia in 1989 and the replacement in June 1991 of the anti-China Foreign Minister Nguyen Co Thach by Nguyen Manh Cam smoothened the process. This was followed by the visit of Le Duc Anh, the second-ranking politburo member, to Beijing in July to end the decade-long "abnormality of relations." In November, the two governments announced the normalization of relations with the visit to Beijing of the VCP's new general secretary, Do Muoi, and of the new prime minister, Vo Van Kiet. The two countries signed numerous agreements for opening border trading points and restoring air, sea, rail, and telecommunications links. However, it took an additional five years before the two countries signed a formal agreement in December 1995 to reopen rail links that had been severed for twenty years following the hostilities of the late 1970s.

Most of Vietnam's disputes with China are territorial: the undemarcated 720-mile land border, rival claims over the Tongking and Beibu Gulfs, the extent of each country's continental shelf, and oil exploration rights and the right to build airstrips on Spratly Islands and to place lighthouses in the area.

Soon after the Communist takeover of South Vietnam, the government attempted to occupy the offshore Spratly Islands—known to the Chinese as the Nansha Islands and to the Vietnamese as the Trung Sa—that had, along with the Paracel Islands, been the subject of disputed claims between China and Vietnam in the nineteenth century. The islands suddenly became valuable in the early 1970s for China, Brunei, Malaysia, Taiwan, the Philippines (only the Spratly group), and South Vietnam because of geological surveys indicating rich oil deposits. When the South Vietnamese government officially incorporated the Spratly Islands through a special decree in 1973 and China contested the claim, the DRV and the NLF maintained silence. Beijing took naval and air action in January 1974 and occupied the Paracel Islands, which were closer to the Chinese naval bases. The Spratlys were beyond the range of Chinese support, which was perhaps why China did not prevent the South Vietnamese occupation of those islands. However, China had been making preparations for some time, resulting in its seizure of a few atolls in the Spratly Island group in 1988.

Four years later, in January 1992, China's National Assembly passed a law on the country's territorial waters, claiming numerous islands in the South China Sea, including the Spratly group. New Chinese maps indicated China's sovereignty over most of the China Sea, including all its seabed oil and gas reserves. In May 1992, China unilaterally proceeded to grant the Colorado-based Crestone Energy Corporation the right to explore for oil within what Vietnam claimed was a part of its continental shelf. Hanoi protested; in 1996, it offered a rival company, Conoco, two exploration blocs adjacent to the areas given to Crestone by China. Hanoi also complained of China's continued occupation of thirty-six small areas along the common land border. Experts from the two countries, beginning in February 1992, met to discuss all territorial disputes, including the offshore islands; this did not help, and the issue has defied any solution. There were serious tensions between the two neighbors in 1994, 1996, and 1997 because of potential gas and oil deposits; diplomacy and negotiations have, however, inhibited the use of force.

A major concern of Vietnam is China's entry into the World Trade Organization in September 2001 and the adverse impacts this would have on Vietnamese exports to Western countries and the ability to attract FDI.

Vietnam and ASEAN

Improvement of ties with ASEAN neighbors was of immense importance to Vietnam, equaled perhaps only by the urge for normalization with the United States. This was not only for economic reasons but also for enhancing security vis-à-vis an aggressive China.

Although in the aftermath of its victory in 1975 Vietnam had impressed most ASEAN members with its desire for peace and good neighborliness, its occupation of Cambodia had made it feared and detested by them. In the late 1980s, when it pulled out of Cambodia, Vietnam's relations with the ASEAN improved markedly. Thus in 1988, Vietnam received foreign ministers of Thailand and the Philippines, indicating to the latter its desire to join the ASEAN as a member. And in November 1990, during President Suharto's visit to Hanoi, Vietnam and Indonesia signed an agreement to establish Indovina, the first joint venture for Vietnam with a foreign country. Its tasks included exploring for oil and gas and developing tourism, transport, forestry, and agriculture.

In October 1991, the Vietnamese prime minister, Vo Van Kiet, visited several ASEAN countries and signed a series of agreements with Indonesia, Thailand, Malaysia, and Singapore involving bilateral trade, long-term credits, new consular offices, and exploitation of oil and gas reserves. He was so impressed by Singapore that he invited the architect of Singapore's prosperity, Lee Kuan Yew, to advise Vietnam in its bid to industrialize.

In July 1992, Vietnam signed the 1976 Bali Treaty of Amity and Concord at the ASEAN ministerial meeting and was granted observer status. During the following year, heads of government of three ASEAN member-states—Singapore, Thailand, and the Philippines—visited Vietnam and signed numerous agreements for promotion of trade, investment, and joint ventures in manufacturing. Thailand and Vietnam agreed to establish a joint body to resolve disputes over maritime boundaries and fishing rights. President Ramos of the Philippines, who shared Vietnam's concern over China's seizure of some atolls in the Spratly Islands and claims to the entire South China Sea area, called for a joint exercise of the six countries with claims in the disputed Spratly group—Brunei, China, Malaysia, Philippines, Taiwan, and Vietnam—to demilitarize the area.

Vietnam's full membership of the ASEAN materialized finally on July 28, 1995, as it became the first Communist member of an organization that was founded almost three decades before as an emphatically anti-Communist body. It will, however, take some time before Vietnam can be fully integrated into the ASEAN in the economic sense. Although the other members of the ASEAN were resolved to reduce their tariffs by the year 2003 to create the AFTA, Vietnam was allowed ten years from January 1, 1996, to bring down its tariff to less than 5 percent. Vietnam's membership opened the doors for Cambodia to be accorded the status of observer and later admitted to full membership of ASEAN on April 29, 1999. A few months previously, in December 1998, the United Nations had reinstated Cambodia's seat in the UN General Assembly.

PEACE SETTLEMENT IN CAMBODIA

An international settlement for peace in Cambodia became a reality in October 1991 because the three major external players in that imbroglio—Vietnam and its ally, the Soviet Union, and their common foe, China—decided that the conflict had for too long soured their bilateral relations. Vietnam had pulled out all its troops from Cambodia by September 1989 in the face of its patron, the Soviet Union, manifesting its inability to fund any longer the costs of the Vietnamese occupation of Cambodia. Vietnam also found it necessary to end the occupation because both China and the United States stipulated withdrawal as one of the essential preconditions for the normalization of their relations with Vietnam. China also insisted on Vietnamese guarantees of a major political role for its protégé, the Khmer Rouge, in the postsettlement government of Cambodia. Moreover, a political settlement in Cambodia would remove the most serious irritant in Vietnam's relations with its ASEAN neighbors.

The path to the Paris Accords on Peace in Cambodia traveled an arduous route. It began with Indonesia's initiative by arranging for Jakarta Informal Meetings, to which the diverse Cambodian factions were invited. From July 1988, the peace process gained real momentum with the major external powers conferring at the nineteen-nation Paris Conference on Cambodia (PCC), cochaired by Indonesia and France. A major breakthrough was marked by the PCC's endorsement in August 1990 of the framework document prepared and approved by the four Cambodian factions. Thereafter, negotiations took another fourteen months at three interdependent levels: the Cambodian factions meeting in Jakarta, Indonesia, and Pattaya, Thailand; the PCC meetings; and the PCC cochairs working jointly with the five permanent members of the UN Security Council and the UN Secretary-General's representative, Rafeeuddin Ahmed. Underlying these developments, however, were cataclysmic changes at the global level that created the climate for an international settlement of the Cambodian conflict: the collapse of the Soviet Union and communist Eastern Europe, the rise of the United States to the status of sole superpower, and the readiness of China and Vietnam to mend their mutual relationship.

Progress followed more quickly in the aftermath of the Seventh Congress of the Vietnamese Communist party in June 1991. At the Pattaya meeting of the Cambodian factions, it was announced in the same month that Sihanouk would return to Phnom Penh as head of the Supreme National Council (SNC) and that the four Cambodian factions, including the Khmer Rouge, would work together there under a UN umbrella. At the second meeting at Pattaya in the last week of August under Sihanouk's chairmanship, attended by representatives of the PCC countries, the SNC announced unanimous agreement on all major points: cease-fire and cessation of foreign military assistance; demobilization of the military forces of the four factions; the relationship between the SNC and the United Nations; UNTAC; Cambodia's future political framework; human rights and principles for a new constitution for Cambodia; and international rehabilitation and reconstruction aid. This came to be known as the Pattaya Consensus, which became the basis of the Paris Accords on the Cambodian Conflict on October 23, 1991.

The Paris Accords on Cambodia represented the most ambitious and elaborate peacekeeping effort ever attempted by the United Nations. It was accepted by all Cambodian parties, though with great reluctance and perhaps under duress by the Khmer Rouge (KR). The settlement created UNTAC for a period of eighteen months to two years with vast powers over the government of Cambodia. The UNTAC would deal with the SNC, which would consist of twelve members—six from the existing government of Cambodia—identified with the ruling party, the Cambodian People's party (CPP)—referred to as the State of Cambodia (SOC), and two each from the three rebel factions: FUNCINPEC (the French acronym for National United Front for an Independent, Neutral, Peaceful, and Co-operative Cambodia), Prince Norodom Sihanouk's party, headed by his son Ranaridh; KPNLF (Khmer People's National Liberation Front) under former Cambodian prime minister Son Sann; and the Khmer Rouge (KR). Norodom Sihanouk would be chairman of the SNC. He, along with UNTAC chief Yasushi Akashi, a former Japanese diplomat with considerable experience in UN peacekeeping operations, would have final decision-making powers. The UNTAC would, through its own senior officials, directly oversee the work of the Ministries of Foreign Affairs, Defense, Finance, Public Security, and Information. It would protect the civil rights of all Cambodians including the estimated 350,000 refugees in Thailand, who would be returned and resettled in Cambodia through the assistance of the UN High Commissioner for Refugees (UNHCR). During the first phase, the UNTAC would separate, "canton," and disarm the forces of the various factions and demobilize 70 percent of each of them; the remaining 30 percent would be allowed to stay in cantonments with weapons under UNTAC control. By mid-1992, the UNTAC had deployed nearly 16,000 troops, 3,500 civilian police, and 3,000 civilian officials including those in charge of organizing the elections. The entire operation was estimated to cost $1.9 billion in addition to $600 million for the repatriation and rehabilitation of refugees by the UNHCR.

On the political plane, the UNTAC was entrusted with the task of holding national elections to a constituent assembly in mid- or late 1993. All Cambodians, including the returning refugees, above the age of 18 would be eligible to vote. After the elections were certified by the UN as fair and free, the constituent assembly would draft a constitution within three months on the lines of democratic liberalism, pluralism, universal franchise, and human rights. Thereafter, the constituent assembly would be transformed into a legislative assembly with a new government responsible to it.

A major flaw in the agreements was that the SOC and the resistance factions were allowed to continue to administer the areas and populations under their respective control. While the FUNCINPEC and KPNLF cooperated, the KR refused the UNTAC teams access to the territories it controlled and would not commit its troops to the cantonments or facilitate their disarmament.

In mid-1992, the KR accused UNTAC of failure to create the neutral political environment envisaged in the Paris Accords. It alleged that the SOC was exercising a degree of control over Cambodian life that made fair political competition for other parties impossible, that there were hundreds of thousands of Vietnamese soldiers in the guise of settlers who could not be distinguished from old genuine settlers, and that therefore all Vietnamese must be expelled from Cambodia in order to make the elections fair. The KR made compliance with its demands a precondition for cooperation with the UNTAC. In fact, the KR launched a campaign to eliminate the *youn,* the pejorative Khmer term for the Vietnamese, which assumed alarming proportions from late 1992. It proved to be popular with the Cambodian masses, whose historical hatred against the Vietnamese was thereby exploited by the KR. Not surprisingly, no individual leader or political party, with the sole exception of Norodom Sihanouk, condemned the atrocities against unarmed Vietnamese civilians. A factor contributing to KR intransigence has been its financial independence, thanks to its lucrative timber and gem trade with Thai businessmen and military leaders across the border.

Despite the lack of cooperation from the KR, the UNTAC went ahead with implementation of the Paris agreements. A crucial boost to its activities was provided by the Security Council's unanimous resolution of October 13, 1992, that elections would be held in Cambodia in May 1993 with or without the participation of the KR. The resolution also authorized the PCC co-chairs, Indonesia and France, to intercede with the KR to allow the UNTAC access to KR territories and help in the process of disarming and demobilizing KR troops. The UN Security Council resolution envisaged economic sanctions including cutting off gasoline supplies to the KR and requested the neighboring states, meaning Thailand, to respect the moratorium on the export of logs, gems, and minerals from Cambodia. Neither the UN resolution nor a subsequent ten-nation conference in Beijing in November 1992 produced any positive reaction from the KR.

Ignoring threats from KR to life and limb, 90 percent of the eligible voters exercised their right to vote in the UNTAC-organized general elections on May 23–28, 1993. A UN international volunteer force of 700 drawn from more than 30 countries helped the process from voter registration to the completion of election. The KR boycotted the elections on grounds that the incumbent CPP would rig the elections. However, it was not the CPP but the FUNCINPEC who won with 45.5 percent of the vote and 58 seats in the National Assembly; the ruling CPP received 38.2 percent of the vote and 51 seats; Buddhist Liberal Democratic party (BLDP) got 10 seats and Moulinaka 1 seat. No one had an absolute majority, let alone the two-thirds majority required for the passing of constitutional proposals.

The transition of authority was not completely peaceful. The ruling CPP challenged the election results in four provinces. The SOC threatened to use the forces under its control—100,000 soldiers and 45,000 police—to retain the status quo and deny the electoral results. The leadership of both CPP and FUNCINPEC were divided in regard to the question and modalities of sharing power. A deputy prime minister in the SOC, Prince Chakrapong (son of Norodom Sihanouk, who had differences with him), led a dissident coup and fled the country but was allowed to return without punishment. The national mood was of reconciliation, a feeling that if the opportunity presented by a peacefully, internationally held election was missed, democracy would be doomed in Cambodia. The only person in the fragmented political spectrum who seemed to command general respect and confidence of the people was Norodom Sihanouk, who in the past had successfully worked out compromises in his nation's interest.

Sihanouk played a crucial role during the transition, emerging as a focal point of national unity and an "indispensable vehicle for national reconciliation." First, he declared on June 3, 1993, that he was officially assuming the functions of head of state, premier, and commander of the armed forces in his capacity as "father of the nation, father of national unity, father of reconciliation."[6] On June 14, the newly elected Assembly ratified the arrangement and gave Sihanouk whatever powers he deemed necessary to "save our nation." Sihanouk reconciled the differences between CPP and FUNCINPEC by creating two coequal deputy premiers, his own son Ranaridh and Hun Sen. The governing coalition, which also included BLDP and Moulinaka (an off-shoot of FUNCINPEC), would be in power until the newly elected Assembly drafted a constitution and formed a regular government.

The new constitution promulgated on September 24, 1993, restored the Royal Kingdom of Cambodia with Norodom Sihanouk as king. It also revived the flag and the national anthem of the Sihanouk era. It may be recalled that in 1995 Sihanouk had abdicated his throne in favor of his own father, Suramarit. After the death of King Suramarit in 1960, the then-Parliament elected Sihanouk as head of state and abolished the monarchy. The new constitution provided for a limited monarchy, a pluralist liberal democracy, a state-guided market economy, and a social system guaranteeing economic, social, cultural, and educational rights to all citizens.

Unstable Government and KR's Intransigence

The government of Cambodia under the new constitution has been a coalition of FUNCINPEC, CPP, and BLDP with Norodom Ranaridh of FUNCINPEC being the First Prime Minister and Hun Sen of CPP the Second Prime Minister. They shared the important ministries and jointly controlled the army and the police. An important center of real power in the coalition government was the CPP's Chea Sim, the chairman of the National Assembly. At least three factors helped to hold the coalition until 1997. The first was the influence of the ailing but alert king, Norodom Sihanouk, who threatened to quit his office every time the coalition was threatened by internal dissentions. The second was the widespread corruption helped by plentiful funds from the international agencies. The third was the KR, which provided a common focal point of hostility for the coalition partners in the government.

Since the Paris Accords, the Cambodian government has been propped up by huge donations from the thirty-two-state International Committee on Reconstruction of Cambodia, which meets every year and pledges loans and grants for debt relief, economic adjustment, and a variety of programs to revitalize the ailing economy. Considerable amounts of these funds remained unused because of Cambodia's inadequate absorption capabilities, but they afforded enormous scope to line the pockets of bureaucrats and politicians. Donor countries have insisted that the funds be spent on social and economic projects, improved fiscal management, reduction of the armed forces from 240,000 to 100,000, judicial reform, poverty reduction, and limitation of illegal logging operations. The external funds continue to provide about US$500 million annually, amounting to 60–70 percent of the country's annual budget. The Cambodian government claims that a reduction in military forces began in May 2000 and that by the end of 2001 more than 16,000 soldiers had been demobilized. The process would be faster if more funds were made available to the government for the demobilization!

From the beginning of the Cambodian Settlement, KR has been most uncooperative. It refused to disarm or "canton" 20 percent of its armed forces as provided by the Paris agreements. Instead of providing UNTAC personnel access to the territory under KR control, the KR fired upon their helicopters, wounded many of them in ambushes and minings, captured some of them, and accused them of spying. KR hindered the voter registration drive, destroyed voter cards, and threatened the voters with dire consequences if they participated in the elections. Indeed, as mentioned earlier, it boycotted the elections. After the elections, it demanded that negotiations be held to share power with FUNCINPEC, oust CPP, and force the ethnic Vietnamese to leave Cambodia. Two major efforts were made to conciliate KR for the sake of national unity, particularly at the instance of King Sihanouk. The first consisted of two meetings in Bangkok between the Government of Cambodia and the KR in January and December 1993, one of which was brokered by the Indonesian foreign minister, Ali Alatas. The second consisted of two roundtable conferences in Phnom Penh in the following June; the negotiations were balked by KR's demand for a power-sharing agreement to precede a cease-fire.

Meanwhile in mid-1993, the government ordered the closure of the KR offices in Phnom Penh, and on July 7 the National Assembly declared KR an outlaw organization. The government offered a six-month amnesty for the KR forces to surrender, failing which they would be subject to a thirty-year sentence. As a reaction, the KR announced a "Provisional Government of National Union and National Salvation" with headquarters in the province of Preah Vihear. Over 2,000 KR soldiers took advantage of the amnesty, but at the end of 1995 an estimated 5,000 to 10,000 remained at bay fighting government forces in western Cambodia.

KR and Pol Pot

The KR's forces were decimated by large-scale defections and the government's success between 1993 and 1998 in destroying KR strongholds in western Cambodia. Remnants of the KR were badly divided; a fairly strong faction under the much-feared KR's chief of staff, Ta Mok, headed the KR "government" in the heavily mined Anlong Veng. In July 1997, Ta Mok brought Pol Pot to "trial" by a "people's tribunal," which sentenced him to life imprisonment. At the trial, Pol Pot refused to accept responsibility for the mass murders and insisted that evidence such as that found at Tuol Sieng prison in Phnom Penh was fabricated by the Vietnamese. A few months later, in March 1998, it was Ta Mok's turn to face mutiny when an estimated 1,000 KR guerrillas rebelled against him. Government troops pushed forward to rendezvous with guerrilla renegades as they pursued Ta Mok and his "prisoner," Pol Pot, east toward Preah Vihear. By the end of the year, virtually all of the KR leadership, including its political chief, Khieu Samphan, and its chief ideologue, Nuon Chea, surrendered to the government forces. Ta Mok was captured on March 6, 1999, on the Thai border, thereby marking the end, after twenty-five years of insurgency, of the KR.

At some point during the government's drive against Ta Mok, he was reported to be considering handing over Pol Pot to the government to stand trial. Reports also indicated that Pol Pot died on April 15, 1998, perhaps by suicide, perhaps by being poisoned by Ta Mok or his men.

Hun Sen Ousts Ranaridh

In July 1997, the same month that Pol Pot was brought to trial, the coalition government fell apart when Second Prime Minister Hun Sen ousted First Prime Minister Prince Ranaridh. The CPP's superior forces overpowered those loyal to the royalist faction, imprisoning and executing forty-three Ranaridh supporters. Hun Sen declared that FUNCINPEC Foreign Minister Ung Huoi had replaced Ranaridh as second prime minister. This "revolution" threatened to wreck the underlying spirit of the coalition government so painstakingly put together by UNTAC and international donors, notably Japan. They now pressed and prevailed upon Hun Sen to hold a show trial of Prince Ranaridh, who had been accused of consorting with the KR and smuggling weapons, and then acquit him through the king's power to pardon.

Cambodian politics is dominated by the durable (since 1985) Prime Minister Hun Sen, a former KR leader who heads the pro-Vietnam ruling party, the Cambodian People's party (CPP). In the 2003 elections to the 123-seat National Assembly, the CPP won 73 seats, and the rivals FUNCINPEC and Sam Rainsy party (SRP) won, respectively, 26 and 24. However, no government could be formed for over a year because the constitution prescribed a two-thirds majority for the ruling party. Neither the FUNCINPEC nor the SRP would conciliate and agree to join the CPP and form a coalition government. Finally, on July 15, 2004, thanks to King Norodom Sihanouk's active intervention, it was agreed that the king appoint Hun Sen prime minister by a royal decree and that the two opposition parties give their consent. Underlying such an "agreement" was a "package deal" that would give the position of president of the National Assembly to Prince Ranaridh of the FUNCINPEC, create 7 positions of deputy prime minister, and appoint as many as 26 cabinet-rank ministers.

A major change in Cambodian politics soon after the installation of the 2004 government was the abdication—not for the first time in Cambodian history—of the popular and much revered King Norodom Sihanouk. His domination of Cambodian politics for more than a half century between 1949 and 2004 was made possible by a combination of his extraordinary ability to play opposing parties domestically and rival powers internationally. Often called mercurial by his critics, he had a steady, charismatic hold over the Cambodian masses, who still regard the monarch as having a divine essence.

Under the current constitution of 1993, the Cambodian monarchy, like its British counterpart, is a constitutional or limited monarchy, with the king having only a ceremonial role. Under that constitution, Norodom Sihanouk had been named king and head of state for life, with no provision for resignation or abdication. Even so, Sihanouk announced on October 7, 2004, that he was abdicating the throne. His fifty-one-year-old son Norodom Sihamoni, who, unlike his father, had lived most of his life in France and Czechoslovakia as a ballet dancer, succeeded him. His name, Sihamoni, is a combination of his father's name, Sihanouk, and his mother's, Monineath. There was then no legal procedure for the selection of the monarch. Therefore, a new law creating a nine-member Royal Throne Council was passed within a week on October 12 by the National Assembly and the Senate. Accordingly, the Royal Throne Council—consisting of the president of the National Assembly, the prime minister, the chiefs of the Orders of Mohanikay and Thammayut, and the first and second vice president of the Assembly—met on October 14 and adopted the recommendation made by King Norodom Sihanouk that his only surviving son, Prince Sihamoni, from his current wife, Queen Monineath, be the next king. On that occasion, the National Assembly bestowed an unprecedented title on the venerable Sihanouk: *preahmahaviraksat,* loosely translated in Khmer as eminent man, in English as king-father, and in French as *roi-pere.*

The KR Trial

With the defeat and capture of the KR leadership in early 1999, domestic and international organizations clamored for legal proceedings against those who had perpetrated torture and mass killings in the country for a quarter century. Since mid-1999, protracted negotiations among Cambodian, UN, and third-party intermediaries have taken place sporadically to work out the modalities of a trial. Prime Minister Hun Sen supported a trial of former KR leaders for crimes against humanity, but with the qualification that those who supported them should also be brought to justice in accordance with the Cambodian judicial system, with international legal assistance, including foreign judges and prosecutors. Against demands from the United States and other Western countries that the trial's focus be on the period of the KR (1975–1979), Hun Sen demanded that the period be extended from 1970 to 1998 so as to include the U.S. bombing of Cambodia in the early 1970s and the years of support by China, Thailand, and the United States to the KR after 1979. Earlier, in December 1998, when major leaders of the KR (Khieu Samphan and Nuon Chea) had surrendered, Hun Sen at first offered amnesty. Thanks to the UN-requested intervention of U.S. Senator Robert Kerry, a tentative agreement was reached over the procedures required to establish a special tribunal. The UN conceded to Cambodia the right to appoint one or two prosecutors and to appoint three to the panel of five judges; the other two would be nominated by the UN. The proposal met the final approval of the Cambodian parliament in January 2001. The cumbersome system provided that Cambodian and foreign prosecutors and judges would constitute a "mixed tribunal" that would prosecute the case. Although foreign judges would be in the minority, they would retain the power of veto. In August 2001, the KR tribunal law was approved by the National

Assembly of Cambodia. It had, however, to be approved by the Senate and ratified by the King and then "examined" by the UN. The UN urged the Cambodian government to make some crucial changes in the law and provide certain clarifications in order for the law to conform with international standards to assure a fair trial. Only then would the UN sign a memorandum of understanding to provide Cambodia with funding, technical support, and international jurists to participate in the proceedings. Without UN support, a KR tribunal would suffer in credibility and funding.

Negotiations between the United Nations and Hun Sen's government dragged on for five years before an agreement was signed on March 17, 2003, to establish an international tribunal consisting of Cambodian and foreign judges to try the surviving Khmer Rouge leaders. The tribunal would consist of a Trial Chamber consisting of Cambodian and international judges. There would additionally be a Supreme Court Chamber consisting of Cambodian and international judges to hear appeals. By May 2006, the two parties agreed to have seventeen Cambodian and ten international judges. The proceedings were expected to last three years, involving an expenditure estimated at $56.3 million, of which the United Nations would pay $43 million and the Cambodian government the balance of $13.3 million. Prolonged debates and dissent marked the preliminaries. Thus, it took another four years, until June 2007, for the tribunal, called the Extraordinary Chambers in the Courts of Cambodia (ECCC), to adopt the 113 articles for governing its operation. By that time, most of the top KR leaders were dead or had been granted amnesty. As former king Norodom Sihanouk remarked, there were only some "old, sickly, unrepentant individuals" from the KR remaining to be tried. Was it worth the effort? In fact, the top KR leader, Pol Pot, primarily responsible for the "killing fields," was dead in 1998 and his top commander, the "Butcher" Ta Mok , died in May 2006. With most of the others including Khieu Samphan and Ieng Sary having been awarded amnesty, only one major KR figure remained in custody in that year: Kang Kek Ieu, nicknamed "Duch."

Economic Reconstruction

The Pol Pot regime's excesses completely destroyed the economic infrastructure of the country, which was hardly developed under French colonial rule. During the Pol Pot period, a whole generation of professionals—teachers, university academics, bureaucrats, businessmen—had been wiped out, leaving a largely young population with little opportunity for guidance from elders and little respect for the country's culture and heritage. KR remnants fighting government forces in the western parts had no respect for heritage and smuggled carvings from Angkor Wat and Angkor Thom across Thailand for sale to dealers in antiquities from the Western world. In the 1990s, with UNESCO's support, the Cambodian government was able to seek the cooperation of enforcement agencies of Western nations and Interpol to arrest the loot of national treasures; in November 1999, Thailand, a member of ASEAN, handed over to the visiting Cambodian foreign minister more than 100 illegally traded antiquities seized by Bangkok authorities from local markets.

The decade of Vietnamese occupation of Cambodia (1979–1989) did little to revitalize the Cambodian economy. In fact, years of sporadic warfare with KR forces did not help the construction of a viable national economy. It is only since the Paris Accords and the infusion of large funds by several Western countries and Japan that the Cambodian economy began to pick up. In the second half of the 1990s, with relative peace prevailing in the country, the economy (based on rice and fish) revived and returned traditional contentment to the peasantry. The infusion of foreign aid and capital helped the growth of the textile and garment manufacturing sectors, with popular Western brand names exploiting Cambodia's low wage structure. More than 100 new factories sprang up to take advantage of the U.S. market. However, the imposition of quotas by the United States toward the end of the 1990s and the signing of the bilateral trade agreement between the United States and Vietnam in July 2000 began to affect industry in Cambodia.

Poor economies often impel the depredation of natural wealth. In 2000, an Asian Development Bank study characterized Cambodia's forest management program as "a total system failure." In January of that year, the government claimed to take stringent measures against illegal logging; opposition parties appealed to foreign aid donors to make any assistance conditional upon the adoption of genuine measures against illegal logging operations in western Cambodia. A major problem in the drive against illegal loggers has been their collusion with army commanders, who have become virtual rulers in some districts, making law enforcement ineffective in those areas. With the progressive demobilization of military forces, the problem may get worse unless the government assists in enforcement with gun-mounted helicopters to survey the affected regions.

27

Tsunami, Cyclone,
Avian Influenza, and
Terrorism in Southeast Asia

TSUNAMI

The tsunami that rolled across the Indian Ocean on December 26, 2004, affected several countries. Although Indonesia, Thailand, Sri Lanka, and South India were hit hardest, several other countries, including Bangladesh, Malaysia, Singapore, Myanmar, and Somalia, sustained damage. The tsunami's epicenter was off the coast of Acheh in West Sumatra, in Indonesia, north of Simulue Island, at a depth of nineteen miles. It took a toll of more than 250,000 people in eleven countries. The worst-hit population center was Banda Acheh in West Sumatra, Indonesia, with 128,000 dead and about 40,000 missing. In some areas, the coastal waves were as high as 100 feet and, as in northwest Sumatra, along a 60-mile sea coast. A second earthquake measuring 8.6 on the Richter scale occurred on March 28, 2005, in northern Sumatra.

The word *tsunami* comes from Japanese, *tsu* meaning harbor and *nami* meaning waves. There is possibly only one other language that has a word for the phenomenon. The word *aazhi peeralai* in the Tamil language in South India speaks of the devastating waves that rose some 700 years ago, among the structures affected being the famous Mahabalipuram temples near Chennai.

Tsunamis are caused by submarine earthquakes. The event of December 26, 2004, is now known as the Great Sumatra–Andaman earthquake (GSAE) or the Asian Tsunami. The magnitude of the earthquake was 9.3, with the longest duration lasting between 8.3 and 10 minutes. It caused the entire planet to rattle briefly, triggering earthquakes in many areas. The GSAE was the most intensive earthquake since 1964 and the second largest since the Kamchatka earthquake of 1737. Seismic experts agree that of all similar events releasing huge volumes of ocean water at the point of ruptures in the previous century, roughly 12 percent, or one-eighth, was released by the GSAE. According to the U.S. Geological Survey

(USGS), the energy released by the GSAE was the equivalent of 23,000 Hiroshima-type atomic bombs.[1]

The GSAE caused an estimated one thousand miles of fault-line slippage along the subduction zone where the India Plate slides under the Burma Plate. The India Plate is the western part of the Indo-Australian Plate that slides toward northeast at an average of 2 inches per year, nearing the Burma Plate at the Sunda Trench, which runs roughly parallel to Sumatra's west coast for about 15 miles and where the India Plate "subducts" beneath the Burma Plate. The latter covers the Indian Nicobar and Andaman Islands as well as West Sumatra. The interface between the two plates resulted in a large fault, called an interplate thrust, located below the region of southwest Sumatra and the Andaman Islands in the area of the Sunda Trench. There were, in fact, two slippages of the plates moving past one another spanning a few minutes. The first one caused a rupture of about 250 miles long and 60 miles wide, beginning off the coast of Acheh, moving northward for about one and a half minutes. The second rupture happened after a lapse of less than two minutes, was somewhat slower than the first, and occurred when the two plates pushed past one another but in the opposite direction.

Predictably, the region was rocked by numerous aftershocks, the largest of them being near the island of Nias, recording 8.7 on the Richter scale. This event was so large that it had its own aftershocks. Some of the islands, for example, the Andaman and Nicobar Islands, may have moved southwest by about four feet, and portions of some of the smaller islands off the coast of West Sumatra have moved below sea level.

The earthquake itself was in the north-south direction, creating tsunami waves in the east-west direction. While northwest Sumatra was immediately affected, it was two hours before Thailand was hit. There was a similar time lapse for it to hit Sri Lanka and Southeast India and as much as seven hours to reach the Somalia coast. Statistics vary, but according to the United Nations, 186,983 people died, and 42,883 were missing. The figures for Myanmar were not available, the government there claiming only 61 dead, although unofficial figures estimate the human loss in Myanmar at ten times that number. Nearly one-third of the dead were children, and possibly four times more women died than men. The losses in Thailand among foreign tourists were the highest, possibly as many as 9,000, many from northern Europe, with 543 from Sweden and an estimated 500 from Germany.

The economic losses—short-term and long-term—were enormous, beyond the comprehension or hope of the sufferers, especially the coastal fishing communities. Loss of boats and trawlers and other accoutrements of the fishing industry all but wiped out export earnings. Maritime trade was similarly affected throughout most of the western Indian Ocean region. The existing buoys and other aids for navigation in the region, including in the vital Strait of Malacca, were displaced both by disastrous waves and the earthquakes. As *National Geographic* reported, "December's tsunami clogged shipping lanes, rearranged coasts, and created new islands."[2] Tourist spots, especially in southern Thailand and Malaya, would not attract foreigners for a considerable time.

The damage done to the environment, yet to be gauged fully, is beyond measure. The subterranean water table has been poisoned from seepage of the ocean saltwater, which has affected both drinking water and irrigation water in the paddies. Considerable areas of cultivable land have been rendered useless for growing crops as the soil micro-organisms have been killed. Both land and sea ecosystems have been severely damaged. As of 2008, no conclusive results of the environmental assessment made by the UN Environment Program (UNEP), which has allocated US$1 million for a study, have been available. The Southeast Asian governments—notably Thailand, Indonesia, Malaysia, and Singapore—have been cooperating with the UNEP and several other study groups sent to the region, primarily by the United States, Australia, Great Britain, and India.

Very few events can equal this tsunami for inspiring so many people in so many countries to feel the pain and donate so much. The humanitarian response in monetary terms amounted to over US$7 billion. Kofi Annan, then UN secretary-general, estimated that it would take five to ten years for completion of the reconstruction and rehabilitation work. The international humanitarian response was astounding. Indonesia's neighbor, Australia, gave an economic aid package of US$760.6 million to Indonesia and another $60 million to the other countries affected; Germany offered $660 million, Japan $500 million, Canada $343 million, Norway and the Netherlands $183 million each, Italy $113 million, the British people about $600 million with a nearly equal amount from their government, and the World Bank $250 million.

Nearer the site of the event, ASEAN members offered assistance. Singapore was moved emotionally. A government minister said: "The tsunami has dramatically changed many people's attitude towards its neighbours. For this generation of Singaporeans, who have rarely experienced hardship, it is a reality check, a grim reminder that they cannot live in isolation from the world outside." Singapore sent a 1,000-member force, including 100 surgeons, to Indonesia and Thailand. A makeshift hospital with sufficient equipment for emergency surgeries was established. The bulk of the assistance went to Acheh province, particularly the worst-hit town, Meulaboh, which had no access because roads were washed away or clogged by debris. Singapore flew in tractors and excavators by heavy Puma and Chinook helicopters from platforms of two naval vessels in order to open roads and to establish a docking port and aircraft landing zones. It was Singapore's largest overseas relief operation, costing the island state S$21 million every two weeks for several months in addition to cash assistance of US$15 million and S$18 million collected by the Red Cross from Singapore's population.

U.S. assistance came in through several announcements over a period of time, totaling $950 million. President Bush announced that the U.S. effort would be led by two former presidents, George Bush Sr. and Bill Clinton. The U.S. Navy's work was outstanding—its rescue and relief work was mounted within hours of the disaster. The United States is a major participant in the West Sumatra International Tsunami Survey Team (ITST), consisting of 12 U.S. and 5 Indonesian scientists. The information they collect and their recommendations will help mitigate damage from future tsunamis in the region. Their suggestions may include management of coastal development, including identification of favorable locations for public buildings or infrastructure. The ITST's work is funded principally by the U.S. Agency for International Development's Office of Foreign Disaster Assistance.

Political Impact

The political impact of the tsunami and earthquakes was clearly established in Acheh in West Sumatra, where for the previous three decades an armed conflict had severely strained the province's relations with the central government. The intensely devout Islamic community of the region regarded the natural catastrophe as Allah's wrath toward Muslims for killing Muslims, a reaction that strengthened the voices advocating peace. The worst tsunami in their memory had hit Acheh's capital, Banda Acheh, leaving a third of its population either dead or missing. The rebel leaders declared a ceasefire within two days of the catastrophe, on December 28, 2004, citing the tsunami as the reason for their conciliatory attitude and agreeing to talks with the Jakarta government. The happy result was the signing of a peace agreement on August 15, 2005, providing for political autonomy for the province and approving a constitutional amendment permitting GAM to function as a party without meeting the requirement of having its headquarters in Jakarta and branch offices in at least half the provinces.

The Future

By April 2005, ASEAN's Subcommittee on Meteorology and Geophysics (SCMG) had set up a technical task force to explore the possibility of collating data from existing and future networks of seismic stations, tide gauges, and buoys in Southeast Asia. The task force identified the seismic stations for "waveform" data exchange and created a mechanism for member states to exchange seismic and tsunami information over the Global Telecommunications System (GTS). This was adopted at the subcommittee's meeting in August 2005.

Of major significance for the future are U.S. efforts to link its existing tsunami warning system in the Pacific with the South and Southeast Asian region. The United States also announced plans to expand tsunami detection and early-warning capabilities as part of its Global Earth Observation System of Systems (GEOSS). The U.S. National Oceanic and Atmospheric Administration (NOAA) declared it would deploy thirty-two new deep-ocean assessment and reporting of tsunami (DART) buoys, extending its coverage throughout the Pacific Ocean Basin and regularly recording sea surface heights and transmitting the data via satellites.

CYCLONE NARGIS

The unfortunate people of Myanmar, already suffering under the continuing military dictatorship and not fully recovered from the 2004 tsunami, experienced yet another disaster on May 2, 2008, when a storm that officials designated as Cyclone Nargis hit the Irrawaddy River Delta. Estimates were that about 146,000 people died and thousands more were missing. Two townships were practically wiped out: Labutta lost about 80,000 persons, and Bogale may have lost over 10,000. Even months later, no one knew the exact numbers of dead and missing or of refugees from the tragedy. Property damage was estimated at US$10 billion.

The name given the cyclone, Nargis, is not Burmese but Urdu and Persian, meaning daffodil, the name of the most-loved and admired Indian cinema actress of yesteryear. According to the Indian Meteorological Department (IMD), it was the first storm of the season, with its origins in the Bay of Bengal on April 27. It moved northwestward, weakening for a day or two and then picking up the pace on May 2 with a speed of 105 miles per hour. It was categorized a cyclone 4 on the standard rating scale and was identified as the eighth-deadliest cyclone ever in the northern Indian Ocean. The cyclone almost bypassed the principal city of Yangon, as it headed northeast and remained a force, albeit weak, until it reached the Myanmar-Thai border.

The IMD had alerted Myanmar on April 30 about the possible development of what it termed "very severe cyclone storm Nargis." The IMD had warned Indian fishermen and other coastal communities in eastern and southeastern parts of the country much earlier. Fishing communities were asked not to sail and the others asked to rush premonsoon agricultural preparedness activities and remain indoors. The Bangladesh government acted likewise. Many observers surmised that Myanmar's authorities may not have heeded the IMD's advice to take advance steps and warn people.

Relief Activities

The event attracted world attention, of governments and charity organizations, of ordinary citizens and major humanitarian bodies, not only because of the magnitude of the suffering but also because of the frustration the Myanmar government caused by closing the doors to all external entities trying to enter the country. The military government had a completely unjustified confidence that it was capable of taking care of all the people's distress. More important, the government was concerned that outsiders would comment adversely on the repressive regime that had kept an unaccounted number of political activists, including the Nobel Prize–winning Aung San Suu Kyi, under restraint for years without the benefit of a trial. President George Bush roundly condemned Myanmar's military leaders for not accepting the U.S. offer to send its naval craft to the region for rescue operations. Many countries approached the Myanmar officials through their ambassadors but to no avail. The first breakthrough came a few days after the tragedy when Myanmar accepted India's request to help. India also urged that Myanmar accept U.S. humanitarian aid; Myanmar agreed.

India launched *Operation Sahayata,* or Operation Assistance. Two Indian Navy ships carrying more than one hundred metric tons, and two Indian Air Force planes carrying a total of eight tons of supplies, brought in the first international assistance to Myanmar. A couple of days later, on May 8, Indian planes flew in an additional thirty-two tons of relief supplies including medicine. The Myanmar government also permitted India to establish two small hospitals in the thickly populated Irrawaddy Delta and to fly about six tons of medicines, mainly painkillers, antibiotics, and vaccines, to the region.

Neighboring countries sent an assessment team and 30 medical personnel per each member state. The states comprising the ASEAN sent additional assistance. The Malaysian government offered a half million Malaysian dollars in the form of blankets, noodles, and medicines. Mercy Malaysia, a nongovernmental organization, sent 180 doctors to South Myanmar. By the fourth week of the month, the

Malaysian Red Crescent Society had sent two disaster relief teams and sent a thousand items each of blankets and mosquito nets, 500 mats, 7,000 mineral water bottles, and 500 first aid kits. Malaysia also served as a conduit for the first U.S. financial aid of US$1 million. In addition to financial assistance, Malaysian aid in the form of relief supplies amounted to over US$4 million. Thailand sent medicines and medical equipment worth about US$31.3 million. It also sent 20 medical teams and 20 communicable-disease suppression units. All this and more in the nature of food supplies, drinking water, and construction materials were flown in to Yangon in C-130 transport planes.

Political Implications

The military junta behaved irrationally and inhumanely in the first few days after the storm. It drastically played down the numbers of people affected and made every effort to see that outsiders would not enter the country, in their view, to use the event to criticize the regime for its suppression of democracy. The government professed its capability to handle any calamity, natural or man-made, and to help its citizens without need for external assistance. It rejected the requests of the Thai prime minister, Samak Sundaravej, as well as the U.K. ambassador to Thailand to visit the country and assess the cyclone damage. The U.S. request to help was rudely turned down, and the UN's warning that Myanmar should not decline international humanitarian assistance was ignored. There was acute international concern that the Myanmar government's inaction might amount to genocide, that there could be a severe outbreak of disease because of thousands of dead bodies left on the ground or floating in flood waters. Fortunately for sufferers, the Myanmar government had excellent relations with the Indian government and agreed with the latter to accept food, drinking water, and medicines from outside. It also agreed to allow India and Malaysia to act as conduits for U.S. assistance.

AVIAN INFLUENZA

The outbreak of avian influenza in mid-2003 made people in all Asian countries, if not around the globe, nervous because of its potential to become a pandemic threat. The virus could just as well be called Asian influenza because the countries reporting it within six months of the first case were all Asian: Vietnam, Japan, Thailand, Cambodia, Laos, Indonesia, South Korea, and China. Malaysia joined the group in August 2004; Russia, Kazakhstan, Turkey, and Romania became the non-Asian countries affected in the second half of 2005 along with Mongolia. Myanmar reported its first outbreak in February 2006. Myanmar's Health Department promptly killed 700,000 chickens and ducks. Of the countries affected by the flu strain (H5N1), three countries have reported control of their poultry outbreaks and were declared by the World Health Organization (WHO) free of disease: Japan, Malaysia, and the Republic of Korea.

Avian influenza, or "bird flu," is a contagious viral affliction for animals, mostly infecting birds and sometimes pigs. It has killed about 150 million birds, including poultry, but it has only rarely crossed the species barrier and infected humans. When it does, however, the virus is usually fatal. To date, it has occurred in eight countries, five of them in Southeast Asia: Cambodia, Indonesia, Myanmar, Thailand, and Vietnam. The worst possibility is that the virus may mutate into a more lethal form that can pass from human to human. Of the avian influenza viruses that have crossed the species barrier, H5N1 has been responsible for causing quick death among humans. In the last five years, more than half those infected by H5N1 died. Almost all the cases involved healthy young adults or children. So far, more than 200 humans have died in Indonesia, Laos, Vietnam, Romania, China, Turkey, and Russia, with the worst affected being Indonesia. The WHO reported on September 10, 2008, that of the 137 cases infected by H5N1 in Indonesia, 112 died: 13 in 2005, 45 in 2006, 37 in 2007, and 17 in 2008; the largest numbers were in Banten with 25; Jakarta, 29; and West Java, 26. The latest case of a human being infected with H5N1 was in Myanmar, which reported its only case of human infection in December 2007 as being a seven-year-old girl from Shan state. Despite serious efforts by the governments of the countries affected to contain the virus, WHO fears that the virus may become pandemic, that the incidence of human to human infection may increase, and that it could be a global risk to humans. WHO estimates it would take several years to control the H5N1 and that it should be done before it becomes pandemic.

TERRORISM

Southeast Asia has, for some time, been a major region for terrorism, particularly in Malaysia, southern Thailand, southern Philippines, and Indonesia. Singapore has also been a target of planned terrorist activity, especially its strategic facilities and U.S. embassy and corporations. Until the turn of the millennium, militant movements in Southeast Asia were not international in scope. The groups asked for autonomy based on ethnicity or religion for a part of the existing state, such as the ethnic minorities in Myanmar and Muslim minorities in southern Thailand and the southern Philippines. In the case of Indonesia, separatist movements were based on neither, such as in Acheh, Papua, or East Timor. After 1999, there was a coalescing of militant movements based particularly on their common religion, Islam, with the goal of creating a pan-Islamic state. Because of the commonality of objectives between such an international Islamic movement and the more widely known Middle East–based Al-Qaeda, some ties were discovered between them. Such connections made Southeast Asia an area of interest to Western countries, particularly the United States after the September 11, 2001, attack on the Twin Towers in New York City. Around the same time, the Singapore government became interested in the phenomenon because of its suspicion that it would be a part of the intended pan-Islamic state, drawing support from the Muslim minority, both of Malaysian and Indian origin. The Singapore government arrested a significant number of terrorists—15 in December 2001 and 18 in September 2002. Its Internal Security Department (ISD) conducted extensive interviews and produced a major White Paper on terrorism in the region, including its causes and what steps the Singapore government was taking to contain and eradicate the threat it poses. Its president's remarks to the opening session of its Parliament on March 25, 2002, still apply to Singapore and other states of Southeast Asia:

The Taleban [*sic*] and Al-Qaeda may have been routed in Afghanistan, but global terrorism is far from defeated. Terrorist cells, linked to global networks, exist in many countries, including in Southeast Asia. The Jemaah Islamiyah terrorist group is a stark reminder that these are not faraway problems, but immediate threats to us here and now. The danger to us is twofold. Firstly, we are directly at risk of terrorist attacks, especially by Islamic terrorist groups originating elsewhere in the region. Such attacks will cause suspicion and arouse enmity between our races. Secondly, the US action against global terrorism may cause repercussions in Muslim countries, and complicate the situation in Southeast Asia.[3]

Of the several terrorist groups operating in diverse countries of Southeast Asia, the Jemaah Islamiyah (JI) is the most powerful. Its current membership may be several thousand, many of them alumni of a religious boarding school, Al Mukmin, founded in the 1970s by Abu Bakar Bashir and the late Abdullah Sungkar. Two decades later, in 1993 or 1994, the duo founded JI as well. When Abdullah Sungkar died in 1999, Abu Bakar Bashir became the spiritual leader of the groups—both Al Mukmin and JI.

Other major JI leaders are Abu Jabril and Riduan Islamuddin, the latter widely known as Hambali. The JI is, in a sense, successor to the well-known organization Darul Islam (House of Islam) in Indonesia's nationalist movement. After fighting the Dutch and participating with other nationalist forces to gain the country's independence in 1949, the Darul Islam continued with an armed movement whose goal was to establish an Islamic state in Indonesia.

The Indonesian government under Sukarno, however, made the Pancasila, which included secularism, its main ideology. His successor, Suharto, continued to follow secularism, and because of his strong anti-Islam attitude toward the Darul Islam and the threat of arrest, some of its leaders, including Bashir and his mentor, Abdullah Sungkar, fled to Malaysia in 1985, where they established the JI. Its long-term goal is to establish a pan-Islamic Daulah Islamiyah, or Islamic state. Centered in Indonesia, the state would embrace Malaysia, the southern Philippines, southern Thailand, and Brunei. The Singapore government argues that such a state would inevitably include Singapore as well, creating thereby an Islamic state that would cover the entire archipelago.

JI formed an extremely well-structured body with four functional committees for fundraising, religious indoctrination, military training, and acquisition of weapons. The JI's armed brigades, four in number, were allotted to four geographical areas in Southeast Asia and were subdivided into battalions, platoons, and squads.[4] The JI's *iqtisod* (economic wing) has many businesses as components, with each pledging to contribute 10 percent of its profits to the *Iqtisod*. Hambali assumed control over the special fund called *Infaq Fisabillah* (Fund for Islamic Cause), which provided money for training JI members in Afghanistan or the southern Philippines. It also pays for recruitment of young members; for support payments to families of members who die in action; for arms and bomb-making materials; and for special Islamic schools (*madrassas*). Hambali maintains that he has refused to take monetary aid from Al-Qaeda. JI's principal executive leader is Hambali, but its chief bomb-maker has been Fathur Rohman Al-Ghozi, an Indonesian.

The Indonesian Islamic militant organizations were suppressed during the Sukarno regime and even more severely during the Suharto regime. After the downfall of Suharto in 1999, the JI became very active and began to nurture its dream of a pan-Islamic state in Southeast Asia. In that year, the JI formed a regional alliance of similar groups, all believing in *jihad* (holy war). Abu Bakar Bashir was named the *amir* (supreme leader) of this alliance called the Rabitaful Mujahidin (RM), or the Coalition of Mujahidin. The coalition would share the resources of its units for training, arms, and finance. The first task RM accomplished was to attack the interests of the Philippines in Indonesia by throwing a bomb at the Philippine ambassador's home in Jakarta in August 2000 and killing two persons. Meanwhile, a JI-associated group, the Majelis Mujahidin Indonesia (MMI), executed its plan to bomb churches in several Indonesian cities on Christmas Eve, 2000. In the same year, the JI bombed the light railway train in Manila, killing 22 persons. It is not clear what the MMI's exact affiliation was to the JI because the MMI's militant wing, known as Laskar Jundullah (Army of Allah), seems to have been specifically charged with targeting churches in the Malukus and Sulawesi islands, which have sizable Christian populations. The anti-Christian attacks also involved a number of radical Arabs, possibly with Al-Qaeda connections.

The JI was specially investigated after Singapore's Internal Security Department in December 2001 discovered two JI cells with elaborate plans to bomb U.S., Australian, British, and Israeli facilities and citizens in the island state. Singapore also discovered JI's links with militant units in the Philippines and Malaysia, the latter being the coordinating unit for bombing attacks in Singapore. Later, the United States found evidence of links between JI and the 9/11 attacks in New York. The FBI claimed proof that Zacharias Moussaoui, who was tried in the United States for his links to the 9/11 hijackers, had visited Malaysia and had been helped financially there.

Bombings in Bali, Indonesia

A major bombing attack on a nightclub in the tourist resort of Bali on October 12, 2002, killing about 200 and injuring about 300 persons, including diverse nationals such as Americans, Australians, Canadians, Europeans, Japanese, as well as Indonesians, attracted world attention to a possible nexus between JI and Al-Qaeda, who were blamed for the reprehensible killings. The incident forced the Indonesian government, for the first time, to take an active role in investigating the JI and its possible links with Al-Qaeda. Indonesia arrested some suspects, including a senior JI commander, Ali Gufron, who was put on trial in the first half of 2003. More significant was the arrest of the topmost "spiritual leader" of the JI, Abu Bakar Bashir, who was charged with past acts of terrorism and involvement with attempts on the life of the then vice president, Megawati Sukarnoputri. After a trial, Bashir received a four-year jail sentence (later reduced by the country's Supreme Court, and Bashir was released in mid-2004). In August 2003, another suspect in the Bali attacks, Amrozi, was sentenced to death. Around the same time, the Indonesian government gained for itself special powers in dealing with terrorism and approached the UN to add JI to its list of terrorist organizations. The suspects were put on trial: Thirty were convicted with sentences of varying length, and three were sentenced to death.

The Bali killings prompted the visits of high-level U.S. officials to Bali, including President Bush's three-hour visit on October 22, 2003, and longer visits by U.S. Attorney General John Ashcroft and Secretary for Homeland Security Tom Ridge. In February 2004, a twenty-six-nation regional conference was held and focused on counterterrorism. An outcome of all such meetings was a comprehensive plan of cooperation between Indonesia and the United States providing funds for the establishment of an Indonesian police counterterrorism unit; training for Indonesian police and security officials; exchange of information between Indonesian intelligence and the U.S. Treasury Department on international money laundering and financing; and training of Indonesian military units in counterterrorism.

J. W. Marriott Hotel Bombing

Equally shocking but with far less loss of human life was the bombing of the J. W. Marriott (JWM) Hotel in Jakarta on August 5, 2003, killing 12 and wounding 150. It was, indeed, designed to drive terror into the hearts of Western tourists and prominent property owners. The JWM entrance lobby was destroyed, and the whole multilevel structure was shaken, unnerving the guests and the staff. This time, the government's security and intelligence officials were active in apprehending the miscreants. Twenty-four suspects were arrested, mostly members of the JI, which was blamed for the bombing. All were put on trial. One of them, Rusman Gunawan (known as "Gun Gun"), was sentenced to four years in prison for facilitating the transfer of funds. He had spent some time in Pakistan and was a member of a special JI cell called Al Ghuraba.

A notable fact that emerged from the investigations of the suspects in the JWM case was that the JI had split into two wings, one supporting Osama bin Laden and his priority to bomb Western, mostly U.S. facilities. The other group's priority was to continue the effort to establish a pan-Islamic state in Southeast Asia.

The Abu Sayyaf Group (ASG) in the Philippines

In the beginning of the new millennium, the Muslim separatist movement in the southern Philippines was led by a particularly vicious Muslim group operating in West Mindanao and the Sulu archipelago. The Abu Sayyaf Group (ASG) became widely known for a series of kidnappings of foreigners, especially Americans. Of the three Americans kidnapped in early 2001, one was killed that June. The other two, the Burnham couple, were missionaries, who revealed in March 2002 that they had arranged, with the knowledge of the FBI, to pay a ransom of US$300,000 to the ASG. The militants denied receiving the payment and alleged it was made to a rival ASG faction. In June, in an encounter between the ASG and Filipino army rangers, the latter found the ASG holding the Burnham couple. In the fracas, Mr. Burnham was killed and Mrs. Burnham was rescued by the rangers. In April 2004, the Arroyo government disclosed that the ASG had bombed a ferry in which more than 100 persons died. The government also announced that it had evidence that the group had a plan to attack parts of Manila, including a popular mall.

While the ASG was showing its muscle, the long-standing and much larger organization of Muslims of Mindanao, the Moro National Liberation Front (MNLF), and the Moro Islamic Liberation Front (MILF) divided the ranks of the

Islamic militants. In June 2003, the MILF signed a peace agreement with the government. Malaysia agreed to monitor the ceasefire. At the same time, there were serious allegations that the MILF and JI had close ties and that a large number of JI recruits who could not be sent to the Middle East for training were, in fact, being trained by the MILF. Malaysia agreed to investigate the existence of such ties and persuade the MILF to sever them.

Part Four Review

DECOLONIZATION AND PEACE IN SOUTHEAST ASIA

In the post–World War II era, Southeast Asia (particularly former French Indochina) earned the dubious distinction of being one of the two most explosive areas of the globe (the other being the Middle East), whose security arrangements were determined more by external powers than by the countries of the region. Apart from Myanmar, Indonesia (until the mid-1960s), and Cambodia (until the end of the 1960s), all others remained dependent in various degrees on bilateral or multilateral agreements with outside powers to enhance their security. Security concerns regarding Southeast Asia predominated—in the mid-1950s, after the withdrawal of French forces from Indochina; in 1968–1969, following the British announcement of withdrawal from east of Suez; and in the early 1970s, following the withdrawal of U.S. forces from Vietnam, Laos, and Cambodia. For the first time in a century, Southeast Asia was rid of any major external military presence. After the Communist victories in Vietnam, Cambodia, and Laos in 1975, it was fervently hoped and believed that it would be possible to preserve peace in the region by keeping external involvement to the minimum and promoting regional cooperation in numerous fields, including education, culture, economics, and communications. Vietnam's march into Cambodia in late 1978 and its decade-long occupation of that country, as well as China's invasion of Vietnam in early 1979, belied those hopes and revived tensions throughout the region.

In the mid-1950s, the Geneva agreements brought temporary peace and freedom to Indochina, though Vietnam was partitioned. The Western (particularly the U.S.) perspective was, however, sharply different from that of the newly independent nations, especially that of India. Two principal security alternatives emerged for Southeast Asia, one propounded by India and the other by the United States.

The Indian alternative played down the Communist threat and completely discounted the U.S.-inspired domino theory, according to which if Vietnam was allowed to go under Communist control, it would not be long before the other Southeast Asian states fell like dominoes to Communist domination. India advocated extension of the Sino-Indian agreement on Tibet of April 29, 1954, which incorporated the five principles—Panchasheel—of peaceful coexistence. India urged a policy of "hands off" in all of Southeast Asia and of neutralization of the region. To Indian Prime Minister Nehru, military alliances spelled increased tensions, and an alliance between a giant power and a tiny state imposed severe limitations on the latter's sovereignty and allowed a return of colonialism by the back door. The five principles of peaceful coexistence were presented as a panacea for political ills of a power-dominated world that was bipolarized between Communist and anti-Communist blocs of nations. Following the Geneva conference, through persistent efforts notably at the Bandung conference, Nehru secured from China and North Vietnam promises of noninterference in neighboring countries. Myanmar and Indonesia enthusiastically adopted the policy of nonalignment; Cambodia abrogated a mutual security pact with the United States in order to join the nonaligned group. China's good behavior at Bandung and thereafter at least until 1959 created enough confidence among most of the newly independent nations of Southeast Asia to spurn the U.S. alternative of enhanced security through military alliances.

The United States held China responsible for the Western defeat in Indochina and believed that only a collective security organization could deter China from advancing further in Southeast Asia. Apprehensive of Communist designs all over the globe, the United States refused to subscribe to the Geneva settlement and instead organized the eight-nation SEATO (Southeast Asia Treaty Organization), which included only Thailand and the Philippines as regional members. However, the U.S. belief in a military containment of communism was not necessarily held by all other members of SEATO. As British Prime Minister Anthony Eden warned in April 1954: "Communism in Asia cannot be checked by military means alone. The problem is as much political as military; if any military combination is to be effective, it must enjoy the widest possible measure of Asian support."[1]

The Sino-Soviet interest until 1958 in a global detente with the United States compelled the Vietnamese Communists to lie low. Thereafter, taking advantage of the Sino-Soviet rift, Hanoi launched the NLF in 1960, reactivating the Communist cadres in the South, which in turn made the United States increase its support of the Saigon government under Ngo Dinh Diem and his successors.

By the mid-1960s, the Vietnam conflict had assumed grave proportions involving a U.S. military build-up to a half million troops by 1968 and deployment of supplies and bombing on a scale surpassing World War II. Although there were token forces from SEATO members, the bulk of the external military assistance came from the United States in response to a "request" from successive South Vietnamese governments. The supply of military goods, including surface-to-air missiles, by the Soviet Union and China to North Vietnam and the NLF made the "undeclared war" an international conflict of the gravest concern to nations around the globe. The Geneva agreements of 1954 were in shambles.

ASEAN, SUPERPOWERS, AND CHINA

Around 1967 to 1969—with the progress of fighting in Vietnam not very flattering to the U.S. military effort, with further ineffectiveness of SEATO thanks to France's virtual nonparticipation in that body's activities, and with Britain's decision to withdraw from east of Suez—there were considerable apprehension and rethinking not only in Southeast Asian capitals but also in Moscow and Washington on questions of the region's security. Among the significant results were the birth of ASEAN (Association of Southeast Asian Nations) in 1967 and its adoption of ZOPFAN (zone of peace, freedom, and neutrality) for Southeast Asia in 1971. More significant were the U.S. and Soviet reactions to the British move as well as to the war in Vietnam. Thus, the general secretary of the Soviet Communist party, Leonid Brezhnev, enunciated a plan in June 1969 for a collective security system for Asia. Not coincidentally, President Richard Nixon proclaimed in July 1969 a doctrine that reiterated U.S. commitments in Asia but emphasized that these would be kept by helping the Asians with money and materiel but not with manpower. Both the superpowers thus implied their readiness to reduce their involvement in Asia and leave the responsibility of securing regional peace to Asians themselves.

For several years from its birth in 1967, the ASEAN (Thailand, Malaysia, Singapore, Indonesia, and the Philippines) was an anti-Communist and anti-China organization. It was more like an association than an alliance, whose members met annually to discuss politics of the region and a few schemes for cultural and economic cooperation. As Thailand's Premier Thanat Khoman said when ASEAN was established, the motivations for "the idea of regional cooperation were less lofty and idealistic but stemmed from more practical and realistic considerations, among them the fact that Southeast Asian nations are comparatively weak and small."[2] In 1971, the ASEAN unanimously resolved to make Southeast Asia a "zone of peace, freedom, and neutrality." In the international councils, the ASEAN members have cooperated closely to present the appearance of a united front. Since 1975, they have used Indonesia's prestigious role in the Non-Aligned Movement (NAM) to obtain respectable positions for themselves in that group of nations.

Four crucial events in the 1970s radically influenced the international relations of Southeast Asian states: President Nixon's visit to China; U.S. withdrawal from Southeast Asia; Communist victories in Vietnam, Cambodia, and Laos; and the Vietnamese occupation of Cambodia. The first two factors augmented the Soviet Union's interest and involvement in Southeast Asia because of their potential for the region coming increasingly under the influence of its rival, China. Moreover, because of the international oil situation and growing needs for markets, Japan's stakes in keeping the Southeast Asian maritime passages open and free have been enhanced more than ever before.

Following the dramatic visit of President Nixon to Beijing in February 1972, most non-Communist Southeast Asian nations took steps to normalize relations with China. By 1975, Malaysia, Thailand, and the Philippines opened diplomatic relations with China. Singapore's Lee Kuan Yew visited Beijing several times, but shied away from establishment of diplomatic relations for fear of potential Chinese consular officials in Singapore influencing its Chinese majority population. Similarly, Indonesia opened the way for diverse trade and cultural contacts, but did not restore diplomatic relations with China until 1990. The memory of Beijing's role in the PKI's coup of 1965 in the minds of Jakarta's ruling generals delayed the decision.

ASEAN AND VIETNAM

The diminution of U.S. influence helped Beijing far more than Moscow in winning friends in the region. Even if Southeast Asians dislike China, they do not deny its legitimate claim to some interest in the region; the Soviet Union is, by contrast, deemed an outsider. The growing Sino-U.S. friendship has removed the risk of offending the United States that improvement of Sino-ASEAN relations would have ordinarily entailed. China's response to ASEAN's approaches has been warm. Thus, China supported the Indonesian-Malaysian declaration in 1969 on their sovereignty over the Strait of Malacca as against Soviet advocacy of internationalization of that maritime passage. Beijing also enthusiastically endorsed ASEAN's 1971 ZOPFAN resolution while Moscow did not. Most important, the Soviet military, economic, and diplomatic support to Vietnam and its consistent opposition to ASEAN's efforts in the United Nations to end the Vietnamese occupation of Cambodia angered the ASEAN members.

From 1978, China's and ASEAN's strategic interests in Southeast Asia more or less converged. China was afraid of being sandwiched between Soviet forces in the north and Soviet-backed Vietnamese forces in the south. Neither China nor the ASEAN wanted to encourage Hanoi to become the capital of a potential Indochina federation, which they feared would be the first step toward extension of Vietnamese power beyond Laos and Cambodia. China would not countenance Soviet hegemony over Vietnam any more than Vietnam's hegemony over the rest of Indochina and Southeast Asia. China made restoration of good relations with the Soviet Union conditional upon the removal of three "obstacles." These were removal of Soviet troops from the Sino-Soviet border, removal of troops from Afghanistan, and withdrawal of Vietnamese troops from Cambodia.

The ASEAN's test of friendship with any country for a decade after 1979 was the latter's policy on the Cambodia question. At the United Nations and other international forums and among members of NAM, the ASEAN proposed a comprehensive political settlement of the Cambodian problem by a complete withdrawal of Vietnamese troops, endorsing the right of the Cambodian people to self-determination, and the need for U.N.-supervised elections. It led the diplomatic offensive also to retain the United Nations seat for the ousted Khmer Rouge regime and to get it represented in other international agencies. On the other hand, Vietnam and the Soviet Union endorsed a rival proposal to hold an international conference of all Southeast Asian states, including the Vietnam-backed Hun Sen government as the sole government of Cambodia, to resolve the problem.

Beneath the facade of a joint policy of the ASEAN in regard to Vietnam and Cambodia lurked serious differences among its members on their perception of the long-term threat posed by China and Vietnam to Southeast Asia. Thailand, the "frontline state," perceives Vietnam as its historical rival for hegemony over Cambodia and wanted the emergence of an independent, neutral Cambodia as a buffer between itself and Vietnam. Historically, Thailand has often allied itself with a strong external power against its enemies. Therefore, it improved its relations with Vietnam's enemy, China, because of the congruence of Sino-Thai strategic interests.

In the 1980s, China funneled military assistance through Thailand to the Khmer Rouge in western Cambodia. Singapore shared Thailand's perception that the immediate threat was posed by Vietnam, because it had already spread its tentacles over Laos and Cambodia, and that the next "domino" in a series could be Thailand. On the other hand, Indonesia and Malaysia regarded China as the main source of long-term threat to the security of Southeast Asia. In 1980, Indonesia and Malaysia enunciated the "Kuantan principle," recognizing Vietnam's legitimate security interest in Cambodia. Such recognition would, in their view, enable Vietnam to withdraw from that country. They also favored normalization of U.S.-Vietnamese relations to enable Vietnam to obtain economic assistance from the Western powers and Japan, thus making it a strong and stable state capable of acting as a buffer between China and Southeast Asia.

CAMBODIA SETTLEMENT

By the mid-1980s, all the parties—ASEAN, Vietnam, China, the Soviet Union, and the United States—agreed that the military stalemate in Cambodia could be resolved only through political means. In November 1985, President Reagan and Secretary-General Gorbachev agreed at Geneva that regional conflicts could best be resolved by the regional states themselves. It seemed that the superpowers had seen the folly and futility of internationalizing the problem in Afghanistan and Cambodia. The escalating costs of the Soviet intervention in Afghanistan drastically reduced Soviet ability to support Vietnam's misadventure in Cambodia. Thus, for varied reasons, all major external powers favored a negotiated settlement of the Cambodian imbroglio. It was such a broad consensus that led to a nineteen-nation agreement in Paris in 1991 whereby a government of national reconciliation was established and elections were held under the auspices of UNTAC in Cambodia.

A CHANGED SOUTHEAST ASIA

Several factors, some of them of global significance, altered the political and strategic thinking in regard to Southeast Asia in the last decade of the twentieth century. First were the sudden collapse of the mighty Soviet Union in August 1991, the emergence of the United States as the sole superpower, and the end of superpower rivalry all over the world, including Southeast Asia. Vietnam was left bereft of external military and economic support and therefore in dire need of mending its relations with the United States and its former adversary, the ASEAN, in order to be able to counter a potential threat from its traditional enemy—China. In the 1970s and 1980s, no ASEAN country liked the presence of U.S. troops within its own borders, but every one of them regarded U.S. military presence in the region as vital for security against communism. In the altered global strategic scenario, there was no need for any of them to include the United States in their security arrangements except to thwart China's aggressive moves in the region.

Second, predating the collapse of the Soviet Union was the admission of failure on the part of the socialist system to raise the standards of living of the people in the Communist countries of Eastern Europe, Soviet Union, China, and Vietnam. The opening of the Chinese economy to Western capitalism, beginning in 1979 under Deng Xiaoping's leadership, followed by Gorbachev's political and economic liberalization of the Soviet Union set in train a trend for the other Communist states to follow. Beginning in 1987 and even more actively after 1991, Vietnam embarked on policies facilitating massive inflows of foreign investment—European, North American, Australasian, and Japanese—into the country. The United States, with its dissatisfaction over Vietnam's inadequate cooperation in securing information about and retrieval of remains of the MIAs, emphatically refused to normalize relations with Vietnam and took action to block the flow of aid to Vietnam from its allies and from international agencies like the IMF and World Bank. As the Vietnamese government's cooperation became increasingly available on the MIA question, the United States relented by increments until it normalized its relations with Vietnam in mid-1995.

Simultaneously, Vietnam was admitted to ASEAN, an organization originally established, inter alia, to oppose Vietnamese hegemonistic ambitions in the region. In 1999, Laos and Cambodia were admitted to ASEAN. The third factor was the emergence in the 1990s of the ASEAN region as one of the best growth areas of the globe, rivaling North America, East Asia, and the European Union (EU). For quite some time, there had been a growing awareness in the United States of the rising importance of trade and investment with the Pacific Rim countries—notably Japan, China, South Korea, Taiwan, Hong Kong, and Singapore—surpassing its traditional trade and investment across the Atlantic in volume and value. Other ASEAN members—notably Thailand, Malaysia, and Indonesia—registered spectacular growth indices consecutively for several years; Malaysia mapped out visions of prosperity by the year 2020. By 1991, Vietnam, too, actively joined the band of ASEAN countries aspiring to be the new "Asian tigers."

Much of this spectacular growth and the plans for expanded economies have been predicated upon massive investments by multinationals from Europe, the United States, and Japan. The common aspirations, based upon pooling of resources in some areas and upon avoidance of competition and conflict in some others, have necessitated numerous agreements arrived at in the annual assemblies of ASEAN economic and foreign ministers as well as those of officials in the fields of education, transport, and communications. Paralleling NAFTA and the EU, ASEAN agreed to accelerate its plans to create the ASEAN Free Trade Area by 2000.

Brunei was admitted to ASEAN in 1984 following independence from Britain; and Myanmar, which had been kept out because of its grossly flawed human rights record, was admitted to ASEAN in 1997. Thus, by the end of the twentieth century, with all Southeast Asian states within the fold, ASEAN truly became the Association of Southeast Asian Nations. In May 2002, East Timor, a former Portuguese colonial outpost that was brought under Indonesian rule as its twenty-seventh province from 1976 to 1999, became, through UN intervention, completely independent. In 2002, East Timor, or Timor Leste, announced its "strategic decision" to join the ASEAN as a member in the future. Three years later, East Timor was recognized by the ASEAN as an observer and allowed to join the ASEAN Regional Forum. It expects to be admitted to the ASEAN before long.

It seems as if international relations in Southeast Asia have come full circle. The polarities of the age of the Cold War and containment of communism that determined the life and politics of the region's people for four decades have given way to a well-founded hope for an enduring peace. In 1971, the then five-member fledgling ASEAN had resolved to establish a zone of peace, freedom, and neutrality in Southeast Asia; in December 1995, all states of Southeast Asia signed, under ASEAN's auspices, a treaty creating a Southeast Asian Nuclear Weapons–Free Zone that prohibits manufacture, possession, or use of nuclear weapons. It covered the land area, territorial waters, the two-hundred-mile exclusive economic zones, and continental shelves of the signatory states. Since none of the Southeast Asian states is a nuclear power, the treaty is symbolic, reflective at best of the desires of a people who have suffered from actual war or from the tensions of a war raging in a neighboring country for decades. Such treaties and, more important, positive attitudes of mutual trust toward neighbors could usher in an era of genuine peace to tense Southeast Asia.

Chronological Chart, B.C.

India and China	Myanmar	Cambodia	Java and Sumatra	Vietnam	Malaya and Thailand
Peking man c.500,000			Java man c.500,000		
			Solo man c.100,000		
Indus Valley civilization c.3000					
				Legend of the birth of Nam Viet c.2800	
					Proto-Malays arrive from southern China 2500
Hsia dynasty 2205–1766					
	Mons arrive in Upper Myanmar c.2000	Khmers arrive in upper Mekong c.2000			
Shang dynasty 1766–1122					
Aryans move into India c.1500					
The Vedas 1500–1000					
The Brahmanas 1000–800					
The Upanishads 600					
Buddha 563–483					
Confucius 551–479					
Ashoka 269–32	Ashoka's missionaries arrive 3rd c.			Dong-son culture c.300	Deutero-Malays arrive from southern China 300

Chronological Chart, B.C. to A.D. 1000

India and China	Myanmar	Cambodia	Java and Sumatra	Vietnam	Malaya and Thailand
Shi Huang-Di 221–07 Unification of China, Great Wall				Nam Viet founded 207	
Han dynasty 202 B.C.–A.D. 220				Nam Viet under Chinese rule 111 B.C.–A.D. 939	
A.D.					A.D.
Buddhist schism: Mahayana and Theravada 1st c.		Funan founded 1st c.		Trung sisters revolt 39	
Mahayana Buddhism adopted 2nd c.	Burmans arrive from eastern Tibet 2nd c.			Champa founded 192	
	Pyus arrive from southern China 3rd c.	Embassies to China and India 3rd c.			
		Chinaís Kíang-tíai visits 3rd c.			
Gupta age 320–550				Mahayana Buddhism from China 5th c.	
A.D. 500–1000		Chenla defeats Funan 6th c.			A.D. 500–1000
Tíang dynasty 618–906					

Islam born 622
(Arabia)

Pyus adopt Vikrama
era 638

Srivijaya founded 7th c.
I-Ching's visit 671

Chenla divided 706

Sailendra founded 8th c.

Thais overrun
Tongking 8th c.

Borobodur built
778–824

Lower Chenla defeated
by Sailendras 790
Jayavarman II 802–50
Unifies Khmers,
adopts Devaraja cult

Sailendra invades
Chenla 790

Pagan founded 849

Sailendra Balaputra
flees to Srivijaya 850

Yasovarman I 889–900
Founds Angkor

Sindok founds
Mataram 929–48

China's rule ended: Dai
Viet founded 939

Chronological Chart, A.D. 1000 to A.D. 1500

India and China	Myanmar	Cambodia	Java and Sumatra	Vietnam	Malaya and Thailand
Northern Sung 960–1126		Suryavarman I 1002–50			
			Srivijaya defeats Mataram 1006		
				Ly dynasty 1009–1225	
			Cholas occupy Srivijaya 1026–45		
			Airlangga divides Mataram into Janggala and Kediri 1042		
	Anawratha 1044–77 Adopts Theravada Buddhism, unifies Myanmar Pagan dynasty 1044–1287				
		Suryavarman II 1113–50 Builds Vishnu temple in Angkor			

Southern Sung
1127–1279

Muslim rule in Delhi
1208

Javavarman VII
1181–1219
Founds Angkor Thom

Ken Angrok defeats
Kediri 1222

Tran dynasty
1225–1400
Tan Thai Tong
1225–58

Mongol invasions
1257–85

Mongols destroy Thai
Nan Chao 1253

Marco Polo in China
1271–91

Yuan (Mongol)
dynasty 1279–1368

Mongols conquer
Pagan 1287

Rama Khamheng
1283–1317
Theravada Buddhism;
Thai alphabet

(*continues*)

Chronological Chart, A.D. 1000 to A.D. 1500 (*continued*)

India and China	Myanmar	Cambodia	Java and Sumatra	Vietnam	Malaya and Thailand
Marco Polo travels through Southeast Asia 1292			Kertanagara defeats Srivijaya 1290		
			Mongols attack Singhasari; Kertanagara killed 1292; Majapahit founded 1292		
Muslim Rule in Gujarat 1297					
			Gajah Mada prime minister 1331–64		Ayuthaya founded; promulgates law code
Ming dynasty 1368–1644					
				China's occupation 1407–28	Malacca founded 1402
		Fall of Angkor 1431 Phnom Penh capital (Vyadhapura) 1434			
	Shin Sawbu 1453–72 Enlarges Shwedagon Pagoda				Trailok 1448–88 Thai palace code

Tun Perak 1456–98

Champa defeated 1471

Vasco de Gama reaches India 1498

Chronological Chart, A.D. 1500 to Present

Events Affecting Southeast Asia	Myanmar	Indonesia, Malaysia, Singapore, and Brunei	Laos, Cambodia, and Vietnam	Thailand	Philippines
1500					*1500*
Alfonso de Albuquerque 1509–15					
		Portuguese conquer Malacca 1511			Magellan killed 1521
			Mac dynasty 1527–1677		
	Tabinshweti 1531–50				
	Myanmar-Thai wars 1531–1605			Thai-Burmese wars 1531–1605	
	Toungoo dynasty 1531–1732				
			Trinh family 1539–1787		
			First partition of Vietnam 1540		
	Bayinnaung 1550–81				First Spanish settlement at Cebu 1565
					Spaniards conquer Manila 1571
					Nareseun 1590–1605

English East India
Company founded 1600

Trinh overthrow Mac
in Tongking 1592

VOC (United East India
Co.) founded 1602

College of St. Thomas
founded 1611

Ambon massacre 1623

Alexandre de Rhodes
1627–49

Ch'ing (Manchu)
dynasty 1644–1911

Dutch conquer
Malacca 1641

Narai 1657–88

Constance Phaulkon
executed 1688

Champa eliminated 1720

Mon rebellion 1740–52

Bohol revolt 1744

(continues)

Chronological Chart, A.D. 1500 to Present (*continued*)

Events Affecting Southeast Asia	Myanmar	Indonesia, Malaysia, Singapore, and Brunei	Laos, Cambodia, and Vietnam	Thailand	Philippines
	Alaungpaya 1752–60 Dagon renamed Rangoon				
	Konbaung dynasty 1752–1885				
					British occupy Manila 1762
	Hsinbyushin 1763–76		Tayson rebellion 1760–1802		
	Occupation of Ayuthaya 1767–82			Ayuthaya sacked 1767 Myanmar's occupation of Ayuthaya 1767–82 Maha Sakarat era adopted	
	Bodawpaya 1781–1819			Chakri dynasty 1782– Rama I 1782–1809	
			Nguyen Anh 1787–1802 Becomes emperor Gia Long 1802		
French Revolution and Napoleonic Wars 1789–1815					

Macartney mission
to China 1793

Symes mission 1795

1800

Unification of Vietnam
1802

Gia Long 1802–20

Nguyen dynasty
1802–1955

Manila Galleon ended
1811

Daendels 1808–10

British occupy Java
1811–16

Peace of Vienna 1815

Singapore founded 1819

Minh Mang 1820–41

Anglo-Dutch treaty 1824

Dipo Negoro revolt
1825–30

First Anglo-Burmese
war 1824–26

Treaty of Yandabo 1826
(British take over
Arakan and Tenasserim)

Crawfurd mission 1827

Culture system begun
1830

1800

(continues)

Chronological Chart, A.D. 1500 to Present (continued)

Events Affecting Southeast Asia	Myanmar	Indonesia, Malaysia, Singapore, and Brunei	Laos, Cambodia, and Vietnam	Thailand	Philippines
East India Co.'s China trade monopoly ends 1833					
	Tharawaddy 1837–46				
Opium War 1840–42			Vietnam occupies Cambodia 1841–45 Thieu-Tri 1841–47		
Treaty of Nanking 1842			Tourane (Da Nang) bombarded 1846 Tu Duc 1847–83		
	Pagan 1846–52				
Revolutions in Europe 1848					
Taiping rebellion 1851–64	Second Anglo-Burmese war 1852 Mindon 1853–78			Mongkut (Rama IV) 1851–68 Anglo-Siamese treaty 1855	
Indian uprising 1857 East India Co. dissolved 1858					

Treaty of Tientsin 1860

Max Havelaar 1860

French occupy Cochin China 1862

De Lagree-Garnier expedition 1866

Straits Settlements under Colonial Office 1867

Protectorate over Cambodia 1867

Phan Boi Chau 1867–1940

Chulalongkorn (Rama V) 1868–1910

Suez canal 1869

The "new imperialism" 1870–1914

Most crops removed from culture system 1870

Ethical policy 1870–1900

Phan Chau Trinh 1871–1926

Garnier killed 1873

Resident system in Malaya begun 1874

Anglo-Perak war 1875

Indian National Congress founded 1885

Third Anglo-Burmese war 1885

France aquires Annam 1885

British annex Upper Myanmar to Indian empire Jan. 1, 1886

(continues)

Chronological Chart, A.D. 1500 to Present (*continued*)

Events Affecting Southeast Asia	Myanmar	Indonesia, Malaysia, Singapore, and Brunei	Laos, Cambodia, and Vietnam	Thailand	Philippines
					Noli Me Tangere published 1887
			Protectorate over Laos 1893		
Japan defeats China 1895		Federation of Malay States 1895			
				Anglo-French declaration 1896	Rizal executed 1896
					Republic proclaimed 1897
			L'Ecole Française d'Extreme Orient founded 1898		
					U.S.-Philippines war 1899–1902
1900					1900
Boxer Rebellion 1900					
			French aquire Battambang and Siem Reap 1904	Loss of Battambang and Siem Reap 1904	
Japan defeats Russia 1905					
	YMBA founded 1906				
Morley-Minto reforms in India 1909	Burma Research Society founded 1909	Four north Malay states under British rule 1909		Loss of four north Malay states 1909	

Ch'ing dynasty overthrown; China becomes a republic 1912

World War I, 1914–1918

Russian revolution 1917

Versailles peace conf. 1919

Montagu-Chelmsford reforms in India 1919

Gandhian movement 1920–48

Chinese Communist party founded 1921

Mao Zedong organizes guerrilla army 1924–25

Communist-KMT alliance, China 1924–27

Sarekat Islam founded 1912

Culture system ended 1917

Dutch introduced legislative reforms 1918

PKI founded 1920

PKI uprising 1926

Chulalongkorn dies 1910

Maha Vajiravudh 1910–25

Chulalongkorn Univ. founded 1917

Prajadhipok (Rama VII) 1925–35

Harrison governor-general 1913–21

(continues)

Chronological Chart, A.D. 1500 to Present (*continued*)

Events Affecting Southeast Asia	Myanmar	Indonesia, Malaysia, Singapore, and Brunei	Laos, Cambodia, and Vietnam	Thailand	Philippines
		PNI founded 1927	VNQDD founded 1927		
			ICP established 1930		
			VNQDD uprising Feb. 1930		
	Saya San rebellion 1930–31		Nghe An uprising 1930–31		
				Bloodless revolution June 24, 1932	
The Long March, China 1934					Tydings-McDuffee Act 1934
Government of India Act 1935					
Japan attacks China 1937–39	Myanmar separated from India 1937 Ba Maw prime minister				
World War II 1939–45					
Japan bombs Pearl Harbor Dec. 7, 1941			Viet Minh founded May 1941		
"Quit India" movement 1942					Hukbalahap founded 1942
Japan occupies Southeast Asia 1942–45					

Indian National Army
1942–45

AFPFL founded 1944

Republic of Indonesia
proclaimed 1945

DRV proclaimed
Sep. 2, 1945

Ho Chi Minh president
N. Vietnam 1945–46;
1954–69

Independence
July 4, 1946

Manuel Roxas
president 1946–48

UMNO founded May
1946

Indonesia–Dutch
conflict 1946–49

France–Viet Minh
agreement Mar. 6, 1946

First Indochina War
1946–54

Parliamentary
democracy restored 1946

King Ananda dies
June 9, 1946

India becomes
independent Aug. 1947

Nehru prime minister
1947–64

Aung San killed
Jan. 1947

Linggadjati agreement
Mar. 1947

Asian Relations
Conference 1947

Independence
Jan. 4, 1948

Communist insurrec-
tion Mar. 1948

Karen rebellion 1948

AFPFL split 1948

Federation of Malaya
Feb. 1, 1948

Communist insurgency
1948–60

Coup; Phibun becomes
prime minister 1948–57

People's Republic of
China 1949

NATO established 1949

MCA founded Feb.
1949

Dutch transfer power
Dec. 27, 1949

Republic of Vietnam
Mar. 1949

Quirino president
1949–53

(continues)

394

Chronological Chart, A.D. 1500 to Present (*continued*)

Events Affecting Southeast Asia	Myanmar	Indonesia, Malaysia, Singapore, and Brunei	Laos, Cambodia, and Vietnam	Thailand	Philippines
1950					1950
Eisenhower president 1952–60	U Nu's four-year plan 1952–56				
Stalin dies 1953	Communist party banned 1953		Cambodia independent 1953		Magsaysay president 1953–57 (dies in plane crash)
Geneva conference, 1954			Dien Bien Phu falls May 7, 1954	Joins SEATO Aug. 1954	
SEATO pact 1954			Geneva agreements July 21, 1954 Vietnam partitioned		
Afro-Asian Bandung conference 1955		Bandung conference 1955	South Vietnam proclaimed republic; Diem president Oct. 26, 1955		
	Buddha's 2,500-year anniversary 1956				
			Government of National Union (Laos) 1957	Phibun overthrown; Sarit Thanarat prime minister 1957–63	Garcia president 1957–60
		Sumatra rebellion 1958			
		Lee Kuan Yew prime minister of Singapore 1959			

Macapagal president 1961–65		Sino-Burmese border agreement 1960	Kong Le's coup Aug. 1960	Emergency ends in Malaya 1960	Kennedy president 1961–63
			NLF established Dec. 1960		
		Buddhism made state religion 1961	Geneva protocol on Laos 1962	Brunei revolt 1962	Sino-Indian war 1962
		Ne Win takes over Mar. 2, 1962		UN administration of West Irian 1962–63	Cuba episode 1962
		U Nu imprisoned 1962–67			
	Thanom Kittikachorn and Prapas Charusathien 1963–1973		Buddhist protests May–Nov. 1963	Malaysia founded Aug. 31, 1963	Lyndon Johnson president 1963–68
			Diem assassinated Nov. 1, 1963	Confrontation policy 1963–66	
			Gulf of Tongking incident Aug. 1964		Nehru dies 1964
Marcos president 1965–86			Bombing of North Vietnam begun Feb. 1965	Singapore a separate state Aug. 9, 1965	Lin Piao doctrine 1965
				Gestapu affair Sept. 30, 1965	
				PKI banned; Suharto takes over	China's Cultural Revolution 1966–68
				Sukarno's power stripped 1967	ASEAN founded 1967

(continues)

Chronological Chart, A.D. 1500 to Present (*continued*)

Events Affecting Southeast Asia	Myanmar	Indonesia, Malaysia, Singapore, and Brunei	Laos, Cambodia, and Vietnam	Thailand	Philippines
Britain decides to pull out of east of Suez 1968			Tet Offensive 1968		
Nixon presidency 1968–74					
	U Nu goes into self-exile 1969	Malay racial riots 1969	Ho Chi Minh dies 1969		
		Parliamentary government in Malaysia suspended 1969–71			
		Tunku Abdul Rahman resigns 1970	Sihanouk overthrown May 1970		
		Sukarno dies 1970			
		Five-power defense amalgam 1971			
Nixon visits China 1972	BSPP's 20-year program 1972				
		Suharto re-elected president 1973	Paris Accords Jan. 27, 1973	Student rebellion; Kittikachorn ordered out of the country; army rule ended Oct. 1973	
				Sanya Thammasak becomes prime minister 1973–75	
	New constitution 1974				Martial law Sept. 23, 1975–Jan. 1981

1975 | | | | | 1975

Mao Zedong dies 1976	Khmer Rouge victory Mar. 31, 1975	Kukrit Pramoj, prime minister 1975–76	East Timor integrated into Indonesia July 1976		
	Communists take over Saigon April 30, 1975		Datak Hussein bin Onn prime minister 1976–80		Tripoli Agreement 1976
	Pol Pot regime 1975–77	Seni Pramoj, prime minister 1976	Suharto re-elected president 1978		
	Vietnam-USSR agreement Nov. 3, 1978				
	Vietnam invades Cambodia Dec. 25, 1978		Mahathir becomes prime minister 1980		
	New constitution for Vietnam 1980	Prem Tinsulanond, prime minister 1980–88			Martial law lifted Jan. 1981
		Pridi Banomyong dies 1983	Suharto re-elected president 1983		Benigno Aquino killed Aug. 21, 1983
			Brunei becomes independent Jan. 1984; joins ASEAN		

(continues)

Chronological Chart, A.D. 1500 to Present (*continued*)

Events Affecting Southeast Asia	Myanmar	Indonesia, Malaysia, Singapore, and Brunei	Laos, Cambodia, and Vietnam	Thailand	Philippines
					Marcos flees; Corazon Aquino becomes president Feb. 1986
					Honasan Revolt 1987
	Ne Win resigns; Sein Lwin succeeds and resigns in 17 days, August 1988	Suharto re-elected president 1988		Chatichai Choonhavan, prime minister 1988–91	Local elections 1988
	National League for Democracy (NLD) established, Sept. 1988	UMNO declared illegal Feb. 1988			
	SLORC established Sept. 24, 1988				
	Aung San Suu Kyi under house arrest July 1989–July 1995				Marcos died Sept. 1989
	SLORC declares martial law July 1990	Indonesia-China relations normalized Aug. 1990			
	National elections held May 1990	General elections, Malaysia, Oct. 1990			
		Singapore-China relations established Oct. 1990			

Soviet Union collapses Aug. 1991

U.S. prepares four-stage normalization plan for relations with Vietnam April 1991

Bill Clinton president 1992–2000

Aung San Suu Kyi awarded Nobel Prize Oct. 1991

Gen. Than Shwe appointed chairman SLORC, April 1992

National Convention opened Jan. 18, 1994

Agreement with Karens, May 1994

Singapore–U.S. defense agreement Nov. 1990

Goh Chok Tong becomes prime minister of Singapore Dec. 1990

General elections, Singapore, Aug. 1991

Massacre at Dili, East Timor, Nov. 12, 1991

Gusmao of Fretilin arrested Nov. 1992

Suharto re-elected president 1993

VCP Seventh Congress June 1991

Paris Peace Agreements on Cambodia Oct. 1991

Vietnam-China relations normalized Nov. 1991

New constitution for Vietnam April 1992

Elections in Cambodia May 1993

General Suchinda Kraprayoon stages coup d'état Feb. 23, 1991

Anand Punyarachan appointed prime minister March 1991

New constitution 1992

General elections March 1992

The Revolt of May 1992

General elections Sept. 1992

Chuan Leekpai appointed prime minister

Mount Pinatubo erupts June 1991

U.S. bases terminated 1991

General elections 1992

Fidel Ramos elected president

(continues)

Chronological Chart, A.D. 1500 to Present (*continued*)

Events Affecting Southeast Asia	Myanmar	Indonesia, Malaysia, Singapore, East Timor, and Brunei	Laos, Cambodia, and Vietnam	Thailand	Philippines
	Agreement with Shans, Oct. 1994				
	Aung San Suu Kyi released, July 1995	General elections Malaysia, April 1995	Vietnam joins ASEAN as a member, July 1995	General elections July 1995	
	NLD boycotts convention, Nov. 1995		Normalization of U.S.-Vietnam relations, July 1995	Banharn Silpa-Archa appointed prime minister	
		Father Belo and Jose Ramos-Horta win Nobel Peace Prize Oct. 1996			Agreement with Moros, July 1996
	SLORC disbanded		First US ambassador to Vietnam arrives May 1997	Baht devalued	
	SPDC constituted Nov. 1997		First elections of Laos National Assembly 1997	Chuan Leekpai becomes PM July 1997	
	Joins ASEAN Dec. 1997				
		Suharto re-elected president March 1998 Suharto forced to resign; Habibie president, May 1998			Estrada president May 1998
		Wahid elected president Oct. 1999	ASEAN Conference at Hanoi Dec. 1998		
		Collapse of Amedeo Group in Brunei 1998			
Currency and economic crisis in Southeast Asia 1987		Anwar removed from Dy PM; jailed and charged—abuse of power			

Suu Kyi under house-arrest; secret talks between Suu Kyi and SLORC Oct. 2000

President Jian Zemin's visit Dec. 2001

Suu Kyi released from house-arrest May 2002

Ne Win dies Dec. 2002

U.S.–Singapore agreement 1998; use of naval base from 2000

Nathan elected president of Singapore 1999

Anwar sentenced 6 years for corruption April 1999

Anwar sentenced 9 years for sodomy August 2000

Wahid impeached Megawati becomes president July 2001

Aceh and Papua get autonomy Jan. 2002

East Timor becomes independent May 2002

Pham Van Dong dies April 2000

US–Vietnam BTA agreement July 2000

Clinton visits Vietnam Nov. 2000

President Putin visits Vietnam, signs agreement Feb. 2001

Boungnang Vorachit becomes PM of Laos March 2001

Thakin Shinawatra PM Jan. 2001

Visiting Forces Agreement May 1999

Estrada impeached Nov. 2000

Estrada forced from office Dec. 2001

(continues)

Chronological Chart, A.D. 1500 to Present (continued)

Events Affecting Southeast Asia	Myanmar	Indonesia, Malaysia, Singapore, East Timor, and Brunei	Laos, Cambodia, and Vietnam	Thailand	Philippines
Currency crisis 1997–1998	Anti-government monks protest 2007	Bali bombing October 2002	Norodom Sihanouk abdicates; Norodom Sihamoni succeeds as king October 2004	Thaksin to step down conditionally April 4, 2006	Gloria Macapagal elected president May 2004
	Referendum on New Constitution May 2008		Marriott Hotel, Jakarta Bombing August 2003	Military coup September 2006	Right of self-determination for Moros recognized March 2007
		Mahathir steps down; Abdulla Ahmad Badawi prime minister October 31, 2003		General elections September 2007	
		Susilo Bambang Yudhoyono president October 2004		Political crisis October–December 2008	
		Tsunami hits Sumatra December 2004			
		Acheh-Jakarta Agreement, August 15, 2005			
		East Timor–Australia Treaty, January 12, 2006			
		E. Timor elections, Xanana Gusmao president, August 2007			

Notes

The following abbreviations are used in the notes and bibliography:

AS	*Asian Survey*
BEFEO	*Bulletin de l'École Française d'Extreme-Orient*
FEQ	*Far Eastern Quarterly*
FEER	*Far Eastern Economic Review*
JAS	*Journal of Asian Studies*
JMBRAS	*Journal Malaya Branch Royal Asiatic Society*
JSEAH	*Journal of Southeast Asian History*
JSEAS	*Journal of Southeast Asian Studies*
JSS	*Journal of the Siam Society*

CHAPTER 1

1. Stephen N. Hay and Margaret H. Case, eds., *Southeast Asian History: A Bibliographic Guide*, New York, Praeger, 1962, p. 3.

2. D.G.E. Hall, *A History of South-East Asia,* 3d ed., London, Macmillan, 1968, p. 3.

3. George B. Cressey, *Asia's Lands and Peoples,* 3d ed., New York, McGraw-Hill, 1963, p. 258.

4. *Ibid.,* p. 269.

5. R. D. Hill, "Rice in Malaya: A Study in Historical Geography," Ph.D. thesis, University of Singapore, 1973, p. 21; D. T. Bayard, "Excavations at Non Nok Tha, Northeastern Thailand, 1968," *Asian Perspectives* 13 (1970), p. 135.

6. P. V. Tobias and G.H.R. von Koenigswald, "A Comparison Between the Olduvai Hominines and Those of Java, and Some Implications for Hominid Phylogeny," *Nature* 204 (1964), pp. 515–518.

7. Franz Weidenrich, *Apes, Giants, and Man,* Chicago, Chicago University Press, 1946, p. 82.

8. T. Jacob, *Some Problems Pertaining to the Racial History of the Indonesian Region,* Utrecht, Drukkerij Neerlandia, 1967, p. 39.

9. Peter Bellwood, *Man's Conquest of the Pacific: The Pre-History of Southeast Asia and Oceania,* New York, Oxford University Press, 1979, p. 42.

10. *Ibid.,* p. 45.

11. *Ibid.,* p. 44.

12. For details see B. Kalgren, "The Date of the Early Dongson Culture," *Bulletin of the Museum of Far Eastern Antiquities* 14 (1942), pp. 1–29.

13. An isolated find of bronze ax, dated around 3500 B.C. in northeast Thailand, has confused scholars of the prehistory of Southeast Asia. D. T. Bayard, "Early Thai Bronze: Analysis and New Dates," *Science* 176 (1972), p. 141.

14. Reginald Le May, *The Culture of South-East Asia,* London, Allen and Unwin, 1954, p. 9.

15. I. W. Mabbett, "The 'Indianisation' of Southeast Asia: Reflections on the Historical Sources," *JSEAS* 8, 2 (September 1977), p. 155.

16. Paul Mus, "Cultes indiens et indigenes au Champa," *BEFEO* 33 (1933), pp. 367–410.

17. J. C. van Leur, *Indonesian Trade and Society,* The Hague, W. van Hoeve, 1955, pp. 103–104.

CHAPTER 2

1. Kenneth R. Hall, *Maritime Trade and State Development in Early Southeast Asia,* Honolulu, University of Hawaii Press, 1985.

2. Paul Pelliot, "Le Fou-nan," *BEFEO* (1903), p. 264.

3. I. W. Mabbett, "Devaraja," *JSEAH* 10 (September 1969), p. 208.

4. I. W. Mabbett, "Varnas in Angkor and the Indian Caste System," *JAS* 36, 3 (May 1977), pp. 429–442.

5. V. Goloubew, "L'hydraulique urbaine et agricole a l'epoque des rois d'Angkor," *Bulletin Economique Indochine,* 1941, fasc. 1.

6. B. P. Groslier, *Angkor et le Cambodge au XVI siecle d'apres les documents portugais et espagnols,* Paris, Presses Universitaires, 1958; and his "Our Knowledge of Khmer Civilization: A Reappraisal," *JSS* 48 (June 1960), pp. 1–28.

7. W. J. Van Liere, "Traditional Water Management in the Lower Mekong Basin," *World Archaeology* 11, 4 (1980), pp. 265–280.

8. Roland Fletcher, "The Water Management System of Angkor: The Implications of New Evidence," keynote address for "Water in Mainland Southeast Asia," Center for Khmer Studies, Siem Reap, Cambodia, November 30–December 2, 2005, p. 5.

9. *Ibid.*

10. Pottier completed his three-volume Ph.D. thesis on the subject at Sorbonne Nouvelle in 1999.

11. Lustig wrote her B.A. thesis on "Water and the Transformation of Power at Angkor" (10th to 13th centuries) at the University of Sydney in 2001.

12. Fletcher, "The Water Management System of Angkor," p. 5.

13. Joseph Buttinger, *Vietnam: A Political History*, New York, Praeger, 1968, p. 29.

14. David G. Marr, *Vietnamese Anti-Colonialism*, 1885–1925, Berkeley, University of California Press, 1971, p. 9.

15. Keith W. Taylor, *The Birth of Vietnam*, Berkeley, University of California Press, 1983, p. 297.

CHAPTER 3

1. L. Ch. Damais, "Pre-Seventeenth Century Indonesian History—Sources and Directions," in Soedjatmoko et al., eds., *An Introduction to Indonesian Historiography*, Ithaca, N.Y., Cornell University Press, 1965, pp. 24–25.

2. Georges Coedes, "Le royaume de Crivijaya," *BEFEO* 18, 6 (1918), pp. 1–36.

3. O. W. Wolters, *Early Indonesian Commerce: A Study of the Origins of Srivijaya*, Ithaca, N.Y., Cornell University Press, 1967, pp. 107–110.

4. J. G. de Casparis, *Selected Inscriptions from the Seventh to the Ninth Century a.d.*, Bandung, Prasasti Indonesia, 1956, pp. 184–185, 204.

5. H. G. Quaritch-Wales, *The Making of Greater India,* 1st ed., London, Bernard Quaritch, 1951, pp. 150–156.

6. de Casparis, *Selected Inscriptions,* pp. 184–187.

7. Georges Coedes, *The Indianized States of Southeast Asia,* Honolulu, East-West Center Press, 1968, p. 126.

8. *Ibid.,* pp. 128–129.

9. The famous Javanese classic *Arjunavivaha,* by the poet Kanva, was composed in 1035 to commemorate this marriage.

10. Jessy Blom, *The Antiquities of Singasari,* Leiden, The Netherlands, Burgersdijk and Niermans, 1939, p. 159.

11. Coedes, *The Indianized States,* p. 199.

CHAPTER 4

1. Yoshikazu Takaya, "An Ecological Interpretation of Thai History," *JSEAS* 6, 2 (1975), pp. 190–195.
2. David K. Wyatt, *Thailand,* New Haven, Yale University Press, 1982, pp. 73–74.
3. G. E. Marrison, "The Coming of Islam to the East Indies," *JMBRAS* 24, part 1 (1951), pp. 35–36, or A. H. Hill, "Hikayat Raja Pasai," *JMBRAS* 33, part 2 (1960), pp. 5–215.
4. Richard O. Winstedt, "Kingship and Enthronement in Malaya," *JMBRAS* 19, parts 3–4 (June 1947), pp. 129–139.
5. J. C. van Leur, *Indonesian Trade and Society,* The Hague, W. van Hoeve, 1955, p. 169.
6. Christopher H. Wake, "Malacca's Early Kings and the Reception of Islam," *JSEAH* 5, 2 (September 1964), pp. 104–128.
7. Tome Pires, *Suma Oriental,* London, Hakluyt Society, 1944, p. 244.

CHAPTER 5

1. J. C. van Leur, *Indonesian Trade and Society,* The Hague, W. van Hoeve, 1955, p. 261.
2. K. M. Panikkar, *Asia and Western Dominance,* London, Allen and Unwin, 1953, p. 49.
3. Kristaf Glamann, *Dutch-Asiatic Trade, 1620–1740,* The Hague, Martinus Nijhoff, 1958.
4. David J. Steinberg, ed., *In Search of Southeast Asia,* New York, Praeger, 1985, p. xiii.
5. D.G.E. Hall, *A History of South-East Asia,* 3d ed., London, Macmillan, 1968, p. 3.
6. John Bowring, *The Philippine Islands,* London, Smith, Elder, 1859, p. 315.

CHAPTER 6

1. *Ramakien* was only partly composed by Rama I. It was completed during the reign of his successor. Georges Coedes, *The Making of South-East Asia,* Berkeley, University of California Press, 1966, p. 165.
2. For a full list, see Dhani Nivat, "The Reconstruction of Rama I of the Chakri Dynasty," *JSS* 43, 1 (1955), pp. 262–265.
3. Bernard B. Fall, *The Two Viet-Nams: A Political and Military Analysis,* rev. ed., New York, Praeger, 1964, p. 21.

PART TWO

1. Charles Boxer, "Some Aspects of Spanish Historical Writing on the Philippines," in D.G.E. Hall, ed., *Historians of Southeast Asia,* London, Oxford University Press, 1961, pp. 200–201.
2. J. C. van Leur, *Indonesian Trade and Society,* The Hague, W. van Hoeve, 1955, p. 261.

CHAPTER 7

1. E. S. de Klerck, *History of the Netherlands East Indies,* vol. 2, Rotterdam, W.L.&J. Brusse, 1938, p. 101.
2. Bernard H. M. Vlekke, *Nusantara: A History of the East Indian Archipelago,* Cambridge, Mass., Harvard University Press, 1943, p. 248.
3. Quoted in C. E. Wurtzburg, *Raffles of the Eastern Isles,* London, Hodder and Stoughton, 1954, p. 461.
4. Vlekke, *Nusantara,* p. 269.
5. J. H. Boeke, "Objective and Personal Elements in Colonial Welfare Policy," in Royal Tropical Institute, ed., *Indonesian Economics: The Concept of Dualism in Theory and Policy,* The Hague, W. van Hoeve, 1961, p. 287.
6. Clive Day, *Policy and Administration of the Dutch in Java,* New York, Macmillan, 1904, p. 13.

7. John S. Furnivall, *Netherlands India: A Study of Plural Economy,* Cambridge, Cambridge University Press, 1944, p. 45.

8. de Klerck, *History of the Netherlands East Indies,* pp. 188–189.

9. Multatuli [E. D. Dekker], *Indonesia: Once More Free Labor,* New York, Exposition Press, 1948, p. 36.

10. Amry Vandenbosch, *The Dutch East Indies,* Berkeley, University of California Press, 1942, p. 59.

11. Multatuli, *Indonesia,* p. 91.

CHAPTER 8

1. C. Northcote Parkinson, *British Intervention in Malaya 1867–1877,* Singapore, University of Malaya Press, 1960, pp. 109–110.

2. Quoted in D. R. SarDesai, *British Trade and Expansion in Southeast Asia, 1830–1914,* New Delhi, Allied Publishers, 1977, pp. 161–162.

3. *Ibid.,* p. 163.

4. W.H.M. Read, *Play and Politics: Recollections of Malaya by an Old Resident,* London, Wells Gardner, Darton, 1901, p. 25.

5. SarDesai, *British Trade and Expansion,* p. 168.

6. John S. Galbraith, "The 'Turbulent Frontier' as a Factor in British Expansion," *Comparative Studies in Society and History* 2, 2 (January 1960), pp. 157–162.

7. C. D. Cowan, *Nineteenth Century Malaya,* London, Oxford University Press, 1961, p. 169.

8. D. R. SarDesai, "Sir Andrew Clarke and Malaya," *Journal of the University of Bombay* 31 (January 1963), pp. 24–38.

9. D. R. SarDesai, *Trade and Empire in Malaya and Singapore, 1869–1874,* Athens, Ohio University International Studies Series, 1970.

10. Parkinson, *British Intervention,* pp. 108–110.

11. A.E.H. Anson, *About Others and Myself, 1845–1920,* London, A. E. Anson, 1920, p. 322.

12. Emily Sadka, *The Protected Malay States 1874–1878,* Kuala Lumpur, University of Malaya Press, 1968, p. 86.

13. R. H. Vetch, *Life of General Sir Andrew Clarke,* London, Murray, 1905, p. 182.

14. D. R. SarDesai, "Resident System in Malaya, 1874–1878," *Journal of the Historical Society* 3 (1964–65), pp. 94–106.

15. Quoted in Sadka, *Protected Malay States,* p. 117.

16. K. G. Tregonning, *A History of Modern Malaya,* New York, David McKay, 1964, pp. 165–166.

CHAPTER 9

1. D. R. SarDesai, *British Trade and Expansion in Southeast Asia, 1830–1914,* New Delhi, Allied Publishers, 1977, p. 102.

2. W. S. Desai, *History of the British Residency in Burma, 1826–1840,* Yangon, Rangoon University Press, 1939, Appendix B. The roots of the "pipal" tree extend over a large terrain.

3. SarDesai, *British Trade and Expansion,* p. 115.

4. Salisbury to Governor General Lawrence, December 10, 1866, Lawrence Papers, F90/27, India Office.

5. Quoted in SarDesai, *British Trade and Expansion,* p. 199.

6. *Ibid.,* p. 201.

7. Htin Aung, *The Stricken Peacock: Anglo-Burmese Relations, 1752–1948,* The Hague, Nijhoff, 1965, p. 119.

8. Compton Mackenzie, *Realms of Silver: One Hundred Years of Banking in the East,* London, Kegan Paul, 1953, p. 87.

9. A. G. Pointon, *The Bombay-Burmah Trading Corporation, 1863–1963,* Southampton, Great Britain, Millbrook Press, 1964, p. 12.

10. SarDesai, *British Trade and Expansion,* p. 207.

11. Htin Aung, *The Stricken Peacock,* p. 81.

12. Dufferin to Churchill, private telegram, October 18, 1885, quoted in SarDesai, *British Trade and Expansion,* p. 217.

CHAPTER 10

1. Henri Blet, *France d'Outre-Mer,* vol. 2, Paris, Arthaud, 1950,p. 281.

2. Bernard Fall, *The Two Viet-Nams: A Political and Military Analysis,* rev. ed., New York, Praeger, 1964, p. 16.

3. Le Thanh Khoi, *Viet-Nam,* Paris, Les Editions de Minuit, 1955, p. 365.

4. David P. Chandler, *A History of Cambodia,* Boulder, Colo., Westview Press, 1983, pp. 123–128.

5. Lois E. Bailey, *Jules Ferry and French Indo-China,* Madison, University of Wisconsin Press, 1946, p. 24.

6. Thomas F. Powers Jr., *Jules Ferry and the Renaissance of French Imperialism,* New York, King's Crown Press, 1944, p. 191.

CHAPTER 11

1. A. B. Griswold, "King Mongkut in Perspective," *JSS* 45, 1 (April 1957), p. 21.

CHAPTER 12

1. W. F. Wertheim, *Indonesian Society in Transition: A Study of Social Change,* The Hague, W. Van Hoeve, 1956, p. 46.

CHAPTER 13

1. Charles Foreman, *The Philippine Islands,* New York, Holt, Rinehart, 1967, pp. 529–531.

2. Rafael Palma, *Pride of the Malay Race: A Biography of José Rizal,* Englewood Cliffs, N.J., Prentice-Hall, 1949, p. 35.

3. Frank C. Laubach, *Rizal, Man and Martyr,* Manila, Community Publishers, 1936, p. 159.

4. Quoted in Austin Craig, *Lineage, Life, and Labors of José Rizal, Philippine Patriot,* Manila, Philippine Education Co., 1913.

5. Quoted in Leon Wolff, *Little Brown Brother: How the United States Purchased and Pacified the Philippine Islands at the Century's Turn,* New York, Doubleday, 1961, p. 46.

6. John Fiske, "Manifest Destiny," *Harper's Magazine* 70 (March 1885), pp. 578–590.

7. J. A. Hobson, *Imperialism,* 3d ed., London, Allen and Unwin, 1938, p. 79.

8. *New York Commercial,* June 1, 1898, quoted in Julius W. Pratt, "American Business and the Spanish-American War," *Hispanic American Historical Review* 14 (May 1934), pp. 192–193.

9. *Congressional Record,* Sixtieth Congress, First Session, vol. 33, part 3, p. 70.

10. Quoted in Francisco Luzviminda, "The First Vietnam: The Philippine-American War," *Bulletin of Concerned Asian Scholars* (December 1973), p. 4.

11. *Ibid.*

12. Quoted in H. Wayne Morgan, *America's Road to Empire,* New York, Wiley and Sons, 1965, p. 104.

13. Edmund Troverso, *The Spanish-American War: A Study in Policy Change,* Lexington, Mass., D. C. Heath, 1968, p. 104.

14. E. L. Laus, *Brief Biographies of the Ten Most Outstanding Filipino National Leaders,* Manila, National Printing, 1951, p. 37.

15. Salvador Lopez, "The Colonial Relationship," in Frank H. Golay, ed., *The United States and the Philippines, 1929–46,* Englewood Cliffs, N.J., Prentice-Hall, 1966, p. 8.

16. Theodore Friend, *Between Two Empires: The Ordeal of the Philippines, 1929–1946,* New Haven, Yale University Press, 1965, p. 6.

CHAPTER 14

1. Robert Van Niel, *The Emergence of the Modern Indonesian Elite,* The Hague, W. van Hoeve, 1960, pp. 233–234.

2. Dorothy Woodman, *The Republic of Indonesia,* New York, Philosophical Library, 1955, p. 366.

3. D.G.E. Hall, *A History of South-East Asia,* 3d ed., London, Macmillan, 1968, p. 851.

4. Jawaharlal Nehru, *Independence and After,* New York, John Day, 1950, p. 332.

CHAPTER 16

1. Quoted by David A. Wilson in George M. Kahin, ed., *Governments and Politics of Southeast Asia,* 1st ed., Ithaca, N.Y., Cornell University Press, 1954, p. 20.

CHAPTER 17

1. For the significance of changes made by the French, see David G. Marr, *Vietnamese Tradition on Trial, 1920–1945,* Berkeley, University of California Press, 1981.

2. P. J. Honey, "Modern Vietnamese Historiography," in D.G.E. Hall, ed., *Historians of South-East Asia,* London, Oxford University Press, 1961, p. 98.

3. Truong Buu Lam, *Patterns of Vietnamese Response to Foreign Intervention, 1858–1900,* New Haven, Yale University, Southeast Asia Studies, 1967, p. 77.

4. David G. Marr, *Vietnamese Anti-Colonialism, 1885–1925,* Berkeley, University of California Press, 1971, pp. 95–97.

5. Quoted from a Viet Minh pamphlet in Jean Lacouture, *Ho Chi Minh: A Political Biography,* New York, Random House, Vantage Books, 1968, p. 88.

6. Ellen Hammer, *The Struggle for Indochina,* Stanford, Calif., Stanford University Press, 1954, p. 102.

7. David Halberstam, *Ho,* New York, Vintage Books, 1971, pp. 84–85.

8. Milton E. Osborne, *Region of Revolt: Focus on Southeast Asia,* Rushcutters Bay, New South Wales, Australia, Pergamon Press, 1970, p. 100.

CHAPTER 18

1. Barbara Watson Andaya and Leonard Y. Andaya, *A History of Malaysia,* London, Macmillan, 1982, p. 259.

CHAPTER 19

1. David J. Steinberg, *Philippine Collaboration in World War II,* Ann Arbor, University of Michigan Press, 1967, p. 93.

2. William J. Pomeroy, *The Forest: A Personal Record of the Huk Guerrilla Struggle in the Philippines,* New York, International Publishers, 1963, p. 19.

3. Caroline G. Hernandez, "The Philippines in 1995: Growth amid Challenges," *Asian Survey* 36, 2 (February 1996), p. 146.

CHAPTER 20

1. *Times of India* (Bombay), November 27, 1995, p. 17.
2. John Badgley, "Myanmar in 1993: A Watershed Year," *Asian Survey* 34, 2 (February 1994), p. 158.

CHAPTER 21

1. Charles Morrison and Astri Suhrke, *Strategies of Survival: The Foreign Policy Dilemmas of Smaller Asian States*, New York, St. Martin's Press, 1978, p. 128.
2. Simon Montlake, "Thailand's Exposed Southern Flank," *FEER*, May 2007, p. 36.
3. Michael H. Nelson, "Bangkok's Elitist Coup," *FEER*, October 2006, p. 28.

CHAPTER 22

1. Yudhoyono's lengthy interview for *BusinessWeek,* July 4, 2005.

CHAPTER 24

1. Abdul Rahman in August 1966, quoted in Michael Leifer, "Astride the Straits of Johore: The British Presence and Commonwealth Rivalry in Southeast Asia," *Modern Asian Studies* 1 (July 1967), p. 293.
2. Charles E. Morrison and Astri Suhrke, *Strategies of Survival: The Foreign Policy Dilemmas of Smaller Asian States,* New York, St. Martin's Press, 1978, p. 156.
3. *Foreign Affairs Malaysia* 1 (June 1970).
4. Colum Murphy, "Abdullah's Imperfect Plan," *FEER,* July–August 2006, p. 19.
5. *Ibid.,* p. 22.
6. Michael D. Barr, "The Charade of Meritocracy," *FEER,* October 2006, p. 18.
7. Linda Y. C. Lim, "Singapore's Success: The Myth of the Free Market Economy," *AS* 23, 6 (June 1983), p. 762.

CHAPTER 25

1. Frances Fitzgerald, *Fire in the Lake*, New York, Vintage Books, 1972, p. 300.
2. D. Gareth Porter, "The Myth of the Bloodbath: North Vietnam's Land Reform Reconsidered," Cornell University International Relations of East Asia Project, Ithaca, N.Y., 1972, mimeo.
3. James P. Harrison, *The Endless War: Fifty Years of Struggle in Vietnam,* New York, Free Press, 1982, p. 126 fn.
4. Jean Lacouture, *Vietnam Between Two Truces,* New York, Vintage Books, 1966, pp. 67–68.
5. William Henderson, "South Vietnam Finds Itself," *Foreign Affairs* 35, 2 (January 1957), p. 285.
6. Douglas Pike, *Viet Cong,* Cambridge, Mass., MIT Press, 1966, p. 76.
7. George M. Kahin and John W. Lewis, *The United States in Vietnam,* New York, Dial Press, 1967, p. 119.
8. Fitzgerald, *Fire in the Lake,* p. 177.
9. U.S. Department of State, *A Threat to the Peace,* Washington, D.C., Government Printing Office, 1961, p. iii.
10. David Halberstam, *The Making of a Quagmire,* New York, Random House, 1965, p. 68.
11. John Galloway, *The Gulf of Tonkin Resolution,* Rutherford, N.J., Fairleigh Dickinson University Press, 1970, pp. 36–37.
12. *Ibid.,* p. 167.

13. Quoted in John C. Pratt, ed., *Vietnam Voices,* New York, Penguin Books, 1984, p. 170.

14. Clark M. Clifford, "A Viet Nam Reappraisal," in Gerald Kurland, ed., *Misjudgment or Defense of Freedom? The United States in Vietnam,* New York, Simon and Schuster, 1975, pp. 121–122.

15. John G. Stoessinger, *Henry Kissinger: The Anguish of Power,* New York, W. W. Norton, 1976, pp. 51–52.

16. "U.S. Foreign Policy for the 1970's: A New Strategy for Peace," report to the Congress by Richard Nixon, February 18, 1970, Washington, D.C., Government Printing Office, pp. 55–56.

17. Norodom Sihanouk, "Cambodia Neutral: The Dictate of Necessity," *Foreign Affairs* 36 (July 1958), pp. 582–586.

18. For short biographies of the eight most prominent members of the Khmer Rouge high command, see John Barron and Anthony Paul, *Murder of a Gentle Land: The Untold Story of Communist Genocide in Cambodia,* New York, Reader's Digest Press, 1977, pp. 43–45.

19. William Shawcross, *Sideshow: Kissinger, Nixon, and the Destruction of Cambodia,* New York, Simon and Schuster, 1979, pp. 16, 236–239.

CHAPTER 26

1. John Lewallen, *Ecology of Devastation: Indochina,* Baltimore, Penguin Books, 1971.

2. Huynh Kim Khanh, "Year One of Post-Colonial Vietnam," *Southeast Asian Affairs 1977,* Singapore, Institute of Southeast Asian Studies, 1977, p. 290.

3. *Ibid.,* p. 294.

4. Michael Vickery, *Cambodia, 1975–1982,* Boston, South End Press, 1984, Chapter 3.

5. Full text of President Clinton's announcement in the *New York Times,* July 12, 1995; Senator McCain's statement quoted in *Keesing's Contemporary Archives, News Digest,* July 1995, p. 40,643.

6. Quoted in *Facts on File* (New York), vol. 53, no. 2741 (June 10, 1993), p. 418.

CHAPTER 27

1. "The Deadliest Tsunami in History?" *National Geographic News,* January 7, 2005.

2. "Tsunami in Southeast Asia: Full Coverage," *National Geographic News,* January 18, 2005.

3. Singapore, Ministry of Home Affairs, *White Paper: The Jemaah Islamiyah Arrests and the Threat of Terrorism,* 2003, p. 2.

4. Zachary Abuza, *Militant Islam in Southeast Asia: Crucible of Terror,* Boulder, Colo., Lynne Rienner, 2003.

PART FOUR REVIEW

1. Anthony Eden, *Full Circle: The Memoirs of Anthony Eden,* Boston, Houghton Mifflin, 1960, pp. 109–110.

2. Charles E. Morrison and Astri Suhrke, *Strategies of Survival: The Foreign Policy Dilemmas of Smaller Asian States,* New York, St. Martin's Press, 1978, p. 265.

Bibliography

This is a selected bibliography. It contains all the items referred to in the notes except archival documentation and collections of personal papers. The bibliography also includes some additional sources that would be useful for a further study of Southeast Asian history. It is divided into five parts: The general section includes reference works and those covering more than one chronological period. The other four sections correspond to the four parts of the book.

GENERAL

Andaya, Leonard Y., and Barbara Watson Andaya, *A History of Malaysia,* London, Macmillan, 1982.

Cady, John F., *Southeast Asia, Its Historical Development,* New York, McGraw-Hill, 1964.

Chandler, David P., *A History of Cambodia,* Boulder, Colo., Westview Press, 1983.

Chen, Anita Beltran, ed., *Contemporary and Historical Perspectives in Southeast Asia,* Ottawa, Canadian Asian Studies Association, 1985.

Chutintaranond, Sunait, and Chris Baker, eds., *Recalling Local Pasts, Autonomous History in Southeast Asia,* Chiang Mai, Silkworm Books, 2002.

Cowan, C. D., and O. W. Wolters, eds., *Southeast Asian History and Historiography,* Ithaca, N.Y., Cornell University Press, 1976.

Cressey, George B., *Asia's Lands and Peoples,* 3d ed., New York, McGraw-Hill, 1963.

de Klerck, E. S., *History of the Netherlands East Indies,* Rotterdam, W. L. & J. Brusse, 1938.

Gross, Max L., *Muslim Archipelago: Islam and Politics in Southeast Asia,* Washington, D.C., Center for Strategic and Intelligence Research, 2007.

Hack, Karl, and Tobias Ratting, eds., *Colonial Armies in Southeast Asia,* London, Routledge, 2006.

Hall, D. G. E., ed., *Atlas of South-East Asia,* New York, St. Martin's Press, 1964.

———, *Historians of South-East Asia,* London, Oxford University Press, 1961.

———, *A History of South-East Asia,* 4th ed., London, Macmillan, 1981.

Hay, Stephen N., and Margaret H. Case, eds., *Southeast Asian History: A Bibliographic Guide,* New York, Praeger, 1962.

James, Helen, *Thailand Culture and Society, Then and Now: A Short History of Thailand's Cultural Development from Pre-historic to Contemporary Times,* Yangon, SEAMEO Regional Center for History and Tradition, 2005, Vol. 1.

Kunstadter, Peter, ed., *Southeast Asian Tribes, Minorities, and Nations,* 2 vols., Princeton, N.J., Princeton University Press, 1967.

Le Thanh Khoi, *Viet-Nam, Paris,* Les Editions de Minuit, 1955.

Ling, Trevor, ed., *Buddhist Trends in Southeast Asia,* Singapore, Institute of Southeast Asian Studies, 1993.

McGee, T. G., *The Southeast Asian City: A Study of the Primate Cities of Southeast Asia,* London, G. Bell & Sons, 1967.

Natham, K.S., and Mohammad Hashim Kamali, eds., *Islam in Southeast Asia: Political, Social, and Strategic Challenges for the Twenty-first Century,* Singapore, Institute for Southeast Asian Studies, 2005.

Peleggi, Maurizio, *Thailand: The Worldly Kingdom,* London, Reaktion, 2007.

Purcell, Victor, *The Chinese in Southeast Asia,* London, Oxford University Press, 1965.

Reynolds, Craig T., *Seditious Histories: Contesting Thai and Southeast Asian Pasts,* Seattle, University of Washington Press, 2006.

SarDesai, D. R., *Vietnam: The Struggle for National Identity,* 2d ed., Boulder, Colo., Westview Press, 1992.

SarDesai, D. R., *Vietnam, Past and Present,* 4th ed., Boulder, Colo., Westview Press, 2005.

Smith, Harold E., Gayla S. Nieminen, and May Kyi Win, eds., *Historical Dictionary of Thailand,* 2d ed., Lanham, Md., Scarecrow Press, 2005.

Soedjatmoko, Mohammad Ali, G. K. Resink, and George M. Kahin, eds., *An Introduction to Indonesian Historiography,* Ithaca, N.Y., Cornell University Press, 1965.

Steinberg, David J., *In Search of Southeast Asia,* New York, Praeger, 1971; 2d ed., 1985.

Tarling, Nicholas, *Corruption and Good Governance in Asia,* London, Routledge, 2005.

Terwiel, B. J., *Thailand's Political History from the Fall of Ayuthaya in 1767 to Recent Times,* Bangkok, River Books, 2005.

Vandenbosch, Amry, *The Dutch East Indies,* 3d ed., Berkeley, University of California Press, 1942.

Vlekke, Bernard H. M., *Nusantara: A History of the East Indian Archipelago,* Cambridge, Mass., Harvard University Press, 1943.

Wang Gungwu, ed., *Nation-building: Five Southeast Asian Histories,* Singapore, Institute of Southeast Asian Studies, 2005.

Woodman, Dorothy, *The Making of Burma,* London, Cresset Press, 1962.

Wyatt, David K., *Thailand,* New Haven, Yale University Press, 1982.

Zurbuchen, Mary S., ed., *Beginning to Remember: The Past in the Indonesian Present,* Seattle, University of Washington Press, 2005.

PART ONE

Adams, J., and N. Hancock, "Land and Economy in Traditional Vietnam," *JSEAH* 1, 2 (1970).

Ahmad Ibrahim, Sharon Siddique, and Yasmin Hussain, eds., *Readings on Islam in Southeast Asia,* Singapore, Institute of Southeast Asian Studies, 1985.

Alatas, Syed Hussain, "On the Need for an Historical Study of Malaysian Islamisation," *JSEAH* 4, 1 (March 1963), pp. 62–74.

Baker, Chris, and Ben Anderson, eds., *Pen and Sail Literature and History in Early Bangkok Including the History of Bangkok in the Chronicles of Ayuthaya,* Chiang Mai, Silkworm Books, 2005.

Bayard, D. T., "Excavations at Non Nok Tha, Northeastern Thailand, 1968," *Asian Perspectives* 13 (1970), pp. 109–144.

———, "The Roots of Indochinese Civilization: Recent Developments in the Prehistory of Southeast Asia," *Pacific Affairs* 53 (1980), pp. 89–114.

———, ed., *Southeast Asian Archaeology at the Fifteenth Pacific Science Congress,* Dunedin, New Zealand, Otago University Studies in Prehistoric Archaeology, 1984.

Briggs, Lawrence P., *The Ancient Khmer Empire,* Philadelphia, American Philosophical Society, 1951.

Buttinger, Joseph, *Vietnam: A Political History,* New York, Praeger, 1968.

Coedes, Georges, *The Indianized States of Southeast Asia,* Honolulu, East-West Center Press, 1968.

———, *The Making of South-East Asia,* Berkeley, University of California Press, 1966.

———, "Le royaume de Crivijaya," *BEFEO* 18, 6 (1918), pp. 1–36.

de Casparis, J. G., *Selected Inscriptions from the Seventh to the Ninth Century a.d.,* Bandung, Prasasti Indonesia, 1956.

Dutton, George Edson, *Tay Son Uprising: Society and Rebellion in Eighteenth Century Vietnam,* Honolulu, University of Hawaii Press, 2006.

Glamann, Kristaf, *Dutch-Asiatic Trade, 1620–1740,* The Hague, Martinus Nijhoff, 1958.

Goloubew, Victor, "L'hydraulique urbaine et agricole a l'epoque des rois d'Angkor," *Bulletin Economique Indochine,* fasc. 1, 1941.

Gomez, Louis, and Hiram Woodward Jr., eds., *Barabudur: History and Significance of a Buddhist Monument,* Berkeley, University of California Press, 1981.

Groslier, Bernard Philippe, *Angkor and Cambodia in the Sixteenth Century: According to Portuguese and Spanish Sources,* trans. Michael Smithies, Bangkok, Orchard Press, 2006.

———, *Angkor et le Cambodge au XVI siecle d'apres les documents portugais et espagnols,* Paris, Presses Universitaires, 1958.

———, "Our Knowledge of Khmer Civilization: A Reappraisal," *JSS* 48 (June 1960), pp. 1–28.

Hall, Kenneth R., *Maritime Trade and State Development in Early Southeast Asia,* Honolulu, University of Hawaii Press, 1985.

Hall, Kenneth R., and John K. Whitmore, eds., *Explorations in Early Southeast Asian History: The Origins of Southeast Asian Statecraft,* Ann Arbor, University of Mich., Center for South and Southeast Asian Studies, 1976.

Hanks, L. M., *Rice and Man: Agricultural Ecology in Southeast Asia,* Chicago, Aldine, 1972.

Heine-Geldern, Robert, "Conceptions of State and Kingship in Southeast Asia," *FEQ* 2 (1942), pp. 15–30.

Higham, Charles, *The Archaeology of Mainland Southeast Asia from 10,000 b.c. to the Fall of Angkor,* Cambridge, Cambridge University Press, 1989.

Hill, A. H., "The Coming of Islam to North Sumatra," *JSEAH* 4, 1 (March 1963), pp. 6–19.

———, "Hikayat Raja Pasai," *JMBRAS* 33, Part 2 (1960), pp. 1–215.

Hill, R. D., "Rice in Malaya: A Study in Historical Geography," Ph.D. thesis, University of Singapore, 1973.

Hoskin, John, *Falcon at the Court of Siam,* Bangkok, Asia Books, 2002.

Jamieson, N., "A Perspective on Vietnamese Pre-History Based upon the Relationship Between Geological and Archaeological Data," *Asian Perspectives* 24 (1981), pp. 187–192.

Janse, J. M., *Archaeological Research in Indo-China: The Ancient Dwelling Site of Dong-S'on,* Cambridge, Mass., Harvard University Press, 1958.

Kalgren, B., "The Date of the Early Dongson Culture," *Bulletin of the Museum of Far Eastern Antiquities* 14 (1942), pp. 1–29.

Kasetsiri, Charnvit, *The Rise of Ayuthaya,* Kuala Lumpur, Oxford University Press, 1976.

Lavy, Paul Andrew, *Visnu and Harihara in the Art and Politics of Early Historic Southeast Asia,* n.p. 2004.

Le Blanc, Marcel, *History of Siam, 1688,* trans. Michael Smithies, Chiang Mai, Silkworm Books, 2003.

Le May, Reginald, *The Culture of South-East Asia,* London, Allen and Unwin, 1954.

Lieberman, Victor B., *Burmese Administrative Cycles: Anarchy and Conquest, c. 1580–1760,* Princeton, N.J., Princeton University Press, 1984.

———, "Ethnic Politics in Eighteenth Century Burma," *Modern Asian Studies* 12, 3 (July 1978), pp. 455–482.

Mabbett, I. W., "Devaraja," *JSEAH* 10 (September 1969), pp. 202–223.

———, "The 'Indianisation' of Southeast Asia: Reflections on Prehistoric Sources," *JSEAS* 8, 1 (March 1977), pp. 1–14.

———, "The 'Indianisation' of Southeast Asia: Reflections on the Historical Sources," *JSEAS* 8, 2 (September 1977), pp. 143–161.

————, "Varnas in Angkor and the Indian Caste System," *JAS* 36, 3 (May 1977), pp. 429–442.

Majumdar, R. C., *Ancient Indian Colonies in the Far East,* Lahore, Punjab Sanskrit Book Depot, 1937.

Marr, David G., and A. C. Milner, eds., *Southeast Asia in the Ninth to Fourteenth Centuries,* Singapore, Institute of Southeast Asian Studies, 1986.

Marrison, G. E., "The Coming of Islam to the East Indies," *JMBRAS* 24, Part 1 (1951), pp. 28–37.

Maspero, M. G., *Le Royaume de Champa,* Paris, Librairie Nationale, 1928.

Maybon, Charles, *Histoire moderne du pays d'Annam, 1592–1820,* Paris, Plon-Nourrit, 1919.

McCoy, Alfred W., and Ed. C. de Jesus, eds., *Philippine Social History: Global Trade and Local Transformations,* Manila, Ateneo de Manila University Press, 1982.

Meilink-Roelofsz, M.A.P., *Asian Trade and European Influence in the Indonesian Archipelago Between About 1500 and 1630,* The Hague, Martinus Nijhoff, 1962.

Mukhom, Wongthes, *Intellectual Might and National Myth: A Forensic Investigation of the Ram Khameng Controversy in Thai Society,* Bangkok, Matichon, 2003.

Mus, Paul, "Cultes indiens et indigenes au Champa," *BEFEO* 33 (1933), pp. 367–410.

Nguyen, Ngoc Huy, *The Le Code: Law in Traditional Vietnam,* Athens, Ohio University Press, 1987.

Nilakanta Sastri, K. A., *History of Srivijaya,* Madras, University of Madras, 1949.

Nivat, Dhani, "The Reconstruction of Rama I of the Chakri Dynasty," *JSS* 43, 1 (1955), pp. 262–265.

O'Harrow, S., "From Co-loa to the Trung Sisters' Revolt: Viet-Nam as the Chinese Found It," *Asian Perspectives* 22, 2 (1979), pp. 140–164.

Pe Maung Tin, U. and G. H. Luce (trans.), *The Glass Palace Chronicle of the Kings of Burma,* London, Oxford University Press, 1923.

Phelan, J. L., *The Hispanisation of the Philippines: Spanish Aims and Filipino Responses, 1565–1700,* Madison, University of Wisconsin Press, 1959.

Pires, Tome, *Suma Oriental,* London, Hakluyt Society, 1944.

Quaritch-Wales, H. G., *Ancient Siamese Government and Administration,* London, Bernard Quaritch, 1934.

————, *The Making of Greater India,* London, Bernard Quaritch, 1951.

Reid, Anthony, and Lance Castles, eds., *Pre-Colonial State Systems in Southeast Asia,* Kuala Lumpur, *JMBRAS* Monograph Series, 1975.

Ruangsilp, Bhawan, *Dutch East India Company Merchants at the Court of Ayuthaya: Dutch Perceptions of the Thai Kingdom, c. 1604–1765,* Leiden, Brill, 2007.

Shrieke, B., *Indonesian Sociological Studies,* 2 vols., The Hague, W. van Hoeve, 1955–1957.

Smith, R. B., and W. Watson, eds., *Early Southeast Asia: Essays in Archaeology, History, and Historical Geography,* London, Oxford University Press, 1979.

Steensgaard, Niels, *Carracks, Caravans, and Companies: The Structural Crisis in European-Asian Trade in the Early Seventeenth Century,* Copenhagen, Scandinavian Institute of Asian Studies, 1973.

Swearer, Donald K., *Becoming the Buddha: The Ritual of Image Consecration in Thailand,* Princeton, N.J., Princeton University Press, 2004.

Takaya, Yoshikazu, "An Ecological Interpretation of Thai History," *JSEAS* 6, 2 (1975), pp. 190–195.

Taufik, Abdullah, and Sharon Siddique, eds., *Islam and Society in Southeast Asia,* Singapore, Institute of Southeast Asian Studies, 1985.

Taylor, Keith W., *The Birth of Vietnam,* Berkeley, University of California Press, 1983.

————, "An Evaluation of the Chinese Period in Vietnamese History," *Journal of Asiatic Studies, Korea University* 23 (January 1980), pp. 139–164.

van Leur, J. C., *Indonesian Trade and Society,* The Hague, W. van Hoeve, 1955.

Veidlinger, Daniel M., *Spreading the Dhamma: Writng, Orality, and Textual Transmission in Buddhist Northern Thailand,* Honolulu, University of Hawaii Press, 2006.

Wake, Christopher H., "Malacca's Early Kings and the Reception of Islam," *JSEAH* 5, 2 (September 1964), pp. 104–128.

Wenk, Klaus, *The Restoration of Thailand Under Rama I,* Tucson, University of Arizona Press, 1968.

Wheatley, Paul, *The Golden Khersonese: Studies in the Historical Geography of the Malay Peninsula Before a.d. 1500,* Kuala Lumpur, University of Malaya Press, 1966.

Winstedt, Richard O., "Kinship and Enthronement in Malaya," *JMBRAS* 19, Parts 3–4 (June 1947), pp. 129–139.

Wolters, O. W., *Early Indonesian Commerce: A Study of the Origins of Srivijaya,* Ithaca, N.Y., Cornell University Press, 1967.

Woodside, Alexander B., *Vietnam and the Chinese Model,* Cambridge, Mass., Harvard University Press, 1970.

PART TWO

Adas, M., *The Burma Delta: Economic Development and Social Change on an Asian Rice Frontier, 1852–1941,* Madison, University of Wisconsin Press, 1971.

———, "From Avoidance to Confrontation: Peasant Protest in Colonial Southeast Asia," *Comparative Studies in Society and History* 23 (1988), pp. 217–248.

Aung, Htin, *The Stricken Peacock: Anglo-Burmese Relations, 1752–1948,* The Hague, Nijhoff, 1965.

Bailey, Lois E., *Jules Ferry and Indo-China,* Madison, University of Wisconsin Press, 1946.

Banerjee, A. C., *The Annexation of Burma,* Calcutta, A. Mukherjee, 1944.

———, *The Eastern Frontier of British India, 1784–1826,* Calcutta, A. Mukherjee, 1946.

Bastin, John, *The Native Policies of Sir Stamford Raffles in Java and Sumatra: An Economic Interpretation,* Oxford, Clarendon Press, 1957.

Blet, Henri, *France d'Outre-Mer,* 2 vols., Paris, Arthaud, 1950.

Boeke, J. H., *The Structure of the Netherlands Indian Economy,* New York, Institute of Pacific Relations, 1942.

Booth, A., W. J. O'Malley, and A. Weidemann, *Indonesian Economic History in the Dutch Colonial Era,* New Haven, Yale University Press, 1990.

Bowring, John, *The Kingdom and People of Siam,* 2 vols., London, Parker, 1857.

———, *The Philippine Islands,* London, Smith Elder, 1859.

Cady, John F., *A History of Modern Burma,* Ithaca, N.Y., Cornell University Press, 1958.

———, *The Roots of French Imperialism in Eastern Asia,* Ithaca, N.Y., Cornell University Press, 1954.

Christian, J. S., *Modern Burma,* Berkeley, University of California Press, 1942.

Coupland, Reginald, *Raffles of Singapore,* 3d ed., London, Collins, 1946.

Cowan, C. D., *Nineteenth Century Malaya,* London, Oxford University Press, 1961.

Cribb, R., ed., *The Late Colonial State in Indonesia: Political and Economic Foundations of the Netherlands Indies, 1800–1942,* Leiden, Royal Institute, 1994.

Day, Clive, *Policy and Administration of the Dutch in Java,* New York, Macmillan, 1904; reprint, Kuala Lumpur, Oxford University Press, 1966.

Desai, W. S., *History of the British Residency in Burma, 1826–1840,* Yangon, Rangoon University Press, 1939.

Dutreb, M., *L'admiral Dupre et la conquete du Tonkin,* Paris, E. Leroux, 1924.

Fasseur, C., *The Politics of Colonial Exploitation: Java, the Dutch, and the Cultivation System,* Ithaca, N.Y., Cornell University Press, 1992.

Foreman, Charles, *The Philippine Islands,* New York, Holt, Rinehart, 1967.

Furnivall, John S., *Colonial Policy and Practice: A Comparative Study of Burma and Netherlands India,* New York, New York University Press, 1956.

———, *Netherlands India: A Study of Plural Economy,* Cambridge, Cambridge University Press, 1944.

Galbraith, John S., "The 'Turbulent Frontier' as a Factor in British Expansion," *Comparative Studies in Society and History* 2, 2 (January 1960), pp. 157–162.

Gillis, E. Kay, *Singapore Civil Society and British Power,* Singapore, Talisman, 2005.

Griswold, A. B., "King Mongkut in Perspective," *JSS* 45, 1 (April 1957), pp. 1–41.

Hahn, Emily, *Raffles of Singapore,* New York, Doubleday, 1946.

Hall, D.G.E., "Anglo-Burmese Conflicts in the 19th Century: A Reassessment of Their Causes," *Asia* 6 (Autumn 1966), pp. 35–52.

Hansen, Anne Ruth, *How to Behave: Buddhism and Modernity in Colonial Cambodia, 1860-1930,* Honolulu, University of Hawaii Press, 2007.

Hobson, J. A., *Imperialism,* 3d ed., London, Allen and Unwin, 1938.

Honey, P. J., "French Historiography and the Evolution of Colonial Vietnam," in D.G.E. Hall, ed., *Historians of South-East Asia,* London, Oxford University Press, 1961.

Laffey, Ella S., "French Adventurers and Chinese Bandits in Tonkin: The Garnier Affair in Its Local Context," *JSEAS* 6 (March 1975), pp. 38–51.

Laubach, Frank C., *Rizal, Man and Martyr,* Manila, Community Publishers, 1936.

Leos, Tamara Lynn, *Subject Siam: Family, Law, and Colonial Modernity in Thailand,* Ithaca, N.Y., Cornell University Press, 2006.

Lewis, Dianne, *Jan Compagnie in the Straits of Malacca, 1641–1795,* Athens, Ohio University Center for International Studies, 1995.

Locher-Scholten, E., "Dutch Expansion in the Indonesian Archipelago Around 1900 and the Imperialism Debate," *JSEAS* 25, 1 (March 1994), pp. 91–111.

Marks, Harry J., *The First Contest for Singapore, 1818–1824,* The Hague, Martinus Nijhoff, 1959.

McIntyre, David, "Britain's Intervention in Malaya: The Origins of Lord Kimberley's Instructions to Andrew Clarke in 1873," *JSEAH* 2, 3 (October 1961), pp. 62–79.

Multatuli [E. D. Dekker], *Max Havelaar,* New York, House and Maxwell, 1967.

Murray, Martin J., *The Development of Capitalism in Colonial Indochina, 1870–1940,* Berkeley, University of California Press, 1980.

Nguyen-Marshall, Van, *In Search of Moral Authority: The Discourse on Poverty, Poor Relief, and Charity in French Colonial Vietnam,* New York, Peter Lang, 2008.

Nguyen, Thua Hy, *Economic History of Hanoi in the Seventeenth, Eighteenth, and Nineteenth Centuries,* trans. Barbara Cohen, Hanoi, National Political Publishing House, 2002.

Osborne, Milton E., *The French Presence in Cochin China and Cambodia: Rule and Response, 1859–1905,* Ithaca, N.Y., Cornell University Press, 1969.

Panikkar, K. M., *Asia and Western Dominance,* London, Allen and Unwin, 1953.

Parkinson, C. Northcote, *British Intervention in Malaya, 1867–1877,* Singapore, University of Malaya Press, 1960.

Powers, Thomas F., *Jules Ferry and the Renaissance of French Imperialism,* New York, King's Crown Press, 1944.

Priestley, H. I., *France Overseas: A Study of Modern Imperialism,* New York, Appleton-Century, 1938.

Rabibhadana, Akin, *The Organisation of Thai Society in the Early Bangkok Period, 1782–1873,* Ithaca, N.Y., Cornell University, Data Paper No. 74, Southeast Asia Program, 1969.

Raffles, Thomas, *Memoirs of the Life and Public Services of Sir Thomas Stamford Raffles,* London, William Clowes and Sons, 1835.

Sadka, Emily, *The Protected Malay States, 1874–1895,* Kuala Lumpur, University of Malaya Press, 1968.

SarDesai, D. R., *British Trade and Expansion in Southeast Asia, 1830–1914,* New Delhi, Allied Publishers, 1977.

———, "Resident System in Malaya, 1874–1878," *Journal of the Historical Society* 3 (1964–1965), pp. 94–106.

———, "Sir Andrew Clarke and Malaya," *Journal of the University of Bombay* 31 (January 1963), pp. 24–38.

———, *Trade and Empire in Malaya and Singapore, 1869–1874,* Athens, Ohio University International Studies Series, 1970.

Singhal, D. P., *The Annexation of Upper Burma,* Singapore, Eastern Universities Press, 1960.

Skinner, G. William, and A. Thomas Kirsh, eds., *Change and Persistence in Thai Society,* Ithaca, N.Y., Cornell University Press, 1975.

Swettenham, Frank, *British Malaya,* London, Allen and Unwin, 1955.

Taboulet, Georges, *La geste francaise en Indochine,* 2 vols., Paris, Adrien-Maison Neuve, 1955–1956.

Tarling, Nicholas, *British Policy in the Malay Peninsula and Archipelago, 1824–1871,* Kuala Lumpur, Oxford University Press, 1969.

Tregonning, K. G., *A History of Modern Malaya,* New York, David McKay, 1964.

Van Kleveren, J. J., *The Dutch Colonial System in the East Indies,* The Hague, Martinus Nijhoff, 1953.

Wilson, Greta D., *Regents, Reformers, and Revolutionaries: Indonesian Voices of Colonial Days,* Honolulu, University of Hawaii Press, 1978.

Wong, Lin Ken, *The Malayan Tin Industry to 1914,* Tucson, University of Arizona Press, 1965.

Wurtzburg, C. E., *Raffles of the Eastern Isles,* London, Hodder and Stoughton, 1954.

PART THREE

Agoncillo, Teodoro A., *The Fateful Years: Japan's Adventure in the Philippines, 1941–1945,* 2 vols., Manila, R. P. Garcia Publishing, 1965.

———, *Filipino Nationalism, 1872–1970,* Quezon City, R. P. Garcia Publishing, 1974.

———, *The Revolt of the Masses: The Story of Bonifacio and the Katipunan,* Manila, University of the Philippines, 1965.

Anderson, B.R.O'G., *Java in a Time of Revolution: Occupation and Resistance, 1944–1946,* Ithaca, N.Y., Cornell University Press, 1972.

Ariffin, Omar, *Bangsa Melayu: Malay Concepts of Democracy and Community, 1945–1950,* Oxford, Oxford University Press, 1993.

Benda, Harry J., *The Crescent and the Rising Sun: Indonesian Islam Under the Japanese Occupation,* The Hague, W. van Hoeve, 1958.

———, "Peasant Movements in Colonial Southeast Asia," *Asian Studies* 3 (1965), pp. 420–434.

Buttinger, Joseph, *A Dragon Embattled: A History of Colonial and Post-Colonial Vietnam,* 2 vols., New York, Praeger, 1967.

Cady, John, *A History of Modern Burma,* Ithaca, N.Y., Cornell University Press, 1958.

Chandler, David P., *The Tragedy of Cambodian History: Politics, War, and Revolution Since 1945,* New Haven, Yale University Press, 1945.

Chesneaux, Jean, *Contribution a l'histoire de la nation Vietnamienne,* Paris, Editions Sociales, 1962.

Christian, John L., and Nobutaka Ike, "Thailand in Japan's Foreign Relations," *Pacific Affairs* 15 (1942), pp. 195–221.

Clancy, G. B., *A Dictionary of Indonesian History Since 1900,* Sydney, Sunda Publications, 1992.

Coates, John, *Suppressing Insurgency: An Analysis of the Malayan Emergency, 1948–1954,* Boulder, Colo., Westview Press, 1992.

Craig, Austin, *Lineage, Life, and Labors of Jose Rizal, Philippine Patriot,* Manila, Philippine Education Co., 1913.

Cribb, R. B., *Modern Indonesia: A History Since 1945,* New York, Longman, 1995.

Devillers, Philippe, and Jean Lacouture, *End of a War: Indochina, 1954,* New York, Praeger, 1969.

Dhiravegin, Likhit, *Siam and Colonialism, 1855–1909: An Analysis of Diplomatic Relations,* Bangkok, Thai Watana Panich, 1975.

Duiker, William J., *The Rise of Nationalism in Vietnam, 1900–1941,* Ithaca, N.Y., Cornell University Press, 1976.

Elsbree, Willard H., *Japan's Role in Southeast Asian Nationalist Movements, 1940–45,* Cambridge, Mass., Harvard University Press, 1953.

Emerson, Rupert, ed., *Government and Nationalism in Southeast Asia,* New York, Institute of Pacific Relations, 1942.

Fall, Bernard B., ed., *Ho Chi Minh on Revolution: Selected Writings, 1920–1966,* New York, Praeger, 1967.

Fenn, Charles, *Ho Chi Minh: A Biographical Introduction,* New York, Charles Scribner's, 1973.

Fiske, John, "Manifest Destiny," *Harper's Magazine* 70 (March 1885), pp. 578–590.

Friend, Theodore, *Between Two Empires: The Ordeal of the Philippines, 1929–1946,* New Haven, Yale University Press, 1965.

Giebel, Christoph, *Imagined Ancestries of Vietnamese Communism: Ton Duc Thang and the Politics of History and Memory,* Seattle, University of Washington, 2004.

Golay, Frank H., ed., *The United States and the Philippines, 1929–46,* Englewood Cliffs, N.J., Prentice-Hall, 1966.

Halberstam, David, *Ho,* New York, Vintage Books, 1971.

Hammer, Ellen J., *The Struggle for Indochina,* Stanford, Calif., Stanford University Press, 1954.

Haseman, John B., *The Thai Resistance Movement During the Second World War,* De Kalb, Northern Illinois Center for Southeast Asian Studies, 1978.

Hindley, Donald, *The Communist Party of Indonesia,* Berkeley, University of California Press, 1964.

Holland, William L., ed., *Asian Nationalism and the West,* New York, Macmillan, 1953.

Ileto, Reynaldo, *Payson and Revolution: Popular Movements in the Philippines, 1840–1910,* Quezon City, Ateneo de Manila Press, 1989.

Jackson, Robert, *The Malayan Emergency: The Commonwealth's Wars, 1948–1966,* New York, Routledge, 1991.

Kahin, George McTurnan, *Nationalism and Revolution in Indonesia,* Ithaca, N.Y., Cornell University Press, 1952.

Kiernan, Ben, *How Pol Pot Came to Power: A History of Communism in Kampuchea, 1930–1975,* London, Verso, 1985.

Kiernan, V. G., "Britain, Siam, and Malaya," *Journal of Modern History* 28 (1956), pp. 1–20.

Kobkua Suwannathat-Pian, *Thailand's Durable Premier: Phibun Through the Decades, 1932–1957,* New York, Oxford University Press, 1995.

Kramer, Paul A., *Blood of Government: Race, Empire, the United States and the Philippines,* Chapel Hill, University of North Carolina Press, 2006.

Lacouture, Jean, *Ho Chi Minh: A Political Biography,* New York, Random House, Vintage Books, 1968.

———, *Vietnam Between Two Truces,* New York, Vintage Books, 1966.

Lam, Truong Buu, *Patterns of Vietnamese Response to Foreign Intervention, 1858–1900,* New Haven, Yale University, Southeast Asia Studies, 1967.

Landon, Margaret, *Anna and the King of Siam,* London, Hamilton, 1956.

Laus, E. L., *Brief Biographies of the Ten Most Outstanding Filipino National Leaders,* Manila, National Printing, 1951.

Leonowens, Anna, *An English Governess at the Court of Siam,* Boston, Osgood and Co., 1870.

Linther, Bertil, *Burma in Revolt: Opium and Insurgency Since 1948,* Boulder, Colo., Westview Press, 1994.

Luzviminda, Francisco, "The First Vietnam: The Philippine-American War," *Bulletin of Concerned Asian Scholars* 5, 4 (December 1973), pp. 2–16.

Marr, David G., *Vietnam 1945: The Quest for Power,* Berkeley, University of California Press, 1995.

———, *Vietnamese Anti-Colonialism, 1885–1925,* Berkeley, University of California Press, 1971.

———, *Vietnamese Tradition on Trial, 1920–1945,* Berkeley, University of California Press, 1981.

May, Glenn Anthony, *Social Engineering in the Philippines: The Aims, Execution, and Impact of American Colonial Policy, 1900–1913,* Westport, Conn., Greenwood Press, 1980.

McAlister, John T., Jr., and Paul Mus, *The Vietnamese and Their Revolution,* New York, Harper and Row, 1970.

McCallum, John, *Leonard Wood: Rough Rider, Surgeon, Architect of American Imperialism,* New York, New York University Press, 2006.

McCormick, Thomas, "Insular Imperialism and the Open Door: The China Market and the Spanish-American War," *Pacific Historical Review* 32 (1963), pp. 155–169.

McVey, Ruth T., *The Rise of Indonesian Communism,* Ithaca, N.Y., Cornell University Press, 1965.

Milner, Anthony Crothers, *The Invention of Politics in Colonial Malaya: Contesting Nationalism and the Expansion of the Public Sphere,* New York, Cambridge University Press, 1995.

Moffat, A. L., *Mongkut, the King of Siam,* Ithaca, N.Y., Cornell University Press, 1961.

Morgan, H. Wayne, *America's Road to Empire,* New York, Wiley and Sons, 1965.

Nehru, Jawaharlal, *Independence and After,* New York, John Day, 1950.

Neumann-Hoditz, Reinhold, *Portrait of Ho Chi Minh,* Berlin, Herder and Herder, 1972.

Ngo Vinh Long, *Before the Revolution: The Vietnamese Peasants Under the French,* Cambridge, Mass., Harvard University Press, 1973.

Nonini, Donald Macon, *British Colonial Rule and the Resistance of the Malay Peasantry, 1900–1957,* New Haven, Yale University Southeast Asia Studies, 1992.

Pabico, Rufino C., *The Exiled Government: The Philippine Commonwealth in the United States during the Second World War,* Amherst, NY., Humanity Books, 2006.

Palma, Rafael, *Pride of the Malay Race: A Biography of José Rizal,* New York, Prentice-Hall, 1949.

Pham Cao Duong, *Vietnamese Peasants Under French Domination, 1861–1945,* Berkeley, Calif., Center for South and Southeast Asian Studies, 1985.

Pike, Douglas, *History of Vietnamese Communism, 1925–76,* Stanford, Calif., Hoover Institution Press, 1978.

Pomeroy, William, *The Philippines: Colonialism, Collaboration, and Resistance,* New York, International Publishers, 1992.

Pratt, Julius W., "American Business and the Spanish-American War," *Hispanic American Historical Review* 14 (May 1934), pp. 163–201.

Rajchagool, Chaiyan, *The Rise and Fall of the Thai Absolute Monarchy,* Bangkok, White Lotus, 1994.

Reddi, V. M., *A History of the Cambodian Independence Movement, 1863–1955,* Tirupati, India, Venkateshwara University, 1970.

Reynolds, E. Bruce, *Thailand's Secret War: The Free Thai, OSS, and SOE During World War II,* New York, Cambridge University Press, 2005.

Rizal, José, *Noli Me Tangere (The Lost Eden)*, trans. Leon Ma Guervero, Bloomington, Indiana University Press, 1961 (originally published 1887).

Roff, William R., *The Origins of Malay Nationalism*, New Haven, Yale University Press, 1967.

Romulo, Carlos P., *I Saw the Fall of the Philippines*, New York, Doubleday, 1942.

——, *I See the Philippines Rise*, New York, Doubleday, 1946.

Sainteny, Jean, *Ho Chi Minh and His Vietnam: A Personal Memoir*, Chicago, Cowles Book Co., 1970.

Salamanca, Bonifacio S., *The Filipino Reaction to American Rule*, Hamden, Conn., Shoe String Press, 1968.

Sarkisyanz, E., *Buddhist Background of the Burmese Revolution*, The Hague, Martinus Nijhoff, 1965.

Shaw, Angel Velasco, and Luis H. Francia, eds., *Vestiges of War: The Philippine-American War and the Aftermath of an Imperial Dream, 1899-1999*, New York, New York University Press, 2002.

Silverstein, J., ed., *Southeast Asia in World War II*, New Haven, Yale University Press, 1966.

Singh, Balwant, *Independence and Democracy in Burma, 1945–1952: The Turbulent Years*, Ann Arbor, Michigan University Press, 1993.

Smith, Malcolm, *A Physician at the Court of Siam*, London, Country Life, 1946.

Sopice, Mohammad Noordin, *From Malayan Union to Singapore Separation: Political Unification in the Malayan Region, 1945–65*, 2d ed., Kuala Lumpur, University of Malaya Press, 2005.

Steinberg, David J., *Philippine Collaboration in World War II*, Ann Arbor, University of Michigan Press, 1967.

Stockwell, A. J., *British Policy and Malay Politics During the Malayan Union Experiment, 1942–1948*, Kuala Lumpur, *JMBRAS*, 1979.

——, *Malaysia, Documents on the End of Empire*, London, H. M.'s Stationery Office, 2004.

Suryadinata, Leo, *Peranakan Chinese Politics in Java, 1917–1942*, Singapore, Institute of Southeast Asian Studies, 1976.

Tai, Hue-Tam, *Radicalism and the Origins of the Vietnamese Revolution*, Cambridge, Mass., Harvard University Press, 1992.

Tan, Tai Yong, *Creating "Greater Malaysia": Decolonization and the Politics of Merger*, Singapore, Institute of Southeast Asian Studies, 2008.

Taylor, George E., *The Philippines and the United States: Problems of Partnership*, New York, Praeger, 1971.

Thomson, R. Stanley, "Siam and France, 1863–70," *FEQ* 5 (1945), pp. 28–46.

Troverso, Edmund, *The Spanish-American War: A Study in Policy Change*, Lexington, Mass., D. C. Heath, 1968.

Tuck, Patrick, *The French Wolf and the Siamese Lamb: The French Threat to Siamese Independence, 1858–1907*, Bangkok, White Lotus, 1995.

Van der Kroef, Justus, *The Communist Party of Indonesia*, Vancouver, University of British Columbia Press, 1965.

Van Niel, Robert, *The Emergence of the Modern Indonesian Elite*, The Hague, W. van Hoeve, 1960.

Vella, Walter F., *Chaiyo! King Vajiravudh and the Development of Thai Nationalism*, Honolulu, Hawaii University Press, 1978.

——, *The Impact of the West on Government in Thailand*, Berkeley, University of California Press, 1955.

——, *Siam Under Rama III*, Locust Valley, N.Y., J. J. Augustin, 1957.

Von der Mehden, Fred, *Religion and Nationalism in Southeast Asia*, Madison, University of Wisconsin Press, 1963.

Warbey, William, *Ho Chi Minh and the Struggle for a Free Vietnam*, London, Merlin Press, 1972.

Wertheim, W. F., *Indonesian Society in Transition: A Study of Social Change*, The Hague, W. van Hoeve, 1956.

Williams, Lorraine, *American Education in the Philippines: The Early Years,* Berkeley, University of California Press, 1991.

Wolff, Leon, *Little Brown Brother: How the United States Purchased and Pacified the Philippine Islands at the Century's Turn,* New York, Doubleday, 1961.

Wyatt, David K., *Politics and Reform in Thailand: Education in the Reign of King Chulalongkorn,* New Haven, Yale University Press, 1969.

Young, Marilyn, *The Vietnam Wars, 1945–1990,* New York, Harper Collins, 1991.

PART FOUR

Albin, David A., and Marlowe Hood, eds., *The Cambodian Agony,* Armonk, N.Y., M. E. Sharpe, 1987.

Artaud, Denise, and Lawrence Kaplan, eds., *Dienbienphu: The Atlantic Alliance and the Defense of Southeast Asia,* Wilmington, Del., Scholarly Resources, 1989.

Ashmore, Harry S., and William C. Baggs, *Mission to Hanoi,* New York, G. P. Putnam, 1968.

Aung San, Suu Kyi, *Freedom from Fear and Other Writings,* New York, Penguin Books, 1991.

Ballard, John R., *Triumph of Self-Determination: Operation Stabilize and United Nations Peacemaking in East Timor,* Westport, Conn., Praeger, 2008.

Banckoff, Greg, and Kathleen Weekley, *Post-Colonial National Identity in the Philippines: Celebrating the Centennial of Independence,* Aldershot, England, Ashgate Publishing, 2002.

Ban Kah Choon, Anna Pakir, and Tong Chee, eds., *Imagining Singapore,* 2d ed., Singapore, Eastern Universities Press, 2004.

Barron, John, and Anthony Paul, *Murder of a Gentle Land: The Untold Story of Communist Genocide in Cambodia,* New York, Reader's Digest Press, 1977.

Barry, Kathleen, ed., *Vietnam's Women in Transition,* Hampshire, England, Macmillan, 1996.

Basu, Samghamitra, *Kampuchea as a Factor in the Sino-Soviet Conflict, 1975–1984,* Calcutta, Firma KLM, 1987.

Becker, Elizabeth, *When the War Was Over: The Voices of Cambodia's Revolution and Its People,* New York, Simon and Schuster, 1986.

Bellows, Thomas, *The People's Action Party of Singapore: Emergence of a Dominant Party System,* New Haven, Yale University, Southeast Asia Studies, Monograph Series no. 14, 1970.

Berman, Larry, *Lyndon Johnson's War,* New York, Norton, 1989.

———, *Planning a Tragedy: The Americanization of the War in Vietnam,* New York, Norton, 1982.

Billings-Yun, Melanie, *Decision Against War: Eisenhower and Dien Bien Phu, 1954,* New York, Columbia University Press, 1988.

Bonner, Raymond, *Waltzing with a Dictator: The Marcoses and the Making of American Policy,* New York, Times Books, 1987.

Bourchier, David, and John Legge, eds., *Democracy in Indonesia: 1950's and 1990's,* Clayton, Australia, Monash University, 1994.

Bouscaren, Anthony, *The Last of the Mandarins,* Pittsburgh, Duquesne University Press, 1965.

Boyce, James K., *The Philippines: The Political Economy of Growth and Impoverishment in the Marcos Era,* Honolulu, University of Hawaii Press, 1993.

Brands, H. W., *Bound to Empire: The U.S. and the Philippines,* New York, Oxford University Press, 1992.

Bresnan, John, ed., *Crisis in the Philippines: The Marcos Era and Beyond,* Princeton, N.J., Princeton University Press, 1986.

Brimmell, J. H., *Communism in Southeast Asia,* London, Oxford University Press, 1959.

Brown, T. Louise, *War and Aftermath in Vietnam,* New York, Routledge, 1991.

Brune, Lester H., *America and the Indochina Wars, 1945–1990,* Claremont, Calif., Regina Books, 1992.

Bui, Diem, *In the Jaws of History,* Boston, Houghton Mifflin, 1987.

Burchett, Wilfred, *The China-Cambodia-Vietnam Triangle,* London, Zed Press, 1981.

Buttinger, Joseph, *A Dragon Embattled: A History of Colonial and Post-Colonial Vietnam,* 2 vols., New York, Praeger, 1967.

Buzzanco, Robert, *Masters of War: Military Dissent and Politics in the Vietnam Era,* Cambridge, Mass., Harvard University Press, 1996.

Cable, James, *The Geneva Conference of 1954 on Indochina,* New York, St. Martin's Press, 1986.

Cady, John, *The History of Post-war Southeast Asia,* Athens, Ohio University Press, 1974.

Campagna, Anthony, *The Economic Consequences of the Vietnam War,* New York, Praeger, 1991.

Carney, Timothy M., ed., "Communist Party in Kampuchea (Cambodia): Documents and Discussion," Cornell University Southeast Asia Program Data Paper, Ithaca, N.Y., 1977.

Castle, Timothy N., *At War in the Shadow of Vietnam: U.S. Military Aid to the Royal Lao Government,* New York, Columbia University Press, 1993.

Chaleemtiarana, Thak, *Thailand: The Politics of Despotic Paternalism,* Bangkok, Thammasat University, Social Science Association, 1979.

Chaliand, Gerard, *The Peasants of North Vietnam,* Harmondsworth, England, Penguin, 1969.

Chan, Heng Chee, *The Dynamics of One-Party Dominance: The PAP at the Grassroots,* Singapore, Singapore University Press, 1976.

Chanda, Nayan, *Brother Enemy: The War After the War—A History of Indochina Since the Fall of Saigon,* San Diego, Calif., Harcourt Brace Jovanovich, 1986.

Chandler, David P., *The Tragedy of Cambodian History: Politics, War, and Revolution Since 1945,* New Haven, Yale University Press, 1991.

Chandler, David P., and Ben Kiernan, eds., *Revolution and Its Aftermath in Kampuchea,* New Haven, Yale University, Southeast Asia Council, 1983.

Chandler, David P., Ben Kiernan, and Chanthou Boua, eds., *Pol Pot Plans the Future: Confidential Leadership Documents from Democratic Kampuchea, 1976–77,* New Haven, Yale University Press, 1988.

Chang, Pao-min, *Kampuchea Between China and Vietnam,* Singapore, Singapore University Press, 1985.

Chen, Peter, ed., *Singapore: Development Policies and Trends,* Singapore, Oxford University Press, 1985.

Clammer, John, *Singapore: Ideology, Society, and Culture,* Singapore, Chapman Publishers, 1985.

Clarke, Jeffrey J., *Advice and Support: The Final Years, 1965–1973,* Washington, D.C., Center for Military History, 1988.

Clements, Alan, *Burma: The Next Killing Fields?* Berkeley, Calif., Odonian Press, 1992.

———, *Burma's Revolution of the Spirit: The Struggle for Democratic Freedom and Dignity,* New York, Aperture, 1994.

Clifford, Clark, "A Vietnam Reappraisal," *Foreign Affairs 47* (July 1969), pp. 601–622.

Clodfelter, Mark, *The Limits of Air Power: The American Bombing of North Vietnam,* New York, Free Press, 1989.

Clutterbuck, Richard, *Conflict and Violence in Singapore and Malaysia, 1945–1983,* Boulder, Colo., Westview Press, 1985.

Conceicao, J. F., *Singapore, the Many-Headed Monster: A Look at Racial Riots Against a Socio-Historical Background,* Singapore, Horizon Press, 2007.

Corfield, Justin J., *Khmers Stand Up! A History of the Cambodian Government, 1970–1975,* Clayton, Australia, Monash University, 1994.

Cotton, James, *East Timor, Australia, and Regional Order: Intervention and Its Aftermath in Southeast Asia,* London, Routledge/Curzon, 2004.

Cottrell, Robert C., *Vietnam, the 17th Parallel,* Philadelphia, Chelsea House Publications, 2004.

Crouch, Harold, *The Army and Politics in Indonesia,* Ithaca, N.Y., Cornell University Press, 1978.

Cullinae, Michael, *Ilusstrado Politico: Filipino Elite Response to American Rulers, 1898-1908,* Quezon City, Ateneo de Manila, University of the Philippines, 2003.

Curtis, Grant, *Transition to What? Cambodia, UNTAC, and the Peace Process,* Geneva, UNRISD, 1993.

Dacy, Douglas C., *Foreign Aid, War, and Economic Development in South Vietnam, 1955–1975,* Cambridge, Cambridge University Press, 1986.

Daniels, Timothy P., *Building Cultural Nationalism in Malaysia: Identity, Representation, and Citizenship,* New York, Routledge, 2005.

Dellinger, David T., *Vietnam Revisited: From Covert Action to Invasion to Reconstruction,* Boston, South End Press, 1986.

Devillers, Philippe, and Jean Lacouture, "The Struggle for the Unification of Vietnam," *China Quarterly* 9 (January–March 1962), pp. 20–23.

Dhiravegin, Likhit, *Demi Democracy: The Evolution of the Thai Political System,* Singapore, Times Academic Press, 1992.

Dirske, Jan-Paul, Frans Huesken, and Mario Rutten, eds., *Indonesia's Experiences Under the New Order,* Leiden, KITLV Press, 1993.

Doronila, Amando, "The Transformation of Patron-Client Relations and Its Political Consequences in Postwar Philippines," *JSEAS* 16, 1 (March 1985), pp. 99–116.

Duiker, William J., *China and Vietnam: The Roots of Conflict,* Berkeley, University of California Press, 1986.

———, *The Communist Road to Power in Vietnam,* Boulder, Colo., Westview Press, 1981.

———, *U.S. Containment Policy and the Conflict in Indochina,* Palo Alto, Calif., Stanford University Press, 1994.

———, *Vietnam: Nation in Revolution,* Boulder, Colo., Westview Press, 1983.

———, *Vietnam Since the Fall of Saigon,* Athens, Ohio University Center for International Studies, 1981.

Dun, Smith, *Memoirs of the Four-Foot Colonel,* Ithaca, N.Y., Cornell University Southeast Asia Program, 1980.

Duran, Frederic, *East Timor, a Country at the Crossroads of Asia and the Pacific: A Geo-Historical Atlas,* Chiang Mai, Silkworm Books, 2006.

Ebihara, May M., *Cambodian Culture Since 1975,* Ithaca, N.Y., Cornell University Press, 1994.

Eden, Anthony, *Full Circle: The Memoirs of Anthony Eden,* Boston, Houghton Mifflin, 1960.

Elliott, David W. P., *The Third Indochina Conflict,* Boulder, Colo., Westview Press, 1981.

———, *Vietnamese War: Revolution and Social Change in the Mekong Delta, 1930–1975,* Armonk, N.Y., M.E. Sharpe, 2003.

———, ed., *Indochina: Social and Cultural Change,* Claremont, Calif., McKenna College Press, 1994.

Ellis, Sylvia, *Britain, America, and the Vietnam War,* Westport, Conn., Praeger, 2004.

Ely, John Hart, *War and Responsibility: Constitutional Lessons of Vietnam and Its Aftermath,* Princeton, N.J., Princeton University Press, 1993.

Etcheson, Craig, *The Rise and Demise of Democratic Kampuchea,* Boulder, Colo., Westview Press, 1984.

Fall, Bernard B., *The Two Viet-Nams: A Political and Military Analysis,* rev. ed., New York, Praeger, 1964.

Falla, Jonathan, *True Love and Bartholomew: Rebels on the Burmese Border,* Cambridge, Cambridge University Press, 1991.

Feith, Herbert, *The Decline of Constitutional Democracy in Indonesia,* Ithaca, N.Y., Cornell University Press, 1962.

Fforde, Adam, *The Agrarian Question in North Vietnam, 1974–1979,* Armonk, N.Y., M. E. Sharpe, 1989.

Fielding, Leslie, *Before the Killing Fields: Witness to Cambodia and the Vietnam War,* London, I. B. Tauris, 2008.

Fifield, Russell, *Americans in Southeast Asia: The Roots of Commitment,* New York, Thomas Y. Crowell, 1973.

Fitzgerald, Frances, *Fire in the Lake,* New York, Vintage Books, 1972.

Fredholm, Michael, *Burma: Ethnicity and Insurgency,* Westport, Conn., Praeger, 1993.

Friend, Theodore, "Marcos and the Philippines," *Orbis* (Fall 1988), pp. 569–586.

Frost, Frank, *The Peace Process in Cambodia,* Queensland, Australia, Griffith University Press, 1993.

———, *Vietnam's Foreign Relations: Dynamics of Change,* Singapore, Institute of Southeast Asian Studies, 1993.

Gaiduk, Ilva N., *Confronting Vietnam: Soviet Policy Towards the Indochina Conflict, 1954–63,* Washington, D.C., Woodrow Wilson Center Press, 2003.

Galloway, John, *The Gulf of Tonkin Resolution,* Rutherford, N.J., Fairleigh Dickinson University Press, 1970.

Gardner, Lloyd C., *Approaching Vietnam: From World War II Through Dienbienphu, 1941–1954,* New York, Norton, 1988.

Gheddo, Piero, *The Cross and the Bo Tree,* New York, Sheed and Ward, 1970.

Gillespie, John, *Transplanting Commercial Law Reform: Developing a "Rule of Law" in Vietnam,* Aldershot, England; Burlington, Vermont; Ashgate Publishing, 2006.

Goh, Keng Swee, *Economics of Modernization,* Singapore, Marshall Cavendish Academic, 2004.

Griffiths, Philip Jones, *Agent Orange: "Collateral Damage" in Vietnam,* London, Trolley, 2003.

———, *Vietnam at Peace,* London, Trolley, 2005.

Haas, Michael, *Cambodia, Pol Pot, and the U.S.,* New York, Praeger, 1991.

Halberstam, David, *The Best and the Brightest,* Greenwich, Conn., Fawcett Publications, 1969.

———, *The Making of a Quagmire,* New York, Random House, 1965.

Hall, Mitchell K., *Vietnam War,* 2d ed., New York, Pearson Longman, 2007.

Hamilton-Merritt, Jane, *Tragic Mountains: The Hmong, the Americans, and the Secret Wars for Laos, 1942–1992,* Bloomington, Indiana University Press, 1993.

Hammer, Ellen J., *A Death in November: America in Vietnam, 1963,* New York, E. P. Dutton, 1987.

Hanna, Willard A., *Eight Nation Makers: Southeast Asia's Charismatic Statesmen,* New York, St. Martin's Press, 1964.

Hardy, Andrew, *Red Hills: Migrants and the State in the Highlands of Vietnam,* Honolulu, University of Hawaii Press, 2003.

Harrison, James P., *The Endless War: Fifty Years of Struggle in Vietnam,* New York, Free Press, 1982.

Hawley, Thomas, *Remains of War: Bodies, Politics, and the Search for American Soldiers Unaccounted for in Southeast Asia,* Durham, N.C., Duke University Press, 2005.

Haycraft, William R., *Unravelling Vietnam: How American Arms and Diplomacy Failed in Southeast Asia,* Jefferson, N.C., McFarland, 2005.

Hayslip, Le Ly, *When Heaven and Earth Change Places: A Vietnamese Woman's Journey from War to Peace,* New York, Doubleday, 1989.

Head, William, and Lawrence E. Grinter, eds., *Looking Back on the Vietnam War,* Westport, Conn., Praeger, 1993.

Heder, Stephen R., *Cambodian Communists and the Vietnamese Model,* Bangkok, White Lotus Press, 2004.

———, *Kampuchean Occupation and Resistance,* Bangkok, Institute of Asian Studies, Chulalongkorn University, 1980.

Henderson, William, "South Vietnam Finds Itself," *Foreign Affairs* 35, 2 (January 1957), pp. 213–294.

Hendon, Bill, *Enormous Crime: The Definitive Account of American POWs Abandoned in Southeast Asia,* New York, Thomas Dunne Books, 2007.

Herring, George C., *America's Longest War: The United States and Vietnam, 1950–1973,* Philadelphia, Temple University Press, 1986.

Hess, Gary R., *Vietnam and the United States: Origins and Legacy of War,* Boston, Twayne, 1990.

Hickey, Gerald C., *Village in Vietnam,* New Haven, Yale University Press, 1964.

Hildebrand, George, and Gareth Porter, *Cambodia: Starvation and Revolution,* New York, Monthly Review Press, 1976.

Hill, Hal, ed., *Indonesia's New Order: The Dynamics of Socio-Economic Transformation,* Honolulu, University of Hawaii Press, 1994.

Hindley, Donald, *The Communist Party of Indonesia,* Berkeley, University of California Press, 1964.

———, "Political Power in the October 1965 Coup in Indonesia," *JAS* 26, 2 (February 1967), pp. 237–249.

Honey, P. J., *Communism in North Vietnam: Its Role in the Sino-Soviet Dispute,* Cambridge, Mass., MIT Press, 1963.

Hood, Steven, *Dragons Embattled: Indochina and the China-Vietnam War,* Westport, Conn., Praeger, 1993.

Hutton, Tim, *Tock Tock Birds: A Spider in the Web of International Terrorism,* Subang Jaya, Selangor, Pelanduk Publications, 2007.

Huyen, N. Khac, *Vision Accomplished? The Enigma of Ho Chi Minh,* New York, Macmillan, 1971.

Huynh Kim Khanh, *Vietnamese Communism, 1925–1945,* Ithaca, N.Y., Cornell University Press, 1982, 1986.

———, "Year One of Post-Colonial Vietnam," *Southeast Asian Affairs,* Institute of Southeast Asian Studies, Singapore, 1977, pp. 287–305.

Jackson, Karl D., ed., *Cambodia, 1975–1978: Rendezvous with Death,* Princeton, N.J., Princeton University Press, 1989.

Jenkins, David, *Suharto and His Generals: Indonesian Military Politics, 1975–1983,* Ithaca, N.Y., Cornell University Southeast Asian Studies Program, 1984.

Kahin, George M., ed., *Governments and Politics of Southeast Asia,* 1st ed., Ithaca, N.Y., Cornell University Press, 1954; 2d ed., 1964.

———, *Intervention: How America Became Involved in Vietnam,* New York, Knopf, 1986.

Karnow, Stanley, *Vietnam, a History: The First Complete Account of Vietnam at War,* New York, Viking Press, 1983.

Keith, Patrick, *Ousted (1963–65),* Singapore, Media Masters, 2005; New York, Routledge, 2003.

Kelley, Gail Paradise, *From Vietnam to America: A Chronicle of the Vietnamese Immigration to the United States,* Boulder, Colo., Westview Press, 1977.

Kervileit, Benedict, and R. Mojares, eds., *From Marcos to Aquino: Local Perspectives on Political Transition in the Philippines,* Honolulu, University of Hawaii Press, 1991.

Kessler, Clive S., *Islam and Politics in a Malay State: Kelantan, 1838–1969,* Ithaca, N.Y., Cornell University Press, 1978.

Khanh, Tran, *The Ethnic Chinese and Economic Development in Vietnam,* Singapore, Institute of Southeast Asian Studies, 1993.

Khoo Book Teik, *Beyond Mahathir: Malaysian Politics and Its Discontents,* London, Zed, 2003.

Kiernan, Ben, *How Pol Pot Came to Power: A History of Communism in Kampuchea, 1930–1975,* London, Verso, 1985.

———, *The Pol Pot Regime,* New Haven, Yale University Press, 1993.

———, ed., *Genocide and Democracy in Cambodia,* New Haven, Yale University, Southeast Asia Studies, 1993.

Kiernan, Ben, and Chantou Boua, eds., *Peasants and Politics in Kampuchea, 1942–1981,* London, Zed Press, 1982.

Kiljunen, Kimmo, ed., *Kampuchea: Decade of the Genocide,* London, Zed, 1984.

Kimball, Jeffrey P., *Vietnam War Files: Uncovering the Secret History of Nixon-Era Strategy,* Lawrence, University Press of Kansas, 2004.

Kipp, Rita Smith, *Disassociated Identities: Ethnicity, Religion, and Class in an Indonesian Society,* Ann Arbor, University of Michigan Press, 1993.

Kissinger, Henry, *Ending the Vietnam War: A History of America's Involvement in and Extraction from the Vietnam War,* New York, Simon and Schuster, 2003.

Klintworth, Gary, *Vietnam's Withdrawal from Cambodia,* Canberra, Australian National University Press, 1987.

Kobkua, Suwannathat-Pian, *Kings, Country, and Constitutions: Thailand's Political Development, 1932–2000,* London, Routledge/Curzon, 2003.

Kramer, Tom, *United Wa State Party, Narco-Army or Ethnic Nationalist Party?* Singapore, Institute of Southeast Asian Studies, 2007.

Kreuzer, Peter, and Rainer Werning, eds., *Voices from Moroland: Perspectives from Stakeholders and Observers on the Conflict in the Southern Philippines,* Petaling Jaya, Strategic Information and Research Development Center, 2007.

Kulick, Elliott, *Thailand's Turn: Profile of a New Dragon,* New York, St. Martin's Press, 1992.

Kurland, Gerald, ed., *Misjudgment or Defense of Freedom? The United States in Vietnam,* New York, Simon and Schuster, 1975.

Lawrence, Mark Atwood, *Vietnam War: A Concise International History,* New York, Oxford University Press, 2008.

Le Hoang Trong, "Survival and Self-Reliance: A Vietnamese Viewpoint," *AS* 15, 3 (March 1975), pp. 281–300.

Lee, Raymond, ed., *Ethnicity and Ethnic Relations in Malaysia,* DeKalb, Northern Illinois University, Center for Southeast Asian Studies, Occasional Papers no. 12, 1986.

Leifer, Michael, *Cambodian Conflicts: The Final Phase?* London, Center for Security and Conflict Studies, 1989.

Lev, Daniel S., *Transition to Guided Democracy,* Ithaca, N.Y., Cornell University Modern Indonesia Project, 1966.

Lewallen, John, *Ecology of Devastation: Indochina,* Baltimore, Penguin Books, 1971.

Lie, Hong, and Sin-Kiong Wong, *Singapore Chinese Society in Transition: Business, Politics and Socio-Economic Change, 1945–65,* New York, Peter Lang, 2004.

Lim, Linda Y. C., "Singapore's Success: The Myth of the Free Market Economy," *AS* 23, 6 (June 1983), pp. 752–764.

Lim, Regina, *Federal-State Relations in Sabah: The Berjaya Administration, 1976–85,* Singapore, Institute of Southeast Asian Studies, 2008.

Linther, Bertil, *Burma in Revolt: Opium and Insurgency Since 1948,* Boulder, Colo., Westview Press, 1994.

Ljunggren, Boerje, ed., *The Challenge of Reform in Indochina,* Cambridge, Mass., Harvard University Press, 1993.

Long, Robert Emmet, ed., *Vietnam Ten Years After,* New York, Wilson, 1986.

Mangold, Tom, *The Tunnels of Cu Chi,* London, Hodder and Stoughton, 1985.

Martin, Marie Alexandrine, *Cambodia: A Shattered Society,* Berkeley, University of California Press, 1994.

Marynov, Gerald, *Politics in Indonesia: An Interpretation,* Kuala Lumpur, University of Malaya Press, 1966.

Masamichi, Royama, *The Philippine Polity,* New Haven, Yale University Press, 1967.

May, Someth, *Cambodian Witness: The Autobiography of Someth May,* ed., James Fenton, London, Faber, 1986.

McCormack, G., "The Kampuchean Revolution, 1975–1978," *Journal of Contemporary Asia* 10 (1980), pp. 75–118.

McGregor, Charles, *The Sino-Vietnamese Relationship and the Soviet Union,* London, International Institute for Strategic Studies, 1988.

McHale, Shawn Frederick, *Print and Power: Confucianism, Communism, and Buddhism in the Making of Modern Vietnam,* Honolulu, University of Hawaii Press, 2004.

McMahon, Robert J., ed., *Major Problems in the History of the Vietnam War: Documents and Essays,* 3d ed., Boston, Houghton Mifflin, 2003.

Mead, Kullada K., *Rise and Fall of Thai Absolutism,* London, Routledge/Curzon, 2004.

Means, Gordon P., *Malaysian Politics: The Second Generation,* Singapore, Oxford University Press, 1991.

Milne, David, *America's Rasputin: Walt Rostow and the Vietnam War,* New York, Hill and Wang, 2008.

Mirante, Edith T., *Burmese Looking Glass: A Human Rights Adventure and a Jungle Revolution,* New York, Grove Press, 1993.

Mokarapong, Thawatt, *History of the Thai Revolution: A Study of Political Behaviour,* Bangkok, Chalermnit, 1972.

Morell, David, and Chai-anan Samudvanij, *Thailand: Reform, Reaction, and Revolution,* Cambridge, Mass., MIT Press, 1981.

Morris, Virginia, with Clive Hills, *Road to Freedom: A History of the Ho Chi Minh Trail,* Bangkok, Orchid Press, 2006.

Morrison, Charles, and Astri Suhrke, *Strategies of Survival: The Foreign Policy Dilemmas of Smaller Asian States,* New York, St. Martin's Press, 1978.

Moyar, Mark, *Triumph Forsaken: The Vietnam War, 1954–1965,* Cambridge, Cambridge University Press, 2006.

Mus, Paul, "The Role of the Village in Vietnamese Politics," *Pacific Affairs* 23 (September 1949), pp. 365–372.

Myint, Soe, *Burma File, a Question of Democracy,* New Delhi, India Research Press, 2003.

Nartsupha, Chatthip, and Suthy Prasartset, *The Political Economy of Siam, 1851–1910,* Bangkok, Social Science Association of Thailand, 1981.

Ng, Tisa, *Ong Teng Cheong: Planner, Politician, President,* Singapore, Editions Didier Millet, 2005.

Ngor, Haing S., *Surviving the Killing Fields: The Cambodian Odyssey,* London, Chatto and Windus, 1988.

Nguyen, Cao Ky, *How We Lost the Vietnam War,* New York, Stein and Day, 1984.

Nguyen, Huy Toan, *Vietnam, the War of Liberation, 1945–1975: Questions and Answers,* Hanoi, Giao Publishers, 2006.

Nguyen, Van Canh, *Vietnam Under Communism, 1975–1982,* Palo Alto, Calif., Hoover Institution Press, Stanford University, 1983.

Nguyen-Vo, Tho-Huong, *Khmer-Viet Relations and the Third Indochina Conflict,* Jefferson, N.C., McFarland, 1992.

Nicholson, Penelope, *Borrowing Court Systems: Experience of Socialist Vietnam,* Leiden, Martinus Nijhoff, 2007.

Noble, Lela Garner, *Government in the Philippines: The Privatization of Politics,* New York, Asia Society, 1989.

———, "The Philippines: Autonomy for the Muslims," in John Esposito, ed., *Islam in Asia: Religion, Politics, and Society,* New York, Oxford University Press, 1987.

Nolting, Frederick, *From Trust to Tragedy,* New York, Praeger, 1988.

Noor, Farish A., *Islam Embedded: The Historical Development of the Pan-Malaysian Islamic Party, PAS, 1951–2003,* 2 vols., Kuala Lumpur, Malaysian Sociological Research Institute, 2006.

Oliver, Kendrick, *My Lai Massacre in American History and Memory,* Manchester, England, Manchester University Press, 2006.

Olson, James S., and Randy Robert, *Where the Dominoes Fell: America and Vietnam 1945–1995,* 5th ed., Malden, Mass., Blackwell, 2008.

Olson, Mari, *Soviet Union–Vietnam Relations and the Role of China, 1949–64, Changing Alliances,* London, Routledge, 2006.

Ooi, Giok Ling, *Beyond the Port City: Development and Identity in 21st Century Singapore,* Singapore, Pearson/Prentice-Hall, 2004.

Ooi, Kea Beng, *Era of Transition: Malaysia after Mahathir,* Singapore, Institute of Southeast Asian Studies, 2006.

Osborne, Milton E., *Before Kampuchea: Prelude to Tragedy,* Sydney, Allen and Unwin, 1979.

———, *Region of Revolt: Focus on Southeast Asia,* Rushcutters Bay, New South Wales, Australia, Pergamon Press, 1970.

Papp, Daniel S., *Vietnam: The View from Moscow, Peking, Washington,* Salisbury, N.C., McFarland, 1981.

Pentagon Papers, New York, Bantam Books, 1971.

Picq, Laurence, *Beyond the Horizon: Five Years with the Khmer Rouge,* New York, St. Martin's Press, 1989.

Pike, Douglas, *History of Vietnamese Communism, 1925–1976,* Stanford, Calif., Hoover Institution Press, 1978.

———, *Viet Cong,* Cambridge, Mass., MIT Press, 1966.

———, *Vietnam and the Soviet Union,* Boulder, Colo., Westview Press, 1987.

Pomeroy, William J., *An American-Made Tragedy,* New York, International Publishers, 1974.

———, *The Forest: A Personal Record of the Huk Guerrilla Struggle in the Philippines,* New York, International Publishers, 1963.

Ponchaud, Francois, *Cambodia Year Zero,* New York, Holt, Rinehart, 1977.

Popkin, S., *The Rational Peasant: The Political Economy of Rural Society in Vietnam,* Berkeley, University of California Press, 1979.

Porter, D. Gareth, "The Myth of the Bloodbath: North Vietnam's Land Reform Reconsidered," Ithaca, N.Y., Cornell University International Relations of East Asia Project, 1972, mimeo.

———, *A Peace Denied: The United States and the Paris Agreements,* Bloomington, Indiana University Press, 1975.

Pratt, John C., ed., *Vietnam Voices,* New York, Penguin Books, 1984.

Quimpo, Nathan Gilbert, *Contested Democracy and the Left in the Philippines after Marcos,* New Haven, Yale University Southeast Asia Studies, 2008.

Race, Jeffrey, *War Comes to Long An,* Berkeley, University of California Press, 1972.

Rajaretnam, M., *The Aquino Alternative,* Singapore, Institute of Southeast Asian Studies, 1986.

Ramage, Douglas E., *Politics in Indonesia: Democracy, Islam, and the Ideology of Tolerance,* New York, Routledge, 1995.

Reid, Anthony, ed., *Verandah of Violence: The Background to the Acheh Problem,* Singapore, Singapore University Press, 2006.

Roff, William R., ed., *Kelantan: Religion, Society, and Politics in a Malay State,* Kuala Lumpur, Oxford University Press, 1974.

Rosenberg, David, ed., *Marcos and Martial Law in the Philippines,* Ithaca, N.Y., Cornell University Press, 1979.

Ross, Robert S., *The Indochina Tangle: China's Vietnam Policy, 1975–1979,* New York, Columbia University Press, 1988.

Rotter, Andrew J., *The Path to Vietnam: Origins of American Commitment to Southeast Asia,* Ithaca, N.Y., Cornell University Press, 1987.

Santos, Soliman M., *Dynamics and Directions of the GRP-MILF Peace Negotiations,* Davao City, Philippines, Alternate Forum for Research in Mindanao, 2005.

SarDesai, D. R., *Indian Foreign Policy in Cambodia, Laos, and Vietnam, 1947–1964,* Berkeley, University of California Press, 1968.

Savage, David, *Dancing with the Devil: A Personal Account of Policy and the East Timor Vote for Independence,* Clayton, Australia, Monash Asia Institute, 2002.

Scaff, Alvin H., *The Philippines Answer to Communism,* Stanford, Calif., Stanford University Press, 1955.

Schanberg, Sydney Hillel, *Death and Life of Dith Pran,* New York, Penguin, 1985.

Schlesinger, Arthur M., Jr., *The Bitter Heritage: Vietnam and American Democracy, 1941–1966,* Boston, Houghton Mifflin, 1967.

Shaplen, Robert, *Bitter Victory,* New York, Harper and Row, 1986.

———, *The Lost Revolution, 1946–1966,* New York, Harper and Row, 1955.

Shawcross, William, *The Quality of Mercy: Cambodia, Holocaust, and Modern Conscience,* New York, Simon and Schuster, 1984.

———, *Sideshow: Kissinger, Nixon, and the Destruction of Cambodia,* New York, Simon and Schuster, 1979.

Short, Anthony, *The Origins of the Vietnam War,* London, Longman, 1989.

Sihanouk, Norodom, "Cambodia Neutral: The Dictate of Necessity," *Foreign Affairs* 36 (July 1958), pp. 582–586.

———, *My War with the CIA,* Harmondsworth, England, Penguin Books, 1973.

Silverstein, Josef, *Burmese Politics: The Dilemma of National Unity,* New Brunswick, N.J., Rutgers University Press, 1980.

Simbulan, Dante C., *Modern Principatia: The Historical Evolution of the Philippines Ruling Oligarchy,* Quezon City, University of the Philippines Press, 2005.

Sison, Jose Maria, *The Implosion of the Communist Party of the Philippines,* Clayton, Australia, Monash University, 1995.

Smith, Roger, *Cambodia's Foreign Policy,* Ithaca, N.Y., Cornell University Press, 1965.

Smythe, Patricia A., *The Heaviest Blow: The Catholic Church and the East Timor Issue,* Munster, Germany, Lit Verlag, 2004.

Snepp, Frank, *Decent Interval: An Insider's Account of Saigon's Indecent End,* New York, Random House, 1977.

Stoessinger, John G., *Henry Kissinger: The Anguish of Power,* New York, W. W. Norton, 1976.

Stuart-Fox, Martin, *The Murderous Revolution: Life and Death in Pol Pot's Kampuchea,* Denver, Colo., Alternate Publishing, 1986.

Stubbs, Richard, *Hearts and Minds in Guerrilla Warfare: The Malayan Emergency, 1948–1960,* Singapore, Oxford University Press, 1989.

Summers, Harry G., Jr., *On Strategy: A Critical Analysis of the Vietnam War,* Novato, Calif., Presidio Press, 1982.

Sutter, Robert G., *The Cambodian Crisis and U.S. Policy Dilemmas,* Boulder, Colo., Westview Press, 1991.

Tan, Teng Lang, *Economic Debates in Vietnam: Issues and Problems in Reconstruction and Development, 1975–1984,* Singapore, Institute of Southeast Asian Studies, 1985.

Tetreault, MaryAnn, *Women and Revolution in Vietnam,* East Lansing, Michigan State University, 1992.

Tham, Seong Chee, *Malays and Modernisation: A Sociological Interpretation,* Singapore, University of Singapore Press, 1977.

Thanet-Aphornsuvan, *Rebellion in Southern Thailand: Contending Histories,* Singapore, Institute of Southeast Asian Studies, 2007.

Thayer, Carlyle A., *Beyond Indochina,* London, Institute for Strategic Studies, 1995.

Thorbecke, Erik, *Rural Indonesia: Socio-Economic Development in a Changing Environment,* New York, New York University Press, 1993.

Thrift, Nigel, and Dean Forbes, *The Price of War: Urbanization in Vietnam, 1954–1985,* London, Allen and Unwin, 1985.

Tilman, Robert O., *Southeast Asia and the Enemy Beyond: ASEAN Perceptions of External Threats,* Boulder, Colo., Westview Press, 1986.

Timberman, David G., *A Changeless Land: Continuity and Change in Philippine Politics,* Singapore, Institute of Southeast Asian Studies, 1991.

Trager, Frank N., ed., *Marxism in Southeast Asia,* Stanford, Calif., Stanford University Press, 1960.

Tran, Dang T., *Vietnam: Socialist Economic Development,* San Francisco, Institute for Contemporary Studies (ICS) Press, 1994.

Truong, Nhu Tang, *Journal of a Vietcong,* London, Cape, 1986.

Turley, William S., ed., *Confrontation or Coexistence: The Future of ASEAN-Vietnam Relations,* Bangkok, Chulalongkorn University, 1985.

———, *The Second Indochina War: A Short Political and Military History,* Boulder, Colo., Westview Press, 1986.

———, ed., *Vietnamese Communism in Comparative Perspective,* Boulder, Colo., Westview Press, 1980.

Unger, Leonard, and Joseph Lasloff, eds., *Laos: Beyond the Revolution,* New York, St. Martin's Press, 1991.

U.S. Department of State, *A Threat to the Peace,* Washington, D.C., Government Printing Office, 1961.

"U.S. Foreign Policy for the 1970's: A New Strategy for Peace," Report to the Congress by Richard Nixon, February 18, 1970, Washington, D.C., Government Printing Office, 1970.

Van der Kroef, Justus, *The Communist Party of Indonesia,* Vancouver, University of British Columbia Press, 1965.

Vatikiotis, Michael, *Indonesian Politics Under Suharto,* New York, Routledge, 1993.

Vickery, Michael, *Cambodia, 1975–1982,* Boston, South End Press, 1984.

Vo, Nhan Tri, *Vietnam's Economic Policy Since 1975,* Sydney, Allen and Unwin, 1990.

von Vorys, Karl, *Democracy Without Consensus: Communalism and Political Stability in Malaysia,* Princeton, N.J., Princeton University Press, 1975.

Voon, Ohin Keong, ed., *Malaysian Chinese and Nation-building: Before Merdeka and Fifty Years After,* Kuala Lumpur, Centre for Malaysian and Chinese Studies, 2007.

Westmoreland, William C., *A Soldier Reports,* New York, Doubleday, 1976.

Willmot, W. E., "Analytical Errors of the Kampuchean Communist Party," *Pacific Affairs* 45, 2 (Summer 1981), pp. 209–227.

Win, Kanbawza, *Comparative Studies of the Two Military Juntas, Thailand and Burma: A Burmese Perspective,* Bangkok, CDSK Publications, 1994.

Woodman, Dorothy, *The Republic of Indonesia,* New York, Philosophical Library, 1955.

Woodside, Alexander B., *Community and Revolution in Modern Vietnam,* Boston, Houghton Mifflin, 1976.

Wright, Martin, ed., *Cambodia: A Matter of Survival,* London, Longman, 1989.

Wurfel, David, *Filipino Politics: Development and Decay,* Quezon City, Ateneo de Manila University Press, 1988.

Yang, Sam, *Khmer Buddhism and Politics from 1954 to 1984,* Newington, Conn., Khmer Studies Institute, 1987.

Yegar, Moshe, *Between Integration and Secession: The Muslim Communities of the Southern Philippines, Southern Thailand and Western Burma,* Lanham, Md., Lexington Books, 2002.

Yoshihara, Kunio, *Foreign Investment and Domestic Response: A Study of Singapore's Industrialization,* Singapore, Eastern Universities Press, 1976.

Young, Marilyn, *The Vietnam Wars, 1945–1990,* New York, HarperCollins, 1991.

Zagoria, Donald, *Vietnam Triangle: Moscow, Peking, Hanoi,* New York, Pegasus, 1967.

Zakaria, Haji Ahmad, ed., *Government and Politics of Malaysia,* Singapore, Oxford University Press, 1987.

Index